A History of English Literature

A HISTORY OF ENGLISH LITERATURE

Peter Quennell
& Hamish Johnson

Ferndale Editions
LONDON

First published 1973 by George Weidenfeld and Nicholson Limited

This edition published 1981 by Ferndale Editions,
Brent House, 24-28 Friern Park, London N12, England,
under licence from the proprietor

Copyright © Peter Quennell 1973

Exclusive North American rights and distribution Marboro Books Corp.

ISBN 0 905746 43 0

Printed and bound in Hong Kong by South China Printing Company

Contents

Preface

Over seventy years have passed since Richard Garnett and Edmund Gosse published the four-volume work that they entitled *English Literature: An Illustrated Record*. This massive survey covers the whole extent of English, Early English and Anglo-Saxon verse and prose from the early days of the eighth until the last decade of the nineteenth century; and later editions were enlarged to include Walter de la Mare and Rupert Brooke. It was an outstanding achievement. Both Garnett and Gosse were distinguished literary scholars in the late-Victorian tradition, perceptive, catholic and widely read; and, although Garnett seems to have been mainly responsible for Volume I, while Gosse alone signed Volumes III and IV, they evolved a singularly homogeneous style. The chief disadvantages of their *Record* are, first, its bulk – together, the four volumes weigh nearly seventeen pounds; second, the somewhat uneven quality of the accompanying illustrations.

In the present volume we have attempted to provide a more compendious type of survey. Here is a single volume – solid enough, it is true, but planned to suit a modern reader's crowded bookshelves, on which we hope that it will occupy a useful position among some of the master-works our text discusses. Throughout, we have assumed that the reader's enjoyment of a book is always increased if he can place its author against the correct historical and social background, and knows something of the personal experiences that may have helped to bring it into being. We have assembled, therefore, a succession of brief biographies, designed to illuminate not only our subjects themselves, but their relationship with other contemporary writers and the ethos of the age in which they lived and worked. We have also, as a pendant to most of our portraits, attached a quotation or quotations. Each section is arranged according to birth-dates, except where a pair of subjects – Johnson and Boswell, Jane and Thomas Carlyle, Elizabeth and Thomas Browning – must necessarily be considered side by side. In our choice of plates we have done our best to supplement the effect of the adjoining text. Surely the pictures of John Donne, young and old – the young adventurer and the melancholy Man of God, depicted in his own prefabricated shroud – sharpen our affection for his genius, and emphasise the dramatic contrast between his youthful love-poems and the fierce sermons and passionate religious sonnets written after he had finally renounced the flesh?

We have had no doctrinaire theories to propose. In a book of this kind, some touches of unreasonable prejudice, some failures of taste and sympathy, must inevitably crop up here and there; but we have endeavoured to counterbalance our private opinions by citing the judgments of better-qualified critics, and permitting Dryden, Johnson, Hazlitt and Coleridge to give their views upon their fellow great men, thus showing the strange vicissitudes of taste that occur in the annals of every literature. No doubt, we have omitted certain writers for whom, despite the limitations of our space, we should have spared at least a paragraph. Now and then we may have erred through inadvertence. Other omissions, we should like to assure the reader, have been made deliberately. Thus, we have excluded Robert Burns because we believe that he was, above all else, a Scottish poet, posthumously adopted into the canon of English literature, whose greatest works belong to a poetic and cultural heritage quite distinct from that of England. Similarly, our account of the nineteenth-century historians ends with Macaulay and Carlyle. Both those great men were devoted to the *art* of history – to history as a form of dramatic narrative or, particularly in Carlyle's case, as a means of political and moral exposition; while their successors learned to regard it as a strictly *scientific* discipline, and mistrusted the literary approach that had originated with historians of the school of Hume and Gibbon.

Our aim here has been to produce a well-documented reference-book, which will enable the reader to draw his own conclusions from the facts we have assembled. Producing it has not been an easy task; we have had to reduce the records of some seventeen centuries into the space of just over five hundred pages. But we have been assisted by the fact that English literature has run a remarkably coherent course. There have been gaps, temporarily barren periods – for instance, between the death of Chaucer and the rise of the early Tudor poets; but, at regular intervals, a man of genius has emerged to give the literary art a new direction; and such artists, besides looking ahead, have kept an attentive eye on the historic past, with the result that Dryden, Pope, Wordsworth, Keats, Tennyson and Matthew Arnold, however much they may differ in method, still seem members of the same family, proud to acknowledge their joint inheritance and glad to remember that they spoke a common language. The slow development of that marvellous language is itself a fascinating theme. 'Englisc', the Anglo-Saxon tongue, was for a while eclipsed by Norman French; and one of our first genuinely native poets was the early thirteenth-century scribe Layamon, a chronicler of 'the noble deeds of the English', who grasped the magnificent possibilities of the hybrid jargon that English everyday people then employed. Layamon, though he read both Latin and French, was a devotee of English vernacular speech and a conscientious artist: 'May the Lord be merciful to him! Pen he took with fingers . . . and the true words set together.' It is to Layamon, the humble parish priest that this book is dedicated.

Acknowledgments

Photographs and illustrations were supplied by or are reproduced by kind permission of the following. The picture on p. 37*t* is reproduced by gracious permission of H.M. the Queen; on p. 37*b* by permission of His Grace the Duke of Norfolk; on p. 53*t* by permission of His Grace the Duke of Portland; on p. 52 by permission of the Marquis of Bath; on p. 53*b* by permission of Lord Montagu of Beaulieu; on pp. 263 and 268*b* by permission of Lord Sackville West; on p. 494*b* by permission of Cecil Beaton; on p. 206 by permission of the Trustees of the Chatsworth Settlement; on p. 31 by permission of the Master and Fellows of Corpus Christi College, Cambridge. Bassano and Vandyk Studios 467*r*, 486*l*, 487*r*; Bodleian Library, Oxford 10, 14, 15, 26, 144*r*, 306; British Museum (photos John Freeman) 13, 19, 20, 23, 28, 33, 34*r*, 35*b*, 36*r*, 39, 41*t*, 44, 47, 49, 67, 68, 73, 75, 80, 82, 83, 86*r*, 89, 91, 92*r*, 95, 98, 99, 102, 105*r*, 107*r*, 109, 111, 113*r*, 114, 120*l*, 122, 124, 126, 130, 135*b*, 139, 142, 143, 144*l*, 147, 151, 158/9, 161, 166, 167, 168, 174*b*, 175, 176, 179, 187, 196, 197*t*, 208, 209, 211, 213, 217*r*, 219, 222, 225, 227*r*, 229, 233, 239, 242, 244, 245, 247, 249*r*, 251, 252, 254, 257, 258, 261, 264, 270, 274, 278, 284*l*, 287*r*, 289, 302, 303, 309, 322, 324, 325, 329, 335, 337*r*, 339*t*, 342, 345, 351, 354, 357, 362*t*, 365*t*, 373, 376, 382, 383, 385*b*, 391, 395, 399, 400, 403, 407, 421, 423, 424, 426, 434, 436*r*, 440, 445; Camera Press 455*b*, 466*b*, 469*r*, 470*t*, 475, 476*r*, 479*b*, 483, 486 *c & r*, 488, 489*r*, 491, 494*c*; Courtauld Institute of Art 36*l*, 52, 210, 255, 284*r*; Fitzwilliam Museum, Cambridge 243; Mark Gerson 469*l*; History Today 34*l*, 53*t*, 54*t*, 113*l*, 163, 198*t*, 385*t*, 428*l*, 430; Henry E. Huntington Library and Art Gallery, California 25, 29; Keats' House, Hampstead, London 319; Keats-Shelley Memorial House 307; Kipling Society 451; Kunstsammlung, Basel 40; Mansell Collection 43, 115, 118, 131*t*, 137, 169, 191*t*, 298, 310, 315, 316, 397, 473*b*, 479*b*; Mary Evans Picture Library 311*t*, 428*r*; Mrs Mary Moorman 299; National Galleries of Scotland 276, 323; National Portrait Gallery 71, 77, 79, 81, 86*l*, 105*l*, 120*t*, 123, 132, 135*t*, 136, 145, 149, 153, 162, 170, 178, 183, 189, 192, 197*b*, 205, 217*l*, 220, 221, 228, 230, 231, 238, 241, 249*l*, 259, 266*l*, 268*t*, 273, 275, 279, 280, 288, 293, 297, 300, 301, 311, 317, 330, 331, 333, 337, 339*b*, 340, 344*l*, 349, 353, 355, 358, 365*b*, 367, 370, 371, 374, 377, 379, 389, 392, 394, 402, 405, 410, 414, 416, 417, 420, 422, 431, 436, 437, 439, 443, 444, 447, 450*l*, 454, 455*t*, 456*t*, 459, 462, 466*t*, 470*b*, 471, 472, 473*t*, 476*l*, 480, 485, 489*l*, 494*t*, 495; National Trust 385*t*, 388; Pepysian Library, Cambridge 177; Pierpont Morgan Library 304, 320; Private Collection 393; Press Association 450*r*; Radio Times Hulton Picture Library 64, 474; Raymond Fortt 35*t*; Reuter Photos Ltd 493; Royal Academy of Arts 487*b*; Salford Art Gallery 287*l*; Tate Gallery 227*b*; University of Nottingham Library 465; Vernon Richards 468*t*; Victoria and Albert Museum 41*b*, 54*b*, 60, 90, 92*l*, 107*l*, 119, 128, 131*r*, 148, 185, 191*b*, 226, 234, 235, 236, 237; Walter Barnes Studio 457, 460, 463, 467*b*, 497.

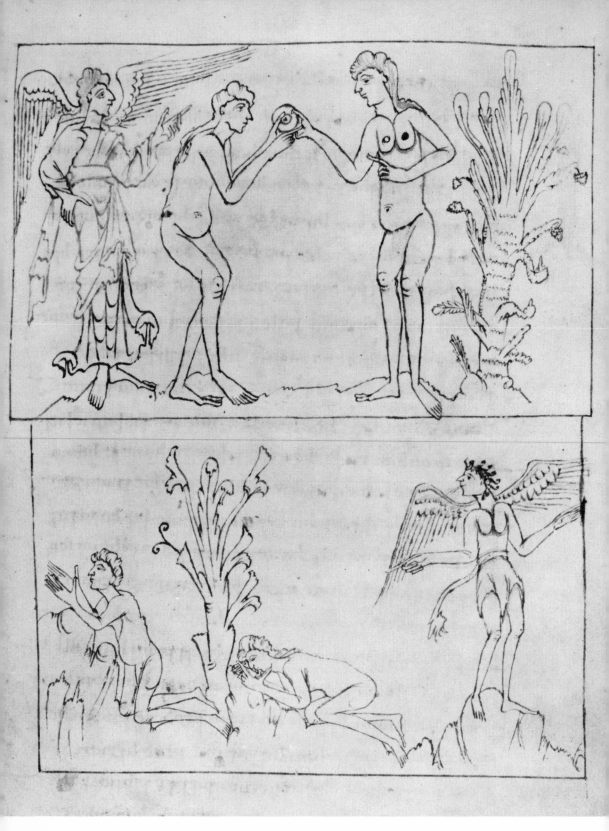

1

Anglo–Saxon Prelude

When Duke William's Norman knights, after a savage day-long struggle, finally defeated King Harold's foot-soldiers near Hastings on 14 October 1066, the English race already possessed a well-developed native literature and a civilization at least as rich and promising as any that, since the fall of Rome, had yet emerged in Northern Europe. CAEDMON, the first English poet whose name we know, is said to have flourished about the year 670; and according to Bede's *Ecclesiastical History*, he was originally a herdsman, but during his later years became a lay-brother at Whitby Abbey. Ashamed because he could not sing to the harp like his fellows, as often as his turn arrived to entertain them, he would rise and leave the hall, until one night he dreamed that he heard a voice that bade him sing of the Creation; and the *Hymn* he composed is quoted by Bede in a Latin rendering. CYNEWULF, the next English poet whose name we know, is a less mysterious figure; several of his poems have escaped destruction; and, although he is no longer credited with *The Dream of the Rood*, the greatest devotional poem of the Anglo-Saxon period, among the works today attributed to him are *Juliana, The Fates of the Apostles, Elene* and *The Ascension*.

The masterpiece of Old English secular verse is unquestionably BEOWULF, an epic poem based on a pre-Christian legend thought to have reached England from the Scandinavian North, and to have been adopted and Christianized, about the beginning of the eighth century, by an Anglo-Saxon Homer. The scenes of the poem are laid in Denmark and Sweden; and the poet relates first how the hero, 'Ecgtheow's son, leader of the Geats', as a young man, faces and slays both the monster Grendel and Grendel's still more monstrous dam beneath the 'bloody and turbid' waters of an enchanted mere.

> Then the sea-wolf dived to the bottom-most depths,
> Swept the prince to the place where she lived,
> So that he, for all his courage, could not
> Wield a weapon; too many wondrous creatures
> Harassed him as he swam; many sea-serpents
> With savage tusks tried to bore through his corslet,
> The monsters molested him. Then the hero saw

(*Opposite*) Adam and Eve; illustration from a manuscript of Caedmon's poem. *c.*1000

I I

That he had entered some loathsome hall –
A vaulted chamber where the floodrush
Could not touch him. A light caught his eye,
A lurid flame flickering brightly.
  Then the brave man saw the sea-monster,
Fearsome, infernal; he whirled his blade,
Swung his arm with all its strength,
And the ring-hilted sword sang a greedy war-song –

(translated Bruce Mitchell, 1968)

Later, as an aged warrior-king, Beowulf kills a treasure-guarding dragon and, having fought his last fight, dies, and his ashes are buried under a royal mound, where the dragon's hoard is also laid to rest.

Two main themes run through *Beowulf*, the heroic and the elegiac. Here, as in other Anglo-Saxon poems, we catch glimpses of a bleak, unfriendly world, where the only source of light and comfort is the high-roofed wooden mead-hall, the meeting-place of the lord and his warriors, who gather round the central hearth to talk and drink and hear the poet's songs. Such an assembly is described by Bede, when he likens human existence to the flight of a bird that enters at one window, dashes wildly across the lighted hall and out again into the surrounding darkness. A sense of doom haunts Anglo-Saxon literature. After 793 the Danes would constantly return, bringing death and desolation; and the English landscape was still strewn with the ruins of abandoned Roman settlements. Thus, in *The Ruin*, we find a poet meditating upon past splendours of an ancient city that 'the strong willed Wyrd' – or Fate – has laid low:

From the raftered woodwork
See, the roof has shed its tiles. To ruin sank the market-place,
Broken up to barrows; many a brave man there,
Glad of yore and gold-bright, gloriously adorned,
Hot with wine and haughty, in war-harness shone . . .

The two most popular short poems of the age, *The Wanderer* and *The Seafarer*, reflect both the Anglo-Saxon poet's passion for the sea and his characteristic melancholy. Thus the author of *The Seafarer* protests that

. . . So haughty of his heart is no hero on the earth . . .
That he was not always yearning unto his seafaring

– yet describes the dreadful hardships he has endured in his battles with the ocean:

All the glee I got me was the gannet's scream,
And the swoughing of the seal, 'stead of mirth of men.

The last great poem that has reached us from the period before the Conquest is *The Battle of Maldon*, the account of a Danish raid

Page from a manuscript
of *Beowulf. c.*1000

on the coast of Essex during the year 991. Others have no doubt
been destroyed. Our knowledge of Old English literature is limited
to a precious handful of manuscripts; but enough remains to show
that Anglo-Saxon poetry, with its bold, dramatic images and its
rich alliterative rhythm, though it owed much to Norse and
Germanic forms, was becoming a strong and independent growth.
English prose, too, had been making powerful strides. THE
VENERABLE BEDE (*c.* 672–735), the greatest scholar of his day,
customarily employed Latin; but when King Alfred, towards the

end of the ninth century, turned his vigorous mind to learning, he commissioned the translation from Latin of both Bede's *Historia Ecclesiastica* and Orosius's world-history, into which he interpolated passages of his own prose, describing the northern voyages of the intrepid adventurers, Othere and Wulfstan. At the same time, Alfred codified the existing laws, and is thought to have inspired the redaction of *The Anglo-Saxon Chronicle.* Latin, he wrote in the preface to his version of Gregory's *Cura Pastoralis*, was a language few had mastered; but many of his countrymen could read 'Englisc'. The long process by which 'Englisc' became English and the new tongue an unequalled literary medium, will be the subject of the following pages.

(*Above*) King Alfred's vision of St Cuthbert; from a 12th-century manuscript.

(*Opposite*) The Venerable Bede writing his book and presenting it to the Bishop of Lindisfarne; from a 12th-century copy of Bede's *Life of St Cuthbert.*

2

The Age of Chaucer

For some two centuries after the Norman Conquest, the English genius remained in servitude. French was the language of the Court and of the Anglo-Norman aristocracy; Latin, that of the Church and of the learned and official classes; while English was reduced to the standing of a 'vulgar tongue', spoken only by the common people. Yet, like the English themselves, it possessed an obstinate strength; and, early in the thirteenth century, a devoted priest named LAYAMON, who lived at the Worcestershire town of Arley, and who was both a poet and a patriot, composed a poem chronicling his countrymen's 'noble deeds', as exemplified in the Arthurian legends, and tracing the origins of the ancient British kingdom back to the Trojan hero, Brutus. His *Brut*, derived from

The coronation of King Harold: detail from the Bayeux Tapestry.

a Norman poem, the *Roman de Brut*, illustrates the gradual development of Anglo-Saxon alliterative style into Middle-English
rhyming verse. Layamon loved books, and had a genuine interest
in the art of literature:

> May the Lord be merciful to him!
> Pen he took with fingers
> And wrote on book-skin;
> And the true words
> Set together . . .

The *Brut*, however, has an historical and philological rather than
a literary value; and more popularly attractive works are the
spirited debate between *The Owl and the Nightingale*, written about
1200, and such early metrical romances as *Havelok the Dane*, produced between 1280 and 1300. But over a hundred-and-fifty years
had passed since the appearance of *The Brut* before three great
poets – the author of *Sir Gawain and the Green Knight*, John Langland
and Geoffrey Chaucer – appeared upon the English scene.

Poets of the Fourteenth Century

By any standards that we apply to it, SIR GAWAIN AND THE
GREEN KNIGHT is one of the greatest early narrative poems in any
European language. The anonymous poet, who is thought to have
worked some time after 1350, was a contemporary of Geoffrey
Chaucer; but whereas Chaucer's works, given a little practice and
occasional reference to a glossary, are not difficult to understand,
Sir Gawain, for the purposes of the ordinary reader must be translated into modern English.[1] While Chaucer spoke the tongue that
would eventually become our own, based on the culture of London, Oxford and Cambridge, the author of *Sir Gawain* was
evidently a native of north-western England, from which he
derived both the dialect he used and the wild landscapes that he
represented. The London poet, moreover, reflects the changing
conditions of fourteenth-century English life. Although he had
inherited many chivalric traditions – among others, the doctrine
of 'courtly love' – he often dared to laugh at chivalry; he inhabited
a world that had begun to lose its sense of awe. His Canterbury
pilgrims are fond of wonderful tales; but there is nothing mysterious about their personalities. Chaucer was a realist and a
brilliant social satirist; a middle-class man of affairs, he had
travelled widely abroad and had a vision of existence that might
almost be described as cosmopolitan.

His fellow poet, by comparison, was a provincial man of genius,
steeped in the chivalric spirit of the Middle Ages, for whom the

---

[1] The excellent translation, from which extracts are quoted below, was made
by Brian Stone and faithfully reproduces the original metre (Penguin Classics,
1959).

court of King Arthur, and the moral code it symbolised, must have seemed very much more real than the existing court at West-minster, which, unlike Chaucer, an important officer of the Crown, he may never, or very seldom, have entered. The back-ground of the opening passages is Camelot, where Arthur, with his 'loyal lords' and 'liegemen peerless', is celebrating Christmas-tide. They are interrupted by the sudden appearance of the mon-strous Green Knight, immensely tall, proportionately broad and massive. 'His vesture was all vivid green'; he is green-bearded and green-haired; and he immediately utters a fantastic challenge, offering to stand up to the blow that any Arthurian champion cares to deal him, provided that, in a year's time, 'I shall have leave to launch a return blow unchecked'. Gawain accepts the challenge, and expeditiously decapitates him. 'Yet the fellow did not fall, nor falter one whit', lifts his severed head (which opens its mouth to remind Gawain of their pact) and 'rushed out at the hall door . . .'

The remainder of the poem describes Gawain's heroic efforts to keep the dreadful promise he has made, and how he rides on his magnificent courser, Gringolet, through the rugged hills of northern England:

> He had death-struggles with dragons, did battle with wolves,
> Warred with wild trolls that dwelt among the crags . . .
> And ogres that panted after him on the highfells . . .
>   Worse was the winter,
> When the cold, clear water cascaded from the clouds
> And froze before it could fall to the fallow earth.
> Half-slain by the sleet, he slept in his armour
> Night after night among the naked rocks,
> Where the cold streams ran clattering from the crests above . . .

Eventually Gawain reaches a castle, a finely decorative piece of fourteenth-century architecture; and there he is exposed to a very different type of trial, in the shape of a beautiful and seductive chatelaine, who makes a determined attack upon his honour. The poet's account of the attempted seduction is at once vividly described and subtly humorous. Gawain refuses to break the chivalric code – not only does he value his own chastity, but the lady's husband has befriended him – and rides away from the warm, luxurious castle, across yet another terrifying wilderness, where

> Under the high clouds, ugly mists
> Merged damply with the moors and melted on the
>   mountains . . .

(*Opposite*) Sir Gawain beheads the Green Knight, watched by King Arthur and Queen Guinevere; from a late 14th-century manuscript.

– until he draws rein at the giant's strong-hold, the mysterious Green Chapel, a cavern dug into the flank of a hillock, possibly an ancient burial-mound. As they have arranged, the Green Knight

then deals him the return blow. But Gawain, wearing a magic girdle with which the lady has presented him – she is, in fact, the Green Knight's consort – triumphantly survives the blow; and the opponents part as friends. Gawain rides quietly home to Camelot. Though he admits that he is ashamed to have accepted the girdle –

> This my bane and debasement, the burden I bear
> For being caught by cowardice and covetousness

– he has, for the most part, preserved his reputation as a truly Christian knight, an example of Continence and Courtesy, Liberality, Loving-kindness 'and Piety, the surpassing virtue'.

The complex symbolism of *Sir Gawain and the Green Knight*

The poet and Pearl, divided by a stream; from a late 14th-century manuscript.

mingles Christian with certain pagan elements; the Green Man
figures in primitive fertility cults; and some anthropologists regard
Gawain himself as a remote descendant of the sun-god. Whatever
the origins of the legend may be, it was transformed by the unknown medieval poet into an extraordinarily rich and varied
poem. Like the Anglo-Saxon bards, he employed alliterative verse,
but inserted a short-lined rhyming refrain at the end of each
strophe. He is also frequently credited with the authorship of
Pearl, a touching allegorical lament for the poet's lost daughter:

> So round, so royal wherever ranged,
> So sweetly small, so wondrous smooth . . .
> I placed my Pearl apart, supreme.
> I lost it – in a garden – alas!
> Through grass to ground 'twas gone from me.

> (Translated by Sir Israel Gollancz, 1921)

But, although both have a gift for evocative imagery – 'I stood as
gentle as hawk in hell', writes the author of *Pearl*, describing how
he had received his mystic vision of the dead child – there seems
otherwise little resemblance between these two unknown fourteenth-century poets.

WILLIAM LANGLAND (*c*.1330–*c*.1400), to whom *The Vision of
Piers Plowman* was first attributed during the fourteenth century, is
thought to have been born in Worcestershire, near Malvern. One
early account makes him the son of a gentleman named Eustace de
Rokayle; and, if that be true, he was probably a bastard, the
offspring of a peasant bondswoman; which would accord with
what we know of his life and with his attitude towards his fellows.
He seems to have received a respectable education; but, despite
the fact that he presently entered the Church, he remained in
Minor Orders. As a young man, he tells us, he visited London,
where he observed the pleasure of the world and indulged his
carnal appetites. He soon repented, however; and much of his
adult life appears to have been passed wandering around the
country, obsessed by his visions of Virtue and Vice, and of the
proper relationship between Man and God. Later he married –
marriage was not forbidden to a clerk in Minor Orders; and, with
his wife, Kit, and his daughter, Calote, shared a miserable London
lodging. Langland was always poor, sometimes apparently close
to destitution. He loved the poor among whom he had dwelt on
his wanderings:

> I have lived long in the land; Long Will men call me,
> But I never found full charity before or after,
> Men are merciful to mendicants and poor folk . . .

And in his great poem he became the self-appointed champion of
the fourteenth-century poor folk, who, although illiterate, had

learned many of his verses by heart. During the summer of 1381, when Wat Tyler led a revolt of the English peasantry against their oppressive feudal overlords, the courageous hedge-priest John Ball (afterwards hung, drawn and quartered) in a versified message that he addressed to the rebels reminded them of Langland's *Vision*. Yet Langland himself was no revolutionary poet; poverty and injustice were merely symptoms of the general turpitude of mankind. His object was not to change a system of government, but to inflame his readers with a true sense of the duties that they owed God; through which, he hoped, they might achieve the Good Life and restore on earth the reign of peace and order. Not that he spares corruption – the worldly pride of the priesthood or the hypocrisy of pilgrims, who journey to a holy shrine with their concubines behind them riding pillion; or the greed and cruelty of prosperous landlords. But, like Bunyan's hero, it is salvation he chiefly seeks; and Piers Plowman is the type of simple man, who suffers not only from poverty and hunger, but from an inextinguishable thirst for righteousness.

Piers Plowman is a dream-poem, which opens on a Shropshire hill:

> In a summer season when the sun was softest,
> Shrouded in a smock, in shepherd's clothing . . .
> I went through this world to witness wonders.
> On a May morning on a Malvern hillside
> I saw strange sights like scenes of Faerie . . .
> By the bank of a brook in a broad meadow.
> As I lay and leaned, and looked upon the water
> I slumbered and slept, so sweetly it murmured.

First, he beholds 'a fair field full of folk', which represents the world as we know it situated betwixt Heaven and Hell, 'Truth's dwelling' and the Devil's kingdom, and speaks with a series of symbolic figures, who gradually become more numerous. These abstractions, which include three potent personages, 'Do Well', 'Do Bet' and 'Do Best', at least from a modern point of view tend to overcrowd the narrative. Part of the poem had evidently been composed as early as 1377; but Langland wrote over a period of many years, possibly until he died; and the result is an extraordinarily intricate and, at times, confusing structure, a spiritual autobiography into which the poet has crammed the experience of a whole life, all his fears and his visionary longings, all his moral indignation and all his gift for human sympathy. His verse is uneven; his rhythms are irregular. He had very little of the urbane distinction of Chaucer, or of the courtly nicety we find in *Sir Gawain and the Green Knight*; his use of the traditional alliterative four-beat mode is a great deal less accomplished. But, besides being a great imaginative writer, he was that rare phenomenon, a genuinely popular poet, who, although he also wrote for the

Late 14th-century manuscript of *Piers Plowman*.

lettered and learned, spoke to the common people of his own day in terms they could immediately understand, and that will continue to be understood by his readers so long as there are rich and poor:

> The needy are our neighbours, if we note rightly;
> As prisoners in cells, or poor folk in hovels,
> Charged with children and overcharged by landlords,
> What they may spare in spinning they spend on rental,
> On milk, or on meal to make porridge
> To still the sobbing the children at mealtime.
> Also they themselves suffer much hunger.

> They have woe in winter time, and wake at mid-night
> To rise and rock the cradle at the bedside,
> To card and to comb, to darn clouts and wash them,
> To rub and to reel and put rushes on the paving.
> The woe of these women who dwell in hovels,
> Is too sad to speak of or to say in rhyme

(From *The Vision of Piers Plowman, newly rendered into modern English*, by Henry W. Wells, 1959.)

GEOFFREY CHAUCER (*c.*1340–*c.*1400) possessed the rare distinction of being both a great poet and a highly successful civil servant. Born in the City of London, son of a prosperous vintner who had once been attached to the court of King Edward III, by 1357 he had joined the household of the King's daughter-in-law, the consort of Prince Lionel. In 1359 he accompanied the English army on an expedition against France, and there was captured and held prisoner until he could collect a ransom, towards which the King himself contributed no less than £16. Five years later, as a valet of the King's household, he received a life-pension; and, in 1368, Prince Lionel having died, he was transferred to the service of Edward's next son, John of Gaunt, the Duke of Lancaster.

Between 1370 and 1386, Chaucer undertook a variety of important diplomatic missions. Thus he made an official journey to Italy towards the end of 1372, where he visited Genoa, Pisa and Florence, and remained for over ten months; in 1377 he was despatched to Flanders and France; and in 1378 he returned to France and, soon afterwards, set forth on another errand to Bernabo Visconti, Duke of Milan. His activities were well-rewarded – not only with such minor privileges as the right to demand a daily jug of wine from the pantry of the royal butler, but with the comptrollership of the duties on wools and skins and, later, the comptrollership of the Petty Customs. In 1386 he became a knight of the shire for Kent. But that same year he suffered a temporary disgrace, lost both his comptrollerships and was obliged to borrow money. In 1389, however, he re-entered the civil service and received several lucrative appointments; and, although in 1399, on the accession of King Henry IV, he addressed a poetic 'Compleynt' to the sovereign, declaring that his purse was empty – at which Henry immediately doubled the pension that his predecessor, King Richard II, had granted him in 1394 – the closing years of Chaucer's existence seem to have been calm and cheerful. Towards the end, he took the lease of a house amid a garden adjoining Westminster Abbey; and there, no doubt, the poet died.

Of Chaucer's private life we have comparatively few records. About 1374 he married a certain Philippa, thought to have been one of the Queen's ladies, who died in 1387, and had a son, possibly illegitimate, the 'litel Lowis', for whose benefit he pre-

Portrait of Chaucer from
the Ellesmere edition of
the Canterbury Tales,
1400–10.

pared his learned *Treatise on the Astrolabe*. 'From the general tenour
of his writings,' observes a late-Victorian biographer, 'it must be
feared that he was neither very constant nor very happy.' For this
bold suggestion we have no solid evidence, except that in 1380 he
appears to have been accused of abducting a woman named
Cecilia Champaigne, who afterwards agreed to drop all legal
proceedings again him, 'whether on account of my carrying off
(*de raptu meo*) or any other cause which I have or may have had . . .'
That Chaucer was fond of women, his poems clearly show. He was
also devoted to his books – which, he informs us, he was always
reluctant to put down – and loved flowers, particularly the common daisy, the 'flower of flowers', with its delicately rose-tipped
petals.

Such was the man who, in addition to his minor works – *The*

Boccaccio (bottom right) takes down a story; from a French edition of *The Decameron*, *c*.1467.

Romaunt of the Rose, a translation from the French; *The Book of the Duchesse; The Parlement of Foules; The Hous of Fame; The Legend of Good Women*, and a quantity of brief lyrics – produced two great masterpieces, *Troilus and Criseyde* and the even more absorbing *Canterbury Tales*. Oddly enough, though Chaucer was one of the most original of English poets, he was also among the most derivative. His contemporaries, like the contemporaries of Shakespeare, did not object to literary borrowing; and it was Chaucer's task, by following French and Italian models, to bring English poetry into line with the civilization of early Renaissance Europe. On his travels abroad he had probably met both Petrarch (1304–74), first and noblest of the Italian humanists, and Boccaccio (1313–75), biographer of Dante and prince of storytellers, on whose *Filostrato* he did not hesitate to found his own *Troilus and Criseyde*. He seldom invented a story – with possibly two exceptions, none of his *Canterbury Tales* has a plot that he had himself conceived; his originality lay in his brilliant rehandling of any story that attracted him, and in his genius for imparting to old material an air of spring-time gaiety and freshness. During the age of Dryden, Chaucer was already acclaimed as the father of modern English poetry; and Pope, when he ascended Dryden's throne, would praise its previous occupant by announcing that Chaucer and

Dryden had performed very much the same task; each had emerged in a period of literary chaos to lay the foundations of a new poetic order.

Although, when he wrote *Troilus and Criseyde*, Chaucer was following Boccaccio's lead, he regarded the three main personages of the ancient legend from a very different point of view. He is less smartly ribald than Boccaccio, but far more intuitive and sympathetic. For the first time in English verse or prose – the Father of English Poetry might also be described as the father of the modern novel – we see a writer attempting to portray, not a succession of well-established types, but a group of individual human characters. His protagonists are shown developing and changing under the influence of their emotional vicissitudes; and their confidant, Pandarus, who abets their unlawful love, is a magnificent piece of serio-comic portraiture. Chaucer's attitude towards the relationship of the sexes would appear to have been based partly on the idea of 'courtly love', with its abstruse system of platonic dalliance and complicated code of honour, partly on his empirical understanding of his fellow men and women. Troilus is the visionary romantic; Pandarus, the good-humoured cynic; and it is the voice of Pandarus that usually prevails. While Troilus submits to the omnipotent power of love, Pandarus urges he should face the facts and, if possible, accept them bravely:

> For thy tak herte, and thenk, right as a knight,
> Thourgh love is broken alday every lawe,
> Kyth[1] now sumwhat thy corage and thy might,
> Have mercy on thy-self, for any awe.
> Let not this wrecched wo thine herte gnaw,
> But manly set the worlde on six and sevene;
> And, if thou dye a martir, go to hevene.

[1] Display. (ed. Skeat; 617–23)

Chaucer's irony does not preclude tenderness; and his cynicism is always friendly. *The Canterbury Tales* reveal not only his knowledge of mankind, and the affection it inspires in him, but his sense of humour and his love of physical grace. The collection is thought to have been begun about 1387, during the period of official obscurity that lasted from 1386 to 1389; and again Chaucer was emulating Boccaccio, whose *Decameron* had been composed between 1348 and 1353. His choice of characters is interesting. The poet had spent much of his life in the precincts of the English court; yet his personages, apart from the Knight, the Squire and the Franklin – and the Knight himself is no military aristocrat, but a wandering mercenary soldier – belong to the middle or the lower classes. As we survey them, we feel that the Age of Chivalry is already passing, and will very soon have vanished. These are commonplace people, notable less for their birth and honours than for the charm that the poet discovers in them as ordinary human beings. Besides Chaucer himself, the cavalcade that sets out from London to St Thomas's shrine at Canterbury includes the *Knight*, his handsome son, the *Squire* and the *Yeoman* who accompanies them; the stately *Prioress*, her attendant *Nun* and *Three Priests*; a *Monk*, a *Friar* and a poor *Parson*, the only member of the gathering to whom the poet gives unstinted praise; a *Merchant*, and a *Man of Lawe*; the *Franklin*, a prosperous land-owner; five craftsmen, the *Haberdasher*, *Carpenter*, the *Webbe* (or weaver) the *Dyer*, the *Tapicier* (an upholsterer) and the *Cook*, whom they have brought along; a *Shipman*, a *Doctor of Physic*, a *Miller* and a *Ploughman* (brother of the virtuous Parson); four sinister personages, the *Manciple* (steward to a learned college), the *Reeve* (a rich lord's crafty bailiff), the *Summoner* (attached to an ecclesiastical court) and the fantastic *Pardoner*; finally, the richly caparisoned *Wife of Bath*, and the threadbare *Clerk of Oxford*, whose devotion to learning is only equalled by the poor Parson's love of good works.

In repeating their stories, Chaucer is well aware that he may perhaps offend a courtly audience. But a poet, he insists, who records another man's tale, must employ the actual words he used, however villainous the speaker's language:

The Wife of Bath; from Caxton's 1492 edition.

> Or elles he moot[1] telle his tale untrewe,
> Or feyne thing[2], or finde wordes newe . . .
> Eek Plato seith, who-so that can him rede,
> The wordes mote be cosin to the dede

[1] must   [2] invent things.   (735–6; 741–2)

He also apologizes for not presenting his characters in their hereditary social order; and once the Knight has told his chivalric tale (borrowed from Boccaccio) of Palamon and Arcite, the huge, uncouth Miller, who has meanwhile got drunk, and who is already reeling in his saddle, insists he should be heard next. The *Miller's Tale* is an exuberant piece of Rabelaisian anecdotage; and it is immediately followed by the *Reeve's Tale*, which proves no less indecent though a little less amusing. These sudden transitions are essential to Chaucer's method; but it is in the portraits he draws, and in the series of vivid details with which he builds them up, that his realism seems most effective. Nothing escapes his eye. The Knight, recently returned from his travels, is wearing a fustian doublet that shows the rust-stains of his armour:

> Of fustian he wered a gipoun,
> Al bismotered with his habergeoun . . .

                                                    (75–6)

As for the Miller, he has a wart on his nose –

> . . . And ther-on stood a tuft of heres,
> Reed as the bristles of a sowes eres . . .

                                                    (555–6)

But to some of his miniature portraits Chaucer also lends an

Here bigynneth the Prioresses tale

Ther was in Asye in a greet citee
Amonges cristene folk a Jewerye
Sustened by a lord of that contree
For foul usure and lucre of vileynye
Hateful to Crist and to his compaignye
And thurgh this strete men myghte ride or wende
For it was free and open at eyther ende

ironic charm, as in his sketch of the gay fastidious Prioress:

> And she was cleped madame Eglentyne.
> Ful well she song the service divyne,
> Entuned in hir nose ful semely;
> And Frensh she spak ful faire and fetisly,[1]
> After the scole of Stratford atte Bowe,
> For Frensh of Paris was to hir unknowe
> At mete wel y-taught was she with-alle;
> She leet no morsel from hir lippes falle,
> Ne wette hir fingres in hir sauce depe . . .
> Ful semely after hir mete she raughte,[2]
> And sikerly[3] she was of greet disport,
> And ful plesaunt, and amiable of port,
> And peyned hir to countrefete chere
> Of court, and been estatlich[4] of manere . . .

[1] elegantly; [2] reached; [3] truly; [4] stately.   (121–9; 136–40)

The fourteenth century was a period of bright colours, splendid clothes and lavish ornament. Even the Knight's yeoman, 'clad in cote and hood of greene', carries a sheaf of 'peacock-arrows' carefully tucked away beneath his belt; the Prioress displays a coral chaplet, 'gauded al with grene', and a golden brooch –

> On which ther was first write a croned A,
> And after, *Amor vincit omnia*

(161–2)

The procession that crosses Chaucer's pages is as bright as the figures of a medieval manuscript. But among the devout pilgrims

there are ominous exceptions – the fat sporting Monk, whose bald
head steams in the sun; the wanton Friar; the piratical Shipman,
who is an occasional pirate and very often drowns his captives; the
lustful, scorbutic Summoner, who keeps a concubine he is not
averse from sharing; and the modish, long-haired Pardoner,
either a eunuch or a homosexual, bearing a cargo of false relics –
'pigges bones' and the like – with which he imposes on the poor.
These are the leeches of medieval society; Chaucer does not forget
the corruption of the world in which he lived, particularly the
corruption of the Church. But he was by no means a simple
satirist; the men and women he depicts are never rudimentary
types of good or evil. He appreciates both their individual complexity and their marvellous diversity. He takes them for what
they are. Chaucer, once Petrarch's disciple, was the first of English
literary humanists, and the earliest poet whose imaginative grasp
of experience was matched by his command of language.

The Canterbury Tales (which Chaucer left unfinished at his death)
throw many sidelights upon the poet's personal character – his
wit, his gaiety and his sensuous love of beauty, which often tempers
his delight in bawdry. Alison, of *The Miller's Tale*, a gay young
woman married to an elderly and superstitious carpenter, is a
thoroughly seductive heroine:

> Fair was this yonge wyf, and ther-with-al
> As any wesele[1] hir body gent and small.
> A ceynt[2] she werede barred[3] al of silk,
> A barmclooth[4] eek as whyt as morne milk
> Up-on hir lendes,[5] full of many a gore,
> Whyt was hir smok and brouded al bifore . . .
> Her filet brood of silk, and set ful hye:
> And sikerly[6] she hadde a likerous[7] yë . . .
> She was ful more blisful on to see
> Than is the new pere-jonette tree[8] . . .
> There nis no man so wys, that coude thenche,[9]
> So gay a popelote[10], or swich a wenche   (3233–8;
>
> [1] weasel; [2] girdle; [3] striped; [4] apron;   3243–4;
> [5] loins; [6] certainly; [7] lecherous eye;   3247–8;
> [8] an early-ripe pear; [9] imagine; [10] darling.   3253–4)

Chaucer assures us, nevertheless, that he himself is a quiet and
modest man; and *The Prologue to Sir Thopas* contains an interesting
self-portrait. After the lady-like Prioress has concluded her tale,
the Host cheerfully accosts him:

> And seyde thus, 'what man artow?' quod he;
> Thou lokest as thou woldest finde an hare,
> For ever up-on the ground I see thee stare.
> Approche near, and loke up merily,
> Now war yow, sirs, and lat this man have place;
> He in the waast[1] is shape as well as I;
> This were a popet[2] in an arm t'enbrace

(*Opposite*) Chaucer reads
aloud from *Troilus and
Criseyde*; early 15th-
century manuscript.

> For any womman, smal and fair of face.
> He semeth elvish[3] by his contenaunce,
> For un-to no wight dooth he daliaunce.

[1] waist; [2] doll; [3] absent-minded.   (1885–94)

Convivial hosts have customarily large waists; and the implication that Chaucer, during middle age, was a somewhat stout person is confirmed by the portrait in an illuminated manuscript that shows him reading his poems aloud, a short white-haired figure with a small forked beard. On this occasion, urged by the Host, he begins to recite *The Tale of Thopas*, a delightful parody of the popular chivalric romance. But after he has got through less than thirty-two stanzas, the Host implores him to desist – 'no more of this, for goddes dignitee' – and Chaucer feels obliged to change his tune and relate the long prose *Tale of Melibeus*, not a very worthy substitute. No doubt, that done, he continued to stare at the ground, yet dart quick sidelong glances at his fellow travellers, until they had passed beneath the gates of Canterbury.

The End of the Middle Ages

Chaucer had had no serious rivals, and left behind no worthy heirs. His contemporary, JOHN GOWER (*c.*1330–1408), though much esteemed during his lifetime, was a learned and energetic versifier – he has been called 'the fourteenth-century Augustan' – rather than a truly gifted poet. As a member of the landed gentry, he very often wrote in French or Latin; and his most important English work, to which he gave a Latin title, *Confessio Amantis*, is a collection of over a hundred stories, for the most part somewhat slow-moving, all more or less illustrative of the power of human love. He had little of Chaucer's easy cynicism, nothing of his grace and gaiety. JOHN LYDGATE, who re-told the legends of Troy and Thebes, and THOMAS HOCCLEVE, author of a vivid autobiographical *Complaint*, seem to have flourished between 1370 and 1450. But they are comparatively uninspiring writers; and, during the later fifteenth century, architecture was the only art that made any significant progress upon English soil. In the later seventeenth century, prefacing Cowley's works, Sir John Denham speaks of the sad condition into which poetry had fallen after Chaucer's disappearance:

> Old Chaucer, like the morning Star
> To us discovers day from far,
> His light those Mists and Clouds dissolv'd,
> Which our dark Nation long involv'd;
> But he descending to the shades,
> Darkness again the Age invades.
> Next (like Aurora) Spencer rose,
> Whose purple blush the day foreshows . . .

A company of pilgrims;
from John Lydgate's
Story of Thebes.

Denham exaggerated; during the reign of Henry VIII, at least
three memorable poets, Skelton, Wyatt and Surrey, helped to
lighten the prevailing darkness; but it is true that the period of the
Wars of the Roses, which intermittently disturbed the kingdom
for thirty years, from 1455 to 1486, was, on the whole, a barren
literary age. It produced a series of stirring popular ballads and
some melodious lyrics, both devotional and secular, but no
great imaginative English verse; and the modern historian who
picks through fifteenth-century prose returns home with a fairly
meagre haul. Strangely enough, the invention of printing – WIL-
LIAM CAXTON (*c.* 1422–*c.* 1491), having acquired the art in the
Low Countries, set up his wooden press at Westminster towards
the end of 1476 – did not precipitate a flood of new writing; the
first English book ever to be published, *The Recuyell of the Historyes
of Troye* (printed in Bruges, a year before Caxton arrived in West-

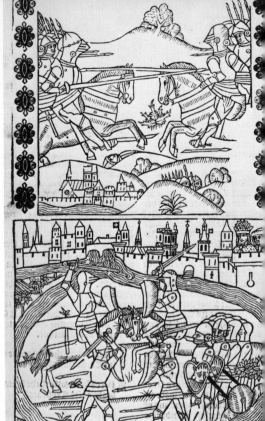

(Above left) The earliest-known representation of Caxton's printing press.

(Above right) Malory's *Morte d'Arthur*; woodcuts of Henry VIII.

minister) was a translation from the French; while the English authors he chose – Chaucer, Gower, and Lydgate – belonged to an earlier generation, except for SIR THOMAS MALORY (*d.*1471); and Malory's famous *La Morte d'Arthur* was itself largely a compilation and masterly reorganization of previous Arthurian texts. Some light on the general barrenness of the age is thrown by a reading of THE PASTON LETTERS (*c.*1421–1503), the private correspondence of a landowning Norfolk family with their kinsmen, agents and retainers. Illuminating as they are from an historical point of view, the cumulative impression these letters make is predominantly grim. Life for the Pastons was an unremitting conflict, in which the tragic dramas of the Wars of the Roses appear as incidental episodes. The Pastons were harsh materialists, inhabiting a dangerous world; and, although among their records a bill survives showing that they occasionally purchased books, they seem to have felt not the smallest interest in contemporary arts and learning. Nor had they the slightest appreciation of beauty; all that concerned them was the security of their own existence, and the constant effort to survive. They give brief accounts of the momentous happenings of the day; but nothing that could possibly be called patriotism coloured their attitude towards society.

3

The English Renaissance

Pre-Elizabethan Verse and Prose

Petrarch, Chaucer's admired acquaintance, had gazed on the splendours of ancient Rome as early as the year 1337; but the Renaissance did not reach England until the beginning of the sixteenth century; and at first its influence was vague and hesitant. When Henry VIII ascended the English throne in 1509, Leonardo da Vinci was already fifty-seven, Michelangelo thirty-four, and Titian thirty-two. Da Vinci and Michelangelo were famous artists; Titian had just executed a series of frescoes with his close contemporary, Giorgione. Yet, in its feeling for the arts, early sixteenth-century England still lagged behind the rest of Europe. The only great painter who appeared at the Tudor court was a German artist, the younger Hans Holbein. Architecture and sculpture had made very little headway; and Nonsuch, King Henry VIII's favourite palace, was a huge and ornate, but somewhat tasteless structure, covered with heraldic gegaws, and generally loaded with superfluous detail. Poets were few, the most distinguished being JOHN SKELTON (1460–1529), SIR THOMAS WYATT (1503?–42) and HENRY HOWARD, EARL OF SURREY (1517?–47).

A celebrated scholar at Oxford, Skelton was one of the tutors

(*Above*) Bas-relief portrait of Henry VIII.

(*Below*) Nonsuch; Henry VIII's huge and ornate palace, also beloved by Queen Elizabeth, who appears in the foreground.

C Here after
foloweth the

boke of Phyllyp Sparowe
compyled by mayſter
Skelton Poete
Laureate.

who superintended the education of the future Henry VIII, and, as his recompense, was granted the living of Diss in Norfolk, where he disregarded his tedious clerical duties and led a carefree literary life. Though his lyrical poems are most often quoted today, for example, his lament over *Philip Sparrow*, a tame bird murdered by a cat, and his affectionate address *To Mistress Margery Wentworth*:

> With margerain gentle,
> The flower of goodlihead,
> Embroidered the mantle
> Is of your maidenhead.
> Plainly I cannot glose;
> Ye be, as I divine,
> The pretty primrose,
> The goodly columbine.
>
> Benign, courteous, and meek
> With wordes well devised;
> In you, who list to seek,
> Be virtues well comprised.
> With margerain gentle,
> The flower of goodlihead
> Embroidered the mantle
> Is of your maidenhead.

his bent was primarily satirical. His uninhibited account of the *Tunning of Eleanor Rummyng* (which caused Pope to describe him as 'beastly Skelton') is a magnificent piece of Rabelaisian narrative; and, later, turning to political subjects, he dared to attack the puissant Cardinal Wolsey, Henry VIII's Lord Chancellor from 1515 to 1529, in *Colin Clout* and *Speke Parrot*. Wolsey, who had at first tolerated these savage lampoons, eventually struck back. Skelton fled to sanctuary at Westminster, where he died in 1529, a year before the Cardinal. A man who loved words, and often employed them with vigorous originality, Skelton belonged in spirit neither to the Renaissance nor to the Middle Ages. He was an individualist, whose extraordinary flow of language reflects his strong and stubborn nature.

Both Wyatt and Surrey, on the other hand, were court-poets; and Wyatt, who was a widely travelled man, had felt the exhilarating influence of Renaissance civilization. It was Wyatt who brought the sonnet to England. At his best, he is a highly original sonneteer and a gifted lyricist. Said once to have been the lover of Anne Boleyn before her marriage to the sovereign, like the Elizabethan sonneteers he was much preoccupied with the themes of hopeless love and corroding sexual jealousy:

(*Above*) Sir Thomas Wyatt; portrait by Holbein.

> They flee from me, that sometime did me seek,
> With naked foot stalking in my chamber:
> I have seen them gentle, tame, and meek,
> That now are wild, and do not once remember,
> That some time they have put themselves in danger
> To take bread at my hand; and now they range
> Busily seeking with a continual change.
>
> Thanked be Fortune, it hath been otherwise
> Twenty times better; but once in special,
> In thin array, after a pleasant guise,
> When her loose gown from her shoulders did fall,
> And she me caught in her arms long and small,
> Therewith all sweetly did me kiss,
> And softly said, 'Dear heart, how like you this?' . . .

(*Below*) Henry Howard, Earl of Surrey; portrait of 1546.

He also produced some delightful songs evidently written to be set to music:

> My lute, awake! perform the last
> Labour that thou and I shall waste,
>   And end that I have now begun;
> For when this song is said and past,
>   My lute, be still, for I have done . . .

Whereas Wyatt has an Italian sweetness and fluency, Surrey's efforts to poeticize the English language, and attune it to Renaissance literary modes, seem a good deal more laborious. His translation of Virgil's *Aeneid*, in which he was the first English poet to employ blank verse – 'a strange meter', he calls it – appeared about 1554. But by temperament, he was a man of the Middle Ages, 'a mirror of knighthood' and the chivalric followers of an idealised mistress, entitled 'The Fair Geraldine'. After the king's marriage to Jane Seymour, Surrey, a member of the opposing faction, headed by his father, the Duke of Norfolk, was disgraced and temporarily imprisoned within the walls of Windsor Castle –

> Where each sweet place returns a taste full sour,
> The large green courts where we wont to rove,
> With eyes cast up unto the Maiden's tower,
> And easy sighs such as folk draw in love . . .

Surrey was one of the King's last victims; the Seymours, a week before Henry's death, eventually brought him down. Accused with his father of high treason, he was executed on 19 January 1547.

Another eminent writer whose death the King decreed was the earliest and most distinguished of English classic humanists, Sir Thomas More (1478–1535), canonized four hundred years after his execution as a martyr of the Roman Catholic Church. Having spent two years at Oxford, he became, before he had reached his twentieth birthday, the friend and associate of Erasmus. A brilliant lawyer, he rose in the royal service and succeeded Cardinal Wolsey as Lord Chancellor; and, during his tenure of the chancellorship, which lasted from 1529 to 1532, he established a high reputation for integrity and industry. The King's divorce from Katherine of Aragon, however, caused him to resign his office; and in 1534, when he had refused to deny the supremacy of the Pope, he was cast into the Tower of London. During the second year of his imprisonment, he was deprived both of his library and of paper, pen and ink; whereat he closed the windows of his cell, exclaiming 'When the wares are gone, and the tools are taken away, it is time to shut up shop'. He was beheaded on 6 July 1535.

More's greatest work, his *Utopia*, of which the Latin text was first published abroad in 1516 – the English translation of the text, the work of Ralph Robynson, appeared in 1551 – is the elaborately detailed account of a Platonic commonwealth, said to have been discovered by the imaginary traveller, Raphael Hythlodaye, who had penetrated its island home. Utopia is the seat of a perfectly civilized community. Here peace reigns, and every form of modern injustice has been banished from the social system. None is unemployed, and none is over-worked. During his own official career, More himself had sometimes prosecuted heretics; but the happy citizens of Utopia enjoy complete religious toleration. Their ruler, we are told, abhors violence. As soon as he gained the throne

(*Opposite*) The Island of Utopia; frontispiece to More's *Utopia*, published at Louvain in 1516.

he made a decree that it should be lawful for every man to favour and follow what religion he would, and that he might do the best he could to bring others to his opinion, so that he did it peaceably, gently, quietly, and soberly, without hasty and contentious rebuking and inveighing

VTOPIAE INSVLAE FIGVRA

Sir Thomas More at home in Chelsea; drawing by Holbein.

against others . . . This law did King Eutopus make not only for the maintenance of peace, which he saw through continual contention and mortal hatred utterly extinguished: but also because he thought this decree should make for the furtherance of religion.

Personally, More's way of life seems to have followed the Utopian pattern. At his country house overlooking the Thames, he was the centre of a harmonious and devoted household; and Holbein's portrait of More among his family, in a finely panelled and elegantly furnished room, is one of the most delightful of early English conversation-pieces.

4

The Elizabethan Age

Henry VIII died in 1547; and, after the brief and difficult reigns of her half-brother, Edward VI, and her half-sister, Queen Mary, in 1558 Queen Elizabeth ascended the throne, which she continued to occupy until 1603. When we speak of the Elizabethan Age, however, as a period of brilliant literary flowering, we must remember that the Queen was already a middle-aged woman before the great Elizabethan Renaissance had begun to take shape. By the time Christopher Marlowe produced his *Tamburlaine*, she was nearly fifty-five years old; and the finest dramatic achievements of the Elizabethan epoch were all crowded into less than two decades. Nor, unlike the Italian Renaissance princes, was Elizabeth a particularly generous supporter either of the visual or of the literary arts; though a learned woman herself and a lover of the modern stage (whose desire 'to see Falstaff in love' is said to have determined Shakespeare to write *The Merry Wives of Windsor*), apart from accepting their effusive dedications she did not habitually encourage writers. That she left to her series of dashing favourites – Southampton, Shakespeare's friend and dedicatee; his rival, Walter Ralegh, the patron of Spenser and Marlowe; and Fulke Greville, 'the master' of Shakespeare and Jonson, as he afterwards informed the world. Ralegh, Greville and Greville's beloved companion, Sir Philip Sidney, were poets in their own right. The courtier-poets of the Elizabethan era form a small distinguished côterie; but, since as aristocrats they seldom published their poems and preferred to pass their manuscripts around a private circle, their influence was somewhat limited; and the majority of famous contemporary writers belonged to a very different social class, Shakespeare being the son of a Warwickshire businessman, Marlowe of a Kentish shoemaker; while the father of Edmund Spenser, the first half of whose allegorical epic, *The Faerie Queen*, appeared in the year 1590, despite the fact that he was descended from gentlemanly stock, during the poet's childhood was obliged to exercise 'the art and mystery of cloth-making'.

(*Above*) Elizabeth R; a silver madallion, commemorating the defeat of the Spanish Armada, 1588.

(*Below*) The Queen hawking with her courtiers; from Turbeville's *Booke of Falconrie*, 1575.

The Rise of the English Drama

Thus Elizabethan literature was an extremely complex growth, in which almost every type of Englishman voiced his passions and his aspirations; but, although the professional players still belonged to a despised caste, it was through drama that the Elizabethans expressed themselves most forcibly and readily. The first English blank-verse play, *Ferrex and Porrex*, or *Gorboduc*, by two young dramatists, Thomas Norton and Thomas Sackville, had been staged as early as 1561. But this was a private performance that had no immediate effect; and, simultaneously, a more popular type of drama, a remote descendant of the medieval Miracle and Morality Plays, with their odd mixture of religious pageantry and scenes of knockabout farce, was filling many London inn-yards, where plank-and-trestle stages were often improvised beneath the galleries.

Besides the inns that leased their yards to players, by 1576 London had two permanent playhouses, the Theatre and the Curtain. They were rowdy places; and the crowds they attracted, and the riots they sometimes caused, frequently alarmed the City magistrates, who distrusted the 'harlotry players' and did their best to put them down. Theatrical companies therefore sought the protection of liberal-minded great men and, having enlisted among their patron's privileged servants, used his name and wore his livery. When Shakespeare reached London, he joined the company called 'Strange's Men', which, when Lord Strange (later Lord Derby) died, was re-entitled 'the Lord Chamberlain's'.

At the outset, the theatres had depended on the services of ill-educated hacks; but during the 1580s a number of intelligent young men – GEORGE PEELE (1558?–97), ROBERT GREENE (1560?–92), THOMAS NASHE (1567–1601) and THOMAS LODGE (1558?–1625) – all set to work producing plays. Nicknamed 'the University Wits', they regarded themselves as poets and men of learning rather than as professional dramatists, and were inclined to approach their new trade with a somewhat supercilious air; they were reluctant, wrote Thomas Lodge, to harness their pens 'to a penny-knave's delight'. Consequently they acquired little sense of the stage; and their tragedies and comedies are nowadays largely forgotten, though their delicate lyrical poems live on in anthologies, and Greene's pamphlets (for example, his posthumous *Groatsworth of Wit*, which included some savage abuse of the upstart playwright, William Shakespeare) have earned him a high position among masters of Elizabethan prose. About the same time, the novelist JOHN LYLY (1554?–1606), inventor of the 'euphuistic' style – the Elizabethan equivalent of nineteenth-century 'fine writing', full of recondite allusions, nicely balanced antitheses and decorative tropes and fancies – whose two romantic tales, *Euphues: the Anatomy of Wit* and *Euphues and His England*, appeared in 1578 and 1581, was writing comedies to be played by boy-actors, the children of the Chapel Royal and the choristers of St Paul's Cathedral. In 1589, the success of the 'Paul's boys' was

(*Opposite*) The Swan Theatre; from a pen-and-ink drawing made in 1596 by a Dutch traveller, Johannes de Witte.

tectum

poebicus

sedilia

orchestra

mimorum
ædes

ingressus

proscænium

planities siue arena

quintum sed ipsam et structuram, bestiarum concertati
oni destinatum, in quo multi vrsi, tauri, & stupenda
magnitudinis canes, distinctis cauriis & septis aluntur; qui
ad

THE

SPANISH TRAGE-
die, Containing the lamentable
end of *Don Horatio,* and *Bel-imperia:*
with the pittifull death of
olde *Hieronimo.*

Newly corrected and amended of such grosse faults as
passed in the first impression.

AT LONDON
Printed by *Edward Allde,* for
Edward White.

Title page of Kyd's
Spanish Tragedy, 1592.

abruptly cut short; a play they enacted having presumed to
touch on 'certain matters of Divinity and of State', any further
performances were summarily prohibited.

Meanwhile, the arrival of a new playwright – a man who loved
and understood his medium – had revolutionised the English
stage. THOMAS KYD (1558?–94?) the son of a London scrivener,
educated at the Merchant Taylors' School, was probably the most
successful, at least with the 'penny-knaves' who crowded the
playhouses, of all the earlier Elizabethan dramatists. His famous

Spanish Tragedy, produced about 1587 – the year that saw the production of Christopher Marlowe's *Tamburlaine the Great* – was still being acted half a century later; and Ben Jonson, we learn, was once commissioned to revamp the text. In Kyd's tragedy as in Marlowe's, Edward Alleyn created the most important rôle, an actor whose 'bent brows', 'furious gestures' and majestic pacings up and down the boards, transported an Elizabethan audience. In *The Spanish Tragedy*, he took the part of the aged Hieronimo, and entered carrying a blazing torch:

> What out-cries pluck me from my naked bed,
> And chill my throbbing heart with trembling fear . . .
> But stay, what murd'rous spectacle is this?
> A man hang'd up and all the murderers gone . . .
> Those garments that he wears I oft have seen:
> Alas, it is Horatio, my sweet son!

At either side of the stage sit Revenge and an attendant Ghost; and, when the Ghost sums up the action of the play, he is able to record no less than nine deaths, three suicides and six particularly atrocious murders. Like *Tamburlaine*, Kyd's drama gratified the Elizabethan taste for the bloody and horrific; and it may have been Kyd who wrote the old-fashioned 'revenge play' upon which Shakespeare founded *Hamlet*. Very little is known of the dramatist's personal existence; but he and Marlowe appear to have been close friends, and to have entertained the same subversive views. In 1593, Kyd was arrested by the authorities and accused of distributing seditious libels; and the admissions he made under torture helped to precipitate his old friend's downfall.

CHRISTOPHER MARLOWE (1564–93), a shoemaker's son from Canterbury, graduated as master of arts at Cambridge in the year 1587. Like other promising 'university wits', he was soon attracted to the London stage, joined the 'Admiral's Men' (afterwards the keenest competitors of the 'Chamberlain's Men', who, about 1592, would secure the services of William Shakespeare) and became a busy playwright. His first important production (which is also the first Elizabethan play that can be considered as a major work of literature) was *Tamburlaine the Great, Parts I & II*, a tremendous swashbuckling drama of pride and ambition and cruelty that reached the boards in 1587 and, with Edward Alleyn performing the chief rôle, at once electrified the public. *The Tragical History of Doctor Faustus* probably appeared in 1588; and it was followed, during the next few years, by *The Jew of Malta* and a fine historical play on the subject of *Edward the Second*, the precursor of Shakespeare's historical dramas. Although they are often attributed to the author of *Tamburlaine*, neither *The Massacre at Paris* nor *Dido, Queen of Carthage* was entirely Marlowe's own work. His only long poem, *Hero and Leander*, remained in manuscript until 1598.

Marlowe had other interests – of a much more dangerous kind.

Before he was awarded his master's degree, he seems to have joined the English secret service, then directed by Sir Francis Walsingham, and to have travelled abroad, investigating the activities of seditious Papist exiles. The Privy Council itself was evidently acquainted with his mission, and in 1587 publicly certified that 'he had done her Majesty good service . . .' He must have enjoyed some measure of official protection. But Marlowe was a rash and impulsive young man, who seldom troubled to conceal his views. Rumours were circulated that he was both an avowed atheist and a notorious homosexual. According to a government informer, he had announced that he could 'show more sound reasons for atheism, than any divine in England is able to give to prove divinity, and that Marlowe told him he hath read the Atheist lecture to Sir Walter Ralegh and others'. It was well known that Ralegh and his friends, the so-called 'School of Night', held extremely heterodox opinions; at their meetings, alleged an English Jesuit, 'both Moses and our Saviour, the Old and New Testament, are jested at, and the scholars taught . . . to spell God backwards'. Such was the dramatist's unfortunate reputation that, when in 1593 his fellow poet, Thomas Kyd, was arrested on a different charge, and, under torture, declared that an essay apparently disputing the godhead of Christ, which had come to light among his papers, had been left behind with him by Marlowe, the Privy Council took immediate action. They summoned Marlowe to appear before them. He 'entered his appearance', but did not obey their order. That same month, he was murdered in a tavern-room at Deptford Strand, beside the Thames. The circumstances of Marlowe's death are mysterious. It was said to have resulted from a tavern-brawl; but one of the three witnesses who saw him stabbed to death had himself been a member of Walsingham's secret service; and the slaying was preceded by an enigmatic conference, while the company dined and walked up and down the garden, that lasted about five hours.

Marlowe's genius, and the 'mighty line' he shaped, made an indelible impression upon Elizabethan literature. Shakespeare quotes from him in *As You Like It*; and a manuscript copy of *Hero and Leander*, which had evidently found its way into his hands several years before its publication, encouraged him to produce his youthful *Venus and Adonis*. With *Tamburlaine*, blank verse came of age. The play is an extravagant melodrama, packed with horrors and absurdities; but in Part I the brutal Scythian conqueror suddenly adopts a poet's rôle, and speaks not only of the meaning and purpose of poetry, but of the artist's devotion to some quintessential beauty that perpetually eludes his grasp:

> What is beauty, saith my sufferings, then?
> If all the pens that ever poets held
> Had fed the feeling of their masters' thoughts,
> And every sweetness that inspir'd their hearts,

TO THE RIGHT
worthy and noble Knight

Sir *VValter Raleigh*, Captaine of her Maiesties
Guard, Lord Wardein of the Stanneries,
and Lieutenant of the Countie of
Cornwall.

(∵)

I R, that you may fee that I am not al-
waies ydle as yee thinke, though not
greatly well occupied, nor altogither
vndutifull, though not precifely of-
ficious, I make you prefent of this fim-
ple paftorall, vnworthie of your high-
er conceipt for the meaneffe of the ftile,
but agreeing with the truth in circumftance and mat-
ter. The which I humbly befeech you to accept in part
of paiment of the infinite debt in which I acknowledge
my felfe bounden vnto you, for your fingular fauours
and fundrie good turnes shewed to me at my late being
in England, and with your good countenance proteЄt a-
gainft the malice of euill mouthes, which are alwaies
wide open to carpe at and mifconftrue my fimple meaning.

A 2   1

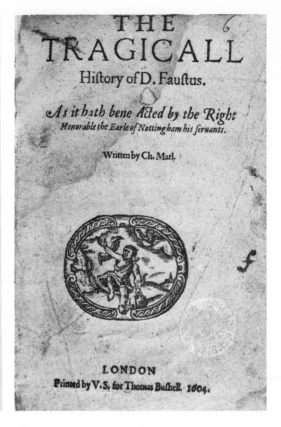

THE
TRAGICALL
Hiftory of D. Fauftus.

As it hath bene Acted by the Right
Honorable the Earle of Nottingham his feruants.

Written by Ch. Marl.

LONDON
Printed by V. S, for Thomas Bufhell. 1604.

Their minds, and muses on admired themes;
If all the heavenly quintessence they still
From their immortal flowers of poesy,
Wherein, as in a mirror, we perceive
The highest reaches of a human wit;
If these had made one poem's period,
And all combin'd in beauty's worthiness,
Yet should there hover in their restless heads,
One thought, one grace, one wonder, at the least,
Which into words no virtue can digest.

(V.i)

(*Above left*) Opening page
of Marlowe's *Edward the
Second*, with a dedication
to Sir Walter Ralegh.

(*Above right*) Title page
of the first edition of
Dr Faustus, 1604.

In *Dr Faustus*, an even more ambitious, but equally imperfect
play, the magician is the type of Renaissance Man, thirsting for
knowledge, whom he had already depicted in *Tamburlaine*:

Nature, that fram'd us of four elements...
Doth teach us all to have aspiring minds:
Our souls, whose faculties can comprehend
The wondrous architecture of the world,
And measure every wandering planet's course,
Still climbing after knowledge infinite,
And always moving as the restless spheres,
Will us to wear ourselves, and never rest...

(Pt 1, II. vii)

Marlowe is the most exquisitely sensuous of all the great Elizabethan poets. Here, for example is Valdes' description of the splendid state with which he and his accomplices, Faustus and Cornelius, if they succeed in their daring magical plan, may presently surround themselves:

> As Indian Moors obey their Spanish lords,
> So shall the spirits of every element
> Be always serviceable to us three;
> Like lions shall they guard us when we please;
> Like Almain rutters with their horsemen's staves,
> Or Lapland giants trotting by our sides;
> Sometimes like women, or unwedded maids,
> Shadowing more beauty in their airy brows
> Than have the white breasts of the queen of love . . .

Hero and Leander, Marlowe's adaptation of a Greek poem supposed to have been written by the half-legendary bard, Musaeus, is one of the finest erotic poems ever written in the English language. Rarely has the consummation of love been depicted with greater fire and eloquence:

> Even as a bird, which in our hands we wring
> Forth plungeth, and often flutters with her wing,
> She trembling strove: this strife of hers, like that
> Which made the world, another world begat
> Of unknown joy. Treason was in her thought,
> And cunningly to yield herself she sought . . .
> Leander now, like Theban Hercules,
> Enter'd the orchard of th'Hesperides;
> Whose fruit none rightly can describe, but he
> That pulls or shakes it from the golden tree.
> Wherein Leander, on her quivering breast,
> Breathless spoke something, and sigh'd out the rest . . .

Marlowe produced his entire literary output between 1587 and 1593; and it was in 1593 that Shakespeare, still a comparatively inexperienced poet, dedicated *Venus and Adonis*, 'the first heir of my invention', to Henry Wriothesley, Lord Southampton.

Shakespearian Heyday

WILLIAM SHAKESPEARE (1564–1616) first emerges from comparative obscurity at the age of twenty-eight, when in a scurrilous pamphlet by the poet Robert Greene, who had died just before its publication, he was denounced as a designing interloper – 'an upstart crow, beautified with our feathers, that . . . supposes he is as well able to bombast out a blank verse as the best of you, and, being an absolute *Johannes fac totum*, is in his own conceit the only Shake-scene in a country'. Shakespeare's friends evidently protested against this savage and ill-considered libel; for soon afterwards the publisher issued an elaborate apology, announcing that

(*Opposite*) Engraved portrait of William Shakespeare, from the First Folio, 1623.

Mr. WILLIAM
SHAKESPEARES

COMEDIES,
HISTORIES, &
TRAGEDIES.

Published according to the True Originall Copies.

Martin Droeshout sculpsit London.

LONDON
Printed by Iſaac Iaggard, and Ed. Blount. 1623.

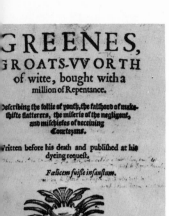

GREENES,
GROATS-VVORTH
of witte, bought with a
million of Repentance.

Defcribing the follie of youth, the falfhood of make-
fhifte flatterers, the miferie of the negligent,
and mifchiefes of deceiuing
Courtezans.

Written before his death and publifhed at his
dyeing request.

Fælicem fuiffe infauftum.

LONDON
Imprinted for William Wright.
1 5 9 2.

he was sorry to have offended a distinguished modern poet, 'because myself have seen his demeanour no less civil than he excellent in the quality he professes. Besides, divers of worship have reported his uprightness of dealing, which argues his honesty, and his facetious grace that approves his art.'

The abusive pamphlet, Greene's *Groatsworth of Wit, bought with a million of Repentance*, appeared in September 1592; and by that time the 'upstart crow' was already well-established among contemporary authors. We know little of Shakespeare's childhood and youth. Born at Stratford-upon-Avon, Warwickshire, on 22 or 23 April 1564, he was the eldest son of John and Mary Shakespeare. His father, an important middle-class citizen of Stratford, is variously described as a glover and a butcher, and seems also to have traded in corn and malt, leather, hides and raw wool. When his son was four, he became Stratford's mayor or 'bailiff'. About 1580, however, he began to lose money, fell foul of the law, suffered a heavy fine and forfeited his seat upon the town-council. Yet he remained a popular local figure; and his neighbours are said to have remembered him as 'a merry-cheeked old man', who declared that his son 'Will was a good honest fellow', and that the two of them would often share a joke.

Stratford had an excellent grammar school; and there, no doubt, the son of a one-time bailiff must have received his education. But Shakespeare's schooling, writes Nicholas Rowe, the poet's earliest biographer and a diligent collector of Stratfordian gossip, was cut short by the decline of his father's fortunes; and John Aubrey tells us that he worked in his father's shop and even learned the butchering trade. Certainly Shakespeare was still at home towards the close of 1582; for that November he was suddenly thrust into marriage with a young woman, eight years older than himself, styled in a legal document 'Anne Hathwey of Stratford', who bore him his first child, a daughter, Susanna, on 26 May 1583. Two further children, the twins Hamnet and Judith, appeared in January 1585. Nothing else is known of Shakespeare's marriage. Perhaps, as James Joyce liked to think, Anne, a 'bold-faced' country girl, had taken advantage of her inexperienced lover; whereupon her indignant relations hastily procured a marriage licence. But since both *Henry VI, Part I*, written at the very beginning of his dramatic career, and *The Tempest*, produced in 1611, when he was about to bid the stage farewell, contain vivid descriptions of the misery and strife that result from 'wedlock forcéd', we may assume that their union was not entirely harmonious, and that Shakespeare proved a restive husband.

Nevertheless, adds Nicholas Rowe, he continued to keep house at Stratford, 'till an extravagance that he was guilty of' – a poaching expedition in a local justice's park – 'forced him out of his country and that way of living . . .' Several different dates have been assigned to Shakespeare's flight, of which 1587 appears the most likely. That year five companies of players passed through Stratford on provincial tours; and one of these companies he may very well have joined. Simultaneously, Richard Field, a fellow Stratfordian whose father was a friend of John Shakespeare, set up in business as a London printer. How Shakespeare earned a living between his departure from Stratford and 1592, when he had begun to make his name, is yet another problem that defies solution. But, about the time the poet left home, Kyd's *Spanish Tragedy* and Marlowe's *Tamburlaine the Great* first appeared upon the London stage; and the theatrical boom these tragedies helped to launch produced a keen demand for new young dramatists, capable of manufacturing blank verse in the popular bombastic mode. *Henry VI*, Shakespeare's first effort, once believed to be the work of several hands, but which critics now believe that he wrote unaided, is a rough, uneven, ill-constructed play. It clearly provided him, however, with much valuable experience; and his next historical play, the tragedy of *Richard III*, shows the remarkably rapid development of his dramatic and poetic gifts. Richard himself, despite his sinister asides, is not by any means a stock villain, but a preliminary sketch for such later Shakespearian personages as Macbeth and Coriolanus – a lonely man penned up in the prison of the Self, condemned to an agonizing isolation against which he struggles like a caged predator.

Shakespeare's literary life is generally divided, though there have been many different divisions, into four main creative periods – the period that lasted until 1594, during which he produced *Henry VI, Parts I, II, and III, Richard III, Titus Andronicus* (a bold attempt to beat Thomas Kyd at his own bloodthirsty game) and a series of comedies, *The Two Gentlemen of Verona, The Comedy of Errors, The Taming of the Shrew,* and, probably, *Love's Labour's Lost,* as well as a couple of ambitious narrative poems, *Venus and Adonis* and *The Rape of Lucrece*; the period between 1594 and 1599, when he wrote *Julius Caesar, Romeo and Juliet, A Midsummer Night's Dream* and *The Merchant of Venice,* and his succession of English historical plays, *King John, Richard II, Henry IV, Parts I and II, Henry V* and (as a complement to *Henry IV, II*) *The Merry Wives of Windsor*; the period of the great tragedies, from 1599 to 1608, that saw the production of *Hamlet, Othello, King Lear* and *Macbeth,* of the majestic Roman dramas, *Antony and Cleopatra* and *Coriolanus,* yet at the same time, of his most successful comedies, *Much Ado About Nothing, Twelfth Night* and *As You Like It,* and of three bitter-sweet plays, *Troilus and Cressida, Measure for Measure* and *All's Well that Ends Well*; finally, his last phase, from 1608 to 1616, when both the dramatist's method and his attitude towards human life seem to have been slowly changing, and he concluded his career with *Timon of Athens, Pericles, Cymbeline, The Winter's Tale, Henry VIII* (which may not have been entirely Shakespeare's) and his finest romantic comedy, *The Tempest.*

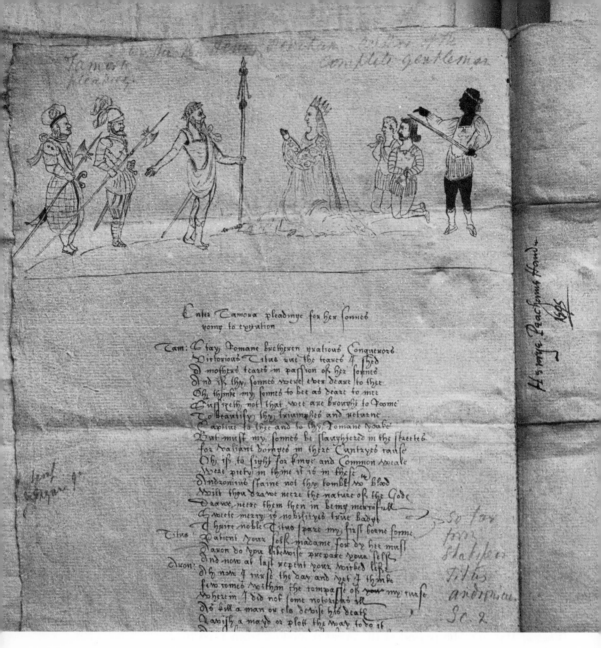

Sketch, made by Henry Peacham about 1594, which shows a scene from *Titus Andronicus*, and disproves the theory that Elizabethan actors always wore contemporary dress.

In each period, Shakespeare moulded his work to suit the tastes of his contemporary audience, and of the different section of society that he happened to be entertaining. Thus his historical plays reflect the mood of heady patriotic sentiment that had coloured English life since the defeat of the Invincible Armada in July 1588; while his courtly comedies were addressed, not so much to the 'groundlings' who filled the theatre's yard, but to a far more distinguished and fastidious audience, among whom the aged Queen herself, painted, bewigged and sparkling with jewels, sometimes occupied the foremost place. After the Queen's death, it was learned that her Scottish successor, the erudite and pedantic

James, took a passionate interest in the Black Arts; and Shakespeare then turned out a Scottish tragedy, mentioning the sovereign's ancient lineage and depicting the conjurations of a group of witches. Shakespeare, the industrious commercial playwright, had a shrewd eye to the main chance. He was, moreover, an exceptionally fortunate man; and, once he had reached London and found his feet on the stage, he seems never to have lacked supporters. His allies, we know, included 'divers of worship'; and about 1593 he secured the patronage and friendship of a dazzling young courtier, Henry Wriothesley, Earl of Southampton, who moved in the inner circles of the Elizabethan aristocracy. During that same year, under the imprint of Richard Field, he dedicated to Lord Southampton his richly decorative, if somewhat clumsy and juvenile poem, *Venus and Adonis* (which, disregarding his work for the stage, he boldly styled 'the first heir of my invention') and, in 1594, *The Rape of Lucrece*. Both dedications have a distinctly personal tone; but the second suggests that the poet and his patron were now on terms of real intimacy; and it is difficult to resist the conclusion that Southampton, a strikingly handsome young man, was the golden youth whom he was to describe in the mysterious *Sonnets*. Through Southampton, Shakespeare would almost certainly have met his close friend and political ally, the even more resplendent Earl of Essex, the last of the ageing Queen's favourites. Each was a compulsive personality; and if Southampton aroused the deep romantic passion that inspired the sonnet-sequence, the fall and death of Essex, who early in 1601 took up arms, not, he protested against the Queen herself, but against the royal government, would appear to have had a profound effect upon the atmosphere of Shakespeare's later tragedies. Essex, though erratic and misguided, had been a gallant, much-loved figure, a friend to the common people – or so they imagined – and the champion of aspiring youth. His death, which saddened his contemporaries and cast a shadow of gloom over the whole Elizabethan court, must, no doubt, for the devoted friend of Southampton (who stood trial at the fallen leader's side) have been a particularly cruel blow.

Meanwhile the dramatist's professional career had proceeded smoothly and successfully. In or around 1592, he had joined the company known as 'Strange's Men', afterwards renamed 'the Chamberlain's Men', who soon became the most popular players of the time; and in 1594, we learn, Shakespeare was among the controllers of his company, a 'sharer', entitled to a proportion of their earnings. In 1599 he received a tenth share of an important piece of theatrical property, the new playhouse, named the Globe, that two adventurous entrepreneurs, the brothers Burbage, had raised above the Bankside marshes. By Elizabethan standards he was now a fairly rich man; two years before the building of the Globe, he had already purchased New Place, one of the most

(*Above*) Henry Wriothesley, 3rd Earl of Southampton, Shakespeare's early patron, and probably the 'golden youth' of his *Sonnets*.

(*Above*) Southampton in later life, as a courtier of James I.

(*Above*) The Earl of Essex, the last of the ageing Queen's favourites.

(*Below*) Frontispiece to Nicholas Rowe's edition of *King Lear*, 1709.

imposing houses in his native town. The fact that Shakespeare was a successful businessman, who did not hesitate to go to law about comparatively small debts, has often puzzled his admirers. But that, after all, was the Elizabethan way – the English sixteenth century was a remarkably litigious age; and Shakespeare was no romantic outcast, but, in his public existence, a thoroughly practical man, who shared the habits and, indeed, many of the failings of the period through which he lived. He was not a rebel like Christopher Marlowe; nor was he a professed agnostic like Sir Walter Ralegh. He had little in common with Ralegh's 'School of Night' (see p. 46), and, so far as we can judge, seems to have accepted the pre-Copernican theory of the universe, which taught that the sun travelled around the earth, and that the earth itself was surmounted by a series of crystalline spheres, revolving one upon the other.

His enquiries into the nature of Man, and into the problems of human destiny, were apt to take a very different form. JOHN FLORIO (1553?–1625) was also a member of Lord Southampton's private circle; and Florio's translation of the essays of Montaigne had evidently been read and enjoyed by Shakespeare. Montaigne's favourite maxim *Que sçais-je?* (What do I know?) he might well have adopted as his own. There was nothing dogmatic about Shakespeare's turn of mind; and we look in vain through his collected works for any evidence that he was either a practising believer or a 'naturally Christian soul'. Though Hamlet's devoted friend, Horatio, speaks of the 'flights of the angels' that may speed the unhappy Prince towards his rest, there seems no hope of moral reconciliation or religious redemption in any of the great tragedies. Endless volumes have been written on Shakespeare's view of tragedy, many illuminating, none conclusive. Here it must be enough to say that, from Richard III to Hamlet, Othello, Macbeth, Lear and Coriolanus, all the tragic heroes he depicts are lonely men, condemned to solitude by some passion or obsession that makes it impossible for them to communicate freely with the rest of mankind – Hamlet by his habitual irresolution, to which he adds a sense of wasted strength; Othello, by his obsessive sexual jealousy; Macbeth, by an accumulating load of guilt; Lear and Coriolanus, by their obstinacy and self-destructive pride. For each, his solitude at length becomes a prison; each is destined to die alone, as the whole structure of his previous life collapses.

During the period about the year 1606, when Shakespeare wrote *King Lear*, his wildest, most despairing play, some critics have suggested that he was close to physical and nervous breakdown. If such a crisis occurred in his life, he evidently surmounted it. He did not cease to write; and *The Tempest*, which William Hazlitt described as 'one of the most original and perfect of his productions', was performed before the King at Whitehall on 1 November 1611. In Shakespeare's nature we observe a constant

balance between two opposing states of mind – the joy of life that he expressed so richly and so beautifully; and a fear and horror of life, that represented Man as nothing more dignified or glorious than a 'poor, bare, forked animal', chance product of 'our dungy earth'. A similar conflict appears in the work of many European writers; but Shakespeare expresses it with greater force and clarity, and in more splendidly memorable images, than any other English poet. Potentially, if not actually, he was a neurotic and a melancholic. Yet, whatever his secret sufferings, he remained, so far as his contemporaries could distinguish, a singularly amiable, well-balanced character. The tributes that he received from his friends are remarkably unanimous; he is described as 'civil', 'gentle', 'friendly', 'sweet'. According to Ben Jonson, who might, given the respective positions they occupied, have envied and disliked him, he was 'honest, and of an open and free nature', a friend whom he had always loved. Shakespeare's appearance, too, was prepossessing. 'He was a handsome, well-shaped man', John Aubrey heard, 'and of a very ready and pleasant, smooth wit.' Among the resorts at which he exercised his wit was the celebrated Mermaid Tavern in Bread Street, just off Cheapside; and among the 'sirenaical gentlemen' he met there may have been Thomas Campion and John Donne.

The Bankside, panoramic view executed by Wenceslaus Hollar, 1647. The Bear-Garden and the Globe have been transposed.

Thus the study of Shakespeare's life, both literary and personal, presents us with a startling paradox. We see a brilliant literary opportunist, who built up a small fortune by studying his public's tastes and cleverly exploiting them, and a poet of immense creative genius who transfigured every subject that he touched. We also confront a man haunted by the terrible visions that he poured out into his last tremendous dramas, but who gave no outward signs of conflict and, once he had abandoned the stage, would quietly settle down as a prosperous middle-class householder in humdrum Stratford. Following Prospero's example, he renounced his magic arts. For, unlike Jonson, a careful self-editor, he made no effort to preserve his plays; and not until 1623, when he had been dead for seven years, would his former associates, Henry Condell and John Heminge, who, no doubt, had acquired the prompt-copies, resurrect them in the First Folio.

Here we cannot attempt to produce a detailed evaluation of Shakespeare's poetic and dramatic gifts. It is a subject that has taxed literary scholarship since the days of John Dryden. Shakespeare took Marlowe's 'mighty line' and soon made of it something, not only mightier, but infinitely more flexible. There are moments when, in the master's hands, despite its basically pentametric form, it almost approximates to 'free verse', so closely, if the occasion demands (as when Juliet's nurse delivers her wonderful monologue) does it reproduce the rhythms of the spoken word. Simultaneously, he mastered the sonnet-form, with which, according to William Wordsworth, he 'unlocked' his heart, and chronicled and analysed the strange romantic passion that had preoccupied his middle years. Finally, Shakespeare was the greatest of all the Elizabethan song-writers. His brief lyrics, especially written for the lute, and designed either to conclude a scene or fill a brief pause in the action, possess a haunting incantatory charm. As has been said of certain Japanese verses, the poem ceases, but the sense goes on.

To his technical mastery of his medium the dramatist added an unequalled grasp of character. Again, this is an immense subject that lies beyond our present scope. Two points, however, are worth making. Shakespeare often accepted a type, then proceeded to develop it into a complex personality. Hamlet, for example, when he set to work reorganizing an old-fashioned revenge play, was the typical Elizabethan 'malcontent', a phenomenon lengthily discussed by physicians and psychologists. The malcontent, frequently a returned traveller, found nothing in modern society to his liking, but, with his hat pulled down above his eyes, his doublet black and hose ungartered, would 'walk melancholy' through the London streets with downcast eyes and folded arms. Hamlet himself is a victim of this well-known form of melancholia; but Shakespeare incorporates its symptoms in an extraordinarily living portrait. To a no less magical change we owe his portrait of

Falstaff. Here Shakespeare combined three separate characters, borrowed from an old play, *The Famous Victories of Henry V*, probably written about 1586. Each was a typical figure of fun; Falstaff, as the dramatist develops him, becomes a personage of heroic size and grandeur, who dominates every scene through which he moves. Equally remarkable is Shakespeare's treatment of Shylock. In 1594 Queen Elizabeth's physician, a learned Jew named Dr Lopez, accused of plotting to poison his royal mistress, had met the hideous death reserved for traitors; and contemporary audiences were bound to welcome a play that introduced a scheming Jewish villain. Shakespeare then obliged by creating the rôle of Shylock. But again the imaginative artist prevailed over the literary opportunist, with results that Heinrich Heine noted. Shakespeare, he observed, may have intended to produce a monster; yet he had clothed his persecuted Jew in an air of tragic dignity; 'the genius of the poet, the universal spirit that inspires him, is always above his individual will'.

Shakespeare's last phase, during which he produced *Timon of*

Pages from the first Quarto of *Hamlet*, with a garbled version of the Prince's famous soliloquy.

The Tragedy of Hamlet

And so by continuance, and weakenesse of the braine
Into this frenfie, which now poffeffeth him:
And if this be not true, take this from this.
    King Thinke you t'is fo?
    Cor. How? fo my Lord, I would very faine know
That thing that I haue faide t'is fo, pofitiuely,
And it hath fallen out otherwife.
Nay, if circumftances leade me on,
Ile finde it out, if it were hid
As deepe as the centre of the earth.
    King. how fhould wee trie this fame?
    Cor. Mary my good lord thus,
The Princes walke is here in the galery,
There let *Ofelia*, walke vntill hee comes:
Your felfe and I will ftand clofe in the ftudy,
There fhall you heare the effect of all his hart,
And if it proue any otherwife then loue,
Then let my cenfure faile an other time.
    King. fee where hee comes poring vppon a booke.
                Enter Hamlet.
    Cor. Madame, will it pleafe your grace
To leaue vs here?
    Que. With all my hart.   *exit.*
    Cor. And here *Ofelia*, reade you on this booke,
And walke aloofe, the King fhal be vnfeene.
    Ham. To be, or not to be, I there's the point,
To Die, to fleepe, is that all? I all:
No, to fleepe, to dreame, I mary there it goes,
For in that dreame of death, when wee awake,
And borne before an euerlafting Iudge,
From whence no paffenger euer retur'nd,
The vndifcouered country, at whofe fight
The happy fmile, and the accurfed damn'd.
But for this, the ioyfull hope of this,
Whol'd beare the fcornes and flattery of the world,
Scorned by the right rich, the rich curffed of the poore?
                                          The

* Prince of Denmarke

The widow being oppreffed, the orphan wrong'd,
The tafte of hunger, or a tirants raigne,
And thoufand more calamities befides,
To grunt and fweate vnder this weary life,
When that he may his full *Quietus* make,
With a bare bodkin, who would this indure,
But for a hope of fomething after death?
Which puffles the braine, and doth confound the fence,
Which makes vs rather beare thofe euilles we haue,
Than flie to others that we know not of.
I that, O this confcience makes cowardes of vs all,
Lady in thy orizons, be all my finnes remembred.
    Ofel. My Lord, I haue fought opportunitie, which now
I haue, to redeliuer to your worthy handes, a fmall remembrance, fuch tokens which I haue receiued of you.
    Ham. Are you faire?
    Ofel. My Lord.
    Ham. Are you honeft?
    Ofel. What meanes my Lord?
    Ham. That if you be faire and honeft,
Your beauty fhould admit no difcourfe to your honefty.
    Ofel. My Lord, can beauty haue better priuiledge than
with honefty?
    Ham. Yea mary may it, for Beauty may transforme
Honefty, from what fhe was into a bawd:
Then Honefty can transforme Beauty:
This was fometimes a Paradox,
But now the time giues it fcope.
I neuer gaue you nothing.
    Ofel. My Lord, you know right well you did,
And with them fuch earneft vowes of loue,
As would haue moou'd the ftonieft breaft aliue,
But now too true I finde,
Rich giftes waxe poore, when giuers grow vnkinde.
    Ham. I neuer loued you.
    Ofel. You made me beleeue you did.
                                          E   Ham.

Athens, Pericles, Cymbeline, The Winter's Tale and *The Tempest*, shows him adapting his art to the conditions of a new dramatic era. In 1608 his company, now re-christened the King's Men, took over the Blackfriars playhouse, where, no longer exposed to wind and rain as in the Globe's old-fashioned wooden oval, they could perform plays of a much more sophisticated kind, on a candle-lit stage, beneath a solid roof. The Jacobean audience enjoyed elaborate spectacles and light poetic entertainment, such as Beaumont and Fletcher had begun to provide, rather than resounding dramas. Thus, *The Winter's Tale*, produced in 1611, contains an attractive 'transformation-scene', and has a plot full of romantic absurdities and amusing flights of fancy, where tragic and comic themes are curiously interwoven. But during the same year, Shakespeare disposed of his shares both in the Blackfriars and in the Globe; and it is said that not long afterwards he retired, temporarily at least, to New Place. Though he returned in 1613, when eight of his plays were produced before the Court at Whitehall, and he bought some London property, he had already uttered his poetic farewell. *The Tempest*, staged five or six months after *The Winter's Tale*, on 1 November 1611, was surely intended to be his valediction. Prospero has 'drowned his books', discarded his magic robes, and in lines of surpassing beauty he speaks of life as a dream, and of the world as an 'insubstantial pageant'.

Home at Stratford, Shakespeare seems to have devoted his attention to various forms of local business. Together with seventy-one of his fellow Stratfordians, he endeavoured to push through the House of Commons a bill for the better repair of the roads, and joined a group of Warwickshire landowners in a profitable scheme for enclosing the common lands at Welcombe. He also married off his younger daughter, Judith – Susanna he had previously married to the learned physician, Dr Hall; poor little Hamnet, a child he deeply loved, had died at the age of eleven in 1596. Soon after Judith's marriage, on 25 March, Shakespeare signed his last will and testament, appointing John and Susanna Hall his executors, and in a famous clause leaving Anne Shakespeare only his 'second-best bed' and the furniture that accompanied it. His will made no mention of any books at New Place. Perhaps they were part of the 'goods, chattels . . . and household stuff' that the Hall family inherited. Did they include the testator's own works – the 'good' and 'bad' quartos of his plays that various booksellers had from time to time produced, presumably without his leave; or a copy of the *Sonnets* that, again without his leave, but accompanied by an enigmatic dedication –

TO.THE.ONLIE. BEGETTER.OF.
THESE.INSUING.SONNETS.
MR W.H . . .

an unscrupulous literary businessman, Thomas Thorpe, had

issued in May or June 1609? Although the 'ever-living poet', referred to by the writer of the dedication, had now finally abandoned literature, he did not forget his literary friends; and John Ward, vicar of Stratford between 1662 and 1681, reports that in the spring of 1616 'Shakespeare, Drayton and Ben Jonson had a merry meeting', during which they 'drank too hard'; for, on 23 April, 'Shakespeare died of a fever there contracted'. He now lies buried in Stratford parish church, his tomb marked by a few lines of singularly uninspiring doggerel; while an almost equally uninspiring bust looks out from the chancel-wall above.

LOVE AND MOONLIGHT
The Merchant of Venice

How sweet the moonlight sleeps upon this bank!
Here will we sit, and let the sounds of music
Creep in our ears; soft stillness and the night
Become the touches of sweet harmony.
Sit, Jessica. Look how the floor of heaven
Is thick inlaid with patines of bright gold;
There's not the smallest orb which thou behold'st
But in his motion like an angel sings,
Still quiring to the young eyed cherubims;
Such harmony is in immortal souls;
But, whilst this muddy vesture of decay
Doth grossly close it in, we cannot hear it.

PERDITA AMONG THE SHEPHERDS
The Winter's Tale

PER: ... Now, my fairest friend,
I would I had some flowers o' the spring that might
Become your time of day; and yours, and yours,
That wear upon your virgin branches yet
Your maidenheads growing. O Proserpina!
For the flowers now, that, frighted, thou letst fall
From Dis's waggon! daffodils,
That come before the swallow dares, and take
The winds of March with beauty; violets dim,
But sweeter than the lids of Juno's eyes
Or Cytherea's breath; pale primroses,
That die unmarried, ere they can behold
Bright Phoebus in his strength, a malady
Most incident to maids; bold oxlips, and
The crown-imperial; lilies of all kinds,
The flower-de-luce being one. – O! these I lack,
To make you garlands of; and, my sweet friend,
To strew him o'er and o'er!
FLO: What! like a corse?
PER: No; like a bank for love to lie and play on;
Not like a corse; or if, – not to be buried,
But quick and in mine arms. Come, take your flowers:
Methinks I play as I have seen them do

Hunting scene on a late
16th-century table-carpet.

In Whitsun pastorals: sure, this robe of mine
Does change my disposition.

FLO: What you do
Still betters what is done. When you speak, sweet,
I'd have you do it ever: when you sing,
I'd have you buy and sell so; so give alms;
Pray so; and, for the ordering your affairs,
To sing them too: when you do dance, I wish you
A wave o' the sea, that you might ever do
Nothing but that; . . .

THE NURSE REMEMBERS JULIET'S AGE
Romeo and Juliet

NURSE: Even or odd, of all days in the year,
Come Lammas-eve at night shall she be fourteen.
Susan and she, – God rest all Christian souls! –
Were of an age. Well, Susan is with God;
She was too good for me. But, as I said,
On Lammas-eve at night shall she be fourteen;
That shall she, marry; I remember it well.
'Tis since the earthquake now eleven years;
And she was wean'd, I never shall forget it,
Of all the days of the year, upon that day.
For I had then laid wormwood to my dug,
Sitting in the sun under the dove-house wall;
My lord and you were then at Mantua.
Nay, I do bear a brain: but, as I said,
When it did taste the wormwood on the nipple
Of my dug, and felt it bitter, pretty fool!

To see it tetchy and fall out with the dug.
'Shake', quoth the dove-house. 'Twas no need, I trow,
To bid me trudge.

BRUTUS AND CASSIUS PART
Julius Caesar

BRU: And whether we shall meet again I know not.
    Therefore our everlasting farewell take:
    For ever, and for ever, farewell, Cassius!
    If we do meet again, why, we shall smile;
    If not, why then, this parting was well made.
CAS: For ever, and for ever, farewell, Brutus!
    If we do meet again, we'll smile indeed;
    If not, 'tis true this parting was well made.
BRU: Why, then, lead on. O! that a man might know
    The end of this day's business, ere it come;
    But it sufficeth, that the day will end,
    And then the end is known. Come, ho! away!

OTHELLO'S FAREWELL TO HIS WIFE
Othello

It is the cause, it is the cause, my soul;
Let me not name it to you, you chaste stars! –
It is the cause. Yet I'll not shed her blood;
Nor scar that whiter skin of hers than snow,
And smooth as monumental alabaster.
Yet she must die, else she'll betray more men.
Put out the light, and then put out the light:
If I quench thee, thou flaming minister,
I can again thy former light restore,
Should I repent me; but once put out thy light,
Thou cunning'st pattern of excelling nature,
I know not where is that Promethean heat
That can thy light relume. When I have pluck'd the rose,
I cannot give it vital growth again,
It needs must wither: I'll smell it on the tree.
O balmy breath, that dost almost persuade
Justice to break her sword! One more, one more.
Be thus when thou art dead, and I will kill thee,
And love thee after. One more, and this the last:
So sweet was ne'er so fatal. I must weep,
But they are cruel tears; this sorrow's heavenly,
It strikes where it doth love.

A YOUNG MAN'S PASSION
Troilus and Cressida

. . . I tell thee I am mad
In Cressid's love: thou answer'st, She is fair;
Pour'st in the open ulcer of my heart
Her eyes, her hair, her cheek, her gait, her voice;
Handlest in thy discourse, O! that her hand,

In whose comparison all whites are ink,
Writing their own reproach; to whose soft seizure
The cygnet's down is harsh, and spirit of sense
Hard as the palm of ploughman: this thou tell'st me,
As true thou tell'st me, when I say I love her;
But, saying thus, instead of oil and balm,
Thou lay'st in every gash that love hath given me
The knife that made it.

THE HORROR OF DEATH
Measure for Measure

Ay, but to die, and go we know not where;
To lie in cold obstruction and to rot;
This sensible warm motion to become
A kneaded clod; and the delighted spirit
To bathe in fiery floods, or to reside
In thrilling region of thick-ribbed ice;
To be imprison'd in the viewless winds,
And blown with restless violence round about
The pendant world; or to be worse than worst
Of those that lawless and incertain thoughts
Imagine howling: 'tis too horrible!
The weariest and most loathed worldly life
That age, ache, penury and imprisonment
Can lay on nature is a paradise
To what we fear of death.

'RIPENESS IS ALL'
King Lear

EDG: Away, old man! give me thy hand: away!
    King Lear hath lost, he and his daughter ta'en.
    Give me thy hand; come on.
GLO: No further, sir; a man may rot even here.
EDG: What! in ill thoughts again? Men must endure
    Their going hence, even as their coming hither:
    Ripeness is all. Come on.
GLO: And that's true too.

MORTAL TRANSIENCE
Antony and Cleopatra

ANT: Sometime we see a cloud that's dragonish;
    A vapour sometime like a bear or lion,
    A tower'd citadel, a pendant rock,
    A forked mountain, or blue promontory
    With trees upon't that nod unto the world
    And mock our eyes with air: Thou has seen these signs;
    They are black vesper's pageants.
EROS: Ay, my lord.
ANT: That which is now a horse, even with a thought
    The rack dislimns, and makes it indistinct,
    As water is in water.
EROS: It does, my lord.

ANT: My good knave, Eros, now thy captain is
Even such a body: Here I am Antony;
Yet cannot hold this visible shape, my knave.

PROSPERO BIDS GOODBYE
The Tempest

Our revels now are ended. These our actors,
As I foretold you, were all spirits and
Are melted into air, into thin air;
And, like the baseless fabric of this vision,
The cloud-capp'd towers, the gorgeous palaces,
The solemn temples, the great globe itself,
Yea, all which it inherit, shall dissolve,
And, like this insubstantial pageant faded,
Leave not a rack behind. We are such stuff
As dreams are made on, and our little life
Is rounded with a sleep. – Sir, I am vex'd:
Bear with my weakness; my old brain is troubled.

FALSTAFF AND SHALLOW
Henry IV, Part II

SHAL: O, Sir John, do you remember since we lay all night in the wind-
mill in Saint George's Fields?
FAL: No more of that, good Master Shallow, no more of that.
SHAL: Ha! it was a merry night. And is Jane Nightwork alive?
FAL: She lives, Master Shallow.
SHAL: She never could away with me.
FAL: Never. never; she would always say she could not abide Master
Shallow.
SHAL: By the mass, I should anger her to the heart. She was then a
bona-roba.[1] Doth she hold her own well?
FAL: Old, old, Master Shallow.
SHAL: Nay, she must be old; she cannot choose but be old; certain she's
old; and had Robin Nightwork, by old Nightwork, before I came
to Clement's inn.
SIL: That's fifty-five year ago.
SHAL: Ha! cousin Silence, that thou hadst seen that that this knight and
I have seen. Ha! Sir John, said I well?
FAL: We have heard the chimes at midnight, Master Shallow.

[1] Attractive woman.

LOVE AND OLD AGE
Henry IV, Part II

FALSTAFF: Thou dost give me flattering busses.
DOLL: By my troth, I kiss thee with a most constant heart.
FALSTAFF: I am old, I am old.
DOLL: I love thee better than I love e'er a scurvy young boy of
them all.
FALSTAFF: What stuff wilt have a kirtle of? I shall receive money o'
Thursday . . . A merry song, come: it grows late, we'll to bed.
Thou'lt forget me when I am gone.

A reconstruction of a
playhouse, *c.*1595.

THE SONNETS
Sonnet LX

Like as the waves make towards the pebbled shore,
So do our minutes hasten to their end;
Each changing place with that which goes before,
In sequent toil all forwards do contend.
Nativity, once in the main of light,
Crawls to maturity, wherewith being crown'd,
Crooked eclipses 'gainst his glory fight,
And Time that gave doth now his gift confound.
Time doth transfix the flourish set on youth
And delves the parallels in beauty's brow,
Feeds on the rarities of nature's truth,
And nothing stands but for his scythe to mow:
  And yet to times in hope my verse shall stand,
  Praising thy worth, despite his cruel hand.

Sonnet LXXIII

That time of year thou mayst in me behold
When yellow leaves, or none, or few, do hang
Upon those boughs which shake against the cold,
Bare ruin'd choirs, where late the sweet birds sang.
In me thou see'st the twilight of such day
As after sunset fadeth in the west,
Which by and by black night doth take away,
Death's second self, that seals up all in rest.
In me thou see'st the glowing of such fire
That on the ashes of his youth doth lie,
As the death-bed whereon it must expire
Consum'd with that which it was nourish'd by.
    This thou perceiv'st which makes thy love more strong,
    To love that well which thou must leave ere long.

ARIEL'S SONG
The Tempest

Full fathom five thy father lies;
    Of his bones are coral made:
Those are pearls that were his eyes:
    Nothing of him that doth fade,
But doth suffer a sea-change
Into something rich and strange.
Sea-nymphs hourly ring his knell:
            ding-dong.
Hark! now I hear them – ding-dong, bell.

AUTOLYCUS' SONG
The Winter's Tale

When daffodils begin to peer,
With heigh! the doxy, over the dale,
Why, then comes in the sweet o' the year;
    For the red blood reigns in the winter's pale.

The white sheet bleaching on the hedge,
    With heigh! the sweet birds, O, how they sing!
Doth set my pugging[1] tooth on edge;
    For a quart of ale is a dish for a king.

The lark, that tirra-lirra chants,
    With, heigh! with, heigh! the thrush and the jay,
Are summer songs for me and my aunts,[2]
    While we lie tumbling in the hay.

                    [1] thievish; [2] mistresses.

CLOWN'S SONG
Twelfth Night

When that I was and a little tiny boy,
With hey, ho, the wind and the rain;
A foolish thing was but a toy,
For the rain it raineth every day.

> But when I came to man's estate,
> With hey, ho, the wind and the rain;
> 'Gainst knaves and thieves men shut their gates,
> For the rain it raineth every day.

> But when I came, alas! to wive
> With hey, ho, the wind and the rain;
> By swaggering could I never thrive,
> For the rain it raineth every day . . .

'The Faerie Queene'

EDMUND SPENSER (1552–99), the first major English poet since Chaucer, was born in London in 1552, the son of a journeyman clothmaker. He was educated first as a 'poor scholar' dependent on the 'spending of the money of Robert Nowell', and then at the newly opened Merchant Taylors' School. In 1569 he matriculated at Pembroke Hall, Cambridge, and in the same year published his earliest work, a translation of Petrarch's *Canzoni*. His main studies were devoted to the classics; and he was profoundly influenced by the then current emphasis on Platonic dialectics. At Cambridge he met Gabriel Harvey and Edward Kirke, who became stimulating friends. Harvey was a Fellow of his college, a scholar and controversialist who lectured on rhetoric and whose great interest was the future of English poetry. After taking his degree, Spenser left Cambridge in poor health, with little money and few material prospects; and, during a visit to his family in Lancashire, he is said to have conceived a passion for a high-born lady. Harvey, however, recalled him to London and introduced him to the Earl of Leicester who offered him employment. At Leicester House he met the great men of the day, including the universally admired Sir Philip Sidney, himself a poet and champion of poetry against its Puritan detractors. This friendship stirred Spenser to serious literary ambition; and in 1579 he published *The Shepherd's Calendar*, a poem that was widely praised.

Spenser had hoped to obtain a post at court; but his hopes were disappointed; and in 1589 he accepted the post of secretary to Lord Grey de Wilton, Lord Deputy of Ireland. He accompanied Grey on his ruthless expeditions against the Irish rebels, and remained in Ireland, occupying various minor official posts, after the Lord Deputy's return. Having finally resigned in 1587, he moved to Kilcolman castle on a confiscated Irish estate near Cork, where he resumed writing. In 1589 he received a visit from Ralegh who, impressed by the opening passages of *The Faerie Queene*, strongly urged that he should finish it. He also persuaded Spenser to accompany him to London, where he presented the poet to their sovereign. The first three books of *The Faerie Queene* appeared in 1590, with a dedication to the Queen; and Spenser was granted a royal pension of fifty pounds a year. This was not enough to

Januarye.   *Fol.1*

Ægloga prima.

ARGVMENT.

I N this fyrſt Æglogue Colin cloute a ſhepheardes boy complaineth him of his vnfortunate loue, being but newly (as ſemeth) enamoured of a coun-trie laſſe called Roſalinde: with which ſtrong affection being very ſore tra-ueled, he compareth his carefull caſe to the ſadde ſeaſon of the yeare, to the froſtie ground, to the froſen trees, and to his owne winterbeaten flocke. And laſtlye, fynding himſelfe robbed of all former pleaſaunce and delights, hee breaketh his Pipe in peeces, and caſteth him ſelfe to the ground.

COLIN Cloute.

A ſhepheards boye (no better doe him call)
when Winters waſtful ſpight was almoſt ſpent,
All in a ſunneſhine day, as did befall,
Led forth his flock, that had bene long ypent.
So faynt they woxe, and feeble in the folde,
That now vnnethes their feete could them vpholo.

All as the Sheepe, ſuch was the ſhepeheards looke,
For pale and wanne he was, (alas the while,)
May ſeeme he lovd, or els ſome care he tooke:
Well couth he tune his pipe, and frame his ſtile.
     A.I.   Tho

The 'fyrst Aeglogue' of Spenser's *Shepherd's Calendar*, 1579.

maintain him in London, and he reluctantly retired to Ireland. In June 1594, he married Elizabeth Boyle, recording the experi-ences of his twelve months' courtship in the sonnet sequence *Amoretti*, and the solemnities of the marriage itself in his *Epithal-amion*. In the winter of 1595 to 1596 he travelled back to London for the publication of books IV to VI of *The Faerie Queene*, and a volume that contained the *Amoretti*. In 1597 he was again at Kil-colman, where he wrote the *Mutabilitie Cantos*, his last surviving work. When, in 1598, Kilcolman was sacked and burned by rebels, the poet barely escaped with his life. In December he once more journeyed home and, soon after he reached London, Spenser died – on 16 January 1599 – not, as legend had it, desperately poor. He was buried in Westminster Abbey, near the tomb of Chaucer.

The Shepherd's Calendar is modelled on the classical eclogues of Theocritus and Virgil, so much admired and so frequently imitated during the Renaissance. It has considerable technical merit; Spenser shows great virtuosity, even at the outset of his

'Aprill', Spenser's 'Aegloga Quarta'.

career, in his clever handling of a variety of stanza forms. The poem consists of twelve eclogues, one for each month of the year, illustrating the course of life and love from youth to age. Spenser deliberately used archaisms to establish a link with the English literary tradition. He was a self-conscious artist, who brought a new freshness into English poetry. The songs in the *Calendar* reveal his lyric gift, as in this extract from 'Aprill':

> See, where she sits upon the grassie green,
>   (O seemly sight)
> Yclad in Scarlet like a maiden Queen,
>   And Ermines white.
> Upon her head a Cremosin coronet,
> With Damask roses and Daffadillies set
>   Bayleaves between,
>   And Primroses green
> Embellish the sweet Violet.

                                 (55–63)

The Amoretti, his sequence of love sonnets, have been overshadowed by Shakespeare's. They are exceptional in that they depart from Petrarch's precedent, and celebrate betrothed love. There is a restrained quality even in the passion they depict – Coleridge called it 'Maidenliness':

> Like as a huntsman after weary chase,
> Seeing the game from him escaped away,
> Sits down to rest him in some shady place,

With panting hounds, beguiled of their prey:
So, after long pursuit and vain assay,
When I all weary had the chase forsook,
The gentle deer returned the self-same way,
Thinking to quench her thirst at the next brook.
There she, beholding me with milder look,
Sought not to fly, but fearless still did bide.
Till I in hand her yet half trembling took,
And with her own good will her firmly tied.
  Strange thing, me seemed, to see a beast so wild
  So goodly won, with her own will beguiled.

                                                  (*LXVII*)

The *Epithalamion*, which forms a conclusion to the sonnets – a
rhapsody on the joys of marriage – has a poetic stateliness, tempered by a strength of feeling, unequalled in Elizabethan verse.

Spenser's masterpiece, *The Faerie Queene*, with its complex
allegorical pattern, is not always an easy poem from the modern
reader's point of view. The poem exists on four levels – literal,
spiritual, moral, and political. Thus when, in Book I, the Red
Cross Knight defends his beloved Una, he is also the Christian
soul defending Truth; and his enemy, Archimago, is at once
Hypocrisy and the Pope of Rome. Spenser had a moral purpose;
the poem's aim, he said, was 'to fashion a gentleman or noble
person in vertuous and gentle discipline'. Spenser completed only
six books of the poem, although he had meant to write twelve,
telling the stories of twelve knights, who symbolized 'the twelve
private moral virtues, as Aristotle hath devised'. The whole poem
was dedicated to the magnification both of England and of her
sovereign lady, who appears as Gloriana, the Faerie Queene. If
the poem is not entirely successful, it is because Spenser tries to do
too much. His moral object conflicts with the demands of the
narrative; and the tale itself is often lost in a labyrinth of moral and
political allegories. The poem holds our attention, however, as an
immense poetic pageant, a long array of rich and luminous
images united by the pervasive dream-like harmony of the slow-
moving nine-line stanza. Spenser's descriptive gifts give poetic life
to even the most outlandish monsters:

And that more wondrous was, in either jaw
  Three ranks of iron teeth enraunged were
In which yet trickling blood and gobbets raw
Of late devoured bodies did appear,
That sight thereof bred cold congealed fear;
Which to increase, and all at once to kill,
A cloud of smothering smoke and sulphur sear
Out of his stinking gorge forth steamed still
That all the air about with smoke and stench did fill.

His blazing eyes, like two bright shining shields,
  Did burn with wrath, and sparkled living fire;

> As two broad Beacons, set in open fields,
> Send forth their flames far off to every shire,
> And warning give, that enemies conspire,
> With fire and sword and region to invade;
> So flam'd his eye with rage and rancorous ire:
> But far within, as in hollow glade,
> Those glaring lamps were set, that made a dreadful shade.
>
> (I, XI. 13, 14)

Spenser has been called 'the poet's poet', which suggests that his talents are of a rarefied kind, only to be appreciated by his fellow poets. Certainly, his influence on English literature has been strong throughout the ages. Dryden, Milton, and even Pope, to whom his vision seems so alien, paid him heartfelt tribute. Keats was greatly indebted to him, most obviously in 'The Eve of St Agnes'; and he deeply affected Tennyson, Browning and William Morris, who admired not only the music of his verse, but the strength of his visual imagery and his rhetorical command of language.

'Rare Ben Jonson'

BEN JONSON (1572–1637) was born in London, and went to Westminster school, and then, about 1589, was apprenticed to his stepfather, a bricklayer. The next few years of his life are obscure, though he is known to have campaigned abroad. He married in 1595, and had a son – 'his best piece of poetry', he afterwards declared – who died of the plague seven years later. In 1597 he was was serving Philip Henslowe, manager of the Fortune theatre, as actor and playwright, and was cast into gaol for his part in a lost satiric comedy, *The Isle of Dogs*. In 1598 *Every Man In His Humour* was played by the Lord Chamberlain's Company, with William Shakespeare in a leading role. Shortly afterwards, having challenged and killed a fellow actor, he again suffered brief imprisonment. His release was followed by the production of *Every Man Out Of His Humour* in 1599. These two comedies enjoyed a great success; and between 1599 and 1601 he wrote experimental plays which he called 'comical satires' – contributions to the 'war of the theatres' that had broken out between the select playhouses in the purlieus of the City and the public playhouses on the Bank-side. In 1603, on the accession of James I, Jonson began to compose court masques and entertainments. In 1605 he once more went to prison, for his share in the comedy *Eastward Ho* that the Scottish faction at Court had found offensive; and he and his collaborators, Chapman and Marston, were threatened with the loss of their ears and noses. In 1606 *Volpone*, the first of his great comedies, was produced at the Globe, followed by *The Alchemist* in 1610, and *Bartholomew Fair* in 1614. But his two Roman tragedies, *Sejanus* in 1603, and *Catiline* in 1611, were, despite his concern with classic 'unity of action' and a knowledge of history that far exceeded

Ben Jonson; portrait by an unknown artist; 'a man passionately kind and angry . . .'

Shakespeare's, considerably less successful. His later comedies, though they have their fine moments, show the gradual decline of his dramatic powers.

The edition of Jonson's collected plays published in 1616 was the first work of its kind to reach the English reader. In 1618 he visited the Scottish poet, Drummond of Hawthornden; and in 1623 he contributed commendatory verses to the Shakespearian First Folio. During his later life he produced further masques at the court of Charles I, and quarrelled violently with the court architect, Inigo Jones, who designed the scenery. In 1628 he was paralysed by a stroke and could no longer leave his room; but his younger disciples, 'The Sons of Ben', continued to visit him. He died in 1637 and was buried in Westminster Abbey, under the epitaph 'O Rare Ben Jonson'.

Jonson's earliest successful comedy, *Every Man In His Humour*, establishes his view of the function of comedy as a method of reforming human weaknesses by ridicule. He considered himself both a moralist and a social realist, and developed the so-called Comedy of Humours, in which each character is seen to be dominated by one particular quirk or trait. Thus in *Volpone, or the Fox*, Jonson depicts a scheming miser who feigns illness that he may watch his equally avaricious neighbours flattering and cajoling him. His servant, Mosca, cunningly manipulates them as they hasten to advertise their deep respect and devotion. Then he, too, decides he will impose on his master; and, at the end, all the characters are suitably exposed and punished. Gold is the centre of the comedy; unbridled lust for it, the driving motive; and the play opens with Volpone's blasphemous daily act of worship:

> Good morning to the day; and next, my gold!
> Open the shrine, that I may see my saint.
> Hail the world's soul, and mine! more glad than is
> The teeming earth to see the longed-for sun
> Peep through the horns of the celestial Ram,
> Am I, to view thy splendour darkening his;
> That lying here, amongst my other hoards,
> Show'st like a flame by night, or like the day
> Struck out of chaos, when all the darkness fled
> Unto the centre.

The very extravagance of this speech indicates the obsessive character of Volpone's ruling passion, which gives it an almost poetic quality. The plot is ingenious; and a sub-plot, concerned with the brainless English tourist, Sir Politick Would-be, adds a further dimension, as well as a topical reference. Sir Politick and his wife are intent upon mimicking Italian manners, themselves shown to be a form of mimicry. The main characters mimic, and become practically indistinguishable from, beasts; and, having violated the basic order of nature, they degenerate into monsters.

The Alchemist is again concerned with deception; and here gold once more provides the bait. A pretended alchemist sets out to exploit the gullible; and among Jonson's dramatis personae is Sir Epicure Mammon, an ambitious but simple-minded voluptuary, whose hedonism matches his command of language. Here he contemplates the rewards of his future riches:

> I will have all my beds blown up, not stuft:
> Down is too hard; and then, mine oval room
> Filled with such pictures as Tiberius took
> From Elephantis, and dull Aretine
> But coldly imitated. Then, my glasses
> Cut in more subtle angles, to disperse
> And multiply the figures, as I walk
> Naked between my succabae. My mists
> I'll have of perfume, vapoured 'bout the room,
> To lose our selves in; and my baths, like pits
> To fall into; from whence we will come forth,
> And roll us dry in gossamer and roses,

The conclusion of *The Alchemist* introduces a surprising twist; for Face, the instigator of the fraud, eventually goes unpunished while his employer, whose absence has enabled Face to hatch his schemes, himself succumbs to temptation on his return home, and accepts the profits of the swindle. Jonson divides mankind not into good and bad, but, more cynically, into knaves and fools.

Frontispiece to *Volpone*
by Aubrey Beardsley
(1872–1898).

In his own day, Jonson was regarded by some of his contemporaries as a finer dramatist than Shakespeare. During the eighteenth and nineteenth centuries, however, he was comparatively neglected. Today, both his superb craftsmanship and his poetic originality, his peculiar blend of delicacy and strength, receive the attention they deserve. Steeped in the classics – unlike Shakespeare he was a genuine classical scholar – he introduced new standards of restraint and unity, and evolved a simple, direct style, based on humanity and commonsense. Rejecting euphemism and unnecessary word-play, he employed 'language such as men doe use'. His most successful lyric poems, though few in number, are both melodious and eloquent:

> Queen and Huntress, chaste and fair
> Now the sun is laid to sleep,
> Seated in thy silver chair
> State in wonted manner keep:
> Hesperus entreats thy light,
> Goddess excellently bright.
>
> Earth, let not thy envious shade
> Dare itself to interpose;
> Cynthia's shining orb was made
> Heaven to clear when day did close:
> Bless us then with wished sight,
> Goddess excellently bright
>
> Lay thy bow of pearl apart
> And thy crystal-shining quiver;
> Give unto the flying hart
> Space to breathe, how short soever:
> Thou that mak'st a day of night.
> Goddess excellently bright!

Some of Jonson's shorter poems are also delightfully comic and ironic, as when he describes '*My Picture Left in Scotland*'.

> I now think Love is rather deaf than blind,
>   For else it could not be
>   That she
> Whom I adore so much should so slight me,
>   And cast my suit behind.
>
> I'm sure my language to her was as sweet,
>   And every close did meet
>   In sentence of as subtle feet,
>   As hath the youngest he,
> That sits in shadow of Apollo's tree
>
>   O! but my conscious fears,
>   That fly my thoughts between,
>   Tell me that she hath seen
>   My hundreds of grey hairs,
>   Told seven-and-forty-years,
> Read so much waste, as she cannot embrace
> My mountain belly and my rocky face,
> And all these, through her eyes, have stopped
>   her ears.

WILLIAM DRUMMOND OF HAWTHORNDEN (1585–1649), a Scottish country gentleman of ancient lineage, though an agreeable minor poet, is now chiefly remembered through his link with Ben Jonson, whose character and sayings he Boswellized, when Jonson paid him a long visit at Hawthornden during the winter months of 1618. Among the opinions Drummond noted down was Jonson's view that Shakespeare had 'wanted art'; among the anecdotes he recorded, his guest's story of how, while campaigning in the Low Countries, he had once fought a duel, single-handed, between the English and the enemy camps, killed his adversary and carried away the spoils. Of the master-poet Drummond's *Conversations* draw a vivid personal portrait: 'A great lover and praiser of himself, a contemner and scorner of others . . . jealous of every word and action of those about him (especially after drink, which is one of the elements in which he liveth) . . . passionately kind and angry, careless either to gain or keep.'

Song-Writers and Sonneteers

Although the Elizabethan Age produced only one distinguished English painter, the incomparable miniaturist, Nicholas Hilliard, it could boast of many fine composers – John Dowland, William Byrd, John Bull and Orlando Gibbons. Queen Elizabeth's subjects had a reverential regard both for music and for dancing; and SIR JOHN DAVIES (1569–1626), a gifted minor poet whose

(*Below left*) Title page of *Parthenia* or *the Maydenhead of the first musicke that ever was printed for the Virginalls*. *c.*1611 by William Byrd, John Bull and Orlando Gibbons.

(*Below right*) Title page of Thomas Campion's *Observations on the Art of English Poesy*, 1602.

Orchestra, or A Poem of Dancing was published in 1596, describes the cosmic dance from which Creation sprang:

> Dancing, bright lady, then began to be
> When the first seeds whereof the world did spring,
> The fire, air, earth and water did agree
> By Love's persuasion, nature's mighty king,
> To leave their first disorder'd combating . . .

The Queen herself danced, with impressive grace and gaiety, even as an old woman; ambitious young gentlemen were recommended by the entertaining autobiographer LORD HERBERT OF CHERBURY to engage the services of an 'accurate' French dancing-master; and actors themselves were trained to 'move in music'. Many composers wrote for the dances of the Court – galliards (of which the Queen was particularly fond), pavanes, corantos and lavoltas. But their greatest achievement was the music they produced for voices, either madrigals executed by several singers, or solo 'ayres' to be accompanied by the lute.

A multitude of *Books of Ayres* were circulated during the Elizabethan period, incorporating words and music; and THOMAS CAMPION (*d.*1620), being at once a skilful composer and a remarkably accomplished poet, set his own verses to music with the help of a contemporary lutanist, Philip Rossiter. Educated at Cambridge, he became a successful London physician and a member of the 'worshipful fraternity of sirenaical gentlemen', including Shakespeare, Jonson, Drayton and the young John Donne, who frequented the famous Mermaid Tavern in Bread Street. Otherwise the details of his life remain obscure; even the date of his birth is unknown; but we learn that he died, no doubt carried off by the plague, on 1 March 1620, and was buried in a City church. Few English poets have had a more sensitive ear; and so deeply was Campion concerned with the alliance between words and music, and with the harmonic construction of his poems – he 'aimed chiefly', he said, 'to couple my Words and Notes lovingly together' – that he believed that English verse could afford, now and then, to discard the use of rhyme, and in 1602 published a scholarly pamphlet entitled *Observations on the Art of English Poesy*, where he attacked 'the custom of rhyming' as both 'vulgar and un-artificial' – 'artificial', of course, in Campion's day, being still a term of high praise. It was not a popular theory – Jonson himself replied with a pamphlet in which he energetically defended rhyme. Some of the unrhymed verses that Campion added to his treatise have a particularly melodious cadence:

(*Opposite*) Masque at a wedding-feast, held by Sir Henry Unton, about 1596.

> Rose-cheeked Laura, come;
> Sing thou smoothly with thy beauty's
> Silent music, either other
>   Sweetly gracing

> Lovely forms do flow
> From concert divinely framed;
> Heaven is music, and thy beauty's
> Birth is heavenly . . .

But, for the most part, despite his literary theories, he preferred to use rhyme, with results that were often memorable:

> When thou must home to shades of underground,
> And there arrived, a new admired guest,
> The beauteous spirit do engirt thee round,
> White Iope, blithe Helen, and the rest,
> To hear the stories of thy finished love
> From that smooth tongue whose music hell can move;

> Then wilt thou speak of banqueting delights,
> Of masques and revels which sweet youth did make,
> Of tourneys and great challenges of knights.
> And all these triumphs for thy beauty's sake:
> When thou hast told these honours done to thee,
> Then tell, O tell, how thou didst murder me.

At the same time, Campion composed masques. Of the five *Books of Ayres* that contain his exquisite lute-songs, the first appeared in 1601.

The Sonnet was a form of verse-writing particularly well-suited to the Elizabethan genius. *Tottel's Miscellany* (1557), which has been described as 'the earliest printed collection of polite verse' intended for the general English reader, contained no less than sixty sonnets; and it prefaced a long series of similar anthologies, the most important being *England's Helicon* (1600), which represented some of the major poets of the day. First employed in England by Sir Thomas Wyatt, who had brought it home from Italy, the sonnet was adapted and refined by Sir Philip Sidney, who imitated not only Italian models, but Ronsard, du Bellay and other members of the French *Pléiade*; and whose *Astrophel and Stella* became the inspiration of all succeeding sonnet-sequences. No doubt the roundness and completeness of the sonnet gave it a peculiar charm. Into fourteen lines the poet was expected to compress an entire emotional episode, with a beginning, a middle and an end, the last couplet rounding off the theme already propounded in the opening passage, varying it, enlarging upon it or administering a subtle twist that transformed the poem's character. Shakespeare's sonnets (see pp. 64–5) present too many problems to be analysed here at any length; but, despite the intricacy of the story they tell, and the writer's acrimonious references to the harsh conditions of his own life, in 1598 a critic called them 'sugared'; while their mid-seventeenth-century publisher informed his readers that they were '*serene*, clear and elegantly plain . . . no intricate or cloudy stuff to puzzle intellect, but perfect eloquence; such as will raise your admiration to (the poet's) praise'.

Besides Shakespeare, the two most gifted Elizabethan sonneteers were SAMUEL DANIEL (1562–1619) and MICHAEL DRAYTON (1563–1631). Shakespeare had evidently read and admired them both; there is a clear connection between his sonnet 106:

> When in the chronicles of wasted time,
> I see descriptions of the fairest wights,
> And beauty making beautiful old rhyme
> In praise of ladies dead and lovely knights . . .

and Sonnet 4 from Daniel's *Delia*:

> Let others sing of knights and paladins
> In aged accents and untimely words,
> Paint shadows in imaginary lines
> Which well the reach of their high wits records . . .

The link between Shakespeare and his friend Drayton is very often no less striking; and he seems actually to be parodying Drayton in his notorious Sonnet 130, where he abuses the so-called 'Dark Lady', whose eyes are 'nothing like the sun', whose skin is discoloured and whose locks are coarse and wiry. Drayton was also a Warwickshire man; and in his native county, while he was attached to a patrician household, he became enamoured of the unknown woman whom he developed into the heroine of *Idea's Mirror*, the sonnet-sequence he published during the year 1594. He was an extremely prolific poet, author of *Poly-Olbion*, a panoramic view of British history; *Nimphidia, or the Court of Faery*, a charming evocation of the world of Queen Mab; and of ballads, pastorals and vigorous satires. Today, however, he is chiefly remembered for two poignant sonnets, where, as in so much Elizabethan verse, his theme is the splendours and miseries of human passion:

> Since there's no help, come let us kiss and part.
> Nay, I have done; you get no more of me,
> And I am glad, yea, glad with all my heart,
> That thus so cleanly I myself can free.
> Shake hands for ever, cancel all our vows,
> And when we meet at any time again,
> Be it not seen in either of our brows
> That we one jot of former love retain.
> Now at the last gasp of Love's latest breath,
> When, his pulse failing, Passion speechless lies,
> When Faith is kneeling by his bed of death,
> And Innocence is closing up his eyes,
> Now, if thou wouldst, when all have given him over,
> From death to life thou might'st him yet recover.

The poem is divided into three paragraphs, each denoting a dramatic change of mood; but the tone, unlike that of a sonnet by Sidney, is so direct and spontaneously eloquent as to seem almost conversational.

Michael Drayton, in 1599, at the age of thirty-six; portrait by an unknown artist.

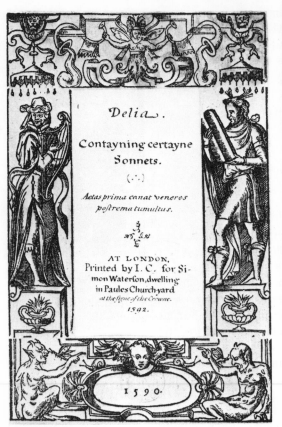

(*Above left*) Samuel Daniel's *Delia*, 1592; the border may have been engraved by the poet himself.

(*Above right*) *Poly-Olbion*, 1612; the title-page represents the tutelary genius of the British Isles.

Elsewhere Drayton enlarges on the pains of love:

> An evil spirit, your beauty haunts me still,
> Wherewith, alas, I have been long possessed,
> Which ceases not to tempt me to each ill,
> Nor gives me once but one poor minute's rest.
> In me it speaks, whether I sleep or wake,
> And when by means to drive it out I try
> With greater torments then it me doth take,
> And tortures me in most extremity.
> Before my face it lays down my despairs,
> And hastes me on unto a sudden death,
> Now tempting me to drown myself in tears,
> And then in sighing to give up my breath.
> Thus am I still provok'd to every evil
> By this good wicked spirit, sweet angel devil.

Courtier Poets

SIR WALTER RALEGH (1552?–1618) was among the most extraordinary of Queen Elizabeth's favourites, and certainly the most gifted. Born at Hayes Barton, the son of a Devonshire country

Sir Walter Ralegh, with
the son he lost during his
expedition to South
America; by an unknown
artist.

gentleman, in 1578 he sailed to America and the West Indies on
a voyage of conquest and exploration led by his half-brother, Sir
Humphrey Gilbert, and later distinguished himself as an officer of
the English forces then battling against the Irish rebels. In 1581 he
returned to Court with despatches, and there immediately
attracted the Queen's attention. Elizabeth was a generous mistress; thanks to estates he received and the commercial monopolies
that she granted him, Ralegh soon grew very rich. Part of his
revenues he devoted to the colonization of the New World, one of
his boldest projects being the settlement of Virginia, which he
named after the Virgin Queen. But a favourite's career had many

(*Opposite*) Ralegh's *History of the World*, 1614, the book that he wrote during his imprisonment in the Tower of London.

drawbacks; Elizabeth would either forbid him to leave her kingdom, or suddenly recall him when he was about to set forth. If she was generous, she was also fiercely jealous; and, when she learned of his liaison with, and secret marriage to Elizabeth Throckmorton, one of her attractive Maids of Honour, she ordered his imprisonment in the Tower of London. Ralegh's cult of the sovereign was extravagant even by Elizabethan standards; and, on seeing her pass by in her royal barge along the Thames beneath his prison window, he fell into a frenzy of amorous despair and attacked his gaoler with a knife. Some of his loveliest lyrics were addressed to the Queen herself; and he bitterly resented the subversive influence of her new favourite, the Earl of Essex, until Essex's tragic downfall in February 1601 at length removed him from the stage.

Under James I, Ralegh's fortunes declined. Accused of having been involved in a conspiracy against the Scottish King's accession, he was once more committed to the Tower, where he spent some fourteen years. His imprisonment, however, was not unduly harsh. With Elizabeth Ralegh, his children and other members of his household, he led a tolerably pleasant life, and began composing a voluminous *History of the World*, the first attempt at such a work in English, which, before his death, he had managed to carry

The Tower of London; drawing by Wenceslaus Hollar, 1647.

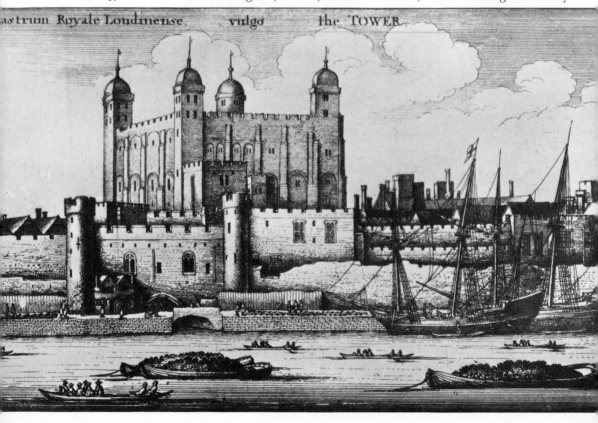

astrum Royale Londinense,   vulgo   the TOWER

on as far as 130 BC. Finally, in 1616, Ralegh launched his last adventure. In 1595 he had already visited Guiana, seeking for 'El Dorado', the fabulous Golden City; and he now suggested that, if he were released from the Tower, he could tap the immense resources of a certain South-American gold-mine, adding the important diplomatic proviso that he would carry off his booty without infringing Spanish territorial rights. He was duly released; but his adventurous scheme miscarried. During the hostilities provoked by his expedition, Ralegh's son and namesake lost his life; and once he had returned to England, the Spanish ambassador insisted he should stand trial. The old charge of treason was thereupon revived; and Ralegh was condemned to death, sentence being pronounced in October 1618 by the Attorney General Francis Bacon.

He had 'risen like a star' his prosecutors reminded him, and like a star he must expect to fall. It was a choice of imagery with which he may well have sympathized; his was essentially a histrionic nature; he shared the Elizabethan view of the world as a stage across which a great man made his fated way. During his years of power and prosperity, Ralegh had had many foes, who denounced him as a 'Machiavel', spoke of his 'bloody pride' and, because he had exploited rich commercial monopolies, styled him a ruthless 'skinner of the poor'. At the same time, he was popularly regarded as a dangerous atheist; for around him he had gathered the small group of free-thinking friends that included Christopher Marlowe and George Chapman, Thomas Harriot, the celebrated mathematician, who was believed to practise the Black Arts, and Northumberland, 'the Wizard Earl'. Ralegh's 'School of Night' alarmed his contemporaries; and Armado in *Love's Labour's Lost*, is thought to represent its founder. Shakespeare had little use for science. Ralegh, on the other hand, seems to have taken a passionate interest in astronomy and chemistry. He was also devoted to literature, and enjoyed the companionship of literary men. He had befriended a series of famous poets from Spenser to Marlowe and Ben Jonson; and, besides being a highly intelligent patron, he was an admirable poet in his own right. The proud, self-seeking adventurer always envisaged the adventures he planned from a poetic point of view. Profit he sought – but something more than profit:

> To seek new worlds, for gold, for praise, for glory,
> To try desire, to try love severed far –

Similarly, the homage that he paid to the Queen he served was based upon romantic motives; and he addressed Elizabeth in a series of perfervid poems, entitled *Cynthia, the Lady of the Sea* (of which only the twenty-first book remains) where the Queen is the Goddess of the Moon, and he himself her moon-struck servant. It is often difficult to distinguish between the poems he wrote for

Cynthia and those inspired by more ephemeral passions. The poem, from which some melodious lines are quoted below, might belong to either category, though the elderly sovereign he adored was more probably the recipient:

'How shall I know your true love,
That have met many one
As I went to the holy land,
That have come, that have gone?'

'She is neither white nor brown,
But as the heavens fair,
There is none that hath form so divine
In the earth or the air . . .

I have lov'd her all my youth,
But now old as you see,
Love likes not the falling fruit
From the witheréd tree.

Know that Love is a careless child,
And forgets promises past;
He is blind, he is deaf when he list
And in faith never fast;

His desire is a dureless content
And a trustless joy;
He is won with a world of despair
And is lost with a toy . . .

But true love is a durable fire
In the mind ever burning;
Never sick, never old, never dead,
From itself never turning.

Ralegh was also a master of English prose, his style being stately and measured, yet comparatively direct and simple, without the ponderous inversions favoured by other Elizabethan prose-writers. In his *History of the World* Ralegh embarked on a subject that, given the historical sources at his disposal, was evidently far beyond his grasp. Nonetheless it was an outstanding achievement; previous English chronicles had been confined to native history; and his *Discoverie of Guiana* is a marvellous evocation of the un-explored Americas in all their primitive innocence and spring-time grace:

I never saw a more beautiful country, nor more lively prospects, hills so raised here and there over the valleys, the river winding into divers branches, the plains adjoining without bush or stubble, all fair green grass, the ground of hard sand easy to march on either for horse or foot, the deer crossing in every path, the birds towards the evening singing on every tree with a thousand several tunes, cranes and herons of white, crimson, and carnation perching on the river's side, the air fresh with a gentle, easterly wind, and every stone that we stooped to take up promised either silver or gold by his complexion.

SIR PHILIP SIDNEY (1554–86) was, like Sir Walter Ralegh, one of the great typical figures of the age in which he lived; but, whereas Ralegh, born some two years earlier, represented not only the fiery spirit of the period but its pride and craft and violence, Sidney personified its romantic idealism and its respect for the chivalric virtues. During his lifetime Sidney became a legend; and the fact that he died young, on a foreign battlefield, helped to keep the legend green. Unlike Ralegh, moreover, the son of a country gentleman, he had been born into the Elizabethan patriciate – his father, Sir Henry Sidney, was a distinguished soldier and statesman, thrice Lord Deputy of Ireland; and he had had no need to fight his way. Sidney was a precocious yet a gentle, grave and remarkably modest youth. 'Though I . . . knew him from a child', wrote his friend and biographer, Fulke Greville, 'I never knew him other than a man; with such staidness of mind, lovely and familiar gravity, as carried grace and reverence above greater years; his talk ever of knowledge, and his very play tending to enrich his mind.' Having left Oxford, he visited the English embassy in Paris, and was made much of by the French court. Later, he travelled through Germany, Italy, Austria, Hungary and Poland; and, on his return home in 1575, he devoted himself both to contemporary political problems and to the cultivation of

(*Below left*) Sir Philip Sidney, the type of Elizabethan hero; portrait by an unknown artist.

(*Below right*) *The Countess of Pembroke's Arcadia*, 1590; the first page of the opening book.

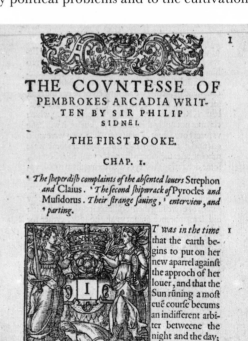

his own imaginative gifts. During his lifetime none of his works was published; his prose romance, *The Countess of Pembroke's Arcadia* (written for his beloved sister's amusement), his famous sonnet-sequence, *Astrophel and Stella* (inspired by his unhappy courtship of Lady Penelope Devereux, who married his rival, Lord Rich) and his *Defence of Poesie* (a counterblast to Puritan critics of the art) appeared in 1590, 1591 and 1598 respectively. But the manuscripts, which were widely circulated, very soon secured him fame; and when in 1586 he joined an English expedition to the Low Countries under the command of his uncle the gallant Earl of Leicester, Queen Elizabeth's long established favourite, and died of the wounds he had received during a skirmish at Zutphen, he was acclaimed as a patriotic hero. Fashionable society at once went into mourning; among 'gentlemen of quality', we are told, 'it was accounted a sin for months afterwards . . . to wear gay apparel in London'.

Sidney's legend has stood the test of time. True, *Arcadia*, despite its many beauties, is not a book we often read today; the pastoral conventions that delighted its author's circle, and that Sidney had borrowed from Spanish and Italian poets, have now lost their poetic freshness; while in his *Defence* (also entitled *An Apologie for Poetrie*) he takes up arms in defence of a cause that no longer needs defending. Here he is at his best, not when he pleads and argues, but when he describes the effect of poetry upon his own mind. Poetry immortalizes every idea and feeling that he himself has learned to value: 'It is not riming and versing that maketh poetry. One may be a poet with versing, and a versifier without poetry.' The art of poetry expresses a state of soul; and even the rudest verse may arouse some deep emotion: 'I never heard the old song of Percy and Douglas that I felt not my heart moved more than with a trumpet . . .'

Astrophel and Stella, a far more rewarding work, must have been written about the time of Penelope Devereux's marriage. Sidney's heroine clearly deserved his interest. The sister of Lord Essex, and a member of the dazzling côterie in which Shakespeare's patron, Lord Southampton, also played a brilliant part, she was to become one of the most wayward of Elizabethan great ladies. As Lady Rich, she would lead a stormy life; and of her twelve children, seven were thought to have been fathered by her husband and five by her young lover, Lord Mountjoy, whom she eventually married in the year 1605. Perhaps Sidney's courtship was a little too platonic to suit this headstrong and ebullient creature; but his sonnets, though based on the convention he had inherited from Surrey and Wyatt, and from the sixteenth-century French poets, suggest a genuine strength of feeling:

> Come, Sleep!; O sleep! the certain knot of peace.
> The baiting-place of wit, the balm of woe,
> The poor man's wealth, the prisoner's release,

> Th'indifferent judge between the high and low;
> With shield of proof shield me from out the prease
> Of those fierce darts Despair at me doth throw:
> O make in me those civil wars to cease;
> I will good tribute pay, if thou do so,
> Take thou of me smooth pillows, sweetest bed,
> A chamber deaf to noise and blind of light,
> A rosy garland and a weary head;
> And if these things, as being thine by right,
> Move not thy heavy grace, thou shalt in me,
> Livelier than elsewhere, Stella's image see.

FULKE GREVILLE (1554–1628) is said often to have remarked that he desired to be remembered 'under no other notions than of Shakespeare's and Ben Jonson's master, Chancellor Egerton's patron . . . and Sir Philip Sidney's friend'. The latter was a friendship that he valued above all else. They had been friends since early childhood, had gone to Shrewsbury School together, and on to Jesus College, Cambridge. In 1577 both arrived at Court; and, after Sidney's early death, Greville decided to remain a courtier, and soon became a royal favourite. He made the most of his luck, and enjoyed, we are told, 'the longest lease and the smoothest time without rub', of any young gentleman who had pleased the Queen. His progress was rapid; and Francis Bacon admits that he had used his influence wisely. In 1583 he was appointed Secretary to the Principality of Wales; in 1597, 'treasurer to the wars'; in 1598, Treasurer of the Navy. During the next reign, under King James I, Greville served as Chancellor of the Exchequer from 1614 until 1621, when he was created Lord Brooke. He had now built up a large fortune, and was the richest landowner of Warwickshire, his native county. But a tragic and ridiculous end awaited him. Seven years later, Greville was stabbed to death, while returning from the privy, by an old and apparently devoted servant, who suspected that his ungrateful employer had omitted to include him in his will.

Greville wrote to amuse a small circle. Though his ambitious *Tragedy of Mustapha* appeared in the year 1609, none of his lyric verses was intended for immediate publication. *Caelica*, which contains a hundred-and-ten poems, all written earlier than 1600, first appeared in 1633. His love-poems, which are among the earliest he wrote, combine an ingenious play of images with an almost conversational directness:

> I with whose colours Myra dressed her head,
> I, that ware posies of her own hand-making,
> I, that mine own name in the chimneys read,
> By Myra finely wrought ere I was waking:
> Must I look on, in hope time coming may
> With turn bring back my time again to play?

I, that on Sunday at the church stile found
A garland sweet with true-love-knots in flowers,
Which I to wear about mine arms was bound
That each of us might know that all was ours:
Must I lead now an idle life in wishes,
And follow Cupid for his loaves and fishes? . . .

Was it for this that I might Myra see
Washing the water with her beauty's white?
Yet could she never write her name to me.
Thinks wit of change when thoughts are in delight?
Mad girls may safely love as they may leave;
No man can *print* a kiss: lines may deceive.

(*Above left*) Fulke Greville, Lord Brooke; from the frontispiece to an early 19th-century edition of his *Life of Sir Philip Sidney*.

(*Above right*) Greville's *Tragedy of Mustapha*, 1609; the title-page.

Greville also produced two ambitious verse-tragedies, *Alaham* and *Mustapha*, in which, observed Charles Lamb, he 'strangely contrived to make passion, character and interest . . . subservient to the expression of State dogmas and mysteries'. The dramatist argues at length about the problems that concern him; but each play is eminently unactable and singularly unreadable. They are redeemed by some splendid bursts of eloquence – in *Alaham*, for instance, by a magnificent Chorus of Priests:

> Oh wearisome Condition of Humanity!
> Borne under one Law, to another bound:
> Vainly begot, and yet forbidden vanity,

Created sick, commanded to be sound:
What meaneth Nature by these diverse laws?
Passion and Reason self-division cause . . .

On his death, he left at Warwick Castle, for many years his country house, a manuscript collection of his verses. Though written by several different hands, its pages bear his own corrections, which show the poet as a conscientious artist, who made frequent efforts to remove the irregularities of his often harsh and tortuous style.

Elizabethan Prose

Richard Hooker; from an early 19th-century edition of Izaak Walton's biography; 'an obscure harmless man . . . in poor clothes . . . of a mean stature and stooping . . .'

RICHARD HOOKER (1554?–1600) was both a noted theologian and a celebrated stylist, who, while he laid down the intellectual foundations of the Anglican establishment, also contrived to set a new standard in the art of English prose-writing. Having obtained a scholarship at Oxford, and afterwards a fellowship, he took orders about 1581, and on a visit to London was married off to his landlady's daughter, with somewhat inharmonious results. His biographer, Izaak Walton, describes Hooker as 'an obscure harmless man . . . in poor clothes, his loins usually girt in a close gown or canonical coat; of a mean stature and stooping . . . his body worn out not with age but with study and holy mortifications; his face full of heat pimples he got by his inactivity and sedentary life.' He evolved, however, a large and grandiose style. The first four books of his great treatise *Of the Lawes of Ecclesiastical Politie* appeared in 1593, the fifth in 1597; and, on his death, he left the work unfinished. Hooker's approach to his subject – the proper basis of church-government – is majestic and authoritative, yet neither intemperate nor overbearing. His periods are finely balanced; he shuns extravagance of thought or language. Here his theme is 'the eternal law of God . . . concerning things natural':

He 'made a law for the rain'; he gave his 'decree unto the sea that the waters should not pass his commandment'. Now if Nature should intermit her course, and leave altogether, though it were but for a while, the observation of her own laws; if those principal and mother elements of the world, whereof all things in this lower world are made, should lose the qualities which they now have; if the frame of the heavenly arch erected over our heads should loosen and dissolve itself; if celestial spheres should forget their wonted motions, and by irregular volubility turn themselves any way as it might happen; if the prince of the lights of heaven, which now as a giant doth run his unwearied course, should, as it were through a languishing faintness, begin to stand and to rest himself; if the moon should wander from her beaten way; the times and seasons of the year blend themselves by disorder and confused mixture; the winds breathe out their last gasp, the clouds yield no rain, the earth be defeated of heavenly influence, the fruits of the earth pine away as children at the withered breasts of their mothers, no longer able to yield them relief: what would become of man himself, whom these things do all now serve? See we not plainly that obedience of creatures unto the law of nature is the stay of the whole world?

Sixteenth-century prose, however, was not always stately and sententious; and the Elizabethan pamphleteers were much akin to modern journalists. Among them was STEPHEN GOSSON (1554–1624), whose *School of Abuse*, an attack on the stage and on poets and players and 'such like caterpillars of a commonwealth', had provoked Sidney to compose his defence of the poetic art. Gosson's best-known pamphlet, which describes among other things the licentious atmosphere said to have prevailed in an Elizabethan play house, is an admirable piece of puritanical invective:

In Rome, when plays or pageants are shown, Ovid chargeth his pilgrims to creep close to the saints whom they serve, and show their double diligence . . . In our assemblies at plays in London, you shall see such heaving and shoving, such itching and shouldering, to sit by women: such care for their garments, that they be not trod on: such eyes to their laps, that no chips light in them: such pillows to their backs that they take no hurt: such masking in their ears, I know not what: such giving them pippins to pass the time: such playing at foot saunt without cards: such ticking, such toying, such smiling, such winking, and such manning them home when the sports are ended, that it is a right comedy . . . Not that any filthiness in deed is committed within the compass of that ground, as was done in Rome, but that every wanton and his paramour, every man and his mistress, even John and his Joan, every knave and his queen, are there first acquainted and cheapen the merchandise in that place, which they pay for elsewhere as they can agree.

The dramatists, too, were sometimes pamphleteers. THOMAS DEKKER, for example, (*c.*1572–*c.*1632), author of *The Shoemaker's Holiday*, *Old Fortunatus* and *The Honest Whore*, also castigated current vices in *The Seven Deadly Sins of London*, *News from Hell* and *The Gull's Hornbook*. Dekker, a hard-worked literary hack, at other times a merchant-tailor, published the pamphlets listed above between 1606 and 1609; but, with his delight in words and flow of picturesque imagery, he shows the true Elizabethan spirit.

History, considered less as an imaginative literary exercise or a collection of old tales, than as a scientific record and analysis of facts, had made little progress under Tudor sovereigns. EDWARD HALL (1498?–1547) was first and foremost an annalist and chronicler. His *Union of the Noble and Illustrious Families of Lancaster and York* came out in 1542, sixteen years before the Queen's accession; and he was succeeded by RAPHAEL HOLINSHED (*d.*1580). His *Chronicles of England, Scotland, Ireland*, on which he had collaborated with two assistants, appeared in 1577; and both Hall and Holinshed provided Shakespeare with invaluable source-books, from which, sometimes paraphrasing whole passages, he hammered out his series of English historical dramas.

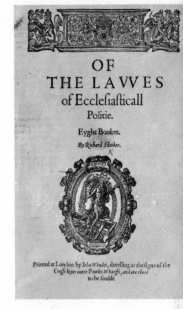

OF
THE LAVVES
of Ecclesiasticall
Politie.

Eyght Bookes.
By Richard Hooker.

Printed at London by *Iohn Windet*, dwelling at the signe of the *Crosse keyes neere Powles Wharffe*, and are there to be foulde

Hooker's *Lawes of Ecclesiastical Politie*, 1593, illustrates his majestic prose-style.

(*Above left*) John Stow, author of the *Chronicles of England* and a *Survay of London*, the greatest antiquarian of his age.

(*Above right*) Title page of Stow's *Chronicles*, showing Queen Elizabeth's descent from Edward III.

Here we must also mention Shakespeare's indebtedness to the excellent translation of a French version of Plutarch's *Lives*, produced in 1570 by SIR THOMAS NORTH (1535?–1601), which the dramatist found equally serviceable when he embarked upon his Roman tragedies.

The chief antiquarian of the age was JOHN STOW (1525–1605) who, besides editing the works of Geoffrey Chaucer, and transcribing and publishing ancient manuscripts, published *The Chronicles of England* in 1580, and the two parts of his fascinating *Survay of London* in 1598 and 1603. Queen Elizabeth's subjects were deeply concerned with their own historic past. At the same time, fired by stories of conquest and adventure, they looked out towards the New World. RICHARD HAKLUYT (1552?–1616), an archdeacon of Westminster and a member of the Virginia Company of London, though a sedentary character himself, greatly enjoyed collecting travellers' tales and, in 1589, issued his *Principal Navagations, Voyages, and Discoveries of the English Nation* – an epic tribute to his countrymen's enterprise which achieved immediate popularity. His narrative has a wonderful directness and, at its best, a sparkling freshness. To the Elizabethans, the New World was still the earthly paradise described by Ralegh, where the wind blew fresh, the meadows were eternally green, and the English adventurer might find bars of solid gold – Spanish loot wrung from the poor Indians – conveniently stacked up on a deserted quayside.

5

The Seventeenth Century

The English seventeenth century was a period of immense achievement. Apart from its contribution to the history of ideas, its rapid progress in the 'natural sciences' and the tremendous advances it made in the art of modern prose-writing, it gave birth to some of the most remarkable poets who have ever used the English language. Milton and Dryden occupy solitary heights. Of their predecessors, the so-called 'Metaphysicals', T. S. Eliot has said – he is referring particularly to John Donne – that they had acquired 'a mechanism of sensibility which could devour any kind of experience'. They were men who suffered, speculated and imagined with equal vivacity and strength of feeling. Seldom have poets been more passionately addicted to thought, or more thoughtful in their analysis of passion; and, when they turned their attention to supernatural themes and studied the relationship between Man and God, they often assumed the attitude and employed the symbolism of earthly lovers.

The seventeenth century was a profoundly religious age. It was also a period of social conflict. The King had raised his standard at Nottingham, and launched his struggle against a rebellious parliament in August 1642; and for many Englishmen, who lived to see the Restoration, the Civil Wars were a catastrophic interlude – the 'Flood' that divided a rich, productive past from a bleak and inharmonious present. Dryden described his Elizabethan and Jacobean ancestors as a legendary 'giant race'; Marvell, while the Deluge was still raging, wrote of England as a devastated garden, where warriors sowed their dragon-seed.

Yet, if the shock was violent, its literary effects were gradual. The catastrophe left many distinguished survivors. Marvell lived on until 1678; Milton, Herrick and Traherne until 1674; Vaughan until 1695. The twelve books of *Paradise Lost* appeared in 1667, and Dryden's *All for Love* in 1678. During the latter decades of the century, however, despite Dryden's magisterial influence, English verse, particularly lyric verse, had begun to slip into a slow decline. Rochester, a neurotic Don Juan who combined Metaphysical ingenuity with Elizabethan eloquence and ardour, died, a broken debauchee, in 1680; Oldham, Flatman, Sedley and Matthew Prior were mellifluous but unimportant rhymers. When

John Dryden wrote his *Secular Masque* in which he bade the century goodbye – he himself would die soon afterwards – English poetry, as contemporary critics agreed, had sunk to a miserably low level. Meanwhile English prose, though it had lost some of the decorative charm cultivated by writers like Sir Thomas Browne, was becoming more and more direct and factual. The second half of the seventeenth century was a scientific age – the Royal Society, under the aegis of Charles II, had been founded in 1662; and Lord Clarendon (whose *History of the Rebellion*, began during the middle of the century, did not appear till 1702) endeavoured to examine the events of the past from a strictly impartial point of view, using a style largely devoid of ornament. It has been said of his *History* that 'we may read pages . . . without lighting upon a single word no longer in use'. He was essentially a modern man.

The Jacobean Drama

From the death of Shakespeare in 1616 to the closing of the London theatres in 1642 by order of a puritanical House of Commons, which had decreed that, 'while these sad causes and set-times of humiliation do continue, public stages should cease and be forborne', the drama that Kyd and Marlowe had founded would continue to pursue its lively course. Among the dramatists it produced were Heywood, Tourneur, Middleton, Webster and Ford. But, as time passed, playwrights came more and more to depend on the extravagant sensationalism of the subjects that they treated.

GEORGE CHAPMAN (1559–1642) was one of the most gifted contemporaries of Ben Jonson. Though he claimed to be self-educated, he probably spent some time at Oxford, afterwards touring Germany with a company of English players. Back in London, he received the patronage of Prince Henry, the short-lived elder son of James I. His first poem, *The Shadow of Night*, had been published in 1594, and from 1595 he was writing comedies for the Admiral's Company. In 1599, with *A Humourous Day's Mirth*, he tried his hand at the Jonsonian comedy of humours. A member of the School of Night and a friend of Ralegh and Marlowe, whose poem *Hero and Leander* he completed with the addition of four new sestiads which do the poem little credit, he produced a series of tragedies based on modern French history, the most successful being *Bussy D'Ambois*, staged in the year 1604. From 1598 to 1616, he worked on his translations of Homer, the achievement that brought him lasting fame and was destined to inspire Keats' famous sonnet. During its preparation, he had a vision of Homer, his breast blazing with poetic fire; and this experience, he felt, entitled him to alter and 'improve' the text. Having completed his translations, Chapman faded away into obscurity and poverty, and died on 12 May 1634.

Mulciber in Troiam.   pro Troia stabat Apollo.

HOMER

THE
WHOLE WORKS
OF
HOMER:
PRINCE OF POETTS
In his Iliads, and
Odysses.
Translated according to the Greeke.
By
Geo: Chapman.
De Ili: et Odiss:
Omnia ab, hisset in his sunt omnia:
sue beati
Te decor eloquij seu rerii pondera
tangunt   Anget.Pol:
At London printed for Nathaniell Butter.
William Hole sculp:

Qui Nil mo-
litur Inepte

ACHILLES   HECTOR

George Chapman's
translations of the *Iliad*
and the *Odyssey*, 1612.

Chapman tended to use literature as a vehicle for his own intellectual interests, with the result that his blank verse is more expository than passionate. In his tragedies, he seems to be doing his best to revive the spirit of his friend Marlowe; each is dominated by a single great man, whose wild and powerful declamations recall the tremendous monologues of Tamburlaine. But Chapman's obsession with the sweeping heroic gesture results in long bombastic passages that are barely intelligible; though Dryden's assessment of *Bussy D'Ambois* – 'uncorrect English, and a hideous mingle of false poetry and true nonsense' – seems a little over-stern.

By the standards of his age, Chapman was an excellent classical scholar. His translation of Homer is not free from the weaknesses that mar his plays; with the authority of his vision to support him, he confidently remodelled Homer's poem, adding some obscurities and touches of rhetorical extravagance. But on the whole the translation is admirably lucid and has moments of real poetic strength:

> And as amidst the sky
> We sometimes see an ominous star blaze clear and dreadfully,

> Then run his golden head in clouds, and straight appear again;
> So Hector otherwiles did grace the vant-guard, shining plain,
> Then in the rear-guard hid himself, and laboured everywhere
> To order and encourage all; his armour was so clear,
> And he applied each place so fast, that, like a lightning thrown
> Out of the shield of Jupiter, in every eye he shone.
> And as upon a rich man's crop of barley or of wheat,
> Opposed for swiftness at their work, a sort of reapers sweat,
> Bear down the furrows speedily, and thick their handfuls fall;
> So at the joining of the hosts ran slaughter through them all.

Chapman was an eccentric, melancholy character whose un-worldliness is reflected in his works. Hence his frequent inability, in Swinburne's expressive phrase, 'to clear his mouth of pebbles and his brow of fog'.

JOHN MARSTON (1576–1634) was a dramatist for only a short period in his life, from 1599 until 1607. He was born in 1576, the son of a lawyer who wished the young man to adopt his own pro-fession; and, after studying at Oxford, Marston entered the Middle Temple in the year 1594. He seems to have remained a lawyer until 1604, but showed little interest in his legal work, and preferred to devote his time to philosophy and literature. In 1598, he published a series of satires notable for their eroticism and wild invective, one of which, *The Metamorphosis of Pigmalion's Image*, was publicly burned by order of Archbishop Whitgift. Marston achieved even greater notoriety through his involvement in the 'War of the Theatres', beginning with a clumsy tribute to Jonson that the older poet interpreted as a deliberate insult. In *Every Man Out of His Humour*, he held Marston up to public ridicule; and the dispute continued through a series of plays, until Jonson effectively ended it, in 1601, with his crushing *Poetaster*. It was almost cer-tainly the events of this period that Jonson was remembering when he declared that he 'beate Marston and took his pistol from him'. The controversy, however, had evidently subsided before 1605. That year, Jonson, Marston and Chapman collaborated on the satirical *Eastward Ho!*, one of the liveliest comedies of the day.

Marston's own plays were written for a company of child-actors, the Paul's Boys. The first were Senecan tragedies – *Antonio and Mellida* (1600), and its sequel, *Antonio's Revenge* (1601), the latter play having a plot somewhat similar to the theme of *Hamlet*. The *Malcontent*, his most ambitious and successful play, was produced in 1604, and followed by *The Dutch Courtesan* and *The Wonder of Women or the Tragdey of Sophonisba* (1606). Shortly afterwards, his career as a dramatist ended; in 1607 he took Holy Orders, and suddenly abandoned writing. Little more is known of him, except that in 1616 he was appointed to the living of Christchurch in Hampshire, which he held until 1631, dying in obscurity three years later.

None of Marston's plays is wholly successful; but all show that he had a considerable, if erratic, literary talent. *The Malcontent* is dominated by Malevole, a cynical, embittered railer, probably derived from Shakespeare's Thersites, whose savage tirades against life and society associate him with the Prince of Denmark, and who has been described as a coarsened version of Shakespeare's mysterious and elusive hero:

Think this: – this earth is the only grave and Golgotha wherin all things that live must rot; 'tis but the draught wherein the heavenly bodies discharge their corruption, the very muckhill on which the sublunary orbs cast their excrements. Man is the slime of this dung-pit, and princes are the governors of these men . . . there goes but a pair of shears betwixt an emperor and the son of a bagpiper – only the dyeing, dressing, pressing, glossing makes the difference.

Though much of his verse is rough and over-written, Marston had a gift for racy dialogue. A contemporary called him a 'ruffian in style'; and he was frequently derided by his fellow authors. Yet he had an important influence on Tourneur, Webster and Ford, and (some literary historians have claimed) on Shakespeare himself. His uneven writing suggests that he had a neurotic personality. He is obsessed by the vices that he pretends to castigate; and it is possible that in the Church he found the peace and security that he had always needed.

We have few records of the life of THOMAS DEKKER (*c.*1572– *c.*1632); but from 1598 onwards he had a hand in many plays and himself wrote seventeen. Much of his enormous output has now been lost; and much of what survives has merely an historical appeal. A commercial dramatist, who wrote to earn his bread, he was an assiduous follower of current fashions. His earliest known play, *The Pleasant Comedie of Old Fortunatus* (1599), remains an entertaining work, while *The Shoemaker's Holiday*, produced in the same year, triumphs by virtue of its rough vitality. Dekker's later plays include his contribution to the 'War of the Theatres', *Satiro-Mastix* (1601), and *The Honest Whore* (1604), in which Thomas Middleton is known to have had a share. Among his other joint efforts are *The Roaring Girl, Westward-Hoe* and *North-ward-Hoe* and *The Witch of Edmonton*, written about 1621, with the help of Ford and Rowley. Despite his struggles, Dekker remained penniless, and passed six years in a debtors' gaol, from 1613 until 1619.

An image of Dekker, albeit probably a distorted one, emerges from the attacks of Ben Jonson – a poor, ignorant vagabond, a 'play-dresser and a plagiary', jealous and conceited, and an inveterate money-grubber. Poor he certainly was; but he was a better playwright, and almost certainly a better man, than Jonson would have had us think. Dekker's plays suggest that he enjoyed life; his lack of learning enabled him to look at life simply and directly, and to record what he observed without prejudice or preconceptions. He was a genuinely popular author, his persistent theme being London, in particular the lower levels of urban society and the world of the crowded London streets.

The Shoemaker's Holiday, adapted from Thomas Deloney's account of the career of Simon Eyre, a fifteenth-century shoe-maker who rose from apprentice to the rank of Lord Mayor, is a happy blend of romance and realism. Dekker's humour is exuberant, and his characters are endearing. The verse, too, is clear and workmanlike, but Dekker is at his best when writing prose, as in Simon Eyre's speeches:

Where be these boys, these girls, these drabs, these scoundrels?
They wallow in the fat brewis of my bounty and lick up the crumbs of my table, yet will not rise to see my walks cleansed.
Come out, you powder-beef queens! What, Nan! What, Madge Mumblecrust!
Come out, you fat midriff swagbelly whores, and sweep these kennels, that the noisome stench offend not the nose of my neighbours.

Besides his plays, Dekker wrote a series of pamphlets on London life, which, in addition to their documentary value, establish him as one of the finest prose writers of the age (see p. 91).

Thomas Heywood's tragedy, *A Woman Killed with Kindness*, explored a new dramatic field.

The prolific THOMAS HEYWOOD (*c.*1570–1641) claimed to have 'had either an entire hand, or at least a maine finger', in some two hundred and twenty plays, of which only twenty-four survive. In 1596, he joined the Admiral's Company as an actor and play-wright, having probably spent some years at Cambridge; and he remained a professional playwright for nearly a quarter of a century. This long experience gave him a mastery of stagecraft. Aware of the limitations of his talent, unlike so many of his fellow dramatists he avoided lofty flights; what interested him were the ordinary problems of existence. Like Dekker, Heywood was closely connected with the city of London, the place he knew and loved best; and his dramas give us a sympathetic impression of contemporary middle-class life. His finest work, *A Woman Killed with Kindness*, was produced in 1602 or 1603. A newly-married couple offer hospitality to a poor gentleman, and, during the husband's absence, the wife allows herself to be seduced. The husband learns of her infidelity, but at first refuses to accept his wife's guilt until he has seen the pair abed:

O God! O God! that it were possible
To undo things done, to call back yesterday!
That Time could turn up his swift sandy glass
To untell the days and to redeem these hours!
Or that the Sun
Could rising from the west, draw his coach backward,

Take from the account of time so many minutes,
Till he had all these seasons called again,
Those minutes, and those actions done in them.
Even from her first offence: that I might take her
As spotless as an angel in my arms!
But oh! I talk of things impossible,
And cast beyond the moon.

Though the wife repents, her husband banishes her to a manor seven miles from London; and there, 'killed by kindness', she eventually dies – but not before her husband has visited her and the drama has closed in a mood of reconciliation. The play is remarkable for the subtlety and poignant restraint with which the separate suffering of man and wife are handled, at a time that also saw the production of *Othello* and *Hamlet*, when the 'revenge play' was still exceedingly popular. Heywood's most individual contribution to the theatre was his introduction of simple domestic themes. During his later years, he wrote poetry and prose translations from the classics, and staged mayoral pageants for the City of London.

Cyril Tourneur (1575?–1626) is perhaps the most obscure of all the Jacobean dramatists. Little is known of his youth; but in 1600 he became secretary to Sir Francis Vere, a post he held for nine years. Afterwards he entered the royal service. On 23 December 1613, he was granted forty-one shillings 'for his charges and paines in carrying letters for his Majestie's service to Brussels'. Then, in 1617, he was arrested, but presently released, on the orders of the Privy Council. Later, in 1625, as Secretary to the Council of War, he joined Sir Edward Cecil on an expedition launched to seize Spanish treasure ships. It missed its quarry, but was attacked by disease on its return, and a hundred and sixty men were put ashore at the Irish port of Kinsale. Among them was Cyril Tourneur, who died there in February 1626.

Though the attribution of his two major plays, *The Revenger's Tragedy* and *The Atheist's Tragedy*, has often been disputed, the case for Tourneur's authorship remains strong; there is a close resemblance of tone and imagery between these plays and his earliest work *The Transformed Metamorphosis* (1600). *The Revenger's Tragedy* (1607) is a tragic burlesque that hovers between tragedy and comedy, with elements that hark back to the tradition of the medieval Morality plays. The atmosphere is one of violence and corruption, permeated by the gloom of death. Tourneur adopts the popular myth of Italianate evil (derived from the legend of the 'develish Machiavel', the bogeyman of sixteenth-century literature), and elaborately refines on it. All recognizable standards of morality disappear, as murder follows murder, and hate, lechery, and ambition rub shoulders. There is no comforting moral, except that every form of evil is ultimately

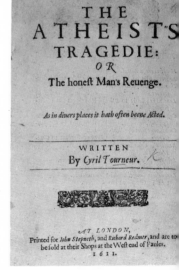

THE
ATHEISTS
TRAGEDIE:
OR
The honeſt Man's Reuenge.

As in diuers places it hath often beene Acted.

WRITTEN
By *Cyril Tourneur.*

AT LONDON,
Printed for *Iohn Stepneth,* and *Richard Redmer,* and are to
be ſold at their Shops at the Weſt end of Paules.
1 6 1 1.

Cyril Tourneur carried on the tradition of the Elizabethan revenge play.

self-destructive. The strength of the play lies in its language; and there are marvellous moments of poetic eloquence:

> Does the silkworm expend her yellow labours
> For thee? For thee does she undo herself?
> Are lordships sold to maintain ladyships,
> For the poor benefit of a bewitching minute?
> Why does yon fellow falsify highways
> And put his life between the judge's lips,
> To refine such a thing, keeps horse and men
> To beat their valours for her?
> Surely we are all mad people, and they
> Whom we think are, are not; we mistake those;
> 'Tis we are mad in sense, they but in clothes.

The Atheist's Tragedy (1611) is less successful. Again the play's structure derives from the Morality tradition, which did not altogether suit the demands of the more naturalistic Jacobean stage. Tourneur's moralising about the inadequacy of atheism dulls the tragedy's dramatic impact.

There is no record of the parentage or early life of JOHN WEB-STER (*c.*1580–*c.*1625). But he was writing for the stage by 1602, when his name appears in Henslowe's account book; and for some years he worked as a collaborator, contributing to the work of Dekker, Heywood and Middleton. Webster's reputation rests on two plays that are said to have taken him several years to write: *The White Devil* (1612) and *The Duchess of Malfi* (1612–1613). His only other completely original play, *The Devil's Law-Case*, is of uncertain date. During his own lifetime, he was an unsuccessful author, and not until the early nineteenth century was he rescued from oblivion.

Both Webster's major plays are concerned with revenge, inspired not, as in *Othello*, by a distorted sense of justice or by injured personal pride, but by an implacable, deep-rooted malice. They depict a world where virtue is impotent before untrammelled self-will. *The White Devil* has a typical theme, based on events that had taken place in Italy only twenty-five years earlier – the criminal career of Vittoria Corombona, a notorious courtesan. It presents numerous bizarre atrocities: a wife dies when she kisses a poisoned portrait of her husband; he, in turn, is killed by having a helmet, charged with poison, rivetted around his head; and, as he expires in agony, he is savagely taunted by his murderers. Almost every device of the contemporary melodrama is woven into Webster's plot; but he manages to combine these crude theatrical conventions with scenes of intense, disturbing drama.

The Duchess of Malfi shows virtue persecuted. The innocent Duchess is driven to madness and death by her brothers, who resent her secret marriage to her steward and employ the ghastliest stratagems with which to torment their victim. Again, what would normally be crude melodrama is redeemed by its poetic treatment, and by the atmosphere of brooding melancholy that permeates the whole play. The portrait of the Duchess is fixed by a series of vivid naturalistic strokes; and she becomes at length a figure of poignant nobility:

> Oh, that it were possible we might
> But hold some two days' conference with the dead!
> From them I should learn somewhat, I am sure,
> I never shall know here. I'll tell thee a miracle;
> I am not mad yet, to my cause of sorrow:
> The heaven o'er my head seems made of molten brass,
> The earth of flaming sulphur, yet I am not mad.
> I am acquainted with sad misery
> As the tann'd galley-slave is with his oar;
> Necessity makes me suffer constantly,
> And custom makes it easy.

Webster's use of language is rich and evocative, his imagery bold and forceful. He seems to have been obsessed with the idea of death and disease, of violence and physical affliction. Yet the gloom of his tragedies is often illuminated by dazzling moments of poetic insight – sometimes conveyed through a single line or phrase – for example, in the words of Vittoria, the White Devil, as she sees her death approaching:

> My soul, like to a ship in a black storm,
> Is driven, I know not whither.

or, during the course of the same drama, in Flamineo's death-speech:

> I do not look
> Who went before, nor who shall follow me;
> No, at myself I will begin and end:
> While we look up to heaven we confound
> Knowledge with knowledge. O I am in a mist.

His ability to distil poetry from melodrama, and the sublime from the grotesque, is typical of Webster's genius.

Although he produced plays that match Webster's for horror, THOMAS MIDDLETON (1580–1627) had a far more realistic talent. The son of a bricklayer, he entered Queen's College, Oxford, in 1598; and there published his first sheaf of poems. By the year 1602 he was already writing for the London stage, his earliest productions being comedies of town-life, notable for their lively pictures of contemporary manners, of which the two best, *A Trick to Catch the Old-one* and *A Mad World, My Masters*, were produced in 1608. For a time he was Chronologer of the City of London, and he was also employed as a public speech-writer. In 1612 he wrote an original tragedy, *Women beware Women*. Elsewhere he collaborated with the literary comedian, WILLIAM ROWLEY (c. 1585–

(*Above left*) 'A true portrait' of Thomas Middleton from an edition of his play, *No Wit Like a Woman's*, published in 1657.

(*Above right*) Middleton's popular play, *A Game at Chess*, was staged in 1624.

1625). Among their joint-productions are some of his finest works, such as *A Fair Quarrel* (1616), *The Changeling* (1622), and *The Spanish Gipsy* (1623). With *A Game at Chess*, staged in 1624, an attack on the pro-Spanish party which introduced some well-known political figures, Middleton achieved great popular renown. But it annoyed the King; and, after the ninth performance, the theatre was obliged to close its doors. Middleton died in poverty at the age of forty-seven.

In his comedies Middleton developed his remarkable naturalistic technique. *A Chaste Maid in Cheapside*, for instance, is a high-spirited, ribald farce with several cleverly interlocking plots. It is his gift of realistic observation that also illuminates his two great tragedies. Thus *Women beware Women* opens with an apparently commonplace scene. A young merchant is about to part from his newly-married bride, the beautiful Bianca. Then the Duke of Venice passes beneath her balcony; she wonders if she has managed to catch his eye, and a note of uneasiness begins to creep in. The Duke has indeed observed the young beauty; and, in a magnificent scene, he successfully attacks her virtue, while, at the front of the stage, her old mother and a designing bawd continue quietly playing chess. The old woman is unaware of the drama that is proceeding in the background; and the game becomes an ironic commentary on the Duke's attempts to 'mate' Bianca.

Although Rowley was responsible both for the opening and closing scenes of *The Changeling* and for the comic sub-plot, the remainder of the play we owe to Middleton. It is one of the finest tragedies of the period – the story of a young and beautiful woman who employs a repulsive agent, the hideous De Flores, to murder the husband she has married against her will. De Flores then blackmails her into becoming his mistress; and, although she afterward marries the man she loves, she finds that her fellow criminal has become 'a wondrous necessary' associate, and that the guilt they share has formed an unbreakable link. Even at a time when she thought she detested De Flores, her obsessive hatred had been close to passion; and, once he has committed the crime she demands, he knows that he can claim her as his prey:

> Look but into your conscience, read me there,
> 'Tis a true book, you'll find me there your equal:
> Push! Fly not to your birth, but settle you
> In what the act has made you, y'are no more now.
> You must forget your parentage to me:
> Y'are the deed's creature; by that name
> You lost your first condition, and I challenge you,
> As peace and innocency has turn'd you out,
> And made you one with me.

Middleton's verse is spare and almost prosaic; the general effect of the drama is dry and hard and cold. It evokes a world exempt from generous emotions, in which the spirit cannot hope to find a place. Middleton, indeed, is the least spiritual of all the Jacobean playwrights.

After Shakespeare's death, the taste of English audiences veered towards a different type of play, more frivolous and less exacting – decorative entertainments like the romantic tragedies and tragicomedies of FRANCIS BEAUMONT (*c.*1584–1616) and JOHN FLETCHER (1579–1625). From 1607 until 1613 these 'twin souls of the drama' were inseparable companions, who, according to Aubrey, 'lived together on the Bankside, not far from the Playhouse, both batchelors; lay together; had one wench in the house between them . . .'. They also shared 'a wonderful consimility of phansy'; and 'it was Mr Beaumont's business to correct the superflowings of Mr Fletcher's wit.' But their alliance ended in 1613, when Beaumont married an heiress and set up an independent household.

John Fletcher was born at Rye in Sussex, the son of Dr Richard Fletcher, afterwards Bishop of London. Having completed his education at Cambridge, he began writing for the stage about 1607, and in 1608 produced a pastoral drama, *The Faithful Shepherdess*. *Philaster*, the first play on which he collaborated with Beaumont, appeared in 1609; and their subsequent productions

included *The Scornful Lady* (1610), *The Maid's Tragedy* (1611),
A King no King (1611), and *Cupid's Revenge* (1612). After Beaumont's marriage in 1613, Fletcher seems to have entered into a
brief collaboration with Shakespeare; and it is generally agreed
that Fletcher wrote parts of *Henry VIII* (1613). Fletcher's own
comedies, of which the best is *The Wild-Goose Chase* (1621), had
some success upon the stage; but throughout his life he continued
to collaborate, and there are few dramatists of the period who did
not, at one time or another, accept his help. Between 1619 and
1622, for example, he wrote a series of ten plays – among them, a
notable tragedy, *The False One* (*c.*1620) – with Philip Massinger
as his lieutenant. He died of a sudden illness on 29 August 1625.

Francis Beaumont, the son of a judge, was educated at Oxford,
and in 1600 entered the Middle Temple with the intention of
himself following the law. Nevertheless he soon strayed into
literature, and in 1602 published a poem, *The Metamorphosis of
Tobacco*. A member of Ben Jonson's circle, he wrote commendatory
verses for some of his plays, including *Volpone* (1606). Beaumont's
earliest known play, a comedy, *The Woman Hater*, was written
about 1606; and soon afterwards he produced *The Knight of the
Burning Pestle*, a riotous comedy in the mock-heroic style. His
partnership with Fletcher, as we have noted above, began during
the year 1607 and lasted until 1613. He died young, at the age of
thirty-two, and was buried in Westminster Abbey.

Beaumont and Fletcher succeeded Shakespeare as principal
dramatists of the Blackfriars Theatre; and their popularity soon
exceeded his. The Blackfriars was one of the new candle-lit
'private' playhouses, that offered greater comfort than the old
Globe and attracted a more affluent and sophisticated audience.
According to James Shirley, it became an 'academy' for the
'young spirits' of the day, who adopted its fashionable playwrights
as their masters. In the new type of drama that Beaumont and
Fletcher popularized, the Elizabethan genius lost much of its
originality and sweeping strength, and its exquisite lyricism
turned 'to favour and to prettiness'. They move in a world of
romantic invention, where technical artistry takes the place of
imaginative art, and inflated grandiloquence of genuine dramatic
poetry. It is an escapist world; and, although the themes they
treat are often sexually 'daring', the effect that their passionate
characters make is, for the most part, strangely superficial. Yet
each dramatist, in his own way, was an accomplished master of
words; witness, this speech from *The Maid's Tragedy*:

> And you shall find all true but the wild island,
> Suppose I stand upon the sea-beach now,
> Mine arms thus, and mine hair blown by the wind,
> Wild as that desert; and let all about me
> Tell that I am forsaken. Do my face
> (If thou hadst ever feeling of a sorrow)

Thus, thus, Antiphila: strive to make me look
Like sorrow's monument; and the trees about me,
Let them be dry and leafless, let the rocks
Groan with continual surges; and behind me,
Make all a desolation. See, see, wenches,
A miserable life of this poor picture.

(*Above left*) John Fletcher, who, with his collaborator Francis Beaumont, established a new form of English drama; by an unknown artist.

Beaumont and Fletcher belonged to a decadent tradition; yet it is worth remembering that their plays once fascinated John Keats, and excited the interest and admiration of a famous modern dramatist, Luigi Pirandello. In 1647 a folio edition of their works appeared, containing thirty-five plays. Of these, however, only about ten are now believed to have been partly Beaumont's work.

(*Above right*) Title page of the third impression of *The Maid's Tragedy*, 1630.

PHILIP MASSINGER (1583–1640), who served his dramatic apprenticeship as John Fletcher's collaborator, was born at Salisbury in 1583 of an old Wiltshire family, his father being house-steward to the Earl of Pembroke. He was educated at Salisbury grammar school, and then at Oxford, where, we are told, 'he applied his mind more to poetry and romances than to logic and philosophy'. In 1613 he was writing plays for the great theatrical manager Philip Henslowe; and, during the next thirty years, he produced or had a hand in some fifty-three plays – of which only nineteen have survived, including a competent tragedy,

The Roman Actor (1626), and two successful comedies, *A New Way to Pay Old Debts* (1626) and *The City Madam* (1632). In 1626 he succeeded Fletcher as chief dramatist for the King's Men. He died on 16 March 1640, and was buried in Fletcher's grave at St Saviour's, Southwark. Massinger is an interesting rather than an inspired dramatist; long passages of moralizing spoil the majority of his plays. His concessions to public taste take the form of crude sensationalism; his borrowings from earlier playwrights were numerous, and as a rule he lacked invention. *A New Way to Pay Old Debts*, however, though Massinger borrows both from Jonson and from Middleton, was to provide Edmund Kean with one of his most splendid rôles – the villainous Sir Giles Overreach – the portrait of a contemporary capitalist, Sir Giles Mompesson, drawn with a savage gusto. *The City Madam*, despite a remarkably improbable plot, is also an effective play; and the spiteful and malicious Frugal seems a character worthy of Ben Jonson.

Massinger was an unequal artist, whose blank verse, as Aldous Huxley once said of Coleridge's, is often 'very blank indeed'. But he has some fine moments. Here, for example, Frugal addresses the snobbish victims he is duping:

> And it shall be
> My glory, nay a triumph to revive
> In the pomp that these shall shine, the memory
> Of the Roman matrons, who kept captive queens
> To be their handmaids. And when you appear
> Like Juno in full majesty, and my nieces
> Like Iris, Hebe, or what deities else
> Old poets fancy; your cramm'd wardrobes richer
> Than various nature's; and draw down the envy
> Of our western world upon you, only hold me
> Your vigilant Hermes with aerial wings,
> My caduceus my strong zeal to serve you,
> Prest to fetch in all rarities may delight you,
> And I am made immortal.

The plays of JOHN FORD (1586–*c*.1639) were written in the reign of Charles I; but they have their roots in the Elizabethan and Jacobean theatre. Born at Ilsington in Devon, after concluding his studies at Oxford, he entered the Middle Temple in the year 1602. Not until 1613 did he begin to collaborate on plays, working with Dekker, Rowley, and Webster. The first play that he wrote unaided, *The Lover's Melancholy*, was staged in 1629; and his three tragedies – *'Tis Pity She's a Whore*, *The Broken Heart* and *Love's Sacrifice* – saw the light in 1633. He died about 1639, shortly after returning to his native Devon. As a dramatist, Ford had been much influenced by Robert Burton's great compendium of human aberrations, *The Anatomy of Melancholy* (see p. 143); and his masterpiece, *'Tis Pity She's a Whore*, unfolds the story of an incestuous passion with rare subtlety and poetic delicacy. The guilty brother and sister, who refuse to renounce their love, die unredeemed and unrepentant:

GIOVANNI: Kiss me. If ever after-times should hear
Of our fast-knit affections, though perhaps
The laws of conscience and of civil use
May justly blame us, yet when they but know
Our loves, that love will wipe away that rigour
Which would in other incests be abhorred.
Give me your hand: how sweetly life doth run
In these well-coloured veins! how constantly
These palms do promise health! but I could chide
With Nature for this cunning flattery.
Kiss me again – forgive me.

Ford, declared Charles Lamb, 'was of the first order of poets', and 'sought for sublimity, not by parcels in metaphors or visible images, but directly where she has her full residence in the heart of man; in the actions and sufferings of the greatest minds . . . Even in the poor perverted reason of Giovanni and Annabella we discover traces of that fiery particle, which, in the irregular starting from out of the road of beaten action, discovers something of a right line . . .'

(*Below left*) Engraved portrait of Phillip Massinger from an edition of *Three New Plays*, 1655.

(*Below right*) The first edition of John Ford's greatest tragedy, '*Tis Pity She's a Whore*, appeared in 1633.

·TIS
Pitty Shee's a Whore

Acted by the *Queenes Maiefties Ser-
uants*, at The Phœnix in
Drury-Lane.

LONDON.
Printed by *Nicholas Okes* for *Richard
Collins*, and are to be sold at his shop
in *Pauls* Church-yard, at the signe
of the three Kings. 1633.

King James's Bible

THE AUTHORIZED VERSION (1611) of the Old and New Testaments, though one of the chief masterpieces of Jacobean prose – indeed, of English prose in general – was a composite production. No less than forty-seven scholars, divided into six groups, labouring at Westminster, Oxford and Cambridge, were employed on this tremendous task; and they themselves made free use of five considerably earlier versions; with the result that the text they published may embody, it is thought, the work of as many as a hundred hands. The Wycliffite Bible, the first complete Bible to appear in English, had been prepared under the direction of John Wyclif (c.1328–84) and his lieutenant, Nicholas Hereford, and completed before the great reformer's death. The earliest Bible to be printed in English, that of Miles Coverdale (1488–1569), appeared during the autumn of 1535; and it was followed by the 'Great Bible' of 1539 on which Coverdale collaborated, and 'Cranmer's Bible', which he helped to edit. None of these versions, however, satisfied King James's bishops. In the year 1604, at the Hampton Court Conference, they declared that previous renderings of the Scriptures were both 'corrupt and not aunserable to the truth of the Originall', and proposed, with their learned sovereign's assent, the undertaking of a fresh translation 'to bee ratified by his *Royall authorite*' so that the whole Church might henceforward 'be bound unto it, and none other'.

As such, despite the Revised Version, launched in 1881, and its painstaking twentieth-century successor, the Authorized Version has continued to hold its place. King James's diligent bishops (who included Lancelot Andrewes) lacked the resources of a modern scholar; and few of them were greatly concerned with the niceties of textual criticism. On the other hand, they shared a sense of style and a firm belief in the literal accuracy of every line and paragraph of Holy Writ. Thus, the Authorized Version possesses a numinous quality impossible to reproduce by means of modern prose, and has remained, age after age, a foundation stone of English literature. Writers who deliberately affect a Biblical style – as Kipling would do in our century – very often strike a false note. But unnumbered Englishmen, believers and atheists alike, have felt the Bible's all-pervading influence and, consciously or unconsciously, have sought to echo the rhythms of its poetic divagations and of its succinct yet always powerful narrative. The conference at Hampton Court, through its efforts to strengthen the Church, had an even more important effect upon the arts of prose and poetry.

(Opposite) The Coverdale Bible of 1535, the earliest translation of the Scriptures to be printed in English.

THE DEATH OF JEZEBEL (II Kings, 9, 30–35)
And when Jehu was come to Jezreel, Jezebel heard of it; and she painted her face, and tired her head and looked out at a window.
And as Jehu entered in at the gate, she said, Had Zimri peace, who slew his master?

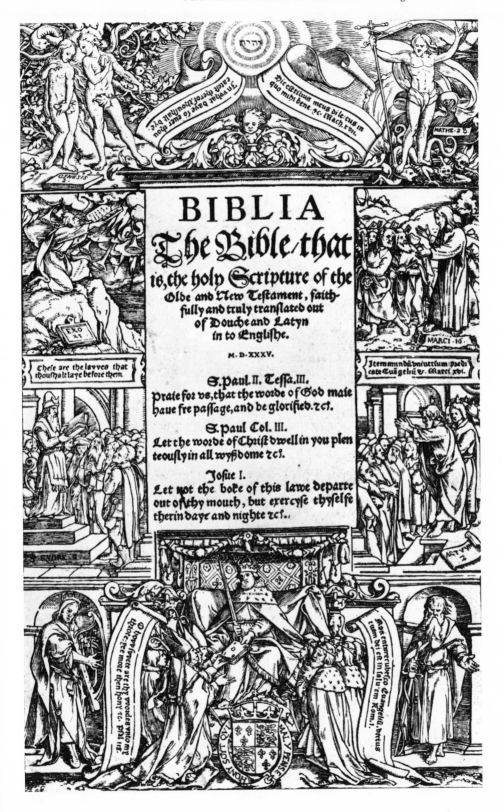

And he lifted up his face to the window, and said, Who is on my side? who? And there looked out to him two or three eunuchs.

And he said, Throw her down. So they threw her down: and some of her blood was sprinkled on the wall, and on the horses: and he trod her under foot.

And when he was come in, he did eat and drink, and said, Go, see now this cursed woman, and bury her: for she is a king's daughter.

And they went to bury her: but they found no more of her than the skull and the feet, and the palms of her hands.

THE MIGHTY BEHEMOTH (Job 40, 15–23)

Behold now behemoth, which I made with thee; he eateth grass as an ox.

Lo now, his strength is in his loins, and his force is in the navel of his belly.

He moveth his tail like a cedar: the sinews of his stones are wrapped together.

His bones are as strong as pieces of brass; his bones are like bars of iron.

He is the chief of the ways of God: he that made him can make his sword to approach unto him.

Surely the mountains bring him forth food, where all the beasts of the field play.

He lieth under the shady trees, in the covert of the reed, and fens.

The shady trees cover him with their shadow; the willows of the brook compass him about.

Behold, he drinketh up a river, and hasteth not: he trusteth that he can draw up Jordan into his mouth.

VANITAS VANITATUM (Ecclesiastes 12, 1–8)

Remember now thy Creator in the days of thy youth, while the evil days come not, nor the years draw nigh, when thou shalt say, I have no pleasure in them.

While the sun, or the light, or the moon, or the stars, be not darkened, nor the clouds return after the rain:

In the day when the keepers of the house shall tremble, and the strong men shall bow themselves, and the grinders cease because they are few, and those that look out of the windows be darkened,

And the doors shall be shut in the streets, when the sound of the grinding is low, and he shall rise up at the voice of the bird, and all the daughters of musick shall be brought low;

Also when they shall be afraid of that which is high, and fears shall be in the way, and the almond tree shall flourish, and the grasshopper shall be a burden, and desire shall fail: because man goeth to his long home, and the mourners go about the streets:

Or ever the silver cord be loosed or the golden bowl be broken, or the pitcher be broken at the fountain, or the wheel broken at the cistern.

Then shall the dust return to the earth as it was: and the spirit shall return unto God who gave it.

Vanity of vanities, saith the preacher; all is vanity.

THE VOICE OF THE BELOVED (The Song of Solomon 2, 10–17)

My beloved spake, and said unto me, Rise up, my love, my fair one, and come away.

For, lo, the winter is past, the rain is over and gone;

(*Opposite*) Early Biblical genealogy; a plate from King James's Bible, 1611.

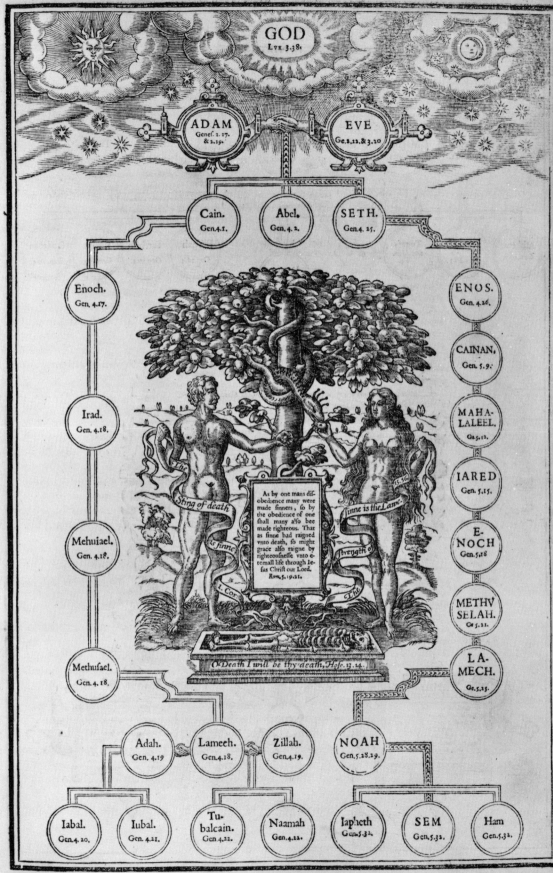

The flowers appear on the earth; the time of the singing of birds is come, and the voice of the turtle is heard in our land;
The fig tree putteth forth her green figs, and the vines with the tender grape give a good smell. Arise, my love, my fair one, and come away.
O my dove, that art in the clefts of the rock, in the secret places of the stairs, let me see thy countenance, let me hear thy voice; for sweet is thy voice, and thy countenance is comely.
Take us the foxes, the little foxes, that spoil the vines: for our vines have tender grapes.
My beloved is mine, and I am his: he feedeth among the lilies.
Until the day break, and the shadows flee away, turn, my beloved, and be thou like a roe or a young hart upon the mountains of Bether.

THE RETURN OF THE LORD (Isaiah 35, 3–10)
Strengthen ye the weak hands, and confirm the feeble knees.
Say to them that are of a fearful heart, Be strong, fear not: behold, your God will come with vengeance, even God with a recompence; he will come and save you.
Then the eyes of the blind shall be opened, and the ears of the deaf shall be unstopped.
Then shall the lame man leap as an hart, and the tongue of the dumb sing: for in the wilderness shall waters break out, and streams in the desert.
And the parched ground shall become a pool, and the thirsty land springs of water: in the habitation of dragons, where each lay, shall be grass with reeds and rushes.
And an highway shall be there, and a way, and it shall be called The way of holiness; the unclean shall not pass over it; but it shall be for those: the wayfaring men, though fools, shall not err therein.
No lion shall be there, nor any ravenous beast shall go up thereon, it shall not be found there; but the redeemed shall walk there:
And the ransomed of the Lord shall return, and come to Zion with songs and everlasting joy upon their heads: they shall obtain joy and gladness, and sorrow and sighing shall flee away.

THE WORD (The Gospel of St John 1, 1–5)
In the beginning was the Word, and the Word was with God, and the Word was God.
The same was in the beginning with God.
All things were made by him; and without him was not any thing made that was made.
In him was life; and the life was the light of men.
And the light shineth in darkness; and the darkness comprehended it not.

CHRIST AND THE ADULTRESS (The Gospel of St John 8, 3–9)
And the scribes and Pharisees brought unto him a woman taken in adultery; and when they had set her in the midst,
They say unto him, Master, this woman was taken in adultery, in the very act.
Now Moses in the law commanded us, that such should be stoned: but what sayest thou?
This they said, tempting him that they might have to accuse him. But

Jesus stooped down, and with his finger wrote on the ground, as though he heard them not.

So when they continued asking him, he lifted up himself, and said unto them, He that is without sin among you, let him first cast a stone at her. And again he stooped down, and wrote on the ground.

And they which heard it, being convicted by their own conscience, went out one by one, beginning at the eldest, even unto the last: and Jesus was left alone, and the woman standing in the midst.

Bacon and the Pursuit of Truth

FRANCIS BACON (1561–1626) was the youngest child of Sir Nicholas Bacon, Elizabeth's Lord Keeper of the Great Seal. Although at the age of thirteen he went to Trinity College, Cambridge, and afterwards to Gray's Inn, it was always assumed by his contemporaries that he would make his name in politics. But his father's sudden death, when he was fifteen, left him with a very small legacy; and he was, therefore, obliged to earn his living as a lawyer. From 1584 he also served in Parliament; but, as he had offended the Queen, his advancement was slow. Elizabeth's successor proved more sympathetic; by 1607 he was Solicitor General; in 1613 he became Attorney General; in 1616 he was appointed a Privy Councillor; in 1617 Lord Keeper of the Great Seal; and, in the same year, Lord Chancellor. In 1618 he received the title of Lord Verulam, and, in 1621, of Viscount St Albans.

(*Below left*) Francis Bacon at eighteen years of age.

(*Below right*) Francis Bacon, a posthumous portrait executed in 1640; from *The Advancement of Learning*.

Title-page of *The Advancement of Learning*.

Then, a few weeks later, he was accused of bribery and corruption in Chancery suits. Found guilty, he was imprisoned in the Tower, fined and debarred from holding public office. The disgrace he suffered hurt Bacon deeply; but it enabled him to settle down to his real life-work as a writer and philosopher. Once he had retired to his father's estate at Gorhambury, 'I found (he wrote) that I was fitted for nothing so well as for the study of Truth'. In 1605 he had already published *The Advancement of Learning*, a study of early

An allegory of the Royal
Society. Fame crowns
the bust of Charles II.

scientific progress; and he now devoted himself to his immensely
ambitious scheme for reconstructing the foundations of all human
knowledge, which he called the *Magna Instauratio*.

Bacon planned to base all knowledge upon scientific observation – an undertaking beyond the powers of any single man; the
first collection of his *Essays*, a by-product of his philosophic studies,
appeared in 1597, to be followed in 1625 by an extended and
revised volume. It was his unremitting pursuit of truth that
eventually caused Bacon's death. One winter's day in 1626, he left
his coach to gather snow, with which he proceeded to stuff the
carcass of a newly eviscerated fowl, that he might study the
effects of cold as a preservative. During this occupation he contracted pneumonia; he died on 9 April 1626.

Bacon has been entitled 'the first modern mind' and the 'father
of inductive reasoning'. In his own day his work was little understood – his characteristic line of thought was both too complicated

and too unfamiliar; but his new conception of knowledge and of its function became increasingly significant later in the century. Bacon was the spiritual founder both of the English Royal Society and of the French Encyclopedist movement. Since his death he has also been regarded as a pernicious and subversive influence, as the man who divorced science from poetry, and reason from imagination. Such criticisms are misleading, however, if we consider his work in its entirety. He aimed to unite rather than to divide. Bacon was no arid materialist. Shelley, indeed, believed that the author of the *Essays* deserved an honoured place among the poets.

Bacon's literary fame rests on his *Essays*; in them he is brief, pithy and brilliant, with a full share of Jacobean 'wit'. There are 'metaphysical' qualities in his prose that link it to early seventeenth-century verse. Thus he writes of our inherent tendency to error –

the force whereof is such, as it doth not dazzle or snare the understanding in some particulars, but doth more generally and inwardly infect and corrupt the state thereof. For the mind of man is far from the nature of a clear and equal glass, wherein the beams of things should reflect according to their true incidence; nay, it is rather like an enchanted glass, full of superstition and imposture, . . .

The swift movement from image to image, and the complex fusion of ideas, are typical of Bacon at his best, when the need to realize certain abstract ideas forces him to make a poetic use of language. Bacon's aphorisms have always been famous: 'men fear death as children fear to go in the dark; and as that natural fear in children is increased with tales, so is the other'; and 'He that hath wife and children hath given hostages to fortune'. The terse openings to his essays recall the opening lines of some of Donne's poems, an excellent example being his essay, 'On Truth':

What is truth? said jesting Pilate, and would not stay for an answer. Certainly there be that delight in giddiness, and count it a bondage to fix a belief; affecting free will in thinking, as well as in acting. And though the sects of philosophers of that kind be gone, yet there remain certain discoursing wits which are of the same veins, though there be not so much blood in them as was in those of the ancients. But it is not only the difficulty and labour which men take in finding out of truth, nor again that when it is found, it imposeth upon men thoughts, that does bring lies in favour; but a natural though corrupt love of the lie itself. One of the later school of Grecians examineth the matter and is at a stand to think what should be in it, that men should love lies; where neither they make for pleasure, as with poets; nor for advantage, as with the merchant; but for the lie's sake. But I cannot tell: this same truth is a naked and open daylight, that doth not shew the masques and mummeries and triumphs of the world, half so stately and daintily as candle lights. Truth may perhaps come to the price of a pearl, that sheweth by day; but it will not rise to the price of a diamond or carbuncle, that sheweth best in varied lights. A mixture of a lie doth ever add pleasure.

The dramatic opening is followed by a sentence that appears to deny the normal logic of prose, so oblique is the movement of the thought. Bacon's last aphorism is typical of his masterly handling of the form: a sudden precise statement, placed after the previous syntactical flow, focuses attention upon its subtle insight. In his varied and exploratory use of language, and in his capacity to recognize and express a complexity of experience, Bacon is excelled by Shakespeare alone.

Poets Sacred and Profane

One of the most splendid aspects of English seventeenth-century literature was its great constellation of religious poets; and among John Donne's noblest successors in this field were George Herbert, Richard Crashaw, Henry Vaughan and Thomas Traherne. But many of the other poets described here also wrote religious verse. Their range was remarkably wide; and, whereas writers of the sixteenth and eighteenth centuries, when they portrayed the relationship of Man and God, customarily adopted the terms of conventional religious faith, the seventeenth-century poet was apt to approach his subject from a far more imaginative point of view. We become aware that he is describing a deeply-felt experience, and that the type of experience he records has been peculiarly individual. The language he employs is sometimes (as in Crashaw) that of an impassioned lover, sometimes (as in Herbert) that of a devoted friend. The pious verses of Pope and Addison are solemn tributes to divine supremacy; George Herbert, however, does not hesitate to rehearse his doubts and fears and hesitations. Here he seems to anticipate the work of the Victorian poet, Gerard Manley Hopkins, who, now and then, actually remonstrates with God, and protests against the grievous injustices he has suffered at the hands of Providence.

The adjective 'metaphysical' is often applied to most of the poets of the earlier seventeenth century, and denotes a school of poetry (wrote a recent authority, the late Herbert J. C. Grierson) 'inspired by a philosophical conception of the universe and the rôle assigned to the human spirit in the great drama of existence'. They were poets of ideas. Donne, for example, was 'familiar with the definitions and distinctions of Mediaeval Scholasticism'; while 'Cowley's bright and alert, if not profound mind' was 'attracted by the achievements of science and the systematic materialism of Hobbes'. Thanks to their preoccupation with ideas, they developed a new kind of sensibility and a novel method of expressing it. In the eighteenth century their style was much abused; and Dr Johnson believed them to have exerted a particularly deleterious effect both on the current use of prosody and on the evolution of the English language. 'They wrote (he declared) rather as beholders than as partakers of human nature';

A prospect of Westminster in 1647; an engraving by Wenceslaus Hollar.

their courtship had been devoid of fondness, and their lamentation of sorrow. 'Their wish was only to say what they hoped had never been said before'. They had missed the sublime, just as they missed the pathetic; since 'they never attempted that comprehension and expanse of thought which at once fills the mind, and of which the first effect is sudden astonishment, and the second rational admiration'. Though Johnson's strictures were undoubtedly prejudiced, they contain a modicum of truth. In the work of the Metaphysical Poets 'the most heterogenous images' are sometimes 'yoked by violence together'. But, whatever they may have lacked, it was not passionate feeling or intellectual curiosity.

JOHN DONNE (1573–1631), who bridges the gap between two different literary ages, was not only one of the most original of Elizabethan and Jacobean lyricists, but, according to his former master, Ben Jonson, 'the first poet of the world in some things . . .' Both his parents belonged to Catholic families, his father being a prosperous citizen of London; and Donne, having taken his degree at Cambridge, followed the example of many other privileged young men, studying Law, cultivating his literary talents and, in 1596 and 1597, accompanying the Queen's favourite, the celebrated Earl of Essex, on two adventurous naval expeditions. He seems, at this period, to have visited Spain and Italy. By the close of 1597, however, Donne was back again in London, where he became private secretary to Sir Thomas Egerton, the Lord Keeper. Donne's intellectual gifts had won him wide renown; but his early poems show that he was also an experienced man of pleasure, who delighted to 'dig love's mine' and had made a variety of flattering conquests. He now fell deeply in love with his employer's sixteen-year-old niece, Anne More; and after an enforced separation and many clandestine meetings, they were secretly married in the year 1601. Their secret was soon detected. Donne was cast off by the Lord Keeper and temporarily thrown

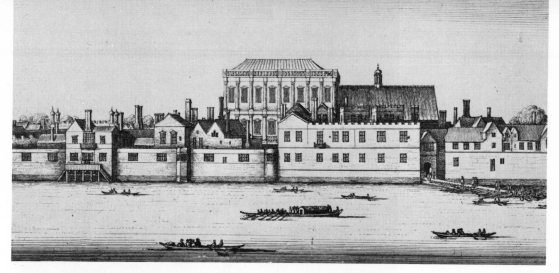

into gaol. Set free and allowed to take up married life, the gay and rakish young poet was reduced to the gloomiest form of domesticity, living amid a brood of noisy and 'gamesome' children in a small, damp country house, from which he despatched imploring letters and eulogistic verses to his former friends and patrons. His health suffered; he lost all joy of life; and about 1608, when he wrote a defence of self-slaying entitled *Biathanatos*, he apparently contemplated suicide.

Although he had often been advised to take Holy Orders, he still hoped to obtain some public office. But James I, himself a learned man, having heard may reports of his subject's erudition, decided that he might 'prove a powerful Preacher'; and in January 1615 Donne gave way and was at last ordained. The King had chosen well; the one-time poet almost immediately developed into the most puissant preacher of his day. Donne did nothing by halves; he was as intemperate in his devotions as he had once been in his passions; and the death of his wife after sixteen years of marriage, during which she had borne him twelve children, further strengthened his ascetic tendency. In 1621 he was appointed Dean of St Paul's. 'Crucified to the world,' he then adopted the existence of an early Christian cenobite among reminders of his own mortality. Towards the end of his life he designed the curious sepulchral monument – a statue of the poet upright, wearing a heavy shroud – that today commemorates him in St Paul's Cathedral. He died, soon after he had delivered his last sermon before King James's successor, the less learned but no less pious Charles I, on 31 March 1631.

Very little of John Donne's work, either sacred or profane, was published in the writer's life-time. His *Poems*, for example, though the manuscripts had been widely circulated and much admired, did not appear until 1633; his *Sermons*, prefaced with a short biography by Izaak Walton, came out between 1640 and 1661. Donne, as a famous divine, would have been greatly distressed had he known that his early verses were to see the light. Some of the

John Donne as a young adventurer; portrait by an unknown artist.

John Donne in the shroud he had made before his death; from *Death's Duel*, 1632.

best, Ben Jonson asserted, had been written before he reached the age of twenty-five – that is to say, some five or six years before the end of the Elizabethan era. Yet the *Songs and Sonnets* he composed as a young man are astonishingly mature productions. True, the effect is very often rugged; and Jonson, whom he had known at the Mermaid Tavern where he may perhaps also have met Shakespeare, once declared that 'for not keeping of accent' the poet had 'deserved hanging'; while Coleridge, two centuries later, would nickname him 'rhyme's sturdy cripple'. Neither critic ventured to deny his strength. Donne, an Elizabethan by birth, adapted and rarified the kind of elaborate conceits that sixteenth-century poets favoured, giving them an entirely new and often strikingly individual twist. He was an extremely *personal* poet; the adventures of his own life – for instance, his stormy relationship with Anne More – are constantly reflected in his verse. He is ribald, passionate, romantic by turns. 'A thought to Donne', wrote T. S. Eliot in his well-known essay on the Metaphysical Poets, 'was an experience; it modified his sensibility.' And every thought that he experienced he immediately began to analyze. The connection between sense and spirit, the interaction of the soul and body, was a subject he always found absorbing. He was a love-poet who insisted that love might be both profoundly spiritual and intensely sensual; and that the 'soul's language' might find a triumphant expression in the ecstatic union of two human bodies:

> I wonder by my troth, what thou and I
> Did, till we lov'd? Were we not wean'd till then
> But sucked on country pleasures, childishly?
> Or snorted we in the seven sleeper's den?
> 'Twas so; but this, all pleasures fancies be.
> If ever any beauty I did see,
> Which I desir'd, and got, 'twas but a dream of thee.
>
> And now good morrow to our waking souls,
> Which watch not one another out of fear;
> For love, all love of other sights controls,
> And makes one little room an everywhere.
> Let sea-discoverers to new worlds have gone,
> Let maps to other, world on worlds have shown,
> Let us possess one world, each hath one, and is one . . .

Donne was a prolific poet. Besides *Songs and Sonnets*, he wrote a series of twenty *Elegies, Satyres, Marriage Songs, Letters to Severall Personages, An Anatomie of the World* (inspired by the idea of death) and *The Progresse of the Soule*, a wonderfully entertaining serio-comic narrative of the various transmigrations of a soul from the apple that hung in the Garden of Eden, through a mandrake, a sparrow, a gigantic fish, an elephant and a 'toyful ape', to Thomech, the sister and wife of Cain, with whom he left the tale unfinished.

Donne's *Divine Poems*, thought to have been the products of his later life, are as fiercely impassioned as his early songs, and often employ the same erotic imagery:

> Batter my heart, three person'd God; for you
> As yet but knock, breathe, shine, and seek to mend;
> That I may rise, and stand, o'erthrow me, and bend
> Your force, to break, blow, burn and make me new.
> I, like an usurpt town, to another due,
> Labour to admit you, but Oh, to no end;
> Reason, your viceroy in me, me should defend,
> But is captived, and proves weak or untrue.
> Yet dearly I love you, and would be loved fain,
> But am betroth'd unto your enemy:
> Divorce me, untie, or break that knot again;
> Take me to you, imprison me, for I
> Except you enthrall me, never shall be free,
> Nor ever chaste, except you ravish me.

Donne's prose-style is no less complex and energetic than the use he made of verse:

Amorous soul, ambitious soul, covetous soul, voluptuous soul, what wouldest thou have in heaven? What doth thy holy amorousness, thy

TO HIS MOST
SACRED MAIESTIE,
CHARLES,
BY THE GRACE OF GOD,
KING OF GREAT BRITAINE,
FRANCE AND IRELAND,
Defender of the Faith, &c.

Moſt dread and gracious Soveraigne,

IN this rumor of *VVarre I am bold to preſent to your ſacred Majeſtie the fruits of Peace, firſt planted by the hand of your moſt Royal Father, then ripened by the ſame gracious influence, and ſince no leſſe cheriſht and protected by your Majeſties eſpeciall favour vouchſafed to the Author in ſo many indulgent teſtimonies of your good acceptance of his ſervice: VVhich grace from your Majeſtie, as he was known to acknowledge with much comfort whilſt he lived, ſo will it give now ſome excuſe to the preſumption of this Dedication, ſince thoſe friends of his, who think any thing of his worthy to out-live him, could not preſerve their piety to him, without taking leave to inſcribe the ſame with your Majeſties ſacred Name, that ſo they may at once give ſo faire a hope of a long continuance both to theſe VVorks of his, and to his gratitude, of which they humbly deſire this Book may laſt to be ſome Monument.*

A 3   I

Dedication page of
Donne's *Sermons*, 1640.

holy covetousness, thy holy ambition, and voluptuousness most carry thy desire upon? Call it what thou will; think it what thou canst; think it something that thou canst not think; and all this thou shall have, if thou have any resurrection unto life; and yet there is a *Better Resurrection*. When I consider what was in my parents loins (a substance unworthy of a word, unworthy of a thought) when I consider what I am now, (a volume of diseases bound up together, a dry cinder, if I look for natural, for radical moisture, and yet a Sponge, a bottle of overflowing Rheums, if I consider accidental; an aged child, a gray-headed infant, and but the ghost of mine own youth) when I consider what I shall be at last, by the hand of death, in my grave, (first, but putrefaction, and then, not so much as putrefaction, I shall not be able to send forth so much as an ill air, not any air at all, but shall be all insipid, tasteless, savourless dust; for a while, all worms, and after a while, not so much as worms . . .). When I consider the past, and present, and future state of this body, in this world, I am able to conceive, able to express the worst that can befall it in nature, and the worst that can be inflicted upon it by man, or fortune; but the least degree of glory that God hath prepared for that body in heaven, I am not able to express, not able to conceive.

(*Sermon XXII*)

The eventful life of EDWARD, LORD HERBERT OF CHERBURY (1583–1648) – philosopher, historian, diplomat, poet and gallant – is recorded in his delightful *Autobiography*. The elder brother of the poet George Herbert (see p. 127), he was educated at Oxford, where he gained a reputation as a linguist, rider, fencer and musician. He went to court, and was knighted by James I; in 1608 he travelled to France, and fought at the siege of Juliers in 1610. He became British ambassador to France in 1619 and, during his embassy, wrote an important treatise, *De Veritate* (1624), setting out his notions of a 'primitive religion' that had become obscured by theology, which provided the basis of seventeenth- and eighteenth-century Deism. Herbert, raised to the peerage by Charles I, was handsome, brave, amorous, and an experienced duellist – apparently the archetypal Cavalier. Yet in the Civil War he took a neutral line, until in 1644, rather than sacrifice his precious library, he surrendered Montgomery Castle to the Parliamentary forces. He then applied to Parliament for a pension, which was granted him a year later.

Lord Herbert of Cherbury, perhaps after a miniature by Isaac Oliver, with the inscription: '*Nulles laides amours ne belles prison.*'

Herbert of Cherbury's poems are characteristic of the taste of the Caroline court, his predominant concern being love and the philosophical questions provoked by it. His most famous poem, *An Ode upon a Question moved, Whether Love should continue for ever?*, is an elegantly casuistic dialogue which concludes with some typically ambiguous quatrains:

> So when from hence we shall be gone,
>   And be no more, nor you, nor I,
>   As one anothers mystery,
> Each shall be both, yet both be one.
>
> This said, in her up-lifted face,
>   Her eyes which did that beauty crown,
>   'Were like two stars, that having faln down,
> Look up again to find their place:
>
> While such a moveless silent peace
>   Did seize on their becalmed sense,
>   One would have thought some influence
> Their ravish'd spirits did possess.

ROBERT HERRICK (1591–1674) was one of those poets whose obvious charm and apparent simplicity tend to obscure their more substantial virtues. His only book, *Hesperides and Noble Numbers*, a collection of poems both sacred and profane, did not appear until he was fifty-seven years old; and much of his life was passed in the country as a quiet parish priest. The son of a London goldsmith, he was apprenticed after his father's death to his uncle, Sir William Herrick, the King's jeweller; but his family must have decided that he would never make a good tradesman; for in 1614 he was sent to Cambridge, where he finally graduated in 1620. About this time Herrick entered the Church; and in 1627 he served as chaplain on Buckingham's disastrous expedition to the Ile de Rhé. Two years later, through the King's patronage, he obtained the living of Dean Prior in south Devon. During the Commonwealth, he was expelled from his parish; but he returned in 1662; and there, though Devon had always bored him, he passed his placid old age.

Portrait of Robert Herrick on the title page of *Hesperides*, 1648.

Although he would evidently have preferred to live in London, he derived unending poetic enjoyment from his life at Dean Prior. Besides a devoted maidservant named Prudence Balwin, he had

HESPERIDES:

OR,

THE WORKS

BOTH

HUMANE & DIVINE

OF

ROBERT HERRICK *Esq.*

OVID.

Effugient avidos Carmina noſtra Rogos.

LONDON,

Printed for *John Williams*, and *Francis Eglesfield*, and are to be ſold at the Crown and Marygold in Saint *Pauls* Church-yard. 1648.

the companionship of a troop of friendly animals which he allowed
to roam about the vicarage, including a spaniel, a lamb and the
domesticated pig that he had taught to use a tankard. He had also
celebrated the charms of a succession of mistresses – whether real
or imaginary we do not know – and took constant delight in all the
pagan festivities with which his parishioners marked the revolution of the seasons, from the gathering of the first spring flowers to
their junketings around the Christmas hearth. As a young man, he
had belonged to the 'tribe of Ben' and formed part of the admiring
circle that Jonson gathered at the Mermaid Tavern; and
Herrick's mellifluous lyricism has a strongly Elizabethan, or
early-Jacobean, cast. But his use of language was far more original
than that of Jonson or most of the sixteenth-century song-writers;
and the deceptive simplicity of his finest lyrics conceals the
exquisite skill with which he uses words and images. The effect is
never merely 'pretty'; it is always redeemed from prettiness,
either by an engaging stroke of wit or by a sudden touch of grim-
ness, when 'the light wax dim' and he begins to think of death and
remembers his own increasing solitude:

TO ANTHEA
Now is the time, when all the lights wax dim;
And thou (Anthea) must withdraw from him
Who was thy servant. Dearest, bury me
Under that holy-oak, or gospel tree:
Where (though thou see'st not) thou may'st think upon
Me, when thou yearly go'st procession:
Or for mine honour, lay me in that tomb
In which thy sacred relics shall have room.
For my embalming (Sweetest) there will be
No spices wanting, when I'm laid by thee.

THE VISION
Sitting alone (as one forsook)
Close by a silver-shedding brook,
With hands held up to Love, I wept,
And after sorrows spent, I slept:
Then in a vision I did see
A glorious form appear to me.
A virgin's face she had; her dress
Was like a sprightly Spartaness.
A silver bow with green silk strung,
Down from her comely shoulders hung:
And as she stood, the wanton air
Dangled the ringlets of her hair.
Her legs were such Diana shows,
When tucked up she a-hunting goes;
With buskins shortened to descry
The happy dawning of her thigh;
Which when I saw, I made access
To kiss that tempting nakedness:

> But she forbad me with a wand
> Of myrtle she had in her hand:
> And chiding me, said, 'Hence, remove,
> Herrick, thou art too coarse to love.'

TO HIS MAID PREW

> These summer-birds did with thy master stay
> The times of warmth; but then they flew away;
> Leaving their poet (being now grown old)
> Exposed to all the coming winter's cold.
> But thou kind Prew did'st with my fates abide,
> As well the winter's as the summer's tide:
> For which thy love, live with thy master here,
> Not two, but all the seasons of the year.

THE AMBER BEAD

> I saw a fly within a bead
> Of amber cleanly buried:
> The urn was little, but the room
> More rich than Cleopatra's tomb.

Herrick bears little or no resemblance to the contemporary Metaphysical poets, some of whom he outlived. The vertiginious flights of fancy in which they loved to engage were utterly beyond his scope; but, like many other great artists, by clinging to a few essential themes, he made a virtue of his limitations.

Henry King's metrical translation of the *Psalmes of David*, 1651.

HENRY KING (1592–1669), like Robert Herrick, was a learned and poetic priest, worthy to be compared with George Herbert. Born in Buckinghamshire and educated at Westminster School and Christ Church, Oxford, he took Holy Orders, and in 1641 was appointed Bishop of Chichester. In 1643, however, when Chichester surrendered to the Parliamentary troops, King's library was seized and his property sequestered. For the next seventeen years, he lived in retirement, but, after the Restoration, resumed his episcopal duties. He died on 30 September 1669.

A close friend of Jonson and Donne, King published his first collection of verses in 1657. It was the loss of his beloved wife, Anne Berkeley, who died at the age of twenty-four, that inspired 'The Exequy', his greatest work. There are few more moving laments in the whole of English literature; King's poem has a sustained intensity of feeling that, elsewhere among the metaphysical poets, only George Herbert and John Donne achieve. Despite the 'witty' conceits he employs – as when he compares his dead wife to 'a little world', doomed, like the great world, to be consumed by the universal conflagration that will precede the Last Day – the tone of King's lament is passionately personal:

> But woe is me! the longest date
> Too narrow is to calculate

These empty hopes: never shall I
Be so much blest as to descry
A glimpse of thee, till that day come
Which shall the earth to cinders doom,
And a fierce fever must calcine
The body of this world like thine,
(My little World!). That fit of fire
Once off, our bodies shall aspire
To our souls' bliss: then we shall rise,
And view our selves with clearer eyes
In that calm region, where no night
Can hide us from each others sight.

King's poem is beautifully organized, both in its exquisite choice of imagery and in the sudden changes of its pace and mood. Having bidden his wife farewell, he remembers his own mortality and compares the pulsation of his heart to the rhythmic bearing of a muffled drum:

'Tis true, with shame and grief I yield
Thou like the van first took the field,
And gotten hast the victory
In thus adventuring to die
Before me, whose more years might crave
A just precedence in the grave.

But hark! My pulse like a soft drum
Beats my approach, tells *thee* I come;
And slow howere my marches be,
I shall at last sit down by *Thee*.

In T. S. Eliot's words, these lines produce a curious 'effect of terror'; and the poet's indirect references to the remembered joys of bodily love give his lines an added force. Behind each image lies an emotion he cannot completely disclose, a sense of loss that still defies expression.

GEORGE HERBERT (1593–1632), born at Montgomery Castle, younger brother of Lord Herbert of Cherbury, came of a prosperous and aristocratic line. Educated at Westminster School and Trinity College, Cambridge, he was elected a fellow of Trinity in 1614, and in 1620 Public Orator, 'the finest place in the University, though not the gainfullest'. He also distinguished himself as a courtier and had originally hoped to enter political life; but he was deterred by his pious mother, long a friend and patroness of John Donne, who encouraged him to join the Church. After a period of doubt and anxiety, which is reflected in some of his most moving poems, he accepted her advice; and, as rector of Fugglestone-cum-Bemerton near Salisbury, he thenceforward led the life of an exemplary parish priest, 'like a saint, unspotted of the world, full of alms-deeds, full of humility'. In 1629 he married his cousin,

Jane Danvers, and four years later died at Bemerton. Soon after his death, his sheaf of poems, *The Temple* – his secular poems he had destroyed when he took Holy Orders – was printed for private circulation only. It achieved a considerable public success, however; and we learn from Izaak Walton that by 1670 it had sold over 20,000 copies.

Herbert's verses constantly remind us that before he had become a saintly clergyman he had been a worldling and a frequenter of the Court. Thus, in 'The Pearl', he speaks of his privileged youth:

> I know the ways of Learning; both the head
> And pipes that feed the press, and make it run;
> What Reason hath from Nature borrowed,
> Or of itself, like a good housewife, spun . . .
>
> I know the ways of Honour, what maintains
> The quick returns of courtesy and wit;
> In vies of favour whether party gains;
> When glory swells the heart, and mouldeth it
> To all expressions both of hand and eye;
> Which on the world a true-love knot may tie . . .
>
> I know the ways of Pleasure, the sweet strains,
> The lullings and the relishes of it;
> The propositions of hot blood and brains;
> What mirth and music mean; what Love and Wit
> Have done these twenty hundred years and more;
> I know the projects of unbridled store:
> My stuff is flesh, not brass; my senses live,
> And grumble oft that they have more in me
> Than He that curbs them, being but one to five:
> 　Yet I love Thee . . .

George Herbert, brother to Lord Herbert of Cherbury; 'like a saint, unspoiled of the world'.

Whereas Donne's address to the godhead often assumes the form of a rough impassioned plea, Herbert's approach is always urbane and courtly; and this attitude is reproduced in a peculiarly grave and gentle music. The poet, we are told, was 'a great musician'; and to call for an instrument and sing one of his own poems was among his last gestures. Just as his work shows nothing of Donne's violence, it lacks the rhetorical complexity, the far-fetched conceits, of Vaughan and Crashaw. His images are usually simple but exquisitely effective; and, although, as in 'The Pearl' and 'The Collar' he may begin by voicing a rebellious impulse, it gradually subsides into a mood of happy reconciliation.

THE COLLAR

I struck the board, and cried, No more;
　I will abroad.
What! Shall I ever sigh and pine?
My lines and life are free; free as the road,
Loose as the wind, as large as store;
　Shall I be still in suit?

Have I no harvest but a thorn
To let me blood, and not restore
What I have lost with cordial fruit?
    Sure there was wine
Before my sighs did dry it; there was corn
Before my tears did drown it.
Is the year only lost to me?
Have I no bays to crown it?
No flowers, no garlands gay? All blasted?
    All wasted?
Not so, my heart; but there is fruit,
    And thou hast hands.
Recover all thy sigh-blown age
On double pleasures; leave thy cold dispute
Of what is fit and not; forsake thy cage,
    Thy rope of sands
Which petty thoughts have made; and made to thee
Good cable to enforce and draw
    And be thy law,
While thou didst wink and wouldst not see.
    Away! take heed;
    I will abroad,
Call in thy death's-head there, tie up thy fears;
    He that forbears
To suit and serve his need
    Deserves his load.
But as I raved and grew more fierce and wild
    At every word,
Methought I heard one calling, 'Child;'
    And I replied, 'My Lord'.

LOVE

Love bade me welcome; yet my soul drew back,
    Guilty of dust and sin.
But quick-eyed Love, observing me grow slack
    From my first entrance in,
Drew nearer to me, sweetly questioning
    If I lacked anything.

'A guest', I answered, 'worthy to be here.'
    Love said, 'You shall be he.'
'I, the unkind, ungrateful? Ah, my Dear,
    I cannot look on Thee.'
Love took my hand, and, smiling, did reply,
    'Who made the eyes but I?'

'Truth, Lord, but I have marred them; let my shame
    Go where it doth deserve.'
'And know you not', says Love, 'who bore the blame?'
    'My Dear, then I will serve.'
'You must sit down,' says Love, 'and taste my meat.'
    So I did sit and eat.

SIR WILLIAM D'AVENANT (1606–68) often claimed, in later life, to have been Shakespeare's illegitimate son by the handsome and intelligent wife of an Oxford inn-keeper. As a young man, he served in the army; and it was during this period that he caught a venereal disease – according to Aubrey, from 'a black, handsome wench that lay in Axe-yard, Westminster' – which left him with a severely mutilated nose, that afterwards excited much unkind derision. Having joined the household of Fulke Greville, he was introduced to Whitehall, and began staging plays for the Court about the year 1630. His first play, *The Wits*, appeared in 1633. Queen Henrietta Maria being determined to introduce the idea of Platonic love to her husband's somewhat wayward court, D'Avenant wrote a play on the subject entitled *The Temple of Love*. He was made Poet Laureate in succession to Ben Jonson in 1638. During the Civil Wars, D'Avenant remained faithful to the royal family, and was knighted in 1643 for his bravery at the siege of Gloucester. He was converted to Catholicism in 1646; and, while visiting France, he started work on his epic poem 'Gondibert'. In 1650, captured by the Parliamentarians, he escaped to Paris. Finally returning home, he set up a semi-legitimate theatre, where he presented plays disguised as 'operas'. These 'musical entertainments' succeeded; but when fears of a counter-revolution swept the country, his theatre was closed and he himself imprisoned. After the Restoration, he was given the managership of the Duke's Playhouse, one of the two licensed theatres, at which he staged some of the first plays to employ actresses and make use of elaborate painted scenery.

Sir William D'Avenant; an early 18th-century portrait, in which the artist has carefully minimised the ugly effect made by his disfigured nose.

D'Avenant has an important place in the history of the theatre; but his own plays, though successful in their time, have become academic curiosities. Dryden, however, called him the founder of 'heroic plays' and used him as his 'guide' in writing *The Conquest of Granada*, inspired by D'Avenant's *The Siege of Rhodes*. As a work of art, the play is marred by its extravagant sensationalism. D'Avenant's comic plays are more interesting, though his humour seldom rises above topicality. His great epic poem, 'Gondibert', is lengthy and dull. But it is of some historical value, since D'Avenant intended it to illustrate the aesthetic theories of Hobbes, which required him to aim at directness and succinctness. He failed in this self-imposed task; but his preface to the poem, and Hobbes' reply, had an important influence on contemporary criticism. D'Avenant is seen at his best in his lyrics, which often possess a gay, ebullient charm:

> Wake all the dead! what ho! what ho!
> How soundly they sleep whose pillows lie low!
> They mind not poor lovers who walk above
> On the decks of the world in storms of love.
> No whisper now nor glance can pass

Through wickets or through panes of glass;
For our windows and doors are shut and barred.
Lie close in the church, and in the churchyard.
    In every grave make room, make room!
    The world's at an end, and we come, we come.

The state is now Love's foe, Love's foe;
Has seized on his arms, his quiver and bow;
Has pinioned his wings, and fettered his feet,
Because he made way for lovers to meet.
    But, O sad chance, his judge was old;
    Hearts cruel grow when blood grows cold.
No man being young his process would draw.
O heavens, that love should be subject to law!
    Lovers go woo the dead, the dead!
    Lie two in a grave, and to bed, to bed!

EDMUND WALLER (1606–87), the son of a rich Buckinghamshire landowner, was said by Clarendon to have been 'nursed in parliaments'. He entered the House of Commons when he was only sixteen. He re-entered it, having survived a period of imprisonment and disgrace, at the outset of the Restoration, and continued his active parliamentary life; so that 'it was no House if Waller was not there'. He had not always distinguished himself. In 1643 Waller and some of his friends hatched a Royalist conspiracy and, when it was detected, the poet is reputed to have lost his nerve and informed on his accomplices, among whom were 'several great ladies'. As a politician, Waller is described by Bishop Burnet as 'a vain and empty, though witty man'. As a poet, he was certainly a light-weight, the kind of poet who is best remembered for a few

(*Above*) Edmund Waller; 'it was no House if Waller was not there'.

(*Left*) The House of Commons during the reign of Charles I.

melodious first lines. Johnson, however, being sternly opposed to the metaphysical school, allotted him an important place in the history of English writing. 'After about half a century of forced thoughts, and rugged metre, some advances towards nature and harmony', he said, had been made by Waller and Sir John Denham. Neither was adventurous; but each had the easy, lucid flow that appealed to an Augustan reader:

> Go, lovely Rose –
> Tell her that wastes her time and me,
> That now she knows,
> When I resemble her to thee,
> How sweet and fair she seems to be.
>
> Tell her that's young,
> And shuns to have her graces spied,
> That hadst thou sprung
> In deserts where no men abide,
> Thou must have uncommended died . . .

John Suckling, portrait after Van Dyck, 1640.

SIR JOHN SUCKLING (1609–41) was a minor poet whom readers of the later seventeenth century found particularly attractive. 'Natural, easy Suckling!' exclaims Congreve's famous heroine, Millamant. A rich young man, of devotedly Royalist stock, Suckling throughout his brief life was the perfect type of cavalier. Having fought abroad under Gustavus Adolphus, he returned to the British court in 1632; and there his 'brisk and graceful look', his 'ready and sparkling wit', and his habit of travelling 'like a young prince for all manner of equipage and convenience, with a cart-load of books', earned him an immediate reputation. At the outbreak of the Civil Wars, Suckling devoted some £12,000 to raising a splendidly caprisoned troop of horse, which put up a poor show when it faced the Roundheads. Later, he was obliged to seek refuge in Paris and, now a ruined and desperate man, committed suicide by taking poison. Meanwhile, he had dashed off a number of plays and a quantity of light occasional verses, among the best-known being the song from *Aglaura*, a play he produced in 1637:

> Why so pale and wan, fond lover?
>   Prithee, why so pale?
> Will, when looking well can't move her,
>   Looking ill prevail?
>   Prithee, why so pale?
>
> Why so dull and mute, young sinner?
>   Prithee, why so mute?
> Will, when speaking well can't win her,
>   Saying nothing do't?
>   Prithee, why so mute?

> Quit, quit for shame! This will not move;
>> This cannot take her.
> If of herself she will not love,
>> Nothing can make her:
>> The devil take her!

Suckling is also remembered as the author of a single couplet:

> Her feet beneath her petticoat
> Like little mice stole in and out

from his delightful 'Ballad upon a Wedding'. There is a pagan gaiety about Suckling's prettiest lyrics, written as the Civil Wars drew near, that recalls the carefree 'age before the Flood'.

RICHARD CRASHAW (1613?–49) led, by comparison with George Herbert, a difficult, stormy and unsettled life. The son of a Puritan divine who strongly opposed the pretensions of the Roman Catholic Church, he went up to Cambridge in 1631, where he became a fellow of Peterhouse in 1637. But in 1644, like many of his contemporaries, he was swept out of his natural orbit by the conflict between King and Parliament. Having lost his fellowship owing to his Royalist and High Church sympathies, he took refuge first at Oxford, where he accepted the Roman Catholic faith, later in Paris and Rome, whither he carried a letter of introduction from the Queen to Cardinal Pallotta, then the Holy City's governor. The Cardinal appointed Crashaw his private secretary; but the English convert was profoundly scandalized both by the wickedness of Rome itself and by the iniquities he detected in his master's own entourage. When he exposed them, he was threatened with assassination; and Pallotta was obliged to despatch his officious secretary to the celebrated shrine of the Virgin at Loretto. There, soon after his arrival, he died, a deeply disappointed man.

Crashaw's collections of secular and religious verse, *Steps to the Temple* and *Delights of the Muses*, appeared as a single volume in 1646. Nowhere else has an English writer reproduced more vividly the spirit of the European Counter-Reformation; and, although it is always dangerous to draw a parallel between literature and the visual arts, Crashaw's 'Hymn to the name and honour of the admirable Saint Theresa' at once recalls Bernini's statue of Saint Theresa in her hour of ecstasy. Both works combine erotic with religious symbolism. The 'Hymn' is essentially a Baroque poem, and Crashaw's description of the saint's 'intolerable joys' brings out all his fiery eloquence. But he was seldom capable of long-sustained flights; and critics who attacked the Metaphysical school have often picked on his more unbalanced fancies – for example, on his ludicrous picture of the weeping Magdalen:

> And now where'er he strays
> Among the Galilean mountains,

> Or more unwelcome ways,
> He's followed by two faithful fountains;
> Two walking baths; two weeping motions;
> Portable and compendious oceans. . . .

In the 'Hymn', to repeat Samuel Johnson's phrase, 'the most heterogeneous images' are, indeed, 'yoked by violence together'.

> O how oft shalt thou complain
> Of a sweet and subtle pain;
> Of intolerable joys;
> Of a death in which who dies
> Loves his death, and dies again,
> And would forever so be slain;
> And lives, and dies; and knows not why
> To live but that he still may die.
>   How kindly will thy gentle heart
> Kiss the sweetly killing dart,
> And close in his embraces keep
> Those delicious wounds, that weep
> Balsam to heal themselves with. Thus
> When these thy deaths, so numerous,
> Shall all at last die into one,
> And melt thy soul's sweet mansion;
> Like a soft lump of incense, hasted
> By too hot a fire, and wasted
> Into perfuming clouds, so fast
> Shalt thou exhale to heaven at last
> In a dissolving sigh, and then
> O what? Ask not the tongues of men.
> Angels cannot tell; suffice
> Thyself shall feel thy own full joys,
> And hold them fast forever. There
> So soon as thou shalt first appear,
> The moon of maiden stars, thy white
> Mistress, attended by such bright
> Souls as thy shining self, shall come,
> And in her first ranks make thee room;
> Where 'mongst her snowy family
> Immortal welcomes wait on thee . . .

ABRAHAM COWLEY (1618–67), the son of a London tradesman and one of the best known Metaphysical poets, like many contemporary writers suffered from the destructive turmoil of the Civil Wars, which, after he had enjoyed a brilliant career at Westminster School and Cambridge, drove him into foreign exile. The next twelve years he was obliged to spend abroad as a Royalist courtier and secret agent; and, when he returned to England in 1656, he was arrested and imprisoned. Once he had been freed, he resumed his literary pursuits – the publication, in 1647, of his collection of lyrics, *The Mistress*, had made him the most famous poet of his day. In 1656 he issued a folio edition of his *Works*; but on the death of Cromwell he again departed for France, where he stayed until the Restoration. The King, however, failed to reward his services; and Cowley, 'weary', he said, 'of the vexations and formalities of an active condition', retired to a modest farm beside the Thames, at which he died in the summer of 1667, having become soaked with dew and caught cold as he directed the operations of his haymakers. Neither Cowley's *Pindaric Odes* – a metrical innovation – nor his sacred epic, the *Davideis*, can be recommended to the modern student of poetry. But much of his lyric verse, published in *The Mistress* certainly deserves re-reading:

> Well then; I now do plainly see,
> This busy world and I shall ne'er agree;
> The very honey of all earthly joy
> Does of all meats the soonest cloy,
> And they (methinks) deserve my pity,
> Who for it can endure the stings,
> The crowd, and buzz, and murmurings
> Of this great hive, the city.
>
> Ah, yet, e'er I descend to th'grave
> May I a small house, and a large garden have!
> And a few friends, and many books, both true,
> Both wise, and both delightful too!
> And since Love ne'er will from me flee,
> A mistress moderately fair,
> But good as guardian angels are,
> Only belov'd, and loving me!...

Abraham Cowley, by
Sir Peter Lely.

('The Wish')

RICHARD LOVELACE (1618–58) born in Woolwich and educated at Charterhouse school and Gloucester Hall, Oxford, was one of the most graceful of the Cavalier poets; and, although he survived the tragedy of the Civil Wars, they left him a ruined and broken-hearted man. During his youth he was so much 'admired and adored by the female sex' that, when he was only eighteen, he received his degree as Master of Arts at the particular request of a distinguished lady who had been struck with his 'most amiable and beautiful person, innate modesty, virtue, and courtly deport-ment'. From the outset an ardent Royalist, in 1642 he presented a petition to Parliament for the restoration of the King, and was cast into the Gatehouse prison, whence he addressed his famous lines 'To Althea'. After the Royalist defeat he quitted England and served under the French King, being seriously wounded at the Siege of Dunkirk. Two years later, he ventured to return to England, where he was again arrested, and spent ten months behind bars. On his release, we are told, he 'grew very melancholy ... went in ragged clothes ... and mostly lodged in obscure and

Richard Lovelace: from
Lucasta, 1662.

dirty places . . .' He is said to have died of consumption 'in a very mean lodging' in Gunpowder Alley, Shoe Lane. His posthumous collection of poems appeared in 1659. He was almost forgotten, however, until 1765, when the celebrated antiquary and church-man, Thomas Percy (1729–1811), published the important work '*Reliques of Ancient English Poetry*'. Lovelace's reputation now rests on one or two delightful lyrics, such as 'To Althea, from prison', with its often-quoted stanza:

> Stone walls do not a prison make,
>   Nor iron bars a cage;
> Minds innocent and quiet take
>   That for an hermitage;
> If I have freedom in my love,
>   And in my soul am free;
> Angels alone that soar above,
>   Enjoy such liberty.

Elsewhere, his verse is often laborious, elliptical in style and over-elaborate, though he was a diligent reviser of his own work. Only now and then, as in 'To Lucasta, going to the warres', does he achieve an effect of ease and grace that reflects his quiet idealism:

> Tell me not (sweet) I am unkind,
>   That from the nunnery
> Of thy chaste breast, and quiet mind,
>   To war and arms I flie.
>
> True; a new mistress now I chase,
>   The first foe in the field;
> And with a stronger faith embrace,
>   A Sword, a Horse, a Shield.
>
> Yet this Inconstancy is such,
>   As you too shall adore;
> I could not love thee (Dear) so much,
>   Lov'd I not Honour more.

Andrew Marvell; 'of a middling stature, pretty strong sett, roundish-faced . . . hazell-eie, browne haire'. Artist unknown.

Richard Lovelace was, above all else, what his French contem-poraries called an *honnête homme* – courtier, lover and polished man of the world, a gallant survivor of the society that the Civil Wars would leave in ruins.

ANDREW MARVELL (1621–78), the son of a Yorkshire school-master, was brought up in the seaport-town of Hull, and, we are told, received his 'first unhappy education among boatswains and cabin-boys', from whom he acquired a fund of coarse invective of which he afterwards made good use when he came to write his satires. When he was only twelve, however, the boy was entered at Trinity College, Cambridge, took his degree in 1638, and then passed some years travelling around Europe. In 1650 he joined

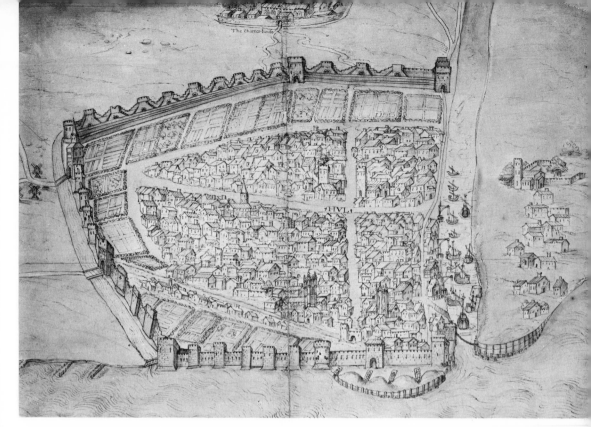

the household of the retired Parliamentary general, Lord Fairfax, as tutor to his twelve-year-old daughter, Mary; and at Nunappleton, his employer's country house, Marvell spent his most productive years. He seems to have conceived a deep and lasting affection not only for his romantic surroundings but for the little girl he tutored. Here he developed into one of the greatest lyrical poets of the English seventeenth century.

He was also an extremely able linguist; and in 1657, at Milton's own suggestion, Marvell became his colleague as Latin Secretary to Cromwell's government. In 1659 he was elected Member of Parliament for Hull, a seat he continued to hold until he died. The diligence and integrity he showed as a public figure are said to have been much respected; and, after the Restoration of the Stuarts in 1660, it is reported that Marvell took 'vigorous' steps to save his former colleague from the scaffold. During his last period, the exquisite lyric poet was transformed into an impassioned satirist; and his *Poems on Affairs of State*, though unpublished until 1689, were widely circulated among his friends. Meanwhile, in 1681, his *Miscellaneous Poems* had themselves been collected and published by a certain Mary Palmer, who claimed to be his widow.

Everything we know about Marvell suggests that he deserved his reputation as a good and kindly man. Physically, writes John Aubrey, he was 'of a middling stature, pretty strong sett, roundishfaced, cherry-cheeked, hazell-eie, browne haire'. He was in his conversation very modest, and of very few words: and though he loved wine he would never drinke hard in company . . . He kept bottles of wine at his lodgeing, and many times he would drinke liberally by himselfe to refresh his spirits and exalt his muse.' Though a believer, Marvell was no bigot and, though a politician, attached to no single political faction. War he detested; and of the Civil War he wrote: 'I think the cause too good to have been fought for. Men ought to have trusted God; they ought to and might have trusted the King.' From an age of ferocious conflict he looked back with exquisite regret to the peaceful world before the Deluge:

> Unhappy! shall we never more
> That sweet militia restore . . .
> When roses only arms might bear,
> And men did rosy garlands wear?
> Tulips, in several colours barred,
> Were then the Switzers of our guard . . .
> But war all this doth overgrow:
> We ordnance plant, and powder sow.

An admirer of Cromwell, the simple country gentleman who

> Could by industrious valour climb
> To ruin the great work of Time
> And cast the kingdoms old
> Into another mould . . .

in his famous 'Horatian Ode upon Cromwell's Return from Ireland' he also paid a noble tribute to the tragic King, and to the unshaken dignity with which he had met his death. But it is as the 'poet of gardens', the author of luminous images that foreshadow the greatest achievements of English Romantic verse, that Marvell will always be remembered. Thus, in 'Appleton House', we follow him between the hedgerows that line Lord Fairfax's garden-walks:

> And through the hazel thick espy
> The hatching throstle's shining eye . . .

while, in 'The Bermudas', we glimpse the richness of a landscape created for the English travellers by the hand of God:

> He hangs in shades the orange bright
> Like golden lamps in a green night,
> And does in the pomegranates close
> Jewels more rich than Ormus shows . . .

Marvell's most sustained effort, however, in which he tempers 'Metaphysical' conceits with a more forceful and spontaneous eloquence, is the well-known poem 'To his Coy Mistress':

> But at my back I always hear
> Time's wingéd chariot hurrying near,

And yonder all before us lie
Deserts of vast eternity.
Thy beauty shall no more be found,
Nor, in thy marble vault, shall sound
My echoing song; then worms shall try
That long-preserved virginity . . .
The grave's a fine and private place,
But none, I think, do there embrace . . .

HENRY VAUGHAN (1622–95) was yet another poet who suffered from the internecine struggles of the English seventeenth century. A Welshman born in Brecknockshire – hence the description 'Silurist', or inhabitant of South Wales, which he used upon the title-page of his first volume of poems – he went up in 1638 to Jesus College, Oxford, whence he and his twin-brother, Thomas, were dislodged by the outbreak of the Civil War. The Vaughans then returned to Wales, and Henry adopted the medical profession; while Thomas Vaughan became a famous alchemist and erudite Rosicrucian, who published a series of learned books. Henry Vaughan's two volumes of poems, *Silex Scintillans* and *Olor Iscanus* were published in 1650 and 1651.

Title page of Henry Vaughan's *Silex Scintillans*, 1650.

The preface that Vaughan attached to the second edition of *Silex Scintillans* contains a warm acknowledgment of the influence of George Herbert – 'the blessed man . . . whose holy life and verse gained many pious Converts', and who had been the first writer to attempt to divert 'the foul and overflowing stream' of irreligious modern poetry. Vaughan, indeed, sometimes borrowed from Herbert; but he was a man of very different genius. A modern critic, D. J. Enright, has suggested that he lacked his master's 'sense of climax'; and there is no doubt that his poems are seldom so complete or so beautifully rounded as the best of the poems in *The Temple*. He is apt to begin with a splendid passage, but afterwards lose his way among accumulated tropes and fancies. His imagination, on the other hand, frequently reminds one of that of the younger Wordsworth. Vaughan, too, was devoted to the idea of childhood, which, like Wordsworth, he equates with a vision of divine innocence. The child is nearer to God than the man; and every step he takes towards maturity carries him further from the original fount of goodness:

Happy those early days, when I
Shined in my angel infancy;
Before I understood this place
Appointed for my second race,
Or taught my soul to fancy aught
But a white, celestial thought;
When yet I had not walked above
A mile or two from my first Love,
And looking back, at that short space,

> Could see a glimpse of His bright face;
> When on some gilded cloud or flower
> My gazing soul would dwell an hour,
> And in those weaker glories spy
> Some shadows of eternity;
> Before I taught by tongue to wound
> My conscience with a sinful sound,
> Or had the black art to dispense
> A several sin to every sense,
> But felt through all this fleshly dress
> Bright shoots of everlastingness.

At the same time, he shares Wordsworth's pantheistic love of natural beauty, and expresses that love in wonderfully vivid and admirably concrete images:

> He that hath found some fledged bird's nest may know
> At first sight if the bird be flown;
> But what fair well or grove he sings in now,
> That is to him unknown.

In another poem, he writes of the dead tree, *The Timber*, that still encloses memories of its youth and grace:

> Sure thou didst flourish once! and many springs,
> Many bright mornings, much dew, many showers,
> Passed o'er thy head; many light hearts and wings
> Which now are dead, lodg'd in thy living bowers.

THOMAS TRAHERNE (1636?–74) remained entirely unknown as a poet until the beginning of the twentieth century when, in 1906, Bertram Dobell first published his poetic works from the original manuscripts. Little is known of the poet's life. But according to John Aubrey, he was the 'son of a shoemaker in Hereford', where Philip Traherne, no doubt a relation, twice served as mayor during the first half of the seventeenth century. Philip Traherne was a keen Royalist, noted 'for his fervent zeal for the Established Church and clergy'; and Thomas Traherne, having gone up to Brasenose College, Oxford, in 1652 and graduated in 1656, took Holy Orders and became rector of Credenhill near Hereford. Then in 1667 he was appointed private chaplain to the Keeper of the Seals, Sir Orlando Bridgman – a post he continued to hold after Bridgman's retirement into private life. Traherne's last years were spent in Bridgman's house at Teddington; and there he wrote his greatest prose work, *Centuries of Meditation*, which Dobell also resurrected. His only published volumes, which are of far less interest, were entitled *Roman Forgeries* and *Christian Ethicks*.

As a poet – and, indeed, as the author of religious meditations – Traherne seems to have foreshadowed many of the ideas of Blake and Wordsworth. 'The world is a pomegranate . . .', he declared in his *Centuries*, 'which God hath put into man's heart . . . It containeth the seeds of grace and the seeds of glory. All virtues lie in the World . . .' And elsewhere: 'Suppose a river or a drop of water . . . an ear of corn, or an herb: God knoweth infinite excellencies in it more than we: He seeth how it relateth to angels and men . . . how it representeth all His attributes . . .' Thus, like Blake, he 'saw the world in a grain of sand' and, like Wordsworth, believed the human child brought with him vivid memories of his celestial heritage, and was himself a heavenly masterpiece.

> These little limbs,
>   These eyes and hands which here I find,
> These rosy cheeks wherewith my life begins,
>   Where have ye been? behind
> What curtain were ye from me hid so long,
> Where was, in what abyss, my speaking tongue?
>
> When silent I
>   So many thousand, thousand years
> Beneath the dust did in a chaos lie,
>   How could I smiles or tears,
> Or lips or hands or eyes or ears perceive?
> Welcome ye treasures which I now receive.
>
> I that so long
>   Was nothing from eternity,
> Did little think such joys as ear or tongue
>   To celebrate or see;
> Such sounds to hear, such hands to feel, such feet,
> Beneath the skies on such a ground to meet.
>
> New burnished joys!
>   Which yellow gold and pearls excel!
> Such sacred treasures are the limbs in boys,
>   In which a soul doth dwell;
> Their organized joints and azure veins
> More wealth include than all the world contains.

('The Salutation')

> A learned and a happy ignorance
>   Divided me
>   From all the vanity,
> From all the sloth, care, pain, and sorrow that advance
>   The madness and the misery
> Of men. No error, no distraction I
> Saw soil the earth or overcloud the sky.
>
> Unwelcome penitence was then unknown,
>   Vain costly toys,
>   Swearing and roaring boys,
> Shops, markets, taverns, coaches, were unshown;
>   So all things were that drowned my joys:
> No thorns choked up my path, nor hid the face
> Of bliss and beauty, nor eclipsed the place.
>
> Only what Adam in his first estate,
>   Did I behold;

Hard silver and dry gold
    As yet lay under ground; my blessed fate
        Was more acquainted with the old
And innocent delights which he did see
In his original simplicity.

Those things which first his Eden did adorn
        My infancy
    Did crown. Simplicity
Was my protection when I first was born.
    Mine eyes those treasures first did see
Which God first made. The first effects of love
My first enjoyments upon earth did prove.

('Eden')

Francis Quarles, from
his *Emblems*, 1635.

Among minor religious poets of the age, FRANCIS QUARLES (1592–1644) certainly deserves a mention. Though an ardent Royalist – during the Civil War his manuscripts were confiscated and destroyed – he was much admired by Puritans, who enjoyed the homeliness of his devotional imagery. Quarles's verses, at their best, have a sober rustic charm; elsewhere, as in his paraphrase of the book of Jonah, *A Feast for Women* (1620) he is intolerably diffuse and awkward. A more original collection, *Emblems*, appeared in 1635. Quarles led a busy public life. Appointed cup-bearer to the Princess Palatine, he visited Germany where he remained for several years; later, he became secretary to an Irish bishop and, in 1639, official Chronologer to the City of London.

Prose Writers

English prose-style, as we understand it today, first began to develop during the second half of the seventeenth century. Many Jacobean and Caroline writers were still close, both in subject and in spirit, to the traditions of the Elizabethan Age.

LANCELOT ANDREWES (1551–1626), successively Bishop of Chichester, Ely and Winchester, was a remarkable linguist, and one of the committee of writers who produced the Authorized Version of the Bible. A foremost representative of Anglican orthodoxy, though he took little part in wordly affairs, he was frequently called into counsel by Queen Elizabeth I and Kings James I and Charles I. Andrewes was primarily a theologian; but his published sermons and his *Manual of Private Devotions* have real literary value. His severe and 'witty' intellectualism finds expression in a condensed, jerky style. His short, packed sentences have a strong cumulative effect; and his arguments are relieved by sudden passages of illuminating imagery:

It was no summer progress. A cold coming they had of it at this time of year, just the worst time of the year to take a journey, and specially a long journey in. The ways deep, the weather sharp, the days short, the sun farthest off, *in solstitio brumali*, 'the very dead of winter'.

This was the passage that inspired T. S. Eliot's 'The Journey of the Magi'. The opening of Andrewes' sermon on Mary Magdalene at the grave of Christ also shows his great dramatic skill:

The Place. In the grave she saw them; and Angels in a grave, is a strange sight, a sight never seen before; not till Christ's body had been there, never till this day; this is the first news of Angels in that place. For a grave is no place for Angels, one would think; for worms rather: blessed Angels, but not in a blessed place. But since Christ lay there, that place is blessed.

Less obviously appealing than those of Donne, Lancelot Andrewes' sermons are, in their own way, no less powerful.

Bishop Lancelot Andrewes, the famous sermonist, who assisted in the preparation of the King James's Bible.

ROBERT BURTON (1577–1640) was the kind of learned eccentric who has played so important a part in the history of English literature. It took him nine years to achieve a degree at Oxford – perhaps because, between 1593 and 1599, he suffered a severe illness, from which he may well have derived his knowledge of the melancholy state. He remained at his Oxford college until he died, employed as tutor and librarian, but also officiating as vicar at the church of St Thomas; and in 1621 he published his vast encyclopedic work, *The Anatomy of Melancholy*. He died on 25 January 1640, near the time he had predicted from his own astrological calculations; and it was whispered among Oxford students that he had committed suicide that his prophecy might be proved true.

Burton is a literary rarity, an author whose fame rests entirely on a single book. The 'melancholy' of his title refers to a genus of mental diseases frequently described during the Renaissance, of which the chief symptom was a sense of fear and sorrow that had no obvious external cause. In expounding his melancholic theme, he drew heavily on earlier writers. The work sets out to be a medical and psychological treatise, but contains so many diversions and digressions, and so many memorable illustrative anecdotes, that it is impossible to fix its character. He cites and quotes the authorities he has consulted, and piles up learned references along the margin, so that, on many pages, his text consists of little else. Burton loved employing synonyms, as this brief passage on ambition shows:

For commonly they that, like Sisyphus, roll this restless stone of ambition, are in a perpetual agony, still perplexed, *semper taciti, tristesque recedunt* (Lucretius), doubtful, timorous, suspicious, loath to offend in word or deed, still cogging and colloguing, embracing, capping, cringing, applauding, flattering, fleering, visiting, waiting at men's doors, with all affability, counterfeit honesty and humility.

Burton's garrulity fits his wide ranging curiosity about human life

(*Above left*) Robert Burton's *The Anatomy of Melancholy*. The first edition of Robert Burton's enormous work had appeared under a pen-name in 1621.

(*Above right*) Pamphlet bequeathed by Robert Burton in 1640 to the Bodleian Library, Oxford.

and his almost irresponsible erudition. His style, loose and informal, rich in homely turns of phrase, gives the impression of fluent and energetic speech. His brain seems to be overcharged with words and ideas which come tumbling and rushing out:

In other countries they have the same grievances, I confess, but that doth not excuse us, wants, defects, enormities, idle drones, tumults, discords, contention, law-suits . . . excess in apparel, diet, decay of tillage, depopulations, especially against rogues, beggars, Egyptians, vagabonds (so termed at least) which have swarmed all over Germany, France, Italy, Poland as you may read in Munster, Cranzius, and Aventinus; as those tartars and Arabians this day do in the eastern countries: yet such has been the iniquity of all ages, as it seems to small purpose.

Burton's book has been plundered by numerous later writers, notably by Laurence Sterne. Burton himself was a secluded clergyman and librarian; but his reading was immense and fed an omnivorous mind, the contents of which he poured into his book. *The Anatomy of Melancholy* is the kind of minor masterpiece, shapeless, diffuse, yet endlessly entertaining, that will never lack admirers.

IZAAK WALTON (1593–1683), though born in Stafford, was apprenticed as a boy to an ironmonger in the City of London. By 1614 he had set up a business on his own, in a shop in Fleet Street, at the time when John Donne was about to become the vicar of St Dunstan's Church. Walton soon gained his friendship; and Donne introduced him to other famous churchmen and writers, including George Herbert. In 1626 he married Rachel Floud; but all their seven children died young and she herself expired in 1640. In 1646 he re-married, and his second wife bore him two sons and a daughter. Walton was a part-time author, even while he continued to keep a shop; and in 1640 his 'Life of Donne' was prefixed to Donne's *LXXX Sermons*. Subsequently he wrote four more 'Lives', each of a distinguished Anglican divine, the subjects he chose being Herbert, Wotton, Hooker and Sanderson. When he retired from business after a successful career, Walton settled down to a carefree existence, which enabled him to enjoy his favourite pastime, fishing.

Izaak Walton, author of *The Compleat Angler* and of important biographies of Donne and Herbert.

His most famous work, *The Compleat Angler, or the Contemplative Man's Recreation*, appeared anonymously in 1653. This is not simply a treatise on angling, but also a prose-pastoral celebrating the beauties of the country. It has an enduring charm and freshness. Walton's wry humour is perpetually creeping through, as when he advises his reader how to catch pike with the help of frogs:

Put your hook into his mouth, which you may easily do from the middle of April till August, and then the frogs mouth grows up, and he continues so for at least six months without eating, but is sustained, none but He whose name is wonderful, knows how; I say, put your hook, I mean the arming wire, through his mouth, and out at his gills, and then with a fine needle and silk sew the upper part of his leg, with only one stitch, to the arming wire of your hook, or the frog's leg, above the upper joint, to the armed wire, and in so doing, use him as though you loved him, that is, harm him as little as you may possibly, that he may live the longer.

Much of Walton's angling lore is worthless. He never aspired to become a professional writer; and for him writing, like fishing, was an occupation with which he entertained his leisure hours.

Among the most learned writers of his day was SIR THOMAS BROWNE (1605–82), the son of a London merchant, educated at Winchester and Pembroke College, Oxford, who, having studied medicine abroad and taken his degree at Leyden, in 1636 settled down as a physician in Norwich, where five years later he married into a well-established Norfolk family, and remained until he died. His earliest book, *Religio Medici*, on which he had started work as early as 1635, was intended primarily for his friends. The manuscript was widely discussed, however; and in 1642, after the publication of a pirated edition, he eventually decided he must print the text. It obtained immediate renown; by 1645 it had reached Paris and been translated into several foreign languages. 'Hardly ever was a book published in Britain that made more noise than the *Religio Medici*', wrote the eighteenth-century bibliographer William Oldys.

Browne's *magnum opus* is indeed an extraordinary book; but it is one that looks back to the Renaissance rather than forward to the Scientific Age. There is nothing that could be described as scientific about the author's style or method. Browne accepts, almost without question, the Protestant faith he had inherited. What concerns him is to show its effect upon the conduct of his own life, and to demonstrate that the practising Christian may, at the same time, be a true humanist. Fanaticism in any form he always strongly opposes; and, though he is a good Protestant, he points out that, just as there have been numerous reformers, so there have been numerous reformations, 'every Country proceeding in a particular way . . . according as their national Interest . . . inclined them; some angrily, and with extremity; others calmly, and with mediocrity, not rending, but easily dividing the community, and leaving an honest possibility of a reconciliation . . .'. He himself has embraced the Protestant faith, merely because 'there is no Church whose every part so squares unto my Conscience . . .'.

Similarly, he deprecates the more elaborate exercises of religious disputation, 'those wingy Mysteries in Divinity and airy subtleties in Religion, which have unhing'd the brains of better heads . . .'. But, despite this attitude, it is typical of Browne that he should admit that 'I love to lose myself in a mystery', and should enjoy rehearsing the 'airy subtleties' – including such problems as 'whether Adam was an Hermaphrodite' – that used to tax the Schoolmen's minds. He is rarely systematic and, if a subject amuses him, he will pursue it through a lengthy paragraph. Though by no means a pedant at heart, he has a pedantic love of curious details; and his book is a repository of theories and legends to which he himself attaches little credence.

Thus the *Religio Medici*, which consists of two parts, the first divided into sixty, the second into fifteen sections, is not so much a treatise as a literary divagation. Browne strays from one topic to another, and is constantly returning to some previous theme. The result is evocative rather than strictly informative; it is the regular recurrence of certain dominant ideas that gives the book a shape and meaning. Browne, for example, is amazed by the strangeness of life, and has adopted the medieval belief that Man is a microcosm, a representation in miniature of the whole created universe:

I could never content my contemplation with those general pieces of wonder, the Flux and Reflux of the Sea, the increase of Nile, the conversion of the Needle to the North; and have studied to match and parallel those in the more obvious and neglected pieces of Nature, which without further travel I can do in the Cosmography of myself. We carry with us the wonders we seek without us: there is all Africa and her prodigies in us; we are that bold and adventurous piece of Nature, which he that studies wisely learns in a *compendium* what others labour at in a divided piece and endless volume.

Simultaneously, he draws a self-portrait. He is 'naturally bashful'; he informs us, 'nor hath conversation, age, or travel, been able to effront or enharden me . . .'. Only in dreams can he talk with ease and zest; for 'I was born in the Planetary hour of Saturn, and I think I have a piece of that Leaden Planet in me. I am no way facetious, nor disposed for the mirth and galliardize of company . . .' There is no doubt that he has experienced pain and despair: 'The heart of man is the place the Devils dwell in: I feel sometimes a Hell within myself . . .' Yet he delights in existence: 'Now for my life, it is a miracle of thirty years, which to relate, were not a History, but a piece of Poetry, and would sound to common ears like a Fable.'

Sir Thomas Browne, from the frontispiece to a later edition of his *Pseudodoxia Epidemica*, which first appeared in 1646.

If Browne's attitude towards life is poetic, so is the prose-style he developed. Above all else, he is a self-conscious stylist, who strove to produce in every paragraph a melodious rhythmic entity. Few prose-writers have been so consistently musical; but the effect is never monotonous, since he is constantly varying his pace. Now he is stately and measured; now he opens or concludes a leisurely passage with a single rapid sentence. He uses language so that every word he drops in arouses a widening circle of associations.

Browne's personal career was placid; and, although a Royalist, he lived without discomfort through the 'drums and tramplings' of the Civil Wars. After issuing the *Religio Medici*, he published in 1646 his *Pseudodoxia Epidemica*, a learned discussion of popular scientific errors, and in 1658 a volume containing two long essays, *Hydriotaphia*, or *Urne-Burial*, and an even more characteristic work, *The Garden of Cyrus*, or *The Quincuncial Lozenge . . . Mystically Considered*, a rare blend of poetic illumination and pedantic erudition:

Life is a pure flame, and we live by an invisible Sun within us. A small fire sufficeth for life, great flames seemed too little after death, while men vainly affected precious pyres, and to burn like Sardanapalus; but the wisdom of funeral Laws found the folly of prodigal blazes, and reduced undoing fires unto the rule of sober obsequies, wherein few could be so mean as not to provide wood, pitch, a mourner, and an Urne.

(*Urne-Burial*, 1658)

But the Quincunx of Heaven runs low, and 'tis time to close the five ports of knowledge. We are unwilling to spin out our awaking thoughts into the phantasms of sleep, which often continueth praecogitations, making Cables of Cobwebs and Wildernesses of handsome Groves. Besides Hippocrates hath spoke so little, and the Oneirocriticall Masters have left such frigid Interpretations from plants, that there is little encouragement to dream of Paradise it self. Nor will the sweetest delight of Gardens afford much comfort in sleep; wherein the dullness of that sense shakes hands with delectable odours; and though in the Bed of Cleopatra, can hardly with any delight raise up the ghost of a Rose.

Though Somnus in Homer be sent to rouse up Agamemnon, I find no such effects in these drowsy approaches of sleep. To keep our eyes open longer were but to act our Antipodes. The Huntsmen are up in America, and they are already past their first sleep in Persia. But who can be drowsy at that hour which freed us from everlasting sleep? or have slumbering thoughts at that time, when sleep it self must end, and as some conjecture all shall awake again?

(*The Garden of Cyrus*, 1658)

John Aubrey; a 19th-century engraving after a drawing by William Faithorne.

JOHN AUBREY (1626–97) was born in Kington, Wiltshire, on 12 March 1626. He went to Trinity College, Oxford, and then on to the Middle Temple, though he was never called to the Bar. In 1652 he inherited his rich father's estate; but he was soon reduced to poverty by his extravagance and lack of business sense. He spent the remainder of his life as a guest in the country houses of his many friends. In 1663 he was nominated as a Fellow of the newly formed Royal Society; and in 1667 he met Anthony a Wood, an Oxford scholar who was preparing his *Athenae Oxoniensis*, a biographical record of Oxford graduates. Aubrey agreed to assist him by preparing a series of 'minutes of lives'. He worked on these and other 'lives' from 1669 until 1696. The only work he published was a volume of *Miscellanies* which appeared in 1696. On his death, he left a large number of manuscripts, including accounts of the natural history of Surrey and Wiltshire written for the Royal Society, and the series of sketches of eminent men that he had originally made for Wood.

Though Aubrey was a careless writer and an unsystematic historian, he had an avid interest in the past and an extraordinarily keen eye. His famous *Brief Lives* were written, he said, 'tumultarily as if tumbled out of a sack'. Any picturesque detail delighted him. Here, for example, is the glimpse he gives us of a certain Dr Butler:

The Dr. lying at the Savoy in London next the water side, where there was a Balcony look'd into the Thames, a patient came to him that was grievously tormented with an Ague. The Dr orders a boat to be in readiness under his window, and discoursed with the patient (a Gent.) in the Balcony, when, on a signal given, two or three lusty Fellows came behind the Gentleman and threw him a matter of 20 feet into the Thames. This surprise absolutely cured him.

Many of his portraits are sharply satirical; but he also praises warmly, as in his note on Charles Cavendish, the Royalist general killed in battle at the age of twenty-three:

A high Extraction to some persons is like the Dropsy, the greatness of the man is his disease, and renders him unwieldy: but here is a Person of Great Extract free from the swelling of Greatness, as brisk and active as the lightest Horseman that fought under him. In some parts of India, they tell us, that a Nobleman accounts himself polluted if a Plebian touch him; but here is a person of that rank who used the same familiarity and frankness amongst the meanest of his Soldiers, the poorest miner, and amongst his equals; and by stooping so low, he rose the higher in the common account, and was valued accordingly as a Prince, and a Great one;

Among Aubrey's greatest assets was his visual imagination. Thus, William Prynne, the Puritan pamphleteer, is far more vividly present in Aubrey's text than in any of his own writings:

His manner of Study was thus: he wore a long quilt cap, which came 2 or 3, at least, inches over his eyes, which served him as an Umbrella to defend his Eyes from the light. About every three hours his man was to bring him a roll and a pot of Ale to refocillate his wasted spirits: so he studied and drank, and munched some bread; . . .

With John Aubrey began the art of biographical portraiture as it is practised at the present day. Like Boswell, he understood that, if we are to depict a personality, we must record not only a character's dominant outlines, but its smallest and most trifling details.

JOHN BUNYAN (1628–88) was born at Elstow, near Bedford, the son of a tinker. He received a rudimentary education; and at about sixteen he was drafted into the Parliamentary army and stationed at Newport Pagnell until 1647. He saw no active service, and his military life was uneventful. But, having been brought up in a small community of staunch Protestants, he was, no doubt, deeply influenced by the preaching captains of the Ironsides, whose religious convictions were backed by a highly-developed theological discipline. Released from the army in 1647, he returned home and followed his father's trade; and, sometime in the next few years, he married. The two devotional volumes that formed his wife's dowry helped to strengthen his religious feelings. But his initial religious fervour was followed by a spiritual crisis, and by a period of darkness and despair. Then, one day, he was introduced to and joined a Separatist church in Bedford. His inner struggles soon worsened; he was assailed by a sense of utter hopelessness, and plagued by whispering voices that consigned him to damnation. Eventually, however, he emerged from his gloom, achieved a state of spiritual serenity, and felt ready to become a preacher. After the Restoration of 1660, independent preachers lost their freedom. On 12 November, Bunyan was brought before a zealous local magistrate and, when he refused to give an assurance that he would not preach again, he was committed to the county gaol. His imprisonment was not quite so rigorous as has often been assumed. He was allowed to visit London to appeal for help in his case, see friends and write several books. He also preached in gaol, and learned to make tag-laces to provide for his family's needs.

John Bunyan by T. Sadler.

With him in prison he had a copy of the Bible and Foxe's famous *Booke of Martyrs*; and, using language largely drawn from these texts, he composed his spiritual autobiography, *Grace Abounding*, written for himself alone. After 1668 Bunyan was granted parole; and, in 1672, the Declaration of Indulgence removed the previous restrictions both on Catholic priests and on dissenting ministers. Bunyan was then released and became pastor of his old church, until, in 1675, Charles II was forced to withdraw the Declaration; and Bunyan suffered a further period of imprisonment. It lasted six months; and, at this time, Bunyan is reputed to have written his masterpiece, *The Pilgrim's Progress*. 'I did it mine own self to gratify,' he declared, insisting that 'manner and matter, too, was all my own'. The book appeared in 1678, and had an enormous success. During his last ten years Bunyan was a public figure whose preaching, at seven o'clock in the morning, drew over a thousand people to a London meeting house. In 1688, on a journey to preach in London, he turned aside to visit Reading, where he hoped to arbitrate in a bitter family quarrel. Having been drenched by a heavy rainstorm, he developed a fever, of which he died on 31 August 1688.

Of Bunyan's numerous books, over sixty were published in his lifetime; but two stand out – *Grace Abounding* and *Pilgrim's Progress*. The former is a record of Bunyan's spiritual development, of the intense mental tortures that he had endured, and of the nervous fantasies that had precipitated his conversion. There are many Puritan self-portraits, but Bunyan's transcends them all. For him, every detail of his career had had some spiritual significance. His passionate integrity is conveyed by the simple directness of his style. Bunyan's search for truth goes far beyond any single system of theology.

The Pilgrim's Progress is a symbolic version of his quest; the good and evil influences that he had described and analyzed in *Grace Abounding*, here take on human personalities. Almost certainly written between 1666 and 1672, the story opens with a picture of his hero, Christian, bearing the burden of his past offences:

As I walk'd through the wilderness of this world, I lighted on a certain place where was a Den, and I laid me down in that place to sleep; and as I slept I dreamed a Dream. I Dreamed, and behold I saw a man clothed with Rags, standing in a certain place, with his face from his own house, a Book in his hand, and a great Burden upon his back. I looked, and saw him open the Book, and read therin; and as he read, he wept and trembled; and not being able longer to contain, he brake out with a lamentable cry, saying, What shall I do?

The vision of Christian's plight dominates the whole narrative, which presents the lonely sufferings of an individual soul. The various characters, whom Christian meets on his journey, represent his own conflicting states of mind, though Bunyan does his

Episode from *The Pilgrim's Progress*; a 17th-century illustration.

best to transform them into 'real' people. His chief purpose is to illustrate the dangers and horrors of a life without faith.

In his description of 'the Valley of the Shadow of Death', Bunyan draws on the worst hallucinations that had obsessed him during his religious crises. But, at the moment of greatest alarm, when he is tormented by a whispering devil, a fine dramatic stroke emphasises the impregnability of Christian's faith:

When Christian had travelled in this disconsolate condition some considerable time, he thought he heard the voice of a man, as going before him, saying, Though I walk through the valley of the shadow of death, I will fear none ill, for thou art with me.

This is the voice of Faithful, whom Christian catches up with next day. They journey onward together, and reach Vanity Fair. There the two pilgrims are imprisoned, exposed in a cage, and finally brought to trial before a jury that includes Mr Blind-Mind, Mr Malice, Mr Love-Lust and Mr Implacable. Though Faithful is condemned to death, Christian escapes with a new companion, Hopeful; and they encounter Mr By-Ends, a temporising parson who makes his personal comment on their rash, obstinate and unruly faith:

They are for hazarding all for God at a clap, and I am for taking all advantages to secure my Life and Estate. They are for holding their notions, though all other men are against them; but I am for religion in what, and so far as the times, and my safety will bear it. They are for religion, when in rags, and contempt; but I am for him when he walks in his Golden Slippers in the Sunshine, and with applause.

When the pilgrims are imprisoned by Giant Despair in his stronghold, Doubting Castle, the narrative becomes a study of spiritual and intellectual malaise. Luckily, Christian discovers that he is carrying a key called 'Promise'. Now the worst of their dangers are over, and we approach a blissful ending, which Bunyan depicts, not in his customary colloquial style, but in language reminiscent of the *Canticles, Isaiah* and *The Revelations*:

In this land also the contract between the Bride and Bridegroom was renewed; yea here, as the Bridegroom rejoiceth over the Bride, so did their God rejoice over them. Here they had no want of Corn and Wine; for in this place they met with abundance of what they had sought in all their Pilgrimage. Here they heard voices from out of the City, loud voices, saying, Say ye to the daughter of Zion, behold thy salvation cometh, behold his reward is with him.

In 1684 Bunyan added a second part to *Pilgrim's Progress*, narrating the pilgrimage of Christian's wife, Christiana. It is a more mellow and placid work than the first part, and suggests a walking tour through the scenes of Christian's former great deeds. But it concludes with a major statement of the heroic splendours of belief. As the pilgrims cross the river of death, they are summoned one by one. Among the blessed is Mr Valiant-for-truth:

Then said he, I am going to my Father's, and though with great difficulty I am got hither, yet now I do not repent me of all the Trouble I have been at to arrive where I am. My Sword I give to him that shall succeed me in my Pilgrimage, and my Courage and Skill to him that can get it. My Marks and Scars I carry with me, to be a witness for me that I have fought His Battles who will now be my Rewarder. When the day that he must go hence was come, many accompanied him to the Riverside, into which as he went he said, Death, where is thy Sting? And as he went down deeper he said, Grave, where is thy Victory? So he passed over, and all the Trumpets sounded for him on the other side.

Bunyan stands at the end of a succession of popular homiletic writers that stretches from the Middle Ages to the heyday of the Puritan preachers, and to the beginnings of the English novel. Although *Pilgrim's Progress* was long regarded as first and foremost a religious manual, we now recognize Bunyan's value as an imaginative writer who made a significant contribution to the modern art of story-telling.

John Milton

JOHN MILTON (1608–74) was the son of a London scrivener, a cultivated and sympathetic man. Sent to St Paul's School, where the curriculum retained many of the characteristics of Renaissance humanistic scholarship, the boy studied Latin, Greek, Hebrew and classical rhetoric. When he went up to Christ's College, Cambridge, in 1625, he was already convinced of his vocation as a great poet. But he disliked the barren disputes of scholastic philosophy that occupied the learned men at Cambridge, and became known as 'the Lady of Christ's', thanks to his puritan idealism and his disdain of the usual undergraduate activities. He wrote some verses at this time – translations and paraphrases of psalms and Latin elegies, and in 1629 his first important poem, the ode 'On the Morning of Christ's Nativity'. At the end of his residence he produced two melodious poetic exercises, 'L'Allegro' and 'Il Penseroso'. Milton graduated in 1632 and then retired to his father's house at Horton, in Buckinghamshire, to complete his literary education. He read extensively and variously, his intention always being to secure a solid basis of knowledge on which to establish his poetic practice. During this period, his output was small; but it included *Comus* and 'Lycidas', the former an aristocratic entertainment, and the latter an elegy for a dead

(*Below left*) John Milton in youth: 'The Lady of Christ's'.

(*Below right*) Milton at the age of sixty-two; engraving by William Faithorne.

friend. After 1630, Milton embarked on an extensive European tour, mostly in Italy, where he visited famous scholars and artists, and absorbed the best of European culture. Among those he met was the aged Galileo.

Milton returned to England in August 1639, and set himself up as the master of a private boarding school; but he soon plunged, on the anti-episcopal side, into the war of pamphlets provoked by the condition of the English church. He produced five pamphlets between April 1641 and March 1642; his central argument being that the Tudor Reformation had been incomplete, and that now the moment had come to carry it a step further. His pamphlets show great rhetorical skill; and he ends the pamphlet *Of Reformation in England* with an extraordinary passionate outburst, revealing his vision of a new and regenerate kingdom. He prophesies a divine deliverance and a brave new world, of which he himself will be the chosen poet.

In the spring of 1642, Milton married Mary Powell, a young girl descended from a family of Royalists. The pair rapidly fell out of love; soon afterwards Mary returned to her parents, and the marriage was not patched up again until 1645. Meanwhile, Milton decided to investigate how he might release himself. The result was a pamphlet, *The Doctrine and Discipline of Divorce*, published in August 1643, that based the plea for divorce upon his own conception of the married state. It aroused considerable dispute; and three pamphlets in reply appeared. By this time the press was being restricted, and all books were required to be licensed by an official censor. Milton defied the censorship; and, although no official action was taken against him, he was stirred into formulating his passionately-held belief that the press should be free in a pamphlet entitled *Areopagitica*, which protests that a man can only present the truth exactly as he sees it, and that controversy is a sign of health and vigour, enabling fragments to be distributed among the various participants:

Truth indeed came once into the world with her divine Master, and was a perfect shape most glorious to look on; but when he ascended, and his apostles after him were laid asleep, then straight rose a wicked race of deceivers, who . . . took the virgin Truth, hewed her lovely form into a thousand pieces, and scattered them to the four winds. From that time ever since, the sad friends of Truth, such as durst appear, imitating the careful search that Isis made for the mangled body of Osiris, went up and down gathering limb by limb still as they could find them. We have not yet found them all, Lords and Commons, nor shall ever do, till her Master's second coming.

Milton's allegiance had now moved from the Presbyterians, who had criticized his *Doctrine and Discipline*, to the Independents, who had gained control of Parliament. At work on a projected history of Great Britain, Milton did not engage in any political activity until the execution of Charles I, in January 1649. Then he almost certainly supported the regicides, and within two weeks had produced a pamphlet concerned with the rights of the people against tyrants, that proclaimed the revocability of supreme power. This treatise pleased the Parliamentary government, and he became a semi-official apologist of their regime. In 1649 he was given an official post, as Latin Secretary to the Council of State; and, in the February of that year, when the Royalists published their mournful *Eikon Basilike*, which purported to be a record of the late King's self-communings, Milton retorted with *Eikonoclastes*, a savage attack on the image of the royal martyr. His next official pamphlet was *A Defence of the English People*, an answer to an attack written by a foreign pedant. In May 1654 he wrote a *Second Defence* . . . in which he explained why he had become involved in controversial pamphleteering:

I saw that a way was opening for the establishment of real liberty; that the foundation was laying for the deliverance of man from the yoke of slavery and superstition; that the principles of religion, which were the first objects of our care, would exert a salutary influence on the manners and constitution of the republic; and as I had from my youth studied the distinctions between religious and civil rights, I perceived that if I ever wished to be of use, I ought at least not to be wanting to my country, to the church, and to so many of my fellow Christians, in a crisis of so much danger; I therefore determined to relinquish the other pursuits in which I was engaged and to transfer the whole force of my talents and my industry to this one important subject.

Milton consistently identified himself with the causes that he supported.

By 1652 he had completely lost his sight; and in 1653 his wife died, leaving behind her three daughters. In 1656 he married Catherine Woodcock; but the following year she expired in childbirth. The death of Cromwell in 1658 was another serious blow. He seemed to think that he could single-handedly argue the nation into maintaining a republican form of government; and throughout the following months he poured out supplicatory letters and pamphlets. In 1670 his *History of Britain* was published; but after thirty years intermittent work, it extended only as far as the Roman Conquest. The destruction of all his political hopes caused him to turn back to his plan for an epic poem, and in 1667 *Paradise Lost* was published. In 1662 he had married his third wife, Elizabeth Minshull. To the poet himself she brought great comfort; but the couple's treatment of his daughters would appear to have been far from kind. Obliged to learn by rote all the languages that their father had himself mastered, they were required to read aloud to him, hour after hour, learned texts they scarcely understood. Milton's last major poems, *Paradise Regained* and *Samson Agonistes*, were published together in 1671. He wrote several more prose works during the interval between the Restoration and his death, which occurred on 8 November 1674.

Milton's first really successful English poem, the ode 'On the Morning of Christ's Nativity', describes the rout of pagan superstition by the advent of the Saviour. At the Nativity, peace descends on the world:

> But peaceful was the night
> Wherein the Prince of light
> His reign of peace upon the earth began:
> The winds, with wonder whist,
> Smoothly the waters kiss'd,
> Whispering new joys to the mild ocean,
> Who now hath quite forgot to rave,
> While birds of calm sit brooding on the charmed wave.

Comus, 'A masque presented at Ludlow castle, 1634', is concerned with the mystical virtues of Chastity – a strange theme for a courtly entertainment. In some ways a complex and difficult work, with many threads and influences running through, it shows Milton's early mastery of different tones. Comus is a magician, who attacks the lady's virtue by celebrating the claims of sensual pleasure:

> Wherefore did Nature pour her bounties forth
> With such a full and unwithdrawing hand,
> Covering the earth with odours, fruits and flocks,
> Thronging the seas with spawn innumerable,
> But all to please and sate the curious taste?
> And set to work millions of spinning worms,
> That in their green shops weave the smooth hair'd silk
> To deck her sons, and that no corner might
> Be vacant of her plenty, in her own loins
> She hutch'd th'all-worshipt ore and precious gems
> To store her children with; if all the world
> Should in a pet of temperance feed on pulse,
> Drink the clear stream, and nothing wear but freize,
> Th'all-giver would be unthankt, would be unprais'd, . . .

In 'Lycidas', prompted by Milton's grief for his friend, Edward King, the lost youth is expanded into a symbolic pastoral character. Milton also seizes the opportunity of voicing his disgust at the present state of England, but concludes with a lyric description of his own existence as a poet:

> Thus sang the uncouth swain to th'oaks and rills,
> While the still morn went out with sandals grey.
> He touch'd the tender stops of various quills,
> With eager thought warbling his Doric lay;
> And now the sun had stretch'd out all the hills,
> And now was dropt into the Western bay.
> At last he rose, and twitch'd his mantle blue:
> Tomorrow to fresh woods and pastures new.

'Lycidas' shows that his genius was already mature, though he continued to suspect that he was still 'unready'; and in *Paradise Lost* Milton at length produced the Christian epic, 'doctrinal to a nation', that, since his boyhood, he had always hoped to write. Here he employs the various resources of the European literary tradition – Biblical, classical, medieval and Renaissance – and uses pagan imagery to serve a Christian purpose, as in the sumptuous picture he draws of the Garden of Eden:

> The birds their choir apply; airs, vernal airs,
> Breathing the smell of field and grove, attune
> The trembling leaves, while universal Pan
> Knit with the Graces and the Hours in dance
> Led on th'Eternal Spring. Not that fair field
> Of Enna, where Proserpin gath'ring flow'rs,
> Herself a fairer flow'r, by gloomy Dis
> Was gather'd, which cost Ceres all that pain
> To seek her through the world; nor that sweet grove
> Of Daphne by Orontes, and th'inspir'd
> Castalian spring, might with this paradise
> Of Eden strive . . .

The sense of infinite and surpassing beauty is combined with tremors of foreboding – Prosepina was captured by the king of the underworld, just as our Mother Eve will be seduced by Satan.

In some respects, the Fallen Angel is the dominant figure of the poem; and William Blake went so far as to assert that he was its real hero. His appearance at the outset is magnificent:

> . . . his ponderous shield
> Ethereal temper, massy, large, and round,
> Behind him cast; the broad circumference
> Hung on his shoulders like the moon, whose orb
> Through optic glass the Tuscan artist views . . .

Satan has many attributes borrowed from the heroic tradition, including certain traces of heroic virtue:

> Darken'd so, yet shone
> Above them all th'Arch-Angel: but his face
> Deep scars of Thunder had intrencht, and care
> Sat on his faded cheek, but under brows
> Of dauntless courage, and considerate pride
> Waiting revenge: cruel his eye, but cast
> Signs of remorse and passion to behold
> The fellows of his crime, . . .

As an epic poet, Milton occasionally nods. Despite his masterly handling of his verse, with its complex and varied use of the extended paragraph, some episodes are dull and slow-moving; as in the seventh book, where Raphael describes the Creation to Adam. But in Book Nine, with a vivid account of the Fall, the work regains its previous level. As Eve parts from her husband,

(*Overleaf*) Illustrations to *Paradise Lost*; from the edition of 1688.

Milton draws on the resources of classical mythology to portray our first parents' grace and innocence:

> Thus saying, from her husband's hand her hand
> Soft she withdrew, and like a wood-nymph light
> Oread or Dryad, or of Delia's train,
> Betook her to the groves, but Delia's self
> In gait surpassed and goddess-like deport,
> Though not as she with bow and quiver armed,
> But with such gardning tools as art yet rude
> Guiltless of fire had formed, or Angels brought.
> To Pales, or Pomona, thus adorned,
> Likest she seemed, Pomona when she fled
> Vertumnus, or to Ceres in her prime,
> Yet virgin of Proserpina from Jove.

When Eve is persuading Adam to eat the apple, she presents it as 'a glorious trial of exceeding love' – a parody of the medieval tradition of *l'amour courtois*. Their formerly innocent relationship now becomes tainted with a sense of guilt and shame. But the poem does not end on that note; after two books in which Michael unfolds the future history of the world to Adam, though the guilty lovers must quit their terrestrial paradise, hope and confidence are reasserted:

> High in front advanc'd
> The brandish'd sword of God before them blaz'd
> Fierce as a comet, which with torrid heat
> And vapour as the Libyan air adust
> Began to parch that temperate clime; whereat
> In either hand the hast'ning angel caught
> Our ling'ring parents, and to th'eastern gate
> Led them direct, and down the cliff as fast
> To the subjected plain, – then disappear'd
> They looking back, all th'eastern side beheld
> Of Paradise, so late their happy seat,
> Wav'd over by that flaming brand, the gate
> With dreadful faces throng'd and fiery arms.
> Some natural tears they dropp'd, but wip'd them soon;
> The world was all before them, where to choose
> Their place of rest, and Providence their guide.
> They hand in hand with wand'ring steps and slow
> Through Eden took their solitary way.

In *Paradise Regained* Milton deals with the Temptation of Christ in the wilderness, which he sees as a redemption of the Fall. Here rhetoric – the art of persuasion – is again upon the side of Evil: Christ's message is comparatively unadorned. There is little of the grand style of *Paradise Lost* in the poem that succeeded it – except in the passage in the fourth book where Satan, with the 'persuasive' eloquence that 'sleek'd his tongue', evokes the worlds of ancient Greece and Rome. The poem echoes Milton's own experience in its identification of Virtue with the private life, and of Evil with the glamour of public life. *Samson Agonistes*, published at the same time, is a Biblical drama in the form of a classical tragedy. There is little dramatic movement; it is built up of a solemn series of dialogues and monologues, with occasional interpositions by the chorus. The whole play has an autobiographical colouring; Milton himself is the blind and helpless Samson, a captive of his Philistine enemies, toiling in the mill at Gaza:

> O loss of sight, of thee I most complain!
> Blind among enemies, O worse than chains,
> Dungeon, or beggary, or decrepit age!
> Light the prime work of God to me is extinct,
> And all her various objects of delight
> Annull'd, which might in part my grief have eas'd,

Milton's family-records, written by himself on the fly-leaf of his Bible.

> Inferior to the vilest now become
> Of man or worm; the vilest here excel me,
> They creep, yet see, I dark in light expos'd
> To daily fraud, contempt, abuse and wrong,
> Within doors, or without, still as a fool,
> In power of others, never in my own;
> Scarce half I seem to live, dead more than half.
> O dark, dark, dark, amid the blaze of noon,
> Irrecoverably dark, total Eclipse
> Without all hope of day!

Milton was not only the most dedicated but the most strictly disciplined of literary artists. At an early age he had set himself the task of producing certain mighty works – a major epic, a minor epic and a Grecian tragedy – and of becoming, despite all the difficulties that confronted him, both public and private, his country's greatest Christian poet. He had, of course, a profoundly Puritan strain; but in his character, as in that of so many great artists, there was an element of contradiction, even perhaps of conflict. Through every poem runs an exquisitely sensuous feeling for human and natural beauty; and no English poet has written lovelier lines or more wonderfully evocative passages, where no single syllable could be changed without damage to the whole harmonious structure, for example in this description of a sinful fallen spirit:

> Thammuz came next behind,
> Whose annual wound in Lebanon allur'd
> The Syrian damsels to lament his fate
> In amorous ditties all a summer's day,
> While smooth Adonis from his native rock
> Ran purple to the sea, suppos'd with blood
> Of Thammuz yearly wounded . . .

Thomas Hobbes; portrait by J. Wright.

Later Seventeenth-Century Prose

THOMAS HOBBES (1588–1679) born in the village of Westport, near Malmesbury in Wiltshire, went up to Oxford at the age of fourteen, and, having taken a degree, in 1608 was appointed tutor to William Cavendish, afterwards first Earl of Devonshire. At Chatsworth he had the opportunity of meeting his employers' famous literary guests, among them Jonson and Lord Herbert of Cherbury; and in its well-stocked library he began his real education. His earliest book, a translation of Thucydides' history of the Peloponnesian Wars, appeared in 1629. But it was his discovery of Euclid and the science of mathematics that inspired him to become a philosophic writer. In 1640 he produced two political treatises, of which manuscripts were widely circulated. Their tendency was strongly Royalist, and Hobbes thought it prudent to retire to France, where he remained for eleven years. In 1645

17th-century picture of
the Great Fire, showing
Old St Paul's in flames.

he was appointed tutor to the exiled Prince of Wales, the future
Charles II; and, in 1651 he issued his masterpiece *Leviathan*. It is a
defence of absolutism; but, by insisting that a subject should
submit to any government with *de facto* control, so long as that
control is firm enough to secure internal peace, he seemed at the
time to offer comfort to the Parliamentarians rather than to the
Royalists. *Leviathan* was also strongly anti-papal and anti-clerical;
and Charles was obliged, albeit reluctantly, to dismiss him from
the court. In 1651 he secretly returned to England, and after the
Restoration Charles II, who is said to have enjoyed his company,
granted him an annual pension of £100. But he was still a suspect
figure; and in 1661 his doctrines were cited in Parliament as one
of the probable causes of the Great Fire, while in 1667 the House
of Commons passed a bill against 'blasphemous' books which
included *Leviathan*. Henceforward, we are told, Hobbes made a
practice of attending church, though he always turned his back
upon the sermon. He was refused permission, however, to publish
any further political or religious works, and his books were banned
and publicly burnt. For the remainder of his long life he lived
quietly with the Cavendish family. At the age of seventy five he
was still playing tennis; and at eighty he produced poetic transla-

tions of the *Iliad* and the *Odyssey*. Asked why he had turned to verse so late, he replied modestly that it was because he had had 'nothing else to do'. He died in 1679 in his ninety-second year.

Hobbes' intellectual career was impeded by the hostile attitude of the English Church, who resented his 'scientific' arguments, such as his account of miracles:

Therefore, if a horse or cow should speak, it were a miracle; because both the thing is strange, and the natural cause difficult to imagine. So also were it to see a strange deviation of nature, in the production of some new shape of living creature. But when a man, or other animal, engenders his like, though we know no more how this is done, than the other; yet because it is unusual, it is no miracle. In like manner, if a man be meta-morphosed into a stone, or into a pillar, it is a miracle; because strange: but if a piece of wood be so changed, because we see it so often, it is no miracle: and yet we know no more by what operation of God, the one is brought to pass, than the other.

The implication is that the mystery of miracles is only a by-product of human ignorance, and that, to explain them, there is no need to look beyond material causes. This kind of thorough-going materialism earned Hobbes the enmity of almost all the leading thinkers of his time; and he became the centre of a con-troversy that lasted for nearly three decades.

The political system of *Leviathan* was derived from Hobbes' mechanistic premises, and built around his pessimistic view of human nature. He denied the existence in human conduct of all but selfish and acquisitive motives, and resolved each virtue into a form of disguised self-interest:

The *value*, or WORTH of a man, is as of all other things, his price; that is to say, so much as would be given for the use of his power: and therefore is not absolute; but a thing dependent on the need and judgment of another. An able conductor of soldiers, is of great price in time of war present, or imminent; but in peace not so. A learned and uncorrupt judge, is much worth in time of peace; but not so much in war. And as in other things, so in men, not the seller, but the buyer determines the price.

Hobbes' cynicism followed logically from his view of the primitive state of man – a creature disposed to violence and war, and fit ultimately for little else. This gloomy vision he expressed in a famous passage:

In such condition, there is no place for industry; because the fruit thereof is uncertain: and consequently no culture of the earth; no navigation, nor use of commodities that may be imported by sea; no commodious building; no instruments of moving, and removing, such things as require much force; no knowledge of the face of the earth; no account of time; no arts; no letters; no society; and which is worst of all, continual fear, and danger of violent death; and the life of man, solitary, poor, nasty, brutish, and short.

To avoid this brutish state of existence, he argued, men have made

Title page of *Leviathan*,
1651.

an implicit contract with each other to surrender their natural
rights to do what they please, so long as their fellows are content
to do the same, and have set up some individual, or group, to
enforce that contract. Thus good becomes what the government
says it is, and the subjects must obey. Peace and order can only be
guaranteed by the institution of an absolute government. Hobbes'
prose is trenchant and admirably lucid; his concern is with matter
rather than with manner. He appears to despise eloquence; yet his

works are full of vivid images. The mind is seen as a spaniel ranging a field, 'the night of our natural ignorance'; men are 'tired of irregular jostling and hewing one another'; the mind may be 'entangled in words, like birds in lime-twigs'. Hobbes' system was a great imaginative conception – a transposition of abstract argument into forceful language; and, as such, it achieves the dignity of art. In his day, he was an isolated phenomenon; his critics were obsessed with his allegedly subversive views, and he was nicknamed the 'Arch-Atheist' and the 'Monster of Malmesbury'. He had no immediate disciples, though Lord Rochester and the poet's libertine circle adopted his cynical opinion of human existence. They borrowed such of Hobbes' ideas as suited them, namely those which, torn from the proper context, appeared to justify their own hedonism and supported their conception of 'natural man', freed from all social and moral constraint. Elsewhere, his influence was more oblique, and even affected contemporary theologians, whom his severe methods of argument and gift of logical precision obliged to adopt the same exacting standards.

Edward Hyde, 1st Earl of Clarendon.

EDWARD HYDE, EARL OF CLARENDON (1609–74), statesman and historian, was originally educated as a lawyer. After attending Magdalen Hall, Oxford, he entered the Middle Temple, and was called to the Bar in 1633. During this period of his existence, he joined Ben Jonson's literary circle, whom he met at Lord Falkland's country house. Having entered Parliament in 1640, he became one of the leaders of the Opposition. But he presently broke with the Parliamentarians and, in 1643, was appointed Chancellor to Charles I. Though Charles ignored his advice – that the Crown should adopt a more lenient attitude towards the rebellious House of Commons – Clarendon remained a loyal subject. Later he shared the exile of Charles II; and during his life abroad he began writing a series of character studies that he later incorporated into his famous history. After the Restoration of the Stuarts, he was re-appointed Lord Chancellor, while his daughter Anne married the Duke of York, the future James II, and bore him a child, also christened Anne, who was destined to become Queen of England. The Chancellor had many enemies; and in 1667, having been accused of treason, he was disgraced and obliged to leave the country. It was in France that he wrote his *History of the Rebellion* (published 1702–4). During his latter years, he grew enormously obese, and died in retirement at Rouen on 9 December 1674.

As an historical writer Clarendon is partial and biased; his object was to plead a cause. But, besides being an invaluable source-book, his *History* contains a succession of extraordinarily vivid portraits. Clarendon's prose tends to be stately and lumbering, with long, digressive, parenthetical sentences, which his disjointed syntax barely holds together. His portraits, on the other hand, are admirably precise and lucid, as in the picture that he draws of Oliver Cromwell:

Without doubt, no man with more wickedness ever attempted anything, or brought to pass what he desired more wickedly, more in the face and contempt of religion, and moral honesty; yet wickedness as great as his could never have accomplish'd those trophies, without the assistance of a great spirit, an admirable circumspection, and sagacity, and a most magnanimous resolution.

When he appeared first in the Parliament he seemed to have a person in no degree gracious, no ornament of discourse, none of those talents which use to reconcile the affections of the standers by: yet as he grew into place and authority, his parts seemed to be renewed, as if he had concealed faculties, till he had occasion to use them; and when he was to act the part of a great man, he did it without any indecency through the want of custom.

JEREMY TAYLOR (1613–67) was born at Cambridge and, after attending the Perse school, went on to Gonville and Caius College as a 'poor scholar'. He took Holy Orders before he was twenty-one; and, in 1634, Archbishop Laud, having heard him preach in St Pauls, granted him a fellowship of All Souls. He remained there until 1638, when he was appointed rector of Uppingham, in Rutland, and during the same year he published his first sermon. On the outbreak of the Civil Wars, he became chaplain to Charles I; and, in 1645, was imprisoned at Cardigan Castle. He was soon released, however, and retired to Wales, where he earned his living as a schoolmaster and served as chaplain to the Earl of Carbery. Some of his finest work was written during this period. But by 1657 he had returned to London; and in 1658 he issued his *Collection of Offices*, a substitute for the Church of England liturgy, the use of which was then forbidden. He next visited Ireland, and ministered to Viscount Conway and the Episcopalians of Lisburn. In 1659, Presbyterian objections to his Anglican practices obliged him to appear before the ecclesiastical commissioners; but after the Restoration, he obtained an Irish bishopric. Having caught a fever while visiting the sick, he died on 13 August 1667.

Jeremy Taylor; portrait by P. Lombart.

Jeremy Taylor wrote profusely; and, though he cannot be ranked with the great minds and original thinkers of the English Church, he has been acclaimed as the 'Shakespeare of English prose'. In his *The Rule and Exercise of Holy Dying* (1651), he draws on a long tradition of religious thought and feeling and, thanks to the splendid luxuriance of his style, invests these old themes with a fresh life:

Take away but the pomps of death, the disguises and solemn bug-bears, the tinsel, and the actings by candle light, and proper and fantastic ceremonies, the minstrels and the noise-makers, the women and the weepers, the swoonings and the shriekings, the nurses and the physicians, the dark room and the ministers, the kindred and the watchers, and then to die is

Frontispiece to Jeremy Taylor's *Golden Grove*; a manual of daily prayers.

easy, ready and quitted from its troublesome circumstances. It is the same harmless thing that a poor shepherd suffered yesterday, or a maid servant today; and at the same time in which you die, in that very night, a thousand creatures die with you, some wise men, and many fools; and the wisdom of the first will not quit him, and the folly of the latter does not make him unable to die.

In his sermons, Taylor, like Milton, combines classical and Christian motifs. He also introduces the imagery of everyday life, his great gift being the strong imagination that enabled him to find concrete illustrations for general ideas, which he often clothed in extended poetic similes. In a sermon describing the effect of anger on prayer, he notes that it causes thoughts to lose their original intention, and then proceeds to illustrate the point:

For so have I seen a lark rising from his bed of grass and soaring upwards singing as he rises, and hopes to get to heaven, and climb above the clouds; but the poor bird was beaten back with the loud sighings of an eastern wind, and his motion made irregular and unconstant, descending more at every breath of the tempest, than it could recover by the libration and frequent weighing of his wings; till the little creature was forc'd to sit down and pant, and still till the storm was over, and then it made a prosperous flight, and did rise and sing as if it had learned music and motion from an Angel as he passed sometimes through the air about his ministries here below: so is the prayers of a good man . . .

As the passage suggests, Taylor was not an exponent of the plain style of preaching that became popular in the later seventeenth century. His sentences are apt to consist of an extended sequence of clauses, with parallel clauses modifying or emphasizing one another. Taylor's achievement, aside from his mastery of prose, was to give added weight and harmony to traditional religious themes.

SIR WILLIAM TEMPLE (1628–99), son of Sir John Temple, Master of the Rolls in Ireland, was born in London in 1628, educated at Cambridge, and, in 1660, elected a member of the Irish Parliament. After undertaking a series of diplomatic missions, he became British Ambassador at the Hague, where he helped negotiate the marriage of William of Orange and the Princess Mary. On his return to England in 1679, he gained the confidence of Charles II, who offered him political office. But his frequent disagreements with the sovereign led him to decline; and he then retired to his country house in Surrey. At Moor Park he passed his leisure writing and gardening; and, with the young Jonathan Swift as his secretary, he wrote his diplomatic memoirs, as well as essays on a

17th-century engraving of the palace at the Hague.

RIA HOLLANDIÆ

INTERIOR.

variety of subjects, including the famous disquisition, *Of Poetry* and his treatise, *Of Ancient and Modern Learning*, which introduced to England the controversy that raged in France over the relative merits of the Ancients and the Moderns. Temple left behind him a substantial body of work, part of which his former secretary published. In 1655, after a long and difficult engagement, he had married DOROTHY OSBORNE (1627–95), an intelligent, sensitive and high-spirited young woman; and her letters to him remain an engaging example of easy, informal seventeenth-century prose.

Temple's own style was clear and unaffected. Much admired during the eighteenth century, it had a strong influence upon the genius of Swift, who seems to have shared the contemporary opinion that Temple had 'advanced our English tongue to as great perfection as it can well bear'. For Samuel Johnson, Temple was 'the first writer who gave cadence to English prose'; and, though he is somewhat less highly regarded today, such passages as the celebrated closing paragraph of his essay *Of Poetry* still support his reputation. Here he discusses the claims of poetry and music:

While this world lasts, I doubt not but the pleasure and request of these two entertainments will do so too; and happy those that content themselves with these, or any other so easy and so innocent; and do not trouble the world, or other men, because they cannot be quite themselves, though nobody hurts them! When all is done, human life is at the greatest and the best but like a froward child that must be played with and humoured a little to keep it quiet till it falls asleep and then the care is over.

JOHN LOCKE (1632–1704) was born at Wrington, in Somerset, and educated at Westminster School and Christ Church, Oxford. A lecturer in Greek in 1662, in 1663 he became censor of Moral Philosophy. He also studied medicine, though he never qualified as a physician. In 1665 he was appointed secretary to Sir Walter Vane, the English ambassador to Brandenburg, and, on his return, he joined the household of Lord Ashley, later first Earl of Shaftesbury and Lord Chancellor in 1673. That same year, Locke received an official post as Secretary to the Board of Trade. In 1682, when Shaftesbury was disgraced and fled the country, Locke's position was extremely difficult; for he himself had been associated with Shaftesbury's alleged conspiracy against the sovereign. He thereupon retired to Holland, where he continued to write the philosophical treatise that he had recently begun, and remained abroad until 1689. He then accepted the Commissionership of Appeals, a near-sinecure that enabled him to prosecute his philosophic work. Latterly, he found a permanent home with his friends, Sir Francis and Lady Masham. He died after a long illness, on 28 October 1704.

Locke was a scholar and a man of the world, who had wide interests and had travelled extensively. His approach to philosophy

John Locke; portrait attributed to Michael Dahl.

was empirical; he worked from experience and distrusted 'systems'. In his *Essay concerning Human Understanding* (1690), he undertook a systematic investigation of its nature, and sought to establish the limits of what the human reason can discover, his object being to concentrate attention on the spheres of knowledge where success was possible. He examined the actual processes of thought, not merely the results of thinking, and this he did largely by examining the mechanism of his own intelligence. The human mind, he concluded, has no knowledge other than that which can reach it through the senses. At birth it resembles a blank page, on which experience inscribes the only real knowledge that we can ever claim.

Locke's prose style is awkward; he deliberately rejects style and rhetorical contrivances; and his *Essay* includes long passages of involved exposition and analysis. He believed, like the founders of the Royal Society, that truth must be arrived at by employing plain language, made up of precisely defined terms. His use of the vernacular when writing philosophy indicates his belief that such studies concerned the whole of mankind. The *Essay* is an experiment in which the reader is invited to partake, himself testing, upon his own account, the facts that are presented to him. As a writer of English prose, his merits are not impressive; it is the idea, rather than the style, that counts:

For, methinks, the understanding is not much unlike a closet wholly shut from light, with only some little openings left, to let in external visible resemblances, or ideas of things without: would the pictures coming into such a dark room but stay there, and lie so orderly as to be found upon occasion, it would very much resemble the understanding of a man, in reference to all objects of sight, and the ideas of them.

For later philosophers, this kind of deceptively simple analogy seems a major weakness of Locke's method. But he exerted considerable influence upon the thinkers of the eighteenth century. Besides the *Essay concerning Human Understanding*, his works included *Some thoughts concerning Education* and *The Reasonableness of Christianity*, published in 1693 and 1695.

ANTHONY ASHLEY COOPER, THIRD EARL OF SHAFTESBURY (1671–1713), grandson of the famous statesman, being a sickly and delicate child, spent his childhood on his family estate, where the private tutor engaged for him was the philosopher John Locke. After five unhappy years at Winchester School, he travelled widely round Europe, and, on his return to England, he attempted a public career and took his seat in Parliament as a member of the Whig Party. But constant ill-health obliged him, in 1698, to give up his seat in the Commons; and, although, when he succeeded to his father's earldom, he became a prominent debater in the House of Lords, by this time his main interests were philosophy and literature. From 1699 onwards he produced a series of treatises which were collected and published in 1711 as *Characteristics of Men, Manners, Opinions and Times*. His chronic asthma often drove him abroad, and in 1713 he died at Naples.

Shaftesbury's existence was uneventful; his infirmity restricted him to a bookish and intellectual life. His works were published anonymously; but they were widely read and much admired, and had a strong effect upon the eighteenth-century cult of 'sensibility'. Champions of the 'Palladian' school, including Lord Burlington and his brilliant protégé, Alexander Pope, adopted Shaftesbury as their guide and mentor. Among the most important aspects of his philosophic creed was the idea of an innate 'moral sense' that gives us an intuitive ability to recognize virtue, this faculty being merely an extension of the aesthetic sense; with the result that good taste and virtue are inextricably connected. Shaftesbury endeavoured to refute Hobbes by demonstrating that men are inherently good; and he was thus forced to explain why so many human beings should be clearly evil. This he did by linking both virtue and taste to the quality of good breeding. Vice, he argued, is a form of bad taste; evil thus is not only a moral, but a social aberration:

Nothing beside ill Humour, either natural or forc'd, can bring a Man to think seriously that the World is govern'd by any devilish or malicious Power. I very much question whether any thing, besides ill Humour, can be the Cause of Atheism. For there are so many Arguments to persuade a Man in Humour that, in the main, all things are kindly and well dispos'd, that one would think it impossible for him to be so far out of conceit with Affairs, as to imagine they all ran at adventures; and that the World, as venerable and wise a Face as it carry'd, had neither Sense nor Meaning in it. This however I am persuaded of, that nothing beside ill Humour can give us dreadful or ill Thoughts of a Supreme Manager.

Though here it is easy and lucid enough, Shaftesbury's prose style frequently becomes obscure; while his attempts at lyric eloquence led one eighteenth century critic to characterize him as the master of the 'sublime of nonsense'.

One of the most penetrating critics of Shaftesbury's slightly specious optimism was BERNARD MANDEVILLE (1670–1733). A physician of Dutch birth, he had come to England 'to learn the language', and remained to practice medicine. In 1705 he published a short satirical poem, *The Grumbling Hive, or, Knaves Turned Honest*, the description of a bee-hive of which the occupants are utterly selfish and venal, though as a social unit it is prosperous and happy; and, in 1714, he republished it as *The Fable of the Bees, or Private Vices, Publick Benefits*, accompanied by a prose essay, 'An Enquiry into the Origin of Moral Virtue', an extended commentary upon his verses. Another edition, with further material added, was issued in 1723, and what had begun as a satirical squib now developed into a series of weighty arguments that provoked a furious controversy. *The Fable of the Bees* was pronounced a 'nuisance' by a Middlesex Grand Jury, and Mandeville himself was denounced as a vicious profligate by the clergy and the press.

The cause of this uproar was his ruthless and unflattering analysis of human prejudices and pretensions. Superficially, the argument of *The Fable of the Bees* is an economic one; it shows that prosperity is always accompanied by vice, and concludes, therefore, that prosperity can only be founded on corruption. Mandeville appears to be recommending vice; but his work has an ironic undertone that most of his detractors missed. His real targets are pride and the hypocrisy that allows men to practise vice under the pretence of virtue. Like Swift, Mandeville saw human nature as fallen; and he hated the self-pride that induced humanity to ignore its natural limitations. His method was to expose our hidden motives: 'The nearer we search into human nature, the more we shall be convinced that the moral virtues are the political offspring which flattery begot upon Pride.' Even the apparently virtuous are not exempt from his scrutiny:

A man of exalted pride may so hide it, that no body shall be able to discover that he has any; and yet receive greater satisfaction from that passion than another, who indulges himself in the declaration of it before all the world. Good manners have nothing to do with virtue or religion; instead of extinguishing, they rather inflame the passions. The man of sense and education never exults more in his pride than when he hides it with the greatest dexterity, and in feasting on the applause which he is sure all good judges will pay to his behaviour; he enjoys a pleasure altogether unknown to the short-sighted, surly alderman, that shews his haughtiness glaringly in his face, pulls off his hat to no body, and hardly deigns to speak to an inferior.

Mandeville was unperturbed by the hostility he aroused, and he continued to promulgate his genially subversive ideas in further pamphlets, including *A Modest Defence of Publick Stews: or, An Essay upon Whoring, as it is now Practis'd in these Kingdoms* (1724), and *The Usefulness of Christianity in War* (1732). We know little of Mandeville's private existence; but he would appear to have been himself a happy man, well-prepared to enjoy life, once it had been cleared of foolish cant. During the nineteenth century, thanks to his reputation for scurrilous cynicism, his works were seldom read; but more recently the subtlety of his paradoxes, and the powerful originality of his iconoclastic mind, have elicited some warm appreciations. Behind his energetic vernacular prose lay a mind capable of philosophical debate at an extremely high level, as we see in one of his last works, *A Letter to Dion* (1732), where he defends his ideas against his most formidable critic, the philosopher George Berkeley. He was particularly admired by those who shared his uncompromising rationalism; and Samuel Johnson, would remark of Mandeville, 'He did not puzzle me; he opened my eyes into real life very much'.

George Berkeley; portrait by J. Smibert.

Title page to *Alciphron*, 1732.

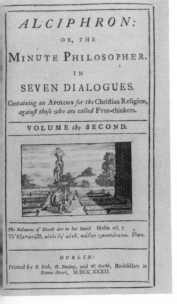

GEORGE BERKELEY (1685–1753) one of the most original of British philosophers, was born in Ireland near Kilkenny. After beginning his education at a local school, he was admitted to Trinity College, Dublin, where he was awarded a Fellowship in 1707. His early interests were mathematics and Greek; and his first publication, the *Essay Towards a New Theory of Vision* (1709) was a mathematical treatise of great originality. In the following year he launched the first of his major philosophical works, the *Treatise concerning the Principles of Human Knowledge* (1710), which contained his famous denial of the existence of matter. His *Theory of Vision* had aroused some controversy; but the *Treatise* brought him ridicule; and one physician went so far as to suggest that the philosopher needed expert medical treatment. Berkeley tried to meet the more reasoned objections to his ideas in the *Three Dialogues between Hylas and Philonous* (1713), a book that he issued through a London publisher. Having reached England, he met Swift and Steele; Addison took him to the first night of his play *Cato*; while Pope presented him with a copy of *Windsor Forest*, and declared that the philosopher had 'every virtue under Heaven'. After a tour of the Continent, Berkeley returned to Ireland and, in 1624, was appointed Dean of Derry. He then decided to found a college in Bermuda – an educational Utopia that would spread Christianity among North-American tribes – and in 1728 sailed to Rhode Island, where for three years he awaited the grant that he had been promised by the British government. During this period, he exerted a profound influence on American philosophy and education, and composed *Alciphron, or the Minute Philosopher* (1732), his polemic against free-thinkers such as Mandeville and Shaftesbury. These dialogues are among his most attractive writings, though the arguments rely for their success on a severe distortion of his opponents' views. In 1734 he became Bishop of Cloyne, where he remained for nearly two decades. In later life, he developed a great enthusiasm for the medicinal properties of tar-water, which, besides being a magnificent panacea, was a beverage, he asserted, that 'cheers but not inebriates'. *Siris: a Chain of Philosophical Reflexions* (1744) is an extraordinary mixture of philosophy and medicine, that starts by celebrating the virtues of tar-water and ends with an exposition of philosophical idealism. In the summer of 1752 Berkeley moved to Oxford, where he died suddenly on 14 January 1753.

Berkeley's most important philosophical works appeared before he was twenty-eight years old, and through them he propounded his 'immaterial hypothesis', in which he denied that there was any such thing as 'matter' existing independently of the intelligence. Reality, he asserts, is merely a product of the human mind – 'sensations are their own reality'. When Dr Johnson claimed to have demolished the bishop's 'ingenious sophistry' by 'striking his foot with mighty force against a large stone, exclaiming "I refute him *thus*",' he ignored the deeper implication of Berkeley's subtle argument. Berkeley founded no school of philosophy, but his ideas exerted a powerful influence on David Hume, who carried them forward into the mainstream of European philosophic thought.

The most complex abstractions become easily understandable when presented in Berkeley's lucid, well-turned prose; his style remains a model for all literary philosophers. In Berkeley's later works his literary artistry is most apparent – sometimes exercised at the expense of his philosophical integrity – as in his witty burlesque of Mandeville in *Alciphron*:

> Drunkenness, for instance, is by your sober moralists thought a pernicious vice; but it is for want of considering the good effects that flow from it. For in the first place it encreases the malt tax, a principal branch of his Majesty's Revenue, and thereby promotes the safety, strength, and glory of the nation. Secondly, it employs a great number of hands, the brewer, the maltster, the ploughman, the dealer in hops, the smith, the carpenter, the brazier, the joiner, with all other atificers necessary to supply those enumerated, with their respective instruments and utensils. All which advantages are procured from drunkenness in the vulgar way, by strong beer.

Diarists

A fine specimen of the seventeenth-century polymath was JOHN EVELYN (1620–1706), a man interested in every branch of knowledge from 'the natural sciences', which he cultivated as a founding member of the Royal Society, to politics, architecture, gardening, forestry and book-collection. Born at Wotton House, Surrey, the son of a prosperous country gentleman, he went up to Balliol College, Oxford, in 1637. During the Civil War, Evelyn supported the King; but he was neither a soldier nor a demagogue, and in 1643 he left England on an extended cultural tour of Europe. French literature influenced him deeply; and his first book was a translation of a political treatise, *De La Liberté et de la Servitude*. Later, he also translated *Advis pour dresser une Bibliothèque*, the work of Mazarin's librarian, Gabriel Naudé, as *Instructions for the Erecting of a Library*. Among the original books that he published after his return to England were *An Apology for the Royal Party* (which he was brave enough to produce just before the Restoration), *Sylva*, his famous treatise on forestry, issued by command of the Royal Society, in the year 1664, monographs on architecture and copper-engraving, and *Fumifugium*, an account of the smoke-nuisance as it affected seventeenth-century London. His best-known production, the private diary he had kept from 1641 to 1706, was not published until 1818.

John Evelyn, the renowned polymath; engraving after a portrait by Kneller.

Evelyn's literary output reveals the breadth of his interests; but, although he did not neglect the political problems of his age, he was always happiest in his own library; for he looked upon a library, he wrote, 'with the reverence of a temple'. Such is the character that his diary exhibits – bookish, learned, sedentary, refined, often profoundly shocked by the social extravagances of the Restoration era, and by the 'luxurious dallying and profaneness' that he noted at King Charles' court. Beside the record kept by his friend Samuel Pepys, who once remarked of Evelyn that 'the more I know him, the more I love him', his diary is a somewhat humdrum chronicle; but he, too, despite his solemn pedantry, had the gift of conveying his experiences in vivid and straightforward prose. Thus he depicts the scene at Whitehall on the eve of Charles II's death:

I am never to forget the inexpressible luxury and profaneness, gaming and all dissoluteness, and as it were total forgetfullness of God (it being Sunday evening) which this day se'nnight I was witness of the King sitting and toying with his concubines, Portsmouth, Cleveland and Mazarine, etc. A French boy singing love songs, in that glorious gallery, while about 20 of the great courtiers and other dissolute persons were at basset round a large table, a bank of at least 2000 in gold before them – six days after was all in the dust!

Samuel Pepys; frontispiece to his *Memoirs of the Royal Navy*.

Unlike John Evelyn, SAMUEL PEPYS (1633–1703) was a worldling and a keen careerist. The son of a London tailor related to Sir Edward Montagu, afterwards first Earl of Sandwich, he received a respectable middle-class education at St Paul's School, and Trinity Hall and Magdalene College, Cambridge, married a penniless girl in 1655, and joined the Admiralty as Clerk of the Acts, a not very distinguished post, in 1660. Thereafter, thanks to his immense energy and natural vitality, he rapidly ascended the official ladder, and became a renowned authority on British naval questions and the trusted adjutant of great men, including the king himself and his brother, the Duke of York. Secretary to the Admiralty in 1673, he was elected member of parliament the same year; and, although at the time of the alleged Popish Plot he suffered imprisonment and political disgrace, in 1683 he was charged with an important mission to Tangiers and, in 1684, reappointed Secretary.

Pepys' range of interests was yet more extensive than Evelyn's; and the Royal Society recognized his scientific distinction by electing him their President. Not only did he shine as a learned historian, who, in 1690, published his authoritative *Memoirs of the Royal Navy*, but he was a celebrated book-collector, a passionate lover of music and an ardent devotee of the seventeenth-century stage. But, above all else, Pepys was a lover of life, an amorist, *bon viveur* and man of the world, who adored the company of attractive women and took his pleasures where he found them. Evelyn returned his friend's affection, though he did not share his worldly tastes. On 26 May 1703, he composed an obituary tribute in his diary: 'This day died Mr Sam Pepys, a very worthy, industrious, and curious person . . .'.

As an essay in self-portraiture, Pepys' *Diary*, kept from 1660 to 1669, when he found his eyesight failing, ranks with the autobiographical works of James Boswell. He shared Boswell's lack of false shame. Since he was writing for his private amusement rather

From Pepys' collection of calligraphy.

than for the edification of posterity, there is nothing that he hesitates to put down, from his desultory amours and frequent quarrels with his wife to his least creditable official dealings. Unlike Evelyn, he was not a littérateur; he merely chronicles in his own words exactly what has befallen him during the course of the last busy day, whether it be an interview with the King, his seduction of a carpenter's wife, a supper-party, a visit to the playhouse, or his exciting glimpse of a royal mistress's underclothes hung out to dry across the Privy Garden. He is rarely sententious, always dramatic and lively, and, whatever the subject he is describing, so far as we can judge, completely candid. Now and then, some momentous public happening – for example, the Great Fire – inspires a splendid flight of eloquence:

Having seen as much as I could now, I away to Whitehall by appointment, and there walked in St James's Park, and there met my wife, and Creed, and Wood and his wife, and walked to my boat; and there upon the water again, and to the fire up and down . . . so near the fire as we could for smoke; and all over the Thames, with one's face in the wind, you were almost burned with a shower of fire-drops . . . When we could endure no more upon the water, we to a little ale-house on the Bankside . . . and stayed till it was dark almost, and saw the fire grow; and, as it grew darker, appeared more and more, and in corners and upon steeples, and between churches and houses, as far as we could see up the hill of the city, in a most horrid, malicious, bloody flame, not like the fine flame of an ordinary fire . . . We stayed till, it being darkish, we saw the flame as only one entire arch of fire from this to the other side of the bridge, and in a bow up the hill for an arch of above a mile long; it made me weep to see it. The churches, houses, and all on fire and flaming at once; and a horrid noise the flames made, and the cracking of houses at their ruin. So home with a sad heart . . .

September 2nd, 1666

In his *Diary* Pepys employed a contemporary form of shorthand, and, when he dealt with his more disreputable adventures, a curious private language he had himself invented. The text was first deciphered at the beginning of the nineteenth century; and two volumes of selections, garbled and bowdlerised, appeared in 1825. The complete work, corrected and unexpurgated, did not begin to reach us until 1970.

Later Seventeenth-Century Verse

Samuel Butler; portrait by E. Lutterel.

SAMUEL BUTLER (1612–80), born at Strensham in Worcestershire, had been a man of many different trades before he finally became a poet. Taken into the service of the local lord of the manor, he did his best to learn painting – apparently with little success, for some of the pictures he produced were afterwards employed to block up disused windows. From 1626 until 1628 he was employed by the Countess of Kent, and he spent much of his time reading in her large library. He also encountered, about this period, the famous antiquarian John Selden, for whom he worked as an amanuensis. When the Stuarts were restored in 1660, Butler was forty-eight and still unknown. Although he had rendered no particular assistance to the Royalist cause, he was now appointed secretary to Lord Carbery and Steward of Ludlow castle. On marrying a rich woman (whose fortune rapidly disappeared) he elected to give up his post; and, in 1663, he published the opening part of *Hudibras*, a violent satire against the Puritans; of which the second part appeared in 1664, and the third in 1678. It delighted both the King and his courtiers; and Charles II is said to have carried around a copy and to have often quoted from it. But Butler himself, who was shy, awkward and tactless, the King found disappointing company; and, despite a royal pension granted him in 1677, he remained comparatively poor. He died of tuberculosis on 25 September 1680.

Hudibras is a mock-heroic satire aimed at the 'caterwauling brethren' who had helped overthrow the monarchy, and, simultaneously, a generalized assault on all the victims of self-righteousness. The title Butler owed to Spenser's *Faerie Queene*; and his model for the character of 'Sir Hudibras' was reputed to be Sir Samuel Luke, one of Cromwell's sternest Presbyterian soldiers.

Don Quixote, too, supplied some hints; and, like Cervantes, Butler contrasts his hero's romantic delusions with the everyday squalor that surrounds him. But it is Butler's skill in comic rhyming that lends the poem its triumphant gusto:

> For his Religion it was fit
> To match his Learning and his Wit:
> 'Twas Presbyterian true blew;
> For he was of that stubborn Crew
> Of errant Saints, whom all men grant
> To be the true Church Militant;
> Such as do build their Faith upon
> The holy Text of Pike and Gun;
> Decide all Controversies by
> Infallible Artillery;
> And prove their Doctrine Orthodox
> By Apostolic Blows and Knocks;
> Call Fire and Sword and Desolation,
> A godly-thorough-Reformation
> Which always must be carried on,
> And still be doing, never done;
> As if Religion were intended
> For nothing else but to be mended;

Some lines from the poem have passed into common usage – 'Look a gift horse in the mouth', 'Spare the rod and spoil the child', 'Devil take the hindmost' – an indication of the popularity it once enjoyed. For Samuel Butler, Puritanism, which has played so important a role in the development of English life and thought, was synonymous both with political tyranny and with personal

Illustration to Canto III of *Hudibras*.

hypocrisy; and its supporters belonged to the numerous tribe of moralists who castigate failings that they cannot themselves enjoy; who

> Compound for sins they are inclined to
> By damning those they have no mind to

In its own burlesque genre, *Hudibras* has few rivals; but unfortunately we know very little of the middle-aged writer who produced it. We are told, however, that he was 'sanguine' choleric, middle-sized, strong', and had a mane of 'lion-coloured' hair.

SIR JOHN DENHAM (1615–69), born in Dublin but brought up in London, entered Trinity College, Oxford, in 1631, and left in 1634. During the Civil War, he took the Royalist side; and, having been discovered carrying letters between the King and Queen, he was forced to flee to France. He returned in 1652; but Parliament had confiscated his properties and until the Restoration he was penniless. Once 'the King enjoyed his own again', Denham was rewarded with a knighthood and appointed Surveyor General of the Royal Works. At Whitehall, we learn from the *Memoirs of the Comte de Grammont*, he cut a somewhat ignominious figure, cuckolded by his young and beautiful wife, who became the mistress of the Duke of York. Her wayward conduct is said to have driven him mad; so that he presented himself before the King and insisted that he was the Holy Ghost. He recovered his wits; but Lady Denham died in 1667; and, for the last two years of his life, he was haunted by persistent rumours that he had poisoned her.

'Cooper's Hill', Denham's only memorable poem, was published in 1642. Greatly admired by eighteenth-century poets, including Alexander Pope, it helped to found a whole new school of descriptive-topographical verse, its celebration of the beauties of a Thames-side landscape being artfully combined with political and moral passages. In the River Thames he finds an image of the harmoniously ordered state:

> No unexpected inundations spoil
> The mower's hopes, nor mock the plowman's toil:
> But God-like his unwearied bounty flows;
> First loves to do, then loves the good he does.
> Nor are his blessings to his banks confined,
> But free, and common, as the sea or wind;
> When he to boast, or to disperse his stores
> Full of the tributes of his grateful shores,
> Visits the world, and in his flying towers
> Brings home to us, and makes both Indies ours;
> Finds wealth where 'tis, bestows it where it wants,
> Cities in deserts, woods in cities plants.
> So that to us no thing, no place is strange,
> While his fair bosom is the world's exchange.
> O could I flow like thee, and make thy stream

> My great example, as it is my theme!
> Though deep, yet clear, though gentle, yet not dull,
> Strong without rage, without o'er-flowing full.

The celebrated last quatrain, which Pope particularly admired, Denham inserted, as a happy after-thought, into the edition of the poem that appeared in 1655. Pope described him as 'majestic Denham'; and, of 'Cooper's Hill', Dryden announced that 'for the majesty of the style it is, and ever will be, the exact standard of good writing'.

MATTHEW PRIOR (1664–1721) is a remarkable example of a literary man whose talents raised him to political eminence. Born near Wimborne in Dorset, he was educated at Westminster School, his education having been financed by a prosperous uncle, a vintner who owned a Rhenish Wine Tavern. The tavern was a gathering place for wits; and it was here, while helping his uncle, that the young man attracted the attention of the Earl of Dorset, a friend of Dryden, who saw him reading Horace and became his patron. With Dorset's assistance, Prior went up to Cambridge, accompanied by a school friend, Charles Montague, later Earl of Halifax; and, in 1687, they collaborated on *The Hind and the Panther Transvers'd to the Story of the Country and the City Mouse*, a parody of Dryden's poem. When he left Cambridge, Prior joined the diplomatic service as an attaché in the English Embassy at the Hague. In 1696 he published his first really distinctive poem, *The Secretary*. His diplomatic career advanced steadily, until, in 1697, he became Secretary of State in Ireland, and, in 1699, Under Secretary of State in England. Meanwhile, his political allegiance had slowly changed from Whig to Tory; and, at the accession of Queen Anne in 1702, he entered the House of Commons as member for East Grinstead. Then, in 1711, he was made Commissioner of Customs by the Tories, and presently played an important part in the formulation of the Treaty of Utrecht. He was ambassador at Paris until the Queen's death; but, once he had returned to England, he was arrested by the Whig government. He spent two years in prison and, after his release, was generously helped by his friends, including Lord Oxford, who gave him four thousand pounds to add to the similar sum he had earned by the publication of a folio edition of his works in 1719. Prior's good fortune, however, was short-lived; he died suddenly in 1721.

Much of Prior's verse was written in his rôle of unofficial laureate for the Tory Party. It is his light and familiar work that survives. But, now and then, he struck a deeper note; and his poem 'On Reading Mezeray's History of France' was one that Sir Walter Scott afterwards declared he could never read without tears:

> . . . Yet for the fame of all these deeds
> What beggar in the Invalides,

With lameness broke, with blindness smitten,
Wished ever decently to die
To have been either Mezeray,
Or any monarch he has written?

It strange, dear Author, yet it true is,
That down from Pharamond to Louis,
All covet life, yet call it pain;
All feel the ill, yet shun the cure:
Can sense this paradox endure?
Resolve me, Combray[1], or Fontaine[2]

The man in graver Tragic known,
Tho' his best part long since was done,
Still on the stage desires to tarry:
And he who play'd the harlequin,
After the jest still loads the scene,
Unwilling to retire, tho' weary.

[1] François de Salignac de La Mothe Fénelon (1651–1715), archbishop of Cambrai and author of *Télémaque*.
[2] Jean de La Fontaine (1621–95), author of the *Fables*.

JOHN WILMOT, EARL OF ROCHESTER (1647–80) was born at Ditchley, near Woodstock, Oxfordshire, the son of a distinguished courtier. A handsome and precocious youth, he entered Wadham College, Oxford, at the age of thirteen, and left with his degree a year later. After touring France and Italy, when he was only seventeen, he himself joined the Court of Charles II and immediately became a royal favourite. As one of Charles's Gentlemen of the Bedchamber, he was exceptionally familiar with his good-natured sovereign, and often lampooned him in his verses. Charles frequently rebuked and dismissed him from court, but regularly called him back. Rochester was a determined hedonist and a practised sensualist, in revolt both against Cavalier romanticism and against Puritan idealism, who based his attitude towards existence on the philosophy of Thomas Hobbes. Many of the stories told of his scandalous exploits are probably picturesque legends. There is no doubt, however, that, in 1665, he carried off a 'melancholy heiress', Elizabeth Malet – an adventure for which he was briefly punished by being committed to the Tower of London. The pair were married in 1667; and, although Rochester was never a faithful husband, he seems always to have treated Elizabeth with particular respect and delicacy; the lyrics that he addressed to his wife are among his finest poems. Meanwhile, he had regained the King's favour, and in 1674 was appointed Ranger of Woodstock Park. There, burned out by debauchery, he died in 1680 – but not before he had been reconverted to the Christian faith, and declared that religion had brought him the sense of 'felicity and glory' that he had missed pursuing worldly pleasures.

At the time, Rochester was thirty-three. His conversion was evidently sincere; but he lived to enjoy it less than two months.

Despite the fact that he has often been represented as the heartless rake par excellence, Rochester was devoted to his friends; and there is unlikely to have been any truth in the report that he had employed a gang of bullies to attack Dryden; he and the master-poet of the age appear to have appreciated one another's talents. For all his professed hedonism, fidelity is a theme that recurs throughout his lyric poems; and he frequently deplores what a French writer has called the 'intermittences' of the human heart:

> All my past life is mine no more,
>   The flying hours are gone:
> Like transitory dreams giv'n o'er,
> Whose images are kept in store,
>   By memory alone
>
> The time that is to come is not,
>   How can it then be mine?
> The present moment's all my lot,
> And that, as fast as it is got,
>   Phillis, is only thine.
>
> Then talk not of inconstancy
>   False hearts and broken vows;
> If I, by miracle, can be
> This live-long minute true to thee,
>   'Tis all that Heav'n allows.

John Wilmot, 2nd Earl of Rochester; portrait attributed to J. Huysmans.

In his more ribald vein, Rochester foresees the future, and presents himself as 'The Maim'd Debauchee', whom he compares to a brave old admiral, looking back upon his past triumphs:

> My pains at last some respite shall afford,
>   While I behold the battles you maintain:
> When fleets of glasses sail around the board,
>   From whose broad-sides volleys of wit shall rain.
>
> Nor shall the sight of honourable scars,
>   Which my too forward valour did procure,
> Frighten new-listed soldiers from the wars,
>   Past joys have more than paid what I endure.
>
> Should some brave youth (worth being drunk) prove nice,
>   And from his fair inviter meanly shrink,
> 'Twould please the ghost of my departed vice,
>   If at my counsel, he repent and drink,
>
> Or should some cold-complexion'd sot forbid
>   With his dull morals, our night's brisk alarms,
> I'll fire his blood by telling what I did
>   When I was strong and able to bear arms, . . .

In his most ambitious, if not his most successful poem, 'A

Satyr against Mankind', he stigmatises man as inferior to the beasts, and makes short work of human reason:

> Reason, an *Ignis fatuus*, in the mind,
> Which leaving light of Nature, Sense behind;
> Pathless and dang'rous wand'ring ways it takes,
> Through errors, fenny-boggs, and thorny brakes;
> Whilst the misguided follower, climbs with pain,
> Mountains of whimseys, heap'd in his own brain:
> Stumbling from thought to thought, falls head-long down,
> Into doubt's boundless sea, where, like to drown,
> Books bear him up awhile, and makes him try,
> To swim with bladders of philosophy, . . .

Rochester's philosophic cynicism did not detract from his romantic lyricism. He remains one of the most original and unconventional love-poets of the later seventeenth century:

> 'Tis not that I'm weary grown
> Of being yours, and yours alone:
> But with what face can I incline
> To damn you to be only mine?
> You, whom some kinder power did fashion
> By merit, and by inclination,
> The joy at least of a whole nation.
>
> Let meaner spirits of your sex,
> With humble aims their thoughts perplex,
> And boast, if, by their arts they can
> Contrive to make *one* happy man;
> While, moved by an impartial sense,
> Favours, like Nature, you dispense,
> With universal influence.
>
> See the kind seed-receiving Earth
> To every grain affords a birth:
> On her no showers unwelcome fall,
> Her willing womb retains 'em all.
> And shall my Celia be confined?
> No, live up to thy mighty mind;
> And be the mistress of mankind.

Tragedy and Comedy

THOMAS OTWAY (1652–85) was one of the last English dramatists who carried on the great traditions of the Elizabethan drama; to which, as the translator of Racine's *Bérénice*, he added a considerable knowledge of the French stage. Born at Trotton in Sussex, he took up residence at Christ Church, Oxford, but was obliged to go down without receiving a degree, when his father died and left him penniless. His first play, *Alcibiades*, was produced in 1675; and the dramatist developed a desperate passion for the actress, Mrs Barry. She rejected him; and, in 1686, the success of *Don Carlos* was overclouded by the discovery that she had accepted the advances of his patron, Lord Rochester. Still suffering from the pangs of frustrated love, he was obliged to watch her rise to fame, and in 1678, he accepted an ensign's commission under the Duke of Monmouth's standard. But a year of unsuccessful service abroad brought him very little profit; and, on his return to England in 1679, he became a heavy drinker. Always in debt and, latterly, sometimes nearly starving, he continued to attribute his misfortunes to the cruelty of Woman. But his plays had some success; both *The Orphan* and *Caius Marius*, produced in 1680, attracted favourable attention, as did *The Soldier's Fortune* (which was semi-autobiographical) and his masterpiece, *Venice Preserv'd*, staged in 1682. Otway's reward was meagre; and what he earned he spent on drink and gambling. Towards the end of his life, which proved an extended tragedy, his favourite resort was an ale-house near Tower Hill; and he is said to have choked to death, after a period of semi-starvation, on a crust of bread that, having unexpectedly obtained a small loan, he was devouring in a London street.

Thomas Otway; from the frontispiece to his *Works*.

Otway's comedies are competent, but usually derivative. The most successful is *The Soldier's Fortune*, with its theme of cuckoldry and unsuccessful marriage:

LADY DUNCE: Die a maid, Sylvia? Fie for shame. What a scandalous resolution's that; five thousand pounds to your portion and leave it all to hospitals, for the innocent recreation hereafter of leading apes in hell? Fie, for shame.

SYLVIA: Indeed such another charming animal as your consort, Sir David, might do much with me; 'tis an unspeakable blessing to lie all night by a horse-load of diseases; a beastly, unsavoury, old, groaning, grunting, wheezing wretch, that smells of the grave he's going to already; from such a curse and hair-cloth next my skin good heaven deliver me.

LADY DUNCE: Thou mistakest the use of a husband, Sylvia; They are not meant for bedfellows; heretofore indeed 'twas a fulsome fashion, to lie o'nights with a husband; but the world's improved and customs altered.

Venice Preserved, which includes a topical caricature of Lord Shaftesbury and references to Titus Oates' alleged discovery of a dangerous Popish plot, has a genuinely moving subject. Two conspirators, Pierre and Jaffeir, seek to overthrow the tyrannical Venetian government; but Jaffeir is persuaded by his beloved Belvidera to betray the friend who trusts him. The play is full of superbly eloquent speeches that reflect the dramatist's own pent-up feelings – his intense preoccupation with the horrors of poverty and with the excruciating pains of hopeless love:

Oh, I will love thee, even in madness love thee.
Though my distracted senses should forsake me,

> I'd find some intervals, when my poor heart
> Should 'suage itself and be let loose to thine.
> Though the bare earth be all our resting-place,
> Its roots our food, some clift our habitation,
> I'll make this arm a pillow for thine head;
> As thou sighing liest, and swelled with sorrow,
> Creep to thy bosom, pour the balm of love
> Into thy soul, and kiss thee to thy rest;
> Then praise our God, and watch thee till the morning.

Restoration Comedy

Otway's genius, though he wrote comedies, was predominantly tragic. The originators of the so-called Restoration Comedy – some of whom lived on into the reign of George I – created an enchanting comic world, where love is represented as a favourite social pastime, and even the most serious and self-destructive passions become grotesque or mildly ludicrous. In 1660, after nearly two decades of Puritan supremacy and military dictatorship, many Englishmen, whatever part they had played during the Civil War, enjoyed an exhilarating sense of freedom; and when the theatres, closed by Parliament in 1642, were re-opened under royal patronage, the drama took a novel turn. It now reflected the tastes of a gaily profligate Court, and of thriving middle-class citizens, like Samuel Pepys, who, although they might disapprove of the 'inexpressible luxury and profaneness' they observed at Whitehall, often imitated courtly habits. They went to the theatre to be entertained; and, while managers enlisted attractive comediennes and provided rich and decorative scenery, the dramatists devised a form of writing that combined verbal wit with social satire. It was not a satire that penetrated very deeply; it had none of Jonson's incisive strength, and lacked any kind of moral message, but played lightly over the surface of existence on the wings of brilliant dialogue. Starting with the assumption that almost every married woman was potentially 'frail', and the average husband a predestined cuckold, the Restoration dramatist built up a picture of society that was neither entirely imaginative nor completely realistic, yet sufficiently close to the facts of real life to keep his worldly audience amused.

Sir George Etherege (c.1634–c.91) would appear to have spent part of his youth abroad, though he may have resided for a while at Cambridge. His first play, *The Comical Revenge; or, Love in a Tub* was produced with great success in 1664; and such were the expectations aroused by his second comedy, *She Wou'd if She Cou'd*, staged in 1668, that Pepys records that over a thousand people had been turned away upon the first night. Nevertheless, it proved a comparative failure; and Etherege then left for

Illustration to Sir George Etherege's *The Man of Mode*.

Constantinople, having received a diplomatic appointment that kept him abroad for three years. In 1676 the last of his three plays, *The Man of Mode, or Sir Fopling Flutter*, was presented at the Duke's House. Again, it succeeded brilliantly; and its eponymous hero became the father of a whole line of stage dandies that culminated in Vanbrugh's Lord Foppington. One of 'the mob of gentlemen who write with ease', Etherege belonged to the circle of rakes and wits gathered around Charles II. In 1685 he was appointed British envoy to the Imperial Diet at Regensburg, whence he wrote some entertaining letters. He found his official duties dreary and tedious, and seems to have scandalised his hosts by his flirtation with a visiting actress. After the fall of James II in 1688, Etherege was obliged to flee to Paris, where he died about 1691.

Etherege's first play is generally held to have marked the beginning of the social Comedy of Manners, the new type of dramatic entertainment that distinguished the literature of the

later seventeenth century. *Love in a Tub* is an uneven mixture of
Jonsonian comedy and modern farce, with the addition of a
serious love story, written in a mixture of prose and rhyming verse.
It broke new ground by portraying the manners of the times, but
(unlike Jonson's 'comedy of humours') avoiding any kind of moral
message. *The Man of Mode* consolidated Etherege's achievement.
The fop of the title remains a peripheral figure, who does not
emerge until the third act; and the main centre of interest is
Dorimant, a cynical and promiscuous rake, said to have been
modelled on Lord Rochester. A master of sexual intrigue, he is
also an 'honest' man, who, following Hobbes and Mandeville,
believes that all human motives are ultimately derived from
appetite. But he meets his match in the equally tough-minded
Harriet. She recognizes him for what he is – 'a man made up of
the forms and commonplaces sucked out of the remaining lees of
the last age' – and yet, despite his vices, loves him. Their lack of
integrity, she knows, is what he really despises in the women whom
he conquers; and that he will certainly hate her, too, 'if ever I do a
thing against the rules of decency and honour'. The witty duels
between Dorimant and Harriet provide the play with its most
amusing scenes. Here, for instance, in the final scene, Dorimant
offers to save Harriet from a marriage she does not desire:

DORIMANT: In this sad condition, Madam, I can do no less than offer
you my service.

HARRIET: The obligation is not great, you are the common sanctuary
for all young women who run from their relations.

DORIMANT: I have always my arms open to receive the distressed. But
I will open my heart and receive you, where none yet did
ever enter – you have fill'd it with a secret, might I but let
you know it –

HARRIET: Do not speak it, if you would have me believe it; your
tongue is so fam'd for falsehood, 'twill do the truth an injury.

DORIMANT: Turn not away then; but look on me and guess it.

HARRIET: Did you not tell me there was no credit to be given to
faces? that women nowadays have their passions as much
at will as they have their complexions, and put on joy and
sadness, scorn and kindness, with the same ease as they do
their paint and patches – are they the only counterfeits?

DORIMANT: You wrong your own, while you suspect my eyes; by all the
hope I have in you, the inimitable colour in your cheeks is
not more free from art than are the sighs I offer.

HARRIET: In men who have been long harden'd in sin, we have
reason to mistrust the first signs of repentance.

DORIMANT: The prospect of such a Heav'n will make me persevere, and
give you marks that are infallible.

HARRIET: What are those?

DORIMANT: I will renounce all the joys I have in friendship and in wine,
sacrifice to you all the interest I have in other women –

HARRIET: Hold – though I wish you devout, I would not have you
turn fanatick.

Though Etherege was an amiable man of the world, who seems, almost by chance, to have become a playwright, within the limitations of the form he launched, he was undoubtedly a true creative artist.

WILLIAM WYCHERLEY (1640–1716), was born near Shrewsbury, educated in France and at Oxford, and, after studying Law at the Inner Temple and serving briefly as a naval officer, became a well-known London wit. His earliest comedy, *Love in a Wood*, was produced in 1671. It was much applauded; and, about the same time, he attracted the attention of the King's reigning mistress, the all-powerful Duchess of Cleveland, who was said to have shown her interest by shouting a ribald remark – 'You, Wycherley, you are the son of a whore', a smart reference to *Love in a Wood* – from the window of her coach. Charles II, however, countenanced the liaison that followed, and planned to make Wycherley his son's tutor. But, when the dramatist contracted a secret marriage – to the widowed Countess of Drogheda – he was banished in disgrace. The marriage proved disastrous. Lady Drogheda was far less rich than he had imagined; she also had a savage temper; and, on her death in 1681, she left him burdened with debts that presently reduced him to a debtor's gaol. He remained a prisoner for some years, until he was rescued by James II, who, having been taken to see *The Plain Dealer* and told of the author's distress, agreed to pay him a modest annual pension. Wycherley lived on, in comparative obscurity, to the age of seventy-six. He had ceased producing plays, but frequently scribbled verses, employing his young friend, Alexander Pope to edit and rewrite his lines. At the end of his existence, he married a young girl, merely, he said, to disappoint his heirs.

William Wycherley; portrait after Lely.

Wycherley's first two plays, *Love in a Wood, or St James's Park* (1671) and *The Gentleman Dancing-Master* (1672) are immature works, though they include some entertaining scenes. His two major works, *The Country Wife* and *The Plain Dealer*, were staged in 1672 or 1673, and 1674 respectively. *The Country Wife* has three separate plots. In one, an ageing rake, who marries an innocent rustic, is successfully out-witted by his bride as soon as she has learned the ways of London. The second concerns the rivalry between an affected fop and a sensible man of the world for the hand of Alithea. The third, and most scandalous, introduces a designing amorist, who lets it be known that, since he contracted the pox abroad, he has become entirely impotent; with the result that jealous husbands gladly trust him in their wives' company, and their wives are delighted to ascertain that poor Mr Horner is still extremely virile. A series of *double entendres* sharpen Wycherley's dialogue. Thus, in the famous 'china scene', Lady Fidget, a party to Horner's deception, arrives at his house, having told her husband that she is going to a so-called China House, a shop selling oriental porcelain. They retire together and, on their reappearance, find Mrs Squeamish, who has not yet discovered Horner's secret, eagerly awaiting them. Lady Fidget emerges holding a piece of china:

LADY FIDGET:	. . . I have been toiling and moiling for the prettiest piece of china, my dear.
HORNER:	Nay, she has been too hard for me, do what I could.
MRS. SQUEAMISH:	Oh, lord, I'll have some china too. Good Mr. Horner, don't think to give other people china, and me none; come in with me too.
HORNER:	Upon my honour, I have none left now.
MRS. SQUEAMISH:	Nay, nay, I have known you deny your china before now, but you shan't put me off so. Come.
HORNER:	This lady had the last there.
LADY FIDGET:	Yes indeed, madam, to my certain knowledge, he has no more left.
MRS. SQUEAMISH:	O, but it may be he may have some you could not find.
LADY FIDGET:	What, d'ye think if he had any left, I would not have had it too? for we women of quality never think we have china enough.
HORNER:	Do not take it ill, I cannot make china for you all, but I will have a roll-wagon for you too, another time.

In the end, Mrs Squeamish herself receives the necessary enlightenment, and the ladies come to terms. So long as 'honour' is preserved, there need be no quarrel; and they can share, and continue to enjoy their friend.

Of all the Restoration dramatists, the author of *The Country Wife* has been most criticised for his alleged indecency. He answered his critics in a scene from *The Plain Dealer*, where his previous play is discussed, and Olivia, an arch-hypocrite, finds obscenity 'in the very name of Horner':

ELIZA:	Truly, 'tis so hidden, I cannot find it out, I confess.
OLIVIA:	O horrid! Does it not give you the rank conception or image of a goat, a town-bull, or a satyr? nay, what is yet a filthier image than all the rest, that of a eunuch?
ELIZA:	What then? I can think of a goat, a bull, or a satyr, without any hurt.
OLIVIA:	Ay: but cousin, one cannot stop there.
ELIZA:	I can, cousin.
OLIVIA:	O no; for when you have those filthy creatures in your head once, the next thing you think is what they do; as their defiling of honest men's beds and couches, rapes upon sleeping and waking country virgins under hedges, and on haycocks. Nay, farther –
ELIZA:	Nay, no farther, cousin. We have enough of your comment on the play, which will make me more ashamed than the play itself.

Such is the prudery, allied to hypocrisy, at which Wycherley so

often tilted. Though he was scarcely a sexual moralist, he was a powerful social satirist; and the fierce energy that he put into his satires frequently anticipates the work of Swift and Pope.

Blenheim Palace, Vanbrugh's masterpiece, presented by the nation to the Duke of Marlborough.

SIR JOHN VANBRUGH (1664–1726) was the son of a 'sugar baker' of Dutch origin. He had been born in London, but, during his childhood, his family moved to Chester to escape the plague. As a young man, he received a military commission, and studied architecture in France, but was arrested at Calais as a British spy; and it was behind the walls of the Bastille that he drafted his first comedy, *The Provok'd Wife*. After his release from imprisonment, towards the end of 1692, Vanbrugh returned home and was soon attracted to the stage. In 1696, he produced *The Relapse*; and the huge success of this play at Drury Lane induced him to continue writing. Meanwhile, his career as an architect prospered; in 1702 he was appointed Comptroller of the Royal Works; and in 1703 Lord Carlisle engaged him to build Castle Howard. He collaborated with Nicholas Hawksmoor on the Clarendon Building in Oxford, and raised his most splendid monument, Blenheim Palace, which an appreciative sovereign and a grateful country bestowed upon the Duke of Marlborough. Vanbrugh was knighted in 1719, and in the same year married a woman many years younger than himself.

Sir John Vanbrugh.

Vanbrugh's plays were written, on his own admission, to 'amuse the gentlemen of the town', and, as a result, often suffer from a certain lack of literary discipline. His two best-known comedies, *The Provok'd Wife* and *The Relapse*, include some singularly brilliant scenes and acutely-drawn characters. In *The Relapse* he provided a ludicrous sequel to Colley Cibber's *Love's Last Shift*, where the rakish Loveless is redeemed at the close of the play through the virtue of his wife Amanda. Vanbrugh starts off with this highly improbable conclusion, and shows Loveless's subsequent fall from grace, when the reformed rake seduces a friend's wife, and Amanda herself is sorely tempted. A secondary plot displays Tom Fashion out-manoeuvring Lord Foppington by marrying his intended consort, Hoyden Clumsey. Lord Foppington, who had also appeared in Cibber's play, as adapted and enlarged by Vanbrugh, is undoubtedly his greatest personage. A dandy, who asserts that his own existence is one 'perpetual stream of pleasure', Foppington gives a marvellously self-complacent account of his customary mode of life:

I rise, madam, about ten a-clack. I don't rise sooner, because 'tis the worst thing in the world for the complexion; nat that I pretend to be a beau; but a man must endeavour to look wholesome, lest he make so nauseous a figure in the side-bax, the ladies should be compelled to turn their eyes upon the play. So at ten a-clack, I say, I rise. Naw if I find 'tis a good day, I resalve to take a turn in the park, and see the fine women; so huddle on my clothes, and get dressed by one. If it be nasty weather, I take a turn in the chocolate-hause: where, as you walk, madam, you may have the prettiest prospect in the world: you have looking glasses all raund you ... from thence I go to dinner at Lacket's, where you are so nicely and delicately serv'd, that, stap me vitals! they shall compose you a dish, no bigger than a saucer, shall come to fifty shillings. Between eating my dinner (and washing my mauth, ladies) I spend my time, till I go to the play; where, till nine a-clack, I entertain myself with looking upon the company; and usually dispose of one hour more in leading 'em aut. So there's twelve of the four and twenty pretty well over. The other twelve, madam, are disposed of in two articles: in the first four I toast myself drunk, and in t'other eight I sleep myself sober again. Thus, ladies, you see my life is an eternal raund of delights.

The baroque energy that Vanbrugh revealed in his buildings found its way into his dramatic works. He was one of the most gifted and vigorous exponents of the English Comedy of Manners.

WILLIAM CONGREVE (1670–1729) came of a Yorkshire family, which, in his early youth, had moved to Ireland. At Kilkenny College, he formed a lifelong friendship with Swift, who was three years older than himself; and in 1686 he went to Trinity College, Dublin, where he began to study drama. In 1688 his family returned to England; and, in 1691, he was entered at the Middle Temple. But he soon abandoned law and, during the same year, published a short novel, *Incognita*. He now became a member of Dryden's literary circle, and made the acquaintance of the publisher, Jacob Tonson. He also joined the famous Kit-Cat Club, a convivial assembly of Whiggish wits and beaux. *The Old Bachelor*, first performed in 1693, proved immediately successful, and was followed by *The Double Dealer* in 1694, and *Love for Love* in 1695. His popularity extended to the Court; and he was granted a small political sinecure, being appointed one of the commissioners for the licensing of hackney coaches. In 1697 he produced his tragedy,

William Congreve; portrait by G. Kneller.

The Mourning Bride; but, in 1700, his last comedy, *The Way of the World*, received a somewhat tepid welcome – the critic John Dennis tells us that it was 'hiss'd by barbarous fools'; and the dramatist was so exasperated that he is said to have harangued his audience from the stage. He thereupon settled down to private life, and did not resume his connection with the drama until 1704, when he briefly joined Vanbrugh in the management of the New Haymarket Theatre. By 1710, when his collected works appeared, Congreve was a sick and ageing man, who suffered from gout, arthritis and a series of cataracts that had left him half-blind. But his political friends did not desert him; and in 1714 he was awarded another sinecure post, the lucrative Secretaryship of the Island of Jamaica. Congreve never married, though for many years he seems to have been the lover of the celebrated actress Mrs Bracegirdle, who was succeeded, towards the end of his life, by Lady Godolphin. He died on 26 January 1729 from injuries he had received in a carriage accident. Congreve was an attractive, good-humoured man, generally admired and liked. Among his intimates, besides Dryden and Swift, were Addison, Steele, Pope and Gay.

In his first plays, *The Old Bachelor*, and *The Double Dealer*, Congreve had already revealed his stage-craft and his mastery of fluent and witty dialogue. *Love for Love* follows a similar pattern, but is a more explicit social satire. Its complicated plot turns on the mercenary motives that were apt to underlie a modern marriage. The play was violently attacked by a non-juring clergyman named Jeremy Collier, and against Collier's accusations of immorality, Congreve defended himself in a sensible, but somewhat ineffective pamphlet. *The Way of the World*, his last play, presents a no less damaging picture of the contemporary social scene. Apart from the witty hero, Mirabell, and the delightful heroine, Millamant, none of the characters portrayed possesses the smallest grain of virtue; avarice, lust and sexual jealousy appear to govern all their actions. The endless intricacies of the plot are handled by Congreve with an almost casual ease; but it is in the creation of character through dialogue that he displays his real dramatic genius. The dialogue is continuously witty and concise; and each character has a distinctive mode of speech – a rhythm and choice of language that is his or hers alone. Thus the wonderfully spirited Millamant describes the conditions she feels obliged to lay down before she will embark on marriage:

MILLAMANT: . . . And d'ye hear, I won't be called names after I'm married; positively I won't be called names.
MIRABELL: Names!
MILLAMANT: Ay, as wife, spouse, my dear, joy, jewel, love, sweetheart, and the rest of that nauseous cant, in which men and their wives are so fulsomly familiar – I shall never bear that – Good Mirabell, don't let us be familiar or fond, nor kiss

LOVE for LOVE:
A
COMEDY.

Acted at the
THEATRE in *Little Lincolns-Inn Fields*,
BY
His Majefty's Servants.

Written by Mr. *CONGREVE*.

Nudus agris, nudus nummis paternis,
Infanire parat certa ratione modoque. Hor.

LONDON:

Printed for *Jacob Tonfon*, at the *Judge's-Head*, near the *Inner-Temple-Gate* in *Fleeftreet*. 1695.

before folks, like my Lady Fadler and Sir Francis: nor go to Hide Park together the first Sunday in a new chariot, to provoke eyes and whispers; and then never been seen there together again; as if we were proud of one another the first week, and ashamed of one another ever after. Let us never visit together, nor go to a play together, but let us be very strange and well bred: let us be as strange as if we had been married a great while; and as well bred as if we were not married at all.

Mirabell, in turn, recites his stipulations:

MIRABELL: Item, when you shall be breeding –
MILLAMANT: Ah! name it not.
MIRABELL: Which may be presumed, with a blessing on our endeavours –
MILLAMANT: Odious endeavours!
MIRABELL: I denounce against all strait lacing, squeezing for a shape, 'till you mould my boy's head like a sugar-loaf; and instead of a man-child, make me father to a crooked billet. Lastly, to the dominion of the tea-table I submit. – But with proviso, that you exceed not in your province; but restrain yourself to native and simple tea-table drinks, as tea, chocolate, and coffee. As likewise to genuine and authorised tea-table talk – such as mending of fashions, spoiling reputations, railing at absent friends, and so forth – but that on no account you encroach upon the men's prerogative, and presume to drink healths, or toast fellows; for the prevention of which, I banish all foreign forces, all auxiliaries to the tea-table, as orange-brandy, all aniseed, cinnamon, citron and Barbado's waters, together with ratafia and the most noble spirit of Clary. – But for the cowslip-wine, poppy-water, and all dormitives, those I allow. – These provisos admitted, in other things I may prove a tractable and complying husband.
MILLAMANT: O horrid provisos! filthy strong waters! I toast fellows, odious men! I hate your odious provisos.
MIRABELL: Then we're agreed.

Congreve himself admitted that *The Way of the World* had been ill-calculated to 'that general taste which seems now to be predominant in the palates of our audience'; and, after its failure, for the remaining thirty years of his life he preferred to be known as a gentleman rather than as a dramatist. The sentimental comedies now becoming popular would scarcely have appealed either to his acute sense of humour or to his astringent sense of style.

GEORGE FARQUHAR (1677–1707) born in Londonderry, the son of an Irish clergyman, attended the Free Grammar School at Londonderry, and, at the age of thirteen, is believed to have witnessed the Battle of Boyne, where William III routed the armies of James II. Having entered Trinity College, Dublin, in 1694, and become a regular visitor to the Smock Alley Theatre, in 1696 he gave up his academic career to earn his living as a proof-reader, but soon afterwards went upon the stage. His first rôle is said to have been that of Othello; but he proved an unsuccessful actor; and, in 1697, he left for England. Though he had few assets apart from the desire to write, he produced his first play, *Love and a Bottle*, at Drury Lane in 1698. His second play, *The Constant Couple* (1699), also staged at Drury Lane, was a resounding popular success, and had a run of fifty-three nights; but the complications of his private life drove him to Holland with the army. On his return, he wrote *Sir Harry Wildair*, which failed. In 1703, Farquhar married Margaret Remell, who was thirty-five, and had no means of her own but two children by a previous marriage; and he then joined Lord Orrery's regiment and was posted to Lichfield to enlist recruits. This experience inspired *The Recruiting Officer*, which appeared in 1706. Lack of money, however, obliged him to sell his commission; and his friend, the actor Robert Wilks, urged him to resume writing. The result was *The Beaux' Stratagem* (1707); but, despite its success, his triumph came too late. Farquhar died on the night of the eleventh performance in a garret above St Martin's Lane.

Farquhar's last two comedies are much superior to any of his early works; and, of the two, *The Beaux' Stratagem* is perhaps the better play. The plot is based on the attempts of two rakes, Aimwell and Archer, to carry off a rich heiress; but the work is most memorable for its gallery of minor personages – Boniface, whose name became the generic term, during the eighteenth-century, for a country inn-keeper; Lady Bountiful, with her over-powering benevolence; Scrub, the simple-minded rustic; Gibbet, the type of stage-highwayman; as well as the drunken Squire Sullen and his miserably ill-treated wife. Mrs Sullen's complaints about the state of marriage have an energetic eloquence:

O Sister, Sister! if you ever marry, beware of a sullen, silent sot, one that's always musing, but never thinks: – There's some diversion in a talking blockhead; and since a woman must wear chains, I wou'd have the pleasure of hearing 'em rattle a little. Now you shall see; but take this by the way :– He came home this morning at his usual hour of four, waken'd me out of a sweet dream of something else, by tumbling over the tea-table, which he broke all to pieces; after his man and he had rowl'd about the room, like sick passengers in a storm, he comes flounce into bed, dead as a salmon into a fishmonger's basket; his feet cold as ice, his breath hot as a furnace, and his hands and his face as greasy as his flannel night-cap. – Oh matrimony! He tosses up the clothes with a barbarous swing over his shoulders, disorders the whole economy of my bed, leaves me half naked, and my whole night's comfort is the tuneable serenade of that wakeful nightingale, his nose! O, the pleasure of counting the melancholy clock by a snoring husband.

The Beaux' Stratagem has been described as one of the last true Restoration comedies. The form was gradually changing.

Frontispiece to *The Beaux'*
Stratagem, 1711 edition.

Farquhar's play is humorous rather than witty, with here and
there a touch of sentiment, and draws its subject-matter not from
fashionable London but from the background of provincial life.
He himself had defined comedy as 'a well-framed tale handsomely
told, as an agreeable vehicle for counsel and reproof' – a definition
that seems less suited to the Comedy of Manners than to the
novels of Henry Fielding and Tobias Smollett.

John Dryden

The master-poet of the later seventeenth-century, JOHN DRYDEN
(1631–1700), was born at Aldwinkle, near Oundle in Northamp-
tonshire, the son of a solid land-owning family, who, during the
Civil War, had supported the Parliamentary cause. A King's
scholar at Westminster School, he went up to Trinity College,
Cambridge, where he received his degree in 1654. As a young
man, he is thought to have had some minor employment in the

THE SEVENTEENTH CENTURY 197

service of the Lord Protector. Certainly, his early sympathies seem to have been with the Commonwealth; and his first substantial poem, published in 1659, was entitled *Stanzas on the Death of Cromwell*. A year earlier, Dryden had gone to London, where he soon became associated with most of the leading intellectuals of the day; and his own standing was confirmed, in 1662, when he was elected a Fellow of the Royal Society. Meanwhile, he had apparently changed his allegiance; for, in 1660, he had welcomed the Restoration of King Charles II by publishing a new poem, *Astrea Redux*. But then, as Dr Johnson observed, if Dryden changed, he changed with the nation. In 1663 Dryden married Lady Elizabeth Howard in circumstances that, according to Johnson's 'Life', did neither of them much credit. The marriage is reported to have turned out ill; and Dryden, we know, was for many years the lover of the actress Ann Reeve. As Lady Elizabeth had brought him no fortune, Dryden tried his hand at writing plays. Having produced a successful first comedy, *The Rival Ladies*, in 1664 he collaborated with his brother-in-law on *The Indian Queen*, a turbulent melodrama with an exotic Mexican background, that established his reputation as a modern dramatist. Of the series of heroic plays he produced, his greatest achievement, his blank-verse tragedy, *All for Love*, appeared in 1678. Meanwhile, he had been appointed Poet Laureate in 1668, and Historiographer Royal in 1670. During the next decade he was commissioned to turn out plays for The King's Theatre, at the rate of one a year.

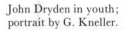

Oliver Cromwell; an illustration to Abraham Cowley's *Works*, 1710.

In 1681 Dryden published the first of his famous political and literary satires, *Absalom and Achitophel*, which he followed with *The Medal* and *MacFlecknoe*. He was now recognized as a great public poet; and, once he had been rewarded with the post of Collector of the Customs, he achieved a large measure of financial independence. Dryden's two puissant theological poems, *Religio Laici* and *The Hind and the Panther*, came out in 1682 and 1687 respectively. The former was ostensibly a defence of the Anglican Church, though its real motives were somewhat more complex; the latter defended the Catholic faith, to which Dryden had been converted at the age of fifty-five. Since Charles II had been succeeded by his Catholic brother, James II, between the publications of the two poems, Dryden was widely accused of time-serving. This charge would appear to have been unjust. When William of Orange replaced James, in the Glorious Revolution of 1688, Dryden refused to swear allegiance; with the result that he lost all his positions and income, and saw his arch-enemy Thomas Shadwell assume his Laureateship. He remained a firm Papist and Jacobite until the end of his existence. In 1690 renewed financial difficulties made him return to writing for the stage; and, during the same year, he produced his translation of Virgil, which is said to have earned him over a thousand pounds. He continued writing

John Dryden in youth; portrait by G. Kneller.

Dryden, the literary patriarch.

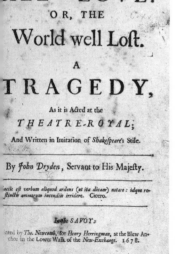

ALL FOR LOVE:
OR, THE
World well Loft.
A
TRAGEDY,

As it is Acted at the
THEATRE-ROYAL;

And Written in Imitation of *Shakefpeare's* Stile.

By *John Dryden*, Servant to His Majefty.

*—facile eft verbum aliquod ardens (ut ita dicam) notare: idque re-
ftinctis animorum incendiis irridere.* Cicero.

In the SAVOY:

Printed by *Tho. Newcomb*, for *Henry Herringman*, at the Blew An-
chor in the Lower Walk of the New-Exchange. 1678.

plays, translations, odes, and critical prefaces; and among them are some of his best work. In his last years Dryden held court in his favourite seat at Will's Coffee House, where the younger writers of the day, including Congreve, Wycherley, Addison and the juvenile Alexander Pope, gathered round to do him honour. Dryden died of gout and gangrene on 1 May 1700, and was buried in Chaucer's grave in Westminster Abbey.

As an emergent writer, Dryden produced a succession of varied and ingenious poems; but for twenty years after the Restoration he was primarily a dramatist. He attempted almost every dramatic mode – comedy, heroic drama and tragedy. Of his comedies, he himself declared that 'reputation in them is the last thing to which I shall pretend'. The finest is undoubtedly *Marriage à la Mode*, a comedy of manners that, although it includes some excellent comic scenes, lacks the conviction and unity of tone we find in Etherege or Congreve; and Dryden, we learn, was among the first to recognize Congreve's superiority. Dryden was also a highly successful author of heroic dramas; and, in this field, he ranges from the baroque splendours of *The Conquest of Granada* (1670) and *Aureng-Zebe* (1675), where he makes a grandiose use of the heroic couplet, to his magnificent blank-verse tragedy, *All for Love*, based on Shakespeare's *Antony and Cleopatra*. It is Dryden's noblest play, and in theme and construction far the simplest, being the only drama, he said, that he had written 'for himself'. Johnson admired it; though, he remarked, 'by admitting the romantick omnipotence of love', the dramatist had 'recommended as laudable and worthy of imitation that conduct which, through the ages, the good have censured as vicious, and the bad despised as foolish'.

Many beautiful songs are scattered through Dryden's comedies and tragedies, sometimes boldly erotic and sometimes dreamily romantic, as in this song from *The Indian Emperor*:

Ah fading joy, how quickly art thou past!
Yet we thy ruin haste.
As if the cares of human life were few,
We seek out new,
And follow fate, which would too fast pursue.

See how on every bough the birds express
In their sweet notes their happiness.
They all enjoy, and nothing spare,
But on their mother nature lay their care:
Why then should man, the lord of all below
Such troubles choose to know
As none of all his subjects undergo?

Hark, hark, the waters fall, fall, fall,
And with a murmuring sound
Dash, dash upon the ground,
To gentle slumbers call.

Dryden's masterly handling of the heroic couplet is seen to the greatest advantage in his satirical and controversial verse. *MacFlecknoe*, the fore-runner of Pope's *Dunciad*, was circulating in manuscript as early as 1678, though not published until 1782. A lampoon on the poetaster Thomas Shadwell, who is presented as the true heir to Richard Flecknoe, a particularly ungifted Irish rhymer, it ridicules its victim by describing him and his pre-posterous literary works in terms of mock-heroic dignity. Flecknoe bestows his crown on the man who most resembles him:

> Shadwell alone my perfect image bears,
> Mature in dullness from his tender years:
> Shadwell alone, of all my sons, is he
> Who stands confirmed in full stupidity.
> The rest to some faint meaning make pretense,
> But Shadwell never deviates into sense.
> Some beams of wit on other souls may fall,
> Strike thro', and make a lucid interval;
> But Shadwell's genuine night admits no ray,
> His rising fogs prevail upon the day . . .

Absalom and Achitophel, which may perhaps have been written at the personal request of Charles II, has a considerably loftier subject. Using a framework of Biblical history, Dryden delivers a furious attack on the Whigs in general, and on Lord Shaftesbury in particular. But such is the poet's art that it tends to enlarge and exalt every personality it touches; so that Shaftesbury himself, 'the false Achitophel', arch-opponent of the Catholic court party and unscrupulous instigator of the London mob against their Papist fellow-citizens, becomes a tragic and impressive figure:

> Of these the false Achitophel was first;
> A name to all succeeding ages curst.
> For close designs, and crooked counsels fit;
> Sagacious, bold, and turbulent of wit:
> Restless, unfixt in principles and place;
> In power unpleas'd, impatient of disgrace.
> A fiery soul, which working out its way,
> Fretted the pigmy body to decay:
> And oe'r informed the tenement of clay.

The Duke of Buckingham, too, is immortalized by Dryden's treatment:

> A man so various, that he seemed to be
> Not one, but all mankind's epitome.
> Stiff in opinions, always in the wrong;
> Was everything by starts, and nothing long:
> But, in the course of one revolving moon,
> Was chemist, fiddler, statesman, and buffoon:
> Then all for women, painting, rhyming, drinking;
> Besides ten thousand freaks that died in thinking.

Religio Laici, or A Layman's Faith, though not the most stimulating of Dryden's poems, shows his remarkable gift of conducting an argument in verse. Here he dwells on the fallibility of human reason and asserts the necessity for revealed religion. The opening passage is particularly characteristic of the poet's weightiest and gravest style:

> Dim as the borrowed beams of moon and stars
> To lonely, weary, wandering travellers,
> Is Reason to the soul; and, as on high
> Those rolling fires discover but the sky,
> Not light us here, so Reason's glimmering ray
> Was lent, not to assure our doubtful way,
> But guide us upward to a better day.
> And as those nightly tapers disappear,
> When day's bright lord ascends our hemisphere;
> So pale grows Reason at Religion's sight;
> So dies, and so dissolves in supernatural light.

During his later years, once he had been deprived of his pension and state appointments, Dryden provided for himself by producing numerous translations, which included a rendering of Virgil's *Aeneid.* These works are somewhat uneven; but they show no sign of mental lassitude; and it was now that he wrote some admirable short poems, among them the ode 'To the Pious Memory of the Accomplished Young Lady, Mrs Anne Killigrew' (1686), and 'Alexander's Feast; or The Power of Musique' (1697). Dr Johnson considered that the first stanza of the former poem marked the highest point in English lyric poetry.

Today Dryden is generally regarded as one of the master-poets of the English language. At the same time, he was a master of prose, and the founder of modern English literary criticism. He wrote for the ordinary reader; his essays, said Johnson, were 'the criticism of a poet; not a dull collection of theorems, nor a rude detection of faults . . . but a gay and vigorous dissertation, where delight is mingled with instruction, and where the author proves his right of judgement, by his power of performance'. His prose is clear, direct and flexible, an ideal instrument for exposition and discussion; witness this extract from his preface to the *Fables,* written in 1700, the year he died:

'Tis with a poet, as with a man who designs to build, and is very exact, as he supposes, in casting up the cost beforehand; but generally speaking he is mistaken in his account, and reckons short of the expense he first intended. He alters his mind as the work proceeds, and will have this or that convenience more, of which he had not thought when he began. So has it happened to me; I have built a house where I intended but a lodge; yet with better success than a certain nobleman, who, beginning with a dog-kennel, never lived to finish the palace he had contrived.

Dryden knew that he could not excel Shakespeare, though he sometimes criticised his methods. But he, too, was a 'myriad-minded' poet; and his handling of dramatic blank verse, as in these quotations from *All for Love*, would alone entitle him to a place among the greatest English writers:

ANTONY TO VENTIDIUS

When first I came to empire, I was borne
On tides of people, crowding to my triumphs;
The wish of nations, and the willing world
Received me as its pledge of future peace;
I was so great, so happy, so belov'd,
Fate could not ruin me; till I took pains
And work'd against my fortune, chid her from me,
And turn'd her loose; yet still she came again.
My careless days, and my luxurious nights,
At length have wearied her, and now she's gone
Gone, gone, divorced for ever.

ANTONY TO CLEOPATRA

Think we have had a clear and glorious day;
And Heav'n did kindly to delay the storm
Just till our close of ev'ning. Ten years' loves
And not a moment lost, but all improv'd
To th'utmost joys: what ages have we liv'd!
And now to die each other's; and, so dying,
While hand in hand we walk in groves below,
Whole troops of lovers' ghosts shall flock about us,
And all the train be ours.

6

The Eighteenth Century

When the elderly <u>Samuel Johnson</u> and his distinguished circle
looked back upon the Age of Anne, they were frequently inclined
to do so in a somewhat condescending spirit. Though they loved
and reverenced the series of great writers – <u>Pope, Swift</u> and
<u>Addison</u> – who had flourished before 1750, they believed that,
since those far-off days English civilization as a whole had been
steadily progressing, and that there was now a close resemblance
between modern London and Rome at the time of the Antonine
emperors.

It was a supremely self-confident age; the present period,
remarked Lord Chesterfield, had 'the honour and pleasure of
being very well with me'; while Horace Walpole asserted that the
reign of George III was an epoch 'in which all arts, all sciences are
encouraged and rewarded'. This feeling of temperate optimism
had a strong effect upon the art of literature. Prose-writers and
poets alike affected an air of classic dignity and harmonious
urbanity, and were at pains to eschew the extravagant whims of
their seventeenth-century predecessors. The second half of this
so-called Augustan Age saw the rise of several brilliantly polished
stylists – David Hume, who sought to deliver his philosophic
opinions with an 'Elegance and Neatness' that would command
'the Attention of the World'; his great adversary, Samuel Johnson,
who invented the peculiarly resounding style that Macaulay nicknamed 'Johnsonese'; and Edward Gibbon, whose 'solemn sneer',
according to *Childe Harold*, would sap the massive foundations of
a no less solemn faith.

Such was the classic facade of <u>English</u> eighteenth-century
literature. But it concealed some very different and much more
irrational tendencies. <u>Pope</u> himself, for a pillar of classicism, had
strikingly <u>Romantic tastes</u> – among them, a passionate devotion
to the architecture of the <u>Middle Ages;</u> and in 1717 he published
his two celebrated 'Gothick' poems, 'Eloisa to Abelard' and his
'Elegy to the Memory of an Unfortunate Lady', which show
his Romantic preoccupation with the darkest and most 'horrid'
sides of Nature. Although the eighteenth century, both English
and French, has been loosely called the 'The Age of Reason', it
was often credulous and superstitious; and in 1760, when James

Macpherson published his *Fragments of Ancient Poetry* and two extensive poems, alleged to be the work of a Gaelic bard named Ossian, despite the protests raised by Johnson and Hume they were widely read and loudly applauded as genuine specimens of antique verse. One of the poets they afterwards fascinated was the youthful William Blake, who had been born in 1757. Meanwhile the cult of sensibility – and the vogue of its exemplar, 'the Man of Feeling' – had begun to sweep across Europe. The adjective 'sentimental' was becoming popular before the middle of the century; and Lawrence Sterne was presently instructing his readers how they should adopt the sentimental mode. 'Grand', 'horrid', 'terrible', 'sublime' were now the epithets that poets applied to any impressive landscape. The Romantic Revolution that threw up Wordsworth and Coleridge was already under way. *Lyrical Ballads*, harbinger of the new movement, appeared in 1798.

Alexander Pope

ALEXANDER POPE (1688–1744) suffered throughout his life from two grievous disabilities, one social and the other physical. The only son of a London linen merchant, he had been born a Catholic, which subjected him to many irritating restrictions and exposed him to much public spite; and, at the age of twelve, he contracted a tubercular infection of the vertebrae that stunted his growth and left him a partially crippled invalid. As an adult, without his periwig and high heels, Pope measured only four foot six inches. He possessed, however, an indomitable spirit and an abundant flow of nervous energy; and, before he was eighteen, when the famous London publisher, Jacob Tonson, expressed an interest in his early pastoral poems, he was already building up a reputation. About that same time, he had become the disciple and friend of the veteran dramatist, William Wycherley, and had made the acquaintance of Congreve, Swift and the literary statesman, Bolingbroke, who consented to read and approve his manuscripts, and assured him of his place among the English poets. His *Pastorals* were published in 1709; and, in 1711, he printed his *Essay on Criticism*, inspired by Boileau's *L'Art Poétique*, a bold attempt to lay down a system of critical rules, written, he claimed, some three years earlier. From Boileau's *Le Lutrin* he also took some hints for his exquisite mock-heroic poem, *The Rape of the Lock*, which appeared in 1712. Then, in 1713, he produced *Windsor Forest*, an imaginative evocation, not unlike Denham's *Cooper's Hill*, of the landscape surrounding his parents' house at Binfield. In 1717, having just celebrated his twenty-ninth birthday, he felt sufficiently well-established to issue his collected *Works*.

A long pause now interrupted his progress as an imaginative literary artist. In 1715 he had undertaken to translate the Iliad into English verse; and once he had completed his rendering of the

Iliad, with the help of two moderately able assistants he embarked upon the *Odyssey*, which occupied him until 1726. His translations involved much arduous labour; and his version of the *Odyssey* provoked many savage criticisms. But together they brought him a modest fortune that enabled him to return to more creative forms of writing. During the second period of his literary life, he was often inclined to look down upon the products of his youth:

> Soft were my Numbers, who could take offence
> While pure Description held the place of Sense?

He now regarded himself as primarily a satirist and a moralist. Since 1711, when a reference in his *Essay on Criticism* had angered the veteran critic, John Dennis, he had been engaged in a series of furious controversies, and his opponents spared neither the alleged shortcoming of his scholarship nor his physical imperfections. Pope was a morbidly sensitive man, who, if he were sufficiently roused, never hesitated to display a strain of almost paranoiac fury; and *The Dunciad*, of which the original version appeared anonymously in 1728, and the complete work, with a different villain and a number of splendid additions, in 1743, is a tremendous attack on the Dunces, the huge tribe of vulgar and conceited scribblers that infested literary London. His *Moral Essays* and *Imitations of Horace*, published between 1731 and 1738, covered a far wider and more fruitful field, being intended to embody both his philosophy of human existence and his attitude towards such contemporary questions as the uses and abuses of modern taste and the proper use of riches. His *Essay on Man*, meant to constitute an introduction to the magnum opus, of which the *Moral Essays* formed a part, was written in 1733 and 1734.

Meanwhile, in 1718, Pope had acquired the villa at Twickenham, where, gardening and building, surrounded by friends and admirers, he was to pass the remainder of his life and spend his happiest and calmest days. But even here he had many painful distractions; and among the worst was his abortive love-affair with a wayward woman of fashion, Lady Mary Wortley Montagu, whom he had long adored and pursued, but who at length became a bitter enemy. A man of passionately sensuous nature, Pope aspired to the commonplace human happiness that had always been denied him. During his later years, however, he was consoled by the faithful attachment, which no doubt was very largely platonic, of his old friend Martha Blount. His life he described as 'a long disease'. Only his immense courage and fund of nervous energy, coupled with an invincible sense of his own genius, enabled him to reach the age of fifty-six.

Pope was one of those poets who dominate a whole period. This he did not only by his extraordinary powers of invention, but by his technical mastery of the forms in which he worked. John Dryden, an earlier master of words, had died when Pope was

Alexander Pope as a young man: portrait by C. Jervas *c.*1715. The figure behind is thought to represent his devoted companion, Martha Blount.

twelve years old. He had had no worthy successors until Pope published his *Essay on Criticism* and, taking the English heroic couplet, began to confer on it a new, more powerful shape. Pope showed that the couplet, if rightly employed, was capable of developing an extraordinarily rich and various music. He was a classicist and a follower of the Palladian School, then headed by Lord Burlington and Burlington's chief employee, William Kent. Yet, simultaneously, he was devoted to medieval architecture, and might possibly be described as the first of the English Romantic poets; for among the collected *Works* that he issued in 1717 are two memorable 'Gothick' poems, 'Eloisa to Abelard' and his 'Elegy to the Memory of an Unfortunate Lady' that, with their air

(*Opposite*) Pope in his Grotto at Twickenham: a sketch by Lady Burlington.

(*Left*) Burlington House, Piccadilly; a citadel of Palladian taste; from a mid-nineteenth-century engraving.

of mystery, melancholy and brooding 'horror', anticipate the spirit of late eighteenth and early nineteenth-century verse.

More typical of this period is the brilliant *Rape of the Lock*, which Johnson regarded as 'the most airy, the most ingenious, and the most delightful' of all the author's compositions. A *jeu d'esprit* intended to reconcile two warring Catholic families, the Petres and the Fermors, who had fallen out when young Lord Petre had secretly snipped off a lock of Miss Arabella Fermor's hair, it soon transcends its immediately frivolous purpose, and soars high into the heavens of lyrical poetry. Seldom has so light a poem possessed so much poetic substance, and so adroitly combined satire, wit and sense with fantastic invention and enchanting social fun.

Later, when he decided to 'moralize his song' and become a scourge of modern sinners, Pope, though a great deal less light-hearted, was no less a literary stylist. *The Dunciad* lacks a genuine theme. Although Pope informed Swift that it was his *chef d'oeuvre*, and had cost him 'as much pains as anything I ever wrote', it is a misbegotten masterpiece. 'Vulgarity, stupidity, futility (suggests a recent biographer) are not themselves enlivening subjects;

Ariel whispers in Belinda's ear; illustration to *The Rape of the Lock*, revised version of 1714; engraving after Du Guernier.

and the poet who devotes over a thousand lines to depicting Dullness . . . evidently runs a grave risk'; while the fact that he changed the identity of his chief villain – in 1743 he substituted Colley Cibber for his previous butt, the odious bookman Lewis Theobald – shows that his satirical motives were not entirely straightforward. What redeem the poem are its fine poetic gusto and the profusion of splendid images with which Pope unfolds his comminatory tale. The effect of the *Moral Essays* is far more concentrated; and here, in his 'Epistle to Dr Arbuthnot' and in his 'Characters of Women', otherwise entitled 'Epistle to a Lady', his adult genius reaches its greatest heights. Less satisfying is his famous *Essay on Man* (1733–44). Bolingbroke seems to have supplied a scheme, which his friend proceeded to versify. But whereas 'the art of Milton works from within (writes a Victorian critic) fusing all the materials into one solid mass', Pope 'begins by elaborating the parts and afterwards endeavours to fit them together by plastering over the interstices'. Pope's attempts to solve the problem of human existence, which he first describes as 'a mighty maze of paths without a plan' – and then re-wrote as 'a mighty maze but not without a plan' – since he was neither a philosopher nor a deep religious thinker, fall a little flat.

Pope often liked to believe that he was primarily a moralist. In fact, he remained essentially an artist, whose love of his art was perhaps even more important to him than his sense of moral right and wrong. Few English poets have been so attached to words, or have harmonised their verse with greater care and skill. Pope's imagery reflects his temperament. Since he was himself a very small man, he was at once attracted by anything small, delicate and beautifully organized, from the spider's web –

> The spider's touch, how exquisitely fine!
> Feels at each thread, and lives along the line . . .
> *(An Essay on Man I)*

to the little golden coins, described in an essay by Addison, that have survived some of the far more massive memorials of the vanished Roman Empire:

> Ambition sigh'd; She found it vain to trust
> The faithless Column and the crumbling Bust . . .
> Convinc'd, she now contracts her vast design,
> And all her Triumphs shrink into a Coin:
> A narrower orb each crowded conquest keeps,
> Beneath her palm here sad Judaea weeps . . .
> A small Euphrates thro' the piece is rolled,
> And little Eagles wave their wings in gold.
> *(Moral Essays V)*

Pope in later life: pencil-drawing by Jonathan Richardson, 1737.

Physical suffering had sharpened his sensitiveness both to pleasure and to pain; and 'His most sensuous descriptive poetry', writes a modern critic, 'is seldom independent of physical irritation. It is the *suffering* eye which stings Pope into his most elaborate luxuriance of vision'. Thus, in *The Rape of the Lock*, Ariel describes the inferno (made up of the apparatus of Belinda's dressing-table) that awaits the disobedient sylph:

> Whatever Spirit, careless of his Charge,
> His Post neglects, or leaves the Fair at large,
> Shall fear sharp Vengeance soon o'ertake his Sins,
> Be stopt in *Vials*, or transfixt with *Pins*;
> Or plung'd in Lakes of bitter *Washes* lie,
> Or wedg'd whole ages in a *Bodkin's* eye
> *Gums* and *Pomatums* shall his Flight restrain,

While clog'd he beats his silken Wings in vain;
Or Alom-*Stypticks* with contracting Power
Shrink his thin Essence like a rivell'd Flower.

With such poetic wealth at hand, Pope's genius is almost as difficult as Shakespeare's to illustrate by brief quotations. An extract from his 'Epistle to a Lady', however, one of the finest of his *Moray Essays*, shows not only his imaginative strength, but his gifts of satirical analysis and dramatic portraiture:

Flavia's a wit, has too much sense to pray;
To toast our wants and wishes is her way;
Nor asks of God, but of her stars, to give
The mighty blessing, 'while we live, to live' . . .
Wise wretch! with pleasures too refin'd to please;
With too much spirit to be e'er at ease;
With too much quickness ever to be taught;
With too much thinking to have common thought:
You purchase pain with all that joy can give,
And die of nothing but a rage to live . . .

Pleasures the sex, as children birds, pursue,
Still out of reach, yet never out of view;
Sure, if they catch, to spoil the toy at most,
To covet flying, and regret when lost.
At last, to follies youth could scarce defend,
'Tis half their age's prudence to pretend:
Asham'd to own they gave delight before,
Reduc'd to feign it, when they give no more,
As hags hold sabbaths less for joy than spite,
So these their merry, miserable night:
Still round and round the ghosts of beauty glide,
And haunt the places where their honour died.

Jonathan Swift: bust by
L. F. Roubiliac.

Swift and the Age of Anne

JONATHAN SWIFT (1667–1745), though born in Dublin, was the child of English parents. From a school at Kilkenny, where he met William Congreve, he went to Trinity College, Dublin; but his academic career was apparently undistinguished; and he obtained a degree only by 'special grace'. His mother, who had lost her husband some while before her son's birth, now procured him a post as secretary to a family connection, Sir William Temple; and at Moor Park, Surrey, Sir William's country house, which included a splendid library, he first became a scholar and a poet. There, too, he contracted Menière's disease, the affliction that would torment him all his life, and encountered Esther Johnson, the illegitimate child of Sir William's housekeeper, whom he afterwards adopted as a beloved friend and pupil. Having left Moor Park, Swift was ordained in 1695 and appointed to a humble Irish living. A year later, Temple called him back; but on

COOKE'S EDITION OF SELECT NOVELS.

TALE OF A TUB,

WRITTEN FOR THE UNIVERSAL
IMPROVEMENT OF MANKIND.

Diu multumque desideratum.

To which are added,

AN ACCOUNT OF A BATTLE
BETWEEN THE
ANCIENT AND MODERN BOOKS.

In St. James's Library.

And a Discourse, concerning the Mechanical

OPERATIONS OF THE SPIRIT.

With the Author's Apology, and Explanatory Notes,

BY W. WOTTON, B.D. AND OTHERS.

Basima eacabasa canaa Irraurista, diarba da caeoraba fobor camelanthi.
Iren. l. i. c. 18.

———— Invatque novos decerpere flores,
Insignemque meo capiti petere Inde coronam,
Unde prius nulli velarunt tempora musae.
Lucret.

Cooke's Edition.

EMBELLISHED WITH SUPERB ENGRAVINGS.

LONDON:
Printed for C. COOKE, No. 17, Paternoster-Row,
And sold by all the Booksellers in
Great-Britain.

TALE OF A TUB.
The arrogance of Peter, in assuming the triple crown
and presenting his foot as an object of salutation.
Vide sect. li. *Page 235.*

his employer's death in 1699 he once more set sail for Ireland as domestic chaplain to a high official. In 1703 his old Dublin college made him Doctor of Divinity, and he was able to revisit London. With him he brought the manuscript of *The Tale of a Tub,* which appeared in 1704, accompanied by *The Battle of the Books.* They established his position as a modern wit; and, through Congreve, he met Steele and Addison. About this time he persuaded Esther Johnson to join him at his Irish place of exile; and she remained his constant companion until she died, though they never lived beneath the same roof. It has been suggested that they may have secretly wed; but there is no solid evidence to support this theory.

Swift paid further long visits to London in 1707 and 1710. It was on the earlier occasion that he drifted into a strange emotional entanglement with Hester (or Esther) Vanhomrigh, the heroine of his enigmatic poem *Cadenus and Vanessa,* a clever, attractive, unbalanced young woman, whose passion for him – which she did not disguise – he seems to have encouraged but felt that he could not return. On his second visit, he changed political parties. Disgusted with the Whigs, who, he believed, had neglected both his

Frontispiece to *Tale of a Tub*; edition of 1798.

own claims to preferment and the welfare of the Irish Church, he allowed Robert Harley, the future Lord Oxford, to enlist his services as a Tory controversialist. Simultaneously, he moved in the world of literature, befriended Pope and Gay, and became one of the founder members of the burlesque 'Scriblerus Club', designed to combat the menacing spread of vulgar pedantry and false taste. He had always hoped that the government would recognize his merits by the grant of an English bishopric or, at least, a deanery. They failed to do so; and the only reward he received was the deanery of St Patrick's, Dublin. During his stay in England, he kept a regular diary for the benefit of Esther Johnson, whom he had left behind across the Irish Channel; and this vivid chronicle of his daily thoughts and feelings, published posthumously as his *Journal to Stella*, shows the fierce and often savage Dean at his tenderest and most playful.

The collapse of the Tory ministry in 1714 obliged him to fall back on Ireland, a country he had never loved; but although he despised the Irish, he generously championed their cause; and the publication of his *Drapier's Letters* in 1724 – a stern protest against the debasement of the Irish coinage – raised him to the rank of national champion. In 1726 he rejoined his London friends, bearing the manuscript of *Gulliver's Travels*, a masterpiece intended to 'vex the world rather than divert it', which came out that same year; and in 1727 he visited London for the last time. In 1728 Esther Johnson died; and Swift's agony is said to have been so great that he could not bring himself to see her while she lay dying or to attend her funeral service. But he paid her a heart-felt tribute. 'With all the softness of temper,' he wrote, 'that became a lady she had the personal courage of a hero.'

Swift lived on until October 1745, continuing to write – his greatest short satire, his ferocious *Modest Proposal* appeared in 1729 – but growing, as the years went by, increasingly wretched and despondent. Among the symptoms of Menière's disease are dizziness, giddiness and nausea; and he now developed a tumour of the brain that gradually unhinged his reason. In 1742 he was declared insane; and before he died he had become an embittered recluse, whose conversation had degenerated into 'mere incessant strains of obscenity and swearing'. He was buried beside Esther in St Patrick's Cathedral, where, as he announced in his own epitaph, *saeva indignatio ulterius cor lacerare nequit* (fierce indignation can no longer lacerate the heart).

Swift's genius has often been misunderstood; and the morbid aspect of his nature is frequently exaggerated. He loved his friends, who returned his deep affection, and was devoted to the patient and gentle Stella, though their odd relationship was almost certainly platonic. It seems clear that, for some unexplained reason, his sexual instincts were inhibited; his attitude towards the women who loved him was that of a master to a favourite pupil.

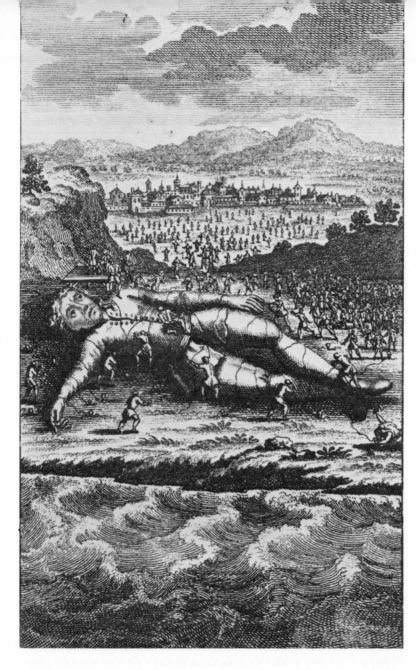

Gulliver in Lilliput; from
the French edition of
1727.

From a secret sense of frustration may have sprung the furious
energy with which he castigated human vices. *The Tale of a Tub*,
his earliest published satire, is an attack on the divisions of the
Christian Church, with subsidiary attacks on the impudent pride
of modern scholars and enthusiasts. *Gulliver's Travels* has a considerably wider scope. When first published, it was presented as a
genuine travel-book. It is, in fact, a devastating parody of the
optimistic travel-tale that, like *Robinson Crusoe*, shows an intrepid
adventurer overcoming every obstacle. Swift sets out to demolish
human pride. Gulliver's first landfall is on the island of Lilliput,

whose tiny inhabitants illustrate all the worst aspects of contemporary society. Much of the satire, being largely topical, may escape a modern reader; but when Gulliver reaches Brobdingnag, the land of the giants, the satirist's range is far less limited. Questioned by the king, a shrewd and upright sovereign, Gulliver does his best to explain and justify the whole system of European government:

I remember very well, in a discourse one day with the King, when I happened to say there were several thousand books among us written upon the art of government, it gave him (directly contrary to my intention) a very mean opinion of our understandings. He professed both to abominate and despise all mystery, refinement, and intrigue, either in a prince or a minister. He could not tell what I meant by secrets of state, where an enemy or some rival nation were not in the case. He confined the knowledge of governing within very narrow bounds; to common sense and reason, to justice and lenity, to the speedy determination of civil and criminal causes; with some other obvious topics, which are not worth considering. And he gave it for his opinion, that whoever could make two ears of corn or two blades of grass grow upon a spot of ground where only one grew before, would deserve better of mankind, and do more essential service to his country, than the whole race of politicians put together.

The gigantic king is completely unimpressed:

I cannot but conclude [he remarks] the bulk of your natives to be the most pernicious race of little odious vermin that nature ever suffered to crawl upon the surface of the earth.

The third voyage, his description of the learned citizens of Laputa, is probably the least satisfying, for the point of the satire is somewhat less sharply defined. It is in his account of Gulliver's fourth voyage that Swift makes his most uncompromising attack on human civilization. The first creatures that Gulliver encounters are the Yahoos, a savage and degenerate species of man. Gulliver, who does not at once recognize their kinship, recoils in horror from these 'abominable animals'. The Yahoos, however, are the subjects of the Houyhnhnms, a race of highly intelligent horses who live according to the laws of 'reason and nature'. Gulliver is gradually forced to acknowledge that mankind, as he knows it in Europe, is nearer to the Yahoos than to their equine masters; and, when he returns home, he finds that he prefers the company of his horse to the kind attentions of his family.

Swift's violent attacks on human pride were inspired not so much by his personal misanthropy as by his religious conviction that Man was a fallen being. His dismisses the idea that men are naturally good, and shows little pity for the weak and abject:

Among the number of those who beg in our streets, [he writes] or are half starved at home, or languish in prison for debt, there is hardly one in a hundred who doth not owe his misfortune to his own laziness or drunkenness, or worse vices.

Swift wrote several pamphlets suggesting to the Irish people how they might undertake their own improvement. He was ignored, and thereupon he presented his *Modest Proposal for Preventing the Children of Poor People in Ireland from being a Burden to their Parents or Country; and for making them beneficial to the Publick*. Here he assumes the character of a modern economist, who thinks in purely economic terms. After a grim assessment of the state of the Irish poor, he outlines a horrid scheme to make some practical use of their superfluous children:

I have been assured by a very knowing American of my acquaintance in London, that a young healthy child well nursed is at a year old a most delicious, nourishing, and wholesome food, whether stewed, roasted, baked, or boiled; and I make no doubt that it will equally serve in a fricassee or ragout.

Since the poor are content to live like beasts, it is as beasts they should be treated. The impersonal, logical tone is maintained throughout; and some of his readers, who missed the irony, decided that Swift must be insane. In fact, his 'savage indignation' does not spare the shrewd economist. But his chief target is the Irish people themselves, whose neglect of reason, decency and Christian precepts had reduced them to their current plight.

Swift was also a considerable poet; and besides his so-called 'obscene' poems which ridicule the romantic view of love – for Swift, most women were 'beasts in petticoats' – he wrote many verses of a far less abrasive kind, among the best being his lightly satirical 'Verses on the Death of Dr Swift':

> My female friends, whose tender hearts
> Have better learned to act their parts,
> Receive the news in doleful dumps:
> 'The Dean is dead *(and what is trumps?)*'
> 'Six deans, they say, must bear the pall
> *(I wish I knew what King to call)*'
> 'Madam, your husband will attend
> The funeral of so good a friend?'
> 'No, Madam, 'tis a shocking sight,
> And he's engaged tomorrow night! . . .
> He loved the Dean *(I led a heart)*
> But dearest friends they say must part.
> His time was come, he ran his race.
> We hope he's in a better place . . .'

JOSEPH ADDISON (1672–1719), the son of a clergyman, was born near Amesbury in Wiltshire. From Charterhouse he went up to Queen's College, Oxford, and was later awarded a fellowship at Magdalen, which he held until 1711. Meanwhile a government pension of £300 per annum – which he had obtained through the influence of his Whig friend, Charles Montague – enabled him to spend four years travelling in France, Germany, and Italy, that he might qualify himself for the diplomatic service. On his return, he achieved brief fame with a poem, *The Campaign*, celebrating Marlborough's victory at Blenheim. It earned him a government sinecure in the Excise; and he soon received a series of far more important offices – as Under-Secretary of State from 1706–8, Secretary to Lord Halifax in 1708, and Chief Secretary in Ireland to Lord Wharton, the Lord Lieutenant. He was also a Whig Member of Parliament for two constituencies from 1708 to 1719, though there is no record of his ever having made a parliamentary speech.

On the fall of the Whig government in 1711, Addison lost his pension, and began to turn to writing. He had already attracted attention as the founder of the *Whig Examiner*, and was a friend of Jonathan Swift and Richard Steele. The latter, who had launched the *Tatler* in 1709, now invited Addison to contribute to his thrice-weekly periodical; and in 1711 Addison and Steele founded the *Spectator*, which ran daily for twenty-one months. Of the 555 essays it published, 274 were written by Addison, including nearly all those on the subject of 'Sir Roger de Coverley'. The paper was a great success, its avowed purpose being to enliven morality with wit, and to temper wit with moral sentiment. The *Spectator* established the role of the magazine as a vehicle for social criticism. In 1713 Addison's tragedy *Cato* was applauded upon the London stage – the play was thought to have a covert political message, and to strike a poetic blow for freedom; but its popularity did not prove lasting. When the Whigs regained power, Addison returned to politics. He was made Secretary to the Lords Justices, Chief Secretary for Ireland again, and a Secretary of State in Lord Sunderland's government. This was the period of his greatest wealth and fame; but it was not a happy one. His health had been failing for some time; and in 1718 he was obliged to give up all his offices. Two years earlier, he had married the Dowager Countess of Warwick, an alliance that, owing to his wife's jealous and possessive nature, seems to have caused him much discomfort; and towards the end of his life he quarrelled with his old friend Steele. They were still unreconciled when Addison died, of asthma and dropsy, on 17 June 1719.

Addison mastered the art of essay-writing in his contributions to the *Tatler*, and perfected it through the more congenial medium of the *Spectator*. The *Tatler* had been a development of the seventeenth-century news sheets – a mixture of gossip, news, and literary essays. The *Spectator*, on the other hand, was concerned with manners and morals, and had a deliberately educational aim. Addison has been aptly described as a lay-preacher, and himself regarded his rôle as primarily instructive:

It was said of Socrates, that he brought philosophy down from heaven, to inhabit among men; and I shall be ambitious to have it said of me, that I have brought philosophy out of closets and libraries, schools and

colleges, to dwell in clubs and assemblies, at tea-tables and in coffee-houses.

I would therefore in a very particular manner recommend these my speculations to all well-regulated families that set apart an hour in every morning for tea and bread and butter; and would earnestly advise them for their good to order this paper to be punctually served up, and to be looked upon as part of the tea-equipage.

This careful lightness of tone is typically Addisonian. He is anxious to avoid any suspicion of overwhelming seriousness. Addison's essays have a remarkably wide range – from ladies' dresses to criticisms of Milton's verse. Common to all the subjects is the writer's literary style – easy and conversational, yet precise and lucid. Johnson saw it as 'the model of the middle style', being 'familiar but not coarse, and elegant but not ostentatious'.

The most enduring creation in the pages of the *Spectator* was the Club to which Mr Spectator belongs, and whose members he reports on. Sir Roger de Coverley, the old-fashioned squire, is a finely comic character:

As Sir Roger is landlord to the whole congregation, he keeps them in very good order, and will suffer nobody to sleep in it besides himself; for if by chance he has been surprised into a short nap at sermon, upon

(*Above left*) Joseph Addison; portrait by Kneller.

'Blest with each Talent and each Art to please,
And born to write, converse and live with ease . . .'

(*Above right*) 'Mrs Hartley in the character of Marcia'; from Addison's tragedy, *Cato*.

recovering out of it he stands up and looks about him, and if he sees anybody else nodding, either wakes them himself, or sends his servant to them.

Sir Roger is a charming anachronism, the point being that he is a typical Tory, harmless and good-natured, but always a little absurd; whereas his opponent at the Club, Sir Andrew Freeport, a Whig merchant 'of indefatigable industry, strong reason, and great experience', is a forward-looking man, an exact personification of the *Spectator*'s editorial policy. Many of Addison's essays are slight enough; as a rule he exerted more influence on social customs than on the art of literature. There are some important exceptions: he praised the old English ballads, notably 'Chevy Chase', at a time when they were considered merely barbarous; and he wrote a series of papers describing 'The Pleasures of the Imagination', that applied Locke's psychological theories to aesthetics.

Personally, Addison was a grave and dignified figure, very unlike the riotous and rollicking Steele. Pope, who had once had a high regard for him, afterwards made him the subject of a brilliantly spiteful sketch, portraying the essayist seated in solemn state among his assembled friends and toadies. The 'Epistle to Dr Arbuthnot' first dismisses the tribe of venal scribblers, but then turns its attention to a vastly more important subject:

> Peace to all such! but were there One whose fires
> True genius kindles, and fair Fame inspires;
> Blest with each Talent and each Art to please,
> And born to write, converse, and live with ease:
> Shou'd such a man, too fond to rule alone,
> Bear, like the *Turk*, no brother near the throne,
> View him with scornful, yet with jealous eyes,
> And hate for Arts that caused himself to rise;
> Damn with faint praise, assent with civil jeer,
> And without sneering, teach the rest to sneer;
> Willing to wound, yet afraid to strike,
> Just hint a fault, and hesitate dislike . . .
> Who but must laugh, if such a man there be?
> Who would not weep, if *Atticus* were he!

SIR RICHARD STEELE (1672–1729) was born in Dublin, the son of an English father and an Irish mother. He was sent to Charterhouse School in 1684, and there he presently met Addison. In 1689 he entered Christ Church College, Oxford, and then transferred to Merton College, but having gone down without a degree, he enlisted in the Horse Guards. He remained in the army for ten years, eventually rising to the rank of captain. As a soldier, he was known for his wild living – he fought two duels, once nearly killing his opponent; and his acquaintances were much amused when, in 1701, he published a moral treatise, *The Christian Hero*, which he was said to have composed on night-duty. During his literary

(*Opposite*) Frontispiece to *The Tatler* of 1710–11.

Sir Richard Steele:
portrait by Jonathan
Richardson, 1712.

apprenticeship Steele produced a number of sentimental comedies; but his connection with modern journalism began in 1707.
He was then appointed to a minor official post, that of Gazetteer.
It involved the editing of official news; and the experience
prompted him to launch a general review of current news and
literature. His object, when he founded the *Tatler* on 12 April
1709, was primarily to make money; and the *Tatler* was followed
by the *Spectator*, run with Addison's assistance. After its death, he
became a politician, but was expelled from the House of Commons for uttering seditious libels. His later periodicals, the
Guardian and *The Englishman*, were more political than literary.
He championed the Whig cause, was rewarded with various
appointments, and in 1715 received a knighthood. Either their
political differences, or his old friend's unwise marriage at length
divided him from Addison; and, in 1719, they continued to abuse
one another through the columns of two short-lived papers, the
Old Whig and the *Plebeian*. In 1722 Steele produced his famous
sentimental comedy, *The Conscious Lovers*. He never fully reformed;
even as an ageing man, he was alternately riotous and repentant,
and often, we are told, 'a little in drink'. Unlike the austere
Addison, he found it impossible to live up to his own lofty ideals,
and he remained a reckless spender. Finally, his debts obliged him
to leave London, and he died in exile at Carmarthen.

Although the *Tatler* owed something to Swift's *Bickerstaff Papers*,
Steele must take credit for inventing the English periodical essay.
His aim was to provide a literary echo of the conversation that he
enjoyed in the London coffee-houses; whence he drew the
'accounts of gallantry, pleasure, and entertainment' with which
he set out to amuse his readers. The *Tatler* contains most of his
best work, including the gently pathetic account of his father's
early death:

The first sense of sorrow I ever knew was upon the death of my father, at
which time I was not quite five years of age; but was rather amazed at
what all the house meant, than possessed with a real understanding why
nobody was willing to play with me. I remember I went into the room
where his body lay, and my mother sat weeping alone by it. I had my
battledore in my hand, and fell a-beating the coffin, and calling Papa;
for, I knew not how, I had some slight idea he was locked up there. My
mother catched me in her arms, and, transported beyond all patience of
the silent grief she was before in, she almost smothered me in her embraces and told me in a flood of tears, 'Papa could not hear me, and
would play with me no more, for they were going to put him under
ground, whence he would never come to us again'.

Steele's *Spectator* essays are less accomplished than Addison's,
and more interesting from an historical than from a literary point
of view. To his contemporaries, he was a reformer who had
initiated great social changes. ''Tis incredible,' wrote Gay in 1712,
'to conceive what effect his Writings have had on the Town; How

many thousand follies they have either quite banish'd or given a very great check to . . .'.

The Birth of the Modern Novel

DANIEL DEFOE (1660–1731) was the son of James Foe, a London butcher, and apparently changed his name by the addition of the first syllable to give it a more aristocratic ring. The family were Presbyterians, and Defoe attended a famous dissenting school at Stoke Newington. After school, he went into business; and when he married in 1684, he was making hosiery. In 1685 he joined Monmouth's rebellion, and in 1688 was a member of the volunteer regiment that acted as escort to the newly arrived King William III. He published a verse satire in 1691, but any further literary ambitions were suppressed by the failure of his business next year, when he went bankrupt to the extent of £17,000. Having managed to avoid a debtors' prison, he became secretary and afterwards manager of a tile factory near Tilbury.

In 1701 he published another verse satire, *The True-Born Englishman*, a defence of the Dutch King William, which proved enormously successful. He followed it with a satire that misfired, *The Shortest Way with Dissenters*. Here Defoe, impersonating a High Anglican Tory, proposed the systematic persecution of dissenting sects. The pamphlet was taken seriously; and though a number of churchmen applauded it, the fraud was eventually discovered, and a warrant was issued for Defoe's arrest. Apprehended and charged with issuing a seditious libel, he was condemned to stand three times in the pillory. The warrant gives a vivid description of his personal appearance, the only description that we have – middle-sized, lean, hair and complexion brown, hooked nose, sharp chin, grey eyes, a large mole near the mouth. He then served seven months in Newgate; and once released, he became a government spy, working in Scotland against the Jacobites. When the Whig administration fell, Defoe did not hesitate to join the Tories. In 1704 he established the thrice-weekly *Review*, which he wrote himself and which marked the beginning of his enormous output of political journalism. He also worked as the subversive editor of a Jacobite paper *Mist's Journal*. Mist, who had found him out, was presently packed off to gaol; and Defoe thereupon adopted fiction as a convenient means of making money. Between 1719 and 1724 he published no fewer than nine novels, including *Robinson Crusoe* in 1719 and *Moll Flanders* in 1722. The success of these works enabled him for a time to live well; but soon his position was again threatened. In 1729 he left the house that he had built at Stoke Newington, and fled to London, a lonely and hunted man. His last works were published under an assumed name. He died of a stroke in Ropemaker's Alley, Moorfields, on 26 April 1731.

Daniel Defoe, business-man, political agent, journalist, pamphleteer, and story-teller.

Friday rescued by Crusoe;
from an early French
translation, published in
Amsterdam.

Defoe's first novel, *The Life and Strange Surprising Adventures of Robinson Crusoe, of York, Mariner,* he wrote at the age of fifty-nine. Presented in the form of a genuine autobiographical novel, it was at first received as such. The most famous part of the novel is the account of Crusoe's twenty-four years' exile on a South American island off 'the Mouth of the Great River of Orinoco'. Defoe combines the main theme – the struggle of the individual against his environment – with an illustration of the elementary processes of political economy as he saw them. At one level, it is an adventure story; at another, a middle-class epic, a celebration of the rising capitalist spirit.

Robinson Crusoe is remarkable for its absorption in concrete realities, and for the verisimilitude of its lavish detail. Defoe derived some of his material from the narratives of shipwrecked sailors, among whom the most famous was Alexander Selkirk. In a moment of anger that he very soon regretted, Selkirk had had himself put ashore on a desert island. His strange experiences, however, had borne little resemblance to those of Crusoe. Distraught and terrified, he had spent eight months, before he began work, in a state of melancholy inertia; and, when he was rescued after four years, he had been so deeply affected by his solitude that one of his first actions on his return to England had been to build himself a cave. With his journalist's instinct, Defoe went in search of Selkirk, though it is doubtful if the two men ever met; and Crusoe's response to his isolation seems psychologically improbable. His firm rationality is never much disturbed. His island is not a wilderness; it suggests a rich estate that still awaits development; and the derelict vessel from which he has swum ashore continues to provide most of the basic necessities of a civilized existence. The healthy-minded Crusoe makes a highly abnormal situation appear comparatively normal. These problems and inconsistencies are swept aside by the author's literary method, which concentrates upon the hero's actions. The style, plain and even clumsy, reflects his attitude towards life:

. . . I made me a table and a chair, as I observ'd above, in the first place, and this I did out of the short pieces of boards that I brought on my raft from the ship. But when I had wrought out some boards, as above, I made large shelves of the breadth of a foot and a half, one over another, all along one side of my cave, to lay all my tools, nails, and iron-work, and in a word, to separate everything at large in their places, that I might come easily at them; I knock'd pieces into the wall of the rock to hang my guns and all things that would hang up. So that had my cave been to be seen, it look'd like a magazine of all necessary things, and I had everything so ready at my hand, that it was a great pleasure to me to see all my goods in such order, and especially to find my stock of all necessaries so great.

Defoe's sentences seem to have no structure other than that imposed by the events they record; and the narrator's characteristic mannerisms – 'as I observed above', 'as above', 'in a word' – coupled with his informal turns of phrase, do much to give his tale its air of sober authenticity.

Moll Flanders, Defoe's most interesting novel apart from *Robinson Crusoe*, is an account, written in the first person, of the heroine's career as a whore and petty thief. The style is plain and straightforward, with here and there, if the story demands it, a fine imaginative touch. Like Robinson Crusoe, Moll Flanders is a confirmed materialist, for whom her sexual attractions are merely a profitable source of income. Her sense of value is usually limited to the amount of money she contrives to earn; and her relationship with her fellow men and women is determined primarily by the degree of wealth they represent. She is continually counting, measuring, evaluating; and, when she looks back on her five marriages, she tots up the profit-and-loss account of each alliance. She is strangely unaffected by her life of crime, and distinguishes between herself, who, as she often reminds us, has been 'bred up tight and cleanly', and the other criminals she encounters, who are merely vicious reprobates. Even her whoring has an economic motive. Governed by a restless, amoral individualism, after one genuinely passionate episode that had disturbed her youth, she lives from adventure to adventure, and opportunity to opportunity. The flaw in Defoe's presentation of her character is that it has very little real depth. Everything happens to Moll, but nothing leaves a permanent scar. She is capable, she tells us, of loving and suffering; but, in later life, her desire for social respectability and financial security replaces every other passion.

The *Journal of the Plague Year*, which Defoe produced in 1722, is a masterpiece of historical reconstruction, and for many years was accepted as a first-hand record of the tragic events of 1665. Defoe uses a wide range of sources – childhood memories, the reminiscences of his parents, official records and statistics – and weaves them into a brilliantly convincing account of the effects of the Plague on London life. Defoe enjoyed reporting for its own sake. Though he was the first great English novelist, he seems to have retained a Puritan distrust of fiction, and to have determined that he would reduce all literature to the status of accurate reportage. The *Journal* is the most successful example of the kind of realism he had in mind.

(*Moll Flanders is tempted to commit murder*)
I went out now by daylight, and wandered about I knew not whither, and in search of I knew not what . . . Going through Aldersgate Street, there was a pretty child had been at a dancing-school, and was agoing home all alone . . . I talked to it, and it prattled to me, and I took it by the hand and led it along till I came to a paved alley that goes into Bartholomew Close, and I led it in there. The child said that was not its way home. I said, 'Yes, my dear, it is; I'll show you the way home.' The child had a little necklace on of gold beads, and I had my eye upon that, and in the dark of the alley I stooped, pretending to mend the child's clog that was loose, and took off her necklace, and the child never felt it, and so led the child on again. Here, I say, the devil put me upon killing the child in the dark alley, that it might not cry, but the very thought frighted me so that I was ready to drop down; but I turned the child about and bade it go back again; for that was not its way home. The child said, so she would; and I went through into Bartholomew Close, and then turned round to another passage that goes into Long Lane, so away into Charterhouse Yard, and out into St John's Street; then

The death-cart; from an early nineteenth-century edition of Defoe's *Journal of the Plague Year*.

crossing into Smithfield, went down Chick Lane, and into Field Lane, to Holborn Bridge, when, mixing with the crowd of people usually passing there, it was not possible to have been found out . . . This string of beads was worth about £12 or £14. I suppose it might have been formerly the mother's, for it was too big for the child's wear, but that, perhaps, the vanity of the mother to have her child look fine at the dancing school, had made her let the child wear it . . .

Eighteenth-Century Verse

EDWARD YOUNG (1683–1765), born at Upham, near Winchester, was educated at Winchester School, and then at Oxford where, in 1708, he was awarded a law fellowship at All Souls. About 1714 he became tutor to the Duke of Wharton's family, a post he held until 1725, when his employer was disgraced and obliged to retire abroad. Meanwhile, he had begun to write verse and had made the acquaintance of the London wits. His continual hunt for a new patron provoked the ridicule of Pope and Swift; but between 1725 and 1728 he published *Love of Fame, or The Universal Passion*, a series of somewhat ineffective satires that, although they

Edward Young: from the frontispiece to his *Works*, 1767.

suffered by comparison with those of Pope, received some favourable notice.

During his late forties, apparently despairing of worldly success, Young decided to take Holy Orders. In 1728 he was appointed Chaplain to King George II, and in 1730 was granted the living of Welwyn in Hertfordshire. Soon afterwards he married Lady Elizabeth Lee, a descendant of the Stuarts. Young was a zealous candidate for preferment, but he never achieved the bishopric he coveted. Then in 1741 his wife died, and he fell into a deep melancholy. This 'pious gloom' inspired him to produce *The Complaint, or Night Thoughts on Life, Death and Immortality*, of which the first part appeared in 1742, and the ninth and last in 1745. The poem was enormously successful; Young was the earliest and most renowned of the English 'graveyard poets'. His fame spread to Europe. Diderot greatly admired his poem; Robespierre slept with it under his pillow; Klopstock preferred it to anything by Milton. Young now had the money and fame that he had long been seeking, and passed his last twenty years in a 'dignified retirement'. He produced one more important work, the remarkable *Conjectures on Original Composition* that came out in 1759, a prose essay on literary inspiration. Young rejected the rules of neo-classicism, and urged that the poet should trust to his innate genius. The blow that he struck there for imaginative freedom exerted a considerable influence on the German literary world.

The subject of Young's *Night Thoughts* is not calculated to arouse much enthusiasm in modern readers. The work is heavy with solemn admonitions, so that it often resembles a versified manual of piety. What recommended his work was the atmosphere in which he clothed its theme, the air of brooding gloom and darkness, of introspective melancholy and romantic sensibility. Young employed a highly ornamented style that, combined with his ponderous didacticism, often makes him difficult to read. But the poem includes some striking lines – 'Death loves a shining mark, a signal blow': 'Man wants but little; nor that little long' – that will always be remembered. His opening description of night is a good example of Young's highly rhetorical style at its most portentous and effective:

> Night, sable goddess! from her ebon throne,
> In rayless majesty, now stretches forth
> Her leaden sceptre o'er a slumbering world . . .
> Nor eye, nor list'ning ear, an object finds;
> Creation sleeps. 'Tis as the general pulse
> Of life stood still, and nature made a pause;
> An awful pause! prophetic of her end.
> And let her prophecy be soon fulfill'd;
> Fate! drop the curtain; I can lose no more.

JOHN GAY (1685–1732), born of a poor family in Barnstaple, was orphaned at the age of ten. When he had completed his education in the West Country, he was apprenticed to a London silk merchant. In 1708 he published a poem called *Wine*, a facetious attack on water-drinkers, and in 1712 joined the household of the Duchess of Monmouth; but two years later, as he paid little attention to his humdrum duties, he was summarily dismissed. Meanwhile, he had dedicated his *Rural Sports*, a series of burlesque pastorals, to Alexander Pope, and the two poets had become friends.

Gay held a series of minor public appointments, and was patronized by various noblemen; but his lazy, self-indulgent nature, which was complicated by a certain vein of pettishness, seems always to have prevented him from making the most of his advantages. Nor was he a lucky man. In 1720 a two-volume collection of his verse, *Poems on Several Occasions*, earned him at least a thousand pounds. But he invested the whole sum in the South Sea Company, and lost it once the Company collapsed. Though his *Fables*, which, hoping to gain a Court appointment, he dedicated in 1727 to the youthful Duke of Cumberland, proved extremely popular with the reading public, his greatest success was *The Beggar's Opera*, produced in 1728. Swift had suggested to Gay that he should write a 'Newgate Pastoral', and even recommended him to visit the ancient London prison in order 'to finish his scenes the more correctly'. Gay's 'ballad opera', which included many spirited songs and picturesque glimpses of contemporary low life, was meant not only to ridicule the ponderous pretensions of the Italian and German operas, but to satirize Sir Robert Walpole's government, Sir Robert himself being represented as the highway-robber Macheath. The Prime Minister

(*Above*) Gay's *Fables*; an illustration by William Kent in the edition of 1787.

(*Left*) Scene from *The Beggar's Opera* by William Hogarth; Polly pleads for the highwayman's life.

(Opposite) *The Seasons*, one of the most popular poems of its age; illustrations engraved in 1770.

took the satire well, and attended the theatre to applaud the play; but its sequel, *Polly*, was suppressed by the Lord Chamberlain. The printed version, however, had enormous sales. Now comparatively rich but still hopelessly improvident, Gay passed his last years under the protection of the devoted Duchess of Queensberry, who quarrelled with King and Court rather than abandon him. He died in 1732, and Pope consecrated to his memory some characteristically euphonious lines. But his own couplet, which appears on his tomb, is perhaps his best epitaph:

> Life is a jest, and all things show it;
> I thought so once, and now I know it.

Gay was a gifted versifier whose handling of rhythm and diction is both sensitive and varied. Though seldom completely serious, he often achieves a nice balance between romantic lyricism and comic realism. *Trivia, of The Art of Walking the Streets of London*, for example, the mock-heroic poem that he published in 1716, presents a lively panorama of city-life at each successive season of the year. After a snow-fall, the noise of traffic is hushed, and the shops are strangely idle:

> On silent wheel the passing coaches roll;
> Oft' look behind, and ward the threat'ning pole.
> In harden'd orbs the school-boy moulds the snow,
> To mark the coachman with a dext'rous throw.
> Why do ye, boys, the kennel's surface spread,
> To tempt with faithless pass the matron's tread?
> How can ye laugh to see the damsel spurn,
> Sink in your frauds, and her green stockings mourn?
> At White's the harness'd chairman idly stands,
> And swings around his waist his tingling hands:
> The sempstress speeds to 'Change with red-tipt nose;
> The Belgian stove beneath her footstool glows;
> In half-whipt muslin needles useless lie,
> And shuttle-cocks across the counter fly.

James Thomson; portrait after J. Patoun, *c.*1746.

JAMES THOMSON (1700–48), one of the most popular and widely esteemed of English eighteenth-century poets, was born at Ednam, Roxburghshire, and in 1715 entered Edinburgh University as a student of divinity. In 1720 he published his first verses, and in 1725 he left for London, where he soon abandoned divinity for literature and became the friend of Pope and Gay. Meanwhile, he earned his living as a tutor in rich families; and the Solicitor General, who had employed him to teach a son, bestowed on Thomson the sinecure post of Secretary of the Briefs in Chancery. *Winter*, the first part of *The Seasons*, appeared in 1726, and the whole poem was published in 1730. In 1736 the poet retired to a small house in Richmond, close to Pope's retreat at Twickenham. Extremely indolent – he never rose until noon – Thomson was also

a greedy man and, even by eighteenth-century standards, unconscionably fat. But like John Gay, he had many good friends; and when he fell into debt, Lord Lyttelton, the dilettante peer, found him another sinecure as Surveyor General of the Leeward Islands. He now spent most of his time constantly revising *The Seasons*, but in 1748 produced *The Castle of Indolence*, an elaborate Spenserian allegory of the way of life that he himself had chosen. Having been drenched with dew while watching a party of hay-makers, he contracted pneumonia and died on 27 August 1748.

Thomson was strongly influenced by Lord Shaftesbury, the Deist philosopher, who saw in the phenomena of Nature a direct revelation of the attributes of God; so that for him contact with Nature was both emotionally uplifting and morally instructive. Such is the philosophy of *The Seasons*, which enables Thomson to make the English landscape the self-sufficient subject of a long, elaborate poem. The poet's classic diction, however, is against him from a twentieth-century point of view. He is determined, at any cost, to avoid 'lowness'. His descriptions must be duly 'elevated'; fish are 'the finny race', birds, 'the plumey people'. He modelled his blank verse on that of Milton, always a difficult master to follow, with the result that Thomson's lines, though often impressively sonorous, are apt sometimes to be dull and turgid, particularly when he decides that the dignity of his theme requires he should reflect or moralize. He is seen at his best, however, in occasional descriptive passages:

> . . . The foodless wilds
> Pour forth their brown inhabitants. The hare,
> Though timorous of heart, and hard beset
> By death in various forms, dark snares, and dogs,
> And more unpitying men, the garden seeks
> Urged on by fearless want. The bleating kind
> Eye the bleak heaven, and next the glistening earth,
> With looks of dumb despair; then, sad-dispersed,
> Dig for the withered herb through heaps of snow.

William Shenstone, gardener and poetaster; portrait by T. Ross, 1760.

WILLIAM SHENSTONE (1714–63) was born, and spent his poetic life, on his family's estate of Leasowes, Halesowen, near Worcestershire. At Pembroke College, Oxford, he was a contemporary of Samuel Johnson, but he took no degree; and once he had inherited Leasowes in 1745, he quietly retired there and passed the remainder of his existence re-modelling and 'improving' it. Shenstone was one of the pioneers of romantic landscape-gardening. He was more famous, indeed, for his walks and streams and prospects than for the occasional verses with which he amused his leisure. His only popular poem, *The School-Mistress*, a light-hearted imitation of Spenser, was published in 1742. Shenstone never married, and he died, like Thomson, as the result of catching a heavy cold, on 11 February 1763.

Much of Shenstone's verse consists of rather tepid moralizing in a gentle, elegaic strain. Some of his lyrics have an attractive simplicity. But it was *The School-Mistress*, originally intended as a literary burlesque, that he would appear to have written with the greatest care. Here he shows an interest in his homely subject not often found among Augustan versifiers, who were seldom bold enough to embark on a theme that might be considered 'low':

> One ancient hen she took delight to feed,
> The plodding pattern of the busy dame;
> Which, ever and anon, impell'd by need,
> Into her school, begirt with chickens, came;
> Such favour did her past deportment claim:
> And, if Neglect had lavish'd on the ground
> Fragment of bread, she would collect the same;
> For well she knew, and quaintly could expound,
> What sin it were to waste the smallest crumb she found.

Usually, as Gray was to point out, it is the too-timid acceptance of current taste that further weakens Shenstone's slight talent: 'He goes hopping along his own gravel-walks, and never deviates from the beaten paths for fear of being lost.'

THOMAS GRAY (1716–71), the son of a London scrivener, was educated at Eton, where he joined Horace Walpole's circle of close friends, and then went up to Cambridge. In Walpole's company he next made the Grand Tour. But they quarrelled – Gray complained of Walpole's aristocratic insolence – and he returned alone to England. For two years he lived with his mother at Stoke Poges, finally deciding to revisit Cambridge and adopt the study of the law. He never became a lawyer; instead, thanks to his classical scholarship, he established a reputation as one of the most erudite of European scholars. His moving 'Ode on a Distant Prospect of Eton College' and his 'Sonnet upon the Death of Richard West' were written in 1742. But not until 1750 did he complete his most famous poem, the *Elegy, written in a Country Churchyard*. He had been working on the text for eight years, and only agreed to publish it in 1751 because he feared that a dishonest printer might issue an unauthorized edition. 'The Progress of Poesy' came out in 1754, and 'The Bard' in 1757.

Though Gray's poetic output was small, the little verse that, after much painstaking revision, he hesitantly presented to the world brought him nation-wide fame; and in 1757 he was offered the laureateship, which he firmly declined, considering it a questionable honour. During later life he devoted himself to an investigation of Celtic and Icelandic verse; and his researches inspired two imitations of ancient poetry, 'The Fatal Sisters' and 'The Descent of Odin'. In 1768 Gray was made Professor of History and Modern Languages at Cambridge; but he had no pupils and never gave a lecture. He died on 30 July 1771 and was

Thomas Gray as a young man; portrait by J.G. Eccardt, 1748.

buried, as he would have wished, at Stoke Poges.

A shy, retiring disposition, combined with a keen scholarly intelligence, seem to have inhibited Gray's approach to poetry. He was never entirely satisfied with his own verse, and always unwilling that it should see the light. In much of it he employs a consciously elevated and stylized diction – for example, in 'The Progress of Poesy', a grandiloquent tribute to the powers of the art, framed as 'A Pindaric Ode', that sweeps us along from Poetry's remote beginnings among the landscapes of ancient Greece –

> Woods, that wave o'er Delphi's steep,
> Isles, that crown th'Aegean deep,
> Fields, that cool Ilissus laves,
> Or where Maeander's amber waves
> In lingering Lab'rinths creep . . .

by way of the New World, where

> She deigns to hear the savage Youth repeat
> In loose numbers wildly sweet
> Their feather-cinctured Chiefs, and dusky Loves

to the triumphs of Shakespeare, Milton and Dryden. Though Johnson criticized Gray's 'Gothic' poems, such as 'The Curse upon Edward', which he considered examples of the 'false sublime', about the famous *Elegy* itself he wrote that it 'abounds with images which find a mirrour in every mind, and with sentiments to which every bosom returns an echo . . .' Reflections on human mortality are an age-old literary commonplace:

> Beneath those rugged elms, that yew-tree's shade,
>   Where heaves the turf in many a mould'ring heap,
> Each in his narrow cell for ever laid,
>   The rude Forefathers of the hamlet sleep.
>
> The breezy call of incense-breathing Morn,
>   The swallow twitt'ring from the straw-built shed,
> The cock's shrill clarion, or the echoing horn,
>   No more shall rouse them from their lowly bed . . .
>
> Oft did the harvest to their sickle yield,
>   Their furrow oft the stubborn glebe has broke;
> How jocund did they drive their team afield!
>   How bow'd the woods beneath their sturdy stroke!
>
> Let not Ambition mock their useful toil,
>   Their homely joys, their destiny obscure;
> Nor Grandeur hear with a disdainful smile
>   The short and simple annals of the poor.

Yet Gray, himself a lonely man, gives these reflections a poignantly personal turn that raises them to the height of pure poetry:

> For who to dumb forgetfulness a prey,
>   This pleasing anxious being e'er resign'd,

Illustration to Gray's *Elegy*, executed by Bentley for Horace Walpole's Strawberry Hill edition.

Left the warm precincts of the cheerful day,
Nor cast one longing ling'ring look behind?

Walpole afterwards regretted his early quarrel with Gray, in which he acknowledged that the fault had been largely his; and the edition of the *Elegy* that he published on the Strawberry Hill Press, decorated by his employee, Richard Bentley, is one of the most delightful of eighteenth-century illustrated books.

WILLIAM COLLINS (1721–59), the son of a prosperous hatter, was born at Chichester and educated at Winchester. As a schoolboy, he began to write verse, and in 1734 he published his first poem, which has since vanished. Six years later he went up to Oxford; but there he lived an idle, dissipated life and very soon got into debt. When he left Magdalen College, he quickly ran through the small fortune that he inherited on his mother's death, and was

William Collins; frontispiece portrait from the *Odes*.

obliged to look for some employment. His relations, considering that he was 'too indolent' even to join the army, advised that he should take Holy Orders. Collins rejected this cynical suggestion. He decided, instead, to try a literary career and, having moved to London in 1744, he met both Samuel Johnson and James Thomson, the famous author of *The Seasons*, who became a close friend. His own literary output was not large, and never sufficient to support him; and in 1749, an uncle having died, bequeathing him two thousand pounds, which enabled him to pay off his debts, he finally returned to Chichester. During the last period of his existence, his reason was clouded by a hopeless melancholy; and it is said that the cloisters of Chichester Cathedral often resounded with his sighs and groans. Meanwhile, his friends had almost forgotten him; in 1759 Goldsmith was surprised to find him 'still alive, happy if insensible of our neglect'. He died in Chichester, at the home of his married sister, on 12 June 1759.

Collins left behind him a very small body of work, and his reputation rests on his *Odes on Several Descriptive and Allegoric Subjects*, a slim volume containing twelve odes, published in 1746. Among them is the 'Ode, Written in the Year 1746', a lament for British soldiers who had fallen during the War of the Austrian Succession:

> How sleep the Brave, who sink to Rest,
> By all their Country's Wishes blest!
> When Spring, with dewy Fingers cold,
> Returns to deck their hallow'd Mould,
> She there shall dress a sweeter Sod,
> Than Fancy's Feet have ever trod.
>
> By Fairy Hands, their Knell is rung,
> By Forms unseen their Dirge is sung;
> There Honour comes, a Pilgrim grey,
> To bless the Turf that wraps their Clay,
> And Freedom shall a-while repair,
> To dwell a weeping Hermit there!

The effect of Collins' threnody is at once classic and romantic; while his celebrated 'Ode to Evening' reveals a similar mastery of form, with its delicate manipulation of assonance and alliteration, and its skilful use of unrhymed Miltonic stanzas:

> Then let me rove some wild and heathy Scene,
> Or find some Ruin 'midst its dreary Dells,
>   Whose Walls more awful nod
>   By thy religious Gleams.
>
> Or if chill blust'ring Winds, or driving Rain,
> Prevent my willing Feet, be mine the Hut,
>   That from the Mountain's Side,
>   Views Wilds, and swelling Floods,
>
> And Hamlets brown, and dim-discover'd Spires,

> And hears their simple Bell, and marks o'er all
> > Thy Dewy Fingers draw
> > The gradual dusky veil.

The whole 'Ode' – its dreamy, pellucid style, drifting movement and its gentle 'dying fall' – is characteristic of the poet's genius. Like all his works, it is a very 'literary' production, inspired by the diction and imagery of Milton's *Lycidas*. Yet, in its stylized way, it is a strangely individual poem, and perfectly evokes not only 'the spirit of place' but the writer's passing mood.

MARK AKENSIDE (1721–70) was a minor poet who, having published one remarkably successful poem, enjoyed briefly far greater fame than his somewhat limited abilities deserved. The son of a butcher, originally intended for the ministry, he preferred to study medicine; and, while a student at Leyden, in 1743, he despatched the manuscript of a poem entitled *The Pleasures of Imagination* to the publisher Dodsley, accompanied by a request for £120 – a ridiculously large sum for an unknown writer's first work. Dodsley consulted Pope, who advised publication, declaring that 'this was no every-day writer'. In 1744 the poem appeared and – didactic poems being then the fashion – was received with loud applause. Its popularity, however, was short-lived. Akenside, who regarded himself as a 'philosophical poet', endeavours to systematize and illustrate the theories of his time, using Addison's papers on the imagination as his framework. The result is frigid and rhetorical, an over-ornamented pastiche of Miltonic blank verse. But one or two of Akenside's lighter poems, notably the lines addressed to 'Amoret' often quoted by anthologists, in which he adds a touch of seventeenth-century 'conceit' to eighteenth-century correctitude, are both harmonious and evocative:

> Behold that bright unsullied smile,
> And wisdom speaking in her mien:
> Yet – she so artless all the while,
> So little studious to be seen –
> We naught but instant gladness know,
> Nor think to whom the gift we owe.

> But neither music, nor the powers
> Of youth and mirth and frolic cheer,
> Add half the sunshine to the hours,
> Or make life's prospects half so clear,
> As memory brings it to the eye
> From scenes where Amoret was by.

> This, sure, is Beauty's happiest part;
> This gives the most unbounded sway;
> This shall enchant the subject heart
> When rose and lily fade away;
> And she be still, in spite of Time,
> Sweet Amoret in all her prime.

Mark Akenside.

Christopher Smart, religious enthusiast and visionary poet; late 18th-century portrait.

CHRISTOPHER SMART (1722–71) was born at Shipborne in Kent in April 1722 and, while he was still young, as an exceptionally precocious poet, he secured the patronage of the Duchess of Cleveland, who granted him a pension in 1742. He went up to Cambridge, where he was a fellow of Pembroke Hall from 1740 to 1749; but he lived a bohemian life and much enjoyed the random conviviality of the local alehouses. Having moved to London, he became a wit and journalist, and a friend of the publisher John Newbery (also the publisher and paymaster of Oliver Goldsmith), whose daughter he married. In 1755 he had left Cambridge and worked for Newbery as a hack writer, usually under the pseudonym 'Ebenezer Pentweazle'. The work was ill-rewarded, and scarcely enabled Smart to pay his debts. He had many friends, including Johnson and Garrick; but despite their help, he found it impossible to provide for his wife and two daughters; and they were obliged to seek refuge with a married sister in Ireland. He never saw them again. His nervous instability – he had already once been committed to Bedlam – now developed into religious mania; and, on his second incarceration, he spent six years almost constantly engaged in prayer. Much of his famous *A Song to David* was scrawled across his prison-walls. When Johnson visited him there, he found him 'harmless'. He was released, but once more fell into debt and died in a debtors' gaol.

Smart was an obscure figure in his own time; and, since his death, his biography has attracted more attention than his poetry. His contemporaries voted him a pious lunatic. 'I have seen his *Song to David*,' wrote Mason to Gray, 'and from thence conclude him as mad as ever.' The Romantics, on the other hand, used him to discredit their eighteenth-century predecessors, seeing in Smart a poetic sensibility crushed by an unpoetic age. But although *A Song to David* lacks the logical, argumentative structure common to most eighteenth-century verse, beneath its abrupt transitions and free associations it has an order all its own:

> He sang of God – the mighty source
> Of all things – the stupendous force
> On which all strength depends;
> From whose right arm, beneath whose eyes,
> All period, pow'r, and enterprize
> Commences, reigns, and ends . . .

> Sweet is the dew that falls betimes,
> And drops upon the leafy limes;
> Sweet Hermon's fragrant air;
> Sweet is the lily's silver bell,
> And sweet the wakeful Taper's smell
> That watch for early pray'r . . .

> Strong is the lion – like a coal
> His eyeball – like a bastion's mole
> His chest against the foes:

> Strong the gier-eagle in his sail;
> Strong against tide th'enormous whale
> Emerges as he goes . . .

In 1939 Smart's unfinished *Jubilate Agno* a product of the poet's religious mania, modelled on ancient Hebrew verse, was published for the first time. Here he summons the whole Creation to join him in an act of worship, and a particularly arresting feature of the work is Smart's description of his beloved cat, Jeffrey. Johnson recorded his impressions of his friend as follows:

I did not think [he said] he ought to be shut up. His infirmities were not noxious to society. He insisted on people praying with him; and I'd as lief pray with Kit Smart as anyone else. Another charge was that he did not love clean linen; and I have no passion for it.

The poetry and criticism of the brothers THOMAS AND JOSEPH WARTON (1728–90 and 1722–1800) is chiefly remarkable for the concern it shows with the literature of earlier ages. Joseph was a clergyman who spent much of his life as the notably unsuccessful headmaster of his old school, Winchester. A friend of the poet Collins, in his own early poetry he reveals an interest in the wilder and more romantic aspects of Nature, which at the time were coming into vogue. Thus *Nature*, published in 1744, draws a comparison between a landscape that has been tamed or 'improved' and the kind of prospect that always delighted eighteenth-century lovers of the sublime and 'picturesque':

> Rich in her weeping country's spoils, Versailles
> May boast a thousand fountains, that can cast
> The tortur'd waters to the distant heav'ns;
> Yet let me choose some pine-topt precipice
> Abrupt and shaggy, whence a foamy stream,
> Like Anio, tumbling roars; or some bleak heath,
> Where straggling stand the mournful juniper,
> Or yew-tree scath'd . . .

Thomas Wharton.

Joseph Warton's *Essay on the Genius and Writings of Mr Pope*, of which the first part appeared in 1756 and the second in 1782, was an important milestone in English literary criticism. Never before had the great man's position been so seriously challenged; for Warton refused to accept Pope as one of the very greatest writers, and claimed that the poetry of reason was inferior to that produced by the 'glowing imagination'.

Educated, like his brother, at Winchester and Oxford, Thomas Warton was also an enthusiast. In his early poem *The Pleasures of Melancholy*, he anticipates some of the wildest excesses of Romantic literature. From a moonlit landscape pierced by the shrieking of an owl, he invites the reader to follow him:

> . . . to cheerless shades,
> To ruin'd seats, to twilight cells and bow'rs,

> Where thoughtful Melancholy loves to muse,
> Her fav'rite midnight haunts.

Naturally he was an admirer of Gothic ruins and a pioneer in the study of the English Middle Ages. His *Observations on the Faerie Queene* (1754) did much to restore Spenser's reputation; while his adventurous *History of English Poetry* (1774–81) opened up areas of English writing that few of his contemporaries had yet troubled to investigate, and presented a whole panorama of literary history from medieval to Elizabethan times. Warton was Professor of Poetry at Oxford between 1757 and 1767, and Poet Laureate from 1785 until 1790. He has been described as a man of 'immense energy and boisterous humour'.

William Cowper:
'But I beneath a
  rougher sea,
And whelm'd in
  deeper gulfs than he.'

WILLIAM COWPER (1731–1800) was born at Great Berkhamsted, Hertfordshire, the son of the local clergyman. He lost his mother when he was only six years old and, a fragile, nervous boy, he was savagely bullied at his first school. At Westminster School, where he remained from 1741 to 1747, thanks to the protection of Charles Churchill he seems to have led a somewhat happier life. He was then placed in a London solicitor's office and entered at the Middle Temple. Though he was called to the Bar, he never practised. Meanwhile, his mental condition was becoming more and more precarious. He had long been addicted to bouts of melancholia; and in 1763, on being offered, through the help of a relation, a sinecure clerkship of the House of Lords, the prospect of a public examination so alarmed him that he broke down and attempted to commit suicide. For two years the poet was confined to a private lunatic asylum; and once he had recovered, he settled down at Huntingdon with his friends, Mr and Mrs Unwin. After his host's death, he moved to Olney with Mrs Unwin; but there, unluckily, he met John Newton, a former slaving-captain turned evangelist, whose influence aggravated his depressive fits. An attack of melancholia caused him to break off his engagement to Mrs Unwin in 1772, and Cowper now become afflicted with an intense religious mania, which produced the conviction that he was irrevocably damned. Newton's departure from Olney, in 1779, temporarily reassured him; and a new friend, Lady Austen, encouraged him to write his most famous poem, *The Task*, which appeared in 1785. In 1787, however, he once more collapsed, though he recovered sufficiently to complete his translation of Homer in 1791. When Mrs Unwin died in 1796, Cowper sunk into a kind of mental stupor. He wrote few poems during his last years; but among them was his memorable lyric, 'The Castaway', a moving record of his distracted state.

The Task opens with a mock-heroic celebration of a sofa, written in a style that parodies eighteenth-century Miltonic diction; but the subject soon changes to Nature and the countryside. The poem is discursive, ranging easily from attacks on political corruption to sketches of rural life, from religious exhortation to a treatise on the cultivation of cucumbers. Part of the poem's originality lies in its lack of any formal structure; the only cohesive element is the poet's personal sensibility. It was a sensibility that disregarded all contemporary poetic laws, and led him to introduce themes previously considered too 'low' for serious treatment. In Cowper's poem we find a novel realism used to present the commonplaces of modern rustic life, as in this vivid sketch of a labourer's winter evening:

> The taper soon extinguish'd, which I saw
> Dangled along at the cold finger's end
> Just when the day declined, and the brown loaf
> Lodg'd on the shelf, half-eaten without sauce
> Or sav'ry cheese, or butter, costlier still;
> Sleep seems their only refuge: for, alas,
> Where penury is felt the thought is chain'd,
> And sweet colloquial pleasures are but few!

'Kate is Craz'd':
illustration to *The Task*;
by Stothard, from the
edition of 1800.

Cowper did not read much poetry; and this may perhaps account for the freshness of his view; he sees suffering labourers, not arcadian swains. He celebrates the pleasures of the countryside without sentimentalizing or idealizing them. Cowper's attacks on city life are a by-product of his humanitarianism. Despite the secluded existence he led, he was sensitive to the most important ideas of his time. In *The Task*, for example, he takes his stand against slavery, cruelty to animals, the Bastille, militarism, and (like William Blake) the destructive effects of industrial development:

> Hence merchants, unimpeachable of sin
> Against the charities of domestic life,
> Incorporated, seem at once to lose
> Their nature; and, disclaiming all regard
> For mercy and the common rights of man,
> Build factories with blood; . . .

The generally placid surface of the poem is disturbed by deep emotion only when Cowper contemplates suffering, whether it be human or animal, or, now and then, his own misery. He had a considerable lyric gift. 'The Castaway', written in 1799, describes a sailor washed from the decks of his ship, and left to drown alone and helpless. It is a reflection of his lifelong nervous terrors; and, at the end, the sailor and the poet are dramatically identified:

> I therefore purpose not, or dream,
>   Descanting on his fate,
> To give the melancholy theme
>   A more enduring date:
> But misery still delights to trace
> Its semblance in another's case.

No voice divine the storm allayed,
  No light propitious shone;
When, snatch'd from all effectual aid,
  We perish'd, each alone:
But I beneath a rougher sea,
And whelm'd in deeper gulphs than he.

CHARLES CHURCHILL (1731–64) was born at Westminster, and went to Westminster School, where it is said that he defended the shy little William Cowper against the attacks of youthful bullies. He was denied entrance to Cambridge, however, when it was discovered that, before he was eighteen, he had already made a secret marriage. His father, a London clergyman, forgave this imprudence on condition that he entered the ministry. Though totally unsuited to such a career, he agreed, and was ordained in 1756, succeeding his father as curate of St John's, Westminster, and took up his duties in September 1758. Finding himself condemned 'to pray and starve on forty pounds a year', Churchill led an unhappy married life. Then in March 1761 he published *The Rosciad*, a collection of satirical portraits of the leading actors and actresses of the day. It was an immediate success; the poem brought him a thousand pounds, which enabled him both to discharge his debts and to pay off his estranged wife. He began to live well, becoming the companion of some of the most notorious rakes of the time and lifelong friend of the 'patriot', John Wilkes; and through Wilkes he was introduced to Sir Francis Dashwood's blasphemous secret fraternity, the Monks of St Francis of Wycombe, the so-called Hell-Fire Club. A lumbering, thick-set, ugly man, Churchill also launched out into a series of disreputable love affairs. By December 1762 he had contracted syphilis; and in January 1763 he was forced to resign his curacy by his scandalized parishioners. His association with Wilkes tempted him to engage in political satire, and write for the fiercely anti-governmental *North Briton*. Wilkes was arrested after the publication of the celebrated No. 45; but Churchill escaped and continued his amorous adventures and high living until the latter months of 1763; when he eloped with Elizabeth Carr, the fifteen-year-old daughter of a Westminster stonemason. Her family threatened violence and punitive legal action. Churchill did not lose his nerve. 'My life I hold for purposes of pleasure', he wrote in a letter to Wilkes; and the short period he spent living quietly with Elizabeth was probably the happiest of his whole existence. But during the autumn of 1764 he set off to visit the exiled Wilkes in France, developed a 'putrid' fever and died in Boulogne on 4 November 1764 at the age of 33.

Churchill achieved his greatest fame as a satirist thanks to his poetic championship of John Wilkes, whose 'martyrdom' by the British government had aroused a tremendous storm of indignation. At the time, he was dubbed 'the British Juvenal'. Much of his verse is therefore inspired journalism, full of personal animosity and current political allusions. His satire is often too vituperative to remain permanently effective; he lashes out left and right, without troubling to preserve a consistent point of view. But his last poems rise above these weaknesses, and, at their best, combine his characteristic vigour and acerbity with a new and imaginative handling of the heroic couplet. 'The Times' (1764) is a lively assessment of the vices of the day, among them Churchill's own failings; and the poem was long neglected owing to the supposed obscenity of its attacks on high-born homosexuals. In 'The Candidate' (1764) he proceeded to castigate Lord Sandwich, who, despite his well-known profligacy and lack of learning, had applied for the High Stewardship of Cambridge. Churchill's diatribe helped to ensure his failure. His most accomplished poem, the 'Dedication to Dr W. Warburton', which appeared after his death, holds an ingenious balance between eulogy and irony:

Charles Churchill, satirist and man of pleasure; portrait by J.S.C. Schaak.

> Health to great Gloster – nor, thro' love of ease,
> Which all priests love, let this address displease.
> I ask no favour, not one note I crave,
> And when this busy brain rests in the grave,
> (For till that time it never can have rest)
> I will not trouble you with one bequest.
> Some humbler friend, my mortal journey done,
> More near in blood, a Nephew or a Son,
> In that dread hour Executor I'll leave,
> For I, alas! have many to receive;
> To give, but little. – To great Gloster Health!
> Nor let thy true and proper love of wealth
> Here take a false alarm – in purse though poor,
> In spirit I'm right proud, nor can endure
> The mention of a bribe – thy pocket's free.

These verses, with their parenthetical interruptions, hesitations and afterthoughts, are very different from the epigrammatic couplets of Pope. Churchill's is a complex style, and a very individual one; and it is unfortunate that he did not live to carry it a step further. He would possibly have disagreed himself; he had no sense of wasted talents, or of having lived his life in vain. 'Life to the last enjoyed, here Churchill lies', were the final words of his own moving epitaph that can still be read above his tomb at Dover. It was a valediction that Byron read and admired just before leaving England as an exile.

THOMAS CHATTERTON (1752–70) is more important for the effect he had on the Romantic conception of the poet than for the poetry that he himself produced. Born in Bristol, the son of a schoolmaster, lay clerk of Bristol cathedral, he had spent long hours delving through the manuscripts preserved among the archives of St Mary Redcliffe church. He created an imaginary

The Death of Chatterton;
after a romantic picture
by William Singleton,
1794.

world around these relics, and began to write verses under the
guise of a fifteenth-century monk, Thomas Rowley, whose works
he professed to have unearthed in a certain 'Mr Canynges'
cofre'. Many of those to whom he showed his rather primitive
forgeries at once accepted them as genuine; and Chatterton was
encouraged to submit some specimens to the great dilettante
Horace Walpole, who was at first attracted but, on the advice of
his friends, Gray and Mason, ultimately returned the papers.
Having journeyed to London in April 1770, Chatterton struggled
without success to earn a living by his pen. Too proud to accept
charity, he poisoned himself with arsenic in a garret above Holborn in August 1770, and was buried in a pauper's grave.

Chatterton, 'the glorious boy who perished in his pride',
appealed to the Romantic poets as the image of outcast poetic
genius, destroyed by an unappreciative society. The romantic
aura that surrounded his short life was soon transferred to his poetic
work; though he is interesting for his potential gifts rather than
for his real achievement. Yet Chatterton undoubtedly possessed
an extraordinarily powerful imagination, which enabled him to
build up a secret world of his own, and to write in the language he
had himself invented. Despite his passion for the Middle Ages,
Chatterton was deeply indebted to Spenser; and some of his
metrical experiments have an almost Elizabethan freshness:

> Oh! sing unto my roundelay;
> Oh! drop the briny tear with me;
> Dance no more at holiday;
> Like a running river be.
> My love is dead,

Gone to his death-bed,
All under the willow-tree.

Black his hair as the winter night,
White his skin as the summer snow.
Red his face as the morning light;
Cold he lies in the grave below.
My love is dead,
Gone to his death-bed,
All under the willow-tree.

Sweet his tongue as the throstle's note,
Quick in dance as thought can be,
Deft his tabour, cudgel stout;
Oh! he lies by the willow tree.
My love is dead,
Gone to his death-bed,
All under the willow-tree.

WILLIAM BLAKE (1757–1827), one of the strangest and most variously gifted figures in the history of English art and writing, was the second son of a London hosier who kept a shop near Golden Square. At school he learned comparatively little; but from a very early age, he used to declare, he had experienced ecstatic visions, during which he had glimpsed the terrible face of God looking through his father's window, and had seen a flight of luminous angels bespangling suburban trees. Yet he was also of a remarkably practical turn; and having been apprenticed to an engraver when he was fourteen, he soon mastered his employer's craft, thus acquiring a means of livelihood that brought him a modest income until the end of his existence. Meanwhile, he had attracted the attention of the well-known sculptor and draughtsman, John Flaxman; and it was Flaxman who, in 1783, helped him to publish his first volume, *Poetical Sketches*, a collection of juvenilia that, besides foreshadowing the young man's original gifts, reveal his indebtedness to the lingering influence of the great Augustan poets. His next effort was considerably more adventurous. Mistrustful of publishers, he decided in 1789 that he would produce a book himself, *Songs of Innocence*, with illustrations that he had designed and engraved, coloured by his own hand. Thereafter he always employed this method, combining the rôles of author, illustrator, engraver and bookseller. *The Book of Thel*, the first of his mysterious 'prophetic books', appeared in the same year as *Songs of Innocence*, and was followed in 1790 by a prose work, *The Marriage of Heaven and Hell* – the greatest of his prophetic publications – and in 1794 by his marvellous *Songs of Experience*, which complemented the *Songs of Innocence*, and gave to the world many of the fascinating lyrics that have since secured him immortality. The last two volumes of the prophetic series, *Milton* and *Jerusalem*, were completed in 1808 and 1820. Though Blake believed that they contained the essence of his philosophy, neither

William Blake on Hampstead Heath, 1821; pencil drawing by his disciple John Linnell.

can today be regarded as a completely valid work of art.

Despite the fact that most of his contemporaries suspected that Blake must be a little mad, his genius did not go unrecognized; and among his admirers were a series of famous artists, including Romney, Flaxman, Fuseli and the powerful Sir Thomas Lawrence, and such distinguished writers as Wordsworth, Coleridge, Southey, Charles Lamb and Walter Savage Landor. Popular success, of course, had failed to come his way; but then the life that the visionary poet led was entirely self-sufficient. He had married young; and his wife Catherine, the uneducated daughter of a Battersea market-gardener, proved a patient and devoted aide, who, although she did not share her husband's visions, tranquilly accepted them. Those visions, which had begun with the apparition of God at a window, accompanied him throughout his whole career. To Blake they remained intensely real; and he always considered himself to be a privileged agent between the eternal

(*Above left*) From *The Book of Thel.*

(*Above right*) Blake's self-portrait; from a note-book.

and the temporal. His prophetic books, he said, he had merely taken down at the bidding of his ghostly visitants, 'without premeditation, and even against my will'. Nevertheless one attribute that most impressed the circle of admirers who gathered around him in his later years was the prophet's air of sanity. Quiet, hardworking, practical, he struck Samuel Palmer as 'a man without a mask, his aim single, his path straightforward, and his wants few'. He seemed frank, utterly unpretentious – '*a new kind of man*', added another disciple, 'wholly original . . . in all things'.

Blake's originality, however, was accompanied by certain disadvantages. Clearly he sometimes mistook the overflowings of his own subconscious mind for voices from the spirit world, and did

A page of *Jerusalem*.

not pause to enquire why the style they often used should so closely resemble mannerisms of James Macpherson's bogus *Ossian*. Almost all the prophetic books, particularly *Jerusalem*, the longest and the most obscure, incorporate fine poetic passages; but as a whole, except for *The Marriage of Heaven and Hell*, they make extraordinarily hard reading, while Blake's endless catalogues of place-names –

Hampstead, Highgate, Finchley, Hendon, Muswell Hill rage loud
Before Bromion's iron Tongs and glowing Poker reddening fierce . . .

– whatever their prophetic significance may be, appear to lack the smallest literary value.

The Marriage of Heaven and Hell, on the other hand, is a master-piece of revolutionary writing. Here Blake, the one-time repub-lican who had worn the scarlet Cap of Liberty, sets forth his creed with unexampled vigour. 'In the line of high poetry and spiritual speculation', Swinburne would declare, it was 'about the greatest work' that the eighteenth century had produced; 'the humour is of that fierce grave sort whose cool insanity of manner is more horrible . . . to the Philistine than any sharp edge of burlesque or glitter of irony . . . The rarity and audacity of thoughts and words are incomparable; not less their fervour and beauty.' Though in his curious private pantheon he had found a niche for Jesus Christ, whom he regarded as a great imaginative artist, Blake's *Marriage of Heaven and Hell* is a bold attack upon some of the main tenets of established Christianity. Here, remembering the ancient Gnostics, he equates Jehovah, 'The Creator of this World', with an obscurantist demiurge (elsewhere entitled Urizen, or 'Your Reason'), and the so-called Devil with the liberating spirit. It is the Devil's aim to break down the arbitrary distinction that Christian moralists have perversely drawn between the human soul and body:

All Bibles, or sacred codes, have been the causes of the following Errors:
1 That Man has two existing principles, Viz: a body and a soul.
2 That Energy, call'd Evil, is alone from the Body, and that Reason, call'd God, is alone from the Soul.
3 That God will torment Man in Eternity for following his Energies.
   But the following Contraries to these are True:
1 Man has no Body distinct from his Soul . . .
2 Energy is the only life, and is from the Body, and Reason is the round or outward circumference of Energy.
3 Energy is Eternal Delight.

The last sentence of 'The Voice of the Devil' is perhaps the most significant. Like D.H. Lawrence, Blake believed in the sanctity of human passion – 'The soul of sweet delight can never be defiled' – and attributed to a divine origin all the various manifestations of sensual energy that Christian believers had combined to damn:

> The pride of the peacock is the glory of God.
> The lust of the goat is the bounty of God.
> The wrath of the lion is the wisdom of God.
> The nakedness of woman is the work of God.

Similarly, 'The road of excess leads to the palace of wisdom', and 'He who desires but acts not, breeds pestilence'. Much of Blake's poetic symbolism has a strongly sexual colouring; the Jerusalem he sought to build on earth was, among other things, a place of sexual freedom, where jealousy is unknown, and

Where every Female delights to give her maiden to her husband . . .
She creates at her will a little moony night and silence

From *Milton*.

> With Spaces of sweet gardens and a tent of elegant beauty,
> Closed in by a sandy desert and a night of stars shining
> And a little tender moon and hovering angels on the wing . . .

Despite the growing complexity of Blake's elaborate religious system, which reaches a climax in the hermetic utterances of *Milton* and *Jerusalem*, it remains a homogeneous edifice; and in his exquisite lyrics, as in his dark prophetic books, he is perpetually re-echoing the same beliefs. His shorter poems may be enjoyed for their own sake; but we cannot understand them fully unless we grasp their intimate relation to his whole ambitious scheme. They express his life-long worship of 'energy' and his hatred of the 'iron laws' that 'the Creator of this World' and the priesthood that serves Urizen have sought to impose upon 'the soul of sweet delight':

> Ah, sun-flower, weary of time,
> Who countest the steps of the sun,

Seeking after that sweet golden clime
Where the traveller's journey is done:

Where the youth pined away with desire,
And the pale virgin shrouded in snow
Arise from their graves and aspire
Where my sun-flower wishes to go!

The Growth of the Novel

SAMUEL RICHARDSON (1689–1761) was born in Devon, the son
of a prosperous cabinet-maker; but his family moved to London
while he was still a child. Though he had little formal education,
he was a precocious, solemn, even priggish boy, whom his friends
had nicknamed 'Serious'. From his early youth he employed his
literary talents by helping the servant-girls of the neighbourhood
to compose their love-letters; and at the age of seventeen he was
apprenticed to a printer. In 1721 he married his master's daughter,
and set up in business on his own account. He soon prospered,
becoming printer to the House of Commons, and presently
Master of the Stationers' Company. In 1731 his wife died, and the
next year Richardson married the daughter of another printer,
who was also the sister of a well-known bookseller. Then in
November 1740, when he had already passed his fiftieth year, this
solid and respectable tradesman suddenly emerged as a brilliant
modern novelist.

Pamela; or, Virtue Rewarded had been written within the space of
two months. Richardson had previously undertaken to produce a
handbook on the art of letter-writing; and the work inspired him
to frame a fictitious narrative consisting of a series of epistles.
Published anonymously, *Pamela* was at once successful, ran
through four editions in six months, and during a period when the
novel often excited the suspicion of moralists, was recommended
and even read from pulpits. Some readers, it is true, regarded its
heroine as a self-seeking humbug; and it was widely parodied, by
Fielding among others in his entertaining *Shamela*. Richardson's
second novel, the voluminous *Clarissa Harlowe*, was issued in three
instalments between 1747 and 1748. It spread the writer's fame
all over Europe; and at home he quietly settled down in a 'flower
garden' of admiring middle-aged ladies. His last novel, *Sir Charles
Grandison*, which portrays his ideal of a high-minded English
gentleman, appeared in 1753–54. Richardson had never forgiven
Fielding for *Shamela*; and, to some extent at least, he planned it as
a counterblast to the immoral tendencies he had detected in
Fielding's *Tom Jones*. Richardson died on 4 July 1761.

Pamela is a simple tale, Richardson's heroine being an innocent
serving-maid whom Mr B, the unscrupulous son of the house,
tries his hardest to seduce by all the graceful arts at his command.
Pamela is poor and unprotected; but, thanks to a rare blend of

virtue and commonsense, she triumphantly resists him; until Mr B learns to value her qualities and, at length, offers her his hand in marriage. Richardson transforms this rudimentary plot into a complex psychological study. *Pamela* has sometimes been described as 'the first modern novel', the first to deal with moral problems in a detailed social context. Although Pamela cannot always grasp her own motives, or understand her secret thoughts and feelings, she presents them forcibly and clearly; and at a certain point the reader begins to perceive that, although she may reject her suitor's courtship, her unacknowledged love threatens to overcome her deep-rooted sense of right and wrong. Only when she has married Mr B and becomes a paragon of every virtue, does the story tend to lose its interest.

Clarissa Harlowe, a novel of daunting bulk – one of the longest in the English language – portrays yet another helpless heroine, whose snobbish and greedy parents have planned a marriage for her, from which she has determined to escape. She accepts the help of a fascinating rake named Lovelace, and he eventually carries her off to a brothel, where she is imprisoned, drugged and ravished. Richardson's portrait of Lovelace is a masterly essay in psychological analysis. He is not all bad; he has many fine qualities besides his charm and gaiety and social grace; but he believes that his task in life is to acquaint the women he seduces with the secrets of their own nature, to show them, by demolishing their false prudery, what it is they really need. Abroad, *Clarissa Harlowe*

(*Above left*) Samuel Richardson; portrait by J. Highmore.

(*Above right*) Illustration for *Clarissa Harlowe;* from a French translation of 1785.

helped to inspire Choderlos de Laclos's extraordinary novel *Les Liaisons Dangereuses* (1782), in which the French writer's rakish protagonist Valmont was evidently based on Richardson's hero-villain.

Richardson's novels often make difficult reading. His was a prolix art. 'Why, Sir,' Johnson once observed, 'if you were to read Richardson for the story, your impatience would be so much fretted that you would hang yourself. But you must read him for the sentiment, and consider the story as only giving occasion to the sentiment.' That sentiment drew floods of tears from Richardson's contemporary readers, some of whom threatened to blow their brains out should Clarissa meet a tragic end. Today it is his psychological acumen – his intuitive knowledge of violent human passions and emotions, unexpected in so staid and virtuous a man – that seems to entitle him to a place among our greatest English novelists.

MR LOVELACE TO JOHN BELFORD, ESQ. LETTER XXVIII. (Lovelace weighs the pros and cons of ravishing Clarissa)

Abhorred be force! – be thoughts of force! There's no triumph over the will in force! This I know I have said. But would I not have avoided it, if I could? Have I not tried every other method? And have I any other recourse left me? Can she resent the *last outrage* more than she has resented a *fainter effort*? And if her resentments run ever so high, cannot I repair by matrimony? She will not refuse me, I know, Jack; the haughty beauty will not refuse me, when her pride of being corporally inviolate is brought down; when she can tell no tales . . . and when that modesty, which may fill her bosom with resentment, will lock up her speech.

But how know I, that I have not made my own difficulties? Is she not a woman? What redress lies for a perpetrated evil? Must she not *live*? Her piety will secure her life. And will not *time* be my friend? . . . She cannot fly me! She must forgive me – and as I have often said, *once forgiven, will be for ever forgiven.*

Why then should this enervating pity unsteel my foolish heart?

It shall not. All these things will I remember; and think of nothing else . . .

I'll teach the dear charming creature to emulate me in contrivance! I'll teach her to weave webs and plots against her conqueror! I'll show her, that in her smuggling schemes she is but a spider compared to me, and that she has all this time been spinning only a cobweb!

HENRY FIELDING (1707–54) was born at Sharpham Park, near Glastonbury, but brought up in Dorset. He was sent to Eton at the age of thirteen, and there acquired the classical knowledge that permeates everything he wrote. By 1728 he had left school and was paying court to a young girl whose guardian, fearing that Fielding might abduct her, at once decided she must be married off. That same year, with the intention of studying law, he entered Leyden University, but very soon returned to London, where he earned his living as a playwright. The plays he produced were mostly burlesques, modelled on the works of Congreve and Wycherley; but often they included a touch of political satire aimed at Sir Robert Walpole's government. In 1734 he married Charlotte Cradock, and passed two years enjoying a country life.

On regaining London in 1736 he leased the Haymarket Theatre, becoming its manager and chief playwright. His theatrical career was brought to an abrupt end when Walpole's Stage Licensing Act of 1737, which Fielding's plays had done much to provoke, curtailed the freedom of the English stage; and he thereupon took up the law and was called to the Bar in 1740. He also turned to journalism as editor of *The Champion* – a periodical that, besides continuing to satirize Walpole, published a number of more literary essays. In 1741 he published an unsigned parody of Richardson's *Pamela*, entitled *An Apology for the Life of Mrs Shamela Andrews*. His first novel, *The Adventures of Joseph Andrews and his friend Mr Abraham Adams*, was intended as a similar parody, but developed into an autonomous work, dominated by the quixotic Parson Adams. *The History of the Life of the Late Mr Jonathan Wild the Great*, which appeared in 1743, is a remarkable piece of sustained irony, once more directed at Robert Walpole and also at the general idea of 'greatness'. In 1744 he lost his beloved wife; and in 1747, apparently to give his children a mother, he married her maid, Mary Daniel.

Henry Fielding: engraving by William Hogarth.

In 1748 Fielding was appointed principal Justice of the Peace for Westminster and Middlesex. He took his duties very seriously and, because he refused to accept fees from the poor, was obliged to seek financial help from Lord Lyttelton and other friends. A year later he became chairman of the Westminster Quarter Sessions, a post in which he was assisted by his blind half-brother, Sir John Fielding. Not only did Fielding organize the first effective London police-force, but he wrote a series of enlightened pamphlets on the causes and the cure of crime. In 1749 he published his greatest novel, *Tom Jones*. He was now a sick and tired man, plagued by the gout from which he had long suffered and afflicted with asthma, jaundice and dropsy. His last novel, *Amelia*, appeared in 1751; and in 1754, having resigned his office, he left England to seek a kindlier climate. From Portugal he sent home his *Journal of a Voyage to Lisbon*. He died soon afterwards at Lisbon, and was buried in the English Cemetery.

Shamela is not only a parody of *Pamela*, but ridicules Richardson's whole point of view. The heroine proclaims her virtue to Mr Booby merely with the purpose of seducing him; and Parson Williams, when he becomes Shamela's paramour, justifies his behaviour by quoting the biblical text 'Be not righteous overmuch'. *Joseph Andrews* is also derived from *Pamela*. Joseph, who happens to be Pamela's brother, advertizes the same moral claims. But after he has been unsuccessfully courted by the lecherous Lady

Illustration for 1742
edition of *Joseph Andrews*.

Booby, who turns out to be Mr B's aunt, the novel develops into a
picaresque travel-story, during which Joseph encounters Parson
Adams. The quixotic parson dominates the tale. Adams is both
comic and admirable; for Fielding saw human virtue as essentially
the product of a sound heart, and believed that pedantic puritanism was the enemy of true goodness. Thus, when Joseph has been
robbed and beaten, and left lying naked by the roadside, the
occupants of a passing coach argue as to whether they should pick
him up. Joseph himself feels deeply ashamed of his nakedness:

The two gentlemen complained they were cold, and could not spare a
rag . . . and the coachman, who had two great-coats spread under him,

refused to lend either, lest they should be made bloody; the lady's foot-
man desired to be excused for the same reason, which the lady herself,
notwithstanding her abhorrence of a naked man, approved; and it is
more than probable poor Joseph, who obstinately adhered to his modest
resolution, must have perished unless the postilion (a lad who hath since
been transported for robbing a hen-roost) had voluntarily stripped off a
great-coat, his only garment, at the same time swearing a great oath (for
which he was rebuked by the passengers) that he would rather ride in
his shirt all his life than suffer a fellow-creature to lie in so miserable a
condition.

In his *History of the Life of the late Mr Jonathan Wild the Great*,
probably the first novel that Fielding wrote, though it was not
published until 1743, Fielding turns the life-story of a notorious
thief into a mordant satire with obvious political overtones. Here
he follows the rise of a particularly successful gangster, and
implies that success and human goodness are very seldom to be
reconciled. *Tom Jones*, however, is built on a larger scale. Fielding,
who asserted that he was 'the Founder of a new Province of
Writing', set out to produce 'a comic-epic in prose'. Tom is a
foundling, brought up by honest Squire Allworthy, who is
banished for offences he has not committed. He takes to the road,
but the daughter of a neighbouring squire, Sophia Western,
follows him; and, after running through numerous adventures,
he is reconciled with Allworthy and wins Sophia's hand. Tom's
lapses and indiscretions – frequently amorous – occupy a good
part of the narrative. He is not a 'respectable' personage; but
the novelist balances his failings against the natural qualities
of his heart. When Tom announces that he would not, 'to pro-
cure pleasure to myself, be knowingly the cause of misery to
any human being', it is clear that he has the novelist's complete
approval. Fielding was a humanitarian and a man of the world,
glad to take human nature as he found it.

For all its detailed presentation of the colour and diversity of
Hanoverian England, *Tom Jones* is not a realistic novel. Its substance is realistic; but the text is interspersed with numerous
passages of exuberant improvisation that constantly remind us of
the author's presence – a device later employed by Thackeray,
who often accosts the reader and buttonholes him in just the same
way. Here as elsewhere, it is Fielding's minor characters that have
most vitality and interest – Squire Western, the traditional
country squire; the accommodating Mrs Waters; Partridge,
Tom's supposed father; the philosopher Square, and the Reverend
Mr Thwackum. The major characters are less vivid since they
frequently serve as the novelist's mouthpiece, and their essential
traits are soon established. In *Amelia*, Fielding's last novel, pathos
replaces the humour and passion that illuminate his earlier books.
The tone is now domestic; and all our attention is focussed upon
the good and gentle heroine. Though as a work of art *Amelia* lacks

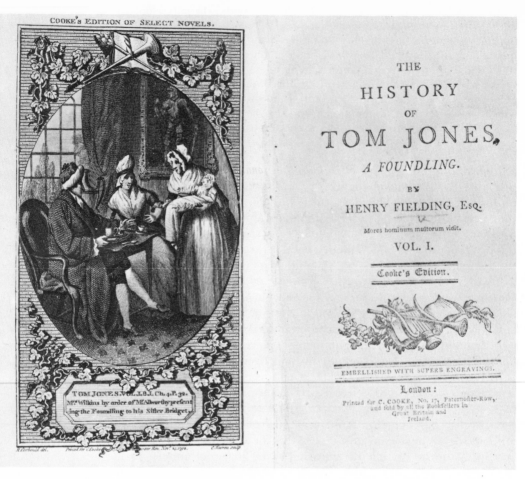

COOKE's EDITION OF SELECT NOVELS.

THE

HISTORY

OF

TOM JONES,

A FOUNDLING.

BY

HENRY FIELDING, Esq.

Mores hominum multorum vidit.

VOL. I.

Cooke's Edition.

EMBELLISHED WITH SUPERB ENGRAVINGS.

London:

Printed for C. COOKE, No. 17, Paternoster-Row, and sold by all the Booksellers in Great Britain and Ireland.

(*Above*) Frontispiece to a late 18th-century edition of *Tom Jones*.

(*Opposite*) Laurence Sterne; painted by Joshua Reynolds, when, as the author of *Tristram Shandy*, he first appeared in London.

vitality, it contains some energetic social diatribes – against the delays of the law, the abuses of the prison-system, the hardships of military services, and the web of corrupt political influence then employed to hold the State together.

LAURENCE STERNE (1713–68), one of the most original of eighteenth-century English writers, could claim to have invented not only a new way of writing but a novel mode of feeling. It was he who popularized the adjective 'sentimental', about which Lady Bradshaigh, an important member of Samuel Richardson's 'flower garden' of admiring ladies, wrote to her idol in 1749 begging for enlightenment. 'Everything clever and agreeable', she said, appeared nowadays to be 'comprehended in that word'. The son of a poor soldier, from whom he afterwards took some hints for his famous character 'Uncle Toby', Sterne led a wandering, poverty-stricken youth. But a more prosperous cousin had him educated at Cambridge; and in 1737 he entered the Anglican Church and then, with the help of an uncle, a canon of York

Minster, left his modest curacy near Huntingdon and moved to a pleasant Yorkshire parsonage. During the eighteenth century the Church of England was an accommodating institution; and Sterne made the most of it. He 'sat down quietly in the lap of the church', and found it a not uncomfortable refuge, which enabled him to enjoy the worldly amusements of York and the company of rakish local squires.

In 1741 he married Elizabeth Lumley, a young woman whom he had long courted; and his first publication was a spirited satire on a certain Dr Topham, the ecclesiastical lawyer of the diocese. The satire was quickly suppressed, but it had whetted the satirist's taste for authorship; and he embarked on the composition of a novel, *The Life and Opinions of Tristram Shandy, Gentleman*, of which the two prefatory volumes came out, and achieved an instantaneous success, towards the end of 1759. Early next year the author travelled to London where he was overwhelmed with praise and flattery. Invitations came ten at a time; fashionable ladies crowded up his staircase. He was welcomed by David Garrick, patronized by Lord Chesterfield, and had his portrait painted by Sir Joshua Reynolds.

Tristram Shandy is indeed an astonishing book – a medley of autobiographical jottings, caustic reflections on life, scandalous anecdotes and strange romantic musings, all thrown together in a lively and eloquent, yet deliberately discontinuous style. The opening chapter contains an account of his own begetting, which had occurred under extremely unfavourable auspices:

I wish either my father or my mother, or indeed both of them, as they were in duty both equally bound to it, had minded what they were about when they begot me: had they duly considered how much depended upon what they were then doing; that not only the production of a rational Being was concerned in it, but that possibly the happy formation and temperature of his body, perhaps his genius, and the very cast of his mind; and for aught they knew to the contrary, even the fortunes of his whole house might take their turn from the humours and dispositions which were then uppermost . . . I am verily persuaded I should have been made a quite different figure in the world from that in which the reader is likely to see me . . .

Pray, my dear, quoth my mother, *have you not forgot to wind up the clock?* – *Good G– – –!* cried my father, making an exclamation, but taking care to moderate his voice at the same time, – *Did ever woman, since the creation of the world, interrupt a man with such a silly question?* Pray, what was your father saying? – Nothing.

There the chapter ends; and the succeeding chapters follow as eccentric a course, the text itself, to make the effect still more bizarre, being scattered with a number of curious typographical devices. Sterne, nevertheless, builds up a vivid picture of the bizarre family he is describing – his opinionated, hot-tempered father and his warm-hearted uncle Toby, a retired soldier, who

Sterne at Ranelagh, with
a fashionable lady on
his arm; a satirical
contemporary print.

spends his days constructing the miniature fortifications among
which, with the assistance of his servant, Corporal Trim, he re-
enacts his memories of Marlborough's campaigns and the sieges
and battles that he had himself observed.

Sterne did not attempt to round off his novel, or carry his hero
much beyond infancy. The last volume of the series was published
in 1767; and in 1762 the novelist had visited Paris, where his
reception was almost as enthusiastic as that accorded David Hume
a year later, and then journeyed to the South of France. From that
and a second tour, in 1765 and 1766, he derived the inspiration for
his most readable and entertaining book, *A Sentimental Journey
through France and Italy*, which came out in 1768; and meanwhile he
had begun to issue a collection of sermons, *The Sermons of Mr*

Tristram Shandy; Uncle Toby's jack-boots are transformed into siege-mortars; illustration by George Cruikshank, 1808.

Yorick, of which the closing instalment appeared in 1769. The *Sentimental Journey* is no regular travel-book but consists, like *Tristram Shandy,* of a succession of luminous images, strung together upon a single thread of feeling. For Sterne, to live was to feel, to sympathize with his fellow creatures, and to explore the secrets of his own heart. 'What a large volume of adventures', he writes, 'may be grasped . . . by him who interests his heart in everything, and who, having eyes to see what time and chance are perpetually holding out to him as he journeyeth on his way, misses nothing he can fairly lay his hands on!'

Sterne displays an exquisite tenderness – sometimes, it is true, a slightly self-conscious tenderness – both towards men and women, and towards beasts and birds; and in Paris, having contemplated the Bastille, he notices a much humbler type of prison. As he is meditating upon the ancient fortress –

I was interrupted . . . with a voice which I took to be of a child, which complained 'it could not get out' – I look'd up and down the passage, and seeing neither man, woman, nor child, I went out . . .

In my return back through the passage, I heard the same words repeated twice over; and looking up, I saw it was a starling hung in a little cage; – 'I can't get out, – I can't get out', said the starling.

Sterne's cult of sensibility extended to his private life. Mrs Sterne, of whom he did not hesitate to admit that he had long ago grown 'sick and tired', soon degenerated into a neurotic invalid; and in heart, if not perhaps in body, he was a singularly unfaithful husband, fascinated first by a young singer named Catherine Fourmantelle, then by an Anglo-Indian lady, Elizabeth Draper. His romantic letters to his beloved 'Bramine' were published after his death as a *Journal to Eliza*.

The tuberculosis of the lungs that eventually killed Sterne may have had some effect upon his literary character, and have helped to give his imagination its peculiarly hectic colouring. He was haunted by the idea of mortal transience:

I will not argue the matter: Time wastes too fast: every letter I trace tells me with what rapidity Life follows my pen; the days and hours of it, more precious, my dear Jenny, than the rubies about thy neck, are flying over our heads like light clouds of a windy day, never to return more – everything presses on – whilst thou art twisting that lock, – see! it grows grey; and every time I kiss thy hand to bid adieu, and every absence which follows it, are preludes to that eternal separation which we are shortly to make. –
Heaven have mercy upon us both!

(Tristram Shandy, Vol. IX)

Like David Hume, whose *Treatise of the Human Understanding* had been published in 1739, he believed that the human personality consisted, at best, of a 'bundle or collection of different perceptions, which succeed each other with an inconceivable rapidity, and are in a perpetual flux and movement'. The task that Sterne had set himself was to describe that state of flux and, when he depicted a character, to break it up into the transient feelings that composed it.

Sterne's last living was at Coxwold in Yorkshire, whither he often retired to enjoy a period of 'sweet retirement'. But he was always devoted to the pleasures of London life; and it was in London that he died on 18 March 1768. His end was characteristic. A 'party of gentlemen', including Hume and Garrick, had sent a messenger to his lodgings to enquire after their friend's health. He entered the sick-room as Sterne was 'just a-dying. I waited ten minutes; but in five he said, "*Now it is come*". He put up his hand, as if to stop a blow, and died . . .'

Tobias Smollet; portrait by an unknown artist, *c.*1770.

TOBIAS SMOLLETT (1721–71) was born on a farm at Dalquhun in Dumbartonshire. His youthful ambition was to be a soldier; but after completing his education at a local school, he went to Glasgow University to study medicine, and was apprenticed for three years to an apothecary and surgeon. In 1739, having become a fully qualified surgeon, Smollett took the road to London, determined not only to set up in practice, but to place his tragedy, *The Regicide*. His efforts failed; and, deeply disappointed, he was obliged to accept a post as ship's surgeon aboard HMS *Chichester*. In that capacity he visited the West Indies under the command of

Admiral Vernon, and witnessed the Admiral's disastrous siege of Cartagena – an experience he afterwards used in *Roderick Random*. As soon as he landed in Jamaica, he left the navy, remaining on the island until 1744, when he returned to London and practised as a surgeon in Downing Street. In 1747 he married Anne Lascelles, a beautiful Jamaican heiress. A year later, the publication of *Roderick Random* brought him sudden literary fame, and he employed his earnings to publish *The Regicide*, which had a somewhat cool reception.

In 1750 Smollett travelled to Aberdeen to take his medical degree, and thence to Paris, where he gathered the subject matter of his second novel, *Peregrine Pickle*, published in 1751. On his return, he settled as a physician in Bath; but his professional career did not succeed, and he moved back to London, and took a house in Chelsea. There he established a remarkable 'literary factory', producing almost any kind of book for which he might receive an order, undertaking many commissions himself but also farming out the work to hacks. Though the business seems to have prospered, his labours ruined his health, while, thanks to his improvidence and extravagant hospitality, he was constantly running into debt. In 1753 he published *Ferdinand, Count Fathom*; and in 1756 he became editor of the *Critical Review*. His popular *History of England* appeared in 1757. After the death of his beloved daughter in 1763, Smollett spent two years abroad, travelling round France and Italy; and on this expedition he encountered Laurence Sterne, to whom he took an instant dislike, and who, in his *Sentimental Journey*, presently caricatured him as 'Smelfungus'. Meanwhile, Smollett's health was steadily deteriorating; and in 1769 he left England for the last time. Though he had contracted arthritis, the benevolent Italian climate enabled him to produce *Humphrey Clinker*, which came out in 1771. During the same year he died, on 17 September, at Monte Nero, near Leghorn.

Smollett was an ill-tempered man who described himself as having an 'over irritable nervous system'; his life was chequered with mishaps, which he usually attributed to the malice and jealousy of his fellow human beings. He quarrelled with almost everyone he knew, and his books very often display the more jaundiced aspect of his nature. In his first novel, *Roderick Random*, Smollett uses the outlines of his own life to form the basis of his narrative, his hero being an impoverished young Scotsman who journeys to London, bent on making his fortune. There is no real plot; it is a story in the established picaresque tradition, and consists of a series of lively episodes in which the hero himself is obviously less important than the striking characters he meets – prostitutes, highwaymen, gamesters, sharks – portrayed against a variety of backgrounds drawn from eighteenth-century low life. An especially memorable episode concerns Roderick's adventures as a surgeon's-mate on a British man-of-war. His graphic descrip-

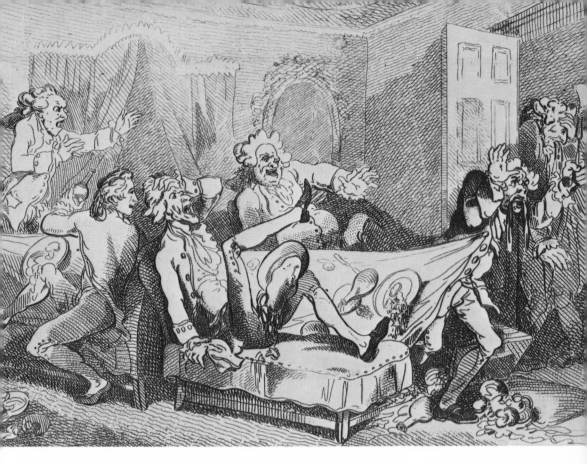

Illustration by
Rowlandson for *Peregrine
Pickle*.

tions of the filthiness of the sick-bay were based on the notes he had himself made during his memorable voyage to Jamaica.

Peregrine Pickle is another picaresque tale, which has a similarly roguish hero and a no less remarkable supporting cast. Peregrine's visit to Paris provides him with a new stage on which to perform, and a fresh opportunity of indulging his favourite vices. The novel has one outstanding comic creation, Commodore Trunnion, whose death-scene shows the story-teller at his best:

Swab the spray from your bowsprit, my good lad, and coil up your spirits. You must not let the toplifts of your heart give way, because you see me ready to go down at these years; many a better man has foundered before he has made half my way, though I trust, by the mercy of God, I shall be sure in port in a very few glasses, and fast moored in a most blessed riding: for my good friend Jolter hath overhauled the journal of my sins, and by the observation he hath taken of the state of my soul, I hope I shall happily conclude my voyage and be brought up in the latitude of heaven . . .

Smollett's last novel, *Humphrey Clinker*, was his most popular achievement and, as a work of literature, has proved the most enduring. Made up of a sequence of letters, it recounts the journey through England and Scotland of a Welsh gentleman named Matthew Bramble. Again there is very little plot; but, as the story proceeds, we watch a fund of latent kindliness gradually emerging in the character of the misanthropic traveller. Here is none of the bitter humour that had distinguished Smollett's earlier novels; and, in the Scotsman, Lismahago, he produced a particularly memorable personage, whose apparently innocuous talk conceals a fund of sharp-edged wit. Though some of Smollett's chamber-pot fun persists, the effect is positively good-natured, as in the misspelt letters of the Welsh maid:

Last Sunday in the parish crutch, if my own ars may be trusted, the clerk called the banes of marriage betwist Opaniah Lashmeheygo and Tapitha Bramble, spinster; he mought as well have called her inkle weaver, for she never spun a hank of yarn in her life. Young Squire Dollison and miss Liddy make the second kipple; and there might have been a turd, but times are changed with Mr Clinker.

OLIVER GOLDSMITH (1730–74) was what would nowadays be called 'a professional Irishman' – gay, imaginative and good-hearted, but extravagant, thriftless, vain and irremediably loquacious. The son of an Irish parish priest, in 1744 he entered Trinity College, Dublin, but made very little academic mark. In 1753, having refused to take Holy Orders, he began to study medicine, left for the Low Countries to continue his studies at Leyden, and then wandered around Europe, returning to England in 1756 'with no more than a few halfpence'. There followed 'eight years of disappointment', during which he endeavoured to earn his living as comedian, school-master, apothecary's assistant, Samuel Richardson's private proof-corrector and 'a physician in a small way'. Finally, Goldsmith became a literary journalist. His first original book, his *Enquiry into the Present State of Polite Learning in Europe*, appeared in 1759; and about 1762, when he published *The Citizen of the World*, a collection of essays that he had already contributed to the *Public Ledger*, he attracted Samuel Johnson's notice.

Johnson was to remain a loyal supporter. 'Dr Goldsmith,' he declared in his friend's lifetime, 'is one of the first men we have as an author'; and, after Goldsmith's death, 'let not his frailties be remembered; he was a very great man'. By his other contemporaries, he was generally regarded as among 'the brightest members of the Johnsonian school'. *The Vicar of Wakefield*, which Johnson claimed to have read, carried off and sold to a publisher, at a moment when the novelist had been held prisoner at his London lodgings by his unpaid landlady, came out in 1766 and achieved an instantaneous success; and in 1768 his comedy *The Good Natur'd Man* was performed at Drury Lane. His second, and even more amusing comedy, *She Stoops to Conquer*, reached the boards in 1773. His two long poems, *The Traveller* and *The Deserted Village*, appeared in 1764 and 1770.

These were not his only publications; he was an exceedingly prolific writer, always improvident, always hard-worked; and

Johnson attributed his early death, on 4 April 1774, to the 'uneasiness' caused by his financial troubles: 'his debts began to be heavy, and all his resources were exhausted'. As poet, novelist and dramatist, Goldsmith had both a charming gift and an enviable facility. Apart from some splendid lines, *The Traveller* now strikes us as a fairly commonplace poem, a nicely turned piece of late-Augustan versifying. But *The Deserted Village* – a lament for one of those English hamlets recently swept away by a rich landlord, anxious to 'improve' his estate, and provide himself with a more spacious view – includes some admirable passages. Goldsmith describes the one-time denizens of the village and their simple rustic pleasures; then depicts its present ruin:

> Along thy glades, a solitary guest,
> The hollow sounding bittern guards its nest;
> Amidst thy desert walks the lapwing flies
> And tires their echoes with unvaried cries.
> Sunk are thy bowers in shapeless ruin all,
> And the long grass o'ertops the mouldering wall . . .

Oliver Goldsmith; portrait by Joshua Reynolds.

Goldsmith's view of his subject, as a contemporary reviewer pointed out, was gracefully imaginative rather than realistic. Very few English villages had lately been reduced to ruin; and 'England now wears a more smiling aspect than she ever did . . .' Nor was *The Vicar of Wakefield* an essay in realism. It was the novelist's simple, easy style that delighted his eighteenth-century readers. Simplicity, observed a reviewer, was his 'characteristic excellence. He appears to tell his story with so much ease and artlessness, that one is almost tempted to think, one could have told it every bit as well without the least study . . . Genuine touches of nature, easy strokes of humour, pathetic pictures of domestic happiness and domestic distress . . . are some of the methods he has made use of . . .' Not only was Goldsmith an artful sentimentalist, who appealed to the eighteenth-century taste for scenes of unspoiled rustic innocence; he was also a sententious moralist. His hero, Dr Primrose, is the type of uncorrupted virtue. He is, nevertheless, one of the most exasperating personages in the whole of English literature, whose copybook maxims seem to be based on the belief that, whereas vice always leads to misery, virtue can be relied upon to pay a good dividend. Primrose is ruined; his beautiful daughter is seduced; but, thanks to a series of highly improbable accidents, 'affluence and innocence' are at length the portion of the afflicted Primrose family.

Goldsmith's 'pathetic pictures of domestic happiness', however, are genuinely touching and amusing. Here, for example, is a glimpse of the Primroses playing hunt-the-slipper at a nearby farmhouse:

Mr Burchell, who was of the party, was always fond of seeing some innocent amusement going forward, and set the boys and girls to blind-

VICAR OF WAKEFIELD.

The Vicar of Wakefield;
from an edition of the
novel published in 1780.

man's buff. My wife, too, was persuaded to join in the diversion, and it
gave me pleasure to think she was not yet too old. In the meantime, my
neighbour and I looked on, laughed at every feat, and praised our own
dexterity when we were young. Hot cockles succeeded next, questions
and commands followed that, and last of all, they sat down to hunt the
slipper. As every person may not be acquainted with this primeval
pastime, it may be necessary to observe, that the company at this play
plant themselves in a ring upon the ground, all except one, who stands
in the middle, whose business it is to catch a shoe, which the company
shove about under their hams from one to another, something like a
weaver's shuttle. As it is impossible, in this case, for the lady who is up to
face all the company at once, the great beauty of the play lies in hitting
her a thump with the heel of the shoe on that side least capable of making
a defence. It was in this manner that my eldest daughter was hemmed in,

and thumped about, all blowzed, in spirits, and bawling for fair play, fair play, with a voice that might deafen a ballad-singer, when, confusion on confusion! who should enter the room but our two great acquaintances from town, Lady Blarney and Miss Carolina Wilelmina Amelia Skeggs!

Probably Boswell's verdict on Goldsmith's literary gifts was less inaccurate than that of Johnson. No modern author, he wrote, 'had the art of displaying with more advantage . . . whatever literary acquisitions he had made'. But 'his mind resembled a fertile, but thin soil', which produced 'a quick but not a strong vegetation, of whatever chanced to be thrown upon it'. Horace Walpole dubbed him an 'inspired ideot'; and the view was shared by those who knew him better. Tales of his fatuity, vanity and unfailing loquacity were always popular among his friends. Yet few members of the brilliant Johnsonian school presumed to doubt that he was a man of genius. Though, as Garrick said, he had 'talked like Poor Poll', he had written 'like an angel'.

FRANCES BURNEY (1752–1840) was the fourth of a family of nine children, her father, Dr Charles Burney, being the famous music-teacher, musician and musicologist so much esteemed by Dr Johnson, who declared that 'my heart goes out to meet him', and that 'Dr Burney is a man for all the world to love'. Frances, better known as Fanny, had been brought up in a bookish household; and although she did not learn to read until she was eight years old, during her adolescence she produced an enormous mass of juvenilia, including 'Elegies, Odes, Plays, Songs, Farces – nay, Tragedies and Epic Poems', of which she made a general bonfire upon her fifteenth birthday. Among the manuscripts she destroyed was the draft of a novel that she afterwards reconstructed from memory to form the basis of her earliest published book. *Evelina, or, a Young Lady's Entrance into the World* appeared anonymously in 1778; and only when her father had heard it praised by his friends, did she at last venture to confess to him that she was herself the unknown author. She now became the literary lion of the day. *Evelina* delighted Dr Johnson, and was publicly described by Sheridan as '*superior* to Fielding'. Sir Joshua Reynolds declared that, having opened the novel and been obliged to put it aside, he 'could think of nothing else'; and Edmund Burke said that, in order to finish it, he had gladly sacrificed a night's sleep.

Today the tremendous success that Miss Burney's novel enjoyed may strike us as somewhat more interesting than the book itself. It arrived at a supremely opportune moment. Fielding had died in 1754; Richardson in 1761; Tobias Smollett ten years later; and the art of the English novel had sunk to a very low ebb. Contemporary novelists were numerous but undistinguished; and by the standard they set, *Evelina* appeared a remarkably original production, with its graphic story of a young girl's misadventures and its

(*Above left*) Fanny
Burney; portrait by her
cousin, Edward Burney.

(*Above right*) Captain
Mirvan enjoys a practical
joke; from the fourth
edition of *Evelina*, 1779.

vivacious scenes of 'low life'. She 'naturally loved a little of the
blackguard', Sir Joshua Reynolds informed his old friend's
daughter. Otherwise how could a well-bred girl have described
such a family as the Branghtons – vulgar but pretentious London
tradespeople, who keep house above a shop near Holborn? It is
the satirical aspect of her narrative that still entertains a modern
reader; the novelist has a sharp eye and a savage sense of fun. But
Evelina, the romantic heroine, destined to triumph over a horrible
French grandmother and her vulgar mercantile companions and,
at length, win the hand of a rich young peer, is a highly unconvincing portrait. Except when she produces a lively caricature of the
kind of people she despises, the novelist's style is often strangely
stilted – an inferior form of 'Johnsonese'; and her subsequent
novels – *Cecilia*, published in 1782, *Camilla* in 1796, and *The
Wanderer* in 1814 – grew progressively more and more unreadable.

Meanwhile, in 1786 Dr Burney, who had an 'almost religious'
respect for the British royal family, had persuaded her to accept a
post at court; and although she hated her years of courtly servitude
as second Keeper of the Robes to Queen Charlotte, and was
bullied and harassed by some of her fellow courtiers, she found
time to carry on her brilliant diary. This private record of her
thoughts and sufferings is undoubtedly her masterpiece; for here,
discarding the grand Johnsonian style, she was free to exercise her
keen satirical wit and her powers of caustic observation.

I stopped him to inquire about Sir Joshua; he said he saw him very often, and that his spirits were very good. I asked about Mr Burke's book.

'Oh,' cried he, 'it will come out next week: 'tis the first book in the world, except my own, and that's coming out also very soon; only I want your help.'

'My help?'

'Yes, madam; you must give me some of your choice little notes of the Doctor's; we have seen him long enough upon stilts; I want to show him in a new light. Grave Sam, and great Sam, and solemn Sam, and learned Sam – all these he has appeared over and over. Now I want to entwine a wreath of the graces across his brow; I want to show him as gay Sam, agreeable Sam, pleasant Sam: so you must help me with some of his beautiful billets to yourself.' . . .

He then told me his *Life of Dr Johnson* was nearly printed, and took a proof sheet out of his pocket to show me; with crowds passing and re-passing, knowing me well, and staring well at him: for we were now at the iron rails of the Queen's Lodge.

I stopped; I could not ask him in: I saw he expected it, and was reduced to apologize, and tell him I must attend the Queen immediately.

He uttered again stronger and stronger exhortations for my retreat, accompanied by expressions which I was obliged to check in their bud. But finding he had no chance for entering, he stopped me again at the gate, and said he would read me a part of his work.

There was no refusing this; and he began, with a letter of Dr Johnson to himself. He read it in strong imitation of the Doctor's manner, very well, and not caricature. But Mrs Schwellenberg was at her window, a crowd was gathering to stand round the rails, and the King and Queen and Royal Family now approached from the Terrace. I made a rather quick apology, and, with a step as quick as my now weakened limbs have left in my power, I hurried to my apartment.

At last released from court in 1791, she presently married a middle-aged French officer, the Comte Alexandre Jean-Baptiste d'Arblay. Their marriage was happy. The Count died in 1818; his widow, a distinguished relic of the age of Johnson, lived on another twenty-two years.

Johnson and Boswell

SAMUEL JOHNSON (1709–84) was never a man who looked back on his own youth with any kind of satisfaction. He would seldom discuss his childhood: 'one has *so* little pleasure', he told his friend Mrs Thrale, 'in reciting the anecdotes of beggary.' Here he drew a somewhat exaggerated picture of his parents' social and financial status. His father, Michael Johnson, though certainly poor, was a hard-working country bookseller; and his mother, christened Sarah Ford, came of honest yeoman stock. When they married, both were middle-aged, and Samuel, their first son, entered the world a sickly, ill-conditioned child. Among other ailments, he soon developed scrofula, a tuberculous infection of the skin and

(*Above*) Earliest known portrait of Samuel Johnson; painted by Joshua Reynolds in 1756, a year after he had completed his *Dictionary*.

(*Below*) Johnson towards the end of his life by Joshua Reynolds; for the last fifty years, he wrote about this time, 'my health has been such as has seldom afforded me a single day of ease'.

lymphatic glands, at that time called 'the King's Evil', which damaged both his sight and his hearing, and left his features scarred for life. Yet he possessed tremendous hidden strength, and grew up at his birthplace, Lichfield in Staffordshire, to become a robust, ungainly boy. His personal character at once inspired respect; and while he attended Lichfield Grammar School, where he received his early education, three of his friends would await him every morning and carry him to school upon their shoulders.

In his nineteenth year Johnson went up to Oxford; and there, too, despite his obstinate idleness, he immediately made his mark and gathered a circle of admiring friends. Then an inherited affliction struck him down. Michael Johnson, his son afterwards declared, was 'a pious and worthy Man', but 'wrong-headed, positive' and troubled with a 'vile melancholy' that pursued him to the grave. This melancholy now descended on Samuel; and during the summer vacation of 1729 he suffered a catastrophic breakdown, accompanied by 'a horrible hypochondria . . . perpetual irritation, fretfulness, and impatience; and . . . a dejection, gloom, and despair' which poisoned the springs of his existence. He recovered at length, but the whole pattern of Johnson's mental life seems to have been fixed before he reached twenty-one. From that moment, he was haunted not only by the fear of madness but by a terrifying sense of guilt. Since his boyhood, he announced as an old man, he had rarely enjoyed 'a single day of ease'.

Meanwhile, he had to earn a living; but his efforts to support himself, first as a country schoolmaster, afterwards at Birmingham as a publisher's hack-writer, proved singularly unsuccessful. Not until 1735 did the clouds show signs of lifting. That year he suddenly fell in love with the widow of a local businessman, whom he married on 9 July. Elizabeth Porter was forty-six and, according to David Garrick, whom Johnson had met at Lichfield and who presently became his pupil, 'a little painted Poppet; full of Affectation and rural Airs of Elegance'. But her husband loved her dearly; and though as an ageing woman she grew coarse and stout and sluggish, and latterly is said to have been much addicted to 'the liberal use of cordials', for Johnson she would never lose her charm. When she died after seventeen years of marriage, he continued to cherish her beloved memory; and she was constantly mentioned in his prayers.

Elizabeth Johnson had brought him a small dowry which amounted to about £700; and with this sum he set up a school at Edial near Lichfield. But only a very few pupils – among them the young David Garrick – ever benefited from Johnson's teaching, and the project soon collapsed. In 1737 he therefore moved to London; and despite his habit of frequently revisiting his birthplace, a Londoner he remained until the end. There followed a long period of bohemian obscurity, during which he earned his bread as a professional journalist, among his chief employers being

Edward Cave, the energetic proprietor of the *Gentleman's Magazine*. At this time, one of his closest friends was the wild and dissipated bohemian, Richard Savage; and the two journalists were sometimes so poor that they could not afford even 'the shelter and sordid comforts of a night cellar', and were obliged to walk the streets till dawn. But Johnson also tried his hand at more imaginative forms of writing. In 1738 he published his poem *London*, an ambitious imitation of a satire by Juvenal on the vices of Imperial Rome, which Alexander Pope saw fit to praise; in 1744 he wrote his *Life of Richard Savage*, who had died in a debtors' gaol a year earlier; in 1746 his unsuccessful tragedy, *Irene*, was staged by Garrick at the Drury Lane Theatre; and in 1749 he produced his second major poem, *The Vanity of Human Wishes*. Finally, in 1750, he began to build up his reputation as a periodical essayist with the famous *Rambler* and *Idler* series. At the same time, he was laying plans for his *Dictionary* – the tremendous work that he launched in 1747 and carried to a triumphant conclusion in 1755.

Johnson's *Dictionary* – a bold attempt to compile 'a dictionary . . . for the use of such as aspire to exactness of criticism or elegance of style', with the help of nearly 2300 pages of definitions and quotations – not only established the lexicographer's fame but secured him financial independence. He was awarded an honorary degree by the University of Oxford and in 1762 granted a royal pension of £300 a year. In 1756 Johnson had been arrested for debt, and in 1759 he had dashed off his Abyssinian novel *Rasselas*, a cautionary tale disguised as a romantic story, to pay his mother's funeral expenses. Henceforward he was an institution, feared, respected, venerated; and the Johnsonian legend, on which Boswell conferred its definitive shape, gradually came into being. But, in 1752, Elizabeth Johnson had died, leaving him, wrote his biographer Sir John Hawkins, 'a childless widower, abandoned to sorrow, and incapable of consolation'. Always a lonely man who feared and detested solitude, he became the most celebrated talker of his day, prepared to discuss any subject, however large or small, with an energy, promptitude and strength of feeling that astonished all his listeners. Even to be snubbed and swept off the board by Johnson was itself regarded as a privilege.

During the early autumn of his life, Johnson made two important friendships. On 16 May 1763 he first encountered James Boswell; and in mid-January 1765 he was presented to Henry and Hester Thrale, a rich brewer and his young and attractive wife, who so much admired his character and conversation that, when he next suffered an attack of melancholia, and described to them the 'horrible' state of his mind, they suggested he should join their household. Boswell remained a life-long friend; Johnson's attachment to Mrs Thrale, for whom he conceived a deeply romantic passion, lasted until her husband's death in 1781. Hester Thrale's remarriage – to the gifted and good-natured Italian musician

Johnson haunts his disciple and biographer; caricature of 1803.

Gabriel Mario Piozzi – was a blow that broke the old man's heart. He died, desperate but resigned and courageous, on 13 December 1784, and was buried in Westminster Abbey.

In his old age Johnson was generally accepted – though there were one or two dissentient voices, none more acrimonious than Horace Walpole's – as the patriarch of modern letters. Yet the achievement that had brought him so much fame was, if not meagre, very far from massive. Among his prose works, many of his periodical essays now seem very dull indeed; his novel *Rasselas* contains some brilliant passages; but unlike Voltaire, whose *Candide* appeared during the same year, Johnson could not tell a story. His political pamphlets are vigorous but wrong-headed. Only in his *Lives of the Poets* (which incorporated his early life of Savage), written between 1779 and 1781, do we feel the full force of the writer's genius; and even there his criticism is frequently prejudiced, and many of the poets he discusses, as he himself would evidently have agreed, have very little real value.

His poetic works are no less unequal in quality. *London* is not a poem that we very often re-read: *The Vanity of Human Wishes*, on the other hand, includes bursts of true poetic eloquence, for example the dozen superb lines that he devotes to 'Swedish Charles'. Nor can we dismiss his occasional lyric verses; his delightful apostrophe to Mrs Thrale's nephew, young Sir John Lade:

> Long-expected one and Twenty
> Ling'ring year at last is flown;
> Pomp and Pleasure, Pride and Plenty,
> Great Sir John, are now your own . . .
> Call the Betsys, Kates, and Jennys,
> Ev'ry name that laughs at Care;
> Lavish of your Grandsire's Guineas,
>   Show the Spirit of an Heir . . .

is said to have fascinated A.E. Housman, with its persuasive lilting rhythm, and been often on his mind when he started to produce his *Shropshire Lad*.

Although almost everything Johnson published was greatly admired by his contemporaries, he seems to have achieved the position he still holds as much through his majestic personal character as through the influence of his writings. Sometimes that influence was definitely deleterious. His peculiar prose style, which Macaulay called 'Johnsonese', was often imitated during the late-eighteenth and early-nineteenth centuries, with extremely bad results. Before they were close friends, Boswell himself had ventured to criticize the great man's 'inflated Rotundity and tumified Latinity of Diction'; and his genius often emerges more clearly in his talk, and in some of his private correspondence, than in the books he left behind him. Luckily his most famous disciple had an extraordinary gift for reportage; while Mrs Thrale and, to a lesser degree, Sir John Hawkins, were highly intelligent observers. Their joint efforts produced a composite portrait of Johnson that resembles nothing else in literary history – that of a man who put his genius into his life and over-shadowed a whole literary age. Despite all his shortcomings, personal or intellectual, we are bound to admit that he was still a giant.

(On Charles XII, King of Sweden, from *The Vanity of Human Wishes*)

> The vanquish'd Hero leaves his broken Bands,
> And shews his Miseries in distant Lands;

Condemn'd a needy supplicant to wait,
While Ladies interpose, and Slaves debate.
But did not Chance at length her Error mend?
Did no subverted Empire mark his End?
Did rival Monarchs give the fatal Wound?
Or hostile Millions press him to the Ground?
His Fall was destin'd to a barren Strand,
A petty fortress, and a dubious Hand;
He left a Name, at which the World grew pale,
To point a Moral, or adorn a Tale.

JAMES BOSWELL (1740–95) was not only a brilliantly gifted reporter, but an accomplished literary strategist; and having recognized his opportunity, he proceeded to exploit it with unfailing skill and perseverance. When he encountered Samuel Johnson for the first time, in the back-parlour of a London bookshop, on 16 May 1763, he was only twenty-two years old. His father, Alexander Boswell, a Scottish law-lord, bore the courtesy title of Lord Auchinleck; and James was proud of his descent from a long line of Scottish landed gentry. But Lord Auchinleck despised his elder son, whom he considered feckless, foolish and extravagant; and the young man, though he respected his father and was desperately determined to do him credit, had very soon begun to hanker after 'the wide speculative scene of English ambition'. Early in 1760 he had already escaped to London, where, like his future opponent Edward Gibbon, he was briefly converted to the Catholic faith; but he also visited Newmarket and cultivated the society of 'the great, the gay, and ingenious'. Finally, towards the end of 1762, he obtained Lord Auchinleck's permission to set out upon the Grand Tour, and once more took the road south. Next year, while sitting behind Tom Davies' shop, he came face to face with Samuel Johnson. Despite a series of sharp preliminary snubs, Boswell was brave enough to visit the old sage at his 'uncouth' London rooms. 'Give me your hand; I have take a liking to you', Johnson announced on 25 June; and from that moment they were fast friends.

In August, however, Boswell was obliged to leave England; and he remained abroad until February 1766, first at Utrecht, endeavouring to study Law, and then exploring Switzerland, Italy, Germany and France, paying effusive court to Voltaire and Rousseau, and, on the island of Corsica, visiting the heroic General Paoli, leader of the Corsican insurgents against the French and Genoese. The visit was well-timed. It was wonderful, he later informed Paoli, what Corsica had done for him; thanks to his visit, he had 'jumped into the middle of life'; and his *Account of Corsica*, published early in 1768, established Boswell as a modern man of letters. It was with the greatest reluctance that he at length returned to Edinburgh; and thenceforward his life was passed between the English and the Scottish capitals. He had two homes, just as he had two fathers – Edinburgh, where in 1769 he married his devoted cousin, Margaret Montgomerie (of whom Johnson somewhat cruelly remarked that she had 'such a person and mind as could not be . . . either admired or condemned'), diligently practised at the Scottish Bar and did his best to settle down; and London, where he enjoyed all the greatest pleasures of life, both sensual and intellectual. Scotland was the home of Lord Auchinleck, his disapproving earthly father; England – and, more particularly, London – was the residence of Samuel Johnson, who had now become a second father, and who accorded him all the paternal affection that the stern Lord Auchinleck refused to give.

James Boswell; portrait by Joshua Reynolds.

Boswell seems to have decided that he would write his hero's life at a very early period of their friendship. As a young man he had contracted a useful habit of recording conversations in his private diaries; and this he applied not only to Johnson's talk but to every incident that appeared to throw some light upon his friend's 'majestic' character. Meanwhile both in London and in Edinburgh, apart from his association with Johnson, he led an extraordinarily active life, scribbling, drinking, making love and struggling against the fits of deep depression that regularly overwhelmed him. He was seldom at rest; his mind and heart and senses were in a state of constant turmoil, his bold ambitions never satisfied. But when in 1773 he was elected to the Club which Sir Joshua Reynolds had founded under Dr Johnson's aegis, and in the same year persuaded his old friend (who loved London and despised and detested Scotland) to accompany him on their famous *Tour of the Hebrides*, he felt that he had achieved two major triumphs. His private life, once they had completed their tour, grew more and more unsatisfactory; he discovered that he was becoming a chronic drunkard; and Johnson's death in 1784 dealt him a blow from which, morally and emotionally, Boswell never quite recovered. His *Journal of a Tour to the Hebrides* came out in 1785, and his *Life of Samuel Johnson*, produced after many delays at the cost of tremendous effort, appeared in 1791. It had worn him out; he died a broken man, exhausted by his drunken habits and haunted by a conviction of personal failure, on 19 May 1795.

The ageing Boswell; an impression by Thomas Lawrence.

His *Life* was immediately acclaimed as a masterpiece, and during the present century the publication of his *Private Papers* – the journal he had been keeping since 1762 – has considerably increased his reputation. Together they form an unequalled self-portrait. Boswell reveals himself as a lifelong manic-depressive – a man with an avid thirst for pleasure, whose cheerful debaucheries were generally succeeded by moods of the profoundest gloom, and who renewed his dissipations merely to escape from the horrors of a 'sickly mind'. He is astonishingly candid; he had 'a kind of strange feeling', he once declared, as if he wished nothing to remain secret that concerned his own existence. His gift of self-analysis is yet the more impressive because he had the gifts of a

Illustrations by Rowlandson for Boswell's *Tour to the Hebrides*.
(*Left*) Johnson arrives in Edinbùrgh.
(*Right*) The great man argùing with Boswell's father, Lord Aùchinleck.

superb reporter. For almost everything we know to his discredit Boswell is our chief authority.

BOSWELL'S FIRST MEETING WITH JOHNSON, 16 MAY 1763

At last, on Monday the 16th of May, when I was sitting in Mr Davies's back-parlour, after having drunk tea with him and Mrs Davies, Johnson unexpectedly came into the shop; and Mr Davies having perceived him through the glass-door in the room in which we were sitting, advanced towards us, – he announced his awful approach to me, somewhat in the manner of an actor in the part of Horatio, when he addressed Hamlet on the appearance of his father's ghost, 'Look, my lord, it comes'. I found that I had a very perfect idea of Johnson's figure, from the portrait of him painted by Sir Joshua Reynolds soon after he had published his Dictionary, in the attitude of sitting in his easy chair in deep meditation; which was the first picture his friend did for him, which Sir Joshua very kindly presented to me, and from which an engraving has been made for this work. Mr Davies mentioned my name, and respectfully introduced me to him. I was much agitated; and recollecting his prejudice against the Scotch, of which I had heard much, I said to Davies, 'Don't tell where I come from'. – 'from Scotland', cried Davies, roguishly. 'Mr Johnson, (said I) I do indeed come from Scotland but I cannot help it.' I am willing to flatter myself that I meant this as light pleasantry to soothe and conciliate him, and not as an humiliating abasement at the expense of my country. But however that might be, this speech was somewhat unlucky; for with that quickness of wit for which he was so remarkable, he seized the expression 'come from Scotland', which I used in the sense of being of that country; and, as if I had said that I had come away from it, or left it, retorted, 'That, Sir, I find, is what a very great many of your countrymen cannot help'. This stroke stunned me a good deal; and when we had sat down, I felt myself not a little embarrassed, and apprehensive of what might come next. He then addressed himself to Davies: 'What do you think of Garrick? He has refused me an order for the play for

Miss Williams, because he knows the house will be full, and that an order would be worth three shillings.' Eager to take any opening to get into the conversation with him, I ventured to say, 'O Sir, I cannot think Mr Garrick would grudge such a trifle to you' 'Sir, (said he, with a stern look), I have known David Garrick longer than you have done; and I know no right you have to talk to me on the subject.' Perhaps I deserved this check; for it was rather presumptuous in me, an entire stranger, to express any doubt of the justice of his animadversion upon his old acquaintance and pupil. I now felt myself much mortified and began to think, that the hope which I had longed for indulged of obtaining his acquaintance blasted. And, in truth, had not my ardour been uncommonly strong, and my resolution uncommonly perservering so rough a reception might have deterred me for ever from making any further attempts.

The Life of Dr Johnson

Eighteenth-Century Prose

In an age that cultivated the art of pleasing, PHILIP DORMER STANHOPE, 4TH EARL OF CHESTERFIELD (1694–1773), wrote nearly seven hundred letters, very largely devoted to the study of its principles. Besides being an arch-snob and a social sage, he was also a political careerist. Having entered parliament at the age of twenty-one, he became Ambassador to the Hague, Lord High Steward, Lord Lieutenant of Ireland and a Secretary of State; and it was during the tenure of the last office that he unluckily fell foul of Samuel Johnson. When Johnson dedicated to him an impressive pamphlet, announcing his *Plan of an English Dictionary*, Chesterfield had contributed £10, but otherwise given little solid help – he was a hard-worked politician; and after the successful publication of the *Dictionary*, Johnson described the unkind treatment he had received in his stateliest and most scathing style. Chesterfield protested that, far from shutting his doors against so distinguished an author, 'he would have turned off the best servant he ever had, if he had known that he had denied him to a man who would always have been more than welcome'. But Johnson would not relent, and afterwards declared that Chesterfield's writings recommended the morals of a whore and the manners of a dancing-master. Chesterfield, however, despite Johnson's abuse, possessed considerable literary talent; and the two series of letters, addressed to his unpromising illegitimate son and to his favoured heir and godson, into whom he seeks to instil his own feeling for the social graces, are fine examples of late-Augustan prose:

Philip Dormer Stanhope, 4th Earl of Chesterfield, arbiter of elegance and professor of the art of pleasing; portrait by Allan Ramsay, 1765.

To his Son
When you come into the House of Commons, if you imagine that speaking plain and unadorned sense and reason will do your business, you will find yourself most grossly mistaken. As a speaker, you will be ranked only

according to your eloquence, and by no means according to your matter; everybody knows the matter almost alike, but few can adorn it. I was early convinced of the importance and powers of eloquence; and from that moment I applied myself to it. I resolved not to utter one word, even in common conversation, that should not be the most expressive and the most elegant that the language could supply me with for that purpose; by which means I have acquired such a certain degree of habitual eloquence, that I must now really take some pains, if I would express myself very inelegantly. I want to inculcate this known truth into you, which you seem by no means to be convinced of yet – that ornaments are at present your only objects. Your sole business is to shine, not to weigh. Weight without lustre is lead. You had better talk trifles elegantly to the most trifling woman, than coarse inelegant sense to the most solid man: you had better return a dropped fan genteelly, than give a thousand pounds awkwardly; you had better refuse a favour gracefully, than grant it clumsily. Manner is all, in everything; it is by manner only that you can please, and consequently rise.

David Hume in later life; like a 'turtle-eating alderman'; portrait by Allan Ramsay.

DAVID HUME (1711–76) was born at Edinburgh of a distinguished Scottish legal family; his father having died in 1713, he was brought up by his devoted mother, 'a woman of singular Merit'. He was an unpromising boy, whom his school-fellows nick-named 'the Clod'; and during his adolescence he suffered from moods of nervous depression that it took him many years to overcome. After studying at Edinburgh University and making an unsuccessful attempt to acquire the secrets of trade at the office of a Bristol merchant, Hume discovered that he had 'an unsurmountable aversion to everything but the pursuits of philosophy and general learning'; and he left for France in 1734, determined to master French and 'l'Art de Vivre, the art of society and conversation'.

At La Flèche, a small Angevin town, Hume produced his great book, A Treatise of Human Nature, the work he had begun to plan while he was still an undergraduate. The Treatise attracted very little notice when the first two volumes appeared in 1739. Its sceptical tendency offended all the critics. But Hume had a courageous and exceptionally resilient nature; disappointments failed to sour him, and he now applied himself to various uninteresting tasks, until in 1748 he could resume his life as an independent man of letters. In 1748 he published his Enquiry concerning the Human Understanding, followed by a series of works on morals, religion and political theory, and finally by his History of England, issued in six volumes between 1754 and 1762. The History established his fame at home; and in 1763 he visited Paris as secretary to the British ambassador, Lord Hertford. There he received a rapturous welcome; he became the darling of French society, courted and flattered despite his stoutness and clumsiness – it is said that he greatly resembled a 'turtle-eating alderman' – by all the smartest women of the day. In 1766 Hume returned to London, where he served as an Under-Secretary of State from

1767 to 1769; and that year he finally retired to Edinburgh. His last years were placid and dignified. He died – having accepted the prospect of extinction with an equanimity that alarmed and puzzled Boswell who, determined to observe an unbeliever confronting death, called on him towards the end – in August 1776.

Hume's aim in his major philosophical works, the *Treatise* and the *Enquiry*, was to investigate the foundations of human knowledge. The conclusion he draws is that human understanding is limited, and can only be trusted to deal with questions that relate to our perceptual experience. Thus he decided, for example, that we can never infer an effect from a cause; we must simply rely on the customary expectation, derived from experience, of one phenomenon following another. When faced by the final implications of his sceptical method, which threaten even reasoning itself, Hume admits to being overcome with a sense of 'pensive melancholy', and turns to the everyday world for comfort:

I dine, I play a game of backgammon, I converse, and am merry with my friends; and when after three or four hours' amusement I would return to these speculations, they appear so cold, and strained, and ridiculous, that I cannot find it in my heart to enter into them any further. Here then I find myself absolutely and necessarily determined to live, and talk, and act, like other people in the common affairs of life.

Hume's sceptical method is perfectly matched by his lucid style and by his characteristic irony:

To reconcile the indifference and contingency of human actions with prescience, or to defend absolute decrees and yet free the Deity from being the author of sin, has been found hitherto to exceed all the power of philosophy. Happy, if she be thence sensible of her temerity when she pries into these sublime mysteries, and, leaving a scene so full of obscurities and perplexities, returns, with suitable modesty, to her true and proper province, the examination of common life, where she will find difficulties enough to employ her enquiries without launching into so boundless an ocean of doubt, uncertainty, and contradiction.

For Hume, philosophy was a department of literature. He was a devotee of literary style; and he wrote not for the specialist but for the educated general reader, to whose experience he frequently appeals, as he is developing his arguments. When he applied his sceptical method to religion, Hume was on dangerous ground. Johnson dubbed him a 'Great Infidel'; and his *Dialogues Concerning Natural Religion* were deliberately held back until the author had died. Organized, with dramatic skill and cunning wit, so that the orthodox believer plays into the sceptic's hands, apart from his youthful *Treatise*, a masterpiece of lucid exposition, they are perhaps his greatest literary work; and the hostility they aroused is a tribute to their effectiveness. Hume's opponents were further exasperated by the testimony of his own life, which appeared to support his contention that humanity and generosity are not always the products of a firm religious faith, and that even a self-proclaimed agnostic may be a good and happy man.

ADAM SMITH (1723–90) is justly regarded as the founder of political economy, though some of his methodology had been adumbrated in the work of earlier writers. A posthumous child – his father had been a Scottish comptroller of customs – he was born in Kirkcaldy, Fife, and after attending the Kirkcaldy Grammar School, he went on to Glasgow University, where he came under the influence of the 'never-to-be-forgotten Dr Hutcheson', a distinguished philosopher who based his system on the benevolent ideas of Shaftesbury. From Glasgow he went up to Balliol College, Oxford, remaining in residence until 1746. At first he considered taking Holy Orders, but in 1751 he was awarded the Chair of Logic at Glasgow, a post he exchanged in the following year for the Professorship of Moral Philosophy. In 1759 he published his *Theory of Moral Sentiments*, which brought him fame and led to his being offered the post of tutor to the young Duke of Buccleuch. He resigned his professorship in 1764, and left for a tour of Europe with his pupil. Smith found little to interest him until he reached Paris; but there he met the group of economists known as the 'Physiocrats', who encouraged him to devote his energies to the great work that he had recently begun 'in order to pass away the time'. Returning to Kirkcaldy, he stayed for nearly ten years with his mother, while he studied and continued to write his book. *An Inquiry into the Nature and Causes of the Wealth of Nations*, a volume that laid the foundations of modern economic theory, appeared in 1776. Appointed Commissioner of Customs at Edinburgh, he spent the remainder of his life in 'the modern Athens', becoming a conspicuous local figure as he perambulated the city with his peculiar swaying walk, holding a bunch of flowers in one hand and carrying his cane across his shoulder. David Hume was a close friend. Elected Lord Rector of the University of Glasgow in 1787, he died in July 1790.

Adam Smith.

Smith's enormous influence can be partly explained both by his extensive and detailed knowledge of his subject, and by the clarity with which he presented his ideas. He supported his analysis of the faults of the English commercial system and his recommendations of commercial freedom – the economic philosophy of *laissez-faire* – with simple, particular instances, set forth in a plain, natural prose:

By what a frugal man annually saves, he not only affords maintenance to an additional number of productive hands, for that or the ensuing year, but, like the founder of a public work-house, he establishes as it were a perpetual fund for the maintenance of an equal number in all times to come. The perpetual allotment and destination of this fund, indeed, is not always guarded, however, by any positive law, by any trust-right or deed of mortmain. It is always guarded, however, by a very powerful principle, the plain and evident interest of every individual to whom any share of it shall ever belong. No part of it can ever afterwards be employed to maintain any but productive hands, without an evident loss to the person who thus perverts it from its proper destination.

EDMUND BURKE (1729–97), was born in Dublin, the son of an Irish lawyer. He was educated with his two brothers at a Quaker school at Ballitore, and then at Trinity College, Dublin, where he took his degree in 1748. His father was anxious he should become a lawyer, and he was entered at the Middle Temple. But he was never called to the Bar; he found history and philosophy more congenial and far more sympathetic than his father's calling, and was presently introduced to the circle of Samuel Johnson and Sir Joshua Reynolds. In 1756 he published an anonymous parody of Bolingbroke, *A Vindication of Natural Society*, and during the same year a treatise on aesthetics entitled *A Philosophical Enquiry into the Origin of our Ideas of the Sublime and the Beautiful*, which had considerable influence abroad. Together with the publisher Dodsley, Burke founded *The Annual Register* in 1759, and wrote a yearly survey of events until 1788. In 1761 he was appointed private secretary to the Chief Secretary for Ireland, and subsequently attached with a similar rôle to the Prime Minister, Lord Rockingham. He entered Parliament as member for Wendover in 1765; and in 1766 he delivered the first of his famous speeches, supporting the rights of the American Colonists. The disturbances caused by the expulsion of John Wilkes from Parliament were the subject of his most impressive early political pamphlet, *Thoughts on the Cause of the Present Discontents* (1770). But he reached the heights of his fame in 1788, when he led the impeachment of Warren Hastings, his speech, which extended over four days, being a masterpiece of oratory. From the outset, he had had misgivings about the French Revolution; and in 1790 he published his *Reflections on the Revolution in France*, a sustained attack upon the new regime. This work provoked Tom Paine (1737–1809) to an equally celebrated reply, *The Rights of Man*. Ironically enough, Paine had derived many of his radical ideas from Burke's early defence of the American cause.

Edmund Burke; portrait by Joshua Reynolds. According to Johnson, his 'stream of mind is perpetual'.

In 1791 Burke denounced his close friend Charles James Fox and deserted the Whig party over the Bill for the division of Canada. He retired on a government pension in 1794; his health slowly failed, and he died at his country house near Beaconsfield on 7 July 1797. Most of his life had been spent in opposition; but his political influence was great and lasting, as the fountain-head of modern British Conservatism, and the articulator of many of its fundamental principles. Johnson deeply admired Burke, though he often differed with him. Burke's 'stream of mind', he declared, was 'perpetual'. And, in 1784, 'Yes, Sir, if a man were to go by chance at the same time with Burke under a shed to shun a shower, he would say – "This is an extraordinary man".'

Burke was first and foremost an orator, known to his contemporaries as 'the Demosthenes of England'; and his prose is that of a great rhetorician, with its declamatory passion, rich imagery, sonorous periods, and deliberately cadenced language. Burke strives for heightened eloquence; he aims at the emotional *tour de force*, as in his celebrated tribute to Queen Marie-Antoinette, and to the ideals of beauty and chivalry that, in Burke's romantic view, she represented:

I thought ten thousand swords must have leaped from their scabbards to avenge even a look that threatened her with insult. But the age of chivalry is gone. That of sophisters, economists, and calculators, has succeeded; and the glory of Europe is extinguished for ever. Never, never more, shall we behold that generous loyalty to rank and sex, that proud submission, that dignified obedience, that subordination of the heart, which kept alive, even in servitude itself, the spirit of an exalted freedom. The unbought grace of life, the chief defence of nations, the nurse of manly sentiment and heroic enterprise, is gone! It is gone, that sensibility of principle, that chastity of honour, which felt a stain like a wound, which inspired courage whilst it mitigated ferocity, which ennobled whatever it touched, and under which vice lost half its evil, by losing all its grossness.

This passage, though it reveals Burke's prose at its most harmonious, also exhibits his rhetorical tendency, which allowed emotion and his love of the grand gesture to overcloud his better judgment. Fanny Burney first heard Burke speak at the trial of Warren Hastings. She was immediately moved by his surpassing eloquence; but, as he proceeded, she writes, 'there appeared more of study than of truth, more of invective than of justice'; and ultimately the shrewd young woman decided that there was 'little of proof to so much passion'. Yet despite the fact that Burke's political and emotional prejudices, and his enjoyment of his own eloquence, may often have carried him away, he remains one of the greatest Anglo-Irishmen of the later eighteenth century.

Edward Gibbon in his younger days; portrait by H. Walton.

EDWARD GIBBON (1737–94) came of a family of country gentlemen which had originated in the Weald of Kent. His parents' other children all died young; Edward himself was a sickly and ugly boy, afflicted by a series of disorders 'both numerous and frequent'; and had it not been for the care of a devoted aunt, he would certainly have gone the same way as his brothers and his sisters. The Gibbons originally lived at Putney, then a pleasant Thameside village; but after his wife's death in 1747, Edward Gibbon senior gave up his London amusements and retired to a Hampshire manor-house named Buriton. At the age of fourteen, he entered his son as a Gentleman Commoner at Magdalen College, Oxford; but the adolescent, who already thirsted after knowledge, was soon deeply disappointed with eighteenth-century academic life; and in 1753 he suddenly departed for London, and was received into the Church of Rome. He had been in a mood of 'blind activity', he afterwards wrote; and a 'momentary show of enthusiasm had raised him above all temporal considerations'. The University then expelled the apostate, and his father, amazed and horrified, ordered that he should leave England at once and remain abroad until he had repented. Exiled to Lausanne, he remained there nearly five years. Meanwhile, he was reconverted to Protestantism and almost forgot how to speak English. At the same time, he fell deeply in love. Mademoiselle Curchod, 'the only woman who could ever have made me happy', was the daughter of a Swiss minister. But once he was allowed to return to Buriton, Mr Gibbon immediately forbade the marriage. The young man submitted after a brief but painful struggle. In his own famous phrase, 'I sighed as a lover, I obeyed as a son . . .'

The failure of his earliest – indeed his only important – love-affair was the first of many adult set-backs. He had established his health, enlarged his knowledge of the world and regained his father's friendship; but once he had quietly settled down at Buriton, and begun a course of steady reading, the outbreak of war between England and France obliged him to accept a commission in a newly formed militia regiment, and embark on a 'wandering life of military servitude', among 'companions who had neither the knowledge of scholars nor the manners of gentlemen'. It was with immense relief that in December 1762 he at length gave up his regimental duties.

He was now free, like other Englishmen of his class, to undertake the Grand Tour. In Paris he attended literary salons and hob-nobbed with the *Philosophes*; in Switzerland he visited Voltaire at Ferney; and, during the spring of 1764, he finally made his way across the Alps. That autumn he entered Rome; and there, on 20 October, he enjoyed the moment of illumination that was to transform his whole existence. As he 'sat musing among the ruins of the Capitol where the barefooted friars were singing vespers in the temple of Jupiter . . . the idea of writing the decline and fall of the city first started to my mind.'

Yet, again, he encountered many reverses. As soon as he returned to England, he found his father ill and his family affairs in a state of sad disorder. Gibbon accepted his responsibilities, both private and public, with his usual philosophic calm. The elder Gibbon died in 1770; and not until he had sold Buriton and acquired a London house could he finally begin work on the tremendous project that had 'started to his mind' in 1764. The first volume of *The History of the Decline and Fall of the Roman Empire* appeared in February 1776. It had a magnificent reception, and soon found its way, Gibbon informs us, to 'every table' and to 'almost every toilette'.

It would continue to occupy him for another eleven years, and during the interval, in September 1783, he severed his connection with the London scene and formed a new establishment with his friend Deyverdun at Lausanne. Gibbon's account of how he finished his work is one of the most moving passages of his autobiography:

It was on the day, or rather night, of the 27th of June, 1787, between the hours of eleven and twelve, that I wrote the last lines of the last page, in a summer house in my garden. After laying down my pen I took several turns in a *berceau*, or covered walk of Acacias . . . The air was temperate, the sky was severe, the silver orb of the moon was reflected from the waters . . . I will not dissemble the first emotions of joy on the recovery of freedom, and perhaps the establishment of my fame. But my pride was soon humbled, and a sober melancholy was spread over my mind by the idea that I had taken an everlasting leave of an old and agreeable companion, and that, whatsoever might be the future date of my history, the life of the historian must be short and precarious.

Among the book's keenest admirers was David Hume, who hastened to inform the author that 'whether I consider the Dignity of your Style, the Depth of your Matter, or the Extensiveness of your Learning, I must regard the Work as equally the Object of Esteem . . .' Johnson and Boswell, on the other hand, both regarded the historian as a noxious infidel; and Boswell, who had taken a personal dislike to him when they met at Sir Joshua Reynolds' celebrated Club, complained that, despite 'its very mellifluous style', it contained much artful infidelity', and asserted that before he encouraged the reader to enter his 'garden of flowery eloquence' Gibbon should have erected a warning notice, 'Spring guns and man-traps set here'. The book's whole tendency, of course, is profoundly anti-Christian; for Gibbon believed that it was the influence of the Christian faith that had gradually brought down the Roman Empire. His agnosticism colours the whole narrative. The man who had once defied his father by deciding to become a Catholic had since developed a passionate suspicion of religious faith in any shape or form. Though the tone he adopted was cool and measured, violent prejudices and prepossessions often boil beneath the surface. He wrote of Christianity, observed the renowned scholar Richard Porson, like a man whom the Christian religion had personally injured. Hence the contemptuous phrase with which he dismissed the Byzantine Empire; it had existed, he wrote, 'one thousand and fifty-eight years, in a state of premature and perpetual decay'.

As an historian, the author of *The Decline and Fall* has now been largely superseded. He lives on as one of our greatest stylists, the creator of a style that exactly reflected the development of his own imagination. No other English historical writer is more nobly panoramic – or, indeed, wherever we open his book, more astonishingly readable. 'Gibbon,' declared Thomas Carlyle, 'is a kind of bridge that connects the antique with the modern ages.

And how gorgeously does it swing across the gloomy and tumultuous chasm of those barbarous centuries . . . The perusal of his work forms an epoch in the history of one's mind.'

Gibbon's method of narration is not only splendidly dramatic but, at times, exquisitely ironic. Here, for example, he is describing the spirit of supreme unworldliness said to have distinguished the early Christians:

There are two very natural propensities which we may distinguish in the most virtuous and liberal dispositions, the love of pleasure and the love of action. If the former be refined by art and learning, improved by the charms of social intercourse, and corrected by a just regard to economy, to health, and to reputation, it is productive of the greatest part of the happiness of private life. The love of action is a principle of a much stronger and more doubtful nature. It often leads to anger, to ambition, and to revenge; but, when it is guided by a sense of propriety and benevolence, it becomes the parent of every virtue . . . To the love of pleasure we may therefore ascribe most of the agreeable, to the love of action we may attribute most of the useful and respectable qualifications. The character in which both the one and the other should be harmonised would seem to constitute the most perfect idea of human nature. The insensible and inactive disposition, which should be supposed alike destitute of both, would be rejected, by the common consent of mankind, as utterly incapable of procuring any happiness to the individual, or any public benefit to the world. But it was not in *this* world that the primitive Christians were desirous of making themselves either agreeable or useful.

The Decline and Fall of the Roman Empire

Gibbon as a be-laurelled celebrity; caricature by Lady Diana Beauclerk.

Once he had completed his masterpiece, Gibbon decided to remain at Lausanne. His last years were spent in 'autumnal felicity', resting quietly on his laurels and doing the honours of his pleasant house to a succession of distinguished tourists. But during the spring of 1793, hearing that his friend Lord Sheffield had recently become a widower, he felt it his duty to return to England; and that winter he was advised by his physicians to undergo an operation. A second operation followed, and although he himself announced that he was good for 'another ten, twelve, or perhaps twenty years', his condition – the result of an abdominal rupture – suddenly deteriorated. He died, quiet and courageous to the end, on 16 January 1794.

Gothic Fantasy

HORACE WALPOLE, afterwards 4th Earl of Orford (1717–97) was a younger son of the great Sir Robert Walpole, who dominated English political life from 1714 to 1742. Horace bore little immediate resemblance to his virile, energetic parent, being effeminate, dreamy, hyper-sensitive and, even as a boy, devoted, not to the life of action, but to the world of art and literature.

(Above right) Horace Walpole, later 4th Earl of Orford; after Joshua Reynolds' portrait of 1757.

(Above left) Frontispiece to 1795 edition of *The Castle of Otranto*.

Thomas Gray was among his dearest friends at Eton, and accompanied him on the Grand Tour that he undertook in 1739. They presently fell out – as the Prime Minister's son, Walpole afterwards admitted, he had treated his middle-class companion with less regard than he deserved. He was also, unlike Gray, a comparatively rich young man; and when he had returned from his tour, he settled down to a life of cultivated ease, writing, collecting, building and pursuing various dilettante studies. In 1746, having purchased Strawberry Hill, a small property beside the Thames, he began to reconstruct it as a miniature Gothic castle. Here he soon established his private printing press, and for the remainder of Walpole's long life, his house, and the vast collection of miscellaneous bric-à-brac he had accumulated beneath its 'pie-crust' battlements, would continue to delight him. It was a fantasy translated into brick and stone, 'built [he said] to please my own taste and . . . realize my own visions'.

At Strawberry Hill he wrote *The Castle of Otranto*, first of those 'Gothick' novels which filled the English circulating libraries between the late 1760s and the appearance of Dickens's earliest books. The story seems to have originated during the summer of

1764 in a particularly vivid dream, of which all he could recover, when he returned to waking life, was that he had thought himself in an ancient castle and 'on the uppermost bannister of a great staircase . . . saw a gigantic hand in armour. In the evening I sat down and began to write, without knowing in the least what I intended to say . . .' The work absorbed him for the next two months, to the exclusion of every interest, and that winter he published his extravagant medieval romance, a fantasia that he had evidently drawn from the depths of his subconscious mind. It was vastly successful; and among the novelists it inspired were William Beckford, Mrs Radcliffe (1764–1823), whose no less celebrated *Mysteries of Udolpho* came out in 1794, Matthew Lewis (1775–1818), notorious author of *The Monk*, the young Shelley and Thomas De Quincey, who published a Gothic novel, *The Avenger*, as late as 1838. Walpole followed it up in 1767 with an alarming blank-verse tragedy, *The Mysterious Mother*. Again it had a rugged Gothic background; but the subject he now chose was an incestuous passion; and it has been conjectured that his youthful affection for his own attractive, wayward mother may perhaps 'explain both his choice of a theme and the intense feeling with which the theme was handled'.

Otherwise, apart from the letters he wrote, Walpole's chief literary productions were either historical or anecdotal, a *Catalogue of Royal and Noble Authors, Anecdotes of Painting in England, Historic Doubts on the Life and Reign of King Richard the Third*, and memoirs of the reigns of George II and George III. Walpole, Johnson remarked, had 'got together a great many curious little things, and told them in an elegant manner'. His masterpiece, however, was his gigantic correspondence. In the letters he addressed to a series of carefully chosen friends – those he despatched to Horace Mann cover the whole period between December 1739, and June 1786 – he drew an extraordinarily vivid picture of his own age. His correspondents were often asked to return his letters; for he himself was well-aware of their historical, perhaps of their literary, value, and employed an appropriately polished style – easy, cursive and conversational, the kind of writing in which 'art conceals art':

THE FUNERAL OF GEORGE II (from a letter to George Montagu, 13 November 1760)
Do you know, I had the curiosity to go to the burying t'other night; I had never seen a royal funeral; nay, I walked as a rag of quality, which I found would be, and so it was, the easiest way of seeing it. It is absolutely a noble sight. The Prince's Chamber, hung with purple, and a quantity of silver lamps, the coffin under a canopy of purple velvet, and six vast chandeliers of silver on high stands, had a very good effect . . . When we came to the chapel of Henry the Seventh, all solemnity and decorum ceased – no order was observed, people set or stood where they could or would, the yeomen of the guard were crying out for help, oppressed by

the immense weight of the coffin, the Bishop read sadly, and blundered in the prayers, the fine chapter, *Man that is born of a woman*, was chanted, not read, and the anthem, besides being unmeasurably tedious, would have served as well for a nuptial. The real serious part was the figure of the Duke of Cumberland, heightened by a thousand melancholy circumstances. He had a dark brown adonis, and a cloak of black cloth, with a train of five yards. Attending the funeral of a father, however little reason he had so to love him, could not be pleasant. His leg extremely bad, yet forced to stand upon it near two hours, his face bloated and distorted with his late paralytic stroke, which has affected, too, one of his eyes, and placed over the mouth of the vault, into which, in all probability, he must himself so soon descend – think how unpleasant a situation! He bore it all with a firm and unaffected countenance. This grave scene was fully contrasted by the burlesque Duke of Newcastle. He fell into a fit of crying the moment he came into the chapel, and flung himself back in a stall, the Archbishop hovering over him with a smelling-bottle – but in two minutes his curiosity got the better of his hypocrisy, and he ran about the chapel with his glass to spy who was or was not there, spying with one hand, and mopping his eyes with t'other. Then returned the fear of catching cold, and the Duke of Cumberland, who was sinking with heat, felt himself weighed down, and turning round, found it was the Duke of Newcastle standing upon his train to avoid the chill of the marble. It was very theatric to look down into the vault, where the coffin lay, attended by mourners with lights. Clavering, the Groom of the Bedchamber, refused to sit up with the body, and was dismissed by the King's order.

WILLIAM BECKFORD (1760–1844) had inherited immense riches. Aesthete, enthusiast, amateur of strange sensations and, above all else, a spoiled child, he was disgraced and driven into social exile before he had reached the age of twenty-six. No one could have entered the world under more auspicious circumstances. Grandson of a prosperous Jamaican planter, son of a plutocratic Lord Mayor, he was educated in harmony by the young Mozart himself, in architecture, by Sir William Chambers, in painting and drawing, by Alexander Cozens. As 'England's wealthiest son', he soon dazzled his contemporaries. But Beckford's nature always ran to extremes; like his hero, Vathek, he combined a thirst for knowledge with a devotion to illicit pleasures; and when he was nineteen, he became violently enamoured of a handsome, effeminate boy named William Courtenay. In 1781 he held a notorious Christmas party at Fonthill, his Wiltshire country house, where, behind closed doors, amid scenes of fantastic splendour, he entertained both his mistress and his boy-favourite; and, in 1784, although a year earlier his family had married him off and he had proved himself a kindly husband, his passion for Courtenay, discovered through an unlucky domestic accident, brought about his social ruin.

His collection of travel sketches, *Dreams, Waking Thoughts and*

Incidents, had been produced in 1783. In 1786 his wife died; he now spent twelve years travelling around Europe; and during this period he gathered material for the brilliant travel-book, *Recollections of an Expedition to the Monasteries of Alcobaca and Batalha*, that he eventually published in 1835. Meanwhile, in 1782, soon after the Fonthill party, he had written his Arabian tale, *The History of the Caliph Vathek*. A proficient linguist, he employed the French language; but in 1786 the story was translated into English and published, without his leave, by a literary clergyman, the Reverend Samuel Henley, to whom he had entrusted it. On his return home, Beckford conceived the plan of rebuilding his father's old house, and began to raise the towering Gothic structure that soon became celebrated as Fonthill Abbey. Here everything was designed on the same prodigious scale. From a lofty central tower (which presently collapsed in ruin) radiated extensive galleries; St Michael's gallery, for example, was over a hundred feet long. And here he installed a magnificent art-collection that included not only French furniture and Renaissance cups and bronzes, but some of the greatest masterpieces of fifteenth-century Italian painting.

Like Walpole's Strawberry Hill, Fonthill Abbey was a visionary edifice. Beckford, however, pleading poverty – his annual income from his West-Indian estates had once amounted to some £155,000, but the Abbey, he said, had cost him more than a quarter of a million – in 1822 abandoned his pleasure-dome, sold the contents and moved to a much more modest house at Bath.

(*Above left*) William Beckford at the age of forty; portrait by Hopper.

(*Above right*) Fonthill Abbey, the gigantic visionary edifice that, with the help of James Wyatt, Beckford built for himself in Wiltshire; the east view.

He died in 1844, lonely, embittered and cantankerous. It was an unhappy life; but at least two of the books he left behind him have secured him a place among English Romantic writers. His travel-book is a wonderfully picturesque narrative; while *Vathek* is both a symbolic self-portrait and an imaginative reflection of his own emotional tragedy. Vathek, a headstrong young prince, a student of all the pleasures and all the sciences – 'even sciences that did not exist' – who had built himself a palace consisting of five pavilions 'destined for the particular gratification of each of his senses', at last, after many terrifying adventures, reaches Eblis, prison-house of lost souls and the 'abode of vengeance and despair'. Vathek's companion is a beautiful woman; around them the hearts of the damned are wreathed in sheets of fire. They are obliged to join the crowd:

At almost the same instant, the same voice announced . . . the awful and irrevocable decree. Their hearts immediately took fire, and they, at once, lost the most precious gift of Heaven: – Hope. These unhappy beings recoiled with looks of the most furious distraction. Vathek beheld in the eyes of Nouronihar nothing but rage and vengeance; nor could she discern aught in his, but aversion and despair . . .

Such was, and should be, the punishment of unrestrained passions and atrocious deeds!

Sheridan and the Comedy of Manners

Richard Brinsley Sheridan; pastel by J. Russell.

RICHARD BRINSLEY SHERIDAN (1751–1816) followed Oliver Goldsmith in the ranks of eighteenth-century dramatists. The son of an actor, he was educated at Harrow and, while still a very young man, met Elizabeth Linley, a beautiful and accomplished singer, with whom in 1773 he eloped to France. After he had fought two duels on her behalf, the romantic pair were married. Sheridan's first play, *The Rivals*, was produced in 1775 when he was only twenty-four. It had a great success; and in 1776 he acquired Garrick's share in the Drury Lane Theatre and succeeded him as its director. *A Trip to Scarborough* and *The School for Scandal* were staged at Drury Lane in 1777; and during the same year Johnson proposed him for membership of the famous Club, announcing that he had written the two best comedies of the age. Sheridan's last original play, a burlesque farce, *The Critic, or a Tragedy Rehears'd*, reached the boards in 1779. Sheridan now turned to politics, entering the House of Commons in 1780. He quickly made his reputation as a brilliant Whig orator; and his speeches against Warren Hastings are said to have rivalled those of Edmund Burke. Besides holding a series of government offices, he became friend and adviser to the Prince of Wales. When he lost his parliamentary seat, however, and his theatrical fortunes began to decline, Sheridan fell on evil days; and the loss of the new theatre he had built – it was burnt down in 1809 – completed his financial ruin. Not only was he hunted by his creditors; but heavy drinking had undermined his health and given him the florid and scorbutic appearance of a veteran drunkard. In Byron's reminiscences of his London life, we catch a curious glimpse of 'poor dear Sherry'. He 'got drunk very thoroughly and very soon', and the poet occasionally had 'to convoy him home – no sinecure, for he was so tipsy that I was obliged to put on his cock'd hat for him; to be sure it tumbled off again, and I was not myself so sober as to be able to pick it up ...' Sheridan died in 1816, the year of Byron's social downfall.

On its first night, *The Rivals* was a failure. Sheridan then withdrew the play, quickly re-wrote it and, ten days later, presented a new version that immediately made his name. It is a derivative work, based on previous English comedies, but enlivened by Sheridan's brilliant dialogue and his mastery of theatrical devices. Here he derided popular theatrical taste, in particular the extravagances engendered by 'The Goddess of the woeful countenance – The Sentimental Muse!'; but he was shrewd enough himself to include a slightly mawkish sub-plot. With his youthful exuberance and his scathing attacks on prudery and humbug, Sheridan brought back to the English theatre something of the

'Lady Teasle, by all that's damnable!'; early 19th-century illustration to *The School for Scandal*.

Sir Peter.—"LADY TEAZLE, BY ALL THAT'S DAMNABLE."—*Act* iv, *scene* 3.

spirit of the Restoration stage. His virtuosity is most evident at the
end of *The Rivals*, as it moves into the realm of farce. The characters, including the incomparable Mrs Malaprop, though threatened with imminent disaster, seem paralysed by their own
verbosity:

MRS MALAPROP: So! So! here's fine work! – here's fine suicide, paracide,
and simulation going on in the fields! and Sir Anthony
not to be found to prevent the antistrophe!

JULIA: For Heaven's sake, Madam, what's the meaning of
this?

MRS MALAPROP: That gentleman can tell – 'twas he enveloped the
affair to me.

LYDIA: Do, Sir, will you, inform us.

FAG: Ma'am, I should hold myself very deficient in every
requisite that forms the man of breeding, if I delayed
a moment to give all the information in my power to a
lady so deeply interested in the affair as you are.

LYDIA: But quick! quick, Sir!

FAG: True, Ma'am, as you say, one should be quick in
divulging matters of this nature; for should we be
tedious, perhaps while we are flourishing on the
subject, two or three lives may be lost!

LYDIA: O patience! – Do, Ma'am, for Heaven's sake! tell us
what is the matter?

MRS MALAPROP: Why! murder's the matter! slaughter's the matter!
killing's the matter! – but he can tell you the per-
pendiculars.

For *The School for Scandal* Sheridan drew on his knowledge of the
modes and manners of the fashionable world of London and Bath.
The play has remained one of the most popular English comedies
ever since its first appearance, when it was 'received by a brilliant
and crowded audience with the most universal and continued
marks of applause'. It has survived thanks to its cleverly constructed scenes, and its admirable dialogue, written in a prose
that, although polished and epigrammatic, is still conversationally
light and rapid. But as in its predecessor, *The Rivals*, the sentimental side is apt to jar. Lamb rightly called it 'a mixture of
Congreve with sentimental incompatibilities'.

7

The Nineteenth Century

Two great movements determined the course of English nineteenth-century life and literature – the Romantic revolution and its Industrial counterpart. Each had originated in England and would reach its highest point on English soil; and for a while they co-existed peacefully. At first, Romantic tourists found as much to admire in mines, factories and blast-furnaces as in torrents, lakes and mountains; both types of landscape might be equally 'picturesque' and afford the same inspiring prospects. Then, before the nineteenth century was well under way, a visionary poet, William Blake, began to perceive the growing evils of industrial civilization. In *Milton*, written and illustrated between 1804 and 1805, Satan himself, 'Prince of the Starry Hosts and of the Wheels of Heaven', is said to turn the factory-wheels day and night, and his labours to symbolize 'Eternal Death'.

During the next age, a long series of English writers, headed by John Ruskin and Thomas Carlyle, were to thunder against the destructive progress of industrial England, which threatened to degrade and destroy every human quality they valued. A strain of protest runs through Victorian literature and a sense of deep anxiety. The world was no longer the safe and ordered place that the Augustans had depicted; it was dark, dangerous, divided, full of hideous doubts and grim forebodings. After 1848, when violent popular revolts had shaken half the thrones of Europe, there was a general fear that worse might follow; and Disraeli's 'two nations' – the rich and the poor – were believed to be drifting slowly towards some savage trial of strength. These fears were echoed by prophets and moralists, and by a number of Victorian novelists, who, like George Eliot, became increasingly preoccupied with contemporary social problems.

Apart from the Romantic revolution, which transformed our view of Man and Nature, the growth of the novel as a literary form was probably the most dramatic development of the age reviewed here. To appreciate the degree of richness and complexity that the novel very soon achieved, one need only glance through some of the novels that had delighted eighteenth-century critics. Men as sophisticated as Johnson, Burke and Gibbon were enchanted by Fanny Burney's *Evelina*, with its primitive plot and

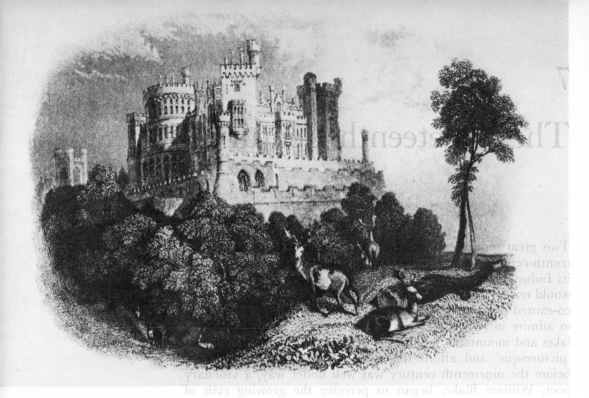

Belvoir Castle: where Crabbe spent two painful years as the Duke of Rutland's private chaplain.

rudimentary set of personages. It is difficult to imagine what they would have made of *Middlemarch*, written less than a hundred years later.

Meanwhile, the Romantic movement had not lost its strength, despite its changing social background. Tennyson and Browning were directly descended from the earlier race of poets. Though Pope shows traces of Romantic feeling, and Walpole and Beckford had written 'Gothick' fantasies, the movement had not finally taken shape, as a decisive literary force, until Wordsworth and Coleridge published their *Lyrical Ballads* in September, 1798. English verse would long remain Romantic; and Wordsworth, Shelley, and Keats still exerted their influence throughout the opening decade of the twentieth century. It required the combined efforts of W.B. Yeats, once he had decided he must modernize his style, and of Ezra Pound's protégé, T.S. Eliot, to give the poetic art a new direction.

Crabbe and the Romantic Revolution

Although he entered the world sixteen years earlier than Wordsworth, GEORGE CRABBE (1754–1832) published most of his major works between 1807 and 1819, and had a view of Nature as strange and arresting as that of any of the great Romantic poets. Born in the East-Anglian fishing village of Aldeburgh, where his father was a minor customs official, at the age of fourteen he was apprenticed to a local surgeon, and, as he later informed Burke, both 'learned to bleed' and eagerly read romances. After a brief

and ill-fated medical career, he set off for London in 1780 to seek his living as a poet. It was a desperate step; and, faced with poverty, hunger and loneliness, he appealed to Edmund Burke, sending him a number of his manuscripts. The great orator recognized his gifts and responded generously, lending him money, introducing him to Reynolds and Dr Johnson, and arranging for him to be ordained. In 1782 Burke also persuaded the reluctant Duke of Rutland to appoint Crabbe as his private chaplain. In later life, Crabbe refused even to speak of the two painful years spent at Belvoir Castle, where he was treated with deliberate condescension, and the family dog was named 'Crabbe'. In 1783, however, he found it possible to marry his beloved Sarah Elmy, after an engagement that had lasted for eleven years.

That May his poem *The Village* was published, Dr Johnson having consented to read it and add a few lines of his own. Here Crabbe opposed the grim realities of English rustic life to the weak pastoralism that still flourished in English poetry, and that had tainted, so he believed, Oliver Goldsmith's famous *Deserted Village*. Though it was well-received, Crabbe published no other important poem until the beginning of the next century. Nevertheless he did not cease from writing; and three novels and a volume of 'romantic' tales were among the many manuscripts that he destroyed. In 1790 he had begun to take opium as a remedy for stomach pains; and he continued to absorb regular small doses for the remainder of his life; with the result that, although his health was uninjured, the dreams that visited him every night grew

(*Above*) Aldeburgh, Crabbe's birthplace; a 19th-century engraving.

(*Below*) George Crabbe; pencil drawing by F. Chantrey.

increasingly fantastic. In 1796, four happy years in Suffolk were brought to a close by the death of a third son; and his wife, whom he had always loved and cherished, became a permanent manic-depressive of the most difficult and tiresome kind.

Then *The Parish Register* appeared in 1807, and was acclaimed as a powerful and highly original work. *The Borough* followed it in 1810, and *Tales in Verse* and *Tales of the Hall* in 1812 and 1819 respectively. In 1813 Mrs Crabbe died, and Crabbe himself fell dangerously ill. But he recovered, and lived on for another ten years, during which he was lionized by London literary society, meeting Wordsworth at Hampstead and visiting his great admirer Sir Walter Scott in Edinburgh. The last period of his life he spent as curate of Trowbridge in Wiltshire, attended by his sons.

Byron's description of Crabbe – 'Nature's sternest painter, yet the best' – underlines the aspect of Crabbe's poetry that was most admired by his contemporaries. His gift of observation and his ability to combine accurate detail with a powerful immediacy of effect led them to compare him with the Dutch genre painters and with the English academician, Sir David Wilkie. But Crabbe's landscapes have a nightmarish life of their own:

> Lo! where the heath, with withering brake grown o'er,
> Lends the light turf that warms the neighbouring poor;
> From thence a length of burning sand appears,
> Where the thin harvest waves its wither'd ears;
> Rank weeds, that every art and care defy,
> Reign o'er the land, and rob the blighted rye:
> There thistles stretch their prickly arms afar,
> And to the ragged infant threaten war;
> There poppies nodding, mock the hope of toil;
> There the blue bugloss paints the sterile soil;
> Hardy and high, above the slender sheaf,
> The slimy mallow waves her silky leaf;
> O'er the young shoot the charlock throws a shade,
> And clasping tares cling round the sickly blade;
> With mingled tints the rocky coasts abound,
> And a sad splendour vainly shines around.

Here, in this extract from *The Village*, Crabbe transcends mere description; his weeds have an actively malevolent life, and their rank luxuriance mocks the hovels of the poor.

In the *Tales* of 1812 we find his noblest imaginative work; for in them he combines the insight of a poet with the talents of a novelist. It is not surprising that Jane Austen admired them greatly, and fancifully pictured herself as Mrs Crabbe. He portrays squires, parsons, merchants and farmers with all the gusto that he had elsewhere devoted to the struggling existence of the peasant. From the standpoint of a moral psychologist, he analyzes the moral failures, the weaknesses and perversities common to all mankind.

Though his view of life is basically sombre, he also excels in astringent comedy, as in his poem 'The Mother', when he introduces a dialogue between an exacting wife and her solicitous husband:

> 'Would she some sea-port, Weymouth, Scarborough, grace?' –
> 'He knew she hated every watering-place.'
> 'The town?' – 'What! now 'twas empty, joyless, dull?'
> – 'In winter?' – 'No; she liked it worse when full'.
> She talk'd of building – 'Would she plan a room?' –
> 'No! she could live, as he desired, in gloom.' . . .
> 'My dear, my gentle Dorothea, say,
> 'Can I oblige you?' – 'You may go away'.

Dealing with a manic-depressive wife must frequently have been an onerous task; but Crabbe was able to use his sad experience impersonally and comically.

In his approach to life, Crabbe resembles Jane Austen, Scott and even Byron, rather than Wordsworth, Coleridge and Shelley. There are, however, numerous passages that suggest powerful emotional impulses, underlying the rational surface of his mind, for example, this extract from 'The Adventures of Richard':

> I loved to walk where none had walked before,
> About the rocks that ran along the shore;
> Or far beyond the sight of men to stray,
> And take my pleasure when I lost my way;
> For then 'twas mine to trace the hilly heath,
> And all the mossy moor that lies beneath:
> Here had I favourite stations, where I stood
> And heard the murmurs of the ocean-flood,
> With not a sound beside, except when flew
> Aloft the lapwing, or the gray curlew . . .

Crabbe's son, who wrote the poet's biography, tells how one summer's day his father was seized with 'so intense a longing to see the sea, from which he had never before been so long absent, that he mounted his horse, rode alone to the coast of Lincolnshire, sixty miles from his house, dipped in the waves that washed the beach of Aldeburgh, and returned to Stathern'.

Crabbe has never lacked admirers. They included Tennyson, Clough, Fitzgerald, Gissing and, in the present century, E. M. Forster, James Joyce, Virginia Woolf and Ezra Pound. Thomas Hardy testified to the deep influence that Crabbe had exerted on his own fiction. Yet today, despite his psychological and sociological probings – 'and closely let me view the naked human heart' – Crabbe is not very often read; and his genius deserves a wider audience. Beneath his disenchanted view of the human condition, we detect a profoundly feeling and understanding spirit, which gives his work its special charm.

WILLIAM WORDSWORTH (1770–1850) was born at Cockermouth in Cumberland, and spent his boyhood at Hawkshead among the English Lakes. There he received the spiritual education to which we owe his greatest poems; for it was during his youth and early manhood – the 'seed-time' of his soul – that he enjoyed almost all the experiences that formed the basis of his adult genius. His life may be divided into two unequal portions – a period of bold imaginative activity, which came to an end about 1816, when he was only forty-six; and what a modern biographer has called his 'long, patient, and dignified old age', when, ruminating over and laboriously moralizing the poetic material he had accumulated in his youth, he became a Grand Old Man of English Literature. By some of his fellow Romantics, once he had renounced the revolutionary principles of his youth, he was regarded as an arch-apostate. In 1818 Shelley dubbed him 'a beastly and pitiful wretch', and likened him to 'Simonides, that flatterer of the Sicilian tyrants'. For Wordsworth, now a staunch conservative, had in 1790 been a keen republican and, during his first visit to revolutionary France, had admired the glorious prospect of a new society:

> France standing on the top of golden hours,
> And human nature seeming born again.

His second visit, in 1791, was marked by a dramatic personal adventure. At Orléans, whither he had gone to learn French, he grew attached to a girl named Annette Vallon, who bore him an illegitimate child. The lovers were parted by the storms of the Revolution; Wordsworth reluctantly returned home; and, although he made a gallant attempt to rejoin Annette in 1793, they did not meet again for ten years, when he was on the eve of marrying Mary Hutchinson. Meanwhile, he had become closely associated with another man of genius, Samuel Taylor Coleridge. The younger poet – Coleridge had been born in 1772 – immediately recognized Wordsworth as 'a very great man, the only man to whom *at all times* . . . I feel myself inferior'; and Wordsworth appreciated Coleridge's gift of 'throwing out . . . grand central truths from which might be evolved the most comprehensive systems'. He said afterwards that Coleridge and his own devoted sister, Dorothy, were the two human beings to whom his intelligence had owed the greatest debt.

Lyrical Ballads, the joint production of Wordsworth and Coleridge, and the volume that introduced 'The Ancient Mariner', appeared in 1798. Wordsworth's contributions were of a very different kind, based on subjects 'chosen from ordinary life', and dealing with 'characters and incidents . . . such as will be found in every village'. Both poets intended to discard the pompous idiom of eighteenth-century verse, and to employ the 'real language' of modern men and women – but of human beings 'in a state of vivid

sensation', when they expressed themselves with natural eloquence.
1798 was Wordsworth's *annus mirabilis*, during which he wrote
Tintern Abbey and began work on a long autobiographical poem
entitled *The Recluse*, that he afterwards renamed *The Excursion*.
His *Ode on Intimations of Immortality from Recollections of Early
Childhood* was published in the year 1807; *The White Doe of
Rylstone*, the last poem that shows some touches of his youthful
genius, appeared in 1815. Five years earlier, he and Coleridge had
quarrelled – Wordsworth was said to have declared that his old
friend was 'a rotten drunkard'; and with his wife, an 'inestimable
fellow-labourer', and Dorothy, his poetic second-self, he now
quietly settled down at Grasmere, where, dignified and 'sedately
confident', producing a large volume of mediocre verse, he would
remain until he died.

The Prelude, never published during its author's lifetime, is
undoubtedly his masterpiece – the story of a poet's education, told
in easy-flowing blank verse, which describes not only the joys of
his childhood, but his 'terrors, pains and early miseries'. Two
passages are especially significant – a picture of the carefree boy
at play:

> All shod with steel,
> We hissed along the polished ice in games
> Confederate, imitative of the chase
> And woodland pleasures, – the resounding horn,
> The pack loud bellowing, and the hunted hare.

Rydal Water and
Grasmere; from an
etching by G. Pickering.

So through the darkness and the cold we flew,
And not a voice was idle; with the din,
Meanwhile, the precipices rang aloud;
The leafless trees and every icy crag
Tinkled like iron, while far distant hills
Into the tumult sent an alien sound
Of melancholy not unnoticed, while the stars,
Eastward, were sparkling clear, and in the west
The orange sky of evening died away.

And this account of a strange and terrifying experience that for
many days, he tells us, had overclouded his imagination. One
evening he had rowed across the lake:

It was an act of stealth
And troubled pleasure, nor without the voice
Of mountain-echoes did my boat move on;
Leaving behind her still, on either side,
Small circles glittering idly in the moon,
Until they melted all into one track
Of sparkling light. But now, like one who rows,
Proud of his skill, to reach a chosen point
With an unswerving line, I fixed my view
Upon the summit of a craggy ridge,
The horizon's utmost boundary; far above
Was nothing but the stars and the grey sky.

She was an elfin pinnace; lustily
I dipped my oars into the silent lake,
And, as I rose upon the stroke, my boat
Went heaving through the water like a swan;
When, from behind that craggy steep, till then
The horizon's bound, a huge peak, black and huge
As if with voluntary power instinct
Upreared its head. I struck and struck again,
And growing still in stature the grim shape
Towered up between me and the stars, and still,
For so it seemed, with purpose of its own
And measured motion like a living thing,
Strode after me.

Wordsworth and Sir
Walter Scott at Newark
Tower; a contemporary
lithograph.

For such eighteenth-century poets as James Thomson, Nature
had been a pleasant playground. For the Romantics, it was a place
both of beauty and of terror, haunted by 'huge and mighty forms'
that inspired the poet with a thrilling sense of dread. The young
Wordsworth had been a fervent Pantheist, he explains in *Tintern
Abbey*:

The sounding cataract
Haunted me like a passion: the tall rock,
The mountain, and the deep and gloomy wood,
Their colours and their forms, were then to me

> An appetite; a feeling and a love,
> That had no need of a remoter charm,
> By thought supplied . . .

But, as both his fears and his ecstasies dwindled, and the 'visionary gleam' that had once irradiated Nature began gradually to die away, he sought to rationalize and, wherever it was possible, to moralize his earlier feelings. He no longer valued his romantic contacts with Nature for their own mysterious sake, but in his impressions found 'types' and 'emblems' of the spiritual and moral world. His spirit hardened; his talents ossified; and Carlyle, who drew so cruel a portrait of the ageing Coleridge, was scarcely less unkind to Wordsworth. Oddly enough, it was over the *French Revolution* and Carlyle's castigation of the vices of the Ancien Régime (which Wordsworth was now inclined to defend) that they principally differed. True, the old poet, Carlyle remembered towards the end of his life, had a direct and forceful way of talking, and was 'a right good old steel-grey figure'. But, at the time, he had remarked that, although 'one finds . . . a kind of sincerity in his speech . . . for prolixity, thinness, endless dilution it excels all other speeches I have heard from mortal. A genuine man (which is much), but also essentially a *small* genuine man . . . I rather fancy he *loves* nothing in the world so much as one could wish'.

Coleridge in youth; portrait by P. Vandyke, 1795.

SAMUEL TAYLOR COLERIDGE (1772–1834), declared William Wordsworth, on receiving the news of his former associate's death, was 'the most *wonderful* man that he had ever known'; and Wordsworth's heart-felt tribute is all the more impressive since they had parted after a bitter quarrel nearly twenty-five years earlier. Yet Coleridge's achievement remained fragmentary; none of the mighty tasks that he had set himself was carried through to a triumphant end; and much of his intellectual strength was dissipated in conversation. He himself would sometimes attribute his failure to the circumstances of his early life. The thirteenth son of a country clergyman, he had lost his father at the age of nine; and 'from infancy to boyhood, and from boyhood to youth', he had been treated, he would exclaim, 'most, MOST cruelly', tormented by an unkind nurse and frequently chastized by his elder brother, Frank. A precocious, but 'fretful and inordinately passionate' boy, he was sent to Christ's Hospital, where, solitary and self-absorbed, he became a 'playless day-dreamer'. In 1791, Coleridge proceeded to Cambridge; but, despite his love of books and consuming thirst for knowledge, he was an extremely idle undergraduate; and having run up debts he could see no means of paying, in desperation he 'fled to Debauchery' and plunged into a drinking bout. Once he had emerged, he decided to join the army and enlisted in the 15th Light Dragoons under the eccentric pseudonym, Silas Tomkyn Comberbache. Coleridge proved a remarkably incompetent trooper, who was perpetually tumbling from the saddle, and never learned to keep his weapons clean. But, his brothers having rallied around him – and also paid his Cambridge debts – he obtained his discharge in April 1794, and, after briefly returning to his old college, Jesus, he left the University in the November of the same year. Meanwhile, he had encountered ROBERT SOUTHEY (1774–1843), the future Poet Laureate and historian, with whom he hatched a chimerical scheme for emigrating to America and founding a small community of like-minded enthusiasts. The scheme miscarried; but Southey persuaded his impressionable friend to marry the sister of the young woman to whom he was himself engaged. The marriage – as it turned out, an extremely unhappy one – took place in October 1795.

In 1796 Coleridge published his first collection of verse, *Poems on Various Subjects*; and in 1797 he began the association with Wordsworth, and with the poet's devoted sister, Dorothy, through which he realized his genius. Wordsworth, he told Southey, was 'a very great man', the only man whom he recognized as a superior being; and Wordsworth admired the majestic scope of Coleridge's intelligence, and his way of throwing out 'grand central truths'. For a time, the two young poets and their families lived side by side among the Somersetshire hills; and during this period Coleridge wrote almost all the poems – 'The Ancient Mariner', the first part of his romantic narrative 'Christabel' (completed in 1800) and the marvellous fragment, 'Kubla Khan' – by which he is today remembered. Their joint-production, *Lyrical Ballads*, appeared in September 1798.

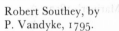

Coleridge in later life; portrait by W. Allston, 1814.

Before the century had ended, however, a major emotional catastrophe was already threatening Coleridge's peace of mind. He had conceived a passionate attachment to Sarah Hutchinson, whose sister was presently to marry Wordsworth; and this passion, and the feelings of guilt it brought with it, accentuated his natural instability. Worse followed. In 1796, as the result of his persistent ill-health, he began to take opium; and the habit, as his dosage increased, gradually destroyed his nervous equilibrium. He was now plagued by incessant nightmares; and the terrible 'night-screams' with which he awoke repeatedly disturbed his household. In 1800 Coleridge moved to the Lake District, whither he was followed by the Wordsworths; and their friendship continued until 1810, when Coleridge learned that Wordsworth had recently described him as a domestic 'nuisance' and denounced his drunken habits. The breach was never completely healed; and, during the last twenty-four years of his life, Coleridge's existence lacked a moral or emotional pivot. More and more detached from his wife and children, he continued to wander round the country, lecturing – his first course of brilliant Shakespearian lectures was delivered in the year 1812 – producing, with Byron's encouragement, a tragedy *Osorio*, at Drury Lane, and writing his major prose-work, *Biographia Literaria*. Finally, in 1816, he entered the

Robert Southey, by P. Vandyke, 1795.

CHRISTABEL.
PART THE FIRST.

THE MIDDLE OF NIGHT BY THE
CASTLE CLOCK,
AND THE OWLS HAVE AWAK,
ENED THE CROWING COCK,
TU—WHIT!—TU—WHOO!
AND HARK, AGAIN! THE CROW,
ING COCK,
HOW DROWSILY IT CREW.

(*Right*) 'Christabel',
edition of 1904.

(*Opposite*) Illustration to
'The Rime of the Ancient
Mariner', 1857.

house of a Highgate surgeon, James Gillman; and under Gillman's patient care he remained until the end. During the last phase, Coleridge had many visitors. Among them were Charles Lamb, who likened him to 'an archangel – a little damaged', and Thomas Carlyle, who described his curious 'corkscrew' gait and his voice, 'a plaintive snuffle and singsong', in which he preached 'earnestly and also hopelessly the weightiest things'. He died at Highgate on 25 July 1834.

The most important part of Coleridge's poetic output was produced between 1797 and 1802; and by the early months of 1801 he already believed that 'the Poet is dead in me . . . I was once a Volume of Gold Leaf rising and riding on every breath of Fancy'. It was not a large output, compared with the achievement of Wordsworth; and it reflects both the strength and the weakness of his radically divided nature. Since he himself was sluggish and irresolute, everything that was light, elusive and evanescent appealed to Coleridge's imagination; and in 'The Ancient Mariner', a symbolic portrayal of his own unhappy wanderings,

it is his love for the beauty of the fire-clad water-snakes, as they wreathe their way round the doomed vessel, that eventually releases the hero from his tragic load of guilt:

> Beyond the shadow of the ship,
> I watched the water-snakes:
> They moved in tracks of shining white,
> And when they reared, the elfish light
> Fell off in hoary flakes.
>
> Within the shadow of the ship
> I watched their rich attire:
> Blue, glossy green, and velvet black,
> They coiled and swam; and every track
> Was a flash of golden fire.
>
> O happy living things! no tongue
> Their beauty might declare:
> A spring of love gushed from my heart,
> And I blessed them unaware:
> Sure my kind saint took pity on me,
> And I blessed them unaware.

Portrait, supposed to be that of Shelley, by E.E. Williams.

Whereas Wordsworth, though he regretted the passing of youth and the fading of his youthful visions, might seek to rationalize his sense of loss, for Coleridge that loss was irreparable, a disaster from which there could be no recovery. Thus, in April, 1802, soon after Wordsworth had begun his famous *Ode on Intimations of Immortality from Recollections of Early Childhood*, he wrote a very different ode, 'Dejection':

> A grief without a pang, void, dark, and drear,
> A stifled, drowsy, unimpassioned grief,
> Which finds no natural outlet, no relief,
>   In word, or sigh, or tear –
> O Lady! in this wan and heartless mood,
> To other thoughts by yonder throstle woo'd,
> All this long eve, so balmy and serene,
> Have I been gazing on the western sky,
> And its peculiar tint of yellow green:
> And still I gaze – and with how blank an eye!
> And those thin clouds above, in flakes and bars,
> That give away their motion to the stars;
> Those stars, that glide behind them or between,
> Now sparkling, now bedimmed, but always seen:
> Yon crescent Moon, as fixed as if it grew
> In its own cloudless, starless lake of blue;
> I see them all so excellently fair,
> I see, not feel, how beautiful they are!

Coleridge had neither Wordsworth's moral resolution nor his gift of concentration. Only here and there, as in 'Frost at Midnight', addressed to his beloved infant son, Hartley, during the winter months of 1798, does he achieve the exquisite intensity of feeling that we find throughout *The Prelude*. Hartley, he suggests, unlike his ill-fated parent, may, through divine help, learn to become one with the surrounding world of Nature:

> Great universal Teacher! he shall mould
> Thy spirit, and by giving make it ask.
> Therefore all seasons shall be sweet to thee,
> Whether the summer clothe the general earth
> With greenness, or the redbreast sit and sing
> Betwixt the tufts of snow on the bare branch
> Of mossy apple-tree, while the night thatch
> Smokes in the sun-thaw; whether the eave-drops fall
> Heard only in the traces of the blast,
> Or if the secret ministry of frost
> Shall hang them up in silent icicles,
> Quietly shining to the quiet Moon.

Though Coleridge's philosophical writings remained fragmentary, modern critics have paid them much attention; and he has been acclaimed as the founder and chief representative of 'the voluntaristic form of idealistic philosophy'. His greatest critical work, *Biographia Literaria*, which has been styled 'almost the bible of modern criticism', appeared in 1817. Here Coleridge presents both his own literary autobiography and his considered views upon the art he practised, with an acumen, a visionary insight and a general breadth of knowledge that still astonish us at each re-reading. True, *Biographia* is an unshapely book, diffuse, divagatory and often ponderous; but here, as in his noble Shakespearian lectures, some brilliant stroke of imaginative perception constantly illuminates the central theme. Coleridge was always the first to admit that he had seldom done himself justice, and that there was little relation between the books he had published and the series of majestic volumes, critical, philosophical, didactic, that existed only in his mind's eye. Few great men have passed through the world with so ineradicable a sense of failure.

PERCY BYSSHE SHELLEY (1792–1822), the personification, according to later Romantics, of brilliant, wayward and rebellious youth, was the son and heir of Timothy Shelley, Member of Parliament and a highly respectable Sussex squire. Educated first at a private school, where he not infrequently alarmed his schoolfellows by his dangerous experiments with gunpowder and which soon became 'a perfect Hell', he was sent to Eton in 1804, and there earned the nickname 'Mad Shelley'. In 1810 he went up to Oxford, full of the revolutionary and atheistic zeal that he had already sought to pass on to his four admiring sisters. His only Oxford friend was Thomas Jefferson Hogg; and in March 1811 both he and Hogg were sent down, for helping to circulate a pamphlet that Shelley had composed under the provocative title, *The Necessity of Atheism*.

Timothy Shelley was no domestic tyrant, but he resolved to take a firm stand; and henceforward Shelley came to regard his father as the epitome of everything he most detested. Similarly, he declared war against Christianity. 'Oh! how I wish I were the Antichrist!' he declared; 'that it were mine to crush the demon; to hurl him to his native hell . . .' Then, his father having reluctantly granted him a small allowance, in 1811, at the age of nineteen, he married Harriet Westbrook, a pretty sixteen-year-old girl. Together they wandered around the country, prosecuting various good causes; and during his first marriage Shelley published *Queen Mab*, his earliest attempt to produce a major work of literature. Alas, though Harriet, he admitted, was 'a noble animal', he had discovered too late that she could neither 'feel poetry' nor 'understand philosophy'; and in 1814 developed a violent passion for Mary Godwin, daughter of the famous reformer William Godwin and the celebrated feminist Mary Wollstonecraft, and suddenly abandoned Harriet. The lovers eloped to France – but not before Shelley had suggested that he, Mary and Harriet might establish a romantic *ménage-à-trois* in which his wife (who was then pregnant) should adopt the rôle of sister. Harriet refused; and two years later Shelley learned that she had committed suicide. The poet's last references to the wretched Harriet were notably ungenerous. He did not blame himself. Everyone 'does *me* full justice', he added with unpleasing unction.

Mary Shelley as a widow; by Eastlake.

Shelley had written his first important long poem, *Alastor*, in August 1815. During the early summer of 1816, beside the Lake of Geneva, he met his fellow exile Byron, with whom he formed a friendship that, despite many differences in their opinions and ways of living, would endure until his death. At the end of 1816 he married Mary Godwin, and made desperate efforts to regain control of his two children by Harriet; but the Lord Chancellor ruled that he was an improper guardian; and in March 1818 he left England for the last time. By his countrymen, he announced 'I am regarded as a rare prodigy of crime and pollution, whose look even might infect'.

The four closing years of Shelley's existence were his most creative period. In 1819 he wrote *The Masque of Anarchy*, an attack on Castlereagh's reactionary administration, and *Peter Bell the Third*, a satirical joke at the expense of Wordsworth. *The Cenci*, a verse tragedy, and *Prometheus Unbound*, a lyrical drama embodying his visionary ideas on the perfectibility of mankind, followed them in 1820; and during this same period he composed his best lyrics, including his magnificent 'Ode to the West Wind'. In 1821 he published a *Defence of Poetry*, a reply to his friend Peacock's *The Four Ages of Poetry*, and hearing that Keats had died – hounded to death, it was said, by brutal reviewers – produced his elegiac *Adonais*, a lament for the fallen poet, which is also a defiant assertion of the

power of art. Shelley himself was dead within little more than a year. On 8 July 1822 he and his friend Edward Williams set sail across the Gulf of Spezia. In a gathering storm their boat vanished; and two weeks later their bodies were washed ashore. Shelley's corpse could only be recognized by the clothes he was wearing, and by the books – volumes of Sophocles and Keats – that he had stuffed into his coat-pockets.

From the point of view of the nineteenth-century reader, Shelley was destined to become the most typical of all the Romantic poets. But just as in his private life he was capable of self-deception, so in his verse he often mistook the poetic attitude for genuine creative effort. His sublime visions are frequently vague and confused; and, like Byron's, his ear was sometimes faulty; he was too concerned with the value of what he was saying to detect, and remove, an inharmonious line. He resembled the English Romantic painter John Martin in his predilection for 'tremendous' imagery, for effects that both amaze and dazzle:

> A sphere, which is as many thousand spheres,
> Solid as crystal, yet through all its mass

Imaginative picture of Shelley, writing *Prometheus Unbound* amid the ruins of the Baths of Caracalla; by Joseph Severn.

> Flow, as through empty space, music and light:
> Ten thousand orbs involving and involved,
> Purple and azure, white, and green, and golden
> Sphere within sphere; and every space between
> Peopled with unimaginable shapes,
> Such as ghosts dream dwell in the lampless deep,
> Yet each inter-transpicuous, and they whirl
> Over each other with a thousand motions,
> Upon a thousand sightless axles spinning . . .

Two preoccupations dominate Shelley's poems – his devotion to Liberty, and his belief in Love as the prime factor in all human progress. Much of his work is visionary and Utopian; and his longer poems, though they include many splendid passages, tend to degenerate into labyrinthine prophesying. But, now and then, he strikes a sharper note, as when he portrays the current plight of 'England':

> An old, mad, blind, despised, and dying king, –
> Princes, the dregs of their dull race, who flow
> Through public scorn, – mud from a muddy spring, –
> Rulers who neither see, nor feel, nor know,
> But leech-like to their fainting country cling,
> Till they drop, blind in blood, without a blow, –
> A people starved and stabbed in the untilled field, –
> An army, which liberticide and prey
> Makes as a two-edged sword to all who wield, –
> Golden and sanguine laws which tempt and slay;
> Religion Christless, Godless – a book sealed;
> A Senate, – Time's worst statute unrepealed, –
> Are graves, from which a glorious Phantom *may*
> Burst, to illumine our tempestuous day.

Shelley's shorter poems are, on the whole, more effective than his ambitious dramas; and in 'Ode to the West Wind' he achieves a degree of concentration that he seldom reaches elsewhere:

> Thou on whose stream, 'mid the steep sky's commotion,
> Loose clouds like earth's decaying leaves are shed,
> Shook from the tangled boughs of Heaven and Ocean,
>
> Angels of rain and lightning: there are spread
> On the blue surface of thine airy surge,
> Like the bright hair uplifted from the head
>
> Of some fierce Maenad, even from the dim verge
> Of the horizon to the zenith's height,
> The lock of the approaching storm. Thou dirge
>
> Of the dying year, to which this closing night
> Will be the dome of a vast sepulchre,
> Vaulted with all thy congregated might
>
> Of vapours, from whose solid atmosphere
> Black rain, and fire, and hail will burst: O hear!

'The Sensitive Plant';
late 19th-century
illustration.

In *Adonais* Shelley followed Keats's advice that he should 'be more of an artist' and 'curb his magnanimity!' He had not known Keats well; but he saw the poet's fate as a reflection of his own existence. The dead man, victimized by his fellow human beings, had triumphed through the strength of art. 'Made one with nature', he had become incorporated into the enduring beauty of the universe, and now, 'among the eternals', enjoyed the vision of transcendent Love:

> That Light whose smile kindles the Universe,
> That Beauty in which all things work and move,
> That Benediction which the eclipsing Curse

> Of birth can quench not, that sustaining Love
> Which through the web of being blindly wove
> By man and beast and earth and air and sea,
> Burns bright or dim, as each are mirrors of
> The fire for which all thirst; now beams on me,
> Consuming the last clouds of cold mortality.

Shelley's portrait has always been difficult to draw. Though he had made a cult of Love, in his relations with other men and women – particularly with those he had once loved – he was sometimes astonishingly insensitive. The form of persecution-mania from which he had suffered since boyhood, and the fantasies and bizarre hallucinations that usually accompanied it, may perhaps have been coloured by his habit of imbibing laudanum (or tincture of opium), which he employed to counteract his nerve-storms; but it may also have been the product of a radically disordered ego. We are 'compelled to perceive', writes a recent biographer, 'that, at least between the ages of twenty and twenty-three, Shelley was on the verge of insanity as it is ordinarily recognized'. Yet Shelley was, at the same time, affectionate, shrewd and modest; and his closest friends adored him. After his death, his cynical associate Byron, whom he had often exasperated beyond endurance, paid a heart-felt tribute to his virtues. 'You were all,' he told his publisher, 'brutally mistaken about Shelley – I never knew one who was not a beast in comparison.'

> Yet now despair itself is mild,
> Even as the winds and waters are;
> I could lie down like a tired child,
> And weep away this life of care
> Which I have borne, and yet must bear,
> Till death like sleep might steal on me,
> And I might feel in the warm air
> My cheek grow cold, and hear the sea
> Breathe o'er my dying brain its last monotony.

('Lines written in Dejection Near Naples, 1818')

George Gordon, LORD BYRON (1788–1824) was one of those writers whose literary productions are so closely connected with the circumstances of their lives that the life itself becomes a work of literature, in which the poet displays his genius far more clearly than in many of his published verses. It was his ancestral heritage, he felt, that had made him what he was – the 'heritage of storms' received from his grandfather, Admiral Byron, nick-named 'Foul-Weather Jack' because, wherever he sailed, he seemed to attract a tempest; from his great-uncle, 'the Wicked Lord', an embittered recluse, who had killed a neighbour in a duel; from his father, 'Handsome Jack', a broken-down military spendthrift; finally, from his mother, an ill-fated Scottish heiress, whom his father had married for money and soon left almost destitute.

Byron in youth; portrait by G. Sanders, 1807.

His father died abroad in 1791, some biographers believe by his own hand. In 1798, on the death of his great-uncle, Byron succeeded to the title, which brought with it Newstead Abbey, a dilapidated Gothic building, 'the melancholy mansion' of his ancestors, and estates that 'the Wicked Lord' had done his best to ruin and despoil. Byron's life was always full of contrasts. During his youth, although he bore an ancient title, he and his mother were often miserably poor; and, although he was handsome, muscular and vigorous, his right leg had been deformed at birth. So long as he lived, his deformity haunted him – it was apparently some form of clubfoot; and he felt that his lameness set him apart from the rest of mankind.

Byron's adult career is so well-known that it scarcely needs recapitulation. After some happy years at Harrow, where he surrounded himself with a bevy of attractive favourites, in 1805 he went up to Trinity College, Cambridge, where, having lived through a period of deep dejection – he could not bear, he said, to think that he was 'no longer a boy' – he acquired a number of valuable friends, the most important being John Cam Hobhouse. *Hours of Idleness*, a collection of somewhat unpromising juvenilia, was issued by a London publisher in 1807; and, when the *Edinburgh Review* gave it a hostile notice, Byron retaliated with the lively satire that he entitled *English Bards and Scotch Reviewers*. His satire appeared in 1809; and, early that same year, he and Hobhouse sailed on a tour of the Near East, which took them to Albania, Athens and Constantinople. Hobhouse presently re-

(*Above*) Newstead Abbey, 'the melancholy mansion of my fathers'; after a picture by T. Allorn.

(*Below*) Byron in Albanian costume; portrait by J. Phillips.

turned home; but Byron remained abroad until July 1811, adopting the habits and sexual *mores* of the Turks, and generally leading an adventurous and carefree life. He regained England, he declared, 'without a hope, and almost without a desire', but, on his travels, he had produced 'a great many stanzas in Spenser's measure relative to the countries I have visited'. These were the first two cantos of *Childe Harold's Pilgrimage* (originally named *Childe Burun's Pilgrimage*). They were published under the imprint of John Murray. Byron awoke and found himself famous one day in March 1812.

The success achieved by the twenty-four-year-old poet was as brilliant as it was unexpected. He became the lion of the day, the hero of fashionable society, a dandy and a bold seducer. His existence was feverish; and among the numerous love-affairs in which he soon became involved, none was more distracting than his liaison with Lady Caroline Lamb, an eccentric and extravagant young married woman, whose vagaries and passionate importunities tried the poet's irritable nerves beyond endurance. From Lady Caroline he took refuge with a middle-aged mistress, Lady Oxford, but then, during the latter part of 1813, plunged into a far more serious 'scrape'. By 'Handsome Jack's' first marriage with the divorced Lady Carmarthen, he had had an only daughter, Augusta, who was now married to her cousin, George Leigh. Byron had hitherto seen little of his half-sister; and, when they met in 1813, a warm sympathy at once sprang up between them. That sympathy gave rise to stronger and, at length, considerably more dangerous feelings. Byron was fascinated by the idea of incest. He loved danger; and his temperament included a wildly self-destructive strain. He had been 'cunning in his overthrow', he admitted at a later stage. He enjoyed the idea that he had ventured to commit a sin 'for which there was no forgiveness in this world, whatever there might be in the next'.

It was to escape from his emotional perplexities that he now embarked on a worldly 'marriage of reason'. But Annabella Milbanke, whom he married in January 1815, was a high-minded and slightly priggish girl, neither pliable nor understanding. There is no doubt that Byron's treatment of his wife was extraordinarily harsh and callous; at the time, tormented by his creditors and hagridden by a secret sense of guilt, he seems to have been close to breakdown. And early in 1816, having borne him a daughter, Ada, Lady Byron left his house. Their separation provoked a major scandal. Byron said goodbye to England, for the second and last time, in April 1816; but, on the eve of departure, he addressed a disingenuous and somewhat self-righteous *Farewell* to his 'unforgiving wife'. He had wept over his wife, then 'wiped his eyes with the public', remarked a cruel contemporary observer.

Equally well-known is the story of Byron's eight long years of exile. From Switzerland, where he first encountered Shelley and

begat an illegitimate daughter, Allegra, he moved to Venice, a city he loved, in which he decided to 'make life an amusement', and plumbed the depths of dissipation; from Venice to Ravenna, the home of his new mistress, the Countess Guiccioli; and thence to Pisa and Genoa. Under Teresa Guiccioli's sobering influence, his way of life grew far more staid; and he played a courageous part in Italian revolutionary politics. He was bored, however; and when, in 1823, the Greek Committee, which his friend Hobhouse had helped to organize with the purpose of assisting the Greek patriots who, three years earlier, had taken up arms against their

Childe Harold; from a water-colour sketch by Westall.

Turkish overlords, elected him their deputy, he was glad to promise his assistance. He sailed from Genoa in July 1823 and landed at Missolonghi, after many delays and hesitations, at the beginning of January 1824. There he died, having accomplished apparently very little, on 19 April 1824. As a man of action, Byron was ineffective; but his death gave a dramatic impetus to the cause of Greek freedom.

During his life-time, Byron dominated contemporary Romantic literature and developed into an almost legendary personage. His fame extended throughout the whole of Europe; and Goethe, in his *Conversations with Eckermann*, shrewdly analyzed both his personal character and the compulsive charm he exercised. Living from mood to mood and passion to passion, Byron, said the elder poet, had understood himself but dimly. He had possessed, how-ever, 'a high degree of that demonic instinct and attraction, which influences others independently of reason, effort and affection, and which succeeds in guiding where the understanding fails'. For his contemporaries, *Childe Harold* represented the sufferings and struggles of an entire generation. Its author was the poet par excellence, solitary, rebellious, persecuted; and innumerable readers felt that he alone could grasp the nature of their deepest problems. Many of his admirers addressed him personally; and a large accumulation of the pleas and demands he received are still stored away among his archives.

As a poet, he had numerous shortcomings – a faulty ear and an imperfect sense of style. The first two cantos of *Childe Harold* contain a ludicrously exaggerated portrait of its sable-suited hero, a young man haunted by the memory of his sins and tormented by the image of an unrequited love:

> For he through Sin's long labyrinth had run,
> Nor made atonement when he did amiss,
> Had sighed to many though he loved but one,
> And that loved one, alas! could ne'er be his.

No less artificial, and even more displeasing from a modern point of view, are the six verse-tales, all with Eastern subjects, *The Giaour, The Bride of Abydos, The Corsair, Lara, The Siege of Corinth* and *Parisina*, that he wrote before he left England. But they greatly increased his popularity; and *The Corsair* sold ten thousand copies on the day of publication. Not until he reached Switzerland, where he began to compose *Manfred* – a symbolical drama in which, under a rather thin disguise, he portrayed his illicit passion for Augusta Leigh – did he reveal his true creative strength. *Manfred* has a tremendous Alpine background; and his recollections of snow peaks and mountain torrents reappear in the Third Canto of *Childe Harold*, planned about the same time. Published towards the end of 1816, it is the masterpiece of Byron's earlier period, and has been described as 'the fullest and noblest

expression of a certain aspect of his genius'. The Fourth Canto, with its vivid pictures of ancient Rome, was to appear in 1818. But Byron himself would always prefer the Third, declaring that it was 'the *best*' that he had ever written:

Don Juan and the 'fair Haidée'; engraving after a drawing by A. Colin.

> From peak to peak, the rattling crags among
> Leaps the live thunder! Not from one lone cloud,
> But every mountain now hath found a tongue,
> And Jura answers, through her misty shroud . . .
>
> And this is in the Night; – Most glorious Night!
> Thou wert not sent for slumber! let me be
> A sharer in thy fierce and far delight, –
> A portion of the tempest and of thee!
> How the lit lake shines a phosphoric sea,
> And the big rain comes dancing to the earth! . . .

Once he had settled down in the enervating climate of Venice, Byron's poetic mood underwent a sudden sea-change. For Childe Harold, the proud and rebellious anarch, he substituted Don Juan, the cynical adventurer, whose story he opened in 1819, but in 1824 would leave unfinished. *Don Juan*, he told his friend Tom Moore, was intended 'to be a little quietly facetious upon everything'; its object, he wrote elsewhere, was to 'strip the tinsel off sentiment'. Yet, besides satire, cynicism and caustic fun, it contains a series of enchanting lyrical passages, such as the description of Juan's brief, but delicious love-affair with the pirate's daughter, Haidée:

> They were alone, but not alone as they
> Who shut in chambers think it loneliness;
> The silent Ocean, and the starlight bay,
> The twilight glow, which momently grew less,
> The voiceless sands and dropping cave, that lay
> Around them, made them to each other press,
> As if there were no life beneath the sky
> Save theirs, and their life could never die . . .

In Italy, as a straightforward satirist, Byron did his best work. *The Vision of Judgment*, an attack on the Laureate, Robert Southey, is an incomparable piece of picturesque invective, which besides manhandling the pompous Laureate himself, ridicules the whole idea of monarchy; while *Beppo*, a lively Venetian tale, strikes a vigorous blow for sexual freedom. Byron, the satirist, frequently imitates Pope. So long as he lived, Pope remained the literary ancestor whom he always sought to follow. Byron's character, both personal and intellectual, was a pattern of conflicting attributes – morose and self-destructive, yet gay and good-humoured; cynical yet soft-hearted; a poet who affected to despise poetry; a Romantic who, in any other age, might well have become a distinguished classic writer. Incidentally, though it was his verses that brought him fame, he had an admirable prose style, as John Ruskin, somewhat unexpectedly, was among the first to point out. His letters and journals, though often dashed off at breakneck speed, form a brilliant self-portrait, which illustrates every aspect, every turn and change, all the virtues and all the vices of his protean personality.

She was always in extremes, either crying or laughing; and so fierce when angered, that she was the terror of men, women and children – for she had the strength of an Amazon, with the temper of Medea . . . That she had a sufficient regard for me in her wild way, I had many reasons to believe. I will mention one. In the autumn, one day, going to the Lido with my gondoliers, we were overtaken by a heavy squall, and the gondola put in peril – hats blown away, boat filling, oar lost, tumbling sea, thunder, rain in torrents, night coming, and wind increasing. On our return, after a tight struggle, I found her on the open steps of the Moconigo palace, on the Grand Canal, with her great black eyes flashing through her tears, and the long dark hair, which was streaming drenched with rain over her brows and breast. She was perfectly exposed to the storm; and the wind blowing her hair and dress about her tall thin figure, and the lightning flashing round her, made her look like Medea alighted from her chariot, or the Sibyl of the tempest . . . Her joy at seeing me again was moderately mixed with ferocity, and gave me the idea of a tigress over her recovered cubs.   (A Venetian Mistress')

Byron on the eve of his departure for Greece; sketch by Count D'Orsay, 1823.

JOHN CLARE (1793–1864) was a poet who had been almost completely forgotten by the beginning of the present century; a four-volume survey of English literature, published in the year 1904, contains no reference to his life and work; and not until 1920, when two modern poets, Edmund Blunden and Alan Porter, edited his *Poems Chiefly from Manuscript*, did he take the place that he deserves in the history of English verse. Born at Helpston, a Northampton-shire village, the son of a country labourer and of a mother who could neither read nor write, Clare was put to work in the fields before he was seven. But he loved the ballads that 'over his horn of ale', he heard his father sing; and a copy of Thomson's *Seasons* that had somehow come his way inspired him with a passionate love of classic poetry. His *Poems Descriptive of Rural Life and Scenery* and *The Village Minstrel* appeared, and were favourably reviewed, in 1820 and 1821. He was introduced to Coleridge, De Quincey and Lamb, and won the approval of John Keats. Two subsequent collections, his *Shepherd's Calendar* and *Rural Muse*, produced between 1827 and 1835, were comparatively unsuccessful. Always wretchedly poor, despite an annual pension of £45 contributed by literary patrons, in later life he developed symptoms of insanity, and was relegated to Northampton County Asylum, where he died in 1864 after twenty years' confinement. At the asylum he did not cease to write; Clare was a true Romantic, exquisitely attuned to the sights and sounds of nature, with a Wordsworthian gift – though he lacked Wordsworth's intellectual powers – of evoking and recording them. Obliged to marry a young woman whom he had got with child, he was haunted by visions of a girl he had known as a boy, but whose affections he had failed to win. His best-known poem 'Written in Northampton County Asylum', has a particularly poignant music:

John Clare; portrait by W. Hilton.

> I am! yet what I am who cares, or knows?
> My friends forsake me like a memory lost.
> I am the self-consumer of my woes;
> They rise and vanish, an oblivious host,
> Shadows of life, whose very soul is lost,
> And yet I am – I live – though I am toss'd
>
> Into the nothingness of scorn and noise,
> Into the living sea of waking dream,
> Where there is neither sense of life, nor joys,
> But the huge shipwreck of my own esteem
> And all that's dear. Even those I loved the best
> Are strange – nay, they are stranger than the rest.
>
> I long for scenes where man has never trod –
> For scenes where woman never smiled or wept –
> There to abide with my Creator, God,
> And sleep as I in childhood sweetly slept,
> Full of high thoughts, unborn. So let me lie, –
> The grass below; above, the vaulted sky.

In youth, as an early portrait shows, Clare had a strangely pre-possessing appearance, with pale, piercing eyes and light straw-coloured hair.

JOHN KEATS (1795–1821) had the unlikeliest family background of all the great Romantic poets. His parents were neither intel-lectual nor, in any way, distinguished. His father, Thomas Keats, having come up from the West Country to work as an ostler at a London livery-stable, had married his employer's daughter, Frances Jennings; and John, their eldest son, was born at the Swan and Hoop Inn, Finsbury Pavement. Thomas Keats, how-ever, a handsome and energetic man, is said to have risen 'much above his station in life'; while Frances, a particularly attractive young woman, was believed by her son to have possessed 'un-common talents'. She was also, though deeply devoted to her children, volatile and pleasure-loving; and when, in 1804, Thomas died after a fall from his horse, his widow remarried less than three months later. But she seems to have deserted her second husband just as swiftly and abruptly, and thereupon vanished in pursuit of new diversions. The Keats children were then entrusted to their maternal grandmother. By the time their mother re-appeared, she had already lost her youth and gaiety. She died, a victim of tuberculosis – the disease that was to carry off two of her sons – early in the year 1810.

John had appointed himself his mother's chivalric protector – once he stood before the door of her sick-room carrying a drawn sword; and her death, we are told, caused him 'impassioned and prolonged grief'. The fact that, since he was an infant, he 'had had no mother' was, he afterwards told his friend Joseph Severn, the greatest misfortune of his whole existence. Yet he grew up strong and self-reliant. At his suburban school, his contemporaries remembered, he had shown few signs of intellectual promise, but had become 'the favourite of all, like a pet prize-fighter, for his terrier courage'. Perhaps it was the shock of his mother's death that helped gradually to change his nature, and set his imagina-tion stirring. At the age of seventeen he began to write verse. Meanwhile his guardian had removed him from school and apprenticed him to an apothecary; and, in 1814, he left the apothecary's shop, and entered a famous London hospital, where he was rapidly appointed ward-dresser. Nevertheless he proceeded to abandon medicine; writing, he had discovered, was his true vocation.

In 1816 he had first met Leigh Hunt, who introduced him to the world of modern literature; and through Hunt, an indifferent poet but an appreciative and sympathetic critic, he enountered Wordsworth and Shelley and the ill-fated artist, Benjamin Robert Haydon (1786–1846). Under their influence, he published a volume of *Poems*, which included some of his finest early sonnets in

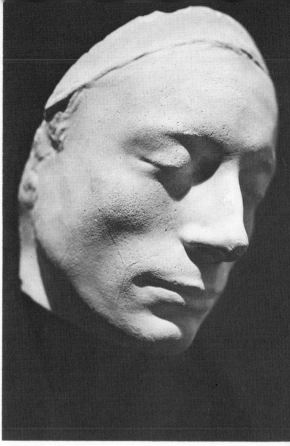

March 1817. It was still-born. Keats felt bitterly downcast, but soon proceeded to compose *Endymion*. It appeared in 1818, only to receive a savage trouncing. Again, Keats rallied, and went on to produce the splendid volume of 1820 – among its contents were his greatest narrative poem, 'The Eve of St Agnes', 'Lamia', 'Isabella', 'Hyperion' and the celebrated 'Odes' – that would establish his poetic status. It attracted much less unfavourable notices; but, alas, they came too late. During February, he had diagnosed in his own case the symptoms of the same disease that, towards the end of 1818, had killed his younger brother, Tom; and, as 1820 progressed, his physical condition grew more and more alarming. To increase his misery, since the autumn of 1818, or the beginning of 1819, Keats had suffered from a desperate passion; his neighbour in Hampstead, Fanny Brawne, whom he had first considered a wayward coquette – 'beautiful and elegant, graceful, silly, fashionable and strange' – now increasingly obsessed his thoughts. An honest and affectionate girl, Fanny returned his love; but Keats seems by turns to have courted and repulsed her. 'I am a Coward,' he declared; 'I cannot bear the pain of being happy'; and, once he knew that he had developed his brother's disease, he felt that marriage was impossible. His physician advised that he should try a warmer climate. Keats landed at Naples on 31 October 1820. He died at Rome, in a little

(*Above left*) Keats; sketches by B.R. Haydon, 1816.

(*Above right*) Haydon's life-mask of Keats.

room above the Spanish Steps, on 23 February 1821. Fanny's
unopened letters lay beside him.

The attacks on Keats's early poems were half-critical and half-
political. Reviewers pointed out his obvious immaturity, as no
doubt they were very right to do. But, simultaneously, in the
person of the young poet, they attacked the so-called 'Cockney
School' headed by the literary Radical, Leigh Hunt. They disliked
his adolescent extravagance, which, indeed, offended fellow poets.
His verse, Byron assured John Murray in October 1820, was 'a
sort of verbal masturbation'; the poet himself was a 'miserable
Self-polluter'. Yet in July 1821 Byron decided that he must make
amends, and requested his publisher, now that Keats was dead,

Manuscript of the opening
lines of *Endymion*.

to 'omit *all* that is said *about him* in any MSS. of mine. His 'Hyperion'
is a fine monument and will keep his name.'

Today we recognize Keats's genius not only in his verse but in
his letters, which show how carefully and critically he scrutinized
his poetic gifts. *Endymion*, he agreed, had been a 'slipshod' poem.

It is as good as I had power to make it . . . Had I been nervous about its
being a perfect piece . . . and trembled over every page, it would not
have been written . . . I will write independently – I have written
independently *without Judgement*. I may write independently, and *with
Judgement* . . . The Genius of Poetry must work out its own salvation in
a man: it cannot be matured by law and precept, but by sensation and
watchfulness . . . that which is creative must create itself.

It is a long process of self-creation that we observe in Keats's
poems. He had certain dominant themes – notably the connection
between Death and Love, inspired by his unhappy mother's fate,
and his view of the beloved woman, symbolized in 'La Belle Dame
Sans Merci' (who may have stood both for his mother and for
Fanny Brawne) as being inevitably a destructive agent; but, at the
same time, he was constantly extending his scope and making his
way into far wider fields. His odes 'To a Nightingale' and 'To a
Grecian Urn' are so well-known that they scarcely need quotation.
Keats's voluptuous nostalgic gloom is best summed up in his 'Ode
to Melancholy', where he bids the reader, if he would enjoy its
baleful influence, to turn to the images of youth and beauty:

> Then glut thy sorrow on a morning rose,
> Or on the rainbow of the salt sand-wave,
> Or on the wealth of globèd peonies;
> Or if thy mistress some rich anger shows,
> Emprison her soft hand, and let her rave,
> And feed deep, deep upon her peerless eyes.
>
> She dwells with Beauty – Beauty that must die;
> And Joy, whose hand is ever at his lips
> Bidding adieu; and aching Pleasure nigh,
> Turning to poison while the bee-mouth sips . . .

During his first poetic period, as he tells us in the 'Ode to a
Nightingale', Keats had been enamoured of the idea of Death:

> Darkling I listen; and for many a time
> I have been half in love with easeful Death,
> Call'd him soft names, in many a musèd rhyme,
> To take into the air my quiet breath;
> Now more than ever seems it rich to die . . .

But when he recognized that Death was rapidly advancing on
him, he took a broader view of human life, which is reflected
in 'Hyperion', the fragment he first inserted into the volume of
1820, and afterwards recast as 'The Fall of Hyperion', making a
large number of revisions, not always with very good results.

Piazza di Spagna, Rome;
Keats' lodgings were on
the right-hand side of the
famous Spanish Steps.

The first version of the poem has a particularly noble opening:

> Deep in the shady sadness of a vale
> Far sunken from the healthy breath of morn,
> Far from the fiery noon, and eve's one star,
> Sat grey-hair'd Saturn, quiet as a stone,
> Still as the silence round about his lair;
> Forest on forest hung about his head
> Like cloud on cloud. No stir of air was there,
> Not so much life as on a summer's day
> Robs not one light seed from the feather'd grass,
> But where the dead leaf fell, there did it rest.
> A stream went voiceless by, still deadened more
> By reason of his fallen divinity
> Spreading a shade: the Naiad 'mid her reeds
> Press'd her cold finger closer to her lips.

And, as it develops, it achieves an effect of Miltonic sonority and gravity, tempered by Romantic undertones:

> As when, upon a trancèd summer-night,
> Those green-rob'd senators of mighty woods,
> Tall oaks, branch-charmed by the earnest stars,
> Dream, and so dream all night without a stir,
> Save from one gradual solitary gust
> Which comes upon the silence, and dies off,
> As if the ebbing air had but one wave:
> So came these words and went . . .

The two poems are especially remarkable, however, not only because the poet appears to be changing his method, and has adopted blank verse, but because he is here concerned less with the woes of the individual than with the Virgilian *lacrimae rerum*, the deeper sorrows of the world at large:

> 'None can usurp this height', returned that shade,
> 'But those to whom the miseries of the world
> Are misery, and will not let them rest' . . .
> 'Are there not thousands in the world', said I . . .
> Who love their fellows even to the death,
> Who feel the giant agony of the world,
> And more, like slaves to poor humanity,
> Labour for mortal good? I sure should see
> Other men here; but I am here alone' . . .

Keats himself – of whom Haydon wrote, 'a genius more purely poetical never existed' – was a strong, attractive young man, only five feet high, but compact and well-built, who had a 'brisk and winning face', with large hazel eyes and curling reddish-golden locks. He loved claret, enjoyed bawdy puns and had a Cockney turn of humour. He adored the art he practised for its own sake; but to the sensuous, imaginative cast of his mind he added a keen critical intelligence.

> She hurried at his words beset with fears,
> For there were sleeping dragons all around,
> At glaring watch, perhaps, with ready spears –
> Down the wide stairs a darkling way they found. –
> In all the house was heard no human sound.
> A chain-droop'd lamp was flickering by each door;
> The arras, rich with horsemen, hawk, and hound,
> Flutter'd in the besieging wind's uproar;
> And the long carpets rose along the gusty floor.

('The Eve of Saint Agnes')

Sir Walter Scott by Andrew Geddes.

The Nineteenth-Century Novel

SIR WALTER SCOTT (1771–1832), the most popular author of the early nineteenth century, both as a poet and as a novelist, was born in Edinburgh, the son of a solicitor. During early childhood he suffered from an illness – probably a form of infantile paraylsis – that permanently lamed his right leg; and, while he was recovering on his grandfather's farm, he first came into contact with the oral traditions of the Border country and its romantic songs and ballads. At the Edinburgh High School, he tells us, he was 'never a dunce, but an incorrigibly idle imp, who was always longing to do something else than that which was enjoined him'. In 1786 he entered his father's office with the intention of becoming a Writer to the Signet; and in 1792, having passed his examinations

Lady of the Lake; frontispiece after Turner.

in both Civil and Scots Law, he joined the ranks of Scottish advocates. Despite his early illnesses, he was now 'a comely creature', vigorous, lively and good-looking. After unsuccessfully pursuing a Scottish girl, who decided to make a more ambitious marriage, in December 1797 he married Miss Charlotte Margaret Carpenter (or Charpentier), a beauty of French descent, for whom his feelings, he admitted at a later time, were 'something short of love in all its fervour'. Simultaneously, he had begun to write poetry. Under the influence of 'Monk' Lewis, he translated the German Romantics and, in 1802 and 1803, published three collections of ballads entitled *Minstrelsy of the Scottish Border*. In 1799 he had been appointed Sheriff-deputy of Selkirkshire, a post that he held for life, with a salary of £300 a year. Thanks to a small inheritance, he also set up a publishing company, nominally headed by James Ballantyne. His first long poem, *The Lay of the Last Minstrel*, written in imitation of the metrical romances of the Middle Ages, came out in 1805, and at once brought him literary fame and fortune. It was followed by *Ballads and Lyrical Pieces* (1806) and *The Lady of the Lake* (1810). Byron's reputation, however, presently threatened to eclipse Scott's; and his later poems, which included *Rokeby* (1813) and *Harold the Dauntless* (1817), attracted much less favourable notice. Scott himself was inclined to dismiss his verse; and his daughter, asked if she had read *The Lay of the Last Minstrel*, is said

The Bride of Lammermoor;
edition of 1888.

to have replied, 'No, papa says there is nothing so bad for young
people as reading bad poetry.'

The profits of his verse-writing enabled Scott to purchase the
estate of Abbotsford, and adopt the rôle of feudal laird. He transformed the great house into a neo-Gothic stronghold, full of
rich baronial detail, helms and hauberks, swords and pikes. It was
an expensive pastime; and the author soon discovered that he
needed another source of income. He therefore resurrected the
manuscript of a novel that he had begun to write in 1805, completed the tale and published it anonymously – he was 'not quite
sure', he remarked, that his contemporaries would approve of a
respectable advocate writing novels – in July 1814. *Waverley; or,
'tis Sixty Years Since* had an immediate and resounding triumph;
and almost equally successful were the string of novels that Scott
hastened to produce between 1815 and 1824 – of which the best-
known are *Guy Mannering, The Antiquary, The Black Dwarf, Old
Mortality, Rob Roy, The Heart of Midlothian, The Bride of Lammermoor, Ivanhoe, Kenilworth* and *Quentin Durward.* Scott was a tireless
worker. But then, in 1825, a sudden financial disaster struck him
down. His publisher went bankrupt; and Scott, being closely connected with the affairs of the firm, was faced with a tremendous
load of debts. The remainder of his life was passed in an unending
struggle to discharge them. Though his health was now failing, he

still laboured indefatigably: and by the summer of 1827 he had paid off some £28,000. The struggle killed him; and the experiences of his declining years are memorably recorded in his *Journal*. He died on 21 September 1832, comforted in his last days, a biographer hopes, by 'the sound of all others most delicious to his ear, the gentle ripple of the Tweed over its pebbles'.

Today it is difficult to understand the popularity of Scott's poems, with their crude German supernaturalism and English eighteenth-century Gothicism. There was little new about their style or content. But, for all his romantic imaginings, the poet continued to aim at an historical accuracy of presentation; and the same spirit of historical exactitude was once admired in Scott's novels. His elaborate reconstructions of an antique background are sometimes less appreciated by the modern reader. Even so, he made an important contribution to the growth of the nineteenth-century novel and laid the foundations of the documentary technique that was to serve the Victorian novelists so well when they applied it to the world beneath their eyes. Scott was only superficially a Romantic story-teller. He eschews fantastic themes and sets out to present facts, based on scholarship and local knowledge. His attitude is cautious and honest; he is against romance and mystery; anything that may appear improbable in his stories is sure to be explained with the help of a long and erudite digression. By combining the roles of novelist and historian, he gave the past a new existence.

Scott's best novels are those which describe eighteenth-century Scotland, from *Waverley* to *The Legend of Montrose*. Here his attitude towards his subject seems, now and then, ambivalent. Although he exalts the primitive life of action, the stuff of the Border ballads he had loved in childhood, at the same time he speaks up for a civilization that, he knew, was bound to supersede it. Thus the Jacobite revolt had been Scotland's last attempt to restore the old heroic values. The novelist does not minimize their appeal; he concludes nevertheless that they are doomed to vanish. *Waverley* sets the pattern. A young Englishman, drawn to the Highlands by romantic curiosity, becomes involved with the rebellious Jacobites. His education – apparently much like Scott's – has inculcated in him a romantic cast of mind that colours everything he sees. The story follows the course of his intellectual development. Edward Waverley becomes a realist and, confronted by the horrors of a real war, at length abandons his delusive dreams. The turning point is reached when he recognizes that the romantic prelude of his existence has ended, and that his adult history has now begun.

Scott was not a great imaginative artist, though undoubtedly a man of great executive gifts. Writing quickly and carelessly for the money he needed to support the way of life that he had chosen, he never fully realized his promise. All his novels have flaws; and most of his later books are pot-boilers. His chief characters are very often dummies. His style is usually undistinguished; much of the dialogue, stiff and stilted. It is his minor personages, drawn from low life, who are apt to monopolize our interest; and when they occupy the centre of the stage, the narrative takes on a new vitality. In *The Heart of Midlothian* (1818), generally agreed to be his best book, he covers a particularly wide field, from personal to political history and, among the characters he depicts, is Queen Caroline, the learned and perspicacious consort of George II. Scott's powerful use of dialect reveals his true dramatic sense.

Here, in *Guy Mannering*, Meg Merrilies curses the Laird of Ellangowan:

Ride your ways, ride your ways, Laird of Ellangowan, ride your ways, Godfrey Bertram! – This day have ye quenched seven smoking hearths – see if the fire in your ain parlour burn the blyther for that. Ye have riven the thack off seven cottar houses – look if your ain roof-tree stand the faster. Ye may stable your stirks in the shealings at Derncleugh – see that the hare does not couch on the hearth-stane at Ellangowan. – Ride your ways, Godfrey Bertram; what do ye glower after our folk for? – There's thirty hearts there, that wad hae wanted bread ere ye had wanted sun-kets, and spent their life-blood ere ye had scratched your finger. Yes – there's thirty yonder, from the old wife of an hundred to the babe that was born last week, that ye have turned out o' their bits o' bields, to sleep with the tod and the black-cock in the muirs! – Ride your ways, Ellan-gowan. – Our bairns are hinging at our weary backs – look that your braw cradle at hame be the fairer spread up – not that 'am wishing ill to little Harry, or to the babe that's yet to be born – God forbid – and make them kind to the poor, and better folk than their father! And now, ride e'en tour ways; for these are the last words ye'll ever hear Meg Merrilies speak, and this is the last reise that I'll ever cut in the bonny woods of Ellangowan.

JANE AUSTEN (1775–1817) was born into just such a family as she herself enjoyed describing. The Austens belonged neither to the mercantile middle class nor to the landed aristocracy; but one relation, who afterwards adopted the novelist's brother, Edward, owned estates in Kent and Hampshire; and Edward's daughter, who became Lady Knatchbull, and whose eldest son would join the House of Lords, during her later life felt obliged to admit 'that Aunt Jane from various circumstances was not so *refined* as she ought to have been'; for the Austens had not been rich, '& the people around them, with whom they chiefly mixed, were not at all high bred, or . . . anything more than *mediocre* . . .'

Jane Austen's father was, in fact, an unambitious country clergyman; and she was born at Steventon, his Hampshire par-sonage. She soon began to write – 'stories of a slight and flimsy nature', and parodies of the fashionable Gothic romances. About the age of seventeen, she dashed off *Lady Susan*, a short novel in the form of letters, and, when she was twenty-one, embarked on *Pride and Prejudice*, which was followed by *Sense and Sensibility* and *Northanger Abbey* between 1797 and 1798. The publisher to whom she submitted *Pride and Prejudice* immediately rejected it; and, although *Northanger Abbey* was purchased for £10, the bookseller to whom she had sold her manuscript never set it up in type. Though she accepted these reverses philosophically, she seems to have been tempted to abandon literature. In 1801 her family removed to Bath and, after her father's death, first to Southampton, then to Chawton Cottage, near Alton. During these years, her only creative effort was an unfinished story named *The Watsons*; and not until she was already thirty-six did she see any of her novels published.

Sense and Sensibility appeared in 1811; *Pride and Prejudice* in 1813; *Mansfield Park* in 1814; *Emma* in 1816. *Persuasion* and *Northanger Abbey* came out a year after the novelist's early death. In 1815, while she was writing *Emma*, her health had begun to break down; and she died at Winchester, at the age of forty-one, on 18 July 1817. It had been a happy life. Jane Austen combined warm affections with a singularly well-balanced disposition. She loved her delightful sister, Cassandra, and was devoted to her various nephews and nieces, being particularly fond of the future Lady Knatchbull. She never fretted against the conditions of her some-what limited existence. Almost all the pleasures she needed she found within her own family; and, although it is said that she was once attached to a young man who vanished from the neighbour-hood before proposing, she seems never to have committed herself to a genuine adult love-affair. In her girlhood, a mildly frivolous young person – once described by the mother of the novelist, Mary Russell Mitford, as a 'husband-hunting butterfly' – she shed no tears over the flight of youth. She had discovered, she told Cassandra Austen in November 1813, that there were 'many Douceurs' attached to the rôle of middle-aged chaperone; 'for I am put on a Sofa near the Fire & can drink as much wine as I like'.

Her six novels fall into two groups, divided by a ten years' interval of silence – *Pride and Prejudice, Sense and Sensibility* and *Northanger Abbey*, succeeded at length by *Mansfield Park, Emma* and *Persuasion*. The effect they produce, nevertheless, is extraordinarily homogeneous. She has had innumerable admirers – among whom were Sir Walter Scott and the future George IV – and a few severe critics, ranging from Charlotte Brontë to D.H. Lawrence. That her view of life was extremely limited, and confined to the doings of a single class, is a point that her detractors have very often made. But one of her chief virtues was the good-natured readiness with which she accepted all her limitations. She regarded herself as a miniaturist, and the material on which she worked was, to use her own expressive phrase, a 'little bit (two inches wide) of ivory'. Jane Austen's books are major works of art, although she was far too sensible a writer to seek to describe sensations or emotions that

(*Opposite*) Portrait by Hoppner, believed to represent Jane Austen as a girl.

Jane Austen; portrait-sketch by her sister, Cassandra; the only authentic likeness that has survived of the novelist as a young woman.

she herself had not observed. The public events of the time are seldom mentioned; and then she allows them only the briefest of reference, as when we learn, during the course of *Mansfield Park*, that Sir Thomas Bertram's ship, while he is returning from the West Indies, has nearly been captured by a French Revolutionary privateer. The subjects she selected were always the subjects that she understood. She had no particularly high opinion of her gifts, and none of the self-conscious airs and graces of the average woman novelist. If a visitor should happen to arrive while she was in the midst of writing, she would slip away the half-written page and quietly resume her social duties.

Yet she possessed an extraordinary dramatic gift, acute imaginative insight, and a wonderful aptitude for evoking a revelatory situation from her knowledge of her characters. In some respects, she was a disciple of Fanny Burney – she owed the title *Pride and Prejudice* to one of Fanny Burney's novels; but, beside Jane Austen's light and penetrating wit, Miss Burney's satirical excursions, at their best, seem a form of heavy schoolgirl humour. With the passage of time, her wit grew increasingly sharp; in *Mansfield Park*, *Emma* and *Persuasion*, it seems to be becoming almost savage, as if she found the follies and vanities she observed more and more difficult to tolerate. She abhorred pretensions – even the pretensions that sometimes accompany exaggerated displays of sorrow. Thus, in *Persuasion*, she depicts a bereaved parent:

They were actually on the same sofa, for Mrs Musgrove had most readily made room for him; – they were divided only by Mrs Musgrove. It was no insignificant barrier indeed. Mrs Musgrove was of a comfortable substantial size, infinitely more fitted by nature to express good cheer and good humour, than tenderness and sentiment; and while the agitations of Anne's slender form, and pensive face, may be considered as very completely screened, Captain Wentworth should be allowed some credit for the self-command with which he attended to her large fat sighings over the destiny of a son, whom alive nobody had cared for.

Jane Austen's narratives are so closely knit that brief quotations seldom do her justice. But this, from the opening paragraph of the same novel, is the portrait she draws of a peculiarly fatuous baronet:

SIR Walter Elliot, of Kellynch-hall, in Somersetshire, was a man who, for his own amusement, never took up any book but the Baronetage; there he found occupation for an idle hour, and consolation in a distressed one; there his faculties were roused into admiration and respect, by contemplating the limited remnant of the earliest patents; there any unwelcome sensations, arising from domestic affairs, changed naturally into pity and contempt, as he turned over the almost endless creations of the last century – and there, if every other leaf were powerless, he could read his own history with an interest which never failed – this was the page at which the favourite volume always opened:
"ELLIOT OF KELLYNCH-HALL".

And this, her description, from *Mansfield Park*, of the squalid and impoverished home to which Fanny Price returns after many years among the prosperous Bertrams:

The sun was yet an hour and a half above the horizon. She felt that she had, indeed, been three months there; and the sun's rays falling strongly into the parlour . . . made her still more melancholy, for sunshine appeared to her a totally different thing in the town and in the country. Here, its power was only a glare: a stifling, sickly glare, serving but to bring forward stains and dirt that might otherwise have slept . . . She sat in a blaze of oppressive heat, in a cloud of moving dust, and her eyes could only wander from the walls, marked by her father's head, to the table cut and notched by her brothers, where stood the tea-board never thoroughly cleaned, the cups and saucers wiped in streaks, the milk a mixture of motes floating in thin blue, and the bread and butter growing every minute more greasy than even Rebecca's hands had first produced it. Her father read his newspaper, and her mother lamented over the ragged carpet . . .

Like Walter Savage Landor, THOMAS LOVE PEACOCK (1785–1866) played no direct part in any of the literary movements of his age; but working from his own reasonable, if idiosyncratic standpoint, he became one of its most gifted satirists. The son of a London glass-merchant, between his eighth and fourteenth years he was educated at a country school. Thereafter, it would seem, he received little formal training; yet he managed to acquire an extensive knowledge of the Greek and Roman classics. In 1804 he published a volume of verse and, in 1806, *The Visions of Love*, a rather tepid poem celebrating the pleasures of domestic affection. Next he was appointed assistant secretary to Admiral Popham on a British man-of-war; but the life of that 'floating inferno' very soon disgusted him. In 1812 he met Percy Bysshe Shelley, and before long the two poets were living together with Harriet Shelley in Edinburgh rooms. Besides introducing Shelley to Greek literature, Peacock did his best to wean his friend from an abstemious vegetarian diet by feeding him on well-peppered chops.

Thomas Love Peacock; portrait by H. Wallis, 1858.

In 1816 he published his first novel, *Headlong Hall*, which was followed by *Melincourt* in 1817, and by *Nightmare Abbey* in 1818. In 1819 the East India Company offered him a clerkship, a post that solved his money problems and enabled him to marry Jane Gryffyth, an attractive Welsh girl. He continued writing at intervals; and with *Maid Marian* (1822) and *The Misfortunes of Elphin* (1829) he temporarily abandoned satire. He returned to his real bent, however, with *Crotchet Castle* (1831). Meanwhile, he was still employed by the East India Company; and in 1836 he persuaded his employers to construct an iron steamship, and himself supervised its design and building – an effort that won him a distinguished mention from the First Lord of the Admiralty. He produced his last novel, *Gryll Grange* at the age of seventy-five, and died in January 1866.

Peacock is a difficult novelist to place – a friend of Shelley, who mocked at Romanticism; an admiring student of the Classics, yet an extremely unconventional writer. His novels depend for their effect less on such traditional ingredients as character and action, than on the interplay of ideas. *Headlong Hall, Nightmare Abbey, Crotchet Castle* and *Gryll Grange* are, first and foremost, brilliant fantasies, where, by means of ingeniously contrived dialogue, the fads, fashions, ideas and problems of the age are mercilessly exposed and ridiculed. The technique seldom changes; a country house-party provides the background for a series of meetings and collisions. The theorist encounters the effect of his theories; and manias overwhelm the maniac. Peacock satirizes every political and social vogue; he attacks economists and liberal doctrinaires, and pillories the excesses and affectations of the contemporary Romantic movement. We behold Scythrop – a caricature of his friend Shelley – quaffing wine from a Byronic skull-cup; Mr Cypress, the quintessence of fashionable Byronism; the Deteriorationist; the Transcendental Logician; the Rational Economist; the Grand Co-operative Parallelogram; and the Steam Intellect Society.

Here, for example, in *Headlong Hall*, Peacock is dealing with early-nineteenth-century landscape-gardeners and their passion for 'improvements':

MR MILESTONE: . . . Now, here is the same place corrected – trimmed – polished – decorated – adorned. Here sweeps a plantation, in that beautiful regular curve: there winds a gravel walk: here are parts of the old wood, left in these majestic circular clumps, disposed at equal distances with wonderful symmetry: there are some single shrubs scattered in elegant profusion: here a Portugal laurel, there a juniper; here a lauristinus, there a spruce fir; here a larch, there a lilac; here a rhododendron, there an arbutus. The stream, you see, is become a canal: the banks are perfectly smooth and green, sloping to the water's edge: and there is Lord Littlebrain, rowing in an elegant boat.

SQUIRE HEADLONG: Magical, faith!

MR MILESTONE: Here is another part of the grounds in its natural state. Here is a large rock, with the mountain-ash rooted in its fissures, overgrown, as you see, with ivy and moss; and from this part of it bursts a little fountain, that runs bubbling down its rugged sides.

MISS TENORINA: O how beautiful! How I should love the melody of that miniature cascade!

MR MILESTONE: Beautiful, Miss Tenorina! Hideous. Base, common, and popular. Such a thing as you may see anywhere, in wild and mountainous districts. Now, observe the metamorphosis. Here is the same rock, cut into the shape of a giant. In one hand he holds a horn, through which that little fountain is thrown to a prodigious elevation. In the other is a ponderous stone, so exactly balanced as to be apparently ready to fall on the head of any person who may happen to be beneath: and there is Lord Littlebrain walking under it.

SQUIRE HEADLONG: Miraculous, by Mahomet!

MR MILESTONE: This is the summit of a hill, covered, as you perceive, with wood, and with those mossy stones scattered at random under the trees.

MISS TENORINA: What a delightful spot to read in, on a summer's day! The air must be so pure, and the wind must sound so divinely in the tops of those old pines!

MR MILESTONE: Bad taste, Miss Tenorina. Bad taste, I assure you. Here is the spot improved. The trees are cut down: the stones are cleared away: this is an octagonal pavilion, exactly on the centre of the summit: and there you see Lord Littlebrain, on the top of the pavilion, enjoying the prospect with a telescope.

Peacock had a Johnsonian hatred of cant, whether it were social, political or intellectual. He is, above all else, the great defender of clarity, sobriety and common sense. His novels look back to the Restoration dramatists and the Jacobean 'comedy of humours'. At the same time, they seem to anticipate the novels of Meredith and Aldous Huxley's *Crome Yellow*.

GEORGE BORROW (1803–81) was, like Laurence Sterne, the son of a poor soldier, and spent many years of his youth wandering with his father's regiment to and fro across the British Isles. He had been born, on 5 July 1803, in East Anglia, at the 'beautiful little town' of East Dereham; and, between 1803 and 1816, his family moved house no less than twenty times, finally settling down at Norwich, where Thomas Borrow decided to retire from the service, having finally risen to the rank of captain. George himself remained a life-long wanderer; and, though Captain Borrow apprenticed him to the law, he soon grew tired of legal drudgery. But he had developed a passion for languages, and, as a young man, could claim to have acquired some knowledge of Latin, Greek, French, Italian, Spanish, German, Danish, Welsh, Hebrew, Armenian, and had learned to converse in Romany, the tongue the gypsies spoke. Simultaneously, under the influence of an older friend, he developed philosophic doubts, which increased his natural pessimism, and became involved 'in a dreary labyrinth', whence, 'whichever way I turned, no reasonable prospect of extricating myself occurred'. Borrow was also subject to bouts of neurotic anxiety that he often called 'the Horrors'.

In 1824 Captain Borrow died; and, having grown weary of his unprofitable life at home, his son decided to descend on London.

George Borrow; portrait by his brother, before his hair had turned white.

But there he failed to find a publisher for the translations of Welsh and Danish poetry that he had brought with him among his luggage, and was obliged to earn his living as a hard-worked publisher's hack. Then, 'after little more than a year's residence', having been prostrated by a fresh onslaught of 'the Horrors', he wandered off again into the country and travelled on foot through Wiltshire, Shropshire and Staffordshire. It was at this stage of his life that Borrow experienced many of the adventures he afterwards described in his picaresque novel *Lavengro*, met Isobel Berners and the 'Flaming Tinman' and was 'drabbed' by Mrs Hearne. A second visit to London proved no more productive than the first; and there followed what his biographers have entitled the 'Veiled Period' of Borrow's life, during which he asserted – how truthfully we cannot say – that he had travelled through Europe and Eastern Russia as far afield as the frontiers of the Chinese Empire. Some of the tales he told were no doubt half-imaginary; and his footloose wanderings produced no reward, either literary or financial. His family at Norwich called him 'poor George'. 'A tall, spare, dark-complexioned man, usually dressed in black', he had prematurely silvered locks.

Salvation came from an unexpected quarter. Through the good offices of one of his Norfolk acquaintances, he was introduced to the directors of the British and Foreign Bible Society, and appointed their representative in St Petersburg. His efforts to distribute a Russian translation of the New Testament were both enterprising and successful; and he was next instructed to proceed to Portugal and Spain, and there carry on the good work. He worked and travelled in Spain – then convulsed by a ferocious civil war – from 1835 to 1840. The result was his first original work, *The Zincali, or The Gypsies of Spain*, which appeared in 1841, and was succeeded, in 1843, by *The Bible in Spain*. The success of that excellent travel-book was 'instantaneous and overwhelming'.

None of his later books had an equally warm reception; and his masterpiece, *Lavengro*, on which he worked between 1842 and 1851, disappointed almost all the critics. Meanwhile, he had married a motherly, middle-aged widow, and been recalled and dismissed by the Bible Society, who had come to dislike his bold and arbitrary methods. With Mrs Borrow, he retired to a Norfolk cottage and published *The Romany Rye*, a sequel to *Lavengro*, but a far less interesting work, another travel-book, *Wild Wales*, and his *Romano Lavo-lil, or Word-Book of the Romany*, a somewhat fragmentary and inadequate essay in linguistic scholarship. He died alone at his cottage near Oulton Broad on 26 July 1881.

Borrow's account of his travels through Spain gives us a wonderfully graphic impression of the wild Iberian peninsula; and, when he visited Toledo and inspected El Greco's famous *Burial of the Count d'Orgaz*, he was among the first travellers since the beginning of the seventeenth century to recognize the artist's genius. An even

more fascinating work is *Lavengro*, which he himself described as 'a dream partly of study, partly of adventure'. It is not autobiographical in the strictest meaning of the word; there is a dreamlike inconsequence about the narrative, which is made up of a series of vivid episodes, drawn from the recollections of his wandering youth. It is full of dramatic portraits and extraordinary natural scenes. Everything he touches, he enlarges; and every human being he meets on his way through life possesses some fantastic or heroic quality, and has some memorable tale to tell.

At one moment, on the eve of a great discovery, he stands contemplating old London Bridge:

London Bridge in 1816, by J.B. Papworth; the huge whale-backed structure that so much impressed Borrow.

A strange kind of Bridge it was; huge and massive, and seemingly of great antiquity. It had an arched back, like that of a hog, and at either side, at intervals, were stone bowers bulking over the river, but open on the other side, and furnished with a semi-circular bench. Though the bridge was wide – very wide – it was all too narrow for the concourse upon it. Thousands of human beings were pouring over the bridge. But what chiefly struck my attention was a double row of carts and wagons, the generality drawn by horses as large as elephants, each row striving hard in a different direction, and not unfrequently brought to a standstill. Oh! the cracking of whips, the shouts and oaths of the carters, and the grating of wheels upon the enormous stones that formed the pavement! . . .

But, if upon the bridge there was a confusion, below it there was a confusion ten times confounded. The tide, which was fast ebbing, obstructed by the immense piers of the old bridge, poured beneath the arches with a fall of several feet, forming in the river below as many whirlpools as there were arches. Truly tremendous was the roar of the descending waters . . . Slowly advancing along the bridge, I came to the highest point, and there stood still, close beside one of the stone bowers, in which, beside a fruitstall, sat an old woman, with a pan of charcoal at her feet, and a book in her hand, in which she appeared to be reading intently. There I stood, just above the principal arch, looking through the balustrade at the scene that presented itself – and such a scene! Towards the left bank of the river, a forest of masts, thick and close, as far as the eye could reach; spacious wharfs, surmounted with the gigantic edifices; and, far away, Caesar's castle, with its White Tower.

BENJAMIN DISRAELI (1804–81) occupies a unique position in the history of English literature, as a famous and distinguished Prime Minister who was also an imaginative and highly successful novelist. Born in London, the son of Isaac D'Israeli, erudite author of the *Curiosities of Literature*, he was descended from Jewish-Italian stock, but had been baptized into the Christian Church at the age of thirteen. After an education said to have been 'somewhat irregular', he entered a London solicitor's office. There he did little good; his aim was to become a poet and a Byronic modern dandy. Through his personal extravagance and reckless speculation he soon accumulated a load of debts; and it was lack of money that, in 1826, encouraged him to publish his first novel, *Vivian Grey*. An absurd and flashy production, the book had a popular *succès de scandale*; and his royalties enabled the young novelist to leave England on an extended tour of Europe and the Near East. Returning in 1831, he decided to stand for Parliament as a New Radical. He failed; and not until he had suffered a series of defeats was he finally elected member for Maidstone in 1837. At first, his exotic appearance and flamboyant mannerisms excited the derision of his fellow members; but soon his intelligence and sharp tongue had begun to earn him the respect that he deserved; and in 1839 he further consolidated his position by marrying a rich widow, Mrs Wyndham Lewis, who was twelve years older than Disraeli and proved, he said, 'the perfect wife'. Assisted by her fortune, he bought an estate at Hughenden and joined the ranks of the land-owning classes.

When he launched the earliest of his group of political novels, *Coningsby*, in 1844, Disraeli had seven years of political experience to draw upon. It was followed by *Sybil* in 1845 and by *Tancred* published in 1847. During that year, Disraeli was leader of the Tory opposition; in 1852 he was appointed Chancellor of the Exchequer, and in 1868 he achieved the great ambition of his life and first served the State as Prime Minister. His second ministry lasted from 1874 to 1880. Meanwhile, in 1870, he had issued *Lothair*. Created 1st Earl of Beaconsfield in 1876, he died in 1881.

Vivian Grey is a lively entertainment; the novelist's brilliant wit makes up for some of the absurdities of the plot and characterization. The hero is a remarkably lucky young man; with a few words he launches a political revolution; duchesses throw themselves at his head; consumptive ladies confess their passion for him as they

EMPRESS AND EARL;

OR, ONE GOOD TURN DESERVES ANOTHER.

LORD BEACONSFIELD. *"Thanks, your Majesty. I might have had it before! Now I think I have EARNED it!"*

expire in his arms; tornadoes leave him unscathed, having swept away everything else in sight. A vein of wild romantic fantasy runs through all Disraeli's novels; and it colours the social and political programme that he puts forward in *Coningsby*, *Sybil* and *Tancred*. Disraeli's schemes for national regeneration were those of the 'Young England' group of Tories; he preached an idealized conservatism that was to unite every section of the social structure. In *Coningsby*, the story of a young man's political education, Disraeli's didactic intentions are particularly obvious; the novel culminates in a symbolic marriage between representatives of the old aristocracy and the new industrialism. The theme of *Sybil* is economic, based on such problems as the Chartist movement and the spread of industrial unrest. The novel has been praised for its pictures of the suffering poor; but, although his descriptions of poverty and squalor are accurate, they were taken largely from official Blue Books; Disraeli had had no real experience of a social world beneath his own. Hatton, the lower-class firebrand, is a clumsy caricature; and the novelist's attempts to demonstrate

(*Above left*) Benjamin Disraeli as a youthful dandy; after a drawing by D. Maclise.

(*Above right*) Disraeli raised to the peerage, 1876; from a *Punch* cartoon.

that the aristocracy was destined to provide the people with leaders is too romantic to be quite convincing. Many of his dramatis personae are animated opinions rather than real men and women. He never pretended to be a realist; and in *Tancred* he adds mysticism to romanticism. Remembering his early visit to the Holy Land, he depicts it as the source of the spiritual renaissance that nineteenth-century England needed to bring about an ideal alliance between people, ruling classes, Crown and Church. *Lothair*, which appeared more than twenty years after *Tancred*, is again concerned with politics; but it is a far mellower and more controlled work. His last novel, *Endymion*, completed just after the Tories had fallen from power and Disraeli had retired to Hughendon, has some of the interest of a self-portrait, its subject being the emergence of an obscure youth who rises to the post of Prime Minister. Disraeli is at his best as a chronicler of political and aristocratic life, which he presented with the mixture of fanciful gusto and satirical wit that continued to distinguish him throughout his whole existence. Though his style improved, it did not radically change; he remained astonishingly young at heart. If *Vivian Grey* is a preposterous juvenile fantasy, *Endymion*, finished when he was over seventy-five, has none of the failings of an old man's book.

Mrs Gaskell (1810–65) was another novelist who dealt with contemporary social problems, and her achievement on this plane seems considerably more impressive than that of either Kingsley or Disraeli. Christened Elizabeth Cleghorn Stevenson, she was the daughter of a Unitarian minister. Her mother had died while giving her birth, and her father then entrusted her to the care of an aunt who lived at Knutsford in Cheshire, where she remained until 1827. In 1832 she met and married the Rev William Gaskell, the Unitarian minister of Cross Street Chapel, Manchester. It was a happy marriage. The Gaskells had seven children; but only four survived; and the death of her only son was a particularly painful blow. To distract her, Mrs Gaskell's husband persuaded her to try her hand at writing. The result was *Mary Barton, a Tale of Manchester Life*, which appeared in 1848. Though regarded by some as a highly subversive production, the book had a considerable success, and gained her the friendship of a number of her fellow-writers, including Charlotte Brontë and Dickens. She now contributed short stories to Dickens's magazines; and *Cranford*, her novel of provincial life, was serialized in *Household Words* between 1851 and 1853. In *Ruth* (1853) and *North and South* (1855) she returned to social problems; and in 1857 she published her controversial *Life of Charlotte Bronte*. Among her later works were *Sylvia's Lovers* (1863), and the unfinished *Wives and Daughters* (1866). With the advance she received on this novel, during the summer of 1865 she bought a country house in Hampshire; and there, that same year, she died of a heart attack on 12 November, quietly and unexpectedly. She was buried at Knutsford, the place she had loved as a girl.

Much of the strength of Mrs Gaskell's best novels lies in their psychological and sociological accuracy. From her observations of the factories and slums of Manchester she had derived the knowledge of modern working-class life that gives *Mary Barton* its disturbing power. The centre of interest is John Barton, Mary's father, a genuine proletarian, unlike many of the working-class characters Kingsley and Disraeli had portrayed. Mrs Gaskell's passionate concern for the poor helps to redeem a story otherwise somewhat crude and melodramatic. But although the novelist shows real imaginative skill in her presentation of John Barton and his struggle against poverty, as a work of literature the book does not quite succeed; and when she provides a conventional happy ending – Barton, who has meanwhile murdered the son of a villainous industrialist, dies in the arms of his reformed employer – she does so at the expense of all that is more interesting about her previous conduct of the story.

Mrs Gaskell, 1851; after George Richmond.

With *Cranford* Mrs Gaskell turned to a very different world, and drew on her recollections of provincial life at Knutsford to create a charming yet penetrating study of the enclosed society of an old-fashioned country town. *Ruth*, on the other hand, published in 1853, is a courageous attempt to lessen the stigma that attached to a 'fallen woman'; while in *North and South* (1855) she returns to the grime and industrial unrest of the North; but again, as in *Mary Barton*, the plot is slightly too contrived. Of her later novels, *Wives and Daughters*, which she did not live to finish, is certainly her best book. It combines a sly, soft humour with a penetrating psychological realism. Mrs Gaskell was undoubtedly a minor novelist. She remains, nevertheless, one of the most gifted women writers who made their mark in the Victorian Age.

William Makepeace Thackeray; drawing by D. Maclise.

WILLIAM MAKEPEACE THACKERAY (1811–63), unlike his greatest rival, Charles Dickens, was brought up in an atmosphere of security and social comfort. His father, a prosperous Anglo-Indian, died when he was only four; but his mother, whose second husband, a retired soldier, Major Carmichael-Smyth, is said to have been the original of 'Colonel Newcome', took a possessive interest in her son's welfare. Though he had detested his schooling at the Charterhouse, Thackeray led a pleasant life at Cambridge, where his friends included Edward Fitzgerald, one day to become the translator of the *Rubáiyát of Omar Khayyám*, but eventually went down without a degree, having over-indulged a juvenile taste for gambling and been fleeced by a card-sharper of £1500. He then travelled abroad and, when he returned to London, began to study for the Law. He was an idle young man, who expected to inherit a moderately substantial fortune. Then, in 1833, the failure

Thackeray in later life;
portrait by Thomas
Lawrence, 1864.

of an Indian agency house, which swallowed up the greater part of his inheritance, at length forced him into active life.

Art was his first love; but his efforts to earn his living as a painter proved completely unsuccessful. Next, he became a journalist, and worked for a variety of publications from *The Times* to *Fraser's Magazine* and *Punch*. Meanwhile, he had married, in 1836, a charming, diminutive, helpless girl named Isabella Shawe, the daughter of an Irish soldier. She bore him three daughters, one of whom died in early childhood. But Mrs Thackeray, to whom her husband – a large, virile, strongly built man, six feet three inches tall – sometimes referred either as 'that diminutive individual' or as 'an anxious little soul', like David Copperfield's child-wife was an extremely inefficient housekeeper; her stews tasted of water and onions; and, again like young Mrs Copperfield, she found it difficult to keep accounts. Finally, after the birth of her last child, she developed melancholia. In 1840 she attempted suicide; her reason collapsed; and Thackeray's married life came to an abrupt and tragic end.

Thackeray's literary career seems to have been shaped by two emotional catastrophes – his wife was pronounced insane and, about 1846, he fell in love with Jane Brookfield. The wife of a close friend, Mrs Brookfield was a gifted and beautiful, but unhappy, languid and neurotic woman. She seems to have welcomed Thackeray's admiration; but she could not, or would not, return the romantic attachment that she had kindled in her devotee; and for many years he was condemned to a state of 'longing passion unfulfilled'. When he wrote *Vanity Fair*, Major Dobbin's passion for Amelia evidently reproduced his own experience. His first important book, *The Yellowplush Correspondence*, a collection of lively satirical sketches, came out under the pseudonym Michael Angelo Titmarsh in 1838; and his enjoyable *Paris Sketch Book* in 1840. His first three novels, *Catherine*, *The Great Hoggarty Diamond* and *Barry Lyndon*, a picaresque story of an eighteenth-century adventurer, evidently much influenced by his admiration for Fielding, appeared between 1839 and 1844. But it was *Vanity Fair*, which, after many false starts, he completed in 1848, that raised him to the heights of fame. The powerful *Edinburgh Review* now acclaimed him as the Fielding of the present age. The novel appeared in instalments; and, before the nineteenth had reached the public, Thackeray was able to inform his mother that he had recently become 'a sort of great man', and was 'all but at the top of the tree', with Dickens as his only rival. Between 1848 and 1859, his other major works, *Pendennis*, *Henry Esmond*, *The Newcomes* and *The Virginians* considerably added to his reputation. His last novels, *Lovel the Widower* and *The Adventures of Philip* were published in 1860 and 1861–2. He died of the heart-disease that had long been undermining his robust constitution on Christmas Eve 1863.

Had Thackeray never written a novel, he would no doubt be remembered as an unusually gifted Victorian journalist, author of *The Yellowplush Papers*, *The Book of Snobs* and the *Paris Sketch Book*, and as the amusing lecturer who had turned *The Four Georges* into a row of historical ninepins, which he proceeded sanctimoniously to knock down. The same faults – moral self-complacency and sentimental loquacity – are present in his major novels, *Vanity Fair*, *Pendennis*, *Henry Esmond* and *The Newcomes*. The Victorian publishers' habit of publishing in parts made it necessary to stuff each part with the kind of literary ingredients that a reader then expected – dramatic interest, sentiment, humour and an over-riding moral message. Thus Thackeray's stories, though cleverly planned and constructed, and full of vivid insights into human nature, are apt to resemble the arrangement of a mid-Victorian dinner-table, surmounted by an elaborate epergne bearing an abundance of fruit and flowers, and scattered with an array of filagree silver dishes containing brightly-coloured bon-bons. There is a little too much of everything; a modern reader might have preferred him to concentrate on a single character or theme – in *Pendennis*, the theme of struggling youth; in *The Newcomes*, of valiant old age. Only in *Vanity Fair* are his talents concentrated upon a single human portrait to which his other personages act as foils – the portrait of a thoroughly amoral woman, Becky Sharp, the determined adventuress whose explosive intervention trans-forms the whole existence of the Osbornes and the Sedleys.

Thackeray loved women; and the women who inspired him seem to have been divided into two opposing types. There were 'women of spirit' – such as his dominant mother, whom he described in his later years as 'O so tender so loving so cruel'; and women, like Amelia Sedley and his own humble, pathetic wife, to whom he affectionately condescended and who aroused his keen, paternal instincts. Amelia is Becky's predestined victim; but, although Thackeray stigmatizes Becky's wickedness and selfish-ness, he finds her none the less attractive, and admires the unscru-pulous courage with which she conducts her long campaign against society. *Vanity Fair* ends on a note of sober disillusionment. Amelia, the 'good woman', has herself a shallow, selfish nature. 'If I had made Amelia a higher sort of woman,' he wrote, 'there would have been no vanity in Dobbin's falling in love with her . . .' At that point, despite his previous moral asides, the novelist lets us draw our own conclusions. His chief object, he said, was 'to convey as strongly as possible the sentiment of reality'. He achieves it in his masterpiece, *Vanity Fair*, which, for all its elaborate Victorian trimmings, remains an extraordinarily 'real' book.

THE MEET AT QUEEN'S CRAWLEY

That was a famous sight for little Rawdon. At half-past ten, Tom Moody, Sir Huddlestone Fuddlestone's huntsman, was seen trotting up

Rebecca's farewell to Miss Pinkerton's Academy; Thackeray's own illustration to the first edition of *Vanity Fair*, 1848.

the avenue, followed by the noble pack of hounds in a compact body – the rear being brought up by the two whips clad in stained scarlet frocks – light hard-featured lads on well-bred lean horses, possessing marvellous dexterity in casting the points of their long heavy whips at the thinnest part of any dog's skin who dares to straggle from the main body, or to take the slightest notice, or even so much as wink, at the hares and rabbits starting under their noses.

Next comes boy Jack, Tom Moody's son, who weighs five stone, measures eight-and-forty inches, and will never be any bigger. He is perched on a large raw-boned hunter, half-covered by a capacious saddle. This animal is Sir Huddlestone Fuddlestone's favourite horse – the Nob. Other horses, ridden by other small boys, arrive from time to time, awaiting their masters, who will come cantering on anon.

Tom Moody rides up to the door of the Hall, where he is welcomed by the butler, who offers him drink, which he declines. He and his pack then draw off into a sheltered corner of the lawn, where the dogs roll on the grass, and play or growl angrily at one another, ever and anon breaking out into furious fight speedily to be quelled by Tom's voice, unmatched at rating, or the snaky thongs of the whips.

Many young gentlemen canter up on thoroughbred hacks, spatter-dashed to the knee, and enter the house to drink cherry brandy and pay their respects to the ladies, or, more modest and sportsmanlike, divest themselves of their mud-boots, exchange their hacks for their hunters, and warm their blood by a preliminary gallop round the lawn. Then they collect round the pack in the corner, and talk with Tom Moody of past sport, and the merits of Sniveller and Diamond, and of the state of the country and of the wretched breed of foxes.

Sir Huddlestone presently appears mounted on a clever cob, and rides up to the Hall, where he enters and does the civil thing by the ladies, after which, being a man of few words, he proceeds to business. The hounds are drawn up to the hall door and little Rawdon descends amongst them, excited, yet half alarmed by the caresses which they bestow upon him, at the thumps he receives from their waving tails, and at their canine bickerings, scarcely restrained by Tom Moody's tongue and lash.

Meanwhile, Sir Huddlestone has hoisted himself unwieldily on the Nob: 'Let's try Sowster's Spinney, Tom,' says the Baronet, 'Farmer Mangle tells me there are two foxes in it.' Tom blows his horn and trots off, followed by the pack, by the whips, by the young gents from Winchester, by the farmers of the neighbourhood, by the labourers of the parish on foot, with whom the day is a great holiday; Sir Huddlestone bringing up the rear with Colonel Crawley, and the whole *cortège* disappears down the avenue.

(Vanity Fair)

CHARLES DICKENS (1812–70) belonged, on both sides of his family, to the urban lower-middle class – a class that rapidly rose into prominence during the first half of the nineteenth century. His paternal grandfather and grandmother had earned their livelihood as upper-servants, privileged retainers of an aristocratic household, with whose help the novelist's father, John, had obtained a clerkship in the Navy Pay Office. In 1809 John Dickens married an attractive and pleasure-loving girl named Elizabeth Barrow. Her origins were slightly more distinguished; but the Barrows had suffered severe financial reverses and looked back wistfully to 'better days'.

Thus Charles Dickens's childhood was passed in an atmosphere of genteel poverty, as his parents, often pursued by their creditors, moved restlessly from place to place – from Portsmouth, where the novelist was born, to various shabby London streets, and thence to the vicinity of the naval dockyards at Chatham. They returned to London in 1822; and soon afterwards John Dickens, a clever and good-natured, but improvident and naturally extravagant man, who contributed many details to his son's portrait of Mr Wilkins Micawber, found himself facing complete financial ruin. Before Charles had reached his thirteenth birthday, his father was cast into the Marshalsea, a debtors' gaol. Meanwhile, he himself had

been condemned to earn a pittance at a London blacking-
warehouse. His salary was only six shillings a week; and it was
kindly suggested to him that he might carry on his education in
the midday break, when the other boys were eating.

Cut off from his family, and from everything he loved and
valued, Charles Dickens was alone and helpless. In later years he
described his first visit to his father at the Marshalsea:

We went up to his room . . . and cried very much. And he told me,
I remember, to take warning . . . and to observe that if a man had
twenty pounds a year, and spent nineteen pounds nineteen shillings and
sixpence, he would be happy; but that a shilling spent the other way
would make him wretched. I see the fire we sat before, now; with two
bricks inside the rusted grate, one on each side, to prevent its burning
too many coals.

It was a crucial period. 'Even now,' he wrote in middle-age,
'famous and caressed and happy, I often forget in my dreams that
I have a dear wife and children . . . and wander desolately back to
that time . . .' He could never forget it; nor could he ever forgive
his mother (who bore some resemblance, not to the devoted Mrs
Micawber, but to the fatuous Mrs Nickleby) because, although
John Dickens eventually agreed that Charles must be allowed to
leave the warehouse, his mother was anxious that he should
remain. Thenceforward the boy determined to stand on his own

feet; and, when John Dickens emerged from the shades of his prison-house not very much the worse for wear, Charles was able to resume his education, and developed during the next few years into a strong-minded and independent youth. In 1828 he set up as a freelance reporter at the ancient Consistory Court of Doctors' Commons; then removed to the public galleries of the Houses of Parliament, where he reported the momentous debates that preceded the passing of the first Reform Bill.

Finally, late in 1833, he slipped a manuscript, the earliest of his *Sketches by Boz*, 'into a dark letter-box in a dark office' – the office of *The Monthly Magazine* – up a dark alleyway off Fleet Street. It was accepted. *Sketches by Boz*, with illustrations by Cruickshank, came out on Dickens's twenty-fourth birthday, 7 February 1836, to be succeeded at the end of March by the opening instalments of the *Pickwick Papers*. The fourth issue, which introduced Samuel Weller, proved extraordinarily successful. *Oliver Twist* was published as a complete volume – and, unlike his previous productions, under his own name – during the latter days of 1838.

Thereafter, triumph was to follow triumph; until the novelist, exhausted by the unsparing energy with which he had pursued success, suddenly collapsed and died. Between 1838 and 1865, he had put forth thirteen major novels – *Oliver Twist, Nicholas Nickleby, The Old Curiosity Shop, Barnaby Rudge, Martin Chuzzlewit, Dombey and Son, David Copperfield, Bleak House, Hard Times, Little Dorrit, A Tale of Two Cities, Great Expectations, Our Mutual Friend* – besides such minor productions as *A Christmas Carol, The Chimes* and *A Cricket on the Hearth*, and a full-length novel, *The Mystery of Edwin Drood*, which he did not live to finish. Both in his literary efforts and in his conduct of his personal life, there was something demonic about Dickens's character. He was never quiescent, but constantly at full stretch, writing, editing, organizing amateur theatricals, travelling, entertaining, dining-out. He enjoyed any kind of public appearance at which he could display his histrionic gifts and, latterly, is said to have killed himself by the popular 'readings' that he organized, where he enacted each of his personages in turn, and particularly excelled in his presentation of one or other of his favourite villains.

Dickens, moreover, was a dandy who affected gaudy waistcoats and a superfluity of jewelled pins and chains. He was also a passionate lover of women; but his early marriage – to Catherine, or Kate, Hogarth, the daughter of a fellow journalist – ran a somewhat dismal course. Mrs Dickens, a quiet, lymphatic, unimaginative woman, soon shrank into the background; and in 1858, after they had been married twenty years and she had borne him ten children, he publicly announced their separation. Meanwhile he had contracted a romantic relationship with a young actress, Ellen Ternan, who eventually became his mistress.

If Dickens's personal vices were characteristic of his age – for

Dickens' first London home at Furnival's Inn.

instance, his unctuous sentimentality that sometimes hid a strain of cruelty – so were the novelist's amazing virtues. He poured out his 'whole heart and soul' into everything he wrote and into every cause he advocated; and many of the campaigns he launched – against poor schooling, the abuses of the English law and the pestiferous London slums – had a lasting effect on the contemporary social structure. True, his heroes and heroines, especially the women he described, seldom rise above the rank of dummies; but as often he looked back to his own youth, and portrayed the shabby genteel world in which he had been born and brought up, with its vast population of strugglers, scroungers, pretenders, oddities and social misfits, he reveals his immense creative genius and, as a story-teller, carries all before him. By comparison, the author of *Vanity Fair* had a staid, prosaic style. Thackeray rarely attempted an elaborate set-piece; but Dickens's descriptive style is almost baroque in its elaboration, whether he is depicting a London fog or the life behind the scenes at a London theatre:

LONDON. Michaelmas Term lately over, and the Lord Chancellor sitting in Lincoln's Inn Hall. Implacable November weather. As much mud in the streets, as if the waters had but newly retired from the face of the earth, and it would not be wonderful to meet a Megalosaurus forty feet long or so, waddling like an elephantine lizard up Holborn-Hill. Smoke lowering down from chimney-pots, making a soft black drizzle, with flakes of soot in it as big as full-grown snow-flakes – gone into mourning, one might imagine, for the death of the sun. Dogs, undistinguishable in mire. Horses, scarcely better; splashed to their very blinkers. Foot passengers, jostling one another's umbrellas, in a general infection of ill tempers, and losing their foot-hold at street-corners, where tens of thousands of other foot passengers have been slipping and sliding since the day broke (if the day ever broke), adding new deposits to the crust upon crust of mud, sticking at those points tenaciously to the pavement, and accumulating at compound interest.

Fog everywhere, fog up the river, where it flows among green aits and meadows; fog down the river, where it rolls defiled among the tiers of shipping, and the waterside pollutions of a great (and dirty) city. Fog on the Essex marshes, fog on the Kentish heights. Fog creeping into the cabooses of collier-brigs; fog lying out on the yards, and hovering in the rigging of great ships; fog drooping on the gunwales of barges and small boats. Fog in the eyes and throats of ancient Greenwich pensioners, wheezing by the firesides of their wards; fog in the stem and bowl of the afternoon pipe of the wrathful skipper, down in his close cabin; fog cruelly pinching the toes and fingers of his shivering little 'prentice boy on deck. Chance people on the bridges peeping into a nether sky of fog, with fog all round them, as if they were up in a balloon, and hanging in the misty clouds.

Gas looming through the fog in divers places in the streets, much as the sun may, from the spongey fields, be seen to loom by husbandman and plough-boy. Most of the shops lighted two hours before their time – as the gas seems to know, for it has a haggard and unwilling look.

(*Bleak House*)

(*Opposite*) Illustration by George Cruikshank to to the 1838 edition of *Oliver Twist*; Bill Sikes at bay.

George Cruikshank

Illustration to Chapter I
of *The Old Curiosity Shop*.

Little Dorrit was almost as ignorant of the ways of theatres as of the ways of goldmines, and when she was directed to a furtive sort of door, with a curious up-all-night air about it, that appeared to be ashamed of itself and to be hiding in an alley, she hesitated to approach it; being further deterred by the sight of some half-dozen close-shaved gentlemen, with their hats very strangely on about the door . . . On her applying to them . . . they made way for her to enter a dark hall . . . where she could hear the distant playing of music and the sound of dancing feet. A man so much in want of airing that he had a blue mould upon him, sat watching this dark place from a hole in a corner like a spider; and he told her he would send a message to Miss Dorrit by the first lady or gentleman who went through. The first lady who went through had a roll of music, half in her muff and half out of it, and was in such a fumbled condition altogether, that it seemed as if it would be an act of kindness to iron her. But as she was very good-natured, she said 'Come with me; I'll soon find Miss Dorrit for you', Miss Dorrit's sister went with her, drawing nearer at every step she took in the darkness, to the sound of music and dancing feet.

At last they came into a maze of dust, where a quantity of people were tumbling over one another, and where there was such a confusion of unaccountable shapes and beams, bulk-heads, brick walls, ropes of gaslight and daylight, that they seemed to have got on the wrong side of the universe . . .

'Why, good gracious, Amy, what ever brought you here? . . .

As her sister said this in no very cordial tone of welcome, she conducted her to a more open part of the maze, where various golden chairs and tables were heaped together, and where a number of young ladies were sitting on anything they could find, chattering. All these young ladies wanted ironing, and all had a curious way of looking everywhere while they chattered.

Just as the sisters arrived there, a monotonous boy in a Scotch cap put

his head around a beam on the left, and said, 'Less noise there, ladies!'
and disappeared. Immediately after which, a sprightly gentleman with a
quantity of long black hair looked round a beam on the right and said,
'Less noise there, darlings!' and also disappeared.

(Little Dorritt)

The real hero of Dickens' novels is London itself, the huge
metropolis he loved and hated, that had threatened to overwhelm
his youth, and, once he had struggled free by dint of herculean
efforts, became his closest friend and dearest enemy.

When the American poet, James Russell Lowell, met ANTHONY
TROLLOPE (1815–82), he found the famous novelist 'a good,
roaring, positive fellow'. Such was the impression that Trollope
usually made. But few distinguished English writers have had a
more unhappy youth. Although his mother, Frances Trollope,
authoress of some entertaining travel-books which included
Domestic Manners of the Americans, published in 1832, was a gay,
bustling, energetic person, his father, an improvident London
barrister, was a gloomy, self-centred and unloving man, whose
absurd misconduct of his financial affairs soon reduced his household to the verge of ruin. At twelve, the boy was sent to Winchester, where he paid the penalty of being poor and awkward –
he felt convinced, he wrote long afterwards, 'that I have been
flogged oftener than any human being alive'; and he grew up idle
and irresolute, obsessed by a sense of his own inferiority. Nor did
he learn much; in 1834, when he applied for a junior clerkship at
the Post Office, he had not yet completely mastered his multipli-
cation tables. Nevertheless he somehow secured the job, and stuck
to it for six years, until his health broke down. On his recovery,
Trollope was despatched to Ireland as a deputy postal surveyor,
with an office at Banagher, beside the River Shannon. His new
life suited him; he enjoyed the company of his Irish neighbours,
and discovered the pleasures of fox-hunting, which became his
favourite pastime. In 1844 he contracted a happy marriage and,
in 1847, published his first novel, *The Macdermots of Ballycloran*.

This book, and its two immediate successors, attracted very
little notice; while *The Warden*, which appeared in 1855, though
well-reviewed, had a disappointing sale. In 1857 he calculated
that he had earned a mere £55 during a whole decade of literary
work. That year, however, the appearance of *Barchester Towers*
brought him sudden fame and fortune; and in 1867 he retired
from the Post Office and devoted his energies to tireless writing.
All his life he worked steadily and regularly. The clerical sequence,
that had begun with *The Warden*, was followed by a series of
political narratives, which opened with *Phineas Finn* in 1869 and
closed with *The Duke's Children* in 1880. At the same time, he continued to hunt – he was a brave but clumsy rider – travelled widely,
visiting America, South Africa, the Antipodes and Iceland, and

Anthony Trollope, by
S. Lawrence, 1865.

became a popular and conspicuous figure in the card-rooms of his London clubs; next to fox-hunting, playing whist was the principal joy of his existence. There was nothing of the aesthete or the dilettante about Anthony Trollope. His honest and unself-conscious *Autobiography*, published in 1883, a year after his death, did some damage to his reputation; for here he insists that success-ful novel-writing is not an art, but a well-managed craft. Certainly, books poured from his desk as from a twentieth-century produc-tion line. Every morning, at half-past-five, he took up his pen, which he did not put down until half-past-eight, working with his watch in front of him and a target of 250 words to be written every quarter of an hour. At the end of October 1859, when Thackeray was preparing to launch the *Cornhill Magazine*, he offered Trollope a fee of £1000 for the serial rights of *Framley Parsonage*, but could allow him only six weeks to produce the text. Trollope set to work; and the manuscript was completed, corrected and delivered within the stipulated time.

Framley Parsonage was part of the succession of Barsetshire novels – *The Warden* (1855), *Barchester Towers* (1857), *Doctor Thorne* (1858), *Framley Parsonage* (1861), *The Small House at Allington* (1864), and *The Last Chronicle of Barset* (1867) – that the novelist constructed around the personages of a quiet cathedral-city, where country gentlemen, local great ladies and genteel provincial clergymen move against a background of ecclesiastical politics. Trollope aimed to depict this world exactly as he had himself observed it, without prejudice or imaginative licence. His novels lack the smallest touch of mystery or ambiguity; there are no unexpected twists of plot or surprising revelations. Thanks to his matter-of-fact approach, Barchester becomes a very real place, calm, orderly, almost idyllic, in which a multitude of modern readers still delight to take refuge. There is no need for suspension of disbelief when we are turning Trollope's pages. Even his heroes are ordinary:

He was a tall thin man, apparently not more than thirty years of age, looking in all respects like a gentleman, but with nothing in his appear-ance that was remarkable. It was a face that you might see and forget, and see again and forget again; and yet when you looked at it and pulled it to pieces, you found that it was a fairly good face, showing intellect in the forehead, and much character in the mouth. The eyes, too, though not to be called bright, had always something to say for themselves, looking as though they had a real meaning. But the outline of the face was almost insignificant, being too thin.

This passage, quoted from *Can You Forgive Her?* (1864), portrays Plantagenet Palliser, the central figure in the series of political novels to which Trollope devoted his creative talents once he had bidden Barchester goodbye. But although Hawthorne described Trollope's works as 'solid and substantial, written on the strength

of beef and through the inspiration of ale', they have also a darker side that becomes increasingly noticeable in his later stories. The quietude of provincial life is disturbed in *The Last Chronicle of Barset* by a glimpse of its underlying harshness, as when the novelist analyses the persecution-complex that afflicts the unhappy Josiah Crawley. In *He Knew He Was Right* (1869), a more extended study of neurosis, he shows the deranging effects of an obsessive and unfounded jealousy – to such effect that many of his previous admirers voted it a highly disturbing book. For the most part,

Frontispiece to *Can You Forgive Her?*

however, Trollope preferred to avoid both the complex and the enigmatic. His chief virtue, according to Henry James – a novelist who always 'loved a mystery' – was his keen 'appreciation of the usual'. He did not 'care for the stars', he freely admitted himself; 'I care, I think, only for men and women.' And it was the human species that, in the forty-seven novels he left behind him on his death, Trollope never tired of observing and delineating. He may not have been among the greatest creative novelists thrown up by the Victorian Age; but he was undoubtedly the age's finest and most conscientious chronicler.

CHARLOTTE (1816–55), EMILY (1818–48) and ANNE (1820–49) BRONTË were extremely dissimilar, both as human beings and as literary artists; but since they were sisters, brought up in close communion, and, during their precocious youth, had collaborated on the same romantic narratives, they must be discussed beneath a single head. The eldest, Charlotte, was the most ambitious – she had, indeed, an iron spirit; Emily, the most brilliant; Anne, the gentlest and the least gifted. Their father was the Reverend Patrick Brontë, an Ulster parish-priest, who since the year 1820 had held the living of Haworth among the Yorkshire moors. In 1821 he had lost his wife; and her death was followed by that of his two elder daughters early in 1825. His four surviving children – a son, Patrick Branwell, had been born just after Charlotte – settled down together at Haworth Parsonage, a bleak, stone-built house overlooking the crowded churchyard, to a secret, self-centred literary life, where they produced a long succession of poems and romantic stories, such as the 'Angrian' chronicles and the endless 'Gondal' histories. Charlotte was Branwell's literary partner, and Anne, Emily's assistant. Each pair created an imaginary country, which they proceeded to populate with beautiful heroines and Byronic heroes. To heighten the effect of mystery and secrecy, they employed the minutest script they could devise.

The Brontës were happy at the Parsonage, but almost always miserable when they were separated and cast forth into the alien world. Teaching was one of the few professions open, at that time, to young women of the Brontës' social rank; and both Charlotte and Emily bitterly resented the servitude that it imposed on them. In 1842, leaving Anne behind, they obtained posts as pupil-teachers at a Brussels girls-school kept by a Madame Héger and her husband; and during a second stay at the *pensionnat Héger*, which lasted throughout 1843, Charlotte is now known to have experienced an acute emotional crisis. She became passionately enamoured of M. Héger; and, although he was middle-aged and happily married and, once he recognized the nature of her feelings, had done his best to check her wild attachment, she wrote him a series of 'desolate and loving letters' that, having been retrieved by Madame Héger from the waste-paper basket, were first pub-

(*Opposite*) The Brontë sisters painted by their brother Patrick Branwell c.1834. Charlotte on the right.

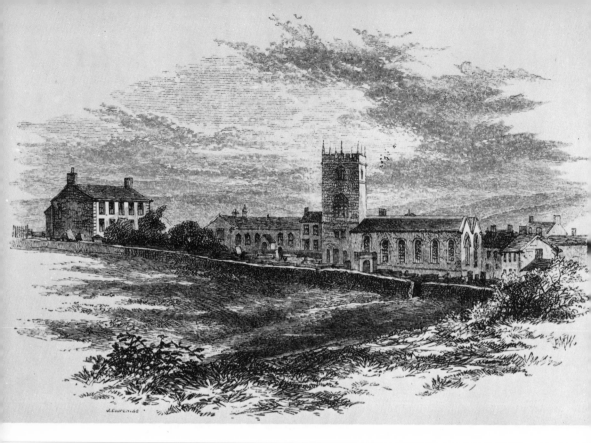

Haworth Church and Parsonage; a 19th-century engraving.

lished nearly sixty years ago. They show the proud, conventional and sternly upright young woman in a strangely unexpected guise, a prey to violent emotions that 'lord it over the mind' and, despite every effort she makes at controlling them, still prevail against her better judgment. Both *The Professor* and *Villette* (a second version of the earlier novel) are based on the experiences of those traumatic twelve months; and there is clearly a close connection between Constantin Héger, who was small and dark and black-browed, and Mr Rochester, Jane Eyre's demon lover.

Yet Charlotte did not lose hope; and, in 1846, she and her sisters, under the androgynous pseudonyms *Currer, Ellis, and Acton Bell*, published a volume of *Poems* at their own expense. It attracted little notice; nor would any of the firms she approached undertake to publish *The Professor*. Nonetheless, she began work on *Jane Eyre*; and, when the book was accepted for publication and appeared in October 1847, 'Currer Bell' at last achieved celebrity. Emily's masterpiece, *Wuthering Heights*, bound up with Anne's innocuous story, *Agnes Grey*, reached the public two months later. Anne's second tale, *The Tenant of Wildfell Hall*, a study of the dangers of alcoholism, came out in 1848. Meanwhile tuberculosis, the hereditary affliction of the Brontë family, had again descended upon Haworth Parsonage; in December 1848 it carried off Emily; and Anne, despite Charlotte's devoted nursing, succumbed early in the summer of 1849. By this time their brother, Patrick Branwell, had also perished of the same disease. As a very young man, he had been his sisters' and his father's pride; more recently, his family's 'drawback' and 'scourge' and their 'skeleton behind the curtain'. Unrequited love was said to have broken his heart; and, before he died, in September 1848, he had become a self-destructive drunkard.

Charlotte herself lived on until 31 March 1855, publishing *Shirley* in 1849 and *Villette*, her most mature achievement, in 1853. Meanwhile she made a series of literary friends, including her future biographer, Mrs Gaskell, and now and then paid a cautious visit to London, though, since she was shy and small and plain, and painfully aware of her own deficiencies, she always shrank from public notice. Had it not been for the benificent interposition of the Reverend Arthur Bell Nicholls, who had come to Haworth as her father's curate, she might well have died a lonely spinster. Two earlier curates had already sought her hand; Nicholls was made of more determined stuff. He declared his love and, after a prolonged struggle against her father's resistance, she eventually accepted him. They were married in June 1854; it was evidently a happy marriage; but, only nine months later, Charlotte died, before she could bear the child that she was carrying.

Charlotte Brontë, 1850, portrait by Richmond.

Every book that Charlotte Brontë wrote was closely connected with her own experience; and, whereas *Villette* is an imaginative distillation of her secret sufferings at Brussels, its predecessor, *Jane Eyre*, is a romanticized self-portrait – the picture of a lonely young woman cast out on the world, who, although small and plain and insignificant, at length runs down the Perfect Lover. The story has many of the shortcomings of a Victorian novelette; but it is redeemed from mediocrity by the strength of Jane Eyre's passion. The novelist herself could never forget her plainness; and, like Jane Eyre, raged at the limitations that her physical circumstances threatened to impose upon her feelings:

Do you think I can stay to become nothing to you? (demands Jane of Mr Rochester.) Do you think I am an automaton? – a machine without feelings? and can bear to have my morsel of bread snatched from my lips, and my drop of living water dashed from my cup? Do you think, because I am poor, obscure, plain, and little, I am soulless and heartless? You think wrong! – I have as much soul as you – and full as much heart! And if God had gifted me with some beauty, and much wealth, I should have made it as hard for you to leave me, as it is now for me to leave you.

Despite its preposterous romantic background, *Jane Eyre* is written in a smooth, well-conducted and fast-flowing style. The descriptive passages have a simple yet sonorous gravity:

I took a book – some Arabian tales; I sat down and endeavoured to read. I could make no sense of the subject. . . I opened the glass door in the breakfast-room: the shrubbery was quite still: the black frost reigned, unbroken by sun or breeze, through the grounds. I covered my head and arms with the skirt of my frock, and went out to walk in a part of the plantation that was quite sequestered: but I found no pleasure in the silent trees, the falling fir cones, the congealed relics of autumn, russet leaves, swept by past winds in heaps, and now stiffened together. I leaned against a gate, and looked into an empty field where no sheep were feeding, where the short grass was nipped and blanched. It was a very grey day; a most opaque sky, 'onding on snaw,' canopied all; thence flakes fell at intervals, which settled on the hard path and on the hoary lea without melting. I stood, a wretched child enough, whispering to myself over and over again, 'What shall I do? – what shall I do?'

By comparison with her sister, Emily, the authoress of *Jane Eyre* had a limited field of vision. Her talents were naturally self-centred. Emily's genius, on the other hand, reached heights where Charlotte could not follow. As her poems show – the only poems written by the Brontës that have stood the test of time – Emily Brontë was a modern mystic:

> Burn then, little lamp, glimmer straight and clear –
> Hush! a rustling wing stirs, methinks the air;
> He for whom I wait thus ever comes to me;
> Strange power! I trust thy might, trust thou my constancy.

And in *Wuthering Heights* the perverse and destructive passion of Catherine and Heathcliff seems more mystical than physical. Heathcliff, even on his death-bed, retains his air of savage splendour:

His eyes met mine so keen and fierce, I started; and then he seemed to smile. I could not think him dead; but his face and throat were washed with rain; the bed clothes dripped, and he was perfectly still . . . I hasped the window; I combed his black long hair from his forehead; I tried to close his eyes; to extinguish, if possible, that frightful, lifelike gaze of exultation . . .

Charlotte even went so far as to doubt whether Emily quite understood the mechanism of the human reproductive processes. She admitted that she found the book alarming – it was haunted, she said, by a 'horror of great darkness'. Yet Catherine was 'not destitute of a certain beauty in her fierceness, or of honesty in the midst of perverted passion and passionate perversity'; and she chose to believe that, had Emily lived, she would gradually have changed her course, and that 'her mind would have grown up like a strong tree, loftier, straighter, wide-spreading . . .'

Wuthering Heights, however, which, when it first appeared with *Agnes Grey*, was generally regarded as an inferior production by the authoress of *Jane Eyre*, remains the greatest of the Haworth novels. It may have owed something to Branwell Brontë, three of whose boon-companions subsequently claimed that they had recognized in the published narrative some of the 'weird fancies of diseased genius' with which he had entertained them while he drank and talked; and he himself asserted that he had written 'a

great portion' of his sister's story. No doubt he lied; but the influence of Branwell's tragedy may have had a strong effect on Emily's imagination; for he had been 'driven to drink', his family believed, by an unhappy love-affair with his employer's wife, who had presently discarded him; and in Branwell's collapse the austere and virginal Emily had had a startling glimpse of naked human passion, as she witnessed the slow destruction of the brother she had loved and admired by his rebellious heart and senses.

Mary Ann Evans, who wrote under the name GEORGE ELIOT (1819–80), was born at South Farm, Arbury, in Warwickshire, on 22 November 1819. Her father, Robert Evans, a staunch Tory, was agent to Sir Roger Newdigate of Arbury Hall. His opinions were the first to influence her; and, as she afterwards wryly admitted: 'I was accustomed to hear him utter the word "Government" in a tone that charged it with awe and made it part of my effective religion, in contrast with the word "rebel", which seemed to carry the stamp of evil in its syllables, and lit by the fact that Satan was the first rebel made an argument dispensing with more detailed inquiry.' As a child, she spent most of her time in close companionship with her brother Isaac. She read a great deal; at the age of eight, a borrowed copy of *Waverley* having been returned before she had leisure to finish it, she decided she would write her own conclusion, which, later, she preferred to Scott's. At school she developed a religious and ascetic tendency; and in 1836, when her elder sister had married, she took over the management of her widowed father's house and farm. But her household duties did not prevent her from learning German and Italian. In the year 1841 Mary Ann and her father moved to Coventry, where she

Wuthering Heights; illustration to Emily Brontë's novel; from an edition of 1872.

George Eliot; portrait by
F.W. Burton, 1865.

found herself living next door to Charles Bray, a distinguished freethinker. She thereupon set out to convert him. The attempt, however, backfired; and the arguments that her neighbour produced led her to abandon Christianity. From 1844 to 1846 she worked on a translation of Strauss's *Das Leben Jesu*. The task threatened to undermine her health; yet once she had completed it, by way of relaxation, she embarked upon an English rendering of Spinoza's *Tractatus Theologico-Politicus*. This new project, she declared, was 'a rest for her mind'. Her three years' work on Strauss's book was rewarded with a fee of £20.

After the death of her father in 1849, Mary Ann spent nearly a year abroad; and when she returned, she lived at the home of John Chapman, editor of *The Westminster Review*. Chapman's household included his wife and his mistress; but apart from a brief period when Mary Ann was passionately attracted to him, the whole group co-existed in apparent harmony for two years. Mary Ann now began contributing articles and reviews to Chapman's paper, and eventually became his co-editor. Through him she met Herbert Spencer and G.H. Lewes. At first she had disliked Lewes, thinking him unduly flippant; but within twelve months she was obliged to admit that 'he has quite won my regard'; and by 1853 regard had changed to love. He was already married; and, though separated from his wife, he was still supporting her and their family of three young children. As divorce was impossible, he and Mary Ann now decided they would live together. In July 1854 they left for Germany, whence they returned to find that they were social outcasts. They had little money – for a while, as an economy, they adopted a vegetarian diet – and poor they remained until Lewes persuaded his consort to publish a story that she had written.

The influence of Lewes on Marian (as she elected to rename herself about 1851) was both powerful and long-lasting. He deliberately permitted her to overshadow him, despite the fact that he himself possessed a brilliant mind; it was the extensiveness of his interests, and the air of flippancy he sometimes assumed, that often caused him to appear superficial. Not only did he produce the standard life of Goethe, but he was a sufficiently learned biologist to win the respect of Charles Darwin. He wrote, moreover, a history of philosophy, and simultaneously exercised his talents as literary and dramatic critic, dramatist, translator, poet and novelist. For Marian, her union with Lewes was a supremely fortunate event. Besides bringing her the devotion she needed, he encouraged her to write a novel.

Marian Evans was thirty-eight when *Amos Barton* began to appear in *Blackwood's Magazine* during January 1857. Emboldened by its favourable reception, she wrote two more stories, *Mr Gilfil's Love Story* and *Janet's Repentance*, and published all three as *Scenes of Clerical Life* in 1858. Their success was immediate; and Marian became famous under her pen-name George Eliot. Dickens wrote to congratulate her, adding that he felt sure that the book had been written by a woman. Her position was consolidated with the appearance of *Adam Bede* in 1859. Lewes now took over their housekeeping, so that the novelist might be free to work; and *The Mill on the Floss* came out in 1860. Having published *Silas Marner* the following year, George Eliot left with Lewes for Florence, to prosecute her researches into the background of the historical novel she was planning. The project became a two-years' nightmare. *Romola*, published in 1863, was a book, she said, that she had embarked on 'as a young woman', and finished as 'an old woman'. Like *Romola*, *Felix Holt* (1866) was an uneven and disappointing work. But her next novel, *Middlemarch* (1871–2), proved to be her masterpiece. Her last novel, *Daniel Deronda* (1876), the portrait of a Jewish idealist, was comparatively unsuccessful. The death of Lewes, on 28 November 1878, struck George Eliot a crushing blow. At first she hoped, and expected to die herself. But presently she came to accept the affection of the doting John Cross, a man some twenty years younger. Their wedding was celebrated in the spring of 1880. That December, George Eliot died after a short illness, and was buried, next to Lewes, in unconsecrated ground.

When, during chapter v of *Amos Barton*, George Eliot states her attitude to her main character, she gives what is virtually a programme for her whole array of novels:

The Rev. Amos Barton, whose sad fortunes I have undertaken to relate, was, you perceive, in no respect an ideal or exceptional character; and perhaps I am doing a bold thing to bespeak your sympathy on behalf of a man who was so very far from remarkable, – a man whose virtues were not heroic, and who had no undetected crime within his breast; who had not the slightest mystery hanging about him, but was palpably and unmistakably commonplace; who was not even in love, but had had that complaint favourably many years ago. 'An utterly uninteresting character!' I think I hear a lady reader exclaim . . .

But, my dear madam, it is so very large a majority of your fellow-countrymen that are of this insignificant stamp. At least eighty out of a hundred of your adult male fellow-Britons returned in the last census are neither extraordinarily silly, nor extraordinarily wicked, nor extraordinarily wise; their eyes are neither deep and liquid with sentiment, nor sparkling with suppressed witticisms; they have probably had no hairbreadth escapes or thrilling adventures; their brains are certainly not pregnant with genius, and their passions have not manifested themselves at all after the fashion of a volcano. They are simply men of complexions more or less muddy, whose conversation is more or less bald and disjointed. Yet these commonplace people – many of them – bear a conscience, and have felt the sublime prompting to do the painful right; they have their unspoken sorrows, and their sacred joys . . .

This commitment to literary realism may have been partly due to the novelist's rationalistic upbringing, under the influence of

Herbert Spencer and the French positivist, Auguste Comte. But its main source was the spontaneous sympathy with the poor and humble that she shared with William Wordsworth. From the relatively simple vignettes of *Scenes of Clerical Life*, George Eliot moved on to a novel of considerable complexity, *Adam Bede*. The story is basically a conventional one of seduction and repentance; but the method in which she presented it, making the portraits of her characters a study of a whole community, added a new dimension to the English novel. Here and there, we observe traces of the novelist's early puritanism; moral choices are shown to have logical and inescapable consequences, so that one lapse brings down nemesis. *The Mill on the Floss* marks a further advance; the first half of the book, with its semi-autobiographical account of the girlhood of Maggie Tulliver, is extraordinarily convincing. She evokes the freshness and intensity of a child's vision and, later, describes the emotional turmoil that overtakes an idealistic young girl, as she struggles to come to terms with the oppressive environment into which she has been born. By comparison, the last section of the novel seems a cramped and hasty piece of writing.

In *Adam Bede* society is the framework of the tale; in *The Mill on the Floss* it is seen as an active agent; in *Middlemarch*, aptly subtitled *A Study of Provincial Life*, it becomes the writer's main preoccupation. George Eliot's masterpiece is remarkable for the width of its scope. The state of medicine in the 1830s; the progress of the 1832 Reform Bill; the problem of emotional frustration in a gifted woman; the spread of the railways; the increasing importance of professional and economic status; the uses and misuses of scholarship – all these subjects, and many more, are drawn into the writer's net. George Eliot describes a society faced by change at every level; but, simultaneously, she portrays a series of characters, each of whom is more or less thwarted – Dorothea, searching for 'some lofty conception of the world which might fairly include the parish of Tipton, and her rule of conduct there', and disastrously supposing that she could find it in marriage to a pedantic older man; Casaubon himself, his life sacrificed to the arid task that he has undertaken; Lydgate, the talented young doctor whose promising career is slowly destroyed by his marriage to a selfish and socially ambitious beauty; the outwardly respectable banker Bulstrode, inevitably destroyed by his dishonest past. Her handling of Bulstrode is one of the novelist's most masterly achievements. Though he is a minor character, his hypocrisy and weakness are subjected to minute and merciless analysis. Yet, at the end, Bulstrode arouses compassion, when after his downfall he comes face to face with his devoted wife:

She locked herself in her room. She needed time to get used to her maimed consciousness, her poor lopped life, before she could walk steadily to the place allotted her. A new searching light had fallen on her husband's character, and she could not judge him leniently: the twenty years in which she had believed in him and venerated him by virtue of his concealments came back with particulars that made them seem an odious deceit. He had married her with that bad past life hidden behind him and she had no faith left to protest his innocence of the worst that was imputed to him . . .

But this imperfectly taught woman, whose phrases and habits were an odd patchwork, had a loyal spirit within her. The man whose prosperity she had shared through nearly half a life, and who had unvaryingly cherished her – now that punishment had befallen him it was not possible to her in any sense to forsake him . . .

When she had resolved to go down, she prepared herself by some little acts which might seem mere folly to a hard onlooker . . .

She took off all her ornaments and put on a plain black gown, and instead of wearing her much-adorned cap and large bows of hair, she brushed her hair down and put on a plain bonnet-cap, which made her suddenly like an early Methodist.

Bulstrode, who knew that his wife had been out and had come in saying that she was not well, had spent the time in an agitation equal to hers . . .

It was eight o'clock in the evening before the door opened and his wife entered. He dared not look up at her. He sat with his eyes bent down, and as she went towards him she thought he looked smaller – he seemed so withered and shrunken. A movement of new compassion and old tenderness went through her like a great wave, and putting one hand on his which rested on the arm of the chair, and the other on his shoulder, she said, solemnly but kindly –

'Look up, Nicholas'.

In the history of the novel, George Eliot was an important innovator; who shifted the emphasis from action to personality, on the inner nature of which her plots depend. Above all else, she brought a new seriousness to the novel, and a wider intellectual range. As Virginia Woolf suggested, she was the first English novelist to write exclusively for grown-ups.

CHARLES KINGSLEY (1819–75), like Disraeli, had a political message to deliver. Born in Devon, the son of a clergyman, after going up to Magdalene College, Cambridge, he was himself ordained in 1842. That year he went to the Hampshire parish of Eversley where, first as curate, then as rector, he remained until his death. When he reached Hampshire, the country was passing through a phase of acute agricultural depression; and the poverty and squalor he saw all around the rectory soon made him a reformer. Under the standard of Christian Socialism he advocated his ideals by means of articles and pamphlets, and through his first two novels, *Yeast, a Problem* (serialised in 1848), and *Alton Locke, Tailor and Poet* (1850). The appearance of *Alton Locke* provoked furious denunciations of Kingsley's socialistic views; and the serialization of *Yeast* in *Fraser's Magazine* caused some outraged readers to cancel their subscriptions. In later books, which included *Hypatia* (1853), an Alexandrian romance, and *Westward*

Charles Kingsley;
portrait from the frontispiece to *Westward Ho!*

Ho! (1855), an Elizabethan saga, the novelist turned his attention to historical subjects. The intense anti-Catholicism of *Westward Ho!* led to a dispute with John Newman, who, ten years earlier, had been received into the Roman Catholic Church; and Newman ended the controversy by writing his own *Apologia pro Vita Sua*.

In 1859 Kingsley was appointed chaplain to Queen Victoria; and in 1860 Professor of Modern History at Cambridge. His famous moralistic fairy-tale, *The Water Babies*, appeared in 1863. Kingsley was an immensely hard-working man, who allowed none of the honours he received to interrupt his duties as a parish priest. In 1873 he became Canon of Westminster. Later, during a lecture-tour of the United States, he grew dangerously ill, and died soon after his return to England, on 23 January 1875.

It is ironic that so zealous a reformer should now be remembered mainly for his historical adventure-stories and his fantastic children's tale. His first two novels, though unevenly written, are his most impressive work; their bitter protests against contemporary social injustice give them a vividness his other novels lack. *Yeast* depicts the squalor and misery in which country-labourers were then condemned to live. *Alton Locke*, the account of a tailor's reluctant conversion to Chartism, increased his reputation as a dangerous social prophet. Much of the narrative is undigested propaganda; but Kingsley's picture of the Victorian clothing-trade, and of the sweated labour it employed, is still a vigorous piece of special pleading.

Kingsley has been described as, at heart, 'a Tory aristocrat tempered by sympathy'. *Westward Ho!* reveals his romantic love of the past; *The Water Babies*, his devotion to nature and fierce hatred of industrialism. He had an over-robust style and, whatever subject he chooses, constantly protests too much. In person, he would appear to have been a typical Victorian enthusiast – tall, wiry and dark-complexioned, with hawk-like eyes, a firm chin and a powerful hook-nose.

George Meredith;
portrait by G.F. Watts,
1893.

GEORGE MEREDITH (1828–1909) deliberately suppressed the details of his early life, and once threatened to haunt any writer who should attempt to publish his biography. He declared himself that he had had an unhappy childhood; with his father, a tailor by profession, he had never had much sympathy; and his mother died when he was only five. In 1842 he was sent to school in Germany, where he remained for two years; and in 1846 he became an articled clerk in a solicitor's office. His employer introduced him to writers and artists; and he soon abandoned the law to earn his living as a freelance journalist. In 1849 his first poem, a commemoration of the battle of Chillianwallah, was published in *Chamber's Edinburgh Journal*; and during the same year he married Mary Ellen Nicolls, the widowed daughter of Thomas Love

Peacock. She was nine years older than Meredith; and their marriage turned out ill. A son was born to them in 1853; but they were always short of money; and Meredith's first few novels, which included *The Shaving of Shagpat* (1856) and *Farina* (1857), had a very poor sale, although the former was hailed by George Eliot as unmistakably 'a work of genius'. In 1858, his marriage broke up; Mrs Meredith had found a lover. Then, for the first time, in 1858, he achieved success with *The Ordeal of Richard Feverel*, which was followed by *Evan Harrington* (1861), *Rhoda Fleming* (1865) and *Vittoria* (1867). In 1866, Meredith remarried – his second wife, Marie Vulliamy, was an agreeable young woman of twenty-four; and soon afterwards he moved to a cottage on Box Hill, Surrey. Meanwhile, he worked as a publishers' reader, and continued to produce novels. *Beauchamp's Career* (1875) and *The Egoist* (1879) established his reputation on a solid basis; and no less admired were *The Tragic Comedians* (1880), *Diana of the Crossways* (1885), and his last novel, *The Amazing Marriage*, which appeared in 1895. Latterly, Meredith was lionized as the venerable 'sage of Box Hill', whom literary enthusiasts loved to visit, and who willingly received their homage. He died, after a long illness, on 18 May 1909.

Meredith's prose style has been aptly described as chaos illumined with flashes of lightning. Avoiding a simple, straight-forward approach, he cultivates intricacy and oddity; so that the reader is either dazzled or bemused by his verbal pyrotechnics:

South-western rain-clouds, too, are never long sullen: they enfold and will have the earth in a good strong glut of the kissing overflow; then, as a hawk with feathers on his beak of the bird in his claw lifts his head, they rise and take veiled feather in long climbing watery lines: at any moment they may break the veil and show soft upper cloud, show sun on it, show sky, green near the verge they spring from, of the green of grass in early dew; or, along a travelling sweep that rolls asunder overhead, heaven's laughter of purest blue among titanic white shoulders: it may mean fair smiling for awhile, or be the lightest interlude; but the watery lines, and the drifting, the chasing, the upsoaring, all in a shadowy fingering of form, and the animation of the leaves of the trees pointing them on, the bending of the tree-tops, the snapping of branches, and the hurrahings of the stubborn hedge at wrestle with the flaws, yielding but a leaf at most, and that on a fling, make a glory of contest and wilderness without aid of colour to inflame the man who is at home in them from old association on road, heath and mountain. Let him be drenched, his heart will sing. And thou, trim cockney, that jeerest, consider thyself, to whom it may occur to be out in such a scene, and what steps of a nervous dancing master it would be thine to play the hunted rat of the elements, for the preservation of the one imagined dry spot about thee, somewhere on thy luckless person!

This is a characteristic example of Meredith's peculiar kind of literary impressionism. Sometimes the effect it produces is brilliant; elsewhere Meredith's method of narration is obscure and over-strained. He seems incapable of stating a fact without some elaborate prefatory arabesque:

The worthy creature's anxiety was of the pattern of cavaliers escorting dames – an exaggeration of honest zeal; or present example of clownish goodness it might seem; until entering the larch and firwood among the beaten heights, there was a rocking and straining of the shallow-rooted trees in a tremendous gust, that quite pardoned him for curving his arm in a hoop about her, and holding a shoulder in front.

The convolutions of Meredith's style, however, had a deliberate literary aim; he set out to evolve a type of prose that would have the lyrical intensity of great verse. Realism he rejected. In the words of his own *Shagpat*, 'Swiftness is mine, and I fly from the sordid'. His first novels were all poetic romances. Those he published after *The Ordeal of Richard Feverel* consist of a series of dramatic moments – great set-pieces of self-discovery and self-realization, illuminated by subtle psychological analysis. His method, wrote Meredith of his own technique, had been to prepare my readers for a 'crucial exhibition of the personnae, and then to give the scene in the fullest of blood and brain under stress of a fiery situation'. The themes that he selected lend themselves to such treatment – the causes and effects of tension in human relationships; the evils of egoism; the search for integrity and self-knowledge. *The Ordeal of Richard Feverel* is an analysis of dishonesty in intimate relationships; *The Egoist* first exposes, and then ruthlessly dissects, the egoism of its hero, Sir Willoughby Patterne. The latter novel shows Meredith's gift for comedy, a gift that also emerges in his picaresque story *Harry Richmond* (1871). His critical essay, *On the Idea of Comedy and the Uses of the Comic Spirit*, is an illuminating exposition of this aspect of his literary work. During his later years as a novelist, Meredith was increasingly concerned with the rôle of modern women, and with the social and emotional disabilities from which he felt they still suffered.

As a poet, Meredith was less ambitious, or at least more orthodox, than as a novelist. He published several collections of verse, by far the best being the dramatic sonnet sequence – his sonnets have sixteen instead of fourteen lines – that he entitled *Modern Love*. Published in 1862, it records the gradual breakdown of his first marriage, caused not so much by any single disaster as by the cumulative effect of minor flaws, and by the growing dissimilarity of husband and wife, both passionate and both frustrated:

> Mark where the pressing wind shoots javelin-like,
> Its skeleton shadow on the broad-back'd wave!
> Here is a fitting spot to dig Love's grave;
> Here where the ponderous breakers plunge and strike,
> And dart their hissing tongues high up the sand:
> In hearing of the ocean, and in sight

Of those ribb'd wind-streaks running into white.
If I the death of Love had deeply plann'd,
I never could have made it half so sure,
As by the unblest kisses which upbraid
The full-waked sense; or failing that, degrade!
'Tis morning: but no morning can restore
What we have forfeited. I see no sin;
The wrong is mix'd. In tragic life, God wot,
No villain need be! Passions spin the plot:
We are betray'd by what is false within.

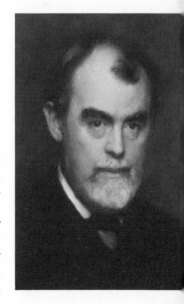

SAMUEL BUTLER (1835–1902) played an important part in the
late nineteenth-century revolt against Victorian moral standards.
The son of a clergyman and the grandson of a bishop, Butler was
himself intended for the Church; but, having received a conventional education at Shrewsbury and St John's College, Cambridge, he discovered that he had lost his faith, refused to take
Holy Orders and, in 1859, emigrated to New Zealand, where he
became a successful sheep-farmer. On his return to London in
1864, he moved into bachelor rooms at Clifford's Inn, which
remained his home until he died. His interests were various; not
only did he paint, and exhibit now and then at the Royal Academy,
but he studied the Greek classics, particularly Homer, and in-
vestigated and criticized the scientific works of Charles Darwin.
His first important book, the fantastic Utopian novel *Erewhon or
Over the Range*, appeared in 1872. His four publications, *Life
and Habit* (1877), *Evolution Old and New* (1879), *Unconscious
Memory* (1880) and *Luck or Cunning* (1887) were concerned with
Darwin's famous theory, and set forth his own views upon

'creative' rather than 'mechanistic' evolution. But in 1897 he reverted to literature, and published *The Authoress of the Odyssey*, a boldly paradoxical attempt to prove that Homer's poetry must have been written by a young woman. Butler's famous novel, *The Way of All Flesh*, came out a year after the author's death.

Erewhon and its lame sequel *Erewhon Revisited* (1901) are travel stories in the style of Jonathan Swift. The traveller's observations of a hitherto unknown land enable Butler to produce a devastating exposé of nineteenth-century life and thought, with special reference to the mechanization of life, which he makes the subject of a brilliantly prophetic section, entitled 'The Book of the Machines'. In Erewhon religion is a banking system, and its Musical Banks pour out worthless currency; while Colleges of Unreason teach a 'hypothetical language' – the language of the Christian Church – that has the great advantage of being altogether meaningless. Here disease is regarded as a crime, and courts punish the sick without discrimination. Victorian England is turned upside down; Butler attacks almost every standard of behaviour that his parents had imposed on him; and when a series of publishers' readers, including George Meredith, had recommended their employers to refuse the manuscript, he issued it anonymously at his own expense.

The Way of All Flesh, derived from Butler's memories of his thwarted and unhappy youth, has an equally destructive purpose. Though it had been written thirty years earlier, its effect in 1903 was still iconoclastic; it was a time-bomb, V.S. Pritchett declares, 'waiting to blow up the Victorian family and with it the whole great pillared and balustraded edifice of the Victorian novel'. The institution of the family is carefully examined and mercilessly ridiculed; Mr and Mrs Pontifex stand for the author's mother and father; and their reign is described as a mixture of sheer stupidity and crushing tyranny that distorts and blights their children's lives. From a literary point of view the book is unbalanced – the propagandist element is far too strong; but it contains some splendid comic passages. Butler chronicles the doings and sayings of three generations of the Pontifex family, whose male offspring are expected to enter the Church, and to make a decent 'Christian marriage'. Here he describes Theobald Pontifex talking over their prospects with his bride-to-be, Christina:

Missionary work indeed in heathen countries was being carried on with some energy, but Theobald did not feel any call to be a missionary. Christina suggested this to him more than once, and assured him of the unspeakable happiness it would be to her to be the wife of a missionary, and to share his dangers; she and Theobald might even be martyred; of course they would be martyred simultaneously, and martyrdom many years hence as regarded from the arbour in the rectory garden was not painful; it would ensure them a glorious future in the next world, and at any rate posthumous renown in this – even if they were not miraculously restored to life again – and such things had happened ere now in the case of martyrs. Theobald, however, had not been kindled by Christina's enthusiasm, so she fell back upon the Church of Rome – an enemy more dangerous, if possible, than paganism itself. A combat with Romanism might even yet win for her and Theobald the crown of martyrdom. True, the Church of Rome was tolerably quiet just then, but it was the calm before the storm, of this she was assured, with a conviction deeper than she could have attained by any argument founded upon mere reason.

'We, dearest Theobald,' she exclaimed, 'will be ever faithful. We will stand firm and support one another even in the hour of death itself. God in His mercy may spare us from being burned alive. He may or may not do so. O Lord' (and she turned her eyes prayerfully to Heaven), 'spare my Theobald, or grant that he may be beheaded'.

'My dearest,' said Theobald gravely, 'do not let us agitate ourselves unduly. If the hour of trial comes we shall be best prepared to meet it by having led a quiet, unobtrusive life of self-denial and devotion to God's glory. Such a life let us pray God that it may please Him to enable us to pray that we may lead.'

ROBERT LOUIS STEVENSON (1850–94) was the only child of a distinguished Scottish engineer and his wife, a 'daughter of the manse'. A frail, excitable child, he owed much to the devoted nurse, Alison Cunningham, 'my second Mother, my first Wife', who guarded him through a series of youthful illnesses, one of which, a gastric fever, nearly carried him off when he was eight years old. His schooling was often interrupted; but, after attending Edinburgh University and studying Law, he was called to the Scottish Bar in 1875. Meanwhile, he had fallen in love with literature and had begun to contribute essays to various London magazines. Though his health was never good, and in 1873 and 1874 he was obliged to spend several months abroad, he remained physically active and travelled widely, often on foot, through the wilder parts of France and Scotland, and published two engaging travel-books, *An Inland Voyage* and *Travels with a Donkey*, which came out in 1878 and 1879. During such an expedition he met the American married woman, then Mrs Osbourne, whose second husband he would presently become. In the year 1879 he followed Fanny Osbourne to California, a difficult expedition that almost cost him his life when he had finally reached San Francisco. They were married, nevertheless, in 1880. But by this time his physical condition was growing more and more precarious; and he spent the next few years wandering, in search of health, from Switzerland to Provence and Hyères, and back again to Southern England. During the summer of 1887, when his father died, Stevenson left England for the last time and, twelve months later, embarked for the South Seas, eventually purchasing a small estate at Vailima in Samoa. There, amid people and surroundings he loved, he became an important local personage; and the disease of the lungs from which he had suffered since youth seems temporarily to have been arrested. His death was sudden; he was

Robert Louis Stevenson, by W.B. Richmond, 1887.

killed by an apoplectic stroke on 3 December 1894. His Samoan friends buried him, in the mountain-top resting-place that he had already pointed out. Behind him he left the manuscript of his unfinished novel, *Weir of Hermiston*.

His early essays, written while he was slowly mastering his craft, tend to be slightly mannered and self-conscious. Even in his later collections, *Virginibus Puerisque* and *Memoirs and Portraits*, there is a certain 'pawkiness' about his style. Stevenson's real gift was for swift dramatic story-telling; and, as a story-teller, he moved on from such fantastic entertainments as *The New Arabian Nights*, published in 1882, to the romantic realism of *Kidnapped*, published in 1886, *The Master of Ballantrae, Catriona* and the unfinished *Hermiston*, which many of the novelist's modern critics hold to be his masterpiece. A little apart stand *Treasure Island*, a book, excellent of its kind, deliberately planned to amuse his juvenile readers, and *Dr Jekyll and Mr Hyde*, a bold attempt, on a far more ambitious plane, to give a symbolic representation of a paranoiac personality. Stevenson, at the same time, was a gifted minor poet; and *A Child's Garden of Verses*, dedicated to the faithful guardian of his own childhood, has a still-unfaded gaiety and freshness.

Kidnapped, however, with its splendidly vivid picture of the feudal Highlands across which the young hero and the Jacobite rebel who accompanies him, the gallant, vain-glorious Alan Breck, flee from Alan's hereditary foes, the Campbells, and the occupying English 'red-coats', is probably his most complete achievement. Stevenson had an imaginative eye for detail, whether he describes a network of mountain-streams as they glitter down a tawny slope, or the distant flash of bayonets; the heat of a summer's day on an isolated rock where the fugitives have taken refuge, or the Cockney twang of the English soldier's voice, overheard by David Balfour:

... You are to remember that we lay on the bare top of a rock, like scones upon a girdle; the sun beat upon us cruelly; the rock grew so heated, a man could scarce endure the touch of it; and the little patch of earth and fern, which kept cooler, was only large enough for one at a time. We took turn about to lie on the naked rock, which was indeed like the position of that saint that was martyred on a gridiron ...

The soldiers kept stirring all day in the bottom of the valley, now changing guard, now in patrolling parties hunting among the rocks. These lay round in so great a number, that to look for men among them was like looking for a needle in a bottle of hay; and being so hopeless a task, it was gone about with the less care. Yet we could see the soldiers pike their bayonets among the heather, which sent a cold thrill to my vitals; and they would sometimes hang about our rock, so that we scarce dared to breathe.

It was in this way that I first heard the right English speech; one fellow as he went by actually clapping his hand upon the sunny face of the rock on which we lay, and plucking it off again with an oath. 'I tell you it's 'ot' says he; and I was amazed at the clipping tones and the odd sing-song in which he spoke, . . .

The pessimistic novels of GEORGE GISSING (1857–1903) reflect his personal misfortunes. The son of a Yorkshire chemist who died in 1870, he won a scholarship to Owens College, Manchester, where he showed considerable promise. His career, however, came to an abrupt end when he fell in love with a seventeen-year-old prostitute. During his efforts to reform her, he was obliged to steal from fellow-students and, having been detected, was not only expelled but sentenced to a month's imprisonment. Thereafter Gissing's life was one of hardship and humiliation. On his release he migrated to America, but failed to earn a living there; and in 1877 he returned and married his first love, now a hopeless alcoholic. She soon resumed her old trade; and the couple eventually separated; she died in a Lambeth slum in 1888.

George Gissing; a photograph of 1901.

Gissing now plunged into Radical politics. His novel, *Workers in the Dawn*, which appeared in 1880, was designed, he wrote, 'to bring home to people the ghastly condition (material, mental, and moral) of our poor classes, to show the hideous injustice of our whole system of society, to give light upon the plan of altering it . . .' *The Unclassed*, on the other hand, published in 1884, shows his Socialist beliefs fading; and, by the time he produced *Demos*, he was an intransigent conservative. Though his novels had little success, he continued to write and earned his bread by private teaching. *The Nether World* (1889), inspired by the shock of his first wife's death, is a deeply pathetic and depressing book; and his two best novels, *New Grub Street* and *Born in Exile*, came out in 1891 and 1892 respectively. During the previous year he married another working-class girl, again with disastrous results; and their miserable life together produced *In the Year of Jubilee* (1894). At last, in 1897, Gissing left his shrewish wife and fled to France. There he achieved some measure of happiness, and published an important critical study of Dickens and *The Private Papers of Henry Ryecroft*, an autobiographical digression. Before he died, his talents had begun to be recognized, at least by certain fellow-writers, who included the sympathetic H.G. Wells. Not until he had died, on 28 December 1903, did he gain a wider popularity.

Gissing's declared intention was to observe and to record; and it is his grim realism that gives his novels their strength. He spares his reader nothing. The London he portrays is a place of unrelieved gloom. Thus, in *The Nether World*, he describes an urban graveyard:

The burial ground by which he had paused was as little restful to the eye as are most of those discoverable in the byways of London. The small trees that grew about it shivered in their leaflessness; the rank grass was wan under the failing day; most of the stones leaned this way or that, emblems of neglect (they were very white at the top, and darkened downwards till the damp soil made them black), and certain cats or dogs were prowling or sporting among the graves. At this corner the east wind blew with a malice such as it never puts forth save where there are poorly clad people to be pierced; it swept before it thin clouds of unsavoury dust, mingled with the light refuse of the streets. Above the shapeless houses night was signalling a murky approach; the sky – if sky it could be called – gave threatening of sleet, perchance of snow. And on every side was the rumble of traffic, the voiceful evidence of toil and poverty; hawkers were crying their goods; the inevitable organ was clanging before a public house hard by; the crumpet-man was hastening along, with monotonous ringing of his bell and hoarse rhythmic wail.

Compared with Gissing's picture of the urban scene, the London that Dickens evokes has a certain raffish picturesqueness, not unrelieved by human jollity:

An evil smell [Gissing records] hung about the butchers' and the fish shops. A public-house poisoned a whole street with alcoholic fumes; from sewer-grates rose a miasma that caught the breath. People who bought butter from the little dealers had to carry it away in a saucer, covered with a piece of paper, which in a few minutes turned oily dark. Rotting fruit, flung out by costermongers, offered a dire regale to the little ragamuffins prowling like the cats and dogs. Babies' bottles were choked with thick-curdling milk, and sweets melted in grimy little hands.

Unlike Dickens, Gissing was no reformer. Having abandoned his early Socialist beliefs, he bitterly despised the masses. His heroes are men who have been dragged down from a higher social level by misfortune or injustice. Here they resemble the novelist himself. The least attractive feature of his books is a persistent note of self-pity. Humour he had always lacked; his emotional range was narrow. Yet, in his semi-autobiographical *New Grub Street* – his account of a serious artist's struggle to realize his gifts in the underworld of modern journalism – he drew not only a vivid self-portrait, but a damning indictment of his own age.

Critics, Essayists and Men of Letters

SAMUEL ROGERS (1763–1855) deserves a small but well-appointed niche among the English men of letters. For over six decades he was an inseparable part of the London literary scene; and having as a youth decided to visit Johnson – when he entered Bolt Court, however, his courage failed him, and he turned away – he lived on to appreciate Byron's genius and, as a very old man, to make the acquaintance of Algernon Charles Swinburne. His own verses, despite the immense care with which he wrote and revised them, now seem curiously undistinguished. Yet Byron was often inclined to prefer them to the works of his fellow Romantic poets; since Rogers, he felt, was a writer in the tradition of Pope, who eschewed all the wild extravagances that had recently come into

Samuel Rogers; chalk drawing by T. Lawrence.

fashion. Rogers' tastes, both in literature and in life, were essentially conservative. The son of a glass manufacturer, he had received a modest education and, still very young, entered a prosperous London bank, where, on his father's death, he inherited a controlling interest. He then built himself a London house, overlooking Green Park, which he filled with splendid bibelots. It was at Park Place that he entertained a long series of celebrated friends, from Byron to the Carlyles; and around his beautifully furnished rooms he hung a choir of caged nightingales.

The book that first established Rogers' fame was *The Pleasures of Memory*, published in 1792. His collected *Poems* appeared in 1812; *Jacqueline*, a narrative poem, of which Byron made quiet fun, in 1814; and the opening sections of *Italy* (completed six years later, and subsequently reissued with magnificent illustrations by Turner) in 1822. Rogers' poems are always 'correct', often pleasing if never definitely inspiring. But he was always a conscientious craftsman; and once, when he had said that he was indisposed, Sydney Smith, the favourite wit of the Holland House côterie, supplied a characteristic explanation. To the question what could ail Rogers,

'Oh, don't you know (Smith responded) he has produced a couplet? When our friend is delivered of a couplet, with infinite labour and pain, he takes to his bed, has straw laid down, the knocker tied up, expects his friends to call and make enquiries, and the answer at the door invariably is "Mr Rogers and his little couplet are as well as can be expected". When he produced an alexandrine he keeps his bed a day longer.'

WILLIAM COBBETT (1768–1835), whom Carlyle once described as 'the pattern of John Bull of the century', was born on his father's Surrey farm, but at an early age decided to join the army. Shipped off with his regiment across the Atlantic, he spent eight years in Canada, and rose to the rank of sergeant-major, a rank that he held with distinction until, in 1791, the regiment was ordered home. Cobbett then purchased his discharge and did his best to organize the prosecution of certain unworthy officers whose peculations he had detected. Failing to do so, he took refuge in France; but, as war was about to break out between France and Great Britain, he soon left for the United States, where he made his name, and earned considerable unpopularity, as a Tory journalist and pamphleteer. By 1800 his position was becoming dangerous, and he hurriedly returned to London. Despite the flattering offers he received from the Tory government, which had appreciated his journalistic gifts, he became an independent editor. *Cobbett's Weekly Political Register*, the magazine he continued to edit for the remainder of his life, was a highly influential publication. In 1806, however, having observed the increasing misery of English country labourers during the Napoleonic Wars, he abandoned his early Toryism and joined the Radicals. His

William Cobbett; by an unknown artist.

attacks on the administration cost him two years' imprisonment; and in 1817 he again retired to the United States. When he reappeared, he resumed his Radical campaign; and, although he was once more prosecuted – and this time acquitted – he was elected member for Oldham in the first reformed parliament of 1832.

Cobbett was an energetic and extraordinarily forceful writer whose best known works are *English Grammar* (1818), *Advice to Young Men* (1829) and *Rural Rides* (1830). The last, a survey of agricultural England from the saddle, shows his prose-style at its best – the style of a self-made man, vigorous, lively and well-turned, but plain, direct and unassuming. Here, for example, is his description of 'a parcel of labourers' obliged to earn their bread by 'parish work':

It is a state of things where all is out of order; where self-preservation, that great law of nature, seems to be set at defiance; for here are farmers unable to pay men for working for them, and yet compelled to pay them for working in doing that which is really of no use to any human being. There lie the hop-poles unstripped. You see a hundred things in the neighbouring fields that want doing. The fences are not nearly what they ought to be. The very meadows, to our right and our left in crossing this little valley, would occupy these men advantageously until the setting in of the frost; and here are they, not, as I said before, actually digging holes one day and filling them up to the next, but, to all intents and purposes, as uselessly employed. Is this Mr Canning's 'sun of prosperity'? Is this the way to increase or preserve a nation's wealth? Is this a sign of wise legislation and of good government? Does this thing 'work well', Mr Canning? Does it prove that we want no change? True, you were born under a Kingly Government; and so was I as well as you; but I was not born under Six Acts,* nor was I born under a state of things like this. I was not born under it, and I do not wish to live under it; and, with God's help, I will change it if I can.

* The notorious Six Acts, passed in 1819 after the Peterloo Massacre, for the maintenance of public order and the repression of radical activities.

WALTER SAVAGE LANDOR (1775–1864) lived through the Romantic Age and well into the Victorian epoch without at any time producing the impression that he belonged to either period. His literary isolation was a corollary of his aggressive personal independence. Born in Warwick, the son of a local physician, he gave a preliminary hint of his turbulent nature by contriving to have himself removed from Rugby School at the early age of ten. Having gone up to Trinity College, Oxford, he became a violent Radical, known as 'the mad Jacobin', and was rusticated in 1794 for firing a gun into the room of a Tory undergraduate. He did not return and, after a quarrel with his father, retreated to Wales, with 'one servant and a chest of books'. His first volume of poems appeared in 1795; and in 1798 he published *Gebir*, a long blank-

Landor's birthplace at Warwick; from a 19th-century engraving.

verse tale that many of his readers held to be completely unintelligible. *Poems from the Arabic and Persian* followed in 1800; and *Poetry, by the Author of Gebir* in 1802.

When his father died in 1805, Landor used part of his inheritance to raise volunteers to fight against Napoleon on Spanish soil, but was thwarted by the unco-operative attitude of both the English and the Spanish governments. Back at home, he exchanged his Warwickshire property for a small estate in Wales, where he soon proceeded to alienate all his neighbours. In 1811 he married a penniless Swiss girl whom he had met at a ball, and the outcome of this sudden move was predictably disastrous. Three years later, threatened with legal proceedings and now almost ruined, Landor was obliged to leave Great Britain; and until 1835 he wandered through France and Italy. The five volumes of his *Imaginary Conversations* came out between 1824 and 1829. In 1835 he finally left his wife, returned to England and settled down in Bath. There he remained for more than two decades; but, at eighty-three, to escape a pending libel action, Landor once more fled the country. At Florence, assisted by Robert Browning – his children had treated him with base ingratitude – the old man found a comparatively peaceful last home; and there he died on 17 September 1864. His friends were devoted to Landor, despite his wild volcanic rages. The diarist Crabb Robinson describes him as 'a man of florid complexion . . . altogether a leonine man', who had 'a fierceness of tone' well suited to the name Savage.

Walter Savage Landor; portrait by W. Bewick.

The unpopularity that Landor courted in his life has extended to his literary reputation. Most of his vast output remains unread, and seems likely to continue so. He was more classical than romantic in spirit; the strictly disciplined form within which he expresses his emotions gives his work a certain air of frigidity, notwithstanding the fresh and vigorous passages that enliven almost all his poems. His lapidary style is seen at its best in a handful of enchanting lyrics, such as the lines he addressed to an early mistress whom he called 'Ianthe':

> Past ruin'd Ilion Helen lives,
>   Alcestis rises from the shades;
> Verse calls them forth; 'tis verse that gives
>   Immortal youth to mortal maids.
>
> Soon shall Oblivion's deepening veil
>   Hide all the peopled hills you see,
> The gay, the proud, while lovers hail
>   In distant ages you and me . . .
>
> *
>
> There is a mountain and a wood between us,
>   Where the lone shepherd and late bird have seen us.
> Morning and noon and eventide repass.
>   Between us now and the mountain and the wood
> Seem standing darker than last year they stood,
>   And say we must not cross – alas! alas!

The long series of *Imaginary Conversations* are a mixture of history, psychology, philosophy, and of Landor's own idiosyncratic ideas, cast in the shape of dialogues between the famous characters of bygone ages. Landor's prose shares the studied artifice of his poetry; and, for all his epigrammatic skill and his eloquent phrases, the overall effect is apt to seem a little too studied. Yet his finest prose has a subtle harmony that recalls his training as a poet:

Laodameia died; Helen died; Leda, the beloved of Jupiter, went before. It is better to repose in the earth betimes than to sit up late; better than to cling pertinaciously to what we feel crumbling under us, and to protract an inevitable fall. We may enjoy the present while we are insensible of infirmity and decay; but the present, like a note in music, is nothing but as it apertains to what is past and to what is to come. There are no fields of amaranth on this side of the grave; there are no voices, O Rhodope, that are not soon mute, however tuneful; there is no name, with whatever emphasis of passionate love repeated, of which the echo is not faint at last.

Landor regarded his isolation and lack of popular success as an index of his literary quality. 'I shall dine late,' he said, 'but the room will be well-lighted, and the guests few but select.' During the writer's own lifetime, however, he was one of Swinburne's greatest idols.

CHARLES LAMB (1775–1834) was brought up in the antique cloisters of the Temple; and something of its quiet old-fashioned atmosphere clung to him throughout his life. His father was a barrister's clerk who lodged at the house of his employer, Samuel

Charles Lamb; portrait by W. Hazlitt, 1804.

Salt, in Crown Office Row. Charles was one of seven children; and the family was by no means rich. But, luckily, when Charles was seven, Salt obtained for him a presentation to the ancient Christ's Hospital. There he met Coleridge, a lonely boy and 'playless day-dreamer', who became a lifelong friend. When he left the school in 1789, Salt's influence helped Lamb to a job as a clerk in South Sea House; and in 1792 he took up a similar post with the East India Company, where he continued to work for the next thirty-three years. His family had a record of mental illness; and in 1795 Lamb himself suffered a breakdown, and spent six weeks in an asylum. The disturbance never recurred. His sister Mary, on the other hand, stabbed their mother to death during a period of derangement. She was confined to an asylum until 1799; but then, their father having died, her brother secured her release by under-taking to become her permanent guardian. Through this act of supreme unselfishness, he lost any hope of personal liberty, and was obliged to put aside his more romantic ambitions. He now began his literary career. His first prose work, *A Tale of Rosamund Gray and Old Blind Margaret*, was published in the summer of 1798. He followed it, in 1802, with *John Woodvil*, an imitation of an Elizabethan tragedy; and in 1806 he and Mary Lamb wrote their famous *Tales from Shakespeare*, Mary composing the larger share of the book. The result was fame – and a fee of sixty guineas.

Between 1807 and 1811 Lamb contributed frequently to periodicals, one of his best essays being *The Genius and Character of Hogarth*, which made its appearance in 1811. In 1820 Hazlitt had introduced him to the editor of *The London Magazine*, which, that August, over the signature 'Elia', published his *Recollections of South-Sea House*. This was the first of the celebrated series of essays that in 1823 were collected as *Essays of Elia*. In 1825, Lamb left the East India House with a comfortable pension; and in 1827 he moved to suburban Enfield. But Enfield bored Lamb; and in 1833 he found a new resting-place at Edmonton. A year later, the death of Coleridge plunged him into deep gloom. His own health now showed signs of failing; and he died the same year on 27 December. His sister Mary, to whom he had sacrificed his life, survived him until 1847.

Lamb deserves recognition as a critic for his pioneering group of studies, *Specimens of English Dramatic Poets who lived About the Time of Shakespeare* (1808), in which he virtually rediscovered many hitherto neglected writers. Elsewhere, his literary criticism is more enthusiastic than perceptive; he has little either of Hazlitt's breadth of vision or of Coleridge's analytic subtlety. Today his reputation rests on his 'Elia' essays. Their most striking feature is the narrowness of Lamb's range; he prefers to avoid major con-temporary issues, but discourses at length on such subjects as whist or chimney-sweeps or the origins of roasted pork. His favourite topic, however, is always himself and his doings – his life

Illustration to *A Midsummer Night's Dream*, in Charles and Mary Lamb's *Tales from Shakespeare*.

with his 'cousin' (who represents Mary Lamb), his college friends, his childhood haunts, his holiday expeditions, his favourite authors, his tastes, his antipathies, and whatever else may happen to come into his head – all with the apparent waywardness of a friendly conversation. His style is mannered and whimsical; it has a smooth, continuous flow, enlivened with learned allusions and literary reminiscences. He is fond of remembering and re-living the past in a vein of gentle humour:

From my childhood I was extremely inquisitive about witches and witch-stories. My maid, and more legendary aunt, supplied me with good store. But I shall mention the accident which directed my curiosity originally into this channel. In my father's book-closet the history of the Bible by Stackhouse occupied a distinguished station. The pictures with which it abounds – one of the ark, in particular, and another of Solomon's Temple, delineated with all the fidelity of ocular measurement, as if the

artist had been on the spot – attracted my childish attention. There was
a picture, too, of the Witch raising up Samuel, which I wish that I had
never seen . . . I have not met with the work from that time to this, but
I remember it consisted of Old Testament stories, orderly set down, with
the *objection* appended to each story, and the *solution* of the objection
regularly tacked to it . . . The *solution* was brief, modest, and satisfactory.
The bane and antidote were both before you. To doubts so put, and so
quashed, there seemed to be an end for ever. The dragon lay dead, for
the foot of the veriest babe to trample on. But – like as was rather feared
than realised from that slain monster in Spenser – from the womb of those
crushed errors young dragonets would creep, exceeding the prowess of
so tender a Saint George as myself to vanquish. The habit of expecting
objections to every passage set me upon starting more objections, for the
glory of finding a solution of my own to them. I became staggered and
perplexed, a sceptic in long-coats. The pretty Bible stories which I had
read, or heard read in church, lost their purity and sincerity of impression
. . . I was not to disbelieve them, but – the next thing to that – I was to
be quite sure that some one or other would or had disbelieved them.
Next to making a child an infidel is the letting him know that there are
infidels at all. Credulity is the man's weakness, but the child's strength.

Lamb's essays are pleasing, but slight in substance. Compared
with Peacock, Hazlitt and De Quincey, he seems at best a secondary figure.

THOMAS MOORE (1779–1852) is generally remembered today as
Byron's friend and first biographer; but at least a decade before,
in 1812, Byron 'awoke to find himself famous', Moore, under the
pseudonym 'Thomas Little', had become a well-known poet. The
son of a Dublin grocer, he had been born above his parents' shop.
He was a promising child and, at the age of four, already loved
reciting verses. Later he shone in amateur theatricals, and he
learned to sing and play on an 'old lumbering harpsicord' which
his father had accepted as part-payment of a bankrupt customer's
debt. In 1794 he entered Dublin University, where he studied law.
But London beckoned him; and in 1799 he set forth across the
Irish Channel, with a scapular sewn into the lining of his coat and
a few guineas secreted beneath the waistband of his pantaloons.
His success was almost immediate. In 1800 he published a translation of the *Odes of Anacreon* and, a year later, his *Poems of the Late
Thomas Little*, which at once endeared him not only to middle-class
reviewers and readers but to aristocratic Whig society. In 1803,
thanks to the good offices of his friend Lord Moira, he was
appointed Admiralty Registrar at Bermuda, where he passed
some agreeable months before returning to England by way of the
United States. The first volume of his *Irish Melodies*, his most
popular collection of poems, appeared in 1807, and *Lalla Rookh*,
an Eastern romance that delighted countless readers, in the year
1817. Meanwhile, hurt by an unkind joke with which Byron had

Thomas Moore as a
youth; by an unknown
artist.

enlivened *English Bards and Scotch Reviewers*, he had challenged the satirist to a duel. Byron, however, had already left England on his famous journey to the Near East; and, when he reappeared, the quarrel was patched up and the two poets formed a lasting friendship. Moore's greatest contribution to English literary history, his *Letters and Journals of Lord Byron*, was published in December 1830. His poetic celebrity never declined – he was still 'Anacreon' Moore; but towards the end of his existence his mental powers slowly dwindled; and he died on 26 February 1852. Eight volumes of his *Memoirs, Journal and Correspondence*, edited by his friend Lord John Russell, were issued between 1853 and 1856.

At the height of his fame, though Moore's poems were renowned for their 'sweetness', they were often criticized – even by the author of *English Bards* – for their unabashed licentiousness. Neither quality has stood the test of time; his sweetness now seems weak and sugary; while the erotic turn of his imagination is unlikely to excite a modern reader. But we must not forget, as he himself reminds us, that his poems were 'intended to be sung rather than read', and should be judged by that standard. Moore had a delightful singing voice, and made a practice of both singing and accompanying the latest verses he had written. Hence his success in fashionable London society, where his accomplished rendering of one of his *Irish Melodies* was, now and then, received with floods of tears. It is to Moore we owe the romantic vision of Ireland that long haunted nineteenth-century literature. He was the first Irishman to revive the Irish legends and give them fresh imaginative substance through the medium of the English language. Moore possessed extraordinary personal charm. He would enter a drawing-room, we are told, and pay his respects to his hostess, 'with a gaiety and an ease, combined with a kind of worshipping deference, that was worthy of a Prime Minister at the court of love'; and such was his habitual gaiety and vivacity that a distinguished American visitor once compared him to a humming-bird. Even in the present century, among authoritative critics, his facile verses have not lacked admirers, including the late Sir Max Beerbohm, who asserted that, in some of his better poems, the true spirit of Irish literature is 'more authentically breathed than it is by Yeats', and our latest Poet Laureate, Sir John Betjeman, who has announced that his love-lyrics are much superior to those of Byron. These are evidently far-fetched claims. But there seems no doubt that Moore deserves an honourable place among Anglo-Irish men of letters.

WILLIAM HAZLITT (1778–1830), son of a Unitarian minister, was born at Maidstone, Kent, and brought up in Shropshire, amid an atmosphere of progressive thought. As his father intended him for the ministry, he was sent to Hackney Theological College;

but becoming preoccupied with social and political problems, when he left the college in 1794 he devoted his attention to philosophy and statecraft. The rich eloquence of Burke's *Letter to a Noble Lord* (1796) made a deep impression on his mind. It was his meeting with Coleridge, however, during the year 1798, that radically changed his life. 'I was at that time dumb, inarticulate', he remembered, 'but now my ideas floated on winged words.' In 1802 he travelled to Paris to study art; and returning home in 1803 he became an itinerant portrait painter. He enjoyed wandering around the country, and he had sufficient skill and self-assurance to earn a living by his brush. Comfort he did not value; and he was delighted should a small commission permit him to dine off sausages and mashed potatoes, 'a noble dish for strong stomachs'. During his travels he had a series of adventurous love affairs, and, once, during his pursuit of a village girl, narrowly escaped being thrown into a horse-pond. Then in 1805 he abandoned the visual arts, and devoted himself to literature. His earliest works were political, among them being an *Essay on the Principles of Human Action*, which appeared in 1805. Through Charles and Mary Lamb, he was introduced to Sarah Stoddart, whom in 1808 he married. But Hazlitt was perpetually falling in and out of love, and the marriage did not succeed.

William Hazlitt; drawing by W. Bewick.

Hazlitt now gradually improved his position in the London literary world, working first as a parliamentary reporter, then as a dramatic critic; and at the same time he began lecturing and contributing to periodicals. Of his collected lectures the most important are *Characters of Shakespeare's Plays* (1817, 1818), *Lectures on the English Poets* (1818, 1819), *Lectures on the English Comic Writers* (1819), and *Lectures on the Dramatic Literature of the Age of Elizabeth* (1820). In 1822 he and his wife were divorced after some years' separation; and during this period he became desperately infatuated with his landlord's daughter – she brought up his daily meals – a 'cold and sullen' girl named Sarah Walker. It was a painful experience; and in *Liber Amoris* (1823), a curiously fascinating piece of self-exposure, he recorded his sensations. Under the title *Table Talk* he now contributed some of his finest essays to the *London Magazine*. Hazlitt had a surprisingly resilient character; and in 1824 he contracted a second marriage – to a Mrs Bridgewater, a widow he had met in a coach, whom he rapidly deserted. In 1825 he published his views on his contemporaries in his ironic and outspoken analysis of *The Spirit of the Age*. His health, which had never been good, deteriorated about 1828; and, two years later, Hazlitt died. 'I have loitered my life away,' he observed, 'reading books, looking at pictures . . . hearing, thinking, writing on what pleased me best. I have wanted only one thing to make me happy; but wanting that, have wanted everything.' Yet he did not regret his strangely erratic existence. 'Well, I've had a happy life,' he remarked to a visitor, not long before he reached its end.

As a professional critic – a career he adopted in 1812 – Hazlitt soon achieved distinction. His essays on Shakespeare are fresh and incisive; and usually he is at his best when praising; his enthusiasm, the sincerity of his commitment and the vigour of his style convey his admiration to the reader. When he attacks, however, he is often wildly prejudiced; with the result that his assessment of his contemporaries, in *On the Living Poets* and *The Spirit of the Age*, sometimes strikes us as absurdly out of focus. His strength lay in his sudden flashes of insight rather than in his powers of reasoning. It was Hazlitt's function to popularize the ideas and methods of his mentor Coleridge; and, though he lacked the older man's poetic percipience and his formidable armoury of learning, he had a far more direct and lucid style. One of his noblest essays, 'My First Acquaintance with Poets', is a vivid account of how Coleridge had originally awakened his intelligence. Later, after the spell had broken and he had come to detest Coleridge's political apostasy, he drew another, no less brilliant portrait in *On the Living Poets*:

But I may say of him here, that he is the only person I ever knew who answered to the idea of a man of genius. He is the only person from whom I ever learnt anything. There is only one thing he could learn from me in return, but *that* he has not. He was the first poet I ever knew. His genius at that time had angelic wings, and fed on manna. He talked on for ever; and you wished him to talk on for ever. His thoughts did not seem to come with labour and effort; but as if borne on the gusts of genius, and as if the wings of his imagination lifted him from off his feet. His voice rolled on the ear like the pealing organ, and its sound alone was the music of thought. His mind was clothed with wings; and raised on them, he lifted philosophy to heaven. In his descriptions, you then saw the progress of human happiness and liberty in bright and never-ending succession, like the steps of Jacob's ladder, with airy shapes ascending, and with the voice of God at the top of the ladder. And shall I, who heard him then, listen to him now? Not I! . . . That spell is broke; that time is gone for ever; that voice is heard no more: but still the recollection comes rushing by with thoughts of long-past years, and rings in my ears with never-dying sound.

'Gusto' is a term that has often been used to characterize Hazlitt's writings; and today it still seems apt. With an eager relish for experience he combined a boundless curiosity. Throughout his works we have frequent glimpses of the mind behind the style – a restive spirit constantly setting forth in pursuit of new adventures.

LEIGH HUNT (1784–1859) was a gifted and industrious man of letters, who spent much of his working life in the company of men of genius. During his earlier years, Keats, Shelley and Byron were among his close friends; at a later stage, he was the Carlyles' Chelsea neighbour, described by the historian as 'one of the most innocent men I ever saw in man's size; a very boy for clear innocence, though his hair is grey, and his face ploughed with many sorrows'. The son of a West-Indian clergyman and an American mother, Hunt, like Coleridge and Lamb, was educated at Christ's Hospital. In 1805 he became a dramatic critic on a paper that his brother edited; and in 1808 he founded the *Examiner*. He remained its editor until 1821, and, being a staunch Radical, took the opportunity of delivering a savage attack upon the Prince Regent, whom he ridiculed as a disreputable idler and 'fat Adonis'. For this offence he was sentenced in 1813 to a period of imprisonment, which he spent not unpleasantly at a London gaol, cheered by the presence of his wife and children, the use of his own piano and a ceiling that he had painted to represent a summer sky. Here Byron visited him and admired his courage and cheerfulness; and, in 1822, he accepted Byron's invitation to join him at his house near Genoa. Shelley encouraged the plan; but it proved a catastrophic mis-step. Byron soon developed a deep distaste both for the sharp-tongued and pretentious Mrs Hunt and for their noisy brood of children; while the *Liberal*, the paper on which all three poets had hoped to collaborate, proved a disappointing venture. Hunt returned to England in 1825, and three years later published a detailed account of his impressions of Byron and Shelley, *Lord Byron and some of his Contemporaries*, which, though it is full of interesting Byronic details, did his reputation no good; the personal animosity that he displayed towards his host is a little too apparent.

For the rest of his life Hunt remained an extraordinarily prolific writer and an energetic editor. Besides launching a succession of magazines that usually failed after a somewhat short career, he poured out an unending flow of prose and verse. Before he left London, Hunt was considered by Tory critics to be a leader of the 'Cockney School', with which they also associated John Keats; and in that rôle the literary taste he showed, as in his most popular poem, the romantic *Story of Rimini*, was frequently deplorable. His prose, however, has far more solid qualities; and his description of his ill-fated visit to Italy is an excellent piece of autobiographical writing. Leigh Hunt was the kind of discursive essayist who flits easily and lightly to and fro amid a large variety of subjects. Though Hunt had pleased the Carlyles, he exasperated Charles Dickens, who, in *Bleak House*, portrayed him as the carefree Mr Skimpole, a frivolous and feckless sponger.

THOMAS DE QUINCEY (1785–1859), son of a prosperous Manchester businessman and his strong-minded Evangelical wife, was one of the oddest and most elusive of nineteenth-century prose-writers. From early manhood to old age he remained a vagrant and a fugitive; though from what he fled, and what he was seeking, seem often equally mysterious. At seventeen he ran away from

Drawing of Thomas de Quincey among his children; by James Archer, 1855.

school and, on the guinea a week his mother allowed him, wandered off alone to London, where he experienced the period of solitary sufferings that he would afterwards describe in his *Confessions of an English Opium-Eater*, his only friend and comforter being a youthful prostitute named Ann, of whom he was presently to lose sight – she vanished one day into the London crowd – but who continued to haunt his dreams until he died. Recaptured and sent to Oxford, he passed some erratic years at the University; then, in 1807, he once again absconded. In 1804 he had become an opium-addict; and henceforward his growing need for opium, which he had first taken as a remedy for neuralgia and tooth-ache, dominated his entire existence. Atrocious stomach-pains, probably caused by a duodenal ulcer, made it impossible to break the habit. As the miseries of addiction increased – like Coleridge, he suffered appalling nightmares – so did the appetite from which they sprang.

About the time De Quincey left Oxford, he visited the English Lakes, gained the friendship of Coleridge and Wordsworth, and purchased a cottage near Grasmere. In 1816 he made one of the few sensible decisions of his life and married Margaret Simpson, the daughter of a neighbouring farmer, who bore him eight children – five boys and three girls – and tended her invalid husband with devoted patience. Despite his private habits, he was now a regular and voluminous contributor to various London periodicals. *The London Magazine* published part of his *Confessions* in 1821; and, in 1826, he joined *Blackwood's Magazine*, which issued a series of his finest essays. In 1828 the De Quinceys moved to Edinburgh; and there he died in 1859. The loss of his wife in 1837 had, for a while, driven him even deeper into the nightmare world of drug-addiction; but during his last years, he had considerably reduced his dosage. Thomas Carlyle has left an admirable description of De Quincey's appearance as a middle-aged man:

De Quincey's last home; 42 Lothian Street, Edinburgh.

He was a pretty little creature, full of wire-drawn ingenuities; bankrupt enthusiasms, bankrupt pride; with the finest silver-toned low, and most elaborate gently-winding courtesies . . . A bright, ready and melodious talker; but in the end inconclusive and long-winded. One of the smallest man-figures I ever saw; shaped like a pair of tongs; and hardly above five feet in all: when he sat, you would have taken him by candle-light, for the beautifullest little Child; blue-eyed, blonde-haired, sparkling face, – had there not been a something too, which said, '*Eccovi*, this Child has been in Hell!'

De Quincey is an uneven writer, at his best superbly eloquent, at his worst, intolerably discursive and unbearably verbose. He had always found it difficult to concentrate his literary gifts; and his autobiography loses much of its dramatic effect because he so often overloads his story with long unnecessary parentheses. Yet his style, when his emotions are strongly aroused and he is exploring the haunted regions of his own past, acquires a strange and solemn music, as he builds up a succession of intricate sentences, each containing some vivid romantic image, into a beautifully balanced whole:

At a vast distance were visible, as a stain upon the horizon, the domes and cupolas of a great city . . . And not a bow-shot from me, upon a stone, shaded by Judean palms, there sat a woman; and I looked, and it was – Ann! . . . Her face was the same as when I saw it last; the same, and yet, again, how different! Seventeen years ago, when the lamplight of mighty London fell upon her face, as for the last time I kissed her lips . . . her eyes were streaming with tears. The tears were no longer seen.

Sometimes she seemed altered; yet again sometimes not altered; and hardly older . . .

Then suddenly would come a dream of far different character – a tumultuous dream – commencing with a music such as I now often heard in sleep – music of preparation and awakening suspense. The undulations of fast-gathering tumults . . . gave the feeling of a multitudinous movement, of infinite cavalcades filing off, and the tread of innumerable armies. The morning was come of a mighty day – a day of crisis and of ultimate hope for human nature . . .

I had the power, and yet had not the power, to decide it. I had the power, if I could raise myself to will it; and yet again had not the power, for the weight of twenty Atlantics was upon me, or the oppression of inexpiable guilt . . . Then like a chorus the passion deepened . . . Then came sudden alarms; hurryings to and fro; trepidations of innumerable fugitives . . . darkness and lights; tempest and human faces; and at last, with the sense that all was lost, female forms, and the features that were worth all the world to me . . . And I awoke in struggles, and cried aloud, 'I will sleep no more!'

The Art of Prose

THOMAS CARLYLE (1795–1881) was the eldest son of an industrious Scottish stone-mason who afterwards became a farmer, and spent an austere youth studying at Edinburgh University (where he failed to take a degree) and as a schoolmaster and tutor of private pupils. His mother, a devout and strong-willed woman, was anxious he should join the ministry, and encouraged his pietistic trend. But it was from his father, said to have been a 'pithy, bitter-speaking body, and an awfu' fighter', that Carlyle must no doubt have inherited his indomitably aggressive spirit. Like Johnson, another bellicose talker, he was afflicted with 'a vile melancholy'; and in 1821, again like Johnson, he seems to have experienced some kind of nervous breakdown when his melancholia almost amounted to madness. During the same year, however, his friend Edward Irving, future divine and founder of the Irvingite sect, introduced him to Jane Baillie Welsh, an attractive and well-bred middle-class girl, 'equally proud (we are told) of her Latin and her eyelashes'. They were an incongruous pair – Thomas, gloomy, saturnine and self-absorbed; Jane, gay, volatile and fond of company. But Jane admired her suitor's craggy intelligence and, because of her respect and admiration, at length decided that she loved him. They were married in 1826, and in 1828 moved from the comparative comfort of Edinburgh to a lonely farm at Craigenputtock. Here his wife suffered but stood firm – she shared her husband's obstinate sense of duty – and Carlyle worked on the strange book that he entitled *Sartor Resartus*, in which, under a somewhat fantastic disguise, he unfolded his intellectual odyssey, related how he had conquered his own destructive despair, and proclaimed the gospel of the 'Everlasting Yea'.

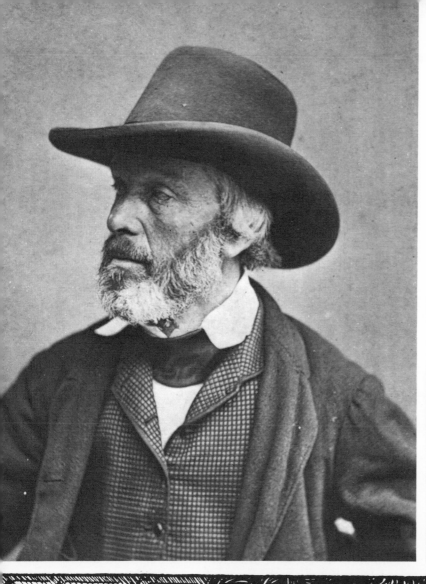

(*Left*) Photograph of Thomas Carlyle in later life.
(*Below bottom*) Illustration to Chapter III of *Sartor Resartus*.
(*Below*) Carlyle's house in Cheyne Row, now the Carlyle Museum.

In 1834, not long after the completion of *Sartor Resartus*, when their prospects seemed a little more hopeful, the Carlyles moved to London; and there, at No. 5 Cheyne Row, Chelsea, a pleasant, roomy, old-fashioned house, the writer would remain until he died. It was not a happy marriage. Both were hypochondriacs, their nervous systems and digestive apparatus in a state of perpetual disarray; while, during later life, Jane Carlyle, whose mind was often clouded by the drugs which she used to combat her incurable insomnia, became unreasonably jealous of Carlyle's platonic infatuation for a brilliant Victorian hostess, Lady Ashburton, who flattered and spoiled the celebrated author, but was apt to patronize his wife. Early in 1866 Jane Carlyle died, suddenly and unexpectedly, as she drove round Hyde Park; and Carlyle, when he looked at her private papers and understood how intense her sufferings had been, received a shock that left him old and wretched, 'the light of his life as if gone out'. Nevertheless he lived on at Cheyne Row, a dyspeptic and embittered sage, for another fifteen years.

Carlyle's last contribution to English historical literature, his huge study of *Frederick the Great*, began to emerge in 1858 and was completed in 1865. It had been preceded, in 1837, by *The French Revolution* (which he was obliged to rewrite after it had been accidentally destroyed, while loaned to John Stuart Mill); in 1841, by *Heroes, Hero-Worship, and the Heroic in History*; in 1843, by *Past and Present*; in 1845, by the work that he himself most heartily approved of, *The Letters and Speeches of Oliver Cromwell*. Carlyle's *Latter-Day Pamphlets*, the fruit of a 'period of deep gloom and bottomless dubitation', saw the light in 1850, and in 1851 his *Life of John Sterling*. As he grew older Carlyle, like his friend John Ruskin, became progressively more and more 'illiberal'. A child of the working-class, he had learned to despise the masses, few of whom, he believed, were fitted for real power; while he continued to celebrate the cult of the Hero, who must be the arbiter of human destiny. Though he hated industrialism and its effects on the modern world, he opposed the idea of parliamentary reform. Had he lived in the twentieth century, Carlyle would probably have degenerated into some type of intellectual fascist.

He survives today, not as a thinker – nor, indeed, as an exact historian: his views about the origins of the French Revolution are absurdly over-simplified – but as a writer who dramatized history, often with magnificent results. His *French Revolution* is a wonderfully dramatic narrative, moving and exhilarating from start to finish. He had also an acute sense of character, and embellished his text with a series of vividly incisive portraits. Elsewhere, Carlyle is at his best in his *Life of John Sterling*, for example, when he records his impressions of the aged Coleridge:

The good man, he was now growing old, towards sixty perhaps; and gave you the idea of a life that had been full of sufferings; a life heavy-laden, half-vanquished, still swimming painfully in seas of manifold physical and other bewilderment. Brow and head were round, and of massive weight, but the face was flabby and irresolute. The eyes, of a light hazel, were as full of sorrow as of inspiration; confused pain looked mildly from them, as in a kind of mild astonishment . . . He hung loosely on his limbs, with knees bent, and stooping attitude; in walking, he rather shuffled than decisively stept; and a lady once remarked, he could never fix which side of the garden walk would suit him best, but continually shifted, in corkscrew fashion, and kept trying both . . . His voice, naturally soft and good, had contracted itself into a plaintive snuffle and singsong; he spoke as if preaching . . .

There was a close resemblance between Carlyle and Ruskin, both in the lives they led and in the messages they uttered. Each had been formed by a pious Scottish mother, and had ultimately rebelled against that mother's faith. Each is said to have suffered from sexual impotence, and was inclined to project his own unhappiness into his attacks upon the world at large. Finally, each had an idiosyncratic style that, as time went by, grew more and more abstruse. But unlike Ruskin's, which recovered its youthful clarity once he had begun to write *Praeterita*, his fellow prophet's style became increasingly dogmatic with every volume he put forth; so that his last major work, *Frederick the Great*, is among the most unreadable biographies ever published by a famous writer.

THE DEATH OF ROBESPIERRE

And so, at six in the morning, a victorious Convention adjourns. Report flies over Paris as on golden wings; penetrates the Prisons; irradiates the faces of those that were ready to perish: turnkeys and *moutons*, fallen from their high estate, look mute and blue. It is the 28th day of July, called 10th of Thermidor, year 1794.

Fouquier had but to identify; his Prisoners being already Out of Law. At four in the afternoon, never before were the streets of Paris seen so crowded. From the Palais de Justice to the Place de la Révolution, for *thither* again go the Tumbrils this time, it is one dense stirring mass; all windows crammed; the very roofs and ridge-tiles budding forth human Curiosity, in strange gladness. The Death-tumbrils, with their motley Batch of Outlaws, some Twenty-three or so, from Maximilien to Mayor Fleuriot and Simon the Cordwainer, roll on. All eyes are on Robespierre's Tumbril, where he, his jaw bound in dirty linen, with his half-dead Brother, and half-dead Henriot, lie shattered; their 'seventeen hours' of agony about to end. The Gendarmes point their swords at him, to show the people which is he. A woman springs on the Tumbril; clutching the side of it with one hand; waving the other Sibyl-like; and exclaims: "The death of thee gladdens my very heart, *m'enivre de joie;*" Robespierre opened his eyes; "*Scélérat*, go down to Hell, with the curses of all wives and mothers!" – At the foot of the scaffold, they stretched him on the ground till his turn came. Lifted aloft, his eyes again opened; caught the bloody axe. Samson wrenched the coat off him; wrenched the dirty linen from his jaw: the jaw fell powerless, there burst from him a cry; – hideous to hear and see. Samson, thou canst not be too quick!

(*The French Revolution*)

Jane Welsh Carlyle as a young married woman, about 1838; drawing by Samuel Laurence.

JANE WELSH CARLYLE (1801–66) never published a book in her lifetime, or seriously contemplated entering the world of literature, though her friend Charles Dickens, delighted by the stories she told, once encouraged her to write a novel. During her lifetime, among her husband's acquaintances, Mrs Carlyle had long been regarded as a remarkably clever and often a formidably sharp-tongued woman; but after her death the publication of the *Letters and Memorials of Jane Welsh Carlyle*, which Thomas Carlyle piously edited, first revealed her original literary gifts. In her private letters, particularly in those she addressed to her youthful cousin, Jeannie Welsh, she found the imaginative outlet that she needed; and there, with unfailing wit and verve, she described the progress of the 'sore life-pilgrimage' (to use her life-companion's own phrase) that she and Thomas Carlyle had been doomed to make together. Both were melancholics; both were hypochondriacs; both, naturally self-centred beings. Yet Jane, despite her unending complaints, was fiercely devoted to her grim and gloomy husband; while Thomas, for all his neglectful ways, had a deep attachment to his ailing neurotic wife, whose true depth of character, he felt, had almost completely escaped him until he looked into her correspondence.

That correspondence has now established her fame. Mrs Carlyle was one of the most brilliant letter-writers of the English nineteenth century. She possessed both a delightfully acute wit and – especially when her subject was 'Mr. C.', and the odd doings of their various friends and servants – a well-developed sense of drama. In some respects she can bear comparison with her great predecessor, Horace Walpole.

THOMAS BABINGTON MACAULAY (1800–59), son of the philanthropist and abolitionist, Zachary Macaulay, even by the high standards of his own age was a remarkably precocious child. When he was only seven, he embarked on a compendium of universal history; at eight he wrote a religious treatise designed to convert the natives of Malabar. In 1818 he went up to Trinity College, Cambridge, where he wrote a prize-poem and eventually gained a fellowship. In 1825 an essay on Milton that he con-contributed to *The Edinburgh Review*, immediately assured him a place among its regular contributors. In 1830 he was elected member of Parliament for Calne, and delivered a maiden speech, supporting the First Reform Bill, that electrified the whole House. Macaulay had no inherited fortune; and, in 1832, owing to various financial reverses, he claimed that he 'did not know where to turn for a morsel of bread'. Soon afterwards, however, he was appointed to the Supreme Council of India with an ample salary. He left England early in 1834, and, during the next three-and-a-half years, he proved himself a gifted colonial administrator, supervising the preparation of a penal code and organizing

Indian education. Once he had returned to England, he re-entered Parliament and began work on his *History of England*. From 1839 to 1841, Macaulay held a Cabinet post as Secretary of State for War. But the fall of the Whig government sent him back to literature; and the first two volumes of his *History* were published in November 1848. They were enormously successful; 13,000 copies were sold in four months; and the fourth and fifth volumes appeared, with no less effect, in December 1855. Meanwhile, his *Lays of Ancient Rome*, the poetic fruit of an Italian tour, and his collection of *Critical and Miscellaneous Essays* had already seen the light, in 1842 and 1843 respectively. His works, both verse and prose, now ran through innumerable editions. In 1857 the author received a peerage. On 28 December 1859 he died as he sat in his library. His *History* he left unfinished.

Macaulay was an immensely erudite man; few of his contemporaries could claim to possess such a prodigious store of information. He was an eloquent talker, said Sydney Smith, often his fellow-guest at Holland House, and not only 'overflowed with learning, but stood in the slop'. As a literary critic and historian, he was more vigorous than subtle; and he regarded the past from the point of view of an enlightened Whig materialist who held a high opinion of the present day. Nineteenth-century England, he believed, had reached a level of civilization unequalled at any other period; and he enjoyed comparing seventeenth-century London with its mid-Victorian counterpart:

Thomas Babington Macaulay, by J. Partridge, 1849.

The town did not, as now, fade by imperceptible degrees into the country. No long avenues of villas, embowered in lilacs and laburnums, extended from the great centre of wealth and civilisation almost to the boundaries of Middlesex and far into the heart of Kent and Surrey. In the east, no part of the immense line of warehouses and artificial lakes which now stretches from the Tower to Blackwall had even been projected. On the west, scarcely one of those stately piles of building which are inhabited by the noble and wealthy was in existence; and Chelsea which is now peopled by more than forty thousand human beings, was a quiet country village with about a thousand inhabitants.

Macaulay's *History* is permeated by the same spirit of Whiggish self-esteem, its basis being the concept of freedom as a guarantee of the enjoyment of private property. The two major achievements on which Britain had founded her greatness were the 'Glorious Revolution' of 1688 and the Industrial Revolution of the late eighteenth and early nineteenth centuries, the former preparing the way for the age of Victoria, the latter advancing the material progress that Macaulay equated with civilization. He planned to reach the widest possible audience – to 'produce something which shall for a few days supersede the last fashionable novel on the tables of young ladies', besides holding the attention of their earnest parents; and, in order to do so, he was apt to simplify his subject, and to introduce some egregious distortions of fact that have since passed into common currency. Though his style is as rotund as Gibbon's, it is less genuinely distinguished. But, whenever an opportunity occurs – for example, in his account of the trial of Warren Hastings – he produces an impressive set piece:

The grey old walls were hung with scarlet. The long galleries were crowded by an audience such as has rarely excited the fears or the emulation of an orator. There were gathered together, from all parts of a great, free, enlightened, and prosperous empire, grace and female loveliness, wit and learning, the representatives of every science and of every art . . . There Siddons, in the prime of her majestic beauty, looked with emotion on a scene surpassing all the imitations of the stage. There the historian of the Roman Empire thought of the days when Cicero pleaded the cause of Sicily against Verres, and when, before a senate which still retained some show of freedom, Tacitus thundered against the oppressor of Africa. There were seen, side by side, the greatest painter and the greatest scholar of the age. The spectacle had allured Reynolds from that easel which has preserved to us the thoughtful foreheads of so many writers and statesmen, and the sweet smiles of so many noble matrons. It had induced Parr to suspend his labours in that dark and profound mine from which he had extracted a vast treasure of erudition. There appeared the voluptuous charms of her to whom the heir of the throne had in secret plighted his faith. There too was she, the beautiful mother of a beautiful race, the Saint Cecilia, whose delicate features, lighted up by love and music, art has rescued from the common decay. There were the members of that brilliant society which quoted, criticised, and exchanged repartees, under the rich peacock hangings of Mrs Montague. And there the ladies whose lips, more persuasive than those of Fox himself, had carried the Westminster election against palace and treasury, shone round Georgiana, Duchess of Devonshire.

Macaulay was no mean versifier, though he remained a minor poet; and his *Lays of Ancient Rome* – a bold attempt to recreate the kind of ballad-poetry that he felt sure Romans must have repeated in the early days of the Republic – have to many of them a fine romantic ring. But his great importance was as the founder of an historical school that his grand-nephew, George Macaulay Trevelyan, would carry on far into the next century. Few English historians have made history so palatable, or literary criticism so entertaining. Yet, despite his bland approval of his own period Macaulay could at times be savage, as when he attacked the British public for driving Byron into exile:

We know no spectacle so ridiculous as the British public in one of its periodical fits of morality. In general, elopements, divorces, and family quarrels pass with little notice. We read the scandal, talk about it for a day, and forget it. But once in six or seven years our virtue becomes outrageous. We cannot suffer the laws of religion and decency to be violated. We must make a stand against vice. We must teach libertines that the English people appreciate the importance of domestic ties. Accordingly some unfortunate man, in no respect more depraved than hundreds whose offences have been treated with lenity, is singled out as

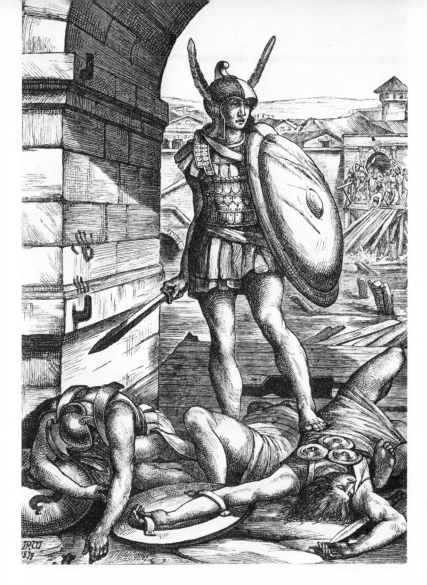

an expiatory sacrifice. If he has children, they are taken from him. If he has a profession, he is to be driven from it. He is cut by the higher orders, and hissed by the lower. He is, in truth, a sort of whipping boy, by whose vicarious agonies all the other transgressors of the same class, are, it is supposed, sufficiently chastised. We reflect very complacently on our own severity, and compare with great pride the high standard of morals established in England with Parisian laxity. At length our anger is satiated. Our victim is ruined and heart-broken. And our virtue goes quietly to sleep for seven years more.

JOHN HENRY NEWMAN (1801–90) was the most distinguished writer and ablest controversialist thrown up by the great religious crisis of the English nineteenth century. The son of a London banker, while still at his private school he fell under the influence of Calvinism; but at Oxford, where he became a fellow of Oriel, he developed far more liberal views. Then, during a journey

Horatius on the Bridge; frontispiece to *Lays of Ancient Rome*.

John Henry Newman,
by G. Richmond, 1844.

abroad, he began to be troubled with fears about the present condition of the Church of England, which, he felt, was being slowly secularized and more and more cut off from its inspired medieval sources. He thereupon hastily returned home and, during the next seven years, from 1833 to 1841, published, with Pusey, Froude and Keble, the famous series of *Tracts for the Times* that launched the so-called Oxford Movement. Newman's advocacy of High Anglicanism was an attempt to mark out a middle-way between the Anglican and Roman faiths. But, little by little, he moved towards Rome, until he had finally made his submission to the Roman Church in October 1845. Two years later, he was ordained priest and established the congregation of the Oratory at Birmingham. The remainder of his existence was spent there; and, as Superior of the Oratory, an ascetic and saintly recluse, he gradually withdrew from public life. His relations with Cardinal Manning, himself one-time supporter of the Oxford Movement but now a far less liberal thinker, concluded in a sharp estrangement. On the other side, Newman was bitterly attacked by Charles Kingsley, to whose Protestant diatribe 'What then does Dr Newman mean?' he replied by composing in 1864 his masterpiece, the *Apologia pro Vita Sua*. In 1870 he followed it with his *Grammar of Assent*. Two books of verse, his long poem, *The Dream of Gerontius*, and a collection, *Verses on Various Occasions*, came out in 1866 and 1868. Newman was at length created a Cardinal in May, 1879, and died, at the age of eighty-nine, on 11 August 1890.

Newman was a sensitive and retiring man, who, beneath his delicate exterior, concealed a tremendous fund of moral courage and intellectual strength. In an age of exuberant stylists, he wrote, at least during his earlier period, a simple, unemphatic prose, more concerned with the message he sought to convey than with linguistic airs and graces. Its grave harmony seems to arise from the writer's own sincerity; and for the most part he prefers to avoid any superfluous dramatic details. When they occur, however, they are often deeply moving, as in this account of how he had left Oxford, and had noted, while he bade his college farewell, the flowers that grew around his door:

I left Oxford for good on Monday, February 23rd, 1846. On the Saturday and Sunday before, I was in my house at Littlemore simply by myself, as I had been for the first day or two when I had originally taken possession of it . . . I called on Dr Ogle, one of my oldest friends, for he was my private Tutor, when I was an undergraduate. In him I took leave of my first College, Trinity, which was so dear to me, and which held on its foundation so many who have been kind to me both when I was a boy, and all through my Oxford life . . . There used to be much snapdragon growing on the walls opposite my freshman's rooms there, and I had for years taken it as the emblem of my own perpetual residence even unto death in my University.

JOHN RUSKIN (1819–1900) was the only child of possessively devoted middle-aged parents; and their attitude towards him was to have a lasting effect upon his personal development. His father had emigrated from Scotland to London, where he had established himself as a prosperous sherry-merchant; and John's youth was passed in the merchant's large suburban villa. Under his parents' strict and anxious charge, the boy learned 'peace, obedi-

Portrait of John Ruskin by John Everett Millais, 1854.

Ruskin in later life; drawing by T.B. Wrigman.

ence, faith', but was denied the companionship of other children and grew up (as he afterwards wrote) to 'lead a very small, perky, contented, conceited, Cock-Robinson-Crusoe sort of life'. His judgements of right and wrong, he said, 'were left entirely undeveloped; because the bridle and blinkers were never taken off me'. Yet his imagination, at least, was never starved; his father, who loved sight-seeing, often took him around England to visit country houses and cathedrals; and, later, the Ruskins journeyed through France and Italy, travelling in their own carriage.

As the result of an unhappy early love-affair, John was threatened with a nervous breakdown. But he slowly recovered and, in 1843, at the age of twenty-four, published the opening volumes of an ambitious treatise, *Modern Painters*, designed to demonstrate their superiority to all the most celebrated Old Masters, '*proved by Examples of the True, the Beautiful, and the Intellectual from the Works of Modern Artists, especially from those of J.M.W. Turner Esq . . .*' Though as art-criticism the book has many failings, it was written in a superbly eloquent style that at once attracted notice. It was followed, in 1849, by *Seven Lamps of Architecture*, a magnificent defence of the Gothic inspiration, and *The Stones of Venice*, which he completed in the year 1853.

Five years earlier he had made a disastrous marriage. In 1848 he wedded Euphemia, or Effie, Gray – an attractive, well-meaning girl, who, although ready enough to share her husband's artistic pursuits, was also fond of pretty clothes and had a natural taste for worldly pleasures. Ruskin had courted her tenderly, but he never sought to consummate their marriage – he suffered apparently from some form of psychological impotence that he could not, or would not seek to overcome; and, when his wife divorced

him, he returned to his parents' household and there quietly resumed his studies, lecturing on art and architecture, and generally seeking to spread the artistic ideals that he had first proclaimed in *Modern Painters*. But he had also a rigorous sense of duty; and, as time went by, he became more preoccupied with social and economic problems. The industrialization of Europe revolted him; it was the antithesis of every value he cherished, either moral or artistic. Thus he protested against the Victorian doctrine of *laissez-faire*, which announced that the industrialist was entitled to engage the largest labour-force he required for the lowest wages he need pay, and that there was no possible relationship between 'the human affections' and the iron laws of nineteenth-century progress. *Unto This Last* (once a text-book of the British Labour Party) appeared in the summer of 1862, and caused universal indignation. It was denounced as 'utter im-

(*Above left*) Drawing by Ruskin of a window in Giotto's campanile; from *Seven Lamps of Architecture*, 1849.

(*Above right*) Drawing by Ruskin, for *The Stones of Venice*.

becility', and said to be an incitement to revolutionary violence.

Unto This Last, which deeply shocked his father, was simply written and contained no 'pretty passages'. It is a splendid piece of controversial writing; and Ruskin might well have developed into one of the most powerful of Victorian polemicists, had not the private troubles that now descended on him helped gradually to warp his judgement. In 1858, when he himself was middle-aged, he had encountered a little girl named Rose La Touche. She was then nine years old; and gradually, in Ruskin's life, Rose became the symbol of everything he desired and loved, and hitherto had failed to grasp. The passion grew; and for seventeen years – until Rose, a precocious, sensitive, neurotic being, died in 1875 – she remained the emotional focus of his whole existence. With his inherited puritanism Ruskin combined a deeply sensuous and romantic nature; and it was the resultant conflict, in which his love of physical beauty warred against a secret horror of the flesh, that was at length to undermine his reason.

The products of his middle period, from 1859 to 1869, *The Two Paths, Sesame and Lilies, The Cestus of Aglaia* and *The Queen of the Air*, are astonishingly uneven books. They are full of brilliant passages, but strangely diffuse and disconnected; the author flits to and fro among a variety of different topics; and when, in 1871, he embarked on a series of letters addressed 'to the working men and labourers of Great Britain', the effect was even more remarkable. Reading *Fors Clavigera*, the mysterious title he chose, was, said Cardinal Manning, like listening to 'the beating of one's own heart in a nightmare!'

During 1878 Ruskin suffered his first serious mental breakdown. Others followed; and by 1888 his condition was so precarious that he felt obliged to retire from public life. Thenceforward, at his house in the Lake District, nursed and carefully watched over by his devoted kinswoman, Joan Severn, he became a remote and solitary figure. His last literary effort, which occupied him at intervals between 1885 and 1889, was his autobiography, *Praeterita*. Though he could not finish it, this fragmentary picture of his childhood and youth is his most delightful, certainly his most moving book. Here he no longer preaches or prophesies, but sets out, across the landscape of his past, '*à la recherche du temps perdu*'. Marcel Proust was a keen admirer of Ruskin, and shared not only his passionate enthusiasm for Gothic architecture but his general attitude towards aesthetic questions. Ruskin, he wrote, had dedicated the better part of his career to an unswerving cult of Beauty. This Beauty, however, 'was not conceived of as a means of embellishing and sweetening existence, but as a reality infinitely more important than life itself'; from that central idea 'Ruskin's whole aesthetic system springs'. Art alone, the prophet believed, if rightly understood, would bring back dignity and harmony to the squalid confusion of industrialized Europe.

Let us, for a moment, imagine the Mediterranean lying beneath us like an irregular lake, and all its ancient promontories sleeping in the sun: here and there an angry spot of thunder, a grey stain of storm, moving upon the burning field; and here and there a fixed wreath of white volcano smoke, surrounded by its circle of ashes; but for the most part a great peacefulness of light, Syria and Greece, Italy and Spain, laid like pieces of a golden pavement into the sea-blue, chased, as we stoop nearer to them, with bossy beaten work of mountain chains, and glowing softly with terraced gardens, and flowers heavy with frankincense, mixed among masses of laurel, and orange, and plumy palm, that abate with their grey-green shadows the burning of the marble rocks, and of the ledges of porphyry, sloping under lucent sand. Then let us pass farther towards the north, until we see the orient colours change gradually into a vast belt of rainy green, where the pastures of Switzerland, and poplar valleys of France, and dark forests of the Danube and Carpathians stretch from the mouths of the Loire to those of the Volga, seen through clefts in grey swirls of rain-cloud and flaky veils of the mist of the brooks, spreading low along the pasture lands: and then, farther north still, to see the earth heave into mighty masses of leaden rock and heathy moor, bordering with a broad waste of gloomy purple that belt of field and wood, and splintering into irregular and grisly islands amidst the northern seas, beaten by storm, and chilled by ice-drift, and tormented by furious pulses of contending tide, until the roots of the last forests fail from among the hill ravines, and the hunger of the north wind bites their peaks into barrenness; and, at last, the wall of ice, durable like iron, sets, deathlike, its white teeth against us out of the polar twilight.

(The Stones of Venice)

WALTER PATER (1839–94) spent much of his adult life behind the walls of Brasenose College, Oxford. Brasenose was, and indeed, still is, one of the more athletic Oxford colleges; and Pater, though he admired athletes as types of masculine beauty, had little interest in manly sports. Nor did Oxford as a whole accord him a particularly friendly welcome; even at Balliol, Benjamin Jowett considered him a possibly subversive influence and regarded him with deep suspicion. Having been educated at King's School, Canterbury, under the shadow of the great Cathedral, Pater had an aesthetic taste for the ceremonies of the Christian Church, but by temperament he remained a pagan; and what he chiefly admired about the Renaissance was its exquisite blending of the sensuous and the spiritual. 'Sensuous' was a word he often employed; and the fact that he was himself an extremely ugly man – his baldness and heavy cavalry moustache are said to have given him the appearance of 'a retired army officer in poor health' – seems to have lent his appreciation of sensuous beauty an especially acute edge. His first published volume, *Studies in the History of the Renaissance*, appeared when he was thirty-four; and there his announcement that 'to burn

Walter Pater by
W. Rothenstein, 1894.

always with this hard, gemlike flame, to maintain this ecstasy is success in life', alarmed his late-Victorian readers. The emphasis he placed on the *pleasure* that we receive from our examination of a painting or a statue struck them as disproportionate; they preferred Ruskin's efforts to detect in every work of art a moral message; and they were disturbed by his references to the picturesque crimes of the Renaissance – 'crime for its own sake, a whole octave of fantastic crime, not only under brilliant fashions but with immaculate grace and discretion about them'. Here as elsewhere, he anticipated Oscar Wilde: though Wilde lacked his belief in 'austerity' and in the value of intellectual discipline.

The Renaissance, which consists of a collection of essays on Pico della Mirandola, Botticelli, Luca della Robbia, the poems of Michelangelo, da Vinci, Giorgione, Raphael and a series of allied subjects, is often brilliantly perceptive. His two-volume novel *Marius the Epicurean*, which describes the gradual fusion of the pagan and Christian worlds, at length emerged in 1885, and was followed by *Imaginary Portraits, Appreciations: with an Essay on Style, Plato and Platonism* and an autobiographical vignette, *A Child in the House*, between 1887 and 1894. Pater was a highly self-conscious stylist; and many of his passages of 'fine writing', for example, his famous description of da Vinci's *Mona Lisa* – 'She is older than the rocks among which she sits; like the vampire, she has been dead many times, and learned the secrets of the grave' – now seem over-elaborate and otiose. Yet Pater possessed a genuine sensibility, which can be enjoyed even in the laborious, slow-moving pages of *Marius the Epicurean*; and, both as an imaginative writer and as a professional art-critic, he throws some gleam of light upon every subject that he touches, whether it be Rome under Marcus Aurelius or the art of seventeenth-century Holland:

THE BACKGROUND OF DUTCH ART

So genially attempered, so warm, was life become, in the land of which Pliny had spoken as scarcely dry land at all. And, in truth, the sea which Sebastian so much loved, and with so great a satisfaction and sense of wellbeing in every hint of its newness, is never far distant in Holland. Invading all places, stealing under one's feet, insinuating itself everywhere along an endless network of canals (by no means such formal channels as we understand by the name, but picturesque rivers, with sedgy banks and haunted by innumerable birds) its incidents present themselves oddly even in one's park or woodland walks; the ship in full sail appearing suddenly among the great trees or above the garden wall, where we had no suspicion of the presence of waters. In the very conditions of life in such a country there was a standing force of pathos. The country itself shared the uncertainty of the individual human life; and there was pathos also in the constantly renewed, heavily-taxed labours, necessary to keep the native soil, fought for so unselfishly, there at all; with a warfare that must still be maintained when the other struggle with the Spaniard was over.

(Imaginary Portraits)

Later Nineteenth-Century Verse

ELIZABETH BARRETT BROWNING (1806–61) and ROBERT BROWNING (1812–89) formed one of the most celebrated partnerships in the history of English literature. But they were imaginative writers of a very different type; and although, when they originally met, Elizabeth was by far the more famous, her poetic reputation has slowly declined, while Robert Browning's has survived a brief eclipse and stands today as high as ever. In the latest *Oxford Book of English Verse*, the poetess is allotted less than two pages; the poet, over fifteen. Elizabeth Barrett Browning, the eldest of a large family, was the daughter of Edward Moulton-Barrett, a rich West-Indian proprietor. Brought up near Malvern, she had begun to write verse before she reached her ninth birthday, and in 1819 completed an epic poem on 'The Battle of Marathon', which her father had printed, and which she followed up with an 'Essay on Mind' that appeared in 1826. During this period she became an invalid; having injured her spine, she was obliged to retire to a sofa, where she lay 'for years upon her back'. In 1833 she published her first adult collection of verse, *Prometheus Bound and Miscellaneous Poems*, and, in 1838, *The Seraphim*. About this time her family moved to a London house, No 50 Wimpole Street, and there, in 1840, the news of her favourite brother's death – he had been drowned at sea, when his sailing-boat foundered – dealt her a traumatic blow. Her invalidism grew more and more pronounced; she seldom left her father's house, and spent most of her time in her airless, overheated bedroom. Such a course of existence suited Mr Barrett, a stern Victorian paterfamilias, who had declared that any daughter of his, should she enter the married state and desert his household, would be guilty of 'unfilial treachery'. But, although forbidden to leave her domestic gaol, she had full permission to continue writing; and in 1844 she published the two volumes of *Poems* that immediately brought her talents into public notice.

Elizabeth Barrett Browning, the last photograph, taken in 1861.

It was these volumes that attracted Robert Browning; and in January 1845 he sent her a warmly appreciative letter. She responded; their friendship quickly developed – she acclaimed her correspondent as 'the king of the mystics'; and, once her affections had been deeply aroused, she found her physical health improving; so that, by 12 September 1846, she had grown strong enough to slip out of Wimpole Street and secretly marry her fellow poet at a nearby London church. A week later, they eloped to Paris, and soon afterwards travelled on to Italy. The refuge they eventually chose was Florence; and there, at the Palazzo Guido, in 1849 Mrs Browning gave birth to their only child, a son. In 1850, she reissued her *Poems*, with the addition of 'Sonnets from the Portuguese', the love-poems she had addressed to her future husband during their engagement. Among her later publications were *Casa Guidi Windows* (1851) and *Poems before Congress* (1860).

WHEN OUR TWO SOULS STAND UP ERECT AND STRONG,
FACE TO FACE, SILENT, DRAWING NIGH AND NIGHER,
UNTIL THE LENGTHENING WINGS BREAK INTO FIRE
AT EITHER CURVED POINT,— WHAT BITTER WRONG
CAN THE EARTH DO TO US, THAT WE SHOULD NOT LONG
BE HERE CONTENDED ? THINK. IN MOUNTING HIGHER,
THE ANGELS WOULD PRESS ON US, AND ASPIRE
TO DROP SOME GOLDEN ORB OF PERFECT SONG
INTO OUR DEEP, DEAR SILENCE. LET US STAY
RATHER ON EARTH, BELOVED,— WHERE THE UNFIT
CONTRARIOUS MOODS OF MEN RECOIL AWAY
AND ISOLATE PURE SPIRITS, AND PERMIT
A PLACE TO STAND AND LOVE IN FOR A DAY,
WITH DARKNESS AND THE DEATH-HOUR ROUNDING IT.

Illustration of 1887 to
Sonnets from the Portuguese.

Her *Last Poems* appeared a year after the writer's death. She died at the Palazzo Guidi on 29 June 1861. Elizabeth Browning was a diminutive, dark-eyed woman, whose abundance of glossy side-curls, framing a small mobile, long-lipped face, gave her a certain resemblance to the beloved spaniel 'Flush' that she had brought with her from Wimpole Street.

'No other woman in England,' we are told by Edmund Gosse, 'has devoted her life so completely to the cultivation of imaginative literature as did Elizabeth Barrett Browning.' But, despite a cultivated feeling for the use of language, she was unmistakably a minor poet, less brilliant than Christina Rossetti, though more accomplished than Christina's brother. The 'Sonnets from the Portuguese', written under Robert Browning's early influence, contain some of her most lasting work:

> I thought once how Theocritus had sung
> Of the sweet years, the dear and wished-for years,
> Who each one in a gracious hand appears
> To bear a gift for mortals, old or young:
> And, as I mused it in his antique tongue,
> I saw, in gradual vision through my tears,
> The sweet, sad years, the melancholy years,

Those of my own life, who by turns had flung
A shadow across me. Straightway I was 'ware,
So weeping, how a mystic Shape did move
Behind me, and drew me backward by the hair;
And a voice said in mastery while I strove,
'Guess now who holds thee?' – 'Death!' I said. But, there,
The silver answer rang, 'Not Death, but Love'.

When Robert Browning carried off Elizabeth, he was in his
mid-thirties. The son of a London bank official who had married
a German-Scottish girl, he had been born at Camberwell, in those
days a pleasant suburban village, still surrounded by woods and
open fields. He was spared much regular education, since he had
early determined to become a poet, and disdained all other
interests. His first published work, *Pauline*, 'subtitled 'Fragment
of a Confession', appeared anonymously in 1833, and proved
entirely unsuccessful; but, two years later, *Paracelsus* attracted the
attention of the critics. His tragedy, *Strafford*, however, produced
in 1837 by the famous actor-manager, William Macready, had a
very short run; and he then plunged into the labyrinthine
Sordello, which he did not publish until 1840, when reviewers and
readers denounced it – not without some justification: it is the
most obscure of all his early poems – as utterly unreadable. For the
next twenty years Browning had little popular success; and, after
his marriage, he long continued to be overshadowed by his wife's
fame. His own works were seldom talked of; he was simply 'the
man who married Elizabeth Barrett'. From this unhappy condition he at last emerged in 1863. His enormous 'murder-poem',
The Ring and the Book, caught the reading public's fancy; and for
the remainder of his life he enjoyed immense fame, second only to
that of Alfred Tennyson. His finest works, however, were almost
all written during the period when he was attracting least notice.
The two volumes of *Men and Women*, which came out in 1855, show
his genius at its height. Two factors – his marriage and his trans-
plantation to Florence – seem to have hastened his development.
One gave him emotional security; the other provided the human
subjects that he needed. Elizabeth's death in 1861 left him temporarily lost and broken. He moved back to England, where he
took up work again. But in 1878 he returned to Italy, and in 1887
purchased a Venetian palace on the Grand Canal. His last years
were happy and industrious; and he much enjoyed his great
celebrity. He died at the Palazzo Rezzonico on 12 December 1889.

The poet had an extraordinarily inquisitive mind – a characteristic observed in 1845 by no less an authority than Walter
Savage Landor, who had admired his early work:

Browning! since Chaucer was alive and hale,
No man hath walk'd along our roads with step
So active, so inquiring eye, or tongue
So varied in discourse . . .

Robert Browning, 1866;
portrait by G.F. Watts.

This enquiring eye he turned both on the old and on the new; and nowhere are past and present so closely bound up together as in the country that he loved best. But, if Italy provided many of his themes, he brought to them a type of literary intelligence – speculative, ruminative, discursive – that appears typically Anglo-Saxon. He welcomed a problem; and, now and then, he himself admitted, his attempts to answer the question he has asked degenerate into 'mere grey argument'. Victorian critics complained of Browning's obscurity; today we are more inclined to dislike his uninhibited verbosity, remembering that a collected edition of his works contains over a thousand crowded double-column pages. Nevertheless, the major poems of his middle period usually display a rare precision. Having evoked a personality, and associated it with the ethos of the age in which that man or woman lived, he allows the protagonist to reveal himself by means of a dramatic monologue. Thus, the Renaissance bishop gives his death-bed instructions, addressed to his ungrateful bastard family, for the construction of his own tomb and, as he does so, voices the mood of the Church, half Christian, half overtly pagan, under the Renaissance pontiffs:

> Nay, boys, ye love me – all of jasper, then! . . .
> There's plenty jasper somewhere in the world . . .
> And then how I shall lie through centuries,
> And hear the blessed mutter of the mass,
> And see God made and eaten all day long,
> And feel the steady candle-flame, and taste
> Good strong thick stupefying incense-smoke!
> For as I lie here, hours of the dead night,
> Dying in state and by such slow degrees,
> I fold my arms as if they clasped a crook,
> And stretch my feet forth straight as stone can point,
> And let the bedclothes, for a mortcloth, drop
> Into great laps and folds of sculptor's work . . .
> Well, go! I bless ye. Fewer tapers there,
> But in a row: and, going, turn your backs
> – Ay, like departing altar-ministrants,
> And leave me in my church, the church for peace . . .

Browning's evocations of the historic or legendary past are never merely picturesque; for he is preoccupied not only with the mood of an age, but with the human condition as a whole. Another character he portrayed in *Men and Women* was the so-called 'Faultless Painter', Andrea del Sarto (1486–1531), who, he learned from Vasari's *Lives*, had been married to a feckless and inconstant beauty:

> How could you ever prick those perfect ears,
> Even to put the pearl there! oh, so sweet –
> My face, my moon, my everybody's moon,
> Which everybody looks on and calls his,

RVMOVR

'I·FOVND·NO
TRVTH·IN
ONE·REPORT
AT·LEAST·'

BYAM·SHAW

Illustration by Byam
Shaw to 'How it strikes a
contemporary'.

And, I suppose, is looked on by in turn,
While she looks – no one's: very dear, no less.
You smile? why, there's my picture ready made,
There's what we painters call our harmony!
A common greyness silvers everything . . .

Browning's use of rhyme was often as subtle and masterly as his
use of blank verse. Among the group of poems he called *Dramatic
Lyrics* – pieces, he wrote, frequently 'lyric in expression', though

'always dramatic in principle, and so many utterances of so many imaginary persons, not mine' – he published 'Two in the Campagna', a glimpse of a modern love-affair played out against the background of the desolate malarial plain, scattered with the ruins of antiquity, that had already fascinated Goethe, Keats and Byron:

> I wonder do you feel today
> As I have felt since, hand in hand,
> We sat down on the grass, to stray
> In spirit better through the land,
> This morn of Rome and May?
>
> For me, I touched a thought, I know,
> Has tantalized me many times,
> (Like turns of thread the spiders throw
> Mocking across our path) for rhymes
> To catch at and let go.
>
> Help me to hold it! First it left
> The yellowing fennel, run to seed
> There, branching from the brickwork's cleft,
> Some old tomb's ruin: yonder weed
> Took up the floating weft,
>
> Where one small orange cup amassed
> Five beetles, – blind and green they grope
> Among the honey-meal: and last,
> Everywhere on the grassy slope
> I traced it. Hold it fast!
>
> The champaign with its endless fleece
> Of feathery grasses everywhere!
> Silence and passion, joy and peace,
> An everlasting wash of air –
> Rome's ghost since her decease. . . .

Browning's verse has always interested novelists; in his auto-biography, Graham Greene records that 'some lines of Browning have stayed in my memory for fifty years and have influenced my life more than any of the Beatitudes'. Browning himself wished to combine the function of poet with the rôles of novelist and dramatist; and, although *The Ring and the Book* – the story of a forgotten crime and a detailed analysis of its psychological origins – is too lengthy, complex and densely written to attract the average twentieth-century reader, he possessed a keen dramatic sense, which, at his best, he translated into passages of pure poetry. Unlike his wife, however, he eschewed 'poetic' language. Often the phrases he employs are deliberately colloquial; the metrical forms he adopted are loosely framed and unexacting. But it is his curiosity, his delight in observation, his passionate concern with the world of ideas, and his efforts to break through the surface of experience and explore the darkest secrets of the subconscious mind, that make him, as a poet, seem so 'modern'. Browning's poems are far closer to modern verse than the works of any of his great contemporaries.

ALFRED TENNYSON, afterwards 1st Lord Tennyson (1809–92) succeeded Wordsworth as Poet Laureate in November 1850. There is a certain resemblance between the two poets; for each, after a stormy and difficult youth, gradually assumed the outlook and attitude of a literary Grand Old Man, overcoming his juvenile doubts and fears, and, at the same time, although he preserved his executive talents, losing a great deal of his early genius. But Tennyson, as a young man, had the heavier burden to bear. The fourth of twelve children, he was the son of the Reverend George Tennyson, rector of Somersby in Lincolnshire. The Tennysons were an ill-omened family. George Tennyson, disappointed by the unsympathetic treatment he had received from his father, a prosperous local notability, who preferred a younger son (afterwards the Right Honourable Charles Tennyson d'Eyncourt M.P.), became a lonely alcoholic; while, of the poet's brothers, Edward grew incurably insane; Charles (Alfred's favourite) was addicted to opium; Frederick proved a rebellious eccentric; and Arthur periodically took to drink. Nor did Septimus turn out very well. He had inherited some kind of nervous disease; and Rossetti used to describe how, when he visited the family, a huge dusky man rose from the heart-rug where he had been lying prone, with the words 'I am Septimus, the most morbid of the Tennysons', uttered in a deep and solemn voice.

Such was the depressing background of the poet's early life. But he escaped, temporarily at least, in 1828, when he and his brother Charles, with whom, during the course of the previous year, he had published a volume entitled *Poems by Two Brothers* – despite the title, Frederick had also contributed – went up to Trinity College, Cambridge. There he produced a second volume, *Poems chiefly Lyrical*, and made a number of important friends. The dearest of these was Arthur Hallam, a brilliant and attractive youth, for whom he developed a deep romantic affection. Having left Cambridge in 1831, Tennyson was obliged to return to Somersby; and in December 1832, he issued a third volume of *Poems* – only 450 copies were printed – which included 'Oenone', 'The Lotos-Eaters', 'Mariana in the South' and 'The Palace of Art'. Then, in September 1833, he heard the news of Hallam's death abroad. It was a violent and shocking blow. But, after Hallam's body had been brought home and buried beside the Severn, Tennyson felt able to return to literature; and in 1834 he began his first Arthurian poem, the 'Morte d'Arthur' and worked on *In Memoriam*, a splendid tribute to the friend he had lost, which appeared at length in 1850. It was the two-volume collection of his verses, new and old, published in 1842, that eventually brought

(*Above top*) Tennyson in 1840; portrait by S. Lawrence.

(*Above*) The old bard; portrait by G.F. Watts; painted in 1873.

him fame. Meanwhile, he had suffered a severe financial reverse, which reduced him to the verge of nervous breakdown. In 1845, however, the Prime Minister, Sir Robert Peel, granted him a pension of £200 a year; and in 1850, after a long engagement – protracted even by Victorian standards – he married the patiently devoted Emily Sellwood. In 1847 he had suffered a further collapse, which required expert medical attention; but 'the peace of God', he wrote in later life, 'came into my life before the altar when I wedded her'.

Peace, alas, does not always encourage the development of an imaginative writer's gifts; and *Maud* – which he himself considered his best work, and into which, his grandson and biographer, Sir Charles Tennyson, tells us, he had 'thrown the whole passion of his being' – was probably his last poem to breathe a spirit of adventure and mark a forward step in his poetic progress. It appeared in 1855; but by that time he had already published an 'Ode on the Death of the Duke of Wellington' and his often-quoted 'Charge of the Light Brigade', and was fast becoming an official poet. The opening series of *The Idylls of the King* – a later edition was prefaced with an obituary tribute to the Prince Consort – came out in 1859; and in 1862 he was presented to the widowed Queen herself, who remained a keen admirer. He took his duties as the Laureate seriously; and he was no less serious in his celebration of the Victorian domestic virtues. Though he never lost his verbal artistry, the series of poems that he continued to produce have a curiously static air. He stood firm on a solid foundation of talent; as an imaginative artist, he had ceased to grow.

The poems by which we remember him best are usually the most despondent. For the great prophet of Victorian optimism, who wrote so reverently of the mysterious ways of Providence and so appreciatively of modern Progress, was a natural melancholic; and melancholy would appear to have been the element in which his genius felt at home. 'His imagination,' writes a recent biographer, Professor Christopher Ricks, 'responded most deeply to the doubtful and dismaying'; and, in 'The Lotos-Eaters', his subject is the supreme futility of the human effort. Here we observe, too, the extraordinarily acute eye that he brought to bear upon the world around him, whether he is describing the waterfalls that stream from the mountainous ramparts of the Lotos-Eater's paradise, or noticing that even the palest face looks dark against a sunset sky:

(*Opposite*) One of Gustave Doré's illustrations to *Idylls of the King*; the body of Elaine is ferried to King Arthur's stronghold.

> A land of streams! some, like a downward smoke
> Slow-dropping veils of thinnest lawn, did go;
> And some through wavering lights and shadows broke,
> Rolling a slumbrous sheet of foam below.
> They saw the gleaming river seaward flow
> From the inner land; far off, three mountain-tops,
> Three silent pinnacles of aged snow,

> Stood sun-set flushed; and, dew'd with showery drops,
> Up clomb the shadowy pine above the woven copse.
>
> A land where all things always seem'd the same!
> And round about the keel with faces pale,
> Dark faces pale against that rosy-flame,
> The mild-eyed melancholy Lotos-eaters came.

No less pensive, and no less exquisitely detailed, is his romantic poem, 'Mariana', where the landscape he depicts is the desolate fen country around his father's house:

> With blackest moss the flower-pots
> Were thickly crusted, one and all:
> The rusted nails fell from the knots
> That held the pear to the gable-wall.
> The broken sheds look'd sad and strange:
> Unlifted was the clinking latch;
> Weeded and worn the ancient thatch
> Upon the lonely moated grange . . .
>
> About a stone-cast from the wall
> A sluice with blacken'd waters slept,
> And o'er it many, round and small,
> The cluster'd marish-mosses crept.
> Hard by a poplar shook alway,
> All silver-green with gnarlèd bark:
> For leagues no other tree did mark
> The level waste, the rounding gray . . .
>
> All day within the dreamy house,
> The doors upon their hinges creak'd;
> The blue fly sung in the pane; the mouse
> Behind the mouldering wainscot shriek'd,
> Or from the crevice peer'd about.
> Old faces glimmer'd thro' the doors,
> Old footsteps trod the upper floors,
> Old voices call'd her from without . . .
>
> The sparrow's chirrup on the roof,
> The slow clock ticking, and the sound
> Which to the wooing wind aloof
> The poplar made, did all confound
> Her sense; but most she loathed the hour
> When the thick-moted sunbeam lay
> Athwart the chambers, and the day
> Was sloping toward his western bower . . .

Probably his richest poem, though not the best organized – he had worked on it over a period of sixteen years – is *In Memoriam*, the long series of carefully-wrought quatrains that he addressed to the beloved memory of Arthur Hallam. He and his friend had been brothers, and more than brothers:

> But thou and I are one in kind,
> As moulded like in Nature's mint;

> And hill and wood and field did print
> The same sweet forms in either mind.

> For us the same cold streamlet curl'd
> Thro' all his eddying coves; the same
> All winds that roam the twilight came
> In whispers of the beauteous world.

Before he has reached the conclusion that his friend now 'lives in God', and that the universe, though apparently barren of meaning, must conceal a sustained creative purpose, he has moved through many darker phases. Either he must believe or completely abandon the struggle:

> Twere best at once to sink to peace,
> Like birds the charming serpent draws,
> To drop head foremost in the jaws
> Of vacant darkness and to cease

An ancient gramophone-disc – one of the earliest that was ever made – reproduces the rusty echo of Tennyson's voice intoning certain lines from *Maud*, for which he evidently had a deep affection. It is not, however, a wholly successful work, and is said to have 'bewildered' contemporary readers. The effort to write a complex drama in verse – he himself subtitled it 'A Monodrama' – employing so large a variety of metrical forms, presented many awkward problems; and the outline of the narrative itself is often somewhat difficult to follow. It was, none the less, a remarkably bold experiment; and the deep personal emotion with which he produced it can be felt throughout the poem. It includes, moreover, some magnificent Tennysonian images:

> None like her, none.
> Just now the dry-tongued laurels' pattering talk
> Seem'd her light foot along the garden walk,
> And shook my heart to think she comes once more;
> But even then I heard her close the door,
> The gates of Heaven are closed, and she is gone.

All the poems from which we have quoted above were written before 1856, when Tennyson was forty-five years old; but this is not to denigrate the quality of such works as *Tiresias* and *Locksley Hall Sixty Years After* which appeared respectively in 1885 and 1886, or, indeed, of his Arthurian *Idylls*. There, on the other hand, his astonishing virtuosity is often more apparent than his genius; and Professor Ricks believes that he can distinguish an inward conflict between the poet's literary self-confidence and a 'faint uneasiness about the extent to which the expertise is . . . purely verbal'.

Meanwhile, Tennyson had become the greatest poetic best-seller since the death of Byron. In 1884 he received a peerage, and lived on, honoured and courted, until October 1892. Physically, the Laureate was a tall and handsome figure, 'a fine, large-featured, dim-eyed, bronze-coloured, shaggy-headed man', wrote Carlyle, 'most restful, brotherly, solid-hearted', whose voice was 'musical, metallic, fit for loud laughter and piercing wail . . .' It is said that he enjoyed improper limericks; and the late T.S. Eliot used to quote a particularly outrageous specimen that Tennyson is reputed to have composed himself. He was also a port-drinker and heavy pipe-smoker; and his loudest wails were drawn from him when he travelled abroad and could discover no shop that sold decent English tobacco.

> Illyrian woodlands, echoing falls
>   Of water, sheets of summer glass,
>   The long divine Peneïan pass
> The vast Akrokeraunian walls,
>
> Tomohrit, Athos, all things fair,
>   With such a pencil, such a pen,
>   You shadow forth to distant men,
> I read and felt that I was there. . . .
>
> For me the torrent ever pour'd
>   And glisten'd – here and there alone
>   The broad-limb'd Gods at random thrown
> By fountain-urns; and Naiads oar'd
>
> A glimmering shoulder under gloom
>   Of cavern pillars; on the swell
>   The silver lily heaved and fell;
> And many a slope was rich in bloom
>
> From him that on the mountain lea
>   By dancing rivulets fed his flocks,
>   To him who sat upon the rocks,
> And fluted to the morning sea
>
> ('To Edward Lear, on his travels in Greece')

EDWARD FITZGERALD (1809–83) was among the very few English nineteenth-century poets who had the means to live a life of leisure, and to write or idle as it pleased him. His father was a Suffolk country gentleman; and Fitzgerald, after some years at Cambridge, where he met Tennyson and became the friend of Thackeray, also settled down in Suffolk. Some part of every year – at least until he had reached the age of sixty-two – he spent on the herring-lugger he had bought for a local fisherman 'knocking about . . . outside Lowestoft'. Otherwise his pursuits were sedentary. A great lover of music, books and flowers, he produced a Platonic dialogue, *Euphranor: A Dialogue on Youth*, and translations from the Greek and Spanish. During the fifties he took up the study of Persian, and, early in 1859, published his famous rendering of the *Rubáiyát of Omar Khayyám*, the collection of quatrains attributed to the Persian poet, mathematician and

Edward Fitzgerald, 1873; by Lady Rivett-Carnac.

philosopher who flourished during the latter half of the eleventh century. It attracted little immediate notice; only the enthusiasm it aroused in the Pre-Raphaelite brotherhood belatedly brought it to the general reader's attention. Today Fitzgerald is probably the best-known, and certainly the most often quoted, of all the minor English poets.

As a translation, the work has many defects. Some passages are oddly garbled. Thus, when the ancient Persian poet speaks of retiring to the wilderness, he asks not for 'a loaf of bread, a jug of wine' and an attractive singing girl, but for a leg of mutton and a handsome boy. Nevertheless, in his own peculiar terms, the translator recreated his original and endowed it with a new existence. He, too, would appear to have exhibited mildly paederastic tastes – his marriage, described as 'a cool affair', soon ended in an amicable parting; and he shared Omar Khayyám's gentle hedonism and his strain of vague reflective melancholy. No one could have been more disturbed than Fitzgerald when, at last, the *Rubáiyát* achieved fame. He was, above all else, a lazy, retiring character; and it seems appropriate that, on 14 June 1883, he should have died quietly in his sleep.

> Ah, Moon of my Delight who know'st no wane,
> The Moon of Heav'n is rising once again:
> How oft hereafter rising shall she look
> Through this same garden after me – in vain.
>
> And when Thyself with shining foot shall pass
> Among the guests star-scatter'd on the grass,
> And in the joyous errand reach the spot
> Where I made one – turn down an empty glass!

ARTHUR HUGH CLOUGH (1819–61) who was born at Liverpool, and spent part of his early youth in the United States, grew up under the sternly uplifting influence of the famous Dr Thomas Arnold. At Rugby, which he entered in 1829 and left in 1837, he distinguished himself not only as an industrious and gifted pupil, but also on the football-field. He then went up to Balliol with a scholarship in October 1837, and was soon taking part in the theological controversies provoked by the Tractarian Movement. John Henry Newman, one of the chief instigators of the Movement, now became his leading light. In 1842 he was elected fellow of Oriel. Yet, despite his apparent success, his inward existence was troubled by his grave religious doubts; and in 1848 he decided to resign his fellowship. He celebrated his resignation not with the theological pamphlet his friends expected, but with a humorous poem, *The Bothie of Tober-na-Vuolich*. That winter he was appointed Principal of University Hall at University College, London; and in 1849 he published his second long poem, a verse-letter entitled *Amours de Voyage*, written during the course of an Italian holiday. Later, on another holiday, he produced a poetic drama *Dipsychus*, which came out in 1850. Finally, having given up his post at University Hall and revisited America, Clough was appointed an examiner in the Education Office. In 1854 he made a happy marriage; but as his health began to break down beneath the strain of work, he was advised to go abroad. While in Europe, he wrote the *Mari Magno* poems, and he died in Florence on 13 November 1861. Matthew Arnold composed his threnody 'Thyrsis' – next to 'The Scholar Gipsy' probably his finest achievement – to commemorate Arthur Clough's death.

Until recently, Clough was often classed among the Victorian minor poets. He possessed, however, unusual literary virtues, including a vein of irony, as we see in his poem 'The Latest Decalogue', a modernized version of the Ten Commandments:

> Thou shalt have one God only; who
> Would be at the expense of two?
> No graven images may be
> Worshipped, except the currency:
> Swear not at all; for, for thy curse
> Thine enemy is none the worse:
> At Church on Sunday to attend
> Will serve to keep the world thy friend:
> Honour thy parents; that is, all
> From whom advancement may befall;
> Thou shalt not kill; but need'st not strive
> Officiously to keep alive:
> Do not adultery commit;
> Advantage rarely comes of it:
> Thou shalt not steal; an empty feat,
> When it's so lucrative to cheat:
> Bear not false witness; let the lie
> Have time on its own wings to fly:
> Thou shalt not covet, but tradition
> Approves all forms of competition.

Thanks to his concern with the central problems of his time, Clough's poetry has long been studied and appreciated by the historians of ideas. But today his verse itself has begun to attract critics; its experimental daring has been recognized, and he receives the attention he deserves. Thus *Amours de Voyage* was described not long ago as one of the high points of Victorian poetry. It is an elaborate speculative poem, written in hexameters – a metre that seems to suit its complex and ambiguous subject. Here Clough has adapted the letter-form, his hero being an intellectual Englishman, vexed by the same doubts that troubled the poet himself, who witnesses, during a leisurely visit to Rome, the French attack upon the Holy City. Like Clough, he remains a detached observer, seeking in vain for any kind of certitude:

Twelve o'clock, on the Pincian Hill, with lots of English,
Germans, Americans, French, – the Frenchmen, too, are protected, –

So we stand in the sun, but afraid of a probable shower;
So we stand and stare, and see, to the left of St Peter's,
Smoke, from the cannon, white, – but that is at intervals only, –
Black, from a burning house, we suppose, by the Cavalleggieri;
And we believe we discern some lines of men descending
Down through the vineyard-slopes, and catch a bayonet gleaming.
Every ten minutes, however, – in this there is no misconception, –
Comes a great white puff from behind Michael Angelo's dome, and
After a space the report of a real big gun, – not the Frenchman's! –
That must be doing some work. And so we watch and conjecture.

Amours de Voyage shows that its dubious and hesitant author was not (as some critics have suggested) a purely intellectual poet with little feeling for the use of language. Here his verse is vividly pictorial; and he draws a dramatic contrast between the movement of the battle and the spectators' paralyzed immobility. The poem is also a destructive examination of many types of modern myth. Each of them is considered; each, at length, is found wanting. Clough's vision of the 'strange disease of modern life' is as penetrative as that of Matthew Arnold.

The poet and critic MATTHEW ARNOLD (1822–88) was the son of Thomas Arnold, the famous headmaster of Rugby School, celebrated in *Tom Brown's Schooldays*. Matthew entered his father's school in 1837. As a boy he was humorous but aloof – his friends at Rugby nicknamed him 'Lofty Matt'; and in 1841, having won the school-prize for a poem, he went up to Oxford with a Balliol scholarship. There he became the friend of the poet Arthur Clough, who was already a Fellow of Oriel. After taking his degree, Arnold taught at Rugby while he waited to become a Fellow himself. After his election, he struck the Oxford world as something of a modern dandy, with his expensive well-cut clothes and fashionable love of all things French. His dandyism increased once he had been appointed Private Secretary to the Liberal peer, Lord Lansdowne. He was much sought after in London drawing-rooms, and exhibited a general air of frivolity and gaiety. His first collection of verses, *The Strayed Reveller and Other Poems*, appeared in 1849 under the initial 'A'; but reviewers paid little attention to the book, and only a very few copies were allowed to reach the public. His next employment was a good deal more onerous. In 1851, when Arnold decided to marry, Lord Lansdowne obtained for his clever young secretary an inspectorship of schools, a somewhat exhausting and depressing occupation. His second volume, *Empedocles on Etna, and Other Poems* came out in 1852, but was also unsuccessful; and, a year later, he published *Poems. A New Edition*, an assembly of all his previous work that he considered worth preserving, accompanied by a preface in which he set forth his ideas of poetic principle and practice. *Poems. Second Series*, followed in 1855, and *New Poems* in 1867. This was his last volume of poetry

Matthew Arnold, by
G.F. Watts.

– he felt that his inspiration had died down, partly no doubt, because his official work absorbed so much of his time and energy. Thereupon he turned to criticism, and issued the first series of *Essays in Criticism* in 1865 – a second series of the essays was published posthumously in 1888. His writings were now increasingly concerned with the problems of his own age; and the publication of *Culture and Anarchy* in 1869 at length established its author as an influential social critic. The subject of his latest works was the conflict that he sought to resolve between rational opinions and religious faith. He retired with a Civil List pension in 1883, and died suddenly, having overtaxed his heart while running for a Liverpool tramcar, on 15 April 1888.

Arnold's finest poems are always personal and elegaic. Thus, 'The Scholar Gypsy' laments the impossibility of realizing 'great actions' in a world overclouded by doubt and disillusionment. From the trials of modern existence he looks longingly back to a period of simple faith, of which his wandering scholar is the image:

> O born in days when wits were fresh and clear,
>   And life ran gaily as the sparkling Thames;
>   Before this strange disease of modern life,
> With its sick hurry, its divided aims,
>   Its heads o'ertax'd, its palsied hearts, was rife –
>   Fly hence, our contact fear!
> Still fly, plunge deeper in the bowering wood!
>   Averse, as Dido did with gesture stern
>   From her false friend's approach in Hades turn,
> Waves us away, and keep thy solitude!

The mood of the poem is one of pensive sadness, only relieved by glimpses of natural beauty and the imaginative joys of recollection. *Thyrsis*, which purports to be 'A Monody, to Commemorate the Author's Friend, Arthur Hugh Clough', follows much the same course. Here Arnold dwells with characteristic nostalgia upon the charm of the country round Oxford, which represents the happiness of youth, as he had experienced it in a fellow poet's company, far from 'the strange disease of modern life', with all its perplexities and inward struggles.

'Dover Beach', Arnold's most famous poem, written during his engagement at a seaside hotel, as he looked out across the ebbing waters, also reflects his yearning for the calm, self-confident religious faith that, despite his father's majestic example, he could somehow never quite achieve:

> . . . The Sea of Faith
> Was once, too, at the full, and round earth's shore
> Lay like the folds of a bright girdle furl'd.
> But now I only hear
> Its melancholy, long, withdrawing roar,
> Retreating, to the breath

Of the night-wind, down the vast edges drear
And naked shingles of the world.

Ah, love, let us be true
To one another! for the world, which seems
To lie before us like a land of dreams,
So various, so beautiful, so new,
Hath really neither joy, nor love, nor light,
Nor certitude, nor peace, nor help for pain;
And we are here as on a darkling plain
Swept with confused alarms of struggle and flight,
Where ignorant armies clash by night.

As a literary critic, though himself a product of Romanticism, Arnold objects to the intense subjectivity of his early nineteenth-century predecessors:

. . . the English poetry of the first quarter of this century, with plenty of energy, plenty of creative force, did not know enough. This makes Byron so empty of matter, Shelley so incoherent, Wordsworth even, profound as he is, yet so wanting in completeness and variety. . . .

Arnold's inclination, as we see from the essay he entitled 'The Study of Poetry', was always to discuss the art in terms of what it is *for*, in a specifically religious sense – an approach that entails the reduction of religion to those elements which it shares with certain kinds of poetry. It was a seminal idea, and has had an important effect upon many twentieth-century critics. *Culture and Anarchy*, Arnold's finest and least diffuse essay in social criticism, was the product of a stirring historical crisis, when England appeared to be threatened with the emergence of dangerous anarchical tendencies. Although he believed that in the organized working class he could detect a potential threat to the whole social system, the essayist's main concern was with spiritual anarchy; and *Culture and Anarchy* is an extended commentary on the closing lines of 'Dover Beach'. The essay is a lay sermon, aimed at the disadvantages of 'doing as one likes', enlivened by the essayist's mischievous humour and his elegant, ironic prose.

COVENTRY PATMORE (1823–96), though he must rank as a Victorian minor poet, possessed a remarkably original gift, which he showed not only in his choice of subjects but in his ingenious use of prosody. The son of an improvident London journalist, he published a collection of poems at the age of twenty-one and, two years later, with the help of Swinburne's friend, Richard Monckton Milnes, obtained a post in the Printed Books Department of the British Museum, where he continued to work for another two decades. In 1847 Patmore married. It was an extremely happy alliance, which inspired a long poetic eulogy, *The Angel in the House*, published as a whole in 1858, on the beauties of the married state. For Patmore there was always a mystic connection between human and divine love; and he attached a prefatory poem to explain his spiritual and literary purpose:

> The richest realm of all the earth
> Is counted still a heathen land:
> Lo, I, like Joshua, now go forth
> To give it into Israel's hand . . .

Emily Patmore's death in 1863 inspired a second collection of verses, *The Victories of Love*. A severe illness now drove the poet abroad. In 1864, he was converted to the Roman Catholic faith; and not long afterwards he remarried. To his new alliance, with a prosperous Catholic lady, we owe *The Unknown Eros and Other Odes*, a more complex version of his views on Christian matrimony, which appeared in 1877. In 1880, however, he lost the second Mrs Patmore; and next year he married his daughter's governess, a shrewd and attractive young person, said to have borne some resemblance to the youthful Becky Sharp. In later life, he became passionately attached to the celebrated poetess Alice Meynell. Patmore died on 26 November 1896. 'What about going to Heaven this time?' are reported to have been among his last words.

Patmore's finest poems are largely concerned with the history of his three marriages; and 'The Angel in the House' is built up of a series of delightful Victorian vignettes:

Coventry Patmore, by J. Sargent, 1894.

> I stood by Honor and the Dean,
> They seated in the London train,
> A month from her! yet this had been,
> Ere now without such bitter pain . . .
> The bell rang, and, with shrieks like death,
> Link catching link, the long array,
> With ponderous pulse and fiery breath,
> Proud of its burthen, swept away.

In later poems, his approach is more mystical, and his use of rhythm and imagery more sophisticated. One or two of his lyrics are rarely moving. But there is a touch of possessive egotism about Patmore's approach to his theme that often strikes a slightly jarring note. Thus, in his description of his beloved wife's death, he seems to reproach her beyond the grave for having left him so abruptly:

> Do you, that have nought other to lament,
> Never, my Love, repent
> Of how, that July afternoon,
> You went with sudden unintelligible phrase,
> And frighten'd eye,
> Upon your journey of so many days
> Without a single kiss, or a goodbye? . . .
> 'Twas all unlike your great and gracious ways.

Patmore's peculiar blend of spiritual and erotic imagery frequently recalls the work of Richard Crashaw; and his admirers, who included Gerard Manley Hopkins, felt that he was drawing close to – and perhaps had even crossed – a dangerous dividing-line; his association of Sacred and Profane Love was becoming slightly suspect. Patmore himself, a typical Victorian sage, opinionated, positive and self-centred, remained entirely unperturbed.

The reputation of GERARD MANLEY HOPKINS (1844–89) was entirely posthumous; his verse remained almost unknown until 1918. The son of a devout Protestant household, he went up to Oxford in 1863; and the years that he passed at Balliol were what Wordsworth, describing his own existence, had called 'the seed-time' of the poet's soul. In 1866 he was received into the Roman Catholic Church; and, having gone down, he stayed for a time with Newman at Birmingham, debating whether he should become a priest. In May 1868 he informed Newman that he had decided to join the Jesuit Order; and, in September, he entered Manresa House, Roehampton, where he began his long and arduous training. From Manresa, he moved on to Stonyhurst, but, after three years spent studying philosophy, he returned to Manresa as Professor of Rhetoric. Between 1874 and 1877, he was a student of theology at St Beuno's College in North Wales; and, while he was there, he learned that the ss *Deutschland* had run aground in the Thames Estuary with the loss of many lives.

(*Below left*) Gerard Manley Hopkins, aged fifteen; by Anne E. Hopkins.

(*Below right*) Photograph of Hopkins in 1880.

Among the dead were five Franciscan nuns, fleeing religious persecution. Hopkins, who since his youth had had an intense interest in poetry, was now persuaded by the rector of the college to break his seven years' silence. The result was 'The Wreck of the *Deutschland*', a startlingly original poem. It proved too original, however, for the editor of the Jesuit magazine to which it was offered; and he immediately refused it. In 1877 Hopkins was ordained, and embarked upon four years of priesthood. His duties took him to various parts of England; and he never found his duties easy. The large industrial cities of Lancashire he particularly detested; for there he observed shocking evidence of 'the hollowness of this century's civilisation'. In October 1881, he returned to Manresa for another period of seclusion, after which he became a teacher at Stonyhurst. And in 1884 he was elected classical fellow of the Royal University in Ireland. He died of typhoid in June 1889.

His Oxford friend, Robert Bridges, who afterwards became his literary executor, failed to appreciate the quality of Hopkins' verse. Its unorthodoxy alarmed him. He considered it perversely odd and obscure. Hopkins was prepared to admit that there might be something in his friend's objections:

No doubt my poetry (he wrote) errs on the side of oddness. I hope in time to have a more balanced and Miltonic style. But as air, melody, is what strikes me most of all in music, and design in painting, so design, pattern, or what I am in the habit of calling inscape is what I above all aim at in poetry. Now it is the virtue of design, pattern, or inscape to be distinctive and it is the vice of distinctiveness to become queer. This vice I cannot have escaped.

When Bridges published the poems in 1918, with an obviously unenthusiastic foreword, the public's lack of response suggested that his caution had been well-advised. It was not until the second edition, introduced by a more sympathetic editor, appeared in 1930, that Hopkin's gifts were generally discovered and acclaimed.

In his early works, Hopkins is clearly indebted both to Keats and to the pre-Raphaelite poets. But even here we notice an extraordinary use of rhythm and syntax, and an entirely original choice of imagery and diction. Take, for example, 'The Habit of Perfection':

> Shape nothing, lips; be lovely-dumb:
> It is the shut, the curfew sent
> From there where all the surrenders come
> Which only makes you eloquent
>
> Be shellèd, eyes, with double dark
> And find the uncreated light:
> This ruck and reel which you remark
> Coils, keeps, and teases simple sight.

In 'The Wreck of the *Deutschland*', Hopkins seems definitely to have broken with the poetic traditions of the past. The poem is a religious meditation on the relationship between Man and God. Here Hopkins was searching for a new form of imaginative expression that would revitalize the art of poetry. He uses conversational idiom, revives Anglo-Saxon words, employs assonance, internal rhyme, alliteration, and a complex rhythmic and linguistic method that he had derived from his study of Welsh poetry:

> Thou mastering me
> God! giver of breath and bread;
> World's strand, sway of the sea;
> Lord of living and dead;
> Thou hast bound bones and veins in me, fastened me flesh,
> And after it almost unmade, what with dread,
> Thy doing: and dost thou touch me afresh?
> Over again I feel thy finger and find thee.
>
> I did say yes
> O at lightning and lashed rod;
> Thou heardst me truer than tongue confess
> Thy terror, O Christ, O God;
> Thou knowest the walls, altar and hour and night:
> The swoon of a heart that the sweep and the hurl of thee trod
> Hard down with a horror of height:
> And the midriff astrain with leaning of, laced with fire of stress.

'The Wreck of the *Deutschland*', though a brilliant experiment, remains a strange and difficult production. Hopkins, we feel, has not quite mastered the novel poetic language he had invented for his own use, and the outline of the narrative is sometimes lost amid its dense linguistic convolutions. More typical of Hopkins are the sonnets that he wrote in 1877, such as 'God's Grandeur', 'The Lantern out of Doors' and 'The Windhover', his most celebrated poem, which evokes the flight of a falcon with persuasive skill:

> I caught this morning morning's minion, king-
> dom of daylight's dauphin, dapple-dawn-drawn falcon,
> in his riding
> Of the rolling level underneath him steady air, and
> striding
> High there, how he rung upon the rein of a wimpling wing
> In his ecstasy! . . .

His last 'dark' sonnets, records of an acute spiritual crisis, which rely less on elaboration and complexity, are among his most powerful and effective works:

> No worst, there is none. Pitched past pitch of grief,
> More pangs will, schooled at forepangs, wilder wring.
> Comforter, where, where is your comforting?
> Mary, mother of us, where is your relief?
> My cries heave, herds-long; huddle in a main, a chief
> Woe, world-sorrow; on an age-old anvil wince and sing –
> Then lull, then leave off. Fury had shrieked 'No lingering!
> Let me be fell: force I must be brief'.

> O the mind, mind has mountains; cliffs of fall
> Frightful, sheer, no-man-fathomed. Hold them cheap
> May who ne'er hung there. Nor does long our small
> Durance deal with that steep or deep. Here! creep
> Wretch, under a comfort serves in a whirlwind: all
> Life death does end and each day dies with sleep.

Hopkins was undoubtedly a great Victorian poet – if not the greatest as was once claimed. He has his limitations. His range is narrow; he was the poetic exponent of dogmatic Christianity, and concentrates on a single area of experience. Yet his modest output includes a handful of poems that stand alone in English nineteenth-century literature.

Francis Thompson; by Neville Lytton, 1907.

FRANCIS THOMPSON (1859–1907) belongs to the great tradition of English religious verse that began early in the seventeenth century; and, during his lifetime, his poems were much admired by Browning, Meredith and Coventry Patmore. The son of a doctor, a Roman Catholic convert, he was born at Preston in Lancashire, educated at Ushaw College and, after an unsuccessful attempt to study medicine, left for London, carrying, as almost his only luggage, volumes of Aeschylus and William Blake. It proved difficult to find work; and he was employed first by a second-hand-book-seller, then by a good-natured bootmaker. During his years of hardship, he became an opium-addict; but, in 1888, the editor Wilfred Meynell, husband of the poetess Alice Meynell, Coventry Patmore's last love, accepted two of his poems, 'Dream Tryst' and 'The Passion of Mary'; and the Meynells then adopted him and undertook his reformation. Thompson's *Poems* appeared in 1893; and in 1895 he published *Sister Songs*. He died of tuberculosis in 1907.

Thompson's verse is fervent yet dreamy, sensuous yet devotional; and, like Crashaw and Patmore, he often mingles the imagery of divine and human love. Among the poems he printed in 1893 was his most celebrated achievement, 'The Hound of Heaven':

> I fled Him, down the nights and down the days;
> I fled Him, down the arches of the years;
> I fled Him, down the labyrinthine ways
>   Of my own mind; and in the midst of tears
>   I hid from Him, and under running laughter.
>   Up vistaed hopes I sped;
>   And shot, precipitated,
> Adown Titanic glooms of chasmed fears,
> From those strong feet that followed, followed after.
>   But with unhurrying chase,
>   And unperturbed pace,
> Deliberate speed, majestic instancy,
>   They beat – and a Voice beat
>   More instant than the Feet –
> 'All things betray thee, who betrayest Me' . . .

The Pre-Raphaelite Poets

DANTE GABRIEL ROSSETTI (1828–82) was the son of a distinguished Italian exile, Gabriele Rossetti. Born in London, he began
to study painting about the age of fifteen and, three years later,
became a student at the Royal Academy. In 1849 he and his
friends, John Everett Millais and William Holman Hunt, established the so-called Pre-Raphaelite Brotherhood and planned a
magazine entitled *The Germ*, of which the opening issue appeared
on New Year's Day, 1850. The Pre-Raphaelites preached a
'childlike submission to nature'; they detested industrialism, wor-
shipped the Middle Ages, and admired above all else the earlier
Italian painters, for example Benozzo Gozzoli (1420–97), whose
'sweet humour' they appraised as positively 'Chaucerian'. At the
same time, Rossetti was writing verse; and it was in *The Germ* that
he published 'The Blessed Damozel', a poem that bears a striking
resemblance to one of his own more elaborate and decoratively
luscious pictures. Among the beautiful women with whom the
Pre-Raphaelites chose to surround themselves, and whom in their

From *The Germ*; Ford
Madox Brown's illus-
tration to a poem by
Rossetti.

Dante Gabriel Rossetti; self-portrait, 1847.

engaging idiom they had nicknamed 'Stunners', was a girl called Elizabeth, or Lizzie Siddall. Rossetti made her acquaintance in 1850, and married her in 1860. Early in 1862, she died a tragic and mysterious death; and, before her coffin was closed, he entered the room and slipped beneath her head the manuscript of his first collection of verses. There it remained until 1869, when the Home Secretary of the day allowed the papers to be disinterred. *Poems* appeared at last in 1870. But although they established the poet's reputation, they attracted the attention of an outraged moralist, Robert Buchanan. Rossetti was described as a modern literary Priapus, arch-exponent of 'the fleshly school of poetry'.

These attacks had hurt Rossetti deeply, and accentuated the bouts of depression, accompanied by insomnia and the dread of losing his eyesight, that had haunted him since Lizzie's death. He also had deeper troubles. Latterly, he had conceived a romantic passion for the wife of his dear friend, William Morris. She dominated his thoughts; and again and again the image of Jane Morris – lovely, languid and melancholy – emerges from the intricate background of his drawings and his pictures. Even his sister, the austere Christina Rossetti, became aware of Jane's pervasive influence:

> One face looks out from all his canvases,
> One selfsame figure sits or walks or leans:
> She found her hidden just behind those screens,
> That mirror gave back all her loveliness.
> A queen in opal or in ruby dress,
> A nameless girl in freshest summer-greens,
> A saint, an angel – every canvas means
> The same one meaning, neither more nor less . . .

('In an Artist's Studio', *New Poems*)

Rossetti's last years, spent at a large, old-fashioned house, No. 16 Cheyne Walk, in Chelsea, were disorderly and overclouded. A succession of model-mistresses, including Fanny Cornforth, whom her lover had affectionately nicknamed 'Jumbo', flitted through his darkened rooms; and his small garden was full of the strange animals he had taken to collecting. But as a remedy for his persistent insomnia, he had begun to drink chloral; and that insidious drug had destructive effects upon his health and mental balance. Soon he became a recluse, and rarely left his house, at least until the hours of darkness. Yet he continued to publish; and his last collection of verses, *Ballads and Sonnets*, which appeared in 1881, was widely discussed and generally praised. He suffered a paralytic stroke, and died on Easter Day, 1882.

Much of Rossetti's verse is too self-consciously 'poetic' to suit a twentieth-century taste. The fact that his talent was a hybrid growth – that he was half-English and half-Italian, and both an artist and a writer – may have had some effect upon his style. His

lengthy sonnet-sequence, *The House of Life*, though it contains many admirable lines, makes difficult reading at the present day. The idea of the poem often fails to separate itself from a web of literary language; the imagery is sumptuous yet strangely lifeless. Rossetti seems more interesting as a literary and artistic personage, one of the liveliest and most versatile of all the Pre-Raphaelite Brothers, than as an imaginative poet in his own right:

Photograph of the Rossetti family about 1864; Dante Gabriel, far left; Christina, on steps; William, far right. Taken by the Rev. C.L. Dodgson, better known as Lewis Carroll.

> Look in my face; my name is Might-have-been;
> I am also called No-more, Too-late, Farewell;
> Unto thine ear I hold the dead-sea shell
> Cast up thy Life's foam-fretted feet between;
> Unto thine eyes the glass where that is seen
> Which had Life's form and Love's, but by my spell
> Is now a shaken shadow intolerable,
> Of ultimate things unuttered the frail scream . . .

(Sonnet XLVI)

CHRISTINA GEORGINA ROSSETTI (1830–94), the last of Gabriele Rossetti's children and the younger of his two daughters, was born in Charlotte Street, Soho. She never went to school, but under the influence of an extremely bookish household she had begun to

write verses about the age of twelve, and, when she was only twenty, contributed a number of poems to *The Germ*. Her earliest collection of verses, *Goblin Market, and other Poems*, did not appear until 1862; and for the next thirty years, despite the numerous illnesses from which she suffered – the worst being a rare and painful malady known as 'exopthalmic goitre' – she maintained a fairly steady output. Her standard was high; there seems no doubt that she was a more gifted poet than her brother, Dante Gabriel, at once more sensitive and more various in her use of words and images. Her emotional range, however, was always narrow; two dominant themes pervade her work; her own deep-rooted sense of frustration and the keen spiritual longings of her 'naturally Christian' soul. A mysterious attachment to a man who could not, or would not return her love – his identity has never

(*Above*) Christina Rossetti; portrait by her brother Dante Gabriel.

(*Right*) *Goblin Market*; title page design by D.G. Rossetti.

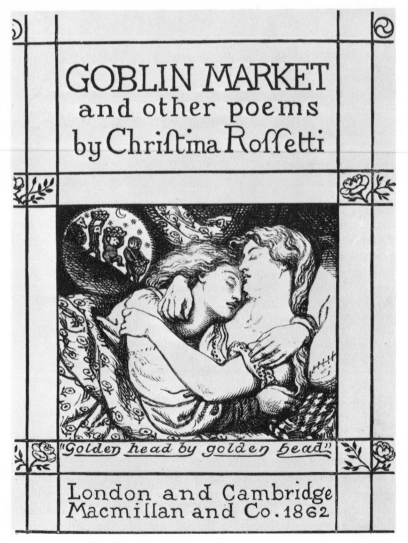

been established, though it is supposed that he may have been a minor member of the Pre-Raphaelite group – seems to have thwarted her entire existence. After the death of her widowed mother and her aunt, with whom she had settled down at 30 Torrington Square, she very seldom left home except to worship at a neighbouring Anglican church. On her death in December 1894, Swinburne composed her funeral elegy, and Edward Burne-Jones designed her monument.

Christina Rossetti's pensive and haggard features, like those of Elizabeth Siddall and Jane Morris, helped to form the Pre-Raphaelite idea of the perfectly beautiful and romantic woman. Her talents also had a distinctly Pre-Raphaelite cast; she, too, adored the Middle Ages and all the delusive visions that they conjured up in the imaginations of the Brotherhood. But she was a genuinely original poet; not only did she carry on the great tradition of seventeenth-century religious verse, but she produced some of the most poignant love-poems written by a woman during the Victorian Age. Her masterpiece, nonetheless, is neither a love-lament nor a record of her passionate religious feelings.

Goblin Market, composed at the outset of her career, is a long poetic fairy-tale that gives imaginative expression to a deep spiritual and moral conflict – the struggle between innocence and experience, between the claims of unsullied maidenly virtue and the rebellious attractions of the flesh. The symbolism of the poem is so closely knit, its stream of fantastic imagery so swift and smooth, that the effect it produces is difficult to illustrate in a single brief quotation. Here, however, is a description of the goblin merchants – strange as the creatures of a medieval bestiary – who offer the two young girls their evil fruit:

> One had a cat's face,
> One whisked a tail,
> One tramped at a rat's pace,
> One crawled like a snail,
> One like a wombat prowled obtuse and furry,
> One like a ratel tumbled hurry skurry.
> She heard a voice like voice of doves
> Cooing all together:
> They sounded kind and full of loves
> In the pleasant weather.
>
> Laura stretched her gleaming neck
> Like a rush-imbedded swan,
> Like a lily from the beck
> Like a moonlit poplar branch,
> Like a vessel at the launch
> When its last restraint is gone.
>
> Backwards up the mossy glen
> Turned and trooped the goblin men,
> With their shrill repeated cry,
> 'Come buy, come buy' . . .

Buy from us with a golden curl

The pictures with which Dante Gabriel embellished early editions of *Goblin Market* are among his finest drawings; and, when he assembled his private menagerie at Cheyne Row, an 'obtuse and furry' wombat, it is interesting to remember, was one of the animals he most valued.

Of all his Pre-Raphaelite associates, WILLIAM MORRIS (1834–96) was not only the most versatile and energetic, but possessed the most engaging character. The son of a prosperous London businessman, he was educated at Marlborough and Exeter College, where he met the artist Edward Burne-Jones; and, having taken his degree, he joined the Oxford offices of the Gothic-revivalist architect G.E. Street. It is said that an early visit to the Great Exhibition of 1851 had already had a profound effect upon his mind. The grotesque ugliness of many of the objects displayed under Paxton's mighty glass roof had astonished and appalled him; and he had formed the conclusion that between art and modern industry there now existed a disastrous gulf, which was rapidly widening as the years went by; 'your manufacturers become base', he wrote at a later period, 'because no well educated person sets hand to them'. Morris was not only a born reformer, but a generally creative spirit. When he was twenty-one, he had begun to write verse; from architecture he moved on to painting; and in 1861 he founded his own firm, which, besides decorating the walls of its clients' houses, was prepared to equip them with furniture, tapestry and even stained glass. Meanwhile in 1857 he had met Dante Gabriel Rossetti; and Rossetti had invited him to join the band of brothers who had been invited to embellish the Oxford Union. Together they produced a series of frescoes illustrating scenes from Malory's *Morte d'Arthur*. Owing to their technical inexperience, their pictures very soon faded. But the artists enjoyed themselves. 'What fun we had!' remembered one of them. 'What jokes! What roars of laughter.'

Enjoyment, indeed, was the keynote of the gospel that William Morris preached and practised. 'One can't get much enjoyment out of life at this rate', he remarked, discussing the kind of daily work through which the vast majority of his fellow men were obliged to earn a livelihood. And the more numerous his occupations, the more enjoyable he found them. If an artist, he said, could not compose an epic poem, weave a tapestry on a handloom, and talk at the same time with his friends and children, he must be a very poor creature. Latterly, he extended his interests to the field of book-production; and after Kelmscott Manor, the beautiful little ancient house that he had bought in Oxfordshire, near Lechlade, he named his newly-founded Kelmscott Press, fount and origin of many splendid volumes. Kelmscott, for a while, was also Rossetti's home. In 1859 Morris had married the Pre-Raphaelite beauty Jane Burden; but, so far as we can tell,

(Opposite) Goblin Market; illustration by D.G. Rossetti.

Rossetti's latter-day passion for Jane did nothing to disturb their friendship. 'Topsy,' as the Pre-Raphaelites had nicknamed Morris, was a naturally generous and unsuspicious man. He was 'pure gold', Ruskin once declared; and his magnificent physical appearance corresponded to his character. He was broad and burly; his beard and whiskers bristled 'like pine needles'; and his hair, particularly when he grew indignant, rose into a 'burning crest'.

Morris had always shared Ruskin's conviction that art could not be dissociated from politics, morality and religion. This belief was at length to make him a Socialist; and between 1884, when he formed the Socialist League, and 1889 when, having broken with the extreme Left Wing of the group, he unwillingly resigned control, he was a courageous champion of the British Labour movement. 'Fellowship is life,' he had once declared, 'lack of fellowship is death.' Morris was a Socialist of the most romantic and idealistic kind; he had little use for the political doctrinaire. 'To speak quite frankly,' he admitted to an audience of working-men, 'I don't know what Marx's theory of value is, and I'm damned if I want to know!' Moreover, although some of his later books, such as *A Dream of John Ball* and *News from Nowhere*, have a definitely propagandist aim, he combined his socialism with a

nostalgic cult of the past, and with a passionate admiration for the art and literature of the English Middle Ages. His first book, *The Defence of Guenevere*, published in 1858, revealed his love of the Arthurian legends; and ten years later, prefacing *The Earthly Paradise*, a loosely-linked series of poetic stories, he enjoined his reader to turn from the harsh industrial present towards his own imaginative – but, it must be admitted, almost wholly delusive – picture of medieval London:

One of the typographical triumphs of the Kelmscott Press.

> Forget six counties overhung with smoke,
> Forget the snorting steam and piston stroke,
> Forget the spreading of the hideous town;
> Think rather of the pack-horse on the down,
> And dream of London, small and white and clean,
> The clear Thames bordered by its gardens green . . .

Morris had an extraordinarily large output, which latterly included translations of the primitive Icelandic sagas. His last major poem, *Sigurd the Volsung*, came out in 1876; his last prose romance, *The Well at the World's End*, appeared in 1896. He died that same year, on 3 October, after a visit to the Arctic coast of Norway. Neither as a poet nor as a prose-writer did Morris reach the highest summits. His talents were too diffuse; his wide-ranging enthusiasm made it difficult for him to achieve the proper degree of intellectual concentration; and his worship of a legendary antique past gives his work, even at its best, a somewhat archaistic air. It has 'dated', like his famous furniture and tapestries. Yet both in literature and in the applied arts he must still be regarded as a genial master-craftsman.

ALGERNON CHARLES SWINBURNE (1837–1909) appeared in the literary heavens like a meteor, then dropped to the earth, where he lay dimly and contentedly smouldering for another three decades. The son of a British admiral, grandson through his mother of the Earl of Ashburnham, he had a comfortable and well-protected childhood; but neither at Eton nor at Balliol did he do his family much credit; and he was obliged to leave Oxford before he had taken a degree. Swinburne now settled down in London as an independent man of letters – though 'settled down' may be scarcely the proper phrase; for, until he had finally retired to the suburbs, he lived an extraordinarily agitated life, writing, declaiming, quarrelling, carousing and pursuing the peculiar erotic pleasures to which his temperament inclined him. His nervous energy seemed all the more remarkable in a man so small and frail. There was something pathetically childlike about the poet's whole appearance. His limbs were perpetually jerking and fluttering; and his huge head, above a slightly receding chin, was crowned by an aureole of wild red hair. At the age of twenty-five, Swinburne made a deep impression upon a young American visitor, Henry Adams, who describes him in his autobiography – 'a tropical bird, high-crested, long-beaked, quick moving, with rapid utterance and screams of humour . . . a crimson macaw among owls'. Swinburne's first major work, *Atalanta in Calydon*, for which he had borrowed the scheme of a Greek tragedy, though its tone was anything but classical, appeared in 1865, and immediately captivated John Ruskin. It was 'the grandest thing', he pronounced, 'ever yet done by a youth – though he is a Demoniac youth'. Its 'power of imagination and understanding simply sweeps me away . . . as a torrent does a pebble. I'm *righter* than he is – and so are the lambs and the swallows, but they're not his match.'

Equally torrential was the effect of *Poems and Ballads: First Series*, which he published next year. Swinburne was now in full spate; and the violent impact of his verse convulsed his readers. Some responded with delight – at Oxford, we are told, undergraduates would walk arm-in-arm up the High Street loudly chanting his most provocative passages – others with intense disgust; and John Morley, statesman and literary historian, abused him as 'the libidinous laureate of a pack of satyrs'. For not only was Swinburne a frankly erotic poet, but the type of eroticism he favoured was seldom discussed, or even allowed a reference, in Victorian society. Through his friend Richard Monckton Milnes,

Algernon Charles Swinburne; caricature of the author of *Songs Before Sunrise*; by 'Ape' in *Vanity Fair*.

who possessed the largest collection of 'rare and curious' books in Europe – and was accustomed to remark of himself, 'Oh! how wide is the diapason of my mind, from what a height to what a depth!' – Swinburne had become acquainted with the works of the notorious Marquis de Sade; and Sade's influence had helped to confirm his own sado-masochistic leanings. In his imagery, pleasure and pain are always closely interwoven; and, as a young poet, he boldly enlarged on themes no other English writer had yet dared to handle. *Poems and Ballads: First Series* marks the highest point of Swinburne's literary achievement. There was then a gradual falling-off. A devoted disciple of Giuseppe Mazzini, he was passionately attached to the cause of European freedom; but his collection of revolutionary poems, *Songs Before Sunrise* (1871), contains more rhetorical rodomontade than genuine poetic eloquence.

Portrait of Swinburne, by G.F. Watts.

During the 1870s, Swinburne's bodily health, undermined by his increasing alcoholism, threatened to collapse completely; and in 1879 Theodore Watts-Dunton, a good-natured associate of the Pre-Raphaelites, removed him from his London rooms, where he was lying almost helpless, to a quiet suburban villa. At 'The Pines' on Putney Hill, Swinburne passed the remainder of his long existence. He did not cease to write; his collected works, which include three poetic dramas, *Chastelard* (1865), *Bothwell* (1874) and *Mary Stuart* (1881), as well as lyrics, narrative poems and learned critical essays, make up a large array of solid volumes. Like other Victorian poetic dramatists, he did not really understand the stage; and even *Chastelard* is seldom acted. As a literary critic, he had the advantage of prodigiously extensive reading; but although at times a remarkably acute judge – he paid, for instance, a magnificent tribute to William Blake's *Marriage of Heaven and Hell* – if he failed to appreciate an author, he often took refuge in vituperation. At the same time, his personal opinions hardened. In 1888 he broke his friendship with Whistler, and solemnly attacked and renounced the aesthetic doctrine of 'Art for Art's Sake'.

No one but a man of genius, T.S. Eliot declared, 'could dwell so exclusively and consistently among words as Swinburne. His language is not, like the language of bad poetry, dead. It is very much alive . . .' Swinburne's employment of words, however, is more vigorous than sensitive. He does not shrink from absurdly awkward rhymes – 'statue' and 'at you' is a particularly odd example – and relies on the headlong rush of his verse, the immediate sensuous effect it produces, rather than on its cumulative shades of meaning. He lacked Tennyson's exquisitely observant eye. Among French poets, his idol was Charles Baudelaire, whom he celebrated in one of his finest later poems, 'Ave Atque Vale'; but he had none of Baudelaire's poignant insight into the essential tragedy of human life or his command of the unforgettable image. Much of Swinburne's verse is merely decorative – here he resem-

bles his fellow Pre-Raphaelite poets; and he shared Rossetti's
enthusiasm for recreating the legendary medieval past:

> I served her in a royal house;
> I served her wine and curious meat.
> For will to kiss between her brows,
> I had no heart to sleep or eat.
>
> Mere scorn, God knows she had of me,
> A poor scribe, nowise great or fair,
> Who plucked back his clerk's hood to see
> Her curled-up lips and amorous hair.

'The Leper', from which this quotation is drawn, was especially
praised by Eliot, and has a simplicity and dramatic directness not
often found among other poems. Elsewhere, he does not develop
his ideas so much as allow them to proliferate, until the basic
outlines of his theme are lost beneath a gathering weight of words.
An artist, the French critic Joseph Joubert once insisted, should
combine a natural facility with 'an acquired difficulty'; and
Swinburne never acquired that difficulty, or learned to restrain
and analyze his prodigious gifts of self-expression. The self he
expressed is always boldly obtrusive; and whether he evokes the
Empress Faustina, enjoying the cruel pleasures of the Circus –

> Nets caught the pike, pikes tore the net;
> Lithe limbs and lean
> From drained-out pores dripped thick red sweat
> To soothe Faustine . . .
>
> All round the foul fat furrow reeked,
> Where blood sank in;
> The circus splashed and seethed and shrieked
> All round Faustine.

– or recalls the melancholic Emperor Julian looking forward to the
supremacy of a martyred Christian Saviour –

> Thou hast conquered, O pale Galilean; the world has grown
>   grey from thy breath;
> We have drunken of things Lethean, and fed on the fullness of death.

– the voice we hear is invariably Swinburne's; he cannot escape
from the magic circle of his own obsessive fantasies. The extravagant turn of the poet's private character was at once his greatest
asset and his chief defect. Everything he set out to do, he over-did;
and because, like Shelley, he had a lifelong passion for the ocean,
he claimed to have swum further out across the English Channel,
and ventured deeper into dangerous submarine caverns, than his
most athletic friends. That aspect of his character, too, is reflected
in his poems, notably in 'Laus Veneris'. Through the claustral
atmosphere that envelops his literary Venusberg, we catch a
sudden sound of winds and waves:

> Ah yet would God this flesh of mine might be

Where air might wash and long leaves cover me,
Where tides of grass break into foam of flowers,
Or where the wind's feet shine along the sea.

The Aesthetic Movement

Robert Browning died in 1889, Alfred Tennyson in 1892; and
with them ended the great age of Victorian poetic literature. But
the last decade of the nineteenth century produced a crop of
rewarding minor poets. All were more or less indebted to contemporary French writers, particularly to Paul Verlaine (1844–96),
who had first sponsored the idea of literary 'decadence', celebrated
the *'poètes maudits'* – poets condemned by the age in which they
lived both to rebellion and to self-destruction – and insisted that
the art a poet practised was both its own justification and its own
reward. Meanwhile, among English writers, Oscar Wilde set out
to popularize the gospel of aestheticism that Walter Pater had
originally preached. 'Not the fruit of experience, (Pater suggested)
but experience itself, is the end . . . What we have to do is to be
for ever curiously testing new opinions and courting impressions,
and never acquiescing in a facile orthodoxy'. The writers of the
'Nineties' had the support of such artists as James McNeill
Whistler (1834–1903) and the brilliant young draughtsman
Aubrey Beardsley (1872–98) in whom the doctrine of 'Art for
Art's Sake' found its ablest exponents; and between the covers of
two short-lived magazines, *The Yellow Book* and its successor *The
Savoy*, artists, poets and prose-writers for some years met on
common ground. Amateurs of 'strange sensations' and, at times,
of curious passions, like the French 'decadents' they were determined to *épater le bourgeois*, to appal and electrify the middle classes.

OSCAR WILDE (1854–1900), arch-prophet of the aesthetic movement, was one of the greatest literary showmen of the English
nineteenth century; and, though his gifts were comparatively
slight, he displayed them with all the panache of a man of genius.
Born in Dublin, the son of a well-known medical specialist and a
pretentious minor poetess who had adopted the pseudonym
'Speranza', Wilde distinguished himself both at Trinity College,
Dublin, and at Magdalen College, Oxford. Once he had gone
down, he plunged into popular journalism and made adventurous
lecture-tours through the United States, where he preached the
gospel of 'Art for Art's Sake', and astonished his audiences both by
his long ambrosial locks and by his velvet breeches and his silk
stockings. At home, he became the type of intransigent modern
aesthete, and gained some useful publicity as the absurd protagonist of Gilbert and Sullivan's operetta *Patience*. In 1884 he married a
pretty, self-effacing young woman, who duly bore him two sons.
Their London house, which Wilde proceeded to equip with nicely

Oscar Wilde two years before his marriage; etching by James Edward Kelly.

chosen modern furnishings, became a citadel of advanced contemporary taste; and in 1892 *Lady Windermere's Fan* brought him the fashionable acclaim that he had always needed.

It was followed by *A Woman of No Importance* in 1893; *An Ideal Husband* in 1895; and, during the same year, by his memorable comedy *The Importance of Being Earnest*. While it was still enjoying a successful run, disaster overtook the dramatist. His infatuation for the young Lord Alfred Douglas – a 'gilded pillar of infamy', as his friend affectionately described him – involved him in a violent quarrel with Lord Alfred's father, the brutal Marquess of Queensberry, which led to a libel action, and, eventually, to Wilde's prosecution and conviction under the Criminal Law Amendment Act. Found guilty of homosexual practices, he was condemned to two years' hard labour. He emerged from prison a ruined and broken man, and, after a period of fruitless exile, died in an obscure Paris hotel at the beginning of the new century. On the eve of the disaster that overwhelmed him, Wilde admitted to his young friend André Gide that he had put his talent into his works, but reserved his genius for his life. He was an inimitable conversationalist; and we are told that his plays and tales and poems were poor reflections of his impromptu verbal triumphs. As dramatist, novelist and poet, he was very largely imitative. Except for his last comedy, all his plays, though laced with glittering veins of wit, are commonplace in thought and structure. His novel *The Picture of Dorian Gray* was partly based on J.K. Huysmans' *A Rebours*. His lyrical poems echo Baudelaire and Verlaine; and, of *The Ballad of Reading Gaol*, he himself wrote that he thought 'bits of the poem very good . . . but I will never again out-Kipling Henley'. As for *De Profundis*, addressed to Lord Alfred Douglas, which he intended as a dignified apologia, and of which his literary executor allowed only the most edifying passages to appear in print, it is spoiled by a certain basis shallowness and by the acrimonious and self-justificatory tone in which he describes his former friend. *The Importance of Being Earnest* alone can claim to be a genuine work of art. A comedy, he said, 'written by a butterfly for butterflies', it shows him as a true descendant of Congreve, with a modern sense of fun. Neither in literature nor in life was tragedy his natural element. His role was not to plumb the depths of feeling, but to flicker delicately across the surface.

Most of the poets of the 'Nineties' were doomed figures; for example, LIONEL JOHNSON (1867–1902), who had developed his aestheticism and his homosexual tastes during his last two years at Winchester. He then went up to New College, where he immediately fell under Walter Pater's influence. At Oxford, his diaphanous good looks and air of grave distinction charmed his fellow undergraduates; and, on going down, he joined 'The Rhymers' Club', an association founded by W.B. Yeats, which met at 'The Cheshire Cheese' off Fleet Street, and had Ernest Dowson and Arthur Symons among its best-known members. In 1891 Johnson was converted to the Roman Catholic faith. But, meanwhile, he had become a desperate alcoholic; and, his consumption of whisky having risen to a couple of pints a day, he eventually died after falling from his chair – the accident fractured his skull – in a London public house. His lines 'By the Statue of King Charles at Charing Cross' certainly deserve quotation:

> Sombre and rich, the skies,
> Great glooms, and starry plains.
> Gently the night wind sighs;
> Else a vast silence reigns . . .
>
> Comely and calm, he rides
> Hard by his own Whitehall.
> Only the night wind glides:
> No crowds, nor rebels, brawl . . .

as does the following extract from one of his devotional poems:

> Dark Angel, with thine aching lust
> To rid the world of penitence:
> Malicious Angel, who still dost
> My soul such subtle violence!
>
> Because of thee, no thought, no thing,
> Abides for me undesecrate:

Dark Angel, ever on the wing,
Who never reachest me too late!

When music sounds, then changest thou
Its silvery to a sultry fire:
Nor will thine envious heart allow
Delight untortured by desire.

ERNEST DOWSON (1867–1900) was another product of what
Yeats in his autobiography called 'the tragic generation'. He
shared Verlaine's taste for absinthe, the notorious '*sorcière glauque*',
and experimented briefly with drugs, including hashish. His
greatest emotional experience seems to have been the passion he
conceived for the very young, and entirely unresponsive daughter
of a Soho restaurant-keeper, the heroine of his most famous poem,
'*Non sum qualis eram bonae sub regno Cytherae*':

(*Below left*) Ernest
Dowson; sketch by
C. Conder.

(*Below right*) Dowson's
Pierrot; frontispiece by
Aubrey Beardsley, 1897.

Last night, ah, yesternight, betwixt her lips and mine
There fell thy shadow, Cynara! thy breath was shed
Upon my soul between the kisses and the wine;
And I was desolate and sick of an old passion,
    Yea, I was desolate and bowed my head:
I have been faithful to thee, Cynara! in my fashion.

All night upon mine heart I felt her warm heart beat,
Night-long within mine arms in love and sleep she lay;
Surely the kisses of her bought red mouth were sweet;
But I was desolate and sick of an old passion,
    When I awoke and found the dawn was grey:
I have been faithful to thee, Cynara! in my fashion.

I have forgot much, Cynara! gone with the wind,
Flung roses, roses riotously with the throng,
Dancing, to put thy pale lost lilies out of mind;
But I was desolate and sick of an old passion,
    Yea, all the time, because the dance was long:
I have been faithful to thee, Cynara! in my fashion. . .

ARTHUR SYMONS (1865–1945), though a graceful and accomplished versifier, who wrote, with the same wistful eroticism, of the chance adventures of the night and the 'Juliets' he met upon the London pavements, is less interesting as a poet than as a literary critic and historian. His *Symbolist Movement in Literature* (1899) first introduced English readers to Rimbaud, Corbière and Laforgue, and would appear to have had an important effect upon the youthful T.S. Eliot.

Arthur Symons as an old man; portrait by R.H. Sauter, 1935.

8

Twentieth-Century Epilogue

'This dreadful gruesome New Year, so monstrously numbered,' wrote Henry James to a woman friend on 1 January 1900. Other observers seem to have experienced very much the same feelings. The century had begun under gloomy auspices, with calamities abroad and a sense of unrest at home. The South African war was less than three months old; but the British forces engaged had already suffered sharp reverses; and, though staunch Imperialists like Rudyard Kipling might defend the justice of the British cause, Lord Salisbury's government, and the bellicose line it pursued, had been fiercely attacked by many liberal thinkers. Meanwhile, there were very few signs of change in the English literary landscape; and the first fourteen years of the new century were, from most points of view, a prolongation of the late-Victorian epoch.

Not until 1914 did a break with the past occur, and novelists and poets enter a period of increasing tension and anxiety, an age of 'repeated shocks' – to borrow Matthew Arnold's phrase – that has continued ever since. Both poetry and fiction were radically transformed between World War I and World War II; poets finally shook off the influence of their Romantic predecessors, and novelists like Joyce and Virginia Woolf did their best to destroy the rigid framework of the orthodox Victorian novel, and substitute for the accepted method of narration a less constricting mode of narrative that would reveal not only a character's actions and his day-to-day relationships but the mysterious recesses of his unconscious mind and the secret storehouse of the human memory. Thus, the novel has tended to become more poetic; and modern verse, with its emphasis on 'wit' and argument, evidently a little more prosaic. The process has not yet ceased; and, before the century ends, it will no doubt have developed even further. The English language is a wonderfully elastic medium, which owes its splendid expressive powers to a millenium of thought and effort.

The Novel

During the first fourteen years of the twentieth century, English fiction continued to derive its standards from a small group of eminent Victorian novelists. Among these, the oldest, Thomas Hardy, had written his last novel, *Jude the Obscure*, five years before the century began; while one of the youngest, H.G. Wells, having already made a name with his brilliant scientific fantasies, in 1900 was just entering his most productive period, when, determined to 'figure as a novelist pure and simple', he would produce his finest realistic books. The cumulative influence of their work was strong. Together they formed a solid block of professional literary expertise.

THOMAS HARDY (1840–1928), the son of a builder and master-mason, was born near Dorchester, Dorset, and educated first at the village school, afterwards at Dorchester High School. In 1856 he was articled to an ecclesiastical architect, and about this period met the Dorset poet, WILLIAM BARNES (1801–86), who kept a school not far from the architect's office. He was also encouraged and assisted by the family of a local clergyman. Besides studying French and Latin, he then began to read the Greek Testament, and, as a result of the various problems it raised, gradually lost his Christian faith. In 1862 Hardy moved to London, where he worked under the well-known architect Reginald Blomfield on the restoration of ancient English churches. He was still undecided whether to become an architect himself or to try his fortunes as a writer. But, his literary efforts having impressed George Meredith, he produced an exciting novel, entitled *Desperate Remedies*, a deliberate bid for popular success, which appeared anonymously in 1872. His second novel, *Under the Greenwood Tree* (1872), was well received; and, two years later, he published *Far From The Madding Crowd* as a serial in *Cornhill Magazine*, at that time edited by Leslie Stephen, the future father of Virginia Woolf. The book brought him popular renown; and, during the same year, Hardy married a clergyman's niece named Emma Gifford. Among his next novels were *The Return of the Native* (1878), *The Mayor of Casterbridge* (1886), *The Woodlanders* (1887), *Tess of the D'Urbervilles* (1891) and *Jude the Obscure* (1895). *Tess*, the story of an innocent village-girl, who gives birth to a bastard child and eventually murders her middle-class seducer, shocked the English reading-public; while *Jude*, the tale of an ambitious young man, whose aspirations towards the life of the spirit are frustrated both by his own shortcomings and by the relentless pressures of modern society, caused an even greater scandal. Its reception so disgusted Hardy that he abandoned novel-writing and set to work on *The Dynasts*, a long ambitious epic-drama; and his last period was devoted to the writing of verse. His wife died in 1912; and in 1914 he remarried. His old age was serene and dignified; and many literary pilgrims made their way to Max Gate, the gaunt and ugly house that he had built himself. He died early in 1928, and was buried in Westminster Abbey.

Thomas Hardy in 1922; portrait by W.W. Ouless.

'Dick Dewy'; illustration to *Under the Greenwood Tree*, 1876.

The finest of Hardy's novels are those which have a Dorset background and describe the characters and landscapes that the novelist had loved since boyhood. They reflect the changing conditions of rural society, as the development of urban industrial life slowly transforms the existence of the placid shires. This theme, which first emerges in *Under the Greenwood Tree*, is treated with yet stronger emphasis in *Far from the Madding Crowd*. Here Bethsheba, a quick-witted country girl, tantalized by her dreams of city-life, finds that she must choose between three very different suitors, a squire, a shepherd and a dashing soldier, the latter a plausible representative of the far-off London world. *The Return of the Native* presents another side of 'Wessex', as Hardy chose to call Dorset – the dark, hostile region of Egdon Heath and the traditional way of life it symbolizes. Hardy's presentation of the Heath is a particularly impressive feature of his book. In *The Mayor of Casterbridge* he returns to a similar conflict – between the old world and the new. But it is in *The Woodlanders* that Hardy introduces one of his most enduring characters – Marty South, an embodiment of rustic virtues, and of the simple community from which she springs, a small group of sturdy self-reliant villagers, 'rooted in one dear perpetual place'.

Tess of the D'Urbervilles, despite its obvious imperfections, is probably Hardy's masterpiece. It contains much of his best writing, as well as some of his worst, and reveals his fatalistic view of a hostile universe, where men and women cannot control their destinies, but are obliged to follow the commands of a destructive demiurge – styled by Hardy 'the President of the Immortals' – at its darkest and its crudest. Poor Tess's misfortunes are too numerous to be altogether credible; the tragic and ironic elements of her story are considerably over-simplified. Yet Tess herself, in her relations with the natural world, remains a touching and commanding figure:

The outskirt of the garden in which Tess found herself had been left uncultivated for some years, and was now damp and rank with juicy grass which sent up mists of pollen at a touch; and with tall blooming weeds emitting offensive smells – weeds whose red and yellow and purple hues formed a polychrome as dazzling as that of cultivated flowers. She went stealthily as a cat through this profusion of growth, gathering cuckoo-spittle on her skirts, cracking snails that were underfoot, staining her hands with thistle-milk and slug-slime, and rubbing off upon her naked arms sticky blights which, though snow-white on the apple-tree trunks, made madder stains on her skin; thus she drew quite near to Clare, still unobserved of him.

Jude the Obscure was fiercely attacked by reviewers, and solemnly burnt by an indignant bishop. It was Hardy's handling of his hero's sexual life – which today seems modest and reticent enough – that had especially offended them. Again, the novel is an uneven piece of work; the dialogue is forced; there are many ponderous locutions and passages of heavy moralizing. Yet the total effect is dramatic; and Hardy's portrait of a lonely, ill-starred man lives on in the reader's imagination.

The sense of tragic loneliness that pervades *Jude the Obscure* reappears in Hardy's verse. It is deceptively unpretentious, concerned with such age-old subjects as the transience of human life, but enlivened by the poet's gift for catching the beauty of the moment. Often memories of the past arise to colour the sensations of the present day:

> Hereto I come to view a voiceless ghost;
>   Whither, O whither will its whim now draw me?
> Up the cliff, down, till I'm lonely, lost,
>   And the unseen waters' ejaculations awe me.
> Where you will be next there's no knowing,
> Facing round about me everywhere,
> With your nut-coloured hair,
> And gray eyes, and rose-flush coming and going.

Yes; I have re-entered your olden haunts at last;
　　Through the years, through the dead scenes I have tracked you;
What have you now found to say of our past –
　　Scanned across the dark space wherein I have lacked you?
Summer gave us sweets, but autumn wrought division?
　　Things were not lastly as firstly well
　　With us twain, you tell?
But all's closed now, despite Time's derision.

I see what you are doing: you are leading me on
　　To the spots we knew when we haunted here together,
The waterfall, above which the mist-bow shone
　　At the then fair hour in the then fair weather,
And the cave just under, with a voice still so hollow
　　That it seems to call out to me from forty years ago,
　　　When you were all aglow,
And not the thin ghost that I now frailly follow!

Ignorant of what there is flitting here to see,
　　The waked birds preen and the seals flop lazily,
Soon you will have, Dear, to vanish from me,
　　For the stars close their shutters, and the dawn whitens hazily.
Trust me, I mind not, though Life lours,
　　The bringing me here; nay, bring me here again!
　　　I am just the same as when
Our days were a joy, and our paths through flowers.

('After a Journey')

Hardy's poetic idiom was idiosyncratic and, now and then, appears clumsy; but that apparent clumsiness, once the poem has been grasped as a whole, serves to underline its meaning. '. . . *There is clarity . . . the harvest of having written* 20 *novels first*', wrote Ezra Pound, reviewing the collected edition of Hardy's poems, issued in 1937.

When the Present has latched its postern behind my tremulous stay,
And the May month flaps its glad green leaves like wings,
Delicate-filmed as new-spun silk, will the neighbours say,
'He was a man who used to notice such things'?

If it be in the dusk when, like an eyelid's soundless blink,
The dewfall-hawk comes crossing the shades to alight
Upon the wind-warped upland thorn, a gazer may think,
'To him this must have been a familiar sight' . . .

If, when hearing that I have been stilled at last, they stand at the door,
Watching the full-starred heavens that winter sees,
Will this thought rise on those who will meet my face no more,
'He was one who had an eye for such mysteries'?

And will any say when my bell of quittance is heard in the gloom,
And a crossing breeze cuts a pause in its outrollings,
Till they rise again, as they were a new bell's boom,
'He hears it not now, but used to notice such things'?

('Afterwards')

A far finer artist than Hardy, and a much more conscientious and deliberate craftsman, was HENRY JAMES (1843–1916) who, between 1902 and 1904, published the three most ambitious books of his later life, *The Wings of the Dove*, *The Ambassadors* and *The Golden Bowl*. His first important novel, *Roderick Hudson*, which appeared in 1876, is a comparatively simple and straightforward narrative; but, since its appearance, he had steadily enlarged his range and improved upon his literary method. James believed himself to be a realist; and what he called 'solidity of specification' was a quality he greatly valued; but he had also a poetic, even a romantic view of life; and realism alone would never have satisfied him or given him the scope he needed. The prefaces that, in 1906, he composed for a collected edition of his works contain the clearest statement of his principles; and, about the same time, his letters to H.G Wells, praising and criticizing Wells' productions, set forth his views with no less point and vigour. He had much admired *Kipps*, he said, as a succulent '*tranche de la vie*'; but the younger man, he knew, mistrusted art, and denigrated the type of 'artist who lives angrily in his stuffy little corner of pure technique'. James, on the other hand, held that only through art could human experience be raised to the height of imaginative literature. Not that he shunned life. 'For myself,' he told his correspondent, 'I live, live intensely and am fed by life, and my value, whatever it be, is my own kind of expression of that'. And elsewhere: art '*makes* life, makes interest, makes importance'; for, as he had already remarked in his preface to *The Spoils of Poynton*, life was 'all inclusion and confusion', while art was 'all discrimination and selection'; and the artist's business was to extract the 'tiny nugget' of gold that he could then 'hammer into a sacred hardness'.

Henry James; portrait by J.S. Sargent, 1913; 'I live, live intensely and am fed by life . . .'

If James's prose-style, as seen in his last three books, tended to grow more and more obscure, it was because his constant attempts to achieve a greater clarity of vision put an undue strain upon the language. When he edited his collected works, besides equipping them with prefaces, he frequently rewrote the text; and, though the results were sometimes unfortunate, we observe how patiently he tried either to introduce a new facet, or to pare a story down to the essential outline. James was a born story-teller; but his method of telling a story became gradually less and less direct. His finest short stories belong to his middle period, among his masterpieces being *Daisy Miller* and *The Aspern Papers*, published in 1879 and 1888 respectively – the decade that saw the production of his greatest early novel, the *Portrait of a Lady*. His sales were never very large; and his efforts to write for the stage proved tragically unsuccessful. But his authority has increased with the passage of years, and can still be felt in the books of most of the novelists who succeeded him, from Conrad to Virginia Woolf. Nor has his subject-matter lost its appeal. 'The secret of his enduring fame', concludes his biographer Leon Edel, 'was a simple one: he had dealt exclusively with the myth of civilization; he had written about men and women and their struggle to control their emotions and passions within the forms and manners of society. He understood human motive and behaviour and was the first of the modern psychological novelists. He had carried his work into a high complexity, and he had endured because he had fashioned a style . . .' We cannot regard him, however, as primarily an artful stylist. James had developed a multitude of human contacts; he loved his fellow men, and loved and enjoyed the world in which they lived. His entire life-work, remarked G. K. Chesterton, was 'made out of sympathy; out of a whole network of sympathy'. He had a mordant wit and a keen satirical verve. Yet it is worth remembering that his last message to his young nephews was to advise them that they should 'be kind'.

Born in New York, the son of a distinguished philosopher and literary figure, Henry James settled down in England during the 1870s and became a naturalized Englishman soon after the outbreak of World War I. Before he died, he received the Order of Merit. His old age was passed in quiet and pleasant rooms, not far from the Carlyles' old house, overlooking the broad sweep of the Thames at Chelsea.

MILLY AND THE PORTRAIT

Once more things melted together – the beauty and the history and the facility and the splendid midsummer glow: it was a sort of magnificent maximum, the pink dawn of an apotheosis, coming so curiously soon. What in fact befell was that, as she afterwards made out, it was Lord Mark who said nothing in particular – it was she herself who said all. She couldn't help that – it came; and the reason it came was that she found herself, for the first moment, looking at the mysterious portrait through tears. Perhaps it was her tears that made it just then so strange and fair – as wonderful as he had said: the face of a young woman, all magnificently drawn, down to the hands, and magnificently dressed; a face almost livid in hue, yet handsome in sadness, and crowned with a mass of hair rolled back and high, that must, before fading with time, have had a family resemblance to her own. The lady in question, at all events, with her slightly Michelangelesque squareness, her eyes of other days, her full lips, her long neck, her recorded jewels, her brocaded and wasted reds, was a very great personage – only unaccompanied by a joy. And she was dead, dead, dead. Milly recognised her exactly in words that had nothing to do with her. 'I shall never be better than this'.

(The Wings of the Dove)

George Moore as the Sage of Ebury Street; by F. Dodd, 1932.

GEORGE MOORE (1852–1933), the unexpected product of a family of sporting Anglo-Irish gentry, was born at Moore Hall, County Mayo, and educated at a Roman Catholic school, but soon revolted against his Irish origins, and began his adult education – which was to occupy him for the next ten or fifteen years – first in London, then in Paris. He had originally hoped to become a painter; and, besides attending a famous Parisian art-school,

where he failed to make much headway, he frequented the great Impressionist artists, including Manet and Degas, who seem to have regarded the odd, inquisitive young Irishman, with his lank blond beard and pale protuberant eyes, as a slightly comic figure. He also fell under the influence of contemporary French story-tellers, Zola, Maupassant and the brothers Goncourt; and, having given up his hopes of succeeding in art, he determined that he would become a writer of the fashionable 'naturalist' school, and did his best to apply the new technique to a variety of English subjects. His early novels, now completely forgotten, are awkward, immature works; but in 1885 he published *A Mummer's Wife*, a painstaking, if uninspired account of the bohemian existence of the modern stage, and in 1894 *Esther Waters*, the portrait of an unfortunate servant-girl, that clearly owed something to the Goncourts' masterpiece, *Germinie Lacerteux* (1865). During the same period, he wrote a diverting autobiographical narrative, *Confessions of a Young Man* (1888), an unselfconscious self-portrait with romantic embellishments, which was followed by his better-written and even more entertaining volume of personal reminiscences, *Memoirs of My Dead Life* (1906). George Moore's character was a curious blend of self-assertion and humility. He spared no pains to improve his own talents, and once declared that he had started life as a literary invertebrate, but slowly, like some primitive organism, had acquired a solid sub-structure. He was never tired of probing and questioning and assimilating useful scraps of knowledge; and Oscar Wilde cracked an unkind joke about his habit of 'conducting his education in public'. Moore did not at length achieve maturity until he published his great autobiographical saga, *Hail and Farewell*, in three sections, *Ave*, *Salve*, and *Vale*, between 1911 and 1914, which relates how, disgusted by the events of the South-African War, he had bidden goodbye to England and tried to settle down again on Irish soil. There he joined Yeats, the visionary poet, 'A.E.', and Yeats' friend and patroness, Lady Gregory, in their bold efforts to revive the Irish drama. They found Moore an unco-operative ally; and *Hail and Farewell* gives a tragi-comic picture of his inevitable disillusionment. When he returned to London, he passed the remainder of his life, quietly and comfortably enough, at a modest house in Ebury Street. Since he published *Hail and Farewell*, he had developed into an accomplished stylist; but, although he wrote some excellent short-stories, the historical romances of his last period, such as *The Brook Kerith* (1916), *Héloise and Abelard* (1921) and *Aphrodite in Aulis* (1930), though carefully organized and finely phrased, are somewhat ponderous and artificial.

Moore's prose-style, achieved despite all the limitations against which he had had to contend, entitles him to a distinguished place among early twentieth-century English writers. Seen at its best in *Hail and Farewell*, it is easy, lively, smooth-flowing and often exquisitely humorous. He makes enchanting fun of himself, just as he delights to satirize his friends and cronies. His long musical sentences are expertly linked together with a grace that often conceals their underlying craftsmanship:

The quays were delightful that day, and I wished Yeats to agree with me that there is nothing in the world more delightful than to dawdle among seagulls floating to and fro through a pleasant dawdling light. 'But how is it, Yeats, you can only talk in the evening by the fire, that yellow hand drooping over the chair as if seeking a harp of applewood?' Yeats cawed; he could only caw that morning, but he cawed softly, and my thoughts sang so deliciously in my head that I soon began to feel his ideas to be unnecessary to my happiness, and that it did not matter how long the clerk kept us waiting. When he appeared he and Yeats walked on together, and I followed them up an alley discreetly remaining in the rear, fearing that they might be muttering some great revolutionary scheme. I followed them up a staircase full of dust, and found myself to my great surprise in an old library. Very like a drawing by Phiz, I said to myself, bowing, for Yeats and the clerk were bowing apologies for our

intrusion to twenty or more shabby-genteel scholars who sat reading
ancient books under immemorial spider webs.

JOSEPH CONRAD (1857–1924) was christened Teodor Jozef
Konrad Korzeniowski at Berdiczew in the Ukraine, the son of an
exiled Polish patriot. Though educated at Cracow and intended
for the university, since his boyhood he had longed to go to sea;
and in 1874 he travelled to Marseilles, whence, in June 1875 he
embarked as an ordinary seaman on a voyage to the West Indies.
After a series of dangerous cruises, smuggling arms between
Marseilles and the Spanish coast, he joined the English steamer
Mavis, and on 18 June 1878 first set foot on English soil. He knew
little English, and had equally little money; but he persisted in his
determination to become a British seaman; and by 1884 he had
gained his master mariner's certificate. Conrad spent the next
twelve years of his life on voyages around the world, accumulating
the strange experiences that he would later turn to literary profit.

In 1884, he changed his citizenship and, as a naturalized
Englishman, decided to take up writing. After his marriage to

Joseph Conrad, by W.
Rothenstein, 1903.

an Englishwoman in 1896, Conrad abandoned the sea, settled down near London and produced a series of romantic novels. *Almayer's Folly* (1895) was followed by *An Outcast of the Islands* (1896), *The Nigger of the Narcissus* (1898) and *Lord Jim* (1900). Despite appreciative reviews, his books had a fairly small sale. From the early months of 1903 until September 1904, he was hard at work on his most ambitious, and greatest novel, *Nostromo* (1904). Meanwhile, he found it difficult to earn a living; and of this period of his existence he would presently write, that he had laboured 'in a great isolation from the world', without amenities or consolations, 'a lonely struggle under a sense of overmatched littleness, for no reward that could be adequate, but for the mere winning of a longitude'. Nothing in his life disappointed him so much as his failure to appeal immediately to a wide public; and he was to write several more novels and tales – including *The Secret Agent* (1907), *A Set of Six* (1908), *Under Western Eyes* (1911), and *'Twixt Land and Sea – Tales* (1912) – before the publication of *Chance* in 1914 brought him popular success, and with it the end of his financial problems. His later works include *Victory* (1915), *The Shadow-line* (1917), *The Arrow of Gold* (1919), and *The Rescue* (1920) He died in 1924.

Apart from his romantic foreign origins, there are several aspects of Conrad's life and work that set him apart as a unique figure in the history of the English novel. While most novelists, who wrote at the same period, have by now undergone some measure of critical revaluation, his reputation has steadily increased; and this is due not only to the virtues of the style he hammered out – at first, though he wrote in English, he seems often to have thought in French, the language he had learned earlier – but to the nature of the themes he handled. A recurrent theme is that of initiation through ordeal, which he uses as a means of investigating the sources and sanctions of morality. In his tales of the sea, the naval tradition is identified with his concept of a moral system, supported by social collaboration and a firmly-established code of duties and responsibilities. Thus, in *Typhoon*, his hero is the courageous but wholly unimaginative Captain McWhirr. The Captain is not a thinking man; but it is his blind commitment to his duty that carries him and his crew through an exhausting and demoralizing storm at sea. *The Secret Sharer*, too, explores the limits of this simple naval discipline, and describes the relationship between law, training, society and the ordinary human affections. The young captain relies confidently upon that discipline, when a complex human situation is suddenly thrown up by the sea.

Conrad's development, from the writing of *Typhoon*, where man is confronted by a tremendous external threat that stimulates his powers of resistance, to the production of *Shadow-line*, where the threat comes as an inward collapse of the will that destroys the ability to plan and act, illustrates his gradual transition from a nineteenth- to a twentieth-century point of view. The shadow-line is the line between youth and maturity; and it is crossed only after a dramatic ordeal in which the young captain is tried and found wanting. The tale is presented with retrospective irony. An older man looks back on his youth; and, while he does so, he reveals the moral inadequacy of the code that he himself had once exemplified. Though the catastrophe was partly due to a predecessor's mis-conduct, his own spiritual unawareness has helped to bring about his fall.

It is impossible here to do more than scant justice to the richness and diversity of Conrad's novels. *Nostromo*, probably his finest work, has a particularly complex structure; the story is told from a succession of different standpoints, both in space and in time. Its theme is the conflict between moral idealism and 'material interests', the second being represented in the novel by the corrupting power of a load of silver that blights everyone it touches. The central crisis of the novel occurs when a lighter, bearing the silver, drifts out into the darkness of the placid Gulf. Nostromo, the picturesque hero-figure, is then abruptly made aware of the real function concealed by his public rôle, while Decoud, the sceptic, finally embraces nihilism. *The Secret Agent* has a London setting – a detective story in which Conrad shows the same grasp of his material as in his stories of the sea, and adds an even subtler insight. *Under Western Eyes* has a no less sombre tone. On the sur-face, an account of revolutionary intrigue, it develops into yet another penetrating study of individual isolation.

RUDYARD KIPLING (1865–1936) was born in Bombay, son of John Lockwood Kipling, a gifted anthropologist and artist. Like other Anglo-Indian children, he was presently sent back to England; but the guardians who undertook his care treated him with a sadistic harshness he could never forget or forgive; and, later, he was initiated into the rigorous tribal system of a minor English public school, where he learned what he would afterwards call 'the law of the jungle', but, before he left, having contributed to and edited the school-magazine, had decided he would become a man of letters. In 1882, Kipling returned to India, and joined the staff of the Lahore *Civil & Military Gazette*. His first book of verse, *Departmental Ditties*, satires on the life of the Indian Civil Ser-vice, appeared in 1886. It was followed, in 1888, by two volumes of Indian short stories, *Plain Tales from the Hills* and *Soldiers Three*, that immediately made his name; and, when he arrived in London a year later, after journeying home by way of America and the Far East, he found himself a well-known literary figure. *Barrack-room Ballads*, a second collection of poems, with a much broader and rougher subject than the first, came out in 1892; and, that same year, he married Caroline Balestier, a young American, the sister of a close friend who had lately died, and whose relations

(*Above left*) The middle-aged Kipling; profile by W. Strang.

(*Above right*) Kipling at the age of sixty-five.

Kipling seems to have accepted as a kind of moral legacy. He now moved to the United States and did his best to settle down in Vermont. There he remained until 1896, publishing further short stories, *Many Inventions* and *The Day's Work*, a novel, *Captains Courageous*, and his two celebrated *Jungle Books*, until an undignified dispute with the Balestier family drove the Kiplings back to England. In 1899, he suffered the most tragic experience – the loss of a daughter he adored; in 1900 he visited and described the South-African battlefields; and in 1901 he crowned his achievement as a novelist by publishing his greatest story, *Kim*. Kipling's later years were spent at the Sussex manor-house he had purchased, amid the fields and hills that provided the background for the romantic historical narratives he assembled in *Puck of Pook's Hill* and *Rewards and Fairies*. In 1907 he received the Nobel Prize for literature. Yet, despite his world-wide reputation and quiet, carefully organized domestic life, his last two books, *Debits and Credits* and *Limits and Renewals*, which appeared in 1926 and 1932, show the writer as a deeply troubled and more and more embittered man. The death of his only son, early in the First World War, was a blow from which he had never quite recovered. A host of fears and dark anxieties haunted his imagination; treachery, disease, madness and death were among the subjects that he now

Illustrations by the author
for his children's book,
Just So Stories, 1902.

described. Had Kipling been a young and unknown writer, the average publisher, one suspects, would have dismissed these stories as perversely morbid. *Something of Myself*, his posthumously published autobiographical sketch, suppresses more than it reveals. Rudyard Kipling emerges at the end of his life as a lonely and mysterious character. He died on 18 January 1936.

The first attempt to restore his standing as a poet was made in 1941, when T.S. Eliot edited his *Choice of Kipling's Verse*, with an enthusiastic introduction. There he pays tribute to Kipling's technical skill, his 'consummate gift of word, phrase and rhythm', and singles out for special praise some of his military ballads, such as the terrifying 'Danny Deever':

'What are the bugles blowin' for?' said Files-on-Parade.
'To turn you out, to turn you out', the Colour-Sergeant said.
'What makes you look so white, so white?' said Files-on-Parade.
'I'm dreadin' what I've got to watch', the Colour-Sergeant said.
'For they're hangin' Danny Deever, you can hear the Dead March play,
The Regiment's in 'ollow square – they're hangin' him today;
They've taken of his buttons off an' cut his stripes away,
An' they're hangin' Danny Deever in the mornin'.

'What makes the rear-rank breathe so 'ard?' said Files-on-Parade.
'It's bitter cold, it's bitter cold', the Colour-Sergeant said.
'What makes that front-rank man fall down?' said Files-on-Parade.
'A touch o' sun, a touch o' sun', the Colour-Sergeant said.
'They're hangin' Danny Deever, they are marchin' of 'im round,
They 'ave 'alted Danny Deever by 'is coffin on the ground;
An' 'e'll swing in 'arf a minute for a sneakin' shootin' hound –
O they're hangin' Danny Deever in the mornin'! . . .

'What's that so black agin the sun?' said Files-on-Parade.
'It's Danny fightin' 'ard for life', the Colour-Sergeant said.
'What's that that whimpers over 'ead?' said Files-on-Parade.
'It's Danny's soul that's passin' now,' the Colour-Sergeant said.
'For they're done with Danny Deever, you can 'ear the quickstep play,
The Regiment's in column, an' they're marchin' us away;
Ho! the young recruits are shakin', an' they'll want their beer today,
After hangin' Danny Deever in the mornin'!

Opposition to Kipling, both as a poet and as a prose-writer, has often been coloured by his opponents' political bias, and by the distaste that even an admirer may feel for the bigoted imperialism and arrogant chauvinism that disfigures so many of his early works. Thus Professor de Sola Pinto declares that his writings exalt the 'vulgar ethics of the crowd'; that, 'like the typical "man of action" of this period, he loved facts but hated and feared reality'; that he ignored 'the fundamental problems of the modern world', and asserted that 'all the world needed was more discipline, obedience and loyalty, and . . . a paternal British Empire . . .'. To this we can only object that mistaken ideas have frequently given birth to admirable works of art. 'If Kipling,' the present writer has suggested in another context, 'failed to become the great modern novelist, the "English Balzac" whom Henry James had foreseen and welcomed, if most of his stories are deformed, here and there, by inexplicable faults of taste and exasperating tricks of style . . . it was not because he had "wrong ideas" or had suffered disabling experiences during childhood . . . but because his genius, in the last resort, was curiously immature. He had known India as a very young man: his famous Indian stories have the clarity of a young man's vision, accompanied by its drawbacks. He simplified his view of life with the help of a schoolboy's code.'

Adult feelings were often beyond his grasp; there are strangely few references in the whole of Kipling's work either to the origins or to the effects of sexual passion. Many of his personages appear to be almost sexless; only in his last tales does he seek to penetrate some of the darkest vagaries of human conduct; and in one of his finest poems, 'McAndrew's Hymn', he describes an engineer's relationship with the machine he serves far more lovingly and elaborately than he had ever described a man's relations with a woman:

The crank-throws give the double-bass, the feed-pump sobs an' heaves,
An' now the main eccentrics start their quarrel on the sheaves:
Her time, her own appointed time, the rocking link-head bides,
Till – hear that note? – the rod's return whings glimmerin' through the
    guides . . .

Kipling remains, nevertheless, at least on his own somewhat restricted level, one of our greatest English story-tellers—a master of language who used the words he loved, not, like Henry James, to analyze his human subjects and establish their moral or their social background, but to fix an extraordinarily vivid impression of any scene he well remembered, with an economy, a precision and acute dramatic sense that immediately summons it up before the reader's eye, as in this description, taken from *Kim*, of the travellers along the Grand Trunk Road:

A solid line of blue, rising and falling like the back of a caterpillar in haste, would swing up through the quivering dust and trot past to a chorus of quick cackling. That was a gang of *changars* – the women who have taken all the embankments of all the Northern railways under their charge – a flat-footed, big-bosomed, strong-limbed, blue-petticoated clan of earth-carriers, hurrying north on news of a job, and wasting no time by the road. They belong to the caste whose men do not count, and they walked with square elbows, swinging hips, and heads on high, as suits women who carry heavy weights. A little later a marriage procession would strike into the Grand Trunk with music and shoutings, and a smell of marigold and jasmine stronger even than the reek of the dust. One could see the bride's litter, a blur of red and tinsel, staggering through the haze, while the bridegroom's bewreathed pony turned aside to snatch a mouthful from a passing fodder-cart. Then Kim would join the Kentish-fire of good wishes and bad jokes, wishing the couple a hundred sons and no daughters, as the saying is. Still more interesting and more to be shouted over it was when a strolling juggler with some half-trained monkeys, or a panting, feeble bear, or a woman who tied goats' horns to her feet, and with these danced on a slack-rope, set the horses to shying and the women to shrill long-drawn quavers of amazement.

H.G. WELLS (1866–1946), whose *Kipps*, despite its author's mistaken views about the art of writing, Henry James considered 'the best novel of the last forty years', had been brought up in Dickensian poverty, between a great English country house where his mother held the post of housekeeper, and his father's small suburban shop. From its basement-kitchen, a sharp, precocious little sandy-haired boy, he watched the feet of pedestrians as they trudged past across the pavement-grating, and noted that the soles of their boots were almost always worn through. Like Kipps, he was first apprenticed to a draper, but soon determined he would become a scientist, took courses at the Royal College of Science, and attended T.H. Huxley's lectures. Wells' scientific training left an indelible mark upon his mind; and his earliest successes – *The Time Machine* (1895), *The Invisible Man* (1897) and *The War of the World* (1898) – were earned in the field of science-fiction. Later he admitted that, during the early years of the new century, he had felt 'a craving to figure as a novelist pure and simple', and produced *Love and Mr Lewisham* (1900), *Kipps* (1905), *Tono Bungay* (1909), and *The History of Mr Polly* (1910), stories of modern life with a strong autobiographical colouring – particularly *Love and Mr Lewisham*, the account of an unhappy youthful marriage, and probably his best book. None of these novels is entirely satisfactory from a literary point of view. Though Wells had a fine Dickensian humour and wrote vigorous, effective prose, he lacked a controlling sense of style; and his attempt to strike a high romantic note, as in the love scenes of *Tono Bungay*, are frequently deplorable. Wells now became more and more concerned to propagate ideas, both in his novels and in his sociological and political treatises, and less and less concerned with art. His last books are difficult to re-read; they exhibit both his artistic and his intellectual limitations. There is a certain cocksureness about his critical method; the problems he examined, and boldly claimed to solve, were apt to seem so wonderfully simple viewed through H.G. Wells' eyes! Lenin, whom he met at the Kremlin, declared that this so-called Socialist was a typical *petit bourgeois*, and bore not the slightest resemblance to a genuine revolutionary. Yet he remains a liberator. 'Wherever a young man . . .' wrote J.B. Priestley, 'was determined to free himself from mental squalor, fear, and ignorance, there was Wells at his side, eager to instruct, startle and inspire'. His books may not be 'great literature'; but they had a profoundly stirring and liberating effect upon a whole generation.

H.G. Wells; pencil drawing by W. Rothenstein, 1912.

Unlike H.G. Wells, ARNOLD BENNETT (1867–1931) was concerned with the novel as a form of art. He produced one or two books into which he put his whole talent, and a multitude of pot-boilers. In the first category his finest achievements are *Anna of the Five Towns* (1902) and *The Old Wives' Tale* (1908). Both describe the life of the Potteries, the grim industrial region where Bennett had been born and brought up; and the latter traces the lives of two women from girlhood to death, and records the inexorable passage of time, as it affects their characters and circumstances. It is a naturalistic novel of the kind that nineteenth-century French novelists had already popularized; and his heroines themselves and their background are depicted in unsparing detail. Bennett's 'Clayhanger' novels – *Clayhanger* (1910), *Hilda Lessways* (1911), *These Twain* (1916) – have the same industrial setting. But, with *Riceyman Steps* (1923) he shifted his attention to a subfusc London scene. Impressive though his best work is, Bennett is seldom an entirely successful novelist, even on his own terms. His masters were Flaubert, Maupassant and the brothers Goncourt; but his appetite for wealth and popular celebrity often distracted his attention from the claims of pure literature.

Arnold Bennett, 1923, at the height of his success.

JOHN GALSWORTHY (1867–1933), shared Arnold Bennett's enthusiasm for the novel as a work of art. His most significant and original book, *The Man of Property* (1906), describes the destructive effects of property-worship on the relationships and capacity for love of individual men and women. Here he introduces the Forsyte family, a middle-class London clan united by bonds of mutual greed and hostility towards outsiders. They exist only through what they possess – through the lucrative alliances they contract and the comfortable fortunes they acquire. Galsworthy then enlarged on the plight of the Forsytes in a long series of novels, entitled 'the Forsyte Saga', beginning with *In Chancery* (1920), and concluding with *On Forsyte-Change* (1930), which he published ten years later. Meanwhile, the author's attitude was shifting; touches of sentimentality crept in; he was less inclined to disapprove. Once an astringent social critic, he developed into a prosperous best-seller; and, when 'the Forsyte Saga' was adapted for television, though it scored a tremendous public success, all its imaginative shortcomings were exposed to view.

John Galsworthy in later life.

Jamesian techniques were adopted by FORD MADOX FORD (1873–1939) whose fame as an enterprising editor and Conrad's devoted collaborator, has tended to obscure his achievement as a novelist. Like James, he was a dedicated literary craftsman; 'I am interested,' he once declared, 'only in how to write, and . . . I care nothing – but nothing in the world – what a man writes about'. His tetralogy of war novels – *Some Do Not* (1924), *No More Parades* (1925), *A Man Could Stand Up* (1926), *The Last Post* (1928) – is built around historical events; it covers a large and complex field, and is constructed with impressive artistry. It is the finest fictional record of the change and disruption brought about by the First World War. Also noteworthy is *The Good Soldier* (1915), a subtle study of intricate personal relationships.

Ford Madox Ford.

The majority of the novels of E.M. FORSTER (1879–1970) appeared before 1914 – *Where Angels Fear to Tread* (1905), *The Longest Journey* (1907), *A Room With a View* (1908), *Howards End* (1910). *Where Angels Fear to Tread* adumbrates the themes and manner of all his later works of fiction; a group of characters, whose mode of life has left them unfulfilled and restless, are brought into contact with a richer, more emotionally primitive civilization, that of Italy, in this particular tale. Two very different cultures are seeking to meet, and overcome the barriers of language; and their efforts broaden into a search for some wider and deeper form of communication. The problem of communication, both between races and between individual human beings, always fascinated E.M. Forster. Thus, in *Howards End* he shows English society broken up by a century of industrial 'progress', so that it has come to form two separate cultural levels, represented by the middle-class conformist Wilcoxes on one side, and by the intellectual Schlegels on the other. Forster's solution, however, is too vague and romantic to provide a satisfactory ending. Of Forster's comparatively small output, only *A Passage to India* (1924) can claim to be a major literary achievement. Again his subject is the necessity of communication and the difficulties that surround the task. Here, on the Indian subcontinent, the rational and practical British face a civilization more spiritual in its ways of thought, but also far more diffuse and weakly organized. Indian characters are often muddle-headed; their efficient and devoted British counterparts are shackled by an insular conservatism and, now and then, by sheer stupidity. At a moment of general crisis, the hero throws in his lot with the Indians, and is denounced as a traitor to his own race. The book has mystical undertones; the dead hostile echo that rumbles in the Marabar Caves, where Miss Quested has her strange adventure, suggests the existence of an alien world beyond the reach of ordinary human reason, and makes a profoundly disturbing impression upon three humdrum Western lives. Forster's novels have a diffident, slightly tentative approach; his native integrity appears to prevent him from hiding his private doubts and weaknesses, with the result that they seem to lack a vital strength. It was the same honest spirit that, after 1924, decided him to publish no more novels: 'I had been accustomed to write about the old-fashioned world,' he tells us, 'with its homes and family lives and comparative peace. All that went, and though I can think about the new world, I cannot put it into fiction.'

Portrait of E.M. Forster, painted about 1940 by Vanessa Bell.

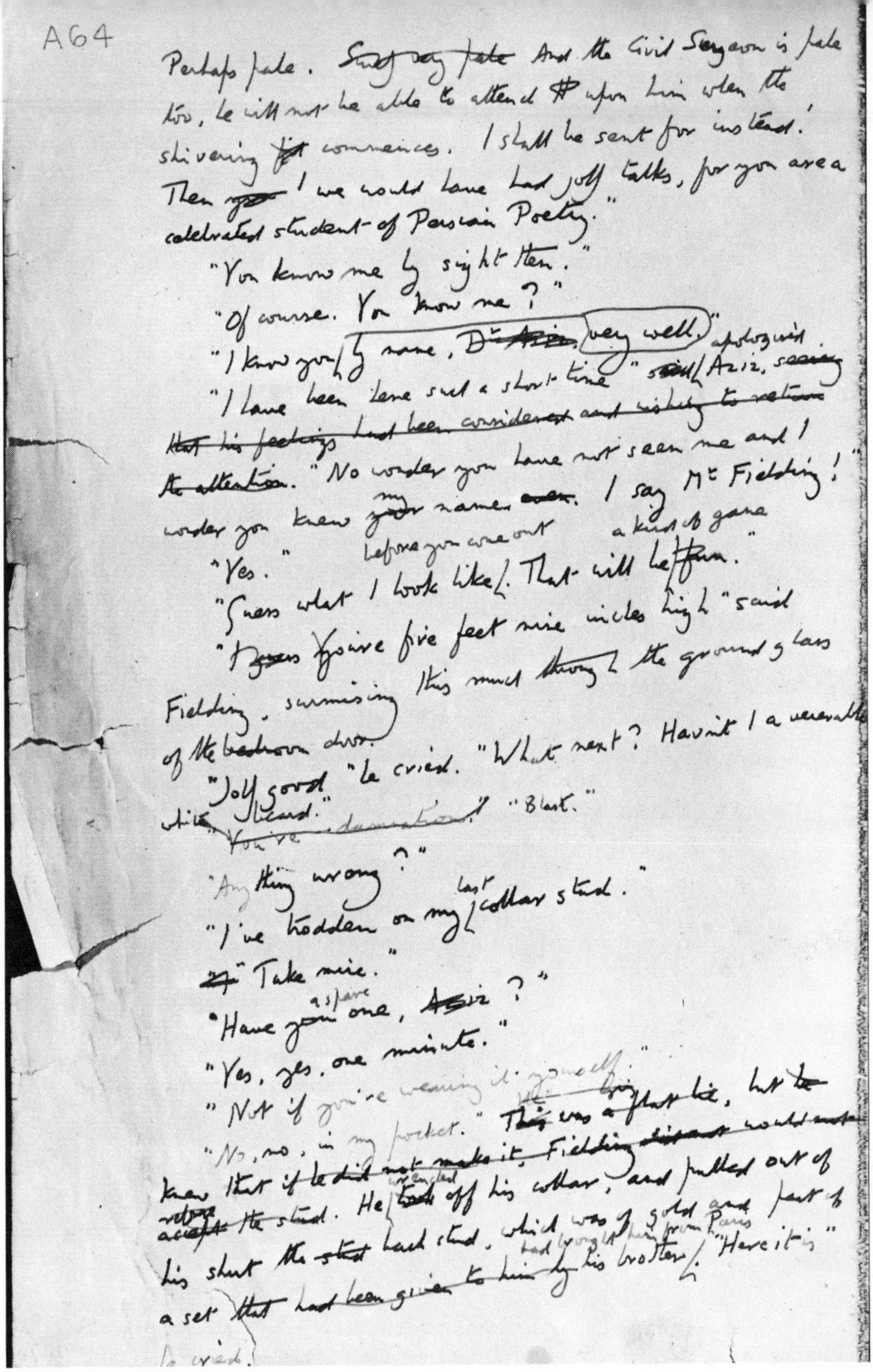

A64

[Manuscript facsimile — handwritten draft, best reading:]

Perhaps fale. ~~Surely say fate~~ And the Civil Surgeon is fale too, he will not be able to attend # upon him when the shivering fit commences. I shall be sent for instead.' Then ~~you~~ / we would have had jolly talks, for you are a celebrated student of Persian Poetry."

"You know me by sight then."

"Of course. You know me?"

"I know your~~ly~~ name, ~~Dr Aziz~~ very well," apologized.

"I have been here such a short time" ~~said~~ Aziz, seeing ~~that his feelings had been considered and wishing to return the attention.~~ "No wonder you have not seen me and I wonder you knew my~~your~~ names ~~over~~. I say Mr Fielding!"

"Yes."

"Guess what I look like. ~~before you are out~~ a kind of game That will be fun."

"~~I guess~~ You're five feet nine inches high" said Fielding, surmising this much through the ground glass of the bedroom door.

"Jolly good," he cried. "What next? Haven't I a venerable white beard." ~~You're~~ ~~damnation~~ "Blast."

"Anything wrong?"

"I've trodden on my last collar stud."

~~I~~ "Take mine."

"Have you a spare one, Aziz?"

"Yes, yes. one minute."

"Not if you're wearing it yourself."

"No, no, in my pocket." This was a flat lie, but he knew that if he did not make it, Fielding ~~distant would~~ accept the stud. He ~~took~~ off his collar, and pulled out of his shirt the ~~stud~~ back stud, which was of gold ~~and~~ part of a set ~~that had been given to him by his brother.~~ "Here it is"

he cried.

The New Novel

All these novelists had inherited the tradition of Victorian story-telling, with its solid characters and well-constructed plots. The advent of James Joyce and Virginia Woolf brings us to the era of the modern novel, which evokes the 'sentiment of reality' by subtler and more incalculable methods.

A page from the manuscript of *A Passage to India*.

JAMES JOYCE (1882–1941), was a single-minded artist. *Dubliners* (1914), his first prose-work, is a collection of relatively straight-forward stories, set in the dilapidated Dublin back-streets. Dublin is also the setting of his autobiographical novel, *A Portrait of the Artist as a Young Man* (1916), which describes the mis-adventures of his own youth and the conflict waged between a young man's romantic sensuality and the influence of a strict religious upbringing. The novel is concerned with Stephen Dedalus's mental and psychological processes. The world of the novel is filtered through Stephen's mind; and much of the narra-tive takes the form of an interior monologue, often apparently loose and aimless, but, in fact, carefully constructed around a succession of recurring motifs.

As early as 1914, Joyce had started work on the short story that, after eight years' labour, he transformed into his gigantic novel, *Ulysses* (1922). Again the background is his native city; the time is 16 June 1904; and Joyce re-lives the events of that summer day through the eyes of Leopold Bloom, his wife, Molly, and the same young Stephen Dedalus who had already figured in *A Portrait*. The story consists of a series of basic episodes, each chronicled by means of an interior monologue, and each typifying a separate character. Stephen's mind is that of a juvenile intellectual, packed with abstruse allusions to philosophy, literature and legend.

In eluctable modality of the visible: at least that if no more, thought through my eyes. Signatures of all things I am here to read, seaspawn and seawrack, the nearing tide, that rusty boot. Snotgreen, bluesilver, rust; coloured signs. Limits of the diaphane. But he adds: in bodies. Then he was aware of them bodies before of them coloured. How? By knocking his sconce against them, sure. Go easy. Bald he was and a millionaire, *maestro di color che sanno*. Limit of the diaphane in. Why in? Diaphane, adiaphane. If you can put your five fingers through it, it is a gate, if not a door. Shut your eyes and see.

Leopold Bloom, on the other hand, a canvasser for advertisements in a Dublin newspaper, is the personification of middle-aged mediocrity. His monologue is loose, unpredictable, but con-siderably less remote from life. At one point, Bloom attends a funeral:

Makes them feel more important to be prayed over in Latin. Requiem mass. Crape weepers. Blackedged notepaper. Your name on the altarlist. Chilly place this. Want to feed well, sitting in there all the morning in the gloom kicking his heels waiting for the next please. Eyes of a toad too. What swells him up that way? Molly gets swelled after cabbage. Air of the place maybe. Looks full of bad gas. Must be an infernal lot of bad gas round the place. Butchers for instance: they get like raw beef-steaks.

(*Opposite*) James Joyce; portrait by J.E. Blanche, 1935.

Molly Bloom, Leopold's lusty and faithless wife, who only appears in the novel when she lies supine upon her bed, is the sensual Earth

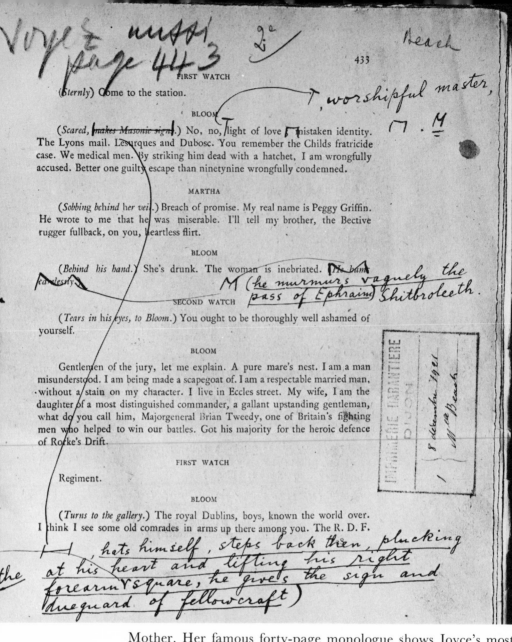

Page proof of *Ulysses*, with the author's corrections.

Mother. Her famous forty-page monologue shows Joyce's most ambitious use of the stream-of-consciousness technique, in which punctuation is abandoned, seemingly swept away by her incessant flow of thoughts and day-dreams:

> . . . frseeeeeeeefronnnng train somewhere whistling the strength those engines have in them like big giants and the water rolling all over and out of them all sides like the end of Loves old sweet sonnnng the poor men that have to be out all the night from their wives and families in those roasting engines stifling it was today Im glad I burned the half of those old Freemans and Photo bits leaving things like that lying around hes getting very careless and threw the rest of them up in the WC . . .

On the surface, *Ulysses* is a carefully-documented naturalistic novel with a very narrow and intense focus; but it includes a series of far deeper strains. Through its complex mythic and symbolic structure, it seeks to transcend its humdrum local background; and its chapters have been planned to correspond with the episodes of Homer's *Odyssey*. Thus Stephen Dedalus, Leopold Bloom and Molly are the modern counterparts of Telemachus, Ulysses and Penelope; and memories of the ancient epic serve to emphasize the greyness and squalor of early-twentieth century Dublin; so that Homer provides a commentary on the Edwardian wasteland. Many other allegories, correspondences and analogies emerge during the course of Joyce's crowded narrative; he had inherited Robert Burton's and Lawrence Sterne's taste for such learned paraphanalia. The result is puzzling, often exhausting. Yet *Ulysses* is less esoteric and perversely 'difficult' than it is sometimes said to be. The author's original intention was to write a comic novel; and as an essay in Rabelaisian comedy, planned and carried out on an heroic scale, it remains a masterpiece.

In *Ulysses*, Joyce's prose style, with its vast apparatus of linguistic and scholarly tricks, and its ingenious employment of learned allusions and quotations, had already begun to resemble a hermetic private language. In *Finnegan's Wake* (1939), a book that Joyce worked on for seventeen years, he carries the process even further. Here he abolishes not only punctuation, but also grammar, syntax and the accepted English vocabulary. It is a strangely original work, where every word, often made up of a number of complex puns, has a precise significance for the author. But the text cannot be read without a glossary; and, if the chief purpose of art is human communication, *Finnegan's Wake* fails to achieve its object. Though it includes magnificent passages of allusive verbal music, it is one of the most unreadable books in the history of modern writing. Joyce was an Irishman, who liked to regard himself as a European artist. He spent most of his adult life abroad, in the self-imposed exile that suited his peculiar creative methods.

Virginia Woolf as a young woman.

An experimental novelist who, in her very different way, invites comparison with James Joyce is VIRGINIA WOOLF (1882–1941). Her first novel, *The Voyage Out* (1915), is a fairly conventional narrative, but one that concentrates on the analysis of character rather than on plot and incident; and the same is true of *Night and Day* (1919). *Jacob's Room* (1922) was the novelist's first attempt to devise a wholly new technique, using a series of disconnected impressions, revealed by an internal monologue, to illuminate her hero's personality. This technique is handled with even greater assurance in *Mrs Dalloway* (1925), and with complete confidence in her most satisfying work, *To the Lighthouse* (1927). Here plot and story-line have been abandoned; unity and coherence are provided by the poetic elements of her subject, and by the elaborate organization of its imagery and symbolism. The restrictions of the novelist's method, however, become apparent in *The Waves* (1931), where pattern and significance are rather too obviously imposed and, despite beautiful passages, her prose is apt to seem a little too self-consciously 'poetic'. Of Virginia Woolf's minor works, *Orlando, a Biography* (1928), inspired by the authoress's devotion to her friend Victoria Sackville-West, in which she follows her hero-heroine through a succession of historic avatars, is certainly the most enjoyable.

D.H. Lawrence in 1920; by J. Juta.

D.H. LAWRENCE (1885–1930) was the son of a Nottinghamshire coal-miner, and grew up in a region, the legendary Sherwood Forest, where industry and agriculture have long existed cheek by jowl. Here pitheads rise amid fields and woodlands; the trees that surround the pits are faintly sooty; and this strange landscape, which he would describe again and again, had a deep and lasting effect upon the novelist's imagination. He was neither a true countryman nor a genuine proletarian; and each aspect of Lawrence's background added something to his literary character. So, indeed, did the contrast between his parents, his father being shrewd, opinionated, coarse; his mother 'a superior soul', who, besides teaching him to despise his father, fired her son with high ambitions. Not for him was the savage life of the pits; he left his ugly native village to become a London schoolmaster; and, at the age of twenty-seven, he carried off the offspring of an aristocratic German family, whom he eventually married on the eve of World War I. Thereafter David and Frieda Lawrence wandered half around the globe, always in search of some spiritual refuge that constantly eluded them. Lawrence developed tuberculosis, of which he died when he was only forty-five.

Lawrence's first novel, *The White Peacock*, appeared in 1911; and, though not a successfully constructed book, it shows his earliest attempts to depict and analyze forces that transcend mere 'personality'. *Sons and Lovers*, published in 1913, is a semi-auto-biographical narrative – the story of Paul Morel, and of his efforts to escape from his mother's overwhelming love into the freedom that he felt he needed. It establishes a number of the novelist's dominant themes – a man's longing to recognize and release the more primitive qualities of his own nature; the importance of restoring to sexual love its original harmony and dignity; and the artist's hatred of the modern industrialized world that destroys all warm spontaneous feeling. At the same time, *Sons and Lovers* is a realistic novel, which gives an extraordinarily vivid account of the divided Morel family. Of the *Rainbow* (1915) Lawrence himself said that, compared with his previous work, it seemed almost to have been written in another language. The scale is considerably less limited; from a single family, in a particular historical period, he moves on to examine a series of generations covering more than half a century. Taken as a whole, the novel presents the state of

"The Breach" took the place of Hell Row. It was a natural succession. Hell Row was a block of some half dozen thatched, ~~subsiding~~ collapsing cottages which stood back in the brook-course by Greenhill Lane. Eastwood had scarcely gathered consciousness when the notorious ~~Hell~~ Row was burned down. The village, was strewed *(spare, meagre and disintegrated)* rather forlornly over hills and the valley, ~~sparse, meagre, and disintegrated~~. Since the seventeenth century the people of Eastwood have scratched at the ~~earth~~ for coal. The old cottage rows along Green-hill Lane were built to accommodate the workers in the ~~old~~, little gin-pits, which were scattered about among the fields, beside Derby Road, and Nottingham Road, and Mansfield Road. To these vanished pits the pasture land in many parts owes its queer configuration. But fifty years ago the pits were busy, and in the four square miles round Eastwood there ~~was~~ perhaps ~~some~~ two or three hundred of ~~the~~ miners' cottages, old and mean, dabbed down

early twentieth-century England, where, as in Hardy's novels, we are shown the destruction of the traditional rustic ways of life. The first half of the book is written in a relatively straightforward style. But, later, the novelist adopts a very different literary mode; and we see him groping for words as he struggles to describe the shadowy life of the unconscious. His language is now mannered, with an insistent pounding rhythm and hypnotic repetition of the same words – 'dark', 'burning', 'fecund', 'hot', 'flow', 'fire', 'obliteration', 'laceration'. Detached from their context such passages are easy to ridicule. But where Lawrence avoids the private mystical jargon that frequently obscures his prose, he succeeds in conveying experiences that a less Dionysiac writer

Manuscript of the first page of *Sons and Lovers.*

might have failed to pin down. A particularly typical passage occurs in *The Rainbow*, when Ursula, walking in the rain and gloomily contemplating her own future, becomes aware of a herd of wild horses:

Yet now her way was cut off. They were blocking her back. She knew they had gathered on a log bridge over the sedgy dike, a dark, heavy, powerfully heavy knot. Yet her feet went on and on. They would burst before her. Her feet went on and on. And tense, and more tense became her nerves and her veins, they ran hot, they ran white hot . . .

Here the horses are a physical embodiment of the conflict within Ursula's mind; and their physicality and sensuality reveals her own barrenness of spirit. The passage, however, is considerably less effective, since it is far more diffuse and pretentious, than a splendid paragraph from *Sons and Lovers*:

The winter of their first year in the new house, their father was very bad. The children played in the street, on the brim of the wide, dark valley, until eight o'clock. Then they went to bed. Their mother sat sewing below. Having such a great space in front of the house gave the children a feeling of night, of vastness, and of terror. This terror came in from the shrieking of the tree and the anguish of the home discord. Often Paul would wake up, after he had been asleep a long time, aware of thuds downstairs. Instantly he was wide awake. Then he heard the booming shouts of his father, come home nearly drunk, then the sharp replies of his mother, then the bang, bang of his father's fist on the table, and a nasty snarling shout as the man's voice got higher. And then the whole was drowned in a swept ash-tree. The children lay in silent suspense, waiting for a lull in the wind to hear what their father was doing. He might hit their mother again. There was a feeling of horror, a kind of bristling in the darkness, and a sense of blood. They lay with their hearts in the grip of an intense anguish. The wind came through the tree fiercer and fiercer. All the cords of the great harp hummed, whistled, and shrieked. And then came the horror of sudden silence, silence everywhere, outside and downstairs.

A similar over-intensity of feeling characterizes Lawrence's later novels. *Twilight in Italy* (1916), nominally a travel-book, but also a picture of the erosion of the Italian soul by northern materialism and mechanical expertise, prepares the way for *Women in Love*, which appeared in 1920. Again, Lawrence is describing a spiritual conflict – between the cold, mechanical world represented by Gerald Crich, and the warm natural life that he opposes. Lawrence's handling of symbols and symbolic scenes was now becoming more assured. Earlier, he had tended to mix, or alternate, naturalistic and symbolic elements; in *Women in Love* the two are combined; and an apparently realistic scene is crystallized around an obviously symbolic detail, as when Birkin throws stones into a pool to shatter the image of the moon. The portrait of Gerald Crich himself is a thoroughly convincing piece of work; there is a central void in his life that no degree of energy can fill; his deep-

D.H. Lawrence and
Aldous Huxley.

rooted incapacity for real human love leads inexorably to his death among the snows.

Lawrence's next novels show a rapid falling off. The style is increasingly vague; mystical elements preponderate; and *Kangaroo* (1923), *The Boy in the Bush* (1924), *St Mawr* (1925) and *The Plumed Serpent* (1926) are over-didactic, and generally ill-constructed. More impressive are *The Virgin and the Gypsy* (1930), *The Man Who Died* (1931), and *Lady Chatterley's Lover* (1928). The suppression of *The Rainbow* on the grounds of its alleged indecency was followed by the public uproar that accompanied the appearance of the last novel, which, until 1960, was banned from sale in English bookshops. This persecution was all the more absurd, considering the passionate puritanism that underlay the novelist's championship of sexual and emotional freedom. In *Lady Chatterley's Lover* Lawrence returned to his main preoccupation, the destructive change of consciousness brought about by modern industrial society. The frank sexual terms he employs here are an honest attempt to humanize the love relationship, which in earlier novels he had treated – with varying degrees of success – in an obscure, apocalyptic style; but the overtly erotic approach proved ultimately no more successful. It is as an imaginative artist, rather than a social prophet, that D.H. Lawrence deserves to be remembered. He had a marvellous gift of evoking any landscape that he had known and loved, whether it was a Derbyshire mining village or the mountain slopes of New Mexico; and the background he provides for Lady Chatterley does much to enliven an otherwise inferior book. Lady Chatterley and her lover themselves remain a pair of talking puppets.

Though the young Evelyn Waugh would take some hints from his novels, RONALD FIRBANK (1886–1926) had no immediate influence upon contemporary writing; but, as an eccentric invert who wrote to amuse himself – Osbert Sitwell describes him sitting alone at the Café Royal, convulsed with amusement at his own private jokes – he created a peculiarly individual style. In spirit he belonged to the 1890s, the age of Oscar Wilde and Aubrey Beardsley, whose studious frivolity he emulated; and his short fantastic novels, of which the best-known are *Valmouth* (1919), *The Flower Beneath the Foot* (1923), *Prancing Nigger* (1924) and *Concerning the Eccentricities of Cardinal Pirelli* (1926), might perhaps be described as improper fairy-tales, intended for exceptionally knowing adults – satirical glimpses of a world where the sexes are often confused, and wit is the only indispensable virtue.

Joyce Cary, a pencil-sketch.

JOYCE CARY (1888–1957) peopled his novels with outlandish extroverts. He is at his best in the trilogy *Herself Surprised* (1941), *To Be a Pilgrim* (1942), and *The Horse's Mouth* (1944), which traces the disorganized life of an unruly man of near-genius. Cary had spent some years in the Nigerian Political service; and *Mister Johnson* (1939), is a wonderfully endearing portrait of one of his African employees.

IVY COMPTON-BURNETT (1892–1969) was a novelist who, before her death, attracted a large band of faithful followers. Her first novel, *Dolores*, appeared in 1911; but it was followed by a long period of silence, and not until 1925, with the appearance of *Pastors and Masters*, did she establish a distinctive style. Her later works include *Men and Wives* (1931), *More Woman Than Men* (1933), *Daughters and Sons* (1937), *Parents and Children* (1941) and *Elders and Betters* (1944), *Manservant and Maidservant* (1947) and, finally, a posthumous volume, *The Last and the First*. The action of Ivy Compton-Burnett's novels appears to take place during the last decade of the nineteenth century, or the beginning of the twentieth; and the story is unfolded, and the atmosphere conveyed, by means of witty and astringent dialogue. Given the limitations of her method and point of view, she is often brilliantly successful. The great disadvantage of her books is that so many of her characters speak in exactly the same tone of voice; parents and children, employers and servants, have an equally polished and allusive turn of phrase.

Ivy Compton-Burnett.

ALDOUS HUXLEY (1894–1963) began his career as a novelist with an admirable light-hearted Peacockian satire, *Crome Yellow* (1921), a diverting caricature of the celebrated Lady Ottoline Morrell and of the salon that she kept at Garsington; and followed it with *Antic Hay* (1923), a more serious, but also a somewhat more cumbrous study of post-war disillusionment. In Huxley's later novels, seriousness becomes solemnity. *Those Barren Leaves* (1925) has little of the freshness and vitality of the first two novels; while *Point Counter Point* (1928), another attempt at a novel of ideas, the savage account of a social system in which the wholesome life of the senses has been paralyzed by an inhibiting morality, is even heavier and worse constructed. Here the novelist's characters have degenerated into mouthpieces for his own ideas, and he is evidently becoming not so much an imaginative artist as an intellectual moralist. *Eyeless in Gaza* (1936) has similarly puppet-like characters; and their development is illustrated by a series of gratuitous horrors, meant to drive home the novelist's moral message. In *Brave New World* (1932), a satirical vision of a scientific Utopia, Huxley manages to regain something of his early fire and gaiety; and the exuberance of his comic invention makes up for the technical weaknesses of the novel, when considered as a work of literary art.

(*Above*) The young Aldous Huxley.

(*Left*) *Brave New World*; a page from the novelist's first draft.

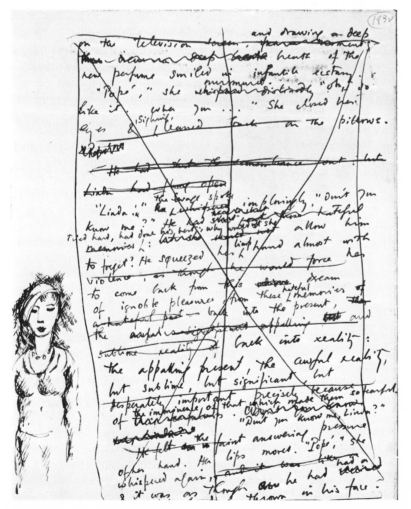

George Orwell (Eric Blair) in 1946.

GEORGE ORWELL, the pen-name of Eric Arthur Blair (1903–50), was a lonely and heroic figure, to whom 'the giant agony of the world', immortalised in Keats' *Hyperion*, was always a 'misery that would not let him rest'. Having broken with his conventional middle-class background, he explored the abysses of poverty and suffering, and published *Down and Out in Paris and London* (1933), an autobiographical account of his adventures. On the outbreak of the Spanish Civil War, he joined the Republican armies, and wrote *Homage to Catalonia* (1938). But Orwell was essentially a humanist, rather than a politician. He loathed the tyranny of an authoritarian government wherever he observed its workings; and from his observations of Communist Russia sprang *Animal Farm* (1945), undoubtedly his best-written and most powerful book. A farmyard fantasy in the style of Jonathan Swift, this absorbing tale satirizes the pretensions of a society that claims to have abolished the idea of 'class' and established a system of perfect social equality, but where, as a character points out, if 'all animals are equal . . . some are more equal than others'. Orwell's last book, *Nineteen Eighty-Four*, a further attack on the totalitarian state – not on totalitarianism as it then existed, but as he imagined that it might soon develop – appeared a year before his end. He died of tuberculosis, the disease that may perhaps have been quickened by the hardships of his early life.

Evelyn Waugh at the age of twenty-one.

CHRISTOPHER ISHERWOOD (*b.*1904), a long-time friend of Auden and Stephen Spender, has always been his own best subject; and it is one that he treats with quietly endearing humour. His early novels, *Mr Norris Changes Trains* (1935) and *Goodbye to Berlin* (1939) are derived from his personal experiences of life in Germany on the eve of World War II; while *Lions and Shadows* (1938) contains a vivid and attractive 'Portrait of the Artist as a Young Man'. They were deservedly popular books, written in a fluent, conversational style, and full of lively scenes and curious characters. Isherwood has also collaborated with W.H. Auden in a series of plays and travel-stories.

EVELYN WAUGH (1903–66), though he himself would have objected to such a description, began his literary career as a social satirist. His first novel, *Decline and Fall* (1928), showed extraordinary promise as a young man's book, genially explosive and destructive; and that promise was realized in *Vile Bodies* (1930), *Black Mischief* (1932), *Scoop* (1938) and *Put Out More Flags* (1942). *Brideshead Revisited* (1945) shows a further development. The story is romantic, with satirical undertones. Waugh describes the decline of an English patrician family, symbolized in the decline and degradation of the splendid house they had inherited. It reveals Waugh as a romantic conservative, a devout Catholic believer and upholder of tradition; while his trilogy of war-novels,

Men at Arms (1952), *Officers and Gentlemen* (1955) and *Unconditional Surrender* (1961) are based on his own military experiences during the Second World War, and reflect the enthusiasm with which he had entered the army and the disillusionment that followed. Waugh was a remarkably accomplished stylist, who employed the rich resources of the English language with easy, unpretentious skill.

(Above left) Evelyn Waugh in 1963.

(Above right) Graham Greene.

GRAHAM GREENE (*b.*1904) describes his early novels as 'entertainments'; they include *The Man Within* (1929), *A Gun For Sale* (1936), *The Ministry of Fear* (1943), and *The Third Man* (1950). They are distinguished by their fugitive heroes and their macabre and shabby backgrounds. Each conveys a haunting sense of sin. As in the books of the French novelist, François Mauriac, his characters' sexual life is almost always repulsive; and Greene's gloomy vision of the world becomes more and more apparent in the serious novels of his later period, *England Made Me* (1935), *Brighton Rock* (1938), *The Power and the Glory* (1940), *The Heart of the Matter* (1948), *The End of the Affair* (1951), *The Quiet American* (1955) and *A Burnt-Out Case* (1961). Graham Greene has defined a novelist's function as 'to try to engage people's sympathy for characters who are outside the official range of sympathy'. A sympathetic writer he certainly is; despite a religious bias that leads him to invest ordinary human weaknesses with an air of almost supernatural horror, he has an exquisitely acute eye; and, during the last twenty years, he has developed into one of the greatest modern English story-tellers.

SAMUEL BECKETT (*b.*1906) has made his mark both as a writer of fiction and as a revolutionary playwright. His first collection of stories, *More Pricks than Kicks*, came out in 1934; his first published novel, *Murphy*, in 1938. Translations from the French original of *Molloy* and *Malone Dies* were published in 1958 and of the *Unnameable* in 1959. Beckett sets out to reduce fiction to the barest essentials of the craft, deriding its accepted techniques and subverting all its traditional standards.

English Verse 1914–45

At the beginning of the twentieth century, the tone of English poetry was still conservative and unadventurous. The most popular poets were Alfred Noyes, William Watson, Henry Newbolt, Alfred Austin (the Poet Laureate) and their mentor, Rudyard Kipling. They were public, rhetorical writers, fond of celebrating the glories of Empire, patriotism, masculine heroism and the public-school spirit. *Clifton Chapel* by Sir HENRY NEWBOLT (1862–1938) is a characteristic specimen of the kind of verse that then found favour, and was most often quoted in anthologies:

Samuel Beckett.

> To set the cause above renown,
>   To love the game beyond the prize,
> To honour, while you strike him down,
>   The foe that comes with fearless eyes:
> To count the life of battle good,
>   And dear the land that gave you birth,
> And dearer yet the brotherhood
>   That binds the brave of all the earth.
>
> My son, the oath is yours: the end
>   Is His, Who built the world of strife,
> Who gave His children Pain for friend,
>   And Death for surest hope of life . . .

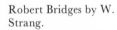

Robert Bridges by W. Strang.

In 1909, the two last great survivors of the Victorian Age, Meredith and Swinburne, both died. Among living poets, born between 1840 and 1865, the more important figures were William Butler Yeats, Thomas Hardy, A. E. Housman and Robert Bridges. But Yeats' finest work was yet to come; Hardy's poetic gifts were largely unrecognized; Housman had published only *A Shropshire Lad*; and Bridges was too learned a poet to interest the ordinary reader.

ROBERT BRIDGES (1844–1930) had long been at work, but had attracted comparatively little notice, when he became Poet Laureate in 1913. His early poems are graceful and well-shaped –

he was a supremely conscientious craftsman. He produced no strikingly original work, however, until in 1929, at the age of eighty-five, he published *The Testament of Beauty*, a long philosophical poem, describing the relationship of man and the universe. It includes some memorable passages; but Bridges' 'loose Alexandrines' seem not quite equal to the task of covering so vast a subject. His scientific disquisitions, for instance, often descend to a somewhat humdrum level.

A. E. HOUSMAN (1859–1936) had a far more individual talent. After an unhappy youth, darkened, when he had gone up to Oxford, by the romantic passion he had conceived for a handsome, unresponsive friend, he joined the Civil Service, where he spent more than ten years of obscure and ill-paid drudgery. Though he had failed at Oxford, in 1892 he was appointed Professor of Latin at University College, London, and in 1911 was granted a professorship and a fellowship at Cambridge. There he remained until he died, a lonely, opinionated, sharp-tongued scholar. Meanwhile, in 1896, he had published *A Shropshire Lad*, a collection of pastoral lyrics; and in 1922 it was followed by *Last Poems*, his farewell to the literary world. Today the fluent pastoralism of *A Shropshire Lad* appears a trifle unconvincing. It is *Last Poems* and his posthumously published *More Poems* that exhibit his real abilities as an imaginative modern poet. Housman's classical training stood him in good stead, and often, in his more epigrammatic verses, for instance, in his 'Epitaph on an Army of Mercenaries', enabled him to achieve an effect of rare emotional compression:

A.E. Housman; pencil portrait by F. Dodd.

> These, in the day when heaven was falling,
> The day when earth's foundations fled,
> Followed their mercenary calling
> And took their wages and are dead.
>
> Their shoulders held the sky suspended;
> They stood, and earth's foundations stay;
> What God abandoned, these defended,
> And saved the sum of things for pay.

In another lyric, he returns to the theme, which haunts all three collected volumes, of thwarted homosexual love:

> Crossing alone the nighted ferry
>   With one coin for fee,
> Whom, on the wharf of Lethe waiting,
>   Count you to find? Not me.
>
> The brisk fond lackey to fetch and carry,
>   The true sick-hearted slave,
> Expect him not in the just city
>   And free land of the grave.

EDWARD (later Sir Edward) MARSH (1872–1953) was a distinguished civil servant, who possessed strong literary leanings; and his anthology, *Georgian Poetry 1911–12*, seemed to herald the beginnings of a new poetic movement; and it was succeeded by similar anthologies in 1915, 1917, 1919 and 1922. The term 'Georgian', as applied to modern verse, would later acquire a pejorative significance; it became associated with a rustic escapism, with descriptions of leisurely rambles around the poet's country cottage. Such attacks were prejudiced; the poets whom Edward Marsh assembled, though one or two were romantic dilettanti, formed a singularly heterogenous group; and all were deeply dedicated to the general improvement of poetic standards. Among writers represented in the closing volume were Walter De La Mare, Edmund Blunden, Robert Graves, Harold Monro and D.H. Lawrence, none of whom deserved the injurious epithets sometimes applied to Georgian poetry as a whole.

WALTER DE LA MARE (1873–1956) was already a well-established poet and story-teller before he appeared in the first Georgian anthology. The atmosphere of his poems is nostalgic, his verse melodious and nicely turned. Many of his earlier poems were expressly written for children; and throughout his life he continued to inhabit a juvenile dream-world of his own imagining, peopled by fairies, witches and ghosts, goblins, sprites and talking animals. Sometimes his literary fantasies degenerate into whimsicality; but elsewhere, as in 'The Song of the Mad Prince', from the volume he entitled *Peacock Pie*, he conveys an adult strength of meaning:

Walter de la Mare.

> Who said, 'Peacock Pie'?
>   The old King to the sparrow:
> Who said, 'Crops are ripe'?
>   Rust to the harrow:
> Who said, 'Where sleeps she now?
>   Where rests she now her head,
> Bathed in eve's loveliness'?
>   That's what I said.
>
> Who said, 'Ay, mum's the word'?
>   Sexton to willow:
> Who said, 'Greek dusk for dreams,
>   Moss for a pillow'?
> Who said, 'All Time's delight
>   Hath she for narrow bed,
> Life's troubled bubble broken'?
>   That's what I said.

JOHN MASEFIELD (1878–1967) one of the oldest poets to figure in the Georgian group, also joined it as a well-known writer. His *Salt Water Ballads* had appeared in 1902, and *Ballads and Poems* in

1910; and both were works that owed much to the heady influence of Rudyard Kipling. Far more original was his long narrative poem, 'The Everlasting Mercy', published three years before the First World War, and 'Dauber', the story of a voyage under sail, which came out in 1913. Their realism and unaccustomed 'coarseness' astonished early-twentieth-century critics; and Masefield was for a while regarded as a revolutionary innovator. By 1919, however, when he produced *Reynard the Fox*, a stirring tale of the hunting-field, he had ceased to cause offence. In 1930, on the death of Robert Bridges, he was appointed Poet Laureate. Finally, the Order of Merit, with which he was invested in 1935, raised him to the literary pantheon.

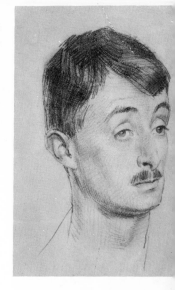

John Masefield in early life; by Henry Lamb.

RUPERT BROOKE (1887–1915), morning-star of the earlier Georgian renaissance, enjoyed a brief but brilliant reputation. During his lifetime he published only one book, *Poems* (1911); the second, *1914 and Other Poems*, was issued in the year of his death by his devoted admirer Edward Marsh. Though it was *1914* that earned him nation-wide fame, his first collection is the more impressive. Brooke, at Cambridge, had been a keen student of the Elizabethan and Jacobean dramatists, from whom he had inherited their taste for the grotesque and their delight in the energetic use of language. But the young poet had also a sentimental and self-consciously romantic strain; and the outbreak of war provided temptations that had a disastrous effect upon his literary judgment. War, which promised to resolve his personal difficulties, he welcomed as a means of spiritual salvation; and he wrote the series of patriotic sonnets that were to become the basis of his literary legend. The most famous of these he called 'The Soldier':

Rupert Brooke in 1913.

> If I should die, think only this of me:
>   That there's some corner of a foreign field
> That is for ever England. There shall be
>   In that rich earth a richer dust concealed;
> A dust whom England bore, shaped, made aware,
>   Gave, once, her flowers to love, her ways to roam,
> A body of England's breathing English air,
>   Washed by the rivers, blest by suns of home.
> And think, this heart, all evil shed away,
>   A pulse in the eternal mind, no less
>   Gives somewhere back the thoughts by England given;
> Her sights and sounds; dreams happy as her day;
>   And laughter, learnt of friends; and gentleness.
>   In hearts at peace, under an English heaven.

He died during the voyage to the Dardanelles, and was buried on the island of Skyros, in April, 1915.

Brooke had never seen the Western Front; and other English poets responded very differently to the idea of international conflict, having themselves experienced the horror, misery and futility

War on the Western Front; Passchendale, 1917.

of modern warfare. The new mood of imaginative disillusion was first expressed by CHARLES SORLEY (1895–1915):

> When you see millions of the mouthless dead
> Across your dreams in pale battalions go,
> Say not soft things as other men have said,
> That you'll remember. For you need not so.
> Give them not praise. For, deaf, how should they know
> It is not curses heaped on each gashed head?
> Nor tears. Their blind eyes see not your tears flow.
> Nor honour. It is easy to be dead.
> Say only this, 'They are dead.' Then add thereto,
> 'Yet many a better one has died before.'
> Then, scanning all the o'ercrowded mass, should you
> Perceive one face that you loved heretofore,
> It is a spook. None wears the face you knew.
> Great death has made all his for evermore.

This was probably Sorley's last poem – he was killed on the Western Front at the age of twenty. But, although he had learned to hate the war, with a strange ambivalence he retained some of the high-minded idealism with which he had originally entered it.

The first war-poems of SIEGFRIED SASSOON (1886–1967) were
almost as enthusiastic as Rupert Brooke's sonnets; but, early in
1916, after he had experienced the life of the trenches, he voiced a
bitter indignation:

> Groping along the tunnel, step by step,
> He winked his prying torch with patching glare
> From side to side, and sniffed the unwholesome air.
>
> Tins, boxes, bottles, shapes too vague to know,
> A mirror smashed, the mattress from a bed;
> And he, exploring fifty feet below
> The rosy gloom of battle overhead.
>
> Tripping, he grabbed the wall; saw some one lie
> Humped at his feet, half-hidden by a rug,
> And stooped to give the sleeper's arm a tug.
> 'I'm looking for headquarters.' No reply.
> 'God blast your neck!' (For days he'd had no sleep,)
> 'Get up and guide me through this stinking place.'
>
> Savage, he kicked a soft, unanswering heap,
> And flashed his beam across the livid face
> Terribly glaring up, whose eyes yet wore
> Agony dying hard ten days before;
> And fists of fingers clutched a blackening wound. . . .

Siegfried Sasson;
portrait by Cecil Beaton,
1928.

Sassoon's personal courage was never in dispute; by his com-
rades he had been nicknamed 'Mad Jack'. At last, however, his
hatred of bloodshed provoked him to defy authority. Anxious not
to make him a martyr, his superior officers arranged that a medical
board should decide that he was suffering from shell-shock; and
in the hospital to which he was relegated he met a fellow-poet who
had reached the same conclusion.

That poet was WILFRED OWEN (1893–1918). 'My subject is
War,' wrote Owen, 'and the pity of War. The Poetry is in the
pity.' He was not primarily concerned with verse as an art,
though he had been writing poems since his boyhood, usually
under the influence of John Keats. Meeting Sassoon had a decisive
effect on his style; for in his new friend's terse, colloquial utterance
he saw the literary medium that suited him, and proceeded to pare
down his own 'poeticality', while preserving his distinctive metrical skill. His last and most celebrated poem, 'Strange Meeting',
describes a situation not unlike that described in Sassoon's 'Rear-
Guard'. Having entered a noisome tunnel, he discovers the corpse
of a slaughtered enemy; and the tunnel he depicts is Hell:

> 'Strange friend,' I said, 'here is no cause to mourn.'
> 'None,' said the other, 'save the undone years,
> The hopelessness. Whatever hope is yours,
> Was my life also; I went hunting wild
> After the wildest beauty in the world,

Which lies not calm in eyes, or braided hair,
But mocks the steady running of the hour,
And if it grieves, grieves richlier than here.
For by my glee might many men have laughed,
And of my weeping something had been left,
Which must die now. I mean the truth untold,
The pity of war, the pity war distilled.'

Wilfred Owen was killed in action on 4 November 1918, only a week before the Armistice.

Like Owen, ISAAC ROSENBERG (1890–1918) was killed in battle not long before the conflict ended. He had had a life of poverty and neglect; and, whereas most of the war-poets held commissioned rank, Rosenberg served as a private soldier. Though his verse is rough and undisciplined compared with the

(*Above left*) Isaac Rosenberg.

(*Above centre*) Edward Thomas in 1905; pencil portrait by his brother.

(*Above right*) Robert Graves.

more conscious art of Owen, he possessed genuine poetic gifts which are seen at their most effective in 'Break of Day in the Trenches'.

Despite the fact that he failed to appear in any of the Georgian anthologies, EDWARD THOMAS (1878–1917) had much in common with the Georgian movement. He did not begin to produce poetry until 1914, having previously tried to earn his living as a prose-writer; and his first collection of poetry was published in 1917, the year he died upon the battlefield. The qualities of his verse – unobtrusive realism, unemphatic, colloquial language, a distinctively personal mode of recording experience – were essentially those which the Georgians aimed at, and, in their most enduring work, achieved.

EDMUND BLUNDEN (b.1896) was one of the literary survivors of
the First World War. In his war-poems and in a prose-narrative
Undertones of War (1928) he records both the horror and pain of
war and its moments of happiness and human warmth. His post-
war poetry is quiet and reflective, deliberately English, inspired
by his love of English country life and its traditions.

ROBERT GRAVES (b.1895) though he began his poetic career
among the Georgians, and his first two volumes of verse, *Over the
Brazier* (1916) and *Fairies and Fusiliers* (1917) have a strongly
Georgian colouring, soon struck out along an individual line. An
obstinate individualist and a dedicated professional poet he has
ever since remained. It was his prose, however – his autobiographical volume *Goodbye to All That* (1929) and his historical novels,
I, Claudius and *Claudius the God* (1934), which he himself has dismissed as 'pot-boilers' – that introduced him to the ordinary
reading public. Graves exalts the poet's rôle, and believes
that every poet must have his muse, and be attached to the
service of the mysterious 'White Goddess' – the name that he has
given to his idea of the sacred Female Spirit, or Mother Goddess
of the Mediterranean world. His verse is vigorous and idiosyncratic, frequently sharpened by an edge of wit. He is an accomplished love-poet – latterly, love has become his chief subject; and
his descriptions of the commerce of the sexes are very often wry
and bitter:

> Twined together and, as is customary,
> For words of rapture groping, they
> 'Never such love', swore, 'ever before was!'
> Contrast with all loves that had failed or staled
> Registered their own as love indeed.
>
> And was not this to blab idly
> The heart's fated inconstancy?
> Better in love to seal the love-sure lips:
> For truly love was before words were,
> And no word given, no word broken.
>
> When the word 'love' is uttered
> (Love, the near-honourable malady
> With which in greed and haste they
> Each other do infect and curse)
> Or, worse, is written down. . .
>
> Wise after the event, by love withered,
> A 'never more!' most frantically
> Sorrow and shame would proclaim
> Such as, they'd swear, never before were:
> True lovers even in this.

It is difficult to see Graves's achievement in perspective. He is
still writing; and every year he makes some important addition to
the massive corpus of his collected works.

The poetry of D.H. LAWRENCE (1885–1930), whose wonderful free-verse picture of a Sicilian snake appeared in the last Georgian Book, is often regarded as a minor byproduct of his work as a prose-writer. Much of his verse is weak and sentimental; but, here and there, he suddenly produced a really memorable poem. His range is wide – from the homely domestic imagery of his early poems, *Love Poems and Others* (1913), through his brilliant explorations of animal life in *Birds, Beasts and Flowers* (1923), to the *Last Poems* (1933), in which, declares their editor Richard Aldington, 'suffering and the agony of departure are turned into music and reconciliation'. The apparent looseness and irregularity of Lawrence's verse is deceptive; his main concern was with the emotional demands of his theme, and with finding a rhythm that would embody it. 'Piano,' for instance, is a poem that displays his technical mastery:

Softly, in the dusk, a woman is singing to me;
Taking me back down the vista of years, till I see
A child sitting under the piano, in the boom of the tingling strings
And pressing the small, poised feet of a mother who smiles as she sings.

In spite of myself the insidious mastery of song
Betrays me back, till the heart of me weeps to belong
To the old Sunday evenings at home, with winter outside
And hymns in the cosy parlour, the tinkling piano our guide.

So now it is vain for the singer to burst into clamour
With the great black piano appassionato. The glamour
Of childish days is upon me, my manhood is cast
Down in the flood of remembrance, I weep like a child for the past.

Lawrence's verse appeared under the banner of the Georgians, but also under that of the Imagists. Whereas the earliest Georgians aimed at improving the standards of poetry while maintaining its popular appeal, the Imagists hoped to launch a revolution; they insisted on writing the kind of poetry that they felt was needed, regardless of the response that it evoked. Imagism originated in the poetry and poetic theory of Edward Storer, F.S. Flint, and T.E. Hulme; but it owed its vitality and the influence it exercised to the young American poet Ezra Pound. Having joined the group in 1909, he had coined the name 'Imagist' to describe the new poets. In 1912 Pound published five Imagist poems by Hulme as an appendix to his own *Ripostes*; and, later, he acquired two protégés, Richard Aldington and H.D., the American poetess Hilda Doolittle. Together, they recommended three poetic principles: (1) 'direct treatment of the thing whether subjective or objective'; (2) 'to use absolutely no word that does not contribute to the presentation'; (3) 'as regarding rhythm: to compose in the sequence of the musical phrase, not in sequence of a metronome'. An anthology, *Des Imagistes*, appeared in 1914, with poems by Aldington, H.D., Flint, James Joyce, Pound and

William Carlos Williams. In subsequent volumes the quality of contributions showed a definite falling-off; by 1917 Pound had moved on to other interests; and the Imagist movement faded away. Very little of the poetry that its followers produced corresponded strictly to their own principles; much of it now seems derivative; but Imagism, in its brief heyday, had an important effect upon the development of modern verse, and, through Pound's example, on the later poetry of Yeats.

Though EZRA POUND (1885–1972) was an American by birth, he deserves a place among the English poets. From Imagism he moved on to write poetry that was complex, tough and 'modern'. But his two masterpieces, *Homage to Sextus Propertius* (1917) and *Hugh Selwyn Mauberley* (1920) were at first greeted with intense hostility by the average English critic. Reviewers pounced upon the former poem, which they dismissed as a hopelessly inaccurate translation of the Latin elegiac poet. In fact, *Sextus Propertius* is a set of variations on a well-known Roman theme, that draws historical parallels between early Imperial Rome and the existing British Empire; while *Hugh Selwyn Mauberley* is an erudite, and consciously 'difficult' attempt to examine the current state of British culture through the biography of a poet:

> For three years, out of key with his time,
> He strove to resuscitate the dead art
> Of poetry; to maintain 'the sublime'
> In the old sense. Wrong from the start –
>
> No, hardly, but seeing he had been born
> In a half-savage country, out of date;
> Bent resolutely on wriging lilies from the acorn;
> Capaneus; trout for factitious bait; . . .

Ezra Pound; the young revolutionary.

Pound left England in 1920; and his subsequent activities, literary and political, cannot be discussed here. Before he left, he had begun his gigantic poem, *The Cantos* – a prodigious imaginative performance that was to occupy him for fifty years. The scale of the work is daunting, as is the method Pound employs; but Pound's command of words and poetic self-assurance carries us through many obstacles. He had a keen ear for the rhythms of living speech; his ideal was what he called 'the musical phrase':

W. B. YEATS (1865–1939) had begun work in the 1880s as a poet of the Irish literary revival. His early poems, published in *The Wanderings of Oisin and Other Poems* (1889), *Poems* (1895), and *The Wind Among the Reeds* (1899), were dreamy and nostalgic:

I would that we were, my beloved, white birds on the foam of the sea!
We tire of the flame of the meteor, before it can fade and flee;
And the flame of the blue star of twilight, hung low on the rim of the sky,
Has awaked in our hearts, my beloved, a sadness that may not die.

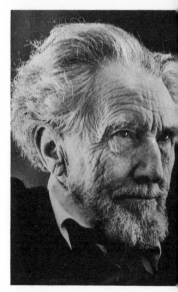

Ezra Pound; the literary veteran.

William Butler Yeats;
etching by Augustus
John, 1907.

A weariness comes from those dreamers, dew-dabbled, the lily and rose;
Ah, dream not of them, my beloved, the flame of the meteor that goes,
Or the flame of the blue star that lingers hung low in the fall of the dew;
For I would we were changed to white birds on the wandering foam: I
    and you!

('The White Bird', 1893)

Once the twentieth century had opened, Yeats deliberately set
about transforming his poetic style; and by 1910, when he published *The Green Helmet and Other Poems*, his aestheticism had given
way to a far more 'modern' manner. Yeats's meeting with Pound,
in the year that he produced *The Green Helmet*, accelerated this
process of modernization; in 1914, on reading *Responsibilities*,

Pound decided that Yeats had at last become a genuinely modern poet. His themes were now public, often political; and his earlier romantic visions had been rejected:

> What need you, being come to sense,
> But fumble in a greasy till
> And add the halfpence to the pence
> And prayer to shivering prayer, until
> You have dried the marrow from the bone?
> For men were born to pray and save:
> Romantic Ireland's dead and gone,
> It's with O'Leary in the grave.
>
> Yet they were of a different kind,
> The names that stilled your childish play,
> They have gone about the world like wind,
> But little time had they to pray
> For whom the hangman's rope was spun,
> And what, God help us, could they save?
> Romantic Ireland's dead and gone,
> It's with O'Leary in the grave . . .
>
> ('September 1913')

In 1916 Yeats found himself confronted with the drama of the Easter Rising; the revolutionaries, whose patriotic fervour he had once despised, had risen to the dignity of tragic heroes. *Easter 1916* is among his greatest works:

> This man had kept a school
> And rode our wingèd horse;
> This other his helper and friend
> Was coming into his force;
> He might have won fame in the end,
> So sensitive his nature seemed,
> So daring and sweet his thought.
> This other man I had dreamed
> A drunken, vainglorious lout.
> He had done most bitter wrong
> To some who are near my heart,
> Yet I number him in the song . . .
> He, too, has been changed in his turn,
> Transformed utterly:
> A terrible beauty is born.

The collection entitled *The Tower* (1928) marks the peak of Yeats's achievement, with the appearance of such poems as 'Sailing to Byzantium', 'Among School Children', and 'Leda and the Swan':

> A sudden blow: the great wings beating still
> Above the staggering girl, her thighs caressed
> By the dark webs, her nape caught in his bill,
> He holds her helpless breast upon his breast.

> How can those terrified vague fingers push
> The feathered glory from her loosening thighs?
> And how can body, laid in that white rush,
> But feel the strange heart beating where it lies?
>
> A shudder in the loins engenders there
> The broken wall, the burning roof and tower
> And Agamemnon dead.
>   Being so caught up,
> So mastered by the brute blood of the air,
> Did she put on his knowledge with his power
> Before the indifferent beak could let her drop?

Of his later poetry, Yeats declared that every poem he wrote had been haunted by the spectres of 'lust and rage'; here a spirit of savage gaiety mingles with anger and resentment. The poems in *Last Poems and Plays* (1940), and, indeed, many in *The Winding Stair* (1929), are somewhat marred by the poet's dependence on esoteric imagery and obscure symbolism. Their significance was so completely clear to himself that he forgot the limitations of his reader.

In 1914, Pound was delighted to discover a poet who had already 'modernized' his verse – T.S. ELIOT (1888–1965). As a young man, Eliot had been deeply indebted to Jules Laforgue and the other French Symbolists, with whom he had first become acquainted through Arthur Symons's enlightening study, *The Symbolist Movement in Literature*. About 1910, while a graduate student at Harvard, he had begun work on *The Love Song of J. Alfred Prufrock*:

> Let us go then, you and I,
> When the evening is spread out against the sky
> Like a patient etherized upon a table;
> Let us go, through certain half-deserted streets,
> The muttering retreats
> Of restless nights in one-night cheap hotels
> And sawdust restaurants with oyster-shells:
> Streets that follow like a tedious argument
> Of insidious intent
> To lead you to an overwhelming question . . .
> Oh, do not ask, 'What is it?'
> Let us go and make our visit.
>
> In the room the women come and go
> Talking of Michaelangelo.

Finished in 1911, the poem did not achieve publication until a year after Eliot had first met Pound – it eventually appeared in 1915 as a contribution to the magazine *Poetry*, and later re-emerged as part of a collection, *Prufrock and Other Observations* (1917). Pound, having become his friend, admirer and propagandist, saw to it that Eliot's work was published; and *Poems* (1919), helped to

T.S. Eliot.

increase his reputation. But it was the appearance of *The Waste Land* (1922) that established him as a major modern poet, and inaugurated his long reign. The immediate response to the poem was hostile; even critics who were inclined to take the poem seriously saw it as a fanciful patchwork of parodies and learned borrowings. The novelty of *The Waste Land*, most apparent in the kaleidoscopic effect produced by its play of contrasts and juxta-positions, baffled many English readers; and they were further baffled and dismayed when they looked through Eliot's mischiev-ous array of annotations. The poem's real originality (as we now see) was derived from the distinctive texture of the verse:

> Phlebas the Phoenician, a fortnight dead,
> Forgot the cry of gulls, and the deep sea swell

> And the profit and loss.
>   A current under sea
> Picked his bones in whispers. As he rose and fell
> He passed the stages of his age and youth
> Entering the whirlpool.
>   Gentile or Jew
> O you who turn the wheel and look to windward,
> Consider Phlebas, who was once handsome and tall as you.

How much the completed text of *The Waste Land* owed to Pound's drastic critical surgery became apparent when the corrected manuscript came to light not long ago.

In 1927 Eliot shocked many of his contemporaries by entering the Church of England, and by going on to proclaim himself an Anglo-Catholic and a Royalist. His struggle towards faith produced *Ash-Wednesday* (1930), a contemplative poem in which a deep devotional earnestness replaces the flippant irony that he had learned from Jules Laforgue. It is not entirely successful; but Eliot regained his mastery with his series of *Four Quartets* – 'Burnt Norton' (1935), 'East Coker' (1940), 'The Dry Salvages' (1941) and 'Little Gidding' (1942). They are carefully organized poems, planned to express shifting, indeterminate states of mind, and to explore the connections between experience and belief, memory and literary fancy. The verse represents a further extension of Eliot's technique, which can accommodate plain abstract statement and, at the same time, generalize personal experience, as in this account of a distant war-time air-raid:

> In the uncertain hour before the morning
>   Near the ending of interminable night
>   At the recurrent end of the unending
> After the dark dove with the flickering tongue
>   Had passed below the horizon of his homing
>   While the dead leaves still rattled on like tin
> Over the asphalt where no other sound was
>   Between three districts whence the smoke arose
>   I met one walking, loitering and hurried
> As if blown towards me like the metal leaves
>   Before the urban dawn wind unresisting.

The author's achievement is still difficult to appraise in its entirety; but there seems no doubt that the period through which he flourished – from 1920 to 1950 – will one day be known to literary historians as 'The Age of T.S. Eliot'.

Meanwhile, during the 1930s, a new young poet had arrived – W.H. AUDEN (*b*.1907). The originality and inventiveness of *Poems*, published in the first year of the decade, immediately struck his readers. His boldly expressive phrases and images, many of them drawn from the mechanical world, his topical urgency and sense of intellectual commitment, made him appear a worthy

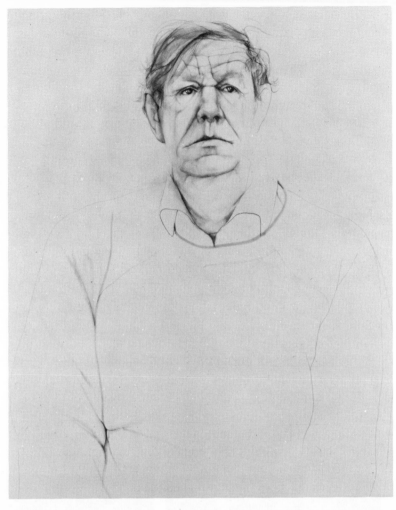

W.H. Auden, 1967.

successor to the now conservative and academically honoured
Eliot. Auden seemed to be reaching out for a popular audience;
and the confident tone in which he treated his subjects recalled the
poets of the pre-war dispensation. His later work had a more
political tendency. At times it was straightforward Marxist propaganda; and the poet today omits such items from collected editions of his work. *Look, Stranger!* (1936) included some highly
original lyrics, among them the well-known love poem, 'Lay your
sleeping head . . .', and showed an increasing technical mastery.
The dogmatic element is less obvious, though it lurks beneath the
surface; and in the last two lines of 'Our Hunting Fathers' he is
directly paraphrasing Lenin:

> Our hunting fathers told the story
>   Of the sadness of the creatures
> Pitied the limits and the lack
>   Set in their finished features;

Saw in the lion's intolerant look,
Behind the quarry's dying glare,
Love raging for the personal glory
    That reason's gift would add,
The liberal appetite and power,
    The rightness of a god.

Who, nurtured in that fine tradition,
    Predicted the result,
Guessed Love by nature suited to
    The intricate ways of guilt,
That human ligaments could so
His southern gestures modify
And make it his mature ambition
    To think no thought but ours,
To hunger, work illegally,
    And be anonymous?

Early in 1939 Auden went to America, where he remained until 1972, the year that saw his triumphant return to his old Oxford College, Christ Church. His new poems may be less stimulating than the old; but they exhibit the same careful craftsmanship, and reveal the same inquisitive and energetic mind.

(*Below left*) Stephen Spender.

(*Below centre*) Cecil Day Lewis.

(*Below right*) Louis MacNeice.

Auden is usually associated with STEPHEN SPENDER (*b.* 1909), CECIL DAY LEWIS (1904–72), and LOUIS MACNEICE (1907–63), who appeared with him in the anthology *New Signatures* (1932). These poets were believed, at the time, to form a propagandist Left-Wing group. In fact, however, there was no such organization, though all four then shared a deep concern with contemporary life and politics. Their joint master was Gerard Manley

Hopkins; but they lacked Hopkins' gift of transforming dogma into poetry; and their political productions, as a whole, have failed to stand the test of time. More lasting are the personal poems they wrote. Stephen Spender, for example, is always at his best when his attitude is least oracular; while MacNeice and Day Lewis – both accomplished literary artists, who possessed a fine taste in language and imagery – are essentially poets of the private life.

EDITH SITWELL (1887–1964) and her brothers OSBERT (1892–1969) and SACHEVERELL (b.1897) belong to no literary school, except the group that they themselves established. Edith Sitwell's first light-hearted volume of verse appeared in 1915; in 1916 she and her brothers issued a poetic miscellany named *Wheels*, and, like Pope, launched a long and hard-fought campaign against the legion of contemporary Dunces. They despised the Georgians. Their joint aim was to revive the art of poetry by introducing a whole new range of arresting images derived from many different sources – from their wide knowledge of foreign art and music, and from their own eclectic interests and tastes, first cultivated in the Derbyshire country house where they had passed a secluded and somewhat unhappy childhood. Their cumulative effect was strong; though at the outset they were often abused and ridiculed, they refused to be ignored; and there is no doubt that they had a highly stimulating, if now and then a somewhat disturbing, influence upon the literary life of Great Britain. Osbert Sitwell, while he continued to write verse, became an accomplished prose-satirist; Sacheverell, despite the fact he is primarily a poet, whose remarkable gifts, during the last few years, seem to have been much neglected, has also produced a multitude of books in prose,

(*Above*) Edith Sitwell, the young poetess.

(*Left*) Sacheverell Sitwell (left) and his brother, Osbert, as children at Renishaw; from Sargent's conversation-piece of the Sitwell family.

Osbert Sitwell in later life.

Sacheverell Sitwell.

imaginative, historical and topographical, including his adventurous essay, *Southern Baroque Art*; and Edith, having begun her career as a fairy-tale lyricist, whose *Rustic Elegies* bear a certain resemblance to Christina Rossetti's *Goblin Market*, gradually developed into a poetic sage. The tone of her later poems, *The Song of the Cold* (1945) and *The Canticle of the Rose* (1949) grew increasingly apocalyptic. But one misses in them the youthful gaiety and freshness that had illuminated her juvenilia.

Edith Sitwell had a succession of protégés, the most brilliant being the young Welsh poet DYLAN THOMAS (1914–53). In the 1930s he published two volumes, *Eighteen Poems* (1934) and *Twenty-Five Poems* (1936). But it was the appearance of *Deaths and Entrances* in 1946 that set him on the road to fame. In his personal life he resurrected the legend of the doomed Bohemian poet. He had a Celtic passion for words – his poems are pyrotechnic displays of word-spinning. Though their content is sometimes obscure, the verbal inspiration never flags; they have a splendid Dionysiac onrush. But these wild outpourings were carefully worked over; and Thomas was well aware of his own literary limitations; he feared, he once confessed, that he was 'a freak *user* of words, not a poet'. Today the element of freakishness seems considerably less alarming than it did twenty or thirty years ago; there is room in modern poetry for both the Dionysiac and the Apollonian. No other English poet since T.S. Eliot has made so deep an impression on young twentieth-century readers:

> The force that through the green fuse drives the flower
> Drives my green age; that blasts the roots of trees
> Is my destroyer.
> And I am dumb to tell the crooked rose
> My youth is bent by the same wintry fever.
>
> The force that drives the water through the rocks
> Drives my red blood; that dries the mouthing streams
> Turns mine to wax.
> And I am dumb to mouth unto my veins
> How at the mountain spring the same mouth sucks.
>
> The hand that whirls the water in the pool
> Stirs the quicksand; that ropes the blowing wind
> Hauls my shroud sail.
> And I am dumb to tell the hanging man
> How of my clay is made the hangman's lime.
>
> The lips of time leech to the fountain head;
> Love drips and gathers, but the fallen blood
> Shall calm her sores.
> And I am dumb to tell a weather's wind
> How time has ticked a heaven round the stars.
>
> And I am dumb to tell the lover's tomb
> How at my sheet goes the same crooked worm.

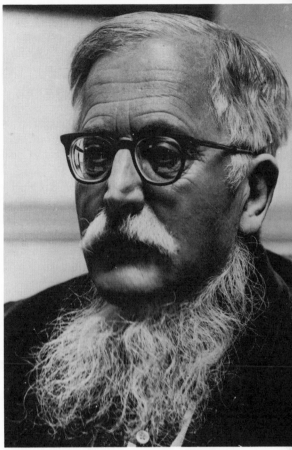

A more intellectual poet is WILLIAM EMPSON (*b.*1906) whose first volume of literary criticism, *Seven Types of Ambiguity*, came out in 1930, to be followed by *Poems* in 1935 and *The Gathering Storm* in 1940. Empson's early poems, which are as much concerned with ideas – often scientific ideas – as with the life of the emotions, are both stylistically assured and intellectually exciting. He works by a process of argument and conceit that recalls the seventeenth-century Metaphysical poets. Later poems exhibit a more static quality. Empson's peculiar blend of musical precision and laconic statement is seen at its most effective in what is probably his finest poem, 'Aubade':

> Hours before dawn we were woken by the quake.
> My house was on a cliff. The thing could take
> Bookloads off shelves, break bottles in a row.
> Then the long pause and then the bigger shake.
> It seemed the best thing to be up and go.
>
> And far too large for my feet to step by.
> I hoped that various buildings were brought low.
> The heart of standing is you cannot fly.

(*Above left*) Dylan Thomas; portrait by Rupert Shepherd.

(*Above right*) William Empson; photograph by Mark Gerson.

It seemed quite safe till she got up and dressed.
The guarded tourist makes the guide the test.
Then I said The Garden? Laughing she said No.
Taxi for her and for me healthy rest.
It seemed the best thing to be up and go.

Two writers who emerged in the 1930s, but who did not achieve immediate recognition, are JOHN BETJEMAN (b.1906) and EDWIN MUIR (1887–1959). Betjeman is a unique phenomenon, a serious contemporary poet with a mass audience. As a wonderfully gifted writer of occasional verse, he resembles WINTHROP MACK-WORTH PRAED (1802–39). But Betjeman's greatest feat is to have invented an entirely new type of personal romanticism. The themes that fascinate him are drawn from the recent past – chiefly from his own past – suburban streets, privet-hedged gardens, Victorian railway stations and parish churches, which he evokes with a strange nostalgic fervour and an ingenious verbal artistry. His language is simple; his rhymes are clearly marked, his rhythms 'catchy' and persuasive. He writes verse that demands to be read aloud:

Rumbling under blackened girders, Midland, bound for Cricklewood,
Puffed its sulphur to the sunset where that Land of Laundries stood.
Rumble under, thunder over, train and tram alternate go,
Shake the floor and smudge the ledger, Charrington, Sells, Dale and Co.,
Nuts and nuggets in the window, trucks along the lines below.

When the Bon Marché was shuttered, when the feet were hot and tired,
Outside Charrington's we waited, by the 'STOP HERE IF REQUIRED',
Launched aboard the shopping basket, sat precipitately down,
Rocked past Zwanziger the baker's, and the terrace blackish brown,
And the curious Anglo-Norman parish church of Kentish Town.
Till the tram went over thirty, sighting terminus again,
Past municipal lawn tennis and the bobble-hanging plane;
Soft and light surburban evening caught our ashlar-speckled spire,
Eighteen-sixty Early English, as the mighty elms retire
Either side of Brookfield Mansions flashing fine French-window fire.

Oh, the after-tram-ride quiet, when we heard a mile beyond,
Silver music from the bandstand, barking dogs by Highgate Pond;
Up the Hill where stucco houses in Virginia creeper drown –
And my childish wave of pity, seeing children carrying down
Sheaves of drooping dandelions to the courts of Kentish Town.

EDWIN MUIR (1887–1958) published his *First Poems* in 1925; but he remained aloof from the mainstream of contemporary writing, and was not acclaimed until the 1940s, when the decline of the 'modern movement', which had laid so much emphasis on technical innovation and linguistic experiment, allowed his plainer virtues to be seen. *Journeys and Places* (1937), *The Narrow Place* (1943) and *The Labyrinth* (1949) revealed him as a master of simple stanza-forms and of lucid and dignified blank verse. He

John Betjeman, at the age
of thirty-one, in a
television programme.

has a narrow range of recurrent images – road and journey,
labyrinth and stronghold – and expresses most movingly, and
seems to have felt most deeply, a sense of tragic aftermath:

> Old gods and goddesses who have lived so long
> Through time and never found eternity,
> Fettered by wasting wood and hollowing hill,
>
> You should have fled our ever-dying song,
> The mound, the well, and the green trysting tree
> They are forgotten, yet you linger still.
>
> Goddess of caverned breast and channelled brow
> And cheeks slow hollowed by millenial tears,
> Forests of autumns fading in your eyes,
>
> Eternity marvels at your counted years
> And kingdoms lost in time, and wonders how
> There could be thoughts so bountiful and wise
>
> As yours beneath the ever-breaking bough,
> And vast compassion curing like the skies.

The 1940s produced a number of accomplished poets, but no
distinctive individual voice. ALUN LEWIS (1915–44) died when
his poetic promise was only beginning to be realized; but 'To
Edward Thomas' is an admirable nature-poem; and 'All Day it
has Rained' and 'The Public Garden' are characterized by a kind
of pensive honesty. KEITH DOUGLAS (1920–44) was another

promising writer, though he left behind him comparatively little verse. Otherwise, the 1940s were a somewhat barren period; but it saw the emergence of GEORGE BARKER, KATHLEEN RAINE, DAVID GASCOYNE, and VERNON WATKINS. At the same time, with the publication of *The North Ship*, PHILIP LARKIN appeared on the literary horizon. A poet who adds to a dry wit a Betjemanesque eye for detail, Larkin was destined to become the most popular poet of the next decade.

The Drama

For drama the period was a poor one, its chief luminary being the Irish playwright, GEORGE BERNARD SHAW (1856–1950). Like Joyce, he came from the Dublin back-streets; but at the age of twenty he moved with his mother to London, where she supported them both by giving singing lessons. He had not thrown himself into the battle of life, he remarked afterwards with characteristic levity; he had thrown his mother in! While she worked, he endeavoured to write novels, and produced no less than five between 1876 and 1885, all of which the publishers rejected. An omnivorous reader and an inveterate music-lover, he then became first a literary and, in 1888, a music critic, writing a series of brilliant reviews under the pseudonym 'Corno di Bassetto'. Even at this period of his life he was calculatedly provocative. Wagner was his musical hero; Ibsen, his favourite modern dramatist; and he dared to criticize Shakespeare as a self-indulgent writer who had lacked 'ideas'. His earliest play, *Widowers' Houses*, was staged in 1892, and, since it dealt with an awkward social problem – nineteenth-century slums and their rapacious landlords – aroused a storm of indignation. Among its successors were *Mrs Warren's Profession* (1893), *Arms and the Man* (1894), *You Never Can Tell* (1895), *The Devil's Disciple* (1896), *Caesar and Cleopatra* (1898) and *Captain Brassbound's Conversion* (1899); and, during the opening decade of the new century, *Man and Superman, John Bull's Other Island, Major Barbara* and *The Doctor's Dilemma. Heartbreak House*, a comedy that shows the influence of Chekhov, was begun in 1913; and *Saint Joan*, a moving historical drama, his greatest popular success, appeared in 1923. Thereafter the value of his plays declined. He was less concerned to use the play as an art-form, and more and more resolved to employ it as a means of disseminating his own theories. He had been converted to Socialism by reading Marx on Capital, and had joined the Fabian Society in 1884. Through its founders, Sidney and Beatrice Webb, he met the rich Irishwoman, Charlotte Payne Townshend, whom, in 1898, he married. Mrs Shaw's fortune brought him financial security; but, although he now lived a comfortable and affluent life, he remained a doctrinaire Socialist.

George Bernard Shaw, the traveller, photographed at Waterloo Station, 1924.

Shaw's plays are easier to enjoy in the theatre than admire upon the printed page. He was the most argumentative and controversial of playwrights, but not the most imaginative; and many of the opinions that his dramatis personae voice – like many of the views he expressed himself – are apt nowadays to seem perverse and foolish. Beside the works of Chekhov, the plays that he produced have little genuine creative substance. He had none of Chekhov's deep poetic insight into the minds of the men and women he portrayed. His own cleverness always dazzled him; he could never resist a startling paradox, or the chance to shock and

Sean O'Casey.

(*Above*) J.B. Priestley at the age of seventy.

(*Right*) Noel Coward at ease; drawing by Cecil Beaton.

surprise his audience. He had a profoundly conceited nature; and the strain of conceit may have prevented him from becoming a literary man of genius. It was as a superb technician, rather than a great artist, that he left his mark upon the age.

Another Irishman who illuminated the English theatre was SEAN O'CASEY (1880–1964). His first play, *The Shadow of the Gunman*, which dealt with the Anglo-Irish conflict of 1920, was produced at the Abbey Theatre, Dublin, in 1923, and brought back to the modern stage the intensity of real experience. It was followed by two similarly powerful dramas, *Juno and the Paycock* (1924), a vivid combination of grotesque comedy and bitter tragedy, set against the background of the Dublin slums, and *The Plough and the Stars* (1926), a sombre chronicle-play that depicts the horror and futility of war, as exemplified in the disastrous Easter Rising. World War I had little immediate effect on the English theatre until 1929, when R.C. SHERRIFF (*b*.1896) produced *Journey's End*, an immensely successful mixture of tragic realism and schoolboy sentiment. A year earlier, O'Casey's play on a comparable theme, *The Silver Tassie*, though it marked a turning point in English dramatic literature, with its strong anti-heroic tone and bold innovatory techniques adapted from the German expressionist theatre, had failed to please a London audience. Of O'Casey's later plays, only *Red Roses for Me* (1942) shows more than glimpses of his early gifts.

During the 1920s and the 1930s, the English stage as a whole was chiefly distinguished by its technical accomplishment. J.B. PRIESTLEY (*b*.1894) wrote a series of 'well-made plays', which achieved the popularity their craftsmanship deserved, as did the undemanding comedies of W. SOMERSET MAUGHAM (1874–1965). Meanwhile NOEL COWARD (*b*.1899) had risen to dizzy

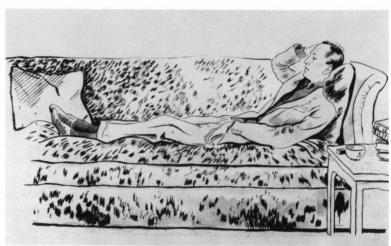

heights of fame. His first play, *The Vortex* (1924) had a serious, if somewhat melodramatic subject; but he followed it with a succession of light-hearted, light-weight comedies, including *Fallen Angels* (1925), *Easy Virtue* (1926), *Bitter Sweet* (1929) and *Private Lives* (1930). *Cavalcade* (1931), on the other hand, was a brave attempt to review Britain's immediate past and sound a patriotic clarion-call. Coward's comedies, ostensibly slight and frivolous, display an unfailing grasp of theatrical ways and means, and a verbal dexterity and wit that he has inherited from the Restoration playwrights.

More ambitious are the plays of T.S. ELIOT (1888–1965) who, for many years between the 1930s and the late 1950s, studied the fascinating problems of poetic drama. His intention was to recreate a drama in which poetry would perform a central rôle, and not serve merely as a type of decorative embellishment. He developed the idea of a ritualized, formalized play – a conception that he worked out most successfully through *Murder in the Cathedral* (1935). His first attempt to write for the popular stage was *The Family Reunion* (1939), an ingenious adaptation of a classical myth to a background of modern everyday life. In *The Cocktail Party* (1950), *The Confidential Clerk* (1954) and *The Elder Statesman* (1958) he continued to use verse – sometimes rather flat verse – to explore a twentieth-century subject. Their humour is occasionally heavy-handed; but, for the most part, Eliot's command of language and his keen poetic imagination carry him triumphantly along.

Critics and Biographers

G.K. CHESTERTON (1874–1936) was the kind of rumbustious littérateur who flourished at the end of the Victorian period and during the first years of the present century, combative, argumentative and immensely energetic. A convert to Catholicism, he shared many of the tastes and prejudices of his old friend HILAIRE BELLOC (1870–1953) – Belloc's hatred of industrial civilization, with its social deceits and democratic frauds, his nostalgia for a bygone Age of Faith, his delight in friendship and his gift for paradox. Chesterton's literary range was wide – from novels and ingenious detective stories to such controversial works as *The Outline of Sanity* and *The Superstition of Divorce*.

G.K. Chesterton, by James Gunn, 1932.

WYNDHAM LEWIS (1884–1957) was both a gifted imaginative writer and a brilliant draughtsman. But he was, above all else, a critic – a self-constituted 'modern Diogenes', who sat 'laughing in the mouth of his tub' and poured forth invective against every passer-by, 'irrespective of race, creed, rank or profession', and who would continue to do so, with undiminished vigour, until a year or two before he died. An early, and highly typical production was the 'Vorticist' magazine he named *Blast*, in which, under the headings 'Blast' and 'Bless', he divided the objects and persons he abominated from those he found deserving of his chary praise. *Blast* was followed by *The Enemy*, a paper he also wrote and edited himself. At the same time, he wrote some highly original novels, including his comic masterpiece *Tarr* (1918) and *The Apes of God* (1930), a savage diatribe directed at certain of his former friends, and a philosophic extravaganza entitled *The Childermass* (1928). His finest books, however, are mainly concerned with literary, artistic and sociological problems. Thus, in *The Lion and the Fox* (1926) he discusses 'the Rôle of the Hero in the plays of Shakespeare'; in *Time and Western Man* (1927), the current obsession with the idea of Time, and its effects upon contemporary literature; in *Paleface* (1929) the cult of Primitive Man, and of the 'dark forces' of the unconscious mind, as popularized by D. H. Lawrence. Lewis ridicules Lawrence's 'Dark Demon', to whom he opposes 'a White Demon or *daimon*; the spirit of the White Race . . .' Each book contains dazzling strokes of wit and valuable passages of critical analysis. If few of the many books he published now seem altogether satisfying, it is because 'the modern Diogenes' was too often carried away by bursts of manic indignation; so that his prose style becomes strangely shapeless. Yet there can be no doubt that he was one of the most original critics to emerge on the English scene since the death of Matthew Arnold.

Portrait of Lytton Strachey, by Vanessa Bell, about 1912.

Of all the friends gathered around Virginia Woolf, who formed the so-called 'Bloomsbury group', LYTTON STRACHEY (1880–1932) was the oddest and the most mercurial. The cultivated product of a well-known Victorian family, during his wide reading he seems to have developed a curious love-hate relationship with the whole Victorian age, which attracted him, yet also symbolized every moral standard that, as an agnostic and a practising hedonist, he himself had long rejected. This attitude towards the nineteenth-century past inspired his first successful book, *Eminent Victorians* (1918). Here, often with a certain disregard for facts, he described and amusingly ridiculed a succession of Victorian worthies; and in his next work, *Queen Victoria* (1921) he began by applying a slightly similar method to the features of their sovereign. Though sometimes deficient from an historical point of view, it is an immensely entertaining volume. But Strachey was out of his depth when he attempted to analyze the complex relationship of *Elizabeth and Essex* (1928). Despite his prejudices, he understood the Victorians; the Elizabethan Court, with its network of political intrigue, its vain-glorious ambitions and violent passions, was utterly beyond his grasp; and his last full-length biography is both an historically misleading and a sadly overwritten narrative.

[Handwritten manuscript facsimile of the last paragraph of Lytton Strachey's Queen Victoria]

Manuscript of the famous last paragraph of Lytton Strachey's *Queen Victoria*.

Strachey, however, founded a new school of biography that had an important effect upon contemporary literature. Many biographers have attempted to follow his lead; and occasionally the result has been disastrous. Literary irony cannot replace judgement; the interpretation of a human character needs a solid basis of established facts, which Strachey's followers have frequently failed to supply. His influence, at the same time, has proved stimulating and enlightening, since it has encouraged the biographer to employ an artist's technique, and give his material a literary shape and finish. This Strachey did in *Queen Victoria*. His portrait may not be entirely accurate; but it has the colouring and gloss of life. Though not a man who much admired women, he seems almost to have loved Victoria. The 'solemn sneer' that he had previously aimed at so many of her famous subjects, before he had reached the end of her long life had become a sympathetic smile.

Manuscript of the famous last paragraph of Lytton Strachey's *Queen Victoria*.

Bibliography

Barber, C. L., *Shakespeare's Festive Comedy* (Princeton, 1959).

Bate, W. J., *The Achievement of Samuel Johnson* (New York, 1955).

Bennett, Joan, *Four Metaphysical Poets* (Cambridge, 1934).

Bennett, Joan, *George Eliot, her mind and her art* (Cambridge, 1962).

Bentley, G. E., *Shakespeare: A Biographical Handbook* (New Haven, 1961).

Booth, Wayne C., *The Rhetoric of Fiction* (Chicago, 1961).

Bradbrook, M. C., *The Growth and Structure of Elizabethan Comedy* (London, 1955).

Bradbrook, M. C., *The School of Night* (London, 1936).

Bradbrook, M. C., *Shakespeare and Elizabethan Poetry* (London, 1951).

Bredvold, Louis I., *The Literature of the Restoration and Eighteenth Century* (Oxford, 1950).

Brower, Reuben A., *Alexander Pope: The Poetry of Allusion* (Oxford, 1959).

Brown, Douglas, *Thomas Hardy* (London, 1954).

Brown, W. C., *The Triumph of Form* (Chapel Hill, 1948).

Butt, J., *The Augustan Age* (London, 1950).

Cassell, R. A., *Ford Madox Ford: A Study of His Novels* (Baltimore and London, 1962).

Chamberlain, Robert L., *George Crabbe* (New York, 1965).

Cobban, A., *Edmund Burke and the Revolt against the Eighteenth Century* (London, 1929).

Crabbe, George, *Tales, 1812, and other selected poems*, ed. Howard Mills (Cambridge, 1967).

Crutwell, Patrick, *The Shakespearian Moment* (London, 1954).

Davie, Donald, *The Late Augustans* (London, 1958).

Dobrée, Bonamy, *English Literature in the Early Eighteenth Century, 1700–1740 (Oxford History of English Literature vol. vii)* (Oxford, 1959).

Dover Wilson, J., *The Fortunes of Falstaff* (Cambridge, 1943).

Eighteenth Century English Literature: Modern Essays in Criticism, ed. J. M. Clifford (Oxford, 1959).

Eliot, T. S., *The Use of Poetry and the Use of Criticism* (London, 1933).

Ellis-Fermor, U., *The Jacobean Drama* (London, 1936).

Ellmann, Richard, *James Joyce* (New York, 1959).

English Romantic Poets: Modern Essays in Criticism, ed. M. H. Abrams (New York and Oxford, 1960).

Essays on the Eighteenth Century presented to David Nicol Smith (Oxford, 1945).

Fergusson, Oliver W., *Jonathan Swift and Ireland* (Urbana, Illinois, 1962).

Ferry, David, *The Limits of Mortality: An Essay on Wordsworth's Major Poetry* (Middletown, Connecticut, 1959).

Foakes, R. A., *The Romantic Assertion* (London, 1958).

Fraser, G. S., *The Modern Writer and His World* (London, 1964).

From Dryden to Johnson, ed. B. Ford (*Pelican Guide to English Literature vol. iv*) (London, 1957).

Galloway, W. F., 'The Sentimentalism of Goldsmith' (*Publications of the Modern Language Association*, xlviii, 1933).

Gittings, R., *John Keats: The Living Year* (London, 1954).

Gleckner, R. F., *The Piper and the Bard: A Study of William Blake* (Detroit, 1959).

Goode, J., Howard, D., and Lucas, W. J., *Tradition and Tolerance in Nineteenth Century Fiction* (London, 1966).

Guerard, A. J., *Conrad the Novelist* (London, 1958).

Hanson, L. & E. M., *The Four Brontës* (Oxford, 1949).

Hardy: A Collection of Critical Essays, ed. Albert J. Guerard (Englewood Cliffs, New Jersey, 1963).

Havens, R. D., *The Mind of a Poet* (Baltimore, 1941).

Hoggart, R., *Auden* (London, 1951).

Hough, Graham, *The Last Romantics* (London, 1947).

House, Humphrey, *The Dickens World* (London, 1941).

Jack, Ian, *Augustan Satire* (Oxford, 1952).

Jacobean Theatre: Stratford-upon-Avon Studies I, ed. J. R. Brown and Bernard Harris (London, 1960).

Jeffares, Norman, *W. B. Yeats, Man and Poet* (London, 1949).

Johnson, E. D. H., *The Alien Vision of Victorian Poetry* (Princeton, 1952).

Kenner, Hugh, *The Invisible Poet* (London, 1959).

Kermode, Frank, *Romantic Image* (London, 1957).

Kettle, Arnold, *An Introduction to the English Novel* (London, 1951).

Knights, L. C., *Drama and Society in the Age of Jonson* (London, 1937).

Knights, L. C., *Some Shakespearian Themes* (London, 1959).

Laurence Sterne: A Collection of Critical Essays, ed. John Traugott (Englewood Cliffs, New Jersey, 1968).

Leavis, F. R., *D. H. Lawrence, Novelist* (London, 1955).

Leech, C., *John Ford and the Drama of his Time* (London, 1957).

Levin, Harry, *James Joyce: A Critical Introduction* (London and New York, 1960).

Lynch, K. M., *The Social Mode of Restoration Comedy* (New York, 1926).

Marchand, L. A., *Byron, a Biography*, 3 vols (London, 1957).

Meredith Now, ed. Ian Fletcher (London, 1972).

Mudrick, M., *Jane Austen: Irony as Defense and Discovery* (Princeton, 1952).

Orwell, George, *Inside the Whale* (London, 1940).

Palmer, J., *The Comedy of Manners* (London, 1913).

Partridge, E. B., *The Broken Compass: A Study of the Major Comedies of Ben Jonson* (London, 1958).

Peter, J., *Complaint and Satire in Early English Literature* (Oxford, 1956).

Praz, Mario, *The Hero in Eclipse in Victorian Fiction* (Oxford, 1956).

Pritchett, V. S., *The Living Novel* (London, 1946).

Quintana, R., *The Mind and Art of Jonathan Swift* (London, 1936).

Raymond, W. O., *The Infinite Moment and other Essays in Robert Browning* (Toronto, 1950).

Ribner, I., *Jacobean Tragedy: The Quest for Moral Order* (London, 1962).

Rossiter, A. P., *Angel with Horns* (London, 1961).

Rudyard Kipling, the man, his work and his world, ed. John Gross (London, 1972).

Sale, Arthur, 'The Development of Crabbe's Narrative Art' (*Cambridge Journal* V, 1952).

Schoenbaum, S., *Middleton's Tragedies* (New York, 1955).

Seventeenth Century English Poetry: Modern Essays in Criticism, ed. W. R. Keast (Oxford, 1962).

Sharrock, R., *John Bunyan* (London, 1954).

Shelley: a Collection of Critical Essays, ed. George M. Ridenour (Englewood Cliffs, New Jersey and London, 1965).

Spacks, P. M., *The Poetry of Vision: Five Eighteenth Century Poets – Thomson, Collins, Gray, Smart, Cowper* (Cambridge, Mass., 1967).

Spiers, J., *Chaucer the Maker* (London, 1951).

Stead, C. K., *The New Poetic* (London, 1964).

Stein, A., *Answerable Style: Essays on Paradise Lost* (Minneapolis, 1953).

Studies in Criticism and Aesthetics 1660–1800, ed. H. Anderson and J. S. Shea (Minneapolis, 1967).

Sutherland, J., *A Preface to Eighteenth Century Poetry* (Oxford, 1948).

The English Mind: Studies in the English Moralists, ed. Hugh Sykes Davies and George Watson (Cambridge, 1964).

Thomas, G., *William Cowper and the Eighteenth Century* (London, 1935).

Trickett, Rachel, *The Honest Muse: A Study in Augustan Verse* (Oxford, 1967).

Trilling, Lionel, *Matthew Arnold* (London, 1939).

Trilling, Lionel, *E. M. Forster* (London, 1944).

Underwood, D., *Etherege and the Seventeenth Century Comedy of Manners*, (New Haven, 1957).

Ure, Peter, *Shakespeare: The Problem Plays* (London, 1969).

Ure, Peter, *Yeats* (London, 1963).

Van Doren, Mark *John Dryden* (Cambridge, 1931).

Victorian Literature: Modern Essays in Criticism, ed. Austin Wright (Oxford, 1961).

Walton, G., *Metaphysical to Augustan* (Cambridge, 1955).

Ward, C. E., *The Life of John Dryden* (London, 1901).

Warnock, G. J., *Berkeley* (London, 1953).

Watkins, W. B. C., *Perilous Balance: The Tragic Genius of Swift, Johnson, and Sterne* (Princeton, 1939).

Watt, Ian, *The Rise of the Novel* (London, 1957).

West, P., *Byron and the Spoiler's Art* (London, 1960).

Willey, B., *The Eighteenth Century Background* (London, 1940).

Wilson Knight, G., *The Wheel of Fire* (London, 1930).

Wilson, B., *The Court Wits of the Restoration* (Princeton, 1948).

Index